MEDIEVAL CENTRAL ASIA

Polity, Economy and Military Organization (Fourteenth to Sixteenth Centuries)

MEDIEVAL CENTRAL ASIA

Polity, Economy and Military Organization
(Fourteenth to Sixteenth Centuries)

MANSURA HAIDAR

CENTRE OF ADVANCED STUDY
Department of History
Aligarh Muslim University

MANOHAR
2004

First published 2004

ISBN 81-7304-554-2

Published by

Ajay Kumar Jain for
Manohar Publishers & Distributors
4753/23 Ansari Road, Daryaganj
New Delhi 110 002

Typeset at

Digigrafics
New Delhi 110 049

Printed at

Lordson Publishers Pvt. Ltd.
Delhi 110 007

To the memory
of my father
Prof. S.M. Zamin Ali

Contents

Acknowledgements

It is my pleasant duty to thank all those persons who have contributed to the completion of this volume.

I owe a deep debt of gratitude to my supervisor (Late) Professor Saiyid Nurul Hasan who had introduced me to this comparatively lesser known Central Asian world and its people. Visionary as he was, he had foreseen that the specialists on Central Asian studies will be needed by the country and the world. As early as 1965, he had tried to get me acquainted with the sources and history of the region—until then a virgin field waiting to be explored. I recollect and gratefully acknowledge the consistent support I received from him at every step without which it would have been well nigh impossible to accomplish my researches on Central Asia. His guidance and assistance had been the means of placing me on the rails of original research.

I also wish to express my sincere thanks to late Professor Bobojon Ghaffurov, a friend of my supervisor Professor S. Nurul Hasan. He took keen interest in the progress of my work and his kind help was always available during my stay in the erstwhile Soviet Union. I am beholden to Professor Goga Abrarovich Hidayatov (the then Dean and Chairman, Department of History and my supervisor in Tashkent), who had been generous in imparting all kind of assistance in my academic pursuits facilitating my access to the relevant libraries throughout the Soviet Union.

I recall with gratitude and a deep sense of personal loss my association with (late) Professor Mrs. Sabahat Azimjanova (the then Director, Oriental Institute, Tashkent) whose affectionate care and concern for my welfare and work was always a source of comfort for me. I learnt much through useful discussions and long scholarly discourses whenever I had a chance to see Professor Bori Ahmedov of Oriental Institute, Tashkent, Professor Razia Muqminova of Institute of History (Tashkent), Professor Mrs. Davidovich, the then Director of Oriental Institute (Moscow), Professor Olga Chekhovich,

Professor Hamid Sulaimanov and Professor Mrs. Razia Sulaimanova and Professor Pugachenkova. I am grateful to them for their academic advices.

I wish to record my grateful thanks to Professor Orinbaev the then Director of Abu Raihan Alberuni Institute of Oriental Studies, Tashkent who had been kindly disposed to me, providing me with all academic help. I also thank (late) Professor Hashimov and Professor Khairullaev of the Institute of Oriental Studies. My boundless gratitude goes to Professor Ahror Mukhtarov of Dushambe, Tajikistan whom I am beholden to in various ways particularly for the constant supply of newly published works which assisted me in updating my knowledge about the latest happenings in Central Asia. My acquaintance with Professor Mansur Bobokhanov, the then Chairman, Department of History, Dushambe and (late) Professor Abdullaev of Institute of History, Dushambe for a short period had left an impact upon me by way of confirming the amicability and generosity of Central Asians.

I had a chance to stay in Central Asia for a longer period of several months at a stretch and to enjoy the hospitality, love and care of my various friends who had turned an alien land into a 'second motherland' for me. Amongst this galaxy of friends were Dr. Mrs. Farida Salimova (an Indologist at the Oriental Institute, Tashkent, a great friend of India and a niece of famous poet Ghaffur Ghulam, well known scholar and writer of several works on Indian customs and traditions and author of monographs on Indira Gandhi, Aruna Asaf Ali and others); Dr. Shirin Jahlova, another reputed Indologist at the Oriental Institute, Tashkent who is well versed in Hindi language and contributed tremendously towards popularizing Indian languages in Central Asia; Mrs. Sorkina, the Russian teacher in Tashkent; and Dr. Yulduz Teshabaev, a well known Indologist from the Oriental Institute. Their constant and active care sustained me during those lonely days in a foreign land. Other friends like Gulsara, and Sewar, both from the Institute of Oriental Studies, Mariam Yuldashaev, French language teacher in Samarqand University, her aunt Borchhin Opa, Ninel Ghaffurova, the daughter of Professor Bobajon Ghaffurov and Reader at the Oriental Institute, Moscow.

I will be failing in my duty if I do not record my thanks to the librarians and library staff of various libraries where I have worked during the long span of my research endeavours. I am grateful to Professor M.H. Rizvi, Professor Nurul Hasan and Professor Shakeel

Ahmad the three successive librarians of Maulana Azad Library who always accorded their wholehearted assistance to all the seekers of knowledge by providing the required material for research. I am also thankful to the librarians at the departmental library of Centre of Advanced Study in History, AMU, Aligarh particularly to Mr. Yusuf Siddiqui who is not only a devoted caretaker of books but also a dedicated person offering all possible assistance to the scholars. I am particularly grateful to Mr. Munirov, the then librarian at Abu Raihan Alberuni Institute of Oriental Studies, Tashkent and Anwar apa the then librarian at the Fundamental Library, Tashkent whose consistently available cooperation went a long way in the completion of my work.

I am grateful to Aligarh Muslim University Vice-Chancellors, particularly to Dr. Mahmoodur Rehman and Mr. Naseem Ahmad who had through their excellent administration provided the peaceful atmosphere and opportunity to the scholars like me to concentrate wholeheartedly on academic works.

I am grateful to the University Grants Commission for providing me the opportunity of visiting erstwhile Soviet Union twice through its Cultural Exchange Programme and also for some financial grant for completing this work.

My thanks are due to the persons who had typed and word processed the script of my research works, namely, Mr. Badar Afroz, Mr. Hamid, Mr. Bahauddin and Mr. Sajjad Abbas.

MANSURA HAIDAR

State and Polity in Turco-Mongol Central Asia

Central Asia has seen the rise and fall of many magnificent dynasties which had ruled over its soil, including the four Sassanid kings who 'excelled in administration as much as the Turks in warfare, Greeks in Sciences and Chinese in handicrafts'. The Arabs too were highly urbanized and their acumen in the affairs of administration was also extraordinary. The Abbasids had given a greatly sophisticated and highly developed administration to the Islamic lands. According to the Islamic principles, 'sovereignty of the Universe belongs to God alone—unshared by anyone. The Muslim public law emerges from the existence of Ummah and not from any well-defined system of state'. The Islamic administrative structure, therefore, comprises almost simultaneously the all-pervading *sharia* rules, which were obligatory as much as *reichsrecht*, and *valksrecht* (i.e. local customary law or *urf o ada*). Complete autocracy or 'unrestricted community sovereignty' was not allowed though the ruling 'obey God, obey Prophet, obey those in authority from amongst you' was the dictum repeated in consonance with the theory of divine kingship.[1] Although *sharia* laws are said to have 'refrained deliberately from providing detailed regulations for all manifold changing requirements of our social existence, the need for temporal legislation was evident'[2] hence independent reasoning necessitated *ijma*. 'Divine law covered all manifestations of human life and it was the purpose of the state to get that law obeyed.' In Ibn-i Khaldun's opinion, 'caliphate in reality substitutes for the lawgiver (Prophet Muhammad) in as much as it serves like him to protect religion and to exercise political leadership of the world'. The community could always 'delegate its legislative powers to a limited number of elected members'[3] hence the view that 'their (the believers) communal business is (to be transacted in consultation among themselves'. And this mass injunction 'was the operative clause of all Islamic thought relating to statecraft reaching to every department'.[4] Like Roman '*consensus prudentum*', the injunction united the will of people (*ijma*) in accordance with *amr i hum shura' bai na hum*, 'the consensus of the learned whose ensured authority was verifying (Konstatierend) rather than normative'.[5]

'The state was, therefore, God's vicegerent on earth to enforce equality, freedom, dignity, personality development and also unity of Islam.' From the very beginning of Perso-Islamic monarchical traditions, the ruler had to be a good supervisor of administrative machinery, organizing state structure, economy digging of canals, underground conduits, construction of bridges, encouragement to cultivation, development of agriculture, florescence of fine arts, beautification of cities and patronage to learning. These duties are enumerated in almost all the *manshurs* issued to the provincial rulers.[6]

During the Abbasid period Transoxiana happened to be a subordinate part of Khurasan. Hereditary governors raised from the native aristocracy were appointed merely because they were well acquainted with the local traditions and inculcated greater confidence amongst the subjects.

In Central administration there were several departments called *dawawin*. In larger provinces also such departments existed. The *Bait-ul mal-i-khassa* was used in defraying such expenses as were made for the benefit of the whole realm. *Majlis-i-amma*, a subsection of *diwan-i-khassa* attended to their problems. *Diwan-i-bait-ul mal* kept accounts of what was paid at *diwan-i-kharaj* and *diwan-i zia*. Its head *sahib-i bait-ul mal* had a right to inspect the *diwan-i-kharaj*. A separate local *bait-ul mal* where taxes from the region were deposited and where current and extraordinary expenses of area were defrayed also existed. This treasury used to send the money realized either in the form of *suftajab* (bills of exchange) or in cash to whichever place the government directed it. Tax was usually paid in dirham though calculated at government bureaus in terms of dinars.[7]

There are references to *rustaq* in some sources. During the Abbasid period the smallest unit of the state was *diya* (*ziya*) or *qura* or *qariya*. A combination of twelve villages formed a *rustaq* and one to twelve *rustaqs* constituted a *taasuq*. All the three subdivisions mentioned above came under the jurisdiction of a town. There were fiscal administrative divisions called *amal*. A region was called a *nahiya*, whereas the provinces were called *kurah* and later on *wilayats*.

Sometimes *kurahs* was confused with the *nahiya* and *amal.*[8] The Mongol Khan Kebek had introduced a unit called *tuman.* In the Mongol empire also both Chingiz and Kublai Khan are said to have appointed twelve barons (officers) for the affairs of the army and twelve others for the general concern of the Empire. These were called Kuran.

The Wazir: The office of *wazir* created by the Abbasids was assigned to the renowned Persian family of Barmakids ever since the days of Caliph Mansur.[9] The office of *wazir* is said to have originated in Persia under Al-Mansur, the first holder of this high office being Khalid Ibn-i Barmak.[10] The best definition of a *wazir* is found in one of Caliph al Nasir (1180-1250)'s letter patent. This 'perfect expression' in summing up of the duties of a *wazir* presents it as the 'divine right of kingship working by proxy'. From Al-Mawardi to Isfahani, almost all the jurists have referred to two types of *wazirs*, namely, *wazir-i tafvizi* (with full authority) and *wazir-i tanfizi* (with executive power though limited only). The former enjoyed de jure powers of sovereignty except in the appointment of his successor whereas the latter only complied with the ruler's orders and enforced them. *Wazir* is said to be, as his name suggests, a 'burden bearer'. In the majestic empires of Abbasids and the Ottomans, there existed but well defined system of *wazirate* with one grand *wazir* with excessive powers and a galaxy of subordinate *wazirs*. In the case of Timurids, however, there is no mention of a full-fledged grand *wazir* with specified powers though there is mention of a grand *wazir*, *wazir* (*wazir-i-azam*) and a number of other *wazirs.*[11] Originally the *wakils* as the incharge of 'domestic affairs of the court' were important enough to be counted as being equal to *amirs* and *wazirs*. Usually *wazirs* were the high officers of state and were selected from amongst the civilian population. The position and authority of the *wazirs* increased and decreased depending upon the state and the *hakim* for whom he worked. Under the early Abbasids, *wazirs* 'were the head of the bureaucracy and virtually incharge of day to day conduct of government. Under the Seljuqid sultans, he happened to be effectively the dignified head of the administration. At another time, he was a relatively minor official'.[12]

The two *wazirs* namely, *wazir-i tanfizi* and *tafvizi* had their different functions. The *tafvizi wazir* was perhaps more independent and powerful having the charge of *Alauddawawin* though without it he was like a clerk.[13] Appointment of a *wazir*, it was believed, did not mean that the Caliph should give up all connections with administration of state 'in the province of politics, it is better to have a co-adjutor rather than one sole person at the helm of affairs'. Frequent references are found to *diwan-ur risail* (the bureaucracy for correspondence) headed by *sahib-ul amal* (responsible for issuing a *kitab*).

The Diwan: Mawardi says that it was King Anusherwan's idea, who, seeing his clerks in the secretariat solving arithmetical sums, called them *diwanah* or mad, as they worked with a frenzy. Another theory is *dewan* (i.e. plural of *dew*—giants) as accountants were like giants in mathematical sums hence the name. Each *dewan* was divided into two sections *majalis-ul asl* or *diwan-ul asl* (commonly known by its short name *asl*) and the *diwan-ul zimma* or *zimam*. While *asl* was the headquarter or main office (lit. rein) hence audit and supervision work was assigned to this special ministry of finance with a supervisory bureau called *diwan-ul ashraf*. The *asl* section had to prepare financial estimates, lists (*amal*) containing the revenue (*irtifa*) of the provincial taxes, the levy of these and so on.[14] A system of checks and balances did exist hence the financial estimates of *asl* had to be checked by the officers of *alzimma* and *usul*. Under the Abbasids, the entire supervisory work was given to the bureau of supreme control called *diwan-uz zimam-ul zimma* or *diwan-ul zimam* or *Alauddawawin*.[15] There used to be a *diwan-ul balad* or *nahiya* in the provinces. There were agents on behalf of the Central government who could be sent to inspect the local *diwans*.

The *diwan-i amid-ul mulk* is said to be identical with the *diwan* of official documents (*diwan-ur rasail* or *diwan-i Insha*) though the two apparently seem to carry two different functions. The *diwan-i amid-ul mulk* seem to be under Muhamad Khwarazm Shah's reign.[16]

As under the Abbasids, an audit or accounts office (*diwan-ul zimam*) introduced by al Mahdi, a board of correspondence or chancellary office (*diwan-ul tawqi*) which took care of all official letters, imperial orders, political documents and a board for inspection of grievances (*diwan-al nazar fil mazalim*) or a supreme court for appeal to set right cases of miscarriage of justice, a police department (known under Abbasids as and under the Turco Mongols as *diwan-al shurtah*) and a postal department (chief *sahib-ul barid*) and a controller of the post and intelligence service (*sahib-ul barid wa Akhbar*) who acted as an inspector general and a direct confidential agent of the Central government.[17]

The *diwan-i mushrif* seems to control the sums allocated for the maintenance of the court. Tusi recounts the duty of the *mushrif* (observer) 'to be aware of all that when on the dargah and report on it when he deemed necessary'.[18] Bayhaqi mentioned that the *mushrif* together with the treasurers used to draw up a report of the court property.[19] There were posts of *qazi-ul quzzat* or *aqzi-ul quzzat* also.

Some compared this post to the *mobidan-i-mobid* (mohutan-mogpetan—mogpet) of Sasanid Persia.[20] The *diwan-i mazalim* was a 'regular, judicial institution with its own rules and procedures'. It was the investigations of grievances or a court of enquiry conducted first by Caliph in person and later by an official nominated or appointed by the king.[21] The *diwan-i jahbada* was an exchange bureau in which old coins were minted in various provinces and where great fluctuations were registered in alloys like that of a private banker. *Jahbada* was responsible for receiving *kharaj* payments, issuing *barat*, receipts, etc.[22]

Other Officers: Although legal matters were solved by the *qazi*, the complaints of high-handedness, tyranny and injustice on the part of officials could be brought to the king himself who looked into the matter personally or appointed his own nominee to examine it. The Abbasid system of two types of *qazis*—the *khassah* and the *ammah mutlaqah* may or may not have existed under the Central Asian kings, but the functions of the *qazis* were almost the same ranging from deciding cases, acting as guardians for orphans, lunatics and minors, managing the *waqf*, punishing the outlaws and violators of *sharia*, appointing *naibs* (judicial deputies in the provinces) and often deputy judges or *qazis*.[23]

Although there were separate departments for *ihtisab* and *auqaf* recommended by the jurists and existing earlier but this separate department of *auqaf* was abolished in later times. Already in the twelfth century the *waqf* establishments were a part of jurisdiction of *qazi*. Being chief of the municipal policy, and an overseer of markets and morals the *muhtasib* was to ensure proper weights and measures to be used in trade, approved morals, abstinence from prohibited acts and so on.

Diwan-al barid was the bureau of the post. Etymologically, the word *barid* originated from semitic language.[24]

The post of *rais* denoted head of the town and this title was often given to certain functionaries whose posts were often hereditary. *Rais* could be the head of a government department. Under Seljuqids, *rais* was a term commonly used for the officer in charge of civil affairs in a city whose duties were those of a notable of the city, recognized and appointed by royal authority or a royal officer.[25] In pre-Mongol Central Asia the *rais* was merely a chief of the town selected from amongst the native gentry, representing the interests of the townsmen on the one hand and on the other hand being an agent of the king through whom the will of the sovereign was made known to the subjects. During the Mongol period some powers of police were also added to his authority.[26] There were *naibs* also (also called *naib-us sultanate*) who were a deputy of the sultan and held the fort in his absence.

The duty of the Muhtasib included maintenance of law and order in the bazaars and, punishing the violators of the sacred law or those who habitually evaded taxes. Tusi confirms that the kings always entrusted this office to someone from the court, either a eunuch or some old turk who evinced partiality towards none and who was feared by the high and the low.[27] Under the Samanids usually learned men held this post.

Occasionally two posts of *sahib-i haras* and *sahib-i shurat* (captain of the watch and captain of the guard respectively) established by Muawiya are noticed in the Central Asian administrative machinery.

The remnants of Sassanid and Arab administration continued to linger in the pattern of governance of later kings though with certain changes. Some of these administrative principles and institutions were adapted or adopted, others were entirely transformed. But traditions of centuries of good management of the affairs of the state could not altogether be obliterated. The Turks, Mongols and Turco-Mongols had thus inherited a strong and well established system from their illustrious predecessors.

Barthold seems to have underevalued the Turks or Turco-Mongol 'nomads'. Commenting upon the Qarakhanids and Seljuqids, he however, concedes that 'it is very probable that under the influence of religion some of these rulers were imbued with a sincere desire to realize the ideals of a just king', and adds, 'the leader of a nomadic people, who had scarcely been distinguished from his warriors by his dress, and who had shared all their labours with them could not suddenly turn into a despot of the same type as Mahmud and Masud'. He further stresses that the 'Persian conception of the monarch as the sole ruler of the state was also foreign to the nomads, in whose eyes the empire was the property of the whole family of the

Khan.[28] In the context of the Qarakhanids, Barthold had surmised that 'as in all nomad Empires the conception of patrimonial property was carried over from the domain of personal law to that of state laws'. Elaborating on the same point, he comments, 'the kingdom was considered the property of the whole family of the Khan and was divided into a number of appanages, the large ones being in turn subdivided into many smaller ones: The authority of the head of the Empire was an occasion entirely disavowed by powerful vassals. The partition system was as always, the cause of personal feuds and of a constant change of rulers.'[29]

The custom of division of Empire into provinces which were assigned to governors variously called in different Empires as (*amirs*, *sahib-i suba*, *muqta*) was as common in Byzantine and Persian States as it was in any Turkish Turco-Mongol, Rajput or Hindu kingdoms. Notwithstanding the methods devised by the Central government to strengthen its control over far-flung and nearby provinces, the difficulty in the means of intercommunication made the restricted delegation of authority and partial decentralization inevitable at least to some extent. Panini and Kautilya's '*Ayudhajibin Sanghas*' or 'Shastropajibin' in the eastern states and the concept of 'per stirpes' which was also not alien to the west proves that inter-territorial division and administrative assignment was a common feature in both east and west alike. The early juridical theorists like Al-Mawardi has described the two distinguished types of governorships, namely: *imarah* by which right of nomination and control of judiciary, taxation, maintenance of law and order, police, and safeguarding of state religion were under the governor's full control, and *khassah* (special or more restricted type in which the governor was devoid of authority over the judiciary, taxation and his powers increased or decreased in proportion to the incompetence or efficiency of the Central ruler). Centrifugal tendencies are said to have been as common in the states of Qarakhanids and Seljudqids as in the kingdom of Ottoman Turks and the Mongols. It is interesting to note that elsewhere. Barthold himself asserts that 'the custom of division of Empire among sons or other members of the ruling family was not purely a characteristic feature of 'all nomad Empires'. On the contrary, it was widely practiced in most of the eastern states and was found occasionally in western states as well.' The Khwarazmshahi dynasty was also no exception.[30]

Under the Sassanids, the Persian governors of provinces enjoyed the title Marzban. Under the later Umayyads, the Marzbans centred only in certain provinces. The *dihqans* were prosperous landlords under the Abbasids, though the highest class of absentee landlords who were drawn from the *dihqan* class and who left their estates to a *wakil* for the supervisory work was known as *tana'ah*, *tunna*. Incidentally the term *tani* in Arabic language means 'settled'. Apart from the financier classes like, *amil*, *dihqan*, *zia* and *tuna*, there were two main classes of agriculturists descending from the Sassanid period namely a destitute class of farm labourers, daily wager (*yom*) and secondly, the class of tenants and metayors. The labourers were the most hard-pressed class whereas the most privileged class was that of *sat'la*—the fruit planters whose hereditary tenancy rights and fixed share in the output was most profitable. The *aris* was another metayor with a shorter period of lease.

The kings were not completely oblivious of their surroundings and kept a vigil and tried to ameliorate the condition of the subjects. In 1091 the Saljuqid Sultan Malik Shah is said to have ordered some of the highly placed officials to 'draw up a report on the state of the kingdom, indicating all defects and possible improvements. Of the works presented to him, the Sultan approved of only of the treatise of Nīzam-ul Mulk which consisted of thirty-nine chapters and decided to adopt it as a guide. It deals with the duties of the various officials, and gives advices on all branches of the administration.'[31] The Saljuqids no longer attached much importance to the espionage system and officers like *sahib-i haras* and *sahib-i khabar* naturally lost their significance.[32] Some of the remnants of Saljuqid era seem to have lingered on in later years also. Not only Nizam-ul Mulk Tusi had considered the *sahib-i khabar* as one of the pillars of order in the state but most of the statesmen like Akbar in his *Dastur-ul arnal*, had particularly emphasized the features found in the Turkish states beyond Hindukush.

Khwarazm Shah's administrative elite included the same Saljuqids officials namely the *wazir*, the *qazi* and *mustauf-i imamalik*. In the twelfth century the terms like *wakils* and *mushir* had somewhat changed in their connotation. The post of *wakil* was bifurcated into the *wakil* of the court and *wakil* of the personal division (which was perhaps corresponding to the *wakil kharji* (*wakil* of tribute) of the Mongol period.[33] The *wakil* controlled the receipts of large sums of money as well as those earmarked for the maintenance of the army; in the provinces, the same duty was performed by the *munshis*.[34]

Sometimes the head of a department at the Centre was authorized to appoint his corresponding post in the provinces.[35]

As earlier in the former dynasties, the *wazirat* on hereditary basis was also not uncommon as Muhammad's *wazir* Nizam-ul Mulk Muhammad b. Masud Alharawi was the son of the *wazir* of Takash. The provincial *wazirs* (occasionally termed as *atabegs* or *ataliqs*) were appointed by the king himself particularly in such provinces which were held by the princes[36] presumably to control the affairs of the state directly.

Thus 'the conception of authority, assertion of power, strict control and iron discipline imbued in the minds of the Mongol tribal people, the heavy superstructure of inflexible bureaucracy naturally strengthened the position of the Turko-Mongol Khan'.

During his own lifetime, Chingiz who was the best physiognomist assigned the various duties regarding the governance to his sons. He had placed with Juji the management of feasts and hunting; Judiciary matters (*yarghu*) and the carrying out of punishment in which administrative government was involved were committed to the wisdom of Chaghatai; Administration of political matters were assigned to Ogedei. The management of military affairs and the protection of the camp were made over to Tuli. The above statement is said to have been recorded between 1203 and 1218.[37]

Chingiz had repeatedly asserted that 'he was the flail of God' (*man azab-i khuda hastam*) sent by Him to punish the people for their sins. In his letter of Nov. 1246 to the Pope, Guyuk referred to the fact that 'Chingiz Khan and Great Khan Ogedei have both transmitted God's order'.[38] Chingiz's orders were conveyed through *payzah* (Chinese Paitzu) or *paitzas* called by Marco Polo as 'tablets of authority' which were both gold and silver tablets and which were hung in the form of a tiger and is described by Chagchun. Wooden *payzahs* were given to minor officials.[39] Chingiz had tried to streamline the administration on the basis of the existing structure, and had probably made certain changes in accordance with his need. It is strange that nomenclature is missing though functions of these ten officials as given in the *Secret History* are the same. These are:

1. Four men whose duty it was 'to carry the bow and arrows; Barthold says that these were the *qurchis* of later times.
2. Three 'oversears of food and drink'; the Mongol text had given their separate categories of morning and evenings. This rank was perhaps called as *bukawul* or *bawurchi*.

3. One 'overseer of sheep pasturage'. In Rashiduddin's work a similar officer referred to as simlar had been described as equerry of the court stud (*akhtachi*).
4. One 'overseer of the preparation of carts (tergen) in later times the office of *yurtchi*. Rashiduddin records that this officer was appointed as captain of a thousand and looked after the mares', though towards the end of his life, he was promoted to become a *bukawul* and *bawurchi*.
5. One *cherbi* ('overseer') of the 'domestic staff'.
6. Four men whose duty was to carry the swords in one place; the head of these was Temuchim's brother Juchi Qasar.
7. Two 'overseers of training horses' (*akhta*, in later times, the office of *akhtachi*), one of these was Temuchim's brother Bilgutay.
8. Four 'overseers of horse pasturage'. Rašhiduddin perhaps refers to the same word '*kotawal*' erroneously interpreted by Berezin as having stemmed from the verb *ketmok* (i.e. to go away). Elsewhere the same word appears in the form *kaytawal*.[40]
9. Four far and near arrows (in chinese *yuan tsien* and *kintsien*, in Mongolian *khota and oira*).
   Presumably these refer to the persons who carried out mission on the personal behests of the Khans, chiefly as envoys. The custom of sending 'messenger arrows' existed in the Ki Empire[41] and in later times there was a special term in the Mongol empire to designate the 'arrows' in which secret letters were enclosed.[42]
10. The elders or the 'guardians' of the assembly. These were the two nobles for whose functions in detail are nowhere to be found. Barthold surmises that they were the chief advisers of the Khan and the duty of maintaining order in meeting devolved upon them. The two persons mentioned in this context occupied 'most honourable posts at Chingiz Khan's court'. Thus Bughurji Noyon sat on his right side above the military leaders, the other Jelme was one of the captains of the guard (*keshik*) and we are told that 'not more than two or three were senior to him'.

Under the Mongol rule, Changchun had noticed an official known as *darukhachi* or *darugha* who was perhaps a representative of the head of the Empire in Almaligh as well as the native ruler. According to the Chinese accounts, the *darugha* or *darukhachi* had to perform the following duties in later times:

(1) Census of the inhabitants, (2) recruitment of an army from the natives, (3) establishment of postal communications, (4) collection of taxes, and (5) delivery of tribute to the court.

He was a military officer, a tax collector, an agent furnishing information to the Central government.[43]

In the contemporary sources, it is mentioned that the first officer appointed by the Mongol rulers in Central Asia was a *basqaq* or a *darugha*.

The custom of appointing *ataliqs* or guide chiefs is also noticed under Chingiz Khan. He had appointed three chiefs each for Juji (namely *runan, mongkeur* and *kete*) and Chaghatai (namely *qarachar*, *mongke* and *idoy udai*). Since Chaghatai was 'hard' and both of a fine nature and busied himself with minutiae, *kokechu* 'was to be at his side and tell (unto him) what he hath thought. For Ogedei and Tolui each he appointed two advisors (namely *iluge* and *degei* and *jadai* and *bala* respectively. For his own mother and *odchigin's* young brethren whom ten thousand people had been assigned', Chingiz appointed four chiefs namely, *guchu*, *kokochu*, *jungsai* and *qorqasun*. For *qasar* and *alchidai* also one advisor each (namely *jebke* and *caurqai*) was appointed respectively. Juvaini further adds that there were officials who 'collect and keep charge of the clothing assigned upon the various provinces; otherwise do likewise with furs, and two of three with gold and silver cash'.[44]

Then there are separate persons to affix *altamghas*, issue *paizas* and supervise the arsenals, there are many persons in charge of hunting birds and beasts and their keepers.[45]

Finally there are one or two persons to deal with the affairs of *imams*, *saiyids*, dervishes, Christians and the holymen (*ahbar*) of every religious community.

All these officials were commanded to be on guard against the stain of usury or covetousness. They were to arrest no one and were to bring each man's case promptly to the Emperor's attention.

They are attended by scribes of every kind for Persian, Uighur Khitayan, Tibetan, Tangut, etc., so that to whatever place a decree had to be issued it should be in the language and script of the people.[46]

The Khauali of Qipchaq or Golden Horde was the western appanage divided later into Blue Horde and White Horde. Though the White Horde held a titular suzerainty, the Blue Horde whose appanage was on the Don and Volga was actually the more powerful and their territories extended from Kune Kieve and the Caucasus to the Aral Sea and Khiva. The administrative excellence of Uzbeg Khan is well reflected through the accounts of Ibn-i Battuta and others. Sultan Uzbeg who reigned from 1312-40 was the greatest of Khans of Blue Horde.[47] Usually the *maliks* over all the territories and sometimes even inside in province were appointed by the Qaan.[48]

A careful study of Mongol sources shows that Mongol Khans were not nomadic bellicose only. On their part, Mongol Khans were keen to improve the administrative affairs and financial management but the distances from the provinces and more often than not tainted reports reaching from the provinces through the Khan's own deputies or provincial magnates gave Khan completely a camouflaged report. Not only *yalavuch* had once threatened to give a bad report if his victim refused to poison Chaghatai but the reports given in accordance with the Emperor's taste, won favour for that messenger though seldom helped the inhabitants[49] as honest reports spoilt the prospects of bad rulers.[50] Occasionally good administrators like Korguz in Khurasan and Mazadran carried out new census for reassessment of taxes founded work shops, spread toiled to justice, removed covetousness of profiteers, forced rendering of accounts in time and distinguished foolish ignorant from capable and wise,[51] protected property.

Similarly, Qaan Mongke appointed Amir Mengeser Noyon with a body of other experienced *amirs* to investigate into the affairs and claims of the people to impart justice. Bulghai Aqa by reason of his past services was commanded to be the chief and leader of the scribes and to be their *wazir*. Like a chamberlain he was to announce the petition of each applicant and to attend to it and it was he who had to draft and to note (*navisad va savad kunad*) the decrees (*amsila*) and mandates. Amir Bulghai was to be assisted in this task by associates appointed by Qaan, e.g. the Moslem Bitikchis, Amir Imad-ul Mulk who had occupied this position at the courts of Ogedei and Guyuk and Amir Fakhr-ul Mulk who had precedence over other officials of the court on account of the length of service together with some other Mongols. To each of them, he assigned a separate task on which after consulting and obtaining the permission of the Amir Bulghai they were to refer their reports to the knot resolving counsel of the Qaan. As for the affairs of the *diwan* such as the assessment of taxes and the conferment of appointments, these are the concern of the Amir Bulghai in conjunction with one or two other persons.[52]

After the Mongols, Timur, the son of an ordinary chieftain of Barlas tribe managed to wrest the sceptre and crown of Central Asia in 1370 after long years of experimentation as a king maker.[53] To establish his sway over the Mongolian Empire, Timur had to contend not only with his rival kinsmen of Turco-Mongol tribes but with a variety of forces eager to overthrow the Mongol regime. They included the displaced members of the former ruling dynasties associated with the Mongol regime by a system of tax farming, a strong religious group of divines (*khwajagan* and *sadát*) well entrenched in Central Asia and actively involved in politics, a militant class of tribal chiefs, a powerful Turco-Mongolian nobility frequently indulging in making and deposing of Khans, a strong merchant class, not only monopolizing the trade but also serving as the financial agents of the Mongolian ruling power and the 'insurgent' revolutionary groups of the *sarbadars*. Such a large number of opponents had emerged under the later Mongol rulers, due to the indifference of the officers of the Mongols to the task of administration which had converted Central Asia into a congeries of state where each 'noble or noyon aspired for kingship and each person possessing a sword became ambitious'.[54] The racial rivalries and clannish prejudices[55] further divided the heterogeneous population of Turks, Mongols, Tajiks, Arabs and others. The complex social structure both facilitated and complicated the task of Timur.

Timur felt the pulse and need of the time for a strong centralized Empire, suppression of Turco-Mongol tribal population particularly Barlas, Sulduz, Jalair, etc., forestalling the growth and development of strong and stable governments in Golden and White Hordes. The state authority of Golden Horde were in the hands of Mongolian nomadic aristocracy from Juji's dynasty operating on military strength, exploiting rich agricultural and cultured regions of Bulgaria, Crimea, and northern Caucasus. The military resources of Golden Horde were very high hence Timur acquired immense booty and captives in his first two invasions. Timur had definite plans to blow up the economic and particularly commercial life of cultured regions of Golden Horde. The task was facilitated due to civil wars when even the military commanders declared independence and twenty-five Khans were deposed within twenty years (1360-80).

Timur moved in a calculated manner quite confident of his success and issuing tokens to those who had helped him during his earlier days, promising them an ample reward as soon as he attained power.[56]

From the very beginning of his career, Timur had been associated with the intrigues of the upper aristocracy and tribal leaders and naturally knew the antidote of any poisonous crisis. In the first place, he strengthened his position by establishing matrimonial relations. In all, he had eighteen wives, two Mughal princesses, two *khatai* (Chinese) and the rest belonging to various other tribes, like Qunghrat Taijut, Dughlat and others.[57] But these much emphasized 'matrimonial alliances were also used by Timur simply as stepping stone and not as a permanent standby for he removed and eliminated all softer bonds soon after extracting the maximum benefits without even a sightest consideration for kinship. Timur tried to open friendship with the leaders of *sarbadars* and sought the help of religious divines'.[58] Since the Mongols formed the bulk of his forces, Timur ensured their support by keeping a puppet Khan on the throne. Ibn-i Arab says that 'the Turks forsooth have tribes and a race like the Arab tribes' and that Timur was one of the four *wazirs* with whom lied the hinge of evil and good since they were the eyes of the kingdoms and by their advice affairs were directed and each of these *wazirs* was to his own tribe a tall wick for the lamp of its counsels in the houses of its habitation.[59] Those four tribes namely Arlat, Jalair, Qauchin and Barlas who were already firmly rooted in Central Asia gave wholehearted support to Timur. Being a good general and an unscrupulous diplomat,[60] Timur conquered and collected wealth but he remembered to kill the kings, for they held 'Sultanates by continuous succession', due to which Timur's kingdom 'would lack a solid foundation'.[61] Like the Ottomans, Timur also preferred to shift the paraphernalia and tribal population, even saints, from the conquered places to prevent the growth of rival centres of power and influence.[62]

Once he had attained power, Timur asserted in one of his letters to Bayazid, 'I am the soldier of Allah, created out of his wrath, to whom dominion is entrusted against those who merit His wrath',[63] and consequently he informed the governor of Haleb 'that all men were subject to his rule and that the one whom he appointed was Khalifa and Imam; that it was fitting that he himself should be the ruler whom all other kings of the world should serve and obey'.[64]

The words amply express Timur's jealousy of power and his desire for conquest. In fact Timur's expansionist policy was dictated by the constant need for booty and an ambition for occupying all trade routes and agricultural zones. Obviously, the state which he built had to be military oriented. Unlike some Chingizide, however, he wanted not only to conquer but to govern and, therefore, administration of the state was as much a part of his ambitious scheme as the desire for conquest. A well-developed administrative machinery had existed in Central Asia earlier but the disintegration which followed the unsuccessful reign of later Mongols had obliterated every sign of it. Timur, therefore, had a difficult task to perform but he did it in a way that his dynasty could rule over the empire for a century more.

A fourteenth century traveller, Al Hasan, the Arab, says that Timur had prepared a code of laws for administration which, however, had not reached us.

From the very beginning Timur involved himself into Central Asian politics and administration with Amir Husain, concentrated upon internal affairs of the state, emphasized his patriotism which sustained him to face the foreigners (Mongols).[65]

Timur possessed the required stature, necessary vision and knew the art of reconciling diverse interests and factions and of negotiating his way out of a deadlock. In the politically fragmented region of Transoxiana, therefore, he easily acquired success. The highly developed superstructure of Timur's Empire was Mongolian in inspiration with a substratum of local traditions and Islamic practices. Timur's Turkish steppe background was neither overshadowed by Mongolian influence nor blurred by the impact of Perso-Islamic milieu. It is a well known fact that in Timur's Empire, Yasaq or the rules of Chingiz co existed with *sharia* and that Timur frequently used them alternately in accordance with his political needs.[66]

It had also been emphasized that the 'Principles enshrined in *tura* were more akin to Timur's personal ideology. It was natural for a despot like him who had a close cathexis with Chingiz to adopt his institutions.'

Timur's deep faith in Tura obviously was a result of his appreciation of Chingiz's statesmanship and his own ambitious plans for power. In his times, *tura* was dominant in many spheres. But the simultaneous existence of sharia cannot be denied. It should be noted here that Timur had simultaneously used both—(*sharia* and *tura*) alternately in accordance with the exigencies of the situation. This explains why Haider Dughlat had occasionally complained that 'the old customs and rights had fallen into disuse.[67] The words of Ibn-i Arab Shah prove beyond doubt the considerable influence of *tura* in Timur's Empire.

Ibn-i Arab says: 'He (Timur) clung to the laws of Chingiz Khan, which are like branches of law from the faith of Islam, and he observed them in preference to the law of Islam. Thus it is also with all the Chaghatais, the people of Dasht, Cathay, Turkestan, all which infidels observe the laws of Chingiz Khan rather than the laws of Islam and accordingly our Maulana Hafizuddin Bazazi and Maulana Saiyyidana Alauddin Mahomed Bukhari and other doctors and banners and leaders of Islam have given an answer to all, that Timur must be accounted an infidel and those also who prefer the laws of Chingiz Khan to the faith of Islam and also for other reasons . . .'.[68] Incidentally the same author had elsewhere commented that Timur was united with the Mongols due to 'double reason': first race, affinity and proximity, second, their religion which is called the law of Chingiz Khan which was spread through both states.[69] A completely different picture of Timur emerges from Yazdi's account where he is depicted as an extremely God fearing deeply religious and righteous sovereign.

Timur took personal and direct interest in administration. Even petty officers had to maintain direct contact and fulfil military and financial obligation.

There did, however, exist certain limitations which the *sharia* laws *tura* or *urf o ada* tradition imposed on the despotism of the king, for example in matters of personal law and judicial process.

The Timurid State, unlike the Ottoman Empire, was fully 'Asiatic'[70] in character and not a theocratic state. In consonance with the prevalent traditions in other Islamic states, the Timurid Empire also followed not only the *sharia* laws but the will of the sovereign and the local unwritten regulations based on traditional customs (*urf o ada*) as well. The *urf o ada* (longstanding conventions) differed in varying degrees from region to region and served as a powerful, extra-canonical but unchangeable and unwritten code of laws.[71]

Apparently there does not seems to be 'a consistent and uniform system', and no mandates clearly defining the responsibilities of various officers seem to exist, enabling the absolute despot to interfere into the affairs arbitrarily. A closer study of various sources, however, reveals that Timur had well-defined regulations for every occasion though flouting them himself whenever the exigencies of situation so demanded.

Timur's theory of sovereignty and views about methods of administration are well reflected through the comments given in various sources including his *Malfuzat-i Timuri*. Timur's gradual rise to power was quite in conformity with the existing socio-political milieu, for sovereignty in medieval times was not always an extensively hereditary privilege. In *Siyasatnama,* Tusi sums up the situation well when he describes how God designated certain outstanding men to be kings, and that practically 'kingship could be acquired through military force, political shrewdness or merely through favourable circumstances'. In fact most of the founders of Islamic dynasties of middle ages originally belonged to humble origins. The subsequent preparation of imaginary exalted geneologies was also common. Any ambitious conqueror and an excellent warrior could rally round himself innumerable plunder seeking needy desperadoes, by guaranteeing for them a share in the booty—an important if not the only source of income in this region. Such self-made sovereigns having no hereditary dynastic claims to the throne were depicted by the contemporary historians as the rightful heir to the throne by virtue of their being the 'defenders of faith, uplifters of religion and protectors of downtrodden' and so on. Yazdi has also tried to glorify Timur as the one with divine status. A general code of rules known as *Tuzukat-i Timuri,* purportedly written by Timur and considered as unauthentic notwithstanding its verifiable and by and large reliable facts, attributes to Timur the following saying that '*din wa Ain-i Islam, Tura and Tuzuk*[72] served as four pillars of a stable government'. A great stickler of law, Timur often stressed the importance of good administration. Ibn-i Arab Shah refers to a speech delivered by Timur at Siwas in which he expressed his views regarding management of a country; necessity of a competent and wise ruler, laws and statutes for the assembly; an Imam for guidance; arrangement of whole society in suitable orders by assigning to each his place of obedience; suitable appointments, justice, unity and harmony among *amirs*.[73] Despite these assertions, Timur, protected his absolute authority. *Tuzukat* adds:

> Therefore it is requisite that the king be not so guided by the conduct of the counsels of others as to make them his associates in his regal authority for although he be obliged to hear good advice from all yet he must not to that

degree attend unto them, as to enable them by their measures their counsels to become his equals, in the end his superior, in the concerns of his government.[74] . . . must not trust the concerns of his government, to other, not deliver over the reins of his authority into the hands of a servant—as it may soon come to pass that the powerful servant shall aspire to regal dignity—seat himself on the throne of his master[75]—nor should he associate any one with him in the administration of his authority.[76]

Timur further asserted that: 'by regulations and by order I so secured my regal authority, that *wazirs*, soldiers, labourers, servants, officers, each one of them being restricted to their proper stations attend with due submission thy command restrain every people tribe under thy dominion within their proper hints failing which there will be corruption, irregularity, disruption.[77]

Timur's one man rule was supported by a galaxy of submissive but competent officers of varied brands. According to the institutes found in *Tuzukat* 12 classes formed the superstructure of Timur's government, namely, (1) theologians, doctors of law, holymen (2) wisemen, *ashab-i kangash*, experienced old men for wise counsel, (3) *orbab-i dua* for imploring their prayers, (4) *amirs*, chiefs commander, (5) soldiers, subjects, treated with dignity and attention and the *ketkhuda* and 'I kept my troops in a state of readiness . . . advanced to them their wages even before it was due. Thus in my expedition against Rum, I gave unto my soldiers seven years wages; part thereof due to the remainder in advance. Such was the discipline established among my troops that the one was never injured or oppressed by the other—and my soldiers of every rank I confined in such sort to their several stations that they could not sit beyond the limits prescribed to them', (6) choicest, wisest and prudent for consultations, (7) *wazirs*, secretary, scribes who kept treasury rich, secured plenty and prosperity to my soldiers, to my subjects, kept in order revenues and expenses of government (8) men learned in medicine, art of healing; astrologers, geometricians, (9) historians, theologians, experts in hadis to hear lives of prophets, patriarchs, history of ancient princes to get knowledge and experience, (10) *Mashaikh*, sufis, arifs for learning word of God, (11) I brought into my place artificers of every sort of denomination and I admitted them into my camp; that both at home and abroad they might supply and keep in readiness the necessaries required for my soldiers (There existed royal workshops about which Clavijo speaks at length.) (12) To travellers and voyagers of every country I gave encouragement that they might communicate unto me the intelligence and transactions of the surrounding nations and appointed merchants, chiefs of caravans, to travel to every kingdom so that they might bring unto me all sorts of valuable merchandize and rare curiosities. That they might give me information of the situations, manners, customs of natives, conduct of princes.[78] Theologians learned in the laws to be respected, their desires fulfilled, 'the soldiers and the genuine descendants of a soldier resolute and brave of whatever tribe or horde he might be, I ordered to be enrolled in the number of my forces to be promoted in proportion to his conduct behaviour pardoned first time before tribunal but that for second and third crimes he should meet with punishment adequate to his offence'.[79]

Elsewhere, Timur emphasizes his choice of officers and style of administration:

> I chose from distinguished ones to whom I give full authority over the moslems. In his hand was the administration of the possessions of churches; he appointed the mulla, decided who in the laws and villages should become mufti, decreed who should be the chief of market, men who control weights measures, see to the supply of necessities of life, determined appointment prebends of saiyids or priests or other persons of merit. This was more than the autonomy of church, surrender of whole public life to spiritual persons. Thence forward, priestly caste stood as one man behind Timur—every mulla, every dervish, a whole hearted adherent a trustworthy experienced spy. Thus did the great calculator establish his realm upon two different mutually hostile elements of population and upon two conflicting law books. He divides the society into 12 classes—highest not generals or ministers but *saiyids*, *shaikhs* and *ulama* but in the domain of army and nomadic tribes only the *yasak* held sway. Timur actually appointed a special judge to regulate disputes between the soldiers and other subjects.[80]

Timur had a cosmopolitan outlook. Prawdin says that he surrounded himself with luxury of Iran but never adopted any of the customary Islamic appellations of the sovereign as protector of faith, etc., though he changed his titles as Empire expanded, he 'remained all the time a true follower of Yasak' though assumed the title of sultan but never that of khan. His successors, biographers tried to make out Timur as a Muslim zealot, a fanatic but most of his campaigns against were fought orthodox Muslim states, his attitude towards Islam was that of Mongol tolerance and indifference though he posed as protector of Islam. Visits to shrines, building of mosques, 'may have been mere policy—the governmental act of a man who was animated by the loftiest ambition possible to an Asiatic sovereign that of reconstituting the empire of Chingiz to be a new Muslim Chingiz Khan'.[81]

Undoubtedly Timur survived to see the metamorphosis of socio-religious scenario of Central Asia in early fifteenth century. In an atmosphere where 'sunni clergy was especially influential, the wide jurisdiction of the religious institution ensured a check on many activities of the state in its various domains. Bukhara became an important centre for sufis and mystics. After the fall of Samanids, they assumed the political as well as the social leadership of the life in the city—the thinking organised into an institution which paralleled the civil government.'[82]

In his letter to the Chinese Emperor, Dai Ming, Shahrukh emphasized that from the time of Ghazan, Uljaitu and Abu Said up to Timur, the Islamic *sharia* was acted upon and men of religion were given an important place. Now that the countries of Khurasan, Transoxiana and Iraq had come down to us the orders throughout the 'country go in accordance with *sharia*, prohibiting the unlawful'. Now the *yarghu* and *qawaidi Chingiz khani* are completely exterminated (*murtafa*).[83] Ibn-i Arab Shah recorded that 'Shahrukh repealed the laws and customs of Chingiz Khan and ordained that they should make his rule flow along the streams of the laws of Islam, but this I do not consider true, since it is considered among them as the purest religion and true faith'.[84] Bahamad Khan also says that Chingiz's book served as a guide to many of the sultans and even Amir Timur kept it safely preserved in the treasury though he did not act upon it; Shahrukh who happened to be the son of justice and faith burnt that book, which was a stock of torment, reducing it to ashes. All the evil customs of Chingiz Khan were given up.[85] Similarly, Abdurrazzaq stresses that since his coronation Shahrukh had done his best to promote religion, abide by the rules of Islam and *sharia*.[86] Elsewhere the same chronicler states that in 907, the *amirs* had advised Mirza Pir Muhammad to bring about a *manshur* from the Abbasid caliphs of Egypt and transform the Moghul *yasaq* (*taghyir-i yasaq-i moghul*).[87] Contradictory information is given by Haider Dughlat. On the one hand, he speaks of 'many of the Moghul *amirs* and notables who were very aged, older indeed than any one else at that time in the Moghul *ulus*, upon all matters such as the *tura* and the *tuzuk* they were consulted and reliance was placed in their discretion and judgement in all important consultations and councils'.[88] On the other, he says, that Mirza Ulugh Beg once asked Amir Khudaidad who knew much about the *tura* of Chingiz to tell him all the regulations. The Amir replied, 'we have completely discarded the infamous *tura* of Chingiz Khan, and have adopted the *shariat*. If, however, sense and good judgement approves the *tura* of Chingiz Khan, I will teach it to him that he may adopt it and forsake the *shariat*.'[89] The Mirza was much perturbed at these words and did not learn the *tura*.[90]

Not only Babur mentions this fact at length saying, 'our forefathers through a long span of time had respected the Chingizi *tura*, doing nothing opposed to it, whether in assembly or in court—though it has no divine authority, still good rules of conduct must be obeyed by whomsoever they are left; just in the same way that if a forefather has done ill, his ill must be changed for good.[91] But the repeated references to *tura* in various context in all the Timurid sources even in India conclusively proves its perpetual application to—certain matters.

Although not only Timur is said to have formed a code of laws, even Sultan Mahmud Mirza is credited with having prepared new rules and regulations of administration the details of such measures are not set out in our sources. It is, therefore, not possible to say categorically whether a formal body of legislation also existed. Probably the kings had at various times enforced certain rules (*yasaq*) to suit their needs without in any way affecting the basic structure which continued to have elements of Turkish institutions with a tinge of Mongolian custom. If Abdurrazzaq is to be trusted, Shahrukh decided in 1417-18 that the system of administration as given in the *Siyasatnama* of Nizam-ul Mulk Tusi and as recorded in Siyaq by Asif should be adopted by his *wazir*[92] as giving the ideal model for administration. In some of his *farmans*, Shahrukh emphasized that there should not be any deviation from the established laws (*qanun-i mahud*). In a different context, however, Sultan Husain is said to have emphasized that it was not binding upon the officers (*bandagan-i diwan-i aala*) of *diwan-i aala* to follow the former Sultans in every matter (*jami 'umur*). Instead the propriety demands that in the sphere of education and training of the experienced servants, innovations should be introduced in accordance with the nature of the authority.[93] Nevertheless, the *tura* seems to have lingered like the Ottoman *kanuni tashrifat*.[94]

The Central Asian rulers enjoyed the title of *Zilullah* (shadow of God), *Imamuzzaman* (Imam of the age), *Khalifat-ur Rahman* (viceregent of God) and *Alkhaqan-al adl* (the just sovereign) and such other titles unlike the Mongol khans who, according to *yasa* preferred their names without lofty titles.[95]

Yazdi described Timur as the 'manifestation of the vestiges of the omnipotence of the old Dignity (*mazhar-i asar-i qadiri qudrat-i qadim*)'.[96]

The ceremonies of the coronation of the *khaqan* were known as *khan kutardilar* (the raising of khan which remained unchanged throughout the thirteenth to fifteenth centuries. A detailed description of the ceremony is available in the accounts of foreign travellers. Babur also mentions it in his memoir.[97]

In this ceremony, the khan was placed on a raised *tushuk* of white felt; all four corners of the felt were held by the military and tribal chiefs, *mullas* and the nobles; and the khan was lifted above the ground. During this ceremony, the khan was supposed to take an oath that he would discharge his functions honestly and properly; that he would rule with justice and dignity, and would also treat the dignitaries of the state in a befitting manner. The nobles in turn promised unquestioning loyalty which were to serve as a sword. After this the treasures were shown to the khan and the distribution of rewards followed.[98]

In accordance with Timurid custom the Sultans sat on a raised cushion (*tushuk*)[99] even in the court. The nobles dismounted some way off. On approaching the king, one had to kneel three times.[100] In return the king often rose to do honour to important dignitaries. Both looked one another in the eyes.[101] Before departure and even while asking after the king's welfare, offering of presents, tributes, etc., by the nobles who had to kneel thrice[102] continued.

The king was indeed despotic and in accordance with Turkish traditions the pivot around whom the entire administrative structure revolved. Babur says that Baqi Beg urged him again and again that two chiefs in one army are a source of fraction and disorder—a foundation of dissensions or ruin for they have said 'ten dervishes can sleep under one blanket but two kings cannot find room in one clime'.[103] Like the Ottoman Janissaries and Saljuqid Mamluks, the Timurid nobility and religious groups played an effective role in the selection of the ruler. But their position in the ruling hierarchy depended entirely upon the personal qualities of the khan. A strong ruler could subdue the nobility as much as a weak ruler could be cowed down by the same nobility.

The Timurid king supervised the civil and military affairs, assigned provinces to princes and the nobles, distributed land grants, issued administrative orders, appointed officers, exercised control over finances, made arrangements for the development of agriculture and economy, led the army in the battlefield, supervised the administration through regular tours[104] and personally planned the disposition of military.

The *qurultai* was organized by Chingiz on every important occasion. Timur also followed in the footsteps of Chingiz. He had a diplomatic way of tackling such assemblies. Ibn-i Arab Shah says that when Timur summoned a *kangash* none dared to avoid. Freedom of speech was granted and views were expressed. But Timur did not accept any of them till the one in his mind was suggested by someone and which he immediately accepted and after discussing it with his sincere associates, he closed the discussion.[105]

The consultative assembly (*majlis-i mashwarat, janqi, qurultai*) had been an important integral part of nomadic administrative structure, also. But the Timurid historians like Yazdi, Abdurrazzaq and others, sensing probably the pulse of the time always stressed that these assemblies were in pursuance of the Islamic principles of *nass shura*[106] and *ijma*.

These assemblies were held both at the centre and in the provinces.[107]

In the *qurultai* or *janqi* the participants comprised the princes, *noyon-i buzurg, amirs* of Tumanat and Hazarjat, *arkan-i daulat* and *ayan-i hazarat.*[108]

The attendance in the *qurultai* was a clear acknowledgement of a noble's obedience, allegiance and submission. Such nobles who wanted to raise the standard of rebellion or even intended to shake off the yoke of subordination usually abstained from such *qurultais.*[109] Timur himself emphasized the need for *janqi* and regularly held such assemblies particularly on all important occasions.

Usually Timur followed the dictates of his own will[110] and never acted upon his nobles' decisions. Several examples go to prove that *kurultai* or *janqi* had become a hoax under Timur who outwitted the participants easily. Either he planted one of his own mouthpiece in the assembly or divined in the holy book and interpreted it in his own favour the text from the Koran.[111] In both the cases decisions were to suit his convenience. The significance of consultative assembly and a regular session of such meetings had been recommended for all statesmen.

Like Chingiz, Timur and his semi-nomadic followers were scornful towards the toiling peasantry but realized the benefits of a settled economy for purposes of revenue. Timur was especially interested in urban and agrarian development. It was in fact Timur's ability to reconcile two contradictory elements satisfying each of them but allowing them to retain their identity. Nevertheless whenever conflict arose, the interests of the Chaghatai nomads were always upheld. Under the Timurids also the hierarchy even in camp courts was strictly maintained. Babur's description of Badiuz Zaman's camp court in 1506 refers to the four *divans* (*tashuks*) placed in the tent. On one of *divans* sat both Badiuz Zaman and Muzaffar Husain—since both were rulers; the *tur* (right hand place of honour was given to Babur and Abul Muhsin and the left side *tushuk* was occupied by Ibn-i Husain and Qasim Sultan Uzbeg. To Babur's right and below his *divan* sat Jahangir Mirza and Abdurrazzaq. To the left of Qasim Sultan and Ibn-i Husain Mirza—'but a good deal lower' sat Muhammad Burunduq Beg, Zulnun Beg and Qasim Beg.[112]

Undoubtedly the empire was divided into *wilayats* (provinces), *buluks* (districts) *tumans qasba* (small subdivisions) and then into *mauza*, *deh* or *qariay* (village).[113] In the fifteenth century Farghana is said to have seven separate *buluks*, namely, Andijan, Aush, Marghainan, Isfara, Khujand, Akhsi and Kashan besides nine *tumans*.[114] Samarqand had seven *tuamans* like *sughd* and *shavdar* besides a number of districts like Bukhara, Kesh Khuzar, Karamina and Qarakul. Asfara has elsewhere been described as a *wilayat* having four *buluks* namely Asfara, Wurukh, Sukh and Hushyar.[115]

But the Central control over the units was both firm and direct. Sometimes the *ayalat* of a place was twice assigned to the same person.[116] Sub-assignments were often done by the emperor himself.[117] But the sub-assignment by the provincial ruler was also not rare as in 853.[118] The provincial *walis* (rulers) were appointed by the ruler along with a *nawab* who was given the charge of entire administrative responsibilities of the state (*zimanm-i hal o aqd o qabz o bist*). A selected group of reliable *amirs* and an army accompanied the *wali*.[119] An *ataliq* was also appointed by the king. In case of the death of an *ataliq*, the next *ataliq* was appointed by the emperor himself. [120] The officials in the Centre and provinces were nominated by the emperor. The relationship between ruler and the other brothers installed as provincial governors was emphasized as that of an *aqa o aini*,[121] the sub-assignments were done even by the weak ruler himself as happened in 858. Abul Qasim Babur assigned Balkh as *suyurghal* to Amir Hisamuddin Shaikh Haji, *wilayat* of San and Charik to Amir Ali Farsi Barlas, Andkhud to Amir Shaikh Zulnun and Amir Ahmad Mushtaqi, Shibarghanto Amir Baba Kukultash, and Qunduz and Baghlan to Pir Sultan.[122]

Shahrukh had inherited from father hostile surrounding regions and territories once ruthlessly devastated by Timur and now burning with a desire of overthrowing enemies and inflicting vendetta. A competing son Ulugh Beg too was very ambitious. The very fact that two blocks of power with their centres in Herat and Samarqand existed under two powerful entities betrays the diametrically opposite local traditions and views not only of the rulers but of the ruled as well. Khalil Sultan also claims to have maintained a 'well-ordered' state and that 'the laws of the kingdom continued according to received custom'.[123]

Even an insignificant ruler like Sultan Mahmud, has been highly praised by Babur for his 'administrative capabilities' that 'the pay of his servants was never disallowed, his assemblies, his gifts, his open tables were all good—everything of his was orderly and well arranged; no soldier or peasant could deviate in the slightest from any plan of his'.[124]

During the emperor's inspection tours, the *toi* was arranged and *tuquz* was offered by the rulers, nobles, officers and others. After celebrations and festivities, the affairs of administration were discussed.[125] The close contact with the commoners either during such inspection tours or during the tour of the city on a *takht-i rawan*, was also preferred. Sometimes such ventures could be hazardous. In complete disregard of politics of kings and ways of sultans, Shahrukh had neither forbidden the common people passing through the streets while moving the royal cavalcade was on the move nor did he refuse to entertain petitioners of justice approach him while on the street. Ahmad Lur who had made an attempt on his (Shahrukh's) life had come closer to him on this very pretext.[126] During Sultan Abu Said's regime however, such administrative tours were effective and enquiry often produced results. The *mubashshirs* from all over the region came to inform the Khan about the affairs of administration. During the sultan's tour of Mazandaran in 866, it was brought to his notice that the Ummal of the *amal* of *qasba* Kosoya had acquired the *amwal-i diwani* in excess. It was ordered that the surplus should be returned to the *raiyyat* immediately from the treasury.[127] In the same way matters were settled in other parts of the Empire also.[128]

While Chingiz Khan had nominated his own successor, he had, however, emphasized that anyone from amongst his sons and grandsons could succeed him provided that such a person was 'worthy of this trust'.[129] Chingiz had selected his third son Ogedei not because of his valour or capacity to fight or organize but because of his 'amiable nature'.[130] Ibn-i Khaldun too stressed that 'Good rulership was equivalent to mildness—a ruler is he who has subjects and subjects are persons who have a ruler'.[131] According to Al Hasan Arabi, Timur had declared that if the prince 'be not born for to be strong in arms, he will not be an effeminate prince that shall preserve the Parthian Empire'.[132] The nomination of the khan was not always respected but the worth of a person always enabled him to contrive his own enthronement. In the absence of a worthy person and an acceptable nomination, certain king-makers raised their own candidate to the *khaqanship*. As worth happened to be the main criterion for accession, aspirations of many energetic and enterprising princes were raised and excited. Consequently civil wars, patricide, fratricide and rebellion were not a rare phenomenon either in Central Asia or in Mughal India. In accordance with the old Turkish traditions, the khanship was not reserved for the sons of the khan only.[133] With the extension of the opportunity to the grandsons and the uncles of the khan,[134] the number of aspirants became very large. Either worth or even popular support could decide the issue of succession.

The Timurid regime is, therefore, characterized generally by civil wars and rebellions. In the absence of any definite custom of succession, either the nomination by the reigning khan or selection of a prince by the nobles decided the matter. In all three situations (i.e. nomination, contrivance and selection), the question of succession had to be formally decided by a *qurultai* which also symbolized an assurance of submission by all the notables. But this does not mean that the Central Asian polity lacked strong solid foundations or Timur's Empire 'tended towards decentralization'.

Timur was brave, a good judge and organizer of men, and not only knew Uzbeg and Tajik languages but was also acquainted simultaneously with nomadic, cattle-breeding life, pastoral economy and agricultural and settled urban life. Similarly, Timur had close contacts with the two diametrically opposite group of *sarbadars*. One comprising militant fighting leaders the other consisting of conciliatory sheikhs, though both having a common aim—the good of people and emancipation from tyrannical Mongol regime.

The name Tamerlang stems from the word *tamar* which in Turkish means iron and true to his name, he was as strong and firm as steel though slightly handicapped hence the term *lang* (lame) was attached to his name. This gallant son of Taragai, son of Abuai, was born in Ilgar village in Kesh. On the night of his birth, strange phenomenon were said to have been seen like: a helmet like object appearing on the sky, flutter in the air; live coals flowing about like glowing ashes; since Timur's palms were full of freshly shed blood, diviners interpreted that he would be a bloodthirsty man, brigand, guardsman or executioner. Both shepherds belonged to a 'mixed horde'.

Timur is described as a fine admixture of wrath and kindness and all his actions have been justified by court historians. Yazdi says that as the 'deputy of God on earth' (Khalifatullah), Timur showed the 'Divine attributes of terror and kindness'—sometimes Timur 'burnt the world' with the 'lightning of his wrath' and sometimes 'lighted a thousands lamps of mercy with his kindness'.[135] Abul Fazl also justifies the terror displayed by Timur 'due to the necessities of conquests', for in his estimation, Timur was inclined towards justice and the promotion of the prosperity of the people and the object of his high ambition was building up of territories which cannot be annexed without punishments and the establishment of prestige.[136] Yazdi says that the tyranny perpetuated in Syria, Rum and Georgia and subsequent massacre, plunder, destruction and enslavement carried 'out of necessity' were the goading factors to lead Timur to holy wars to 'compensate for all these sins'.[137]

Yazdi describes Timur as a perfect man[138] (*kamil-ulzat*), who was 'divinely appointed', 'divinely protected',[139] 'divinely guided', and his tongue was 'divinely inspired'.[140] Timur is called a 'manifestation of the signs of audacity of archaic omnipotent' God (*mazhar-i asar-i qudrat-i qadiri qadim*).[141] Timur's principle '*Rasti rusti*' (Truth is deliverance) was also emphasized not only during his lifetime as it was inscribed on his palace gate in Shahr-i Sabz and on his coins but after his death by the chroniclers also.[142] He was 'distinguished amongst all contemporary rulers in strengthening of the religion and promoting Islam'.[143]

The Persian historians like Hafiz Abru, Yazdi not only call Timur a *dindar* (pious, religious) but claims that: Timur removed the rust of *bidat* (heresy), respected *shara* and held the *ahl-i bait* dear; was devoted to *sadat*, *ulama*, pious, *ahl-i dastar,* muftis, recluses, saints;[144] visited the holy tombs and gave away charities, spent his time in prayers *(nawafil, tilawat-i Quran)* instead of pleasure seeking,[145] offered prayers before every campaign, regularly attended Friday prayers in congregations, observing *roza* (fasting).[146] Timur is presented as the one engrossed in the elevation of the signs of faith and Sharia rules under whose reign Islam was so exalted that nowhere a hundredth part of it was visible. Even a twentieth century traveller Polovtsoff calls Timur as 'half human half divine' Timur was given the title of '*Mujaddad o murawwujdin*'.[147]

Other Timurid historians also attribute to Timur the desirable qualities in a leader of their age, e.g. of being a God fearing man, respecting sadats, learned men, saints, and spreading and maintaining laws of Islam, protecting and providing for the poor students.[148]

Yazdi goes to the extent of attributing holy war to Timur against India and China which is hardly in consistency with the accounts of and even with Timur's own attitude.

Even a hostile chronicler like Ibn-i Arab Shah showers admiration on Timur for his 'strength, love, diligence, firmness of purpose, truthfulness of knowledge, courage, fearlessness and wonderful nature'. The inscription of his seal was '*Rasti rusti*', i.e. Truth is safety and for a brand on his beasts and centremark on his coins[149] he used three rings placed in this way. Although Timur did not know the Arabic language at all and had just sufficient knowledge of Persian, Turkish and Mongol, he was an avid listener and reader of annals and histories of the Prophets[150] and had a very sharp memory. Timur had his own curious and strange ways to keep in touch with the neighbouing countries. His informers and spies appointed abroad included *amirs*, *fakirs* at Damascus among the sufis in the college of Shamisatia or traders seeking a living by some craft, illminded wrestlers, criminal, athletes, hermits, physicians, sailors, singers and even crafty old women.[151] Similarly, Timur excelled in various arts of leading others into error.[152]

Apart from the fact that in Transoxiana, the population of agricultural zones and cities craved for unification, stability and security, Timur himself realized the advantages of trade, urban development, occupation of world caravans routes.

In fact, Timur's expansionist policy was dictated by the constant need for booty and an ambition for occupying all trade routes and agricultural zones. Obviously, the state which he built had to be military in its orientation. Unlike nomadic rulers, however, he wanted not only to conquer but also to govern. A well-developed administrative machinery had existed in Central Asia earlier but the disintegration which followed the unsuccessful reign of later Mongols had obliterated every sign of it. Timur, therefore, had a difficult task to perform but he did it in a way that his dynasty could rule over the empire for a century more.

A fourteenth century traveller, Al Hasan, an Arab, says that Timur had prepared a code of laws for administration which, however, has not reached us. Ibn-i Arab, however, refers to a speech of Timur delivered at Siwas to a general assembly containing his general views.[153]

The dominant groups in Timur's Empire, were no more than pawns on a chessboard whom he cleverly moved in order to win the game. The ruling classes in Timur's Empire comprised three groups of upper, middle and lower strata:

(a) Members of the ruling family, the upper aristocracy at the centre consisting of nobles and high officials, the *noyons*, the religious groups of *khwajagan* and *sadat*.
(b) The middle strata consisted of provincial aristocracy with nobles, officers and landed proprietors.
(c) The third group of lower aristocracy consisting of *rais*, *dehdars* (chiefs of villages) and petty officials. A landholding class also existed in lower aristocracy.

The hierarchy was always emphasized and everywhere maintained religiously. In military array, in court, in festive ceremonies, each man knew his place and position for any change (deliberately or inadvertently) could have disastrous consequences.[154]

Although a large number of officers were appointed by Timur, a system of checks and balances existed at all levels. Manz nicely sums up the situation when she says that Timur 'was more eager to prevent independent action than to use his men efficiently' and that 'he controlled his subordinates not by fitting them into defined places within a system but by a series of shifts and combinations which prevented them from gaining too secure a foothold'.[155] Accordingly, a campaign was led by a group and not by an individual to avoid the bestowing of laurels upon one. Timur changed his *naibs* (deputies) in Samarqand everytime he was out. This 'impermanence of appointments' was deliberate. So was the 'evenhanded attitude' of Timur towards his sons and grandsons.[156]

In the upper aristocracy the highest officer in civil affairs was the Prime Minister known as *diwan-i aala* or *wazir*. Apparently the two posts were synonymous, and the distinction between the *diwan* and *wazir* existing in the Ottoman Empire was not always found in Timur's domain. Each *diwan-i aala* or *wazir* had a number of *diwans, ahl-i diwans* or *sahib-i diwans, mubashir, zabitan, bitakchi, navisandagan, muhassils* and others to help him.

Ibn-i Arab Shah refers to a number of officials involved in Timur's administration like the *diwans*, the *munshi* (secretary), the chief *sadr*, judges, *qazis*, and the commander-in-chief of the army. Among his *khassan-i dargah,* Arab Shah mentions the names of Sulaiman Shah Qumari, Saifuddin Allahadad, Shah Malik, Shaikh Nuruddin.[157] In Samarqand, however, Ali Sher, the *naib* was held in high esteem by Timur who consulted him in all affairs and preferred his advice on others.[158]

The entire empire was divided into provinces assigned to the members of the ruling family. The chief units of the empire were *wilayat, buluk* (districts), *mauza, qariya* (*deh* or village).[159] The rulers or mayors of the cities were called *naiban-i shahr*.[160] The headman of the town was called *rais* and that of village a *dehdar*.[161]

The *wilayats* were called *suyurghals* though they were hardly different from the military grants (*iqta*) of the Turks. The first reference to *suyurghal* in the sense of *iqta* is found in the state of Jalairs in the second half of the fifteenth century. [162] The *yirlighs* with royal seal *altamgha* were issued at the time of assignment to the princes. An *ataliq*, *nawab* or deputy of the king was nominated 'to look after and supervise the big and small administrative affairs of the province'. An army and a group of *umra-i uzzam* also were appointed to assist the prince and his *nawab* in arranging the affairs.[163] This delegation of power by Timur to his sons and nobles was to solve administrative problems, to ensure a regular *mal o kharaj* to treasury and to facilitate the maintenance of a regular army. Barthold says that the princes were more powerful than the *ataliqs* or nawabs as the latter could not assert much because the army was controlled by the prince.[164] Manz, however, believes that though princes had a small personal army, they did not have command over all the troops levied in their provinces.[165] A study of the sources reveals that *suyurghal* holders were fully controlled by the centre, since their appointment was liable to termination at any time.

The big *suyurghals* were assigned only to princes. The towns or smaller *suyurghals* could be assigned to the nobles also by Timur personally.[166] In all the big and small *suyurghals,* both civil and military officers were appointed by Timur. His governors had 'elastic powers'.[167] But even the princes were tried, and punished ruthlessly for faults.[168] The nobles were given such *suyurghals* as were usually far away from their native places so as to rule out local influence. The governorship, *niyabat* of a province or town, was transferable.[169] After the death of a governor, his successor, be he a son was appointed by Timur himself.[170]

In addition to the *suyurghal* holder, and *naib*, a *darugha* was also appointed in the provinces for the maintenance of law and order, supervision of public works and for the collection of taxes.[171] Jean Aubin's view that the governor of a province might be called either *hakim* or *darugha*[172] can be true of the rulers of small places only. Since there is no mention of *darugha* in connection with extortion, it seems that they were not directly dealing with finance or collection of revenue. Manz's view that *darugha's* presence in his jurisdiction was not necessary simply because certain officers appointed as *darugha* are later on described as participating in the campaigns of Timur leads to two inferences. First, that the posts were frequently transferred from one person to another and the *darugha's* term might end before his joining the campaign. Secondly, that the *darugha* was the prefect of a town and the commander of the forces and this necessitated his presence in the campaigns.

Arab Shah categorically says that the rulers of the provinces and the governors 'stayed on the thresholds of servitude and slavery'.[173] Promotions were not easily granted.[174] Timur had a network of spies outside and inside the empire.[175] *Suyurghals* were assigned either in lieu of salary or as gift to the nobles but such *inam* grants were few.

It seems that Timur maintained close contact with people by constantly touring his empire meeting the officers and discussing personalities.[176]

Like the *wazirs* in the Ottoman Empire, Timur's *wazirs* were also exposed to severe punishments. We have the example of Ismail who had to beg from people at the palace daily and whatever he acquired was not more than the *kharj-i muhassilan.*[177] Contemporary accounts are full of such examples of deterrent punishments. Calvijo says that Timur's ambassadors and officers were quite a terror for the population, that villagers 'knowing of their arrival forthwith take a flight with all speed as though a devil is after them. Merchants close their shutters taking to flight. As they go they will call out to one another *elchi* for with the arrival of ambassadors they know that a black day is on them ... those men always behave thus ... for they boast that in carrying out the commands of their lord Timur they may press to his service even to kill and any for none may oppose them a marvel to note how throughout the countryside everyone lived in terror of these messengers.'[178]

Clavijo noticed how brutally the 'Tartars' treated the Persian peasants. The guides and various officers from the court sent to meet and conduct the ambassadors everywhere enforced their demands with the whip and a shower of blows.[179] At Ferricor, a large town, Clavijo saw that the inhabitants had run away due to the mistrust of the soldiers of Timur's army and that it was now about 12 days since he and his Tartar hordes had passed through this place where in truth very visibly the troops had wrought much havoc.[180]

Nobility

Temuchin was raised to the throne in the year of the Tiger in the spring of 1206 and given the title of Chingiz Khan by the priest Kokchu Shaman. According to Rashiduddin, the word Chingiz was the plural of Ching which means strong and hard. Chingiz had proved himself to be true to his title. In the same *qurultai* of 1206 Chingiz is credited with setting up a 'white *tauqinuh* paya (standard) having nine feet' symbol of his absolute authority.[181] On a day chosen by the practitioners of the science of *qam* the accession day was determined.[182] The oath of unquestioning loyalty and complete submission was taken by the aristocracy and commoners alike in a *qurultai*. In accordance with the ancient custom of the Mongols, 'they (aristocracy) removed their hats and sling their belt across their backs. One took his right hand, another the left, and by the resolution of aged counsel and support of youthful fortune established him upon the throne. The title (such as *Qaan*, *Khan*) were determined. They also had to give declarations in writing that they would not change his (Chingiz's) word or command and uttered prayers for his welfare. The ruler Chingiz was a representative of God *Ssuto Bogdo,* divinely appointed 'Heaven assisted' and 'powerful'[183] 'Orion-like' princes who girdled the zone of service about loins of affection in the court, enjoyed full control over his nobility whom he could reward or exile, kill or destroy along with their families. Ladies also sat on the left side.[184] In the distribution of treasure which followed *khan kutardilar*, the hierarchy was determined—the first to receive their share were princes and princesses and all present of the race and lineage of Chingiz Khan as his family was Altan Urugh the 'golden family' and in the words of Ibn-i Arab Shah like the 'Qurayesh of the Turks'. Then their servants, attendants nobles and base, greybeard and suckling, then in due order *noyons*, commander of *tuman*, thousands, hundreds and tens—according to the census, the sultans, the maliks, scribes, officials and their dependants.[185] *Elchis* were sent beforehand to every nook and corner to ensure that from the maliks to secretaries all received the edicts of summons.[186] The khan took a cup and all present in and outside the court thrice knelt down and uttered prayers saying 'May the kingdom prosper by his being khan'. All the princes in services and obeisance to Qaan, knelt three times to the sun outside the *ordu* then returning they held an assembly of mirth and sport.[187]

The theory of kingship as propounded by the Mongols for Chingiz and inferred from *The Secret History of the Mongol Dynasty*[188] hints not only to the divine powers but also makes khan all powerful and especially privileged. The passage is being reproduced here: Aitan, Khuchar, Sacha Beki and all of them after consulting together, said to Temujin 'we appoint you as our *khan*. If you will be our *khan*, we will go as vanguard against the multitude of your enemies. All the beautiful girls and married women that we capture and all the fine horses, we will give to you. When hunting is afoot, we will be the first to go to the battle and will give you the wild beasts that we surround and catch. If in times of battle we disobey your orders or in time of peace we act contrary to your interests, part us from our wives and possessions and cast us out into the wilderness' such was the oath they made to serve him. They made him Great Khan with the name Chingiz.[189]

The Mughul regulation permitted only the sovereign to carry his quiver in his own hands and his hunting ground (being reserved) was also a taboo (*qurq*) and if anyone dared to trespass or enter into it he was reduced to slavery, even if the *amir* may be highly placed or the head of his tribe. The *amirs* take seat in the high *diwan* and sit further off and on both sides of him (khan) and are at bow's length away.[190]

Hierarchy was maintained not only in the distribution of treasury after the accession but in any other *qurultai* also. The first to receive their share were the princes and princesses that were present of the race and lineage of Chingiz; also all their servants and attendants, nobles, and base, grey beard and suckling; and then in due order the noyons, the commanders for *tuman*, thousands hundreds and tens, according to the census, the sultans, maliks, scribes, officials, and their dependants.

The Mongols and the Turks however believed in bureaucratic set-up and added much importance to the development, growth and preservation of aristocratic privileges. In the Orkhan inscriptions, therefore, the *begs* have been described as highly placed officers quite in contrast to the 'black people'. Even Manghits are said to have been mighty nobles who could share hardly in sovereign power though they cooperated in taking administrative responsibility.

In Chingiz's Empire the much emphasized and widely criticized institution was that of Tarkhani—a symbol and not proof of privileges of nobility. The term '*tarkhan*' is well known and elaborately explained by the medieval historians. The *Tarkhan Nama* gives its literal meaning as 'blood thirsty' and also offers a technical explanation as 'free (*mutlaq-ul inam*) who does what he pleases, is exempted from service and is forgiven till nine generations from all sins'.[191] The *Tarikh-i Rashidi* refers to the seven ceremonial and other such privileges bestowed upon Urtubu the ancestor of Amir as Tarkhan Khudaidad by Chingiz. These were *tabal* or *nakkara* (drum), *alam* (standard) also called *tuman tugh* (ten thousand standards), two of his servants to wear *qushun tugh* or *chapar tugh*, he might wear the *kur* (girdle, garter or quiver?) in the councils of khan—a privilege exclusively enjoyed by the khans. Several privileges in connection with the khan's hunt were also granted; he was to be an *amir* over all the Mughals and in the *farmans*, his name was to be entered as *sirdar* of the *ulus* of the Mughals. In the presence of the khan, the other *amirs* were to sit at bow's length farther than he from the khan. In addition to these privileges, two more were added later on, that he should have the power of dismissing or appointing *amirs* of Qushuns (100 *amirs* of followers without applying to or consulting with the khan; and the second was that he and his descendants should be permitted to commit nine crimes without being tried. On committing the tenth offence, trial should be conducted under the following conditions: The accused should be set upon a white two-year old horse; under the hoofs of the horse, nine folds of white felt should be placed—as a token of reward and he should in that position address to khan, while the khan should speak to him with elevation. After investigation and when the crimes are proved against him, watch him while his viens were opened and all his blood drawn from his body. Thus he should perish and the two amirs, waiting and lamenting should carry his body out. Haider Dughlat further adds that these privileges were contained in a *farman* issued under the seal of the khan, written in the Mughal language and character and bearing the date and place of the year. Later on three more privileges are described of allowing *tarkhan* to set his seal on all *farmans* with khan's seal above that of his own and certain privileges on the occasion of festivals.[192]

Abul Fazl also gives almost the same details regarding the system of *tarkhani*. According to him, under Timur, 'just rulers exempted some among their servants from certain injunctions and prohibitions and distinguished them by this name. A *tarkhan* of Timur was one whom his ushers (*chawushan*) did not keep out of any place, and from whom and from whose children, no enquiry was made upto the number of nine faults. Abul Fazl further adds that Chingiz had exalted *qishliq* and *bana* to this rank and from his abundant graciousness relieved them from the burden of attendance (*bar-i-farmaish*) and did not exact from them the royal share of booty. He, however, criticized the provision 'about not enquiring until nine faults have been committed, of whatever nature they may be', for 'If far-seeing princes are engaged in testing men and take care that no evil deed be committed by them and if such orders have been issued for the exaltation of some persons then it is something comprehensible. But as for that provision that no enquiry is to be made for nine generations, it would look as if the almighty had given him (khan) the power of knowing the future.'[193]

The privileges thus granted could be hereditary though subject to the renewal by every new khan. According to Haider Dughlat, the privileges granted by Chingiz to the ancestors of Amir Khudaidad were restored only during the reign of Khizr Khwaja when the old customs and rights, which had fallen into disuse or oblivion (under the usurption of Kamruddin and the ascendancy of Amir Timur) were revived. From that time onwards, the privileges descended upon

Amir Khudaidad's successors. Haider Dughlat claims that the seven privileges 'were in force from before the year 625 of the Hijra which is the date of Chingiz Khan, down to the death of the khan and the murder of my uncle, the date of which was 1st of Muharram 940 of the Hajra when the khanship came to Sultan Rashid, the customs of our forefathers were exchanged for other and very different practices'.[194] The privileges of *tarkhani* seem to have continued as not only Babur refers to them but even Abul Ghazi describes such favours.

It can not be denied that Chingiz had often taken special measures to bestow favours upon his most reliable loyalists. Chingiz had given Muqali the high sounding title of *Quiong* (Prince of the Realm) in 614.[195] Privileges were granted to various people in accordance with their loyalties and services[196] to this khan. Baorchu and Muqali who had helped Chingiz in 'attaining' his throne were 'given the opportunity to sit on seats over all others' and they were not to be punished 'into nine transgressions—seed into seed'. Moreover, Muqali and Boorchu were given the honour of governing 10,000 of those to their left and right respectively. Boroyul and Jelme were not 'subject to punishment until nine transgressions.[197] While distributing favours, appointing commanders of ten to ten thousand and bestowing *tarkhani*, Chingiz had concentrated upon 'those who had set up the nation with him and who had suffered with him'. Custom was of sprinkling the standard with mare's milk,[198] drinking of *otog* (wine which was offered in the court on special occasions as a mark of favour,[199] and the offer of *tuquz*.[200] When Amir Bulagi raised Tughlaq Timur to the the throne of the Khanate, there was conferred up on him the right of appointing and dismissing officers upto the rank of one thousand (*hazari*). It was also ordered that no enquiry should be held about (the offences) of his children up to nine generations. When the offences exceeded nine in number an inquiry was to be held. Then when retribution for this was to be inflicted he was to be placed on a two-year old white horse and a white cloth was to be put under the horse's feet. His representation was to be conveyed to the khan by one of the chiefs of the Barlas tribe and the answer by one of the chiefs of Arkiwat tribe. Then his neck vein was opened and the two *amirs* stood on each side and watched until he died. Then he removed him from the presence and buried him with lamentations. When Khizr Khwaja raised Amir Khudaidad to this rank he added three other privileges, i.e. (1) On feast days when all the grandees stood and one *yasawul* of the ruler was on horseback to keep order, the Tarkhan also had a horse. (2) As when in that feast of joy the cup of *qumiz* was held on the khan's right hand so also did a cup bearer hold one on the left hand for the Tarkhan, (3) his seal appeared on the face of the *farmans* but the seal of the king is put at the head of the last line and that of the Tarkhan below that.[201]

For a while Tarkhans had the following privileges, viz. (1) a *tabb* (kettle drum), (2) a *tuman tugh*, (3) *naqqan* (also a drum), (4) a Tarkhan could confer on two of his select servants a *qushun tugh* (the standard of a squadron), (5) he also could carry a *chatna tugh*, and (6) he had a *qur*.[202]

A Tarkhan of Timur was one whom his ushers (*chawashan*) did not keep out of any place, and from whom and from whose children, re-inquiry was not made up to the number of nine faults.

Timur's *wazirs* and generals were like the pawns of chess though they were the real prop of Timur's power. Ibni Arab aptly comments on their real status. The passage is being quoted here due to its significance. The nobles were the 'planets in sphere of that army' of Timur and 'by whose aid its sky shone, by whose counsels it was led and to whose experience it owed its light. Truly, difficult tasks had trained them, and they had been fashioned by the efforts of Timur, who by their aid had opened closed doors and by their onslaughts widened narrow places and by their attacks escaped from the stress of every melee and by their constancy obtained what he needed and by their counsel reached the hidden treasures of his desires. He had been the moon, they its halo; he the craftsman, they the instruments; he the spirit, they the senses; they had been members, he the head.'[203]

There were many hereditary nobles like Qalich Khan of Andijan. His ancestors had been for many years serving under the Timurids. His grandfather was a noble at Sultan Husain Baiqra's court. Badauni says he belonged to the tribe of Jani Qurbani.[204] Out of expediency, Timur was initially kind to the nobles.

According to Yazdi one of the reasons for the unpopularity of Amir Husain, the last Mongol Khan, was his desire for accumulating treasures so much so that he coveted the wealth of his nobles and demanded large sums from them.[205] On the contrary, Timur had opened the doors of the treasury and the 'riches accumulated by Amir Husain in his military tyrannical manner' to the high and low officers.[206] Timur tried to win over the nobles 'by increasing their estates, making them feel his liberality to bind them unto him, drew great stove of money yearly for tribute of Muscovite but distributed it within the same country for to maintain his authority these by means of giving unto them'.[207] But the phase was soon over and having fully established himself, Timur adopted a policy of reconciliation and of force. If Kucha Malik could be given a *suyurghal*, and *tarkhani* for his acts of bravery, Barat Khwaja Kukultash was given humiliating punishment for ignoring his duties.[208] Cowardice in war was punished by an enquiry, litigation (*yarghu*) in the *diwan-i buzurg* followed by whiplashes, fines and execution.[209] Shaikh Abullais was exiled from his *wilayat* to Hejaz and Zinda Hasham was house arrested.[210]

The position of the nobility was not more than the other satellites of the king. The *qurultai* was attended by the nobles and the *noyons*.[211] Timur had a diplomatic way of tackling such assemblies. Ibn-i Arab says that Timur summoned a Kangash and none dared to abstain. Freedom of speech was granted to all and views were expressed. But Timur did not accept any of them till the one in his mind was suggested by someone which he immediately accepted and after discussing it with his close circle, closed the discussion.[212] Timur seldom granted *tarkhani* for he preferred to use the surplus revenue in empire building and developmental works rather than wasting them on rebellious nobles. The *tarkhani* given by Timur was usually limited to few privileges, e.g. *muhr*, *parwana*.[213] Nevertheless on happy occasions, exemption from taxes was granted to the population. The *tarkhan amirs*, however, were privileged for they could have matrimonial relations with the sovereign[214] which in turn strengthened the khan. Certain other classes of *amirs* like *wujuh-i umara*[215] and *umara-i tuman umara-i uzzam*[216] have also been mentioned. The nobility was however, kept under strict control. Ibn-i Arab quotes the incident of Muhammad Qauchin who was intimate with Timur and enjoyed an exclusive status and was distinguished from and superior to all other *wazirs* and rulers in rank. Conscious of his hold over Timur and led by the persuasions of nobles, Qauchin once pointed out to Timur to think over his decision of a campaign once again. Timur at once ordered that he should be deprived of his riches, property, slaves and that a social boycott should be observed in his case. If anyone violated the order even by giving him he would also meet a similar fate.[217] Timur, however, had a cluster of intelligent nobles also whom he considered a boon for himself. There were a number of nobles whose families held various posts.[218] But Timur was very careful not to allow them to increase their influence. Notwithstanding Timur's claims that 'for still in physiognomy, I am like Ilyas and all my judgments are conclusive'[219] Timur had to face a number of rebellions. Ibn-i Arab says that whenever he went on a campaign, in his early years 'the string of pearls was broken' and disturbance created by the unruly elements of Samarqand were ruthlessly suppressed by Timur. 'He was compelled to put some to death, remove some from office, wooing others with presents and rewards.' And after nine revolts 'his kingdom was cleared of enemies and rebels for none was left in Transoxiana disobedient to him or ready to resist him.'[220] Even then, Timur tried to catch the culprits by trickery and not only made the nobles to confess their rebellious intentions and thus managed to prevent the catastrophie, but also spread the false rumour of his death to know about would be deserters.[221] Strange though such things may seem, they helped Timur in forestalling danger.

It would be wrong to presume that Timur wanted to preserve or 'maintain the tribal character of his polity'. There was a chasm, a persistent cleavage between the settled people and tribal nomads, both of whom wanted to live upon each other, survive at the expense of the other. Whereas the nomadic outlaws were a permanent threat to the security of a big empire with its frequent aggressions against trade, agriculture and law and order, the settled population was always an asset to a better empire building. Being an extremely ambitious sovereign, Timur naturally wanted a very strong stable empire in which the share of nomadic elements was restricted to their being exploited for military recruitments only. With his usual despotic and autocratic attitude, Timur suppressed the rebellious tribal population due to which they could never grow into a militant ruling group. The attitude of Timur towards the Jalair clan typifies his general outlook towards tribal people.

Although the tribal population still formed a considerable part of his subjects, and often created problem for the stability of Timur's Empire,[222] the policy of Timur kept them at a low ebb. Al Hasan, the Arab says that Timur 'caused the head of the chief leaders smitten off not by cruelty but for necessity knowing well that the means to cut off the civil wars is to punish the heads of the same for they be Hydras which grow up too fast'.[223]

Timur personally appointed the leaders of the tribes.[224] Even then if they resisted, strong punishment was meted out to them. The entire *ulus* of Jalair was disbanded and distributed among the nobles and even the identity of the *ulus* was obliterated.[225] Likewise any resistance to follow the orders of Timur brought his wrath. Although two of the Kalantars of Qara Tartar surrendered but were reluctant to go to Transoxiana. Likewise any resistance to follow the orders of Timur invited his wrath. Consequently the entire tribe which comprised 34,000 Khanawars were split into groups or distributed among *tuman amirs* to be sent to Transoxiana. Strict orders were issued that none should buy their sheep and goat lest they become light in weight and fly away.[226] The tribes also had to supply military to the khan at his command. Yazdi says that Kalatiyan, a powerful tribe, was overrun and devastated for not complying with the *yirligh* and for not sending their army to comply with the royal order.[227] A number of tribes and their leaders have been mentioned by Yazdi.[228] Speaking about the Chaghatais, Clavijo says that 'clavsmen were free of all burdens and paid no government taxes but served Timur constantly in his armies and acted as his guard'.[229] These special privileges enjoyed by the Chaghatai soldiers were quite in conformity with Turkish customs as the Ottoman Kullars also enjoyed similar privileges.[230]

The reunification of the Jalair tribe[231] was never desired or facilitated by Timur. The dispersed tribe soon reassembled on its own simply because the society was clan oriented and according to the clan norms, the clan members on entering in any other clan (either voluntarily or forcibly) forfeited their tribal status and clannish privileges. Timur was wise enough not to exterminate them (by killing at mass scale) to avoid violation of tribal norms not to alienate but preserve fellow fighters for using their valour to his benefit and to prevent their small antagonistic groups playing havoc with the friendly tribal people with whom they were associated during their disgrace. At every step, Timur stressed his own authority. Timur's personal relationship were always governed by the political exigencies of the situation. The much hammered 'matrimonial alliances' were also a continuation of the same programme and these allies were used by Timur as stepping stone and not as a permanent standby for he removed them soon after extracting the maximum advantage without even a slightest consideration for kinship. Undoubtedly, hereditary tribal chieftainship is noticed in the Empire of Timur Adil Shah had been entrusted with the tribe of Jalair on the death of his father Bahram Jalair. The best proof of predominance of Timur over the tribes was that the tribal leaders were appointed by Timur himself.[232]

Amongst his *khassan-i dargah,* Arab Shah mentions the names of Sulaiman Shah Qumari, Saifuddin Allahadad, Shah Malik, Shaikh Nuruddin.[233] In Samarqand, however, Ali Sher, the *naib*, was held in high esteem by Timur who consulted him in all affairs and preferred his advice than that of others.[234] The resources of the nobles were not meagre. Amir Firuz Shah, a noble of Shahrukh, had built a number of *madrasas*, *khanqahs*, *rabat*, and *hauzes* in every place.[235] From amongst the hereditary nobles of Sultan Ahmad Mirza may be mentioned the names of Saiyyid Yusuf Aughlaqachi whose grandfather originated from the Muhul horde and his father was 'favoured' by Ulugh Beg Mirza. Babur also showered upon him 'great favor and in truth he was worthy of favor'. 'He was an accomplished man, his judgment and counsel were excellent and he had courage too.'[236] Darwesh Beg who was of the line of Aiku Timur—a favourite of Timur Beg, excelled in music and poetry, though his greatest recommendation was that he happened to be 'a disciple of Khwaja Ubaidullah Ahrar and Sultan Ahmad Mirza was latter's devotee'. The Tarkhan family of nobles dominated the later Timurid dynasty partly due to the weak Timurid princes who ascended the throne in the last quarter of the fifteenth century and matrimonial relations established by the Tarkhans with the ruling family which was torn by mutual dissensions and partly due to collective strength of the nobles heightened by mutual military and marital alliances among the Tarkhan nobles themselves. Babur gives a very detailed account of these 'Pharaohs' (Tarkhan nobles) who 'devoured' the entire revenues and not a farthing reached the Timurid ruler. They laid tables like those of kings, put their seal over that of the king and even became the kingmakers keeping the various princes on the bargaining counter, making opportunistic alliances and even denigrating the sons of Khwaja Ubaidullah Ahrar.

Another class whose extraordinary privileges have been blown out of proportion was the group of Turko-Mongol tribes erroneously called as the 'Chaghatais' perhaps because they claimed to have followed Chaghatai traditions by virtue of being the descendants of Qarachar Noyon, the *ataliq* of Chaghatai. These were large hordes loitering in the plains and deserts of Transoxiana, Turko-Mongol by origin sometimes called Tatars, sometimes Chaghatai, by no means belonging to the royal dynasty of Chaghatai and formed the core of

Timur's military force. Being a product of clan-oriented age—Timur drew the leaders of his army from his own clan—the Barlas. These clan people like their counterparts in Transoxiana and Moghulistan were still semi settled. With their faithful adherence to the principle of *tura*, aversion to settled life in the towns, proud but devoted to their sovereign, they kept on enjoying certain privileges. Rubruck states that 'they esteem themselves lords and think that nothing should be denied to them by any man'. An echo of the same is heard in the account of Clavijo. He says that: 'Chaghatais is a privileged folk enjoying special favours of Timur, allowed to herd their flocks wheresoever they will, may seek pasture and sow their crops in all districts.'[237]

This could misguide people to believe that these were the hereditary prerogative of the successors of the Chaghatais instead of being military privileges. The misconception that these Chaghatais were outlaws and on them military discipline was not enforced or they were with regard to the king more powerful needs to be allayed. Both Rubruck and Clavijo speak of extreme discipline, regularity and order being enforced not only in the court and army but even in winter and summer pasturage as they all knew and maintained their decorum only too well. A lack of proper knowledge of sources or quick conclusion might lead one to a wrong assessment and interpretation of these two quotations. Apparently they seem to refer to the Chaghatais as 'favored' people enjoying certain 'special privileges' which may provide the much sought after evidence of special status of the successors of Chaghatais and to 'hereditary privileges' but after a dispassionate examination of source material it may be seen that the term Chaghatais did not denote the successors of the Chaghatais. Instead this word was applied to all the Mongol or Turko-Mongol population living in the Chaghatai's domain and particularly to the Turko-Mongol military clans like Barlas, Arlat, Jalair and Qauchin, living in Central Asia since the enthronement of Mubarak in 1266. Being the core military group and the most supporting strength of Timur, Chaghatais were the 'favoured' ones, but any default on the part of these favoured kinsmen infuriated Timur. Arab Shah mentions that once the Chaghatais plundered the town after Timur had acquired *mal-i amani* and security had been declared, an enraged Timur ordered that all Chaghatais should be crucified in the silk market.[238] Besides, Timur's favours shown to the Chaghatais were military prerogatives and not hereditary privileges.

Clavijo himself points to the fact that the artisans were forced to sell the goods at nominal rates to the soldiers in general all of whom enjoyed immense privileges. It should be noted that the term 'Chaghatais' in the sources does not in fact refer to the successors or descendants of Chaghatais who are usually referred to as Chaghatai Nazadan. As already stated the term Chaghatais was applied loosely to the entire population living in Central Asia in the thirteenth century and particularly to the people of four Turko-Mongol tribes namely Jalair Arlat, Qauchin, and Barlas, none of whom were successors of Chaghatais nor purely Mongols. The term is applied by a traveller like Clavijo in the then contemporary sense for those Turko-Mongols who were Timur's own kith and kin that 'this Chaghatais was a privileged folk'.

A careful study of various sources shows that the privileges, whether hereditary or acquired, were given or retained only on the king's sweet will and on a reciprocal basis as these *yarlighs* and *paizas* were frequently annulled, abrogated (*algha, abtala, qaza, ata*) or discarded and abandoned (*nabaza* or *taraka*). All the new khans asked for the scrutiny of such documents. Mongke Khan ordered that 'any *yarlighs* and *paizas* from the time of Chingiz Khan, Ogedei, Guyuk and other princes should be returned'.[239] To avoid a morass of conflicting landownership and also to facilitate the abrogation of any privileges, an yearly renewal of such papers was essential. Ghazan had declared, 'Before this time, past Sultans and Chingiz Khan in all their *farmans* and *yarlighs* made mention that thirty year old claims should not be listened to'[240] presumably because he was a devout Muslim and Islamic laws recommended a thirty years' period.[241] Timur, however, preferred annual renewal. The other privileges and even *tarkhani* was easily terminated. After the accession of a new khan the *yirlighs* and *paizas* were usually retrieved from the holders, subjected to review and reconsideration, and then reissued.[242]

There are very explicit orders regarding the punishment to a rebellious noble. Chingiz had given instructions in *yasaq* that if someone from his *urugh* opposed (or revolted?), he should be given *sage cousel.* If a second time he repeated, he should be thoroughly questioned and reprimanded (*bazkhwasti baligh*), a third time he should be sent to a far off *mauza* Olchin Qulchin. If on his return he had been fully warned and behaved well, alright, if not he should be thrown into prison, and if he improves then fine—if not his *aqa* and *aini* should be assembled to do consultations and *kangameshi* and then decide in this matter.[243] There were various ways adopted by the Mongols and the Turks to put down rebel amirs with a high hand and inflict torture up on them. Juvaini says that it was the custom of the Mongols that in the case of a criminal who is worthy of death but whose life has been spared, was to be send to wars, arguing that if he was fated to be killed he will be killed in the fighting. Or else they would send him on an embassy to a foreign land who they were not entirely certain would send him back; or again they would send him to hot countries whose climate is unhealthy.[244] 'Similar instances are found in later sources of fifteenth and seventeenth centuries.' Thus nobles were punished in myriad ways.

Sultan Mahmud's attitude towards his Mongol chiefs and his putting to death five of these influential *amirs* and extirpating their families[245] is an example in question. The various categories and titles of nobles seems to have existed as they have been mentioned in the sources, e.g. *uzma-i arkan-i mamlakat*,[246] *umara-i kabbar, umara-i uzzam, muqarraban-ul hazrat*, but they were all not safe from the king's wrath. The confiscation of property at all levels was not unknown in the Muslim world and at times this forfeiture of possessions was followed by the loss of life. A special 'bureau of confiscation' also existed on a regular basis. But these confiscations were merely undertaken as a punitive measure. Those who fell from imperial grace, committed embezzlement, resorted to treachery, disobedience or dishonesty also were subjected to such punishment.[247] The *ankari* or law of escheat was not prevalent among the Turko-Mongols.

Another form of seizure of property is noticed in the form of present day death duty. The sources show that whenever a noble, spiritual guide or a potentate of any category died, his survivors prepared the list of all his precious possessions. Whenever the ruler visited the place on a condolence spree, the list was shown to him and possession were offered to him as a courtesy gift. The ruler merely picked a few things and left the rest for the family. The only class which enjoyed both the king's favours and financial benefits in the form of tax-free land grants and political power to some extent was the religious group. The *Dastur-ul katib* writes, 'be it known to all that the armies of the rulers are of two types/categories: One is the *lashkar-i zahiri* (the evident army). This group comprises the nobles and the military aristocracy who receives from the king's stipend, robes or the *iqta* so that they may defend the empire from the onslaught of rebels and opponents. The other group is the internal army (*lashkariyan-i batini*) who do not possess the power of *amirs* because they enjoy from the benevolence of just king's prosperity and happiness and night and day they are continuously engaged in the prayers for the longevity and perpetuity of the kingdom and the ruler's grandeur.'[248]

Land Control and Revenue System

As has already been discussed, the financial administration under the Mongols was at a primitive level in the beginning. Neither accounts and proper recording of receipts and expenditure were maintained nor safeguarding and distribution of treasures was properly organized. The treasurers received and spent the amount collectively, putting down the treasure in the open covered with felt and giving them to the *amirs* at their demand. Obviously no proportionate distribution was possible and annually eight tenths of these treasures were squandered and only 2 per cent was spent according to the instructions of the king.[249] The evils of usury, bonded labour leading to slavery, embezzlement and extortion were prevalent. Similarly the soldiers in accordance with the old tradition collected the *qopchuq* on horses, cattle, etc., for the benefit of the army camps and soldiers without means and Mongol troops as a rule neither received wages or salaries nor fiefs. The provision quotas thus drafted on the provinces encouraged exploitation, ruined peasants and was not even plentiful for the soldiers partly because the 'administrators of finance were malevolent, intendants were dilatory and court secretaries failed to make out the drafts in time'. With the accession of Timur, the old revenue arrangement was revived.

There may or may not have been a systematic clearcut definite revenue reckoning as under the Ottomans in their *timar*, *ziamat* and *khassa*[250] but an efficient well thought out and planned system inherited by the Mongols from their predecessors did exist and perhaps was not being followed in initial stages by the Mongols. The head of the ruling institutions, the bureaucracy under and next to the 'Sultan was the office of the *diwan-i aala*, the other important officers being the *diwan-i mushrif* and *wazir dastur-i aazam*.[251] As in other Turkish states, the *diwan-i aala* was a general administrative and supervisory body. Occasionally the ruler or his nominee—a prince and lower *wazirs* sat in the *diwan-i aala*. Abdurrazzaq mentions how in 820, Shahrukh had personally attended to the affairs there.

As the designation of *wazir* (burden bearer) itself denotes, the post carried multifarious responsibilities and the 'pen of both the Empire and the religion' were in the hands of the *wazirs*. Abdurrazzaq described the *wazir* as the 'hand, heart, tongue, eyes and ears of the Emperor' and that 'after the sovereignty, no post was higher than that of a *wazir*'.[252]

Apparently it seems that *wazirs* and the *diwans* were appointed from amongst the Barlas clan. Abdurrazzaq says that since the sons of Firuz were young, the new *amir-i diwan* Muzaffaruddin Sultan Barlas older then whom there was none in the Barlas *urugh* (clan) was appointed[253] in his stead. Though many other instances prove that the Persian element equally dominated mainly in Khurasan and Persia under Abusaid Mirza and Sultan Husain Mirza.[254]

The *wazirs* and the *diwans* were subservient to the *sahib-i diwan*, the former called as *sahib-i aazam* and the latter as *sahib-i dastur-i aazam*.[255] The *diwans* played an important role in the prosperity of the state. Under the *diwan-i aala* and the *diwans* were the *sahib-i taujih* (accountant officer in charge of pipe-office) some of whom due to their competence could have a direct access to the king without the help of *wazirs*,[256] several auditors (*mustaufi*), *zabit* who controlled the district level state exchequer and were often promoted to the rank of *wazir*.[257] The *munshis* and *navisandagan* of the *diwans* also existed.[258] From the rank of scribe (*mansab-i insha*) one could be directly promoted to the *wizarat* as happened in the case of Majduddin Mohd. b. Ghayasuddin Ahmad Alkhwafi.[259] The *mansab* of the *diwan* could be held for several years.[260] The *diwani* could be hereditary[261] and a son could receive the *mansab* of *imarat-i diwan-i aala* of his father.[262] Even if young, the sons could be appointed in their father's stead and another officer *amir-i diwan* was appointed to supervise.[263] Nematullah was the *wazir* and *mushrif-i khazana-i amera* of Timur. His son Naimul Haq served as *wazir* during Shahrukh's regime.[264] Shahrukh's *wazir* Ghayasuddin Pir Muhammad Khwafi called Yakqalam held the office for thirty years and his son Majduddin Muhammad became *wazir* and *diwan* of Husain Baiqra.[265] When Amir-i Aazam Hasan Sufi Tarkhan died, his son Amir Mahdi Tarkhan—a generous and brave youth was awarded his father's *mansab* of *imarat-i diwan-i aala* in 827.[266] Another *diwan-i aala* Khwaja Qutubuddin Taus Simnani had held the office of the *diwan* of Mirza.

Abul Qasim Babur for several years was temporarily replaced by Khwaja Abdullah. The latter's high-handedness led to the uprising by the people and their demand for Simnanis reinstatement. Simnani was reappointed in 866 and his efforts which resulted in the affluence of Khurasan were appreciated in 871. He was also appointed in Fars and Iraq for the realization of *amwal-i diwani* and *jihat-i sultani*.[267]

Nevertheless the vast responsibilities shouldered by the *wazir* or the high *diwan* often exposed him to severe punishments and even execution as under the Ottomans and the Saljuqids. Amir Shaikh Abusaid (the controllor of affairs of state of Shah Medina) appointed Khwaja Kalan Tarkash as *wazir* and he had imposed a large amount by way of *sarshumar* on the *muhallat* (quarters) of Herat. *Tahsilat* (collections) were noted down and the *muhassils* (tax collectors) resorted to abuses and coercion by torture so that 'life consuming fumes arose from the houses of poor subjects and wails of men and women reached the sky'. Amir Shir Haji, an important *amir* of Mirza Shah Mahmud, brought him to the city from his garden of Zaghan and it was announced in every corner that no living being should pay any thing by way of *sarshumar* (lit. to counting of heads—tax on cattle) and those who have already paid it should take it back and the servants of Amir Shaikh Abusaid should be destroyed. The common men, the people (*awamunnas*) therefore, caused the devastation of many of the servants including the two *wazirs* of Amir Abusaid driving the latter to flight. A large number of commoners (*mardum-i aam*) joined hands and in the northern part of Mukhtar mountains put him to death. Later on Khwaja Kalan Tarkash was brought to book and tortured.[268] The appointments of *wazir* or *diwan* could be done by the central *sahib-i diwan*[269] also and the latter sometimes was so powerful that his decisions could not be altered.[270] The appointment and promotion of *diwans* was usually done by the king or the provincial rulers.[271] The *diwans*, if expelled from one province could easily get job in another state. Khwaja Abdullah Akhtab for whom Sultan Husain had ordered imprisonment due to extortion leading to a people's uprising fled to Hesar Shadman where Mirza Sultan Mahmudsaïd had given him the post of *wizarat*.[272] Although Khwaja Shamsuddin Marwarid, a refugee from Kirman, had been given the *wizarat* of Herat by Abusaid, the latter during his Iraq expedition ordered the efficient *wazir* to move over to Samarqand. After the death of Abusaid, Khwaja Marwarid returned to Herat and was given the *wizarat* of Herat by Sultan Husain Baiqara.[273] The promotions from the post of *diwan* to *sahib-i diwan* and thereafter even to the postion of *diwan-i aala* have been mentioned.[274]

Since Saiyid Fakhruddin was the only *sahib-i diwan* in 1417-18, he amassed much wealth and gained power. Shahrukh had tried to improve the situation by asking Mirza Baisunqur in 819 to sit in the *diwan-i aala* personally to keep a check on the transactions and prevent extortion and oppression.[275] Like the Ottoman grand *wazir*, the Timurid grand *wazir* also had to perform civil, military and judicial duties though with much less power. The *diwan-i aala* had other '*sharik*'[276] *diwans* or *sahib-i diwans* who were directly and separately appointed by the sovereign.[277] A *diwan-i aala* therefore, had to put up with any *sahib-i diwan* even though the latter was not much liked by him.[278] Khwand Mir says that the *wazir* of Shahrukh sometimes enjoyed absolute authority but on other occasions, there were more than one *wazir* or *sahib-i diwans*, who proved to be a check upon the authority of one another. Even under Shahrukh, a *wazir* like Khwaja Ghayasuddin Pir Ahmad Alkhwafi had in Khwaja Ahmad Daud a minister with competing authority.[279] Similarly, Sultan Husain had two principal *wazirs*, besides a few others. Sometimes misunderstandings arose between the *wazirs*. Khwand Mir[280] reports how Shahrukh has ordered that Kh. Ghayasuddin Pir Ahmad should confiscate the *sarkar* of Amir Ali and the latter should take steps to investigate into the *sarkar* of the former when the two had started opposing each other. Khwaja Pir Ahmad had even protested by not coming to the *diwan-i aala* for three days in 845, when a new undesirable *sharik* for Khwaja Shamsuddin Simnani had been appointed but finally had to surrender and Simnani continued till the end of Shahrukh's reign.[281] Khwaja Ghayasuddin Pir Ahmad held an independent charge of *wizarat* of a vast empire (extending from Khita borders up to Rum) with all the delegated powers from the ruler Shahrukh for forty years till the end of Shahrukh's reign. Later on khwajas continued to enjoy the position even under Alauddaula and Sultan Muhammad.[282] In 810 Shahrukh had assigned him with the reigns of entire affairs of government finances, confiscation, receipts, business transactions of (*zimam-i halo aqd o qabz o bist o maham-i mulk o mal*) money and country because he is said to have 'even surpassed Asaf and Tusi'[283] in the affairs of the *diwani*. As aginst his long span of service Asifi, son of Khwaja Neamat, held the charge of *wizarat* under Abusaid only for a short period (*chandgah*).[284] The extraordinary powers enjoyed by the *wazirs* were also curtailed to some extent. Pir Muhammad is said to have ordered in 807 that the expenditure of travellers (*ikhrajat-i sadir o warid*) in the *wilayats* was to be out of the *mal* of that particular place and that no one was allowed to take away even a maund of hay without imperial orders.[285]

Crisis in the revenue and agrarian system was not rare. In Sultan Husains's finance office, there was no proper order or method at first resulting in wastage and extravagance; the peasants did not prosper and the soldier was not satisfied. The situation came to such a pass that once when Sultan Husain was urgently in need of money he asked the finance officers for it, he was told that 'none had been collected and that there was none'. It is said that one of the nobles of Sultan Majduddin thereupon told the sultan that if Mirza strengthened his hands by not opposing his orders, it shall so be before long that the country shall prosper, the peasants be content and the soldiers well off, and the treasury full. Encouraged by these promises, Sultan Husain put Majduddin in authority throughout Khurasan and entrusted all public business to him, with diligence and efforts. Majduddin 'made soldiers and peasants grateful and content, filled the treasury to abundance and made the districts habitable and cultivated'. The reforms in the *diwani* and extermination of extortion, were successfully carried out. He did all this, however, in the face of opposition from the *begs* and men of high ranks. Babur says that opponents of Majduddin 'all out of temper with what Majduddin Muhammad had effected', and led by Ali Sher Navoi the famous Uzbeg poet and a favourite noble of Sultan Husain, manipulated the arrest and dismissal of Majduddin. Likewise his successor Nizam-ul Mulk of Khwaf, the *diwan*, was in a short time arrested and put to death. Later on Khwaja Afzal of Iraq was made the *diwan*, *beg* and allowed to impress the seal in the diwan.[286]

If the *diwans* were efficient, they became very powerful. Majduddin due to his competence and favours of the sovereign was able to dominate not only on the administration and financial affairs but the domination over matters connected with the soldiers and the subjects as well as nobles and *wazirs* also came under his sway.[287] The influence of Majduddin had increased so considerably that during his region none dared to say any thing regarding small and big affairs of finance to the Emperor without the knowledge of Majduddin.[288] While discussing the competence of Khwaja Qutubuddin Taus Simnani, Khwand Mir states that due to the former's efforts towards the amelioration of *dihqans*, development of agriculture, annually in Khurasan also 7,000 assload of seeds were sown and such a thing was never noticed in any other region.[289] Even Sultan Husain's *wazir*, Majduddin, who enjoyed the power to put his stamps on the orders and *manshurs,* 'sat at the foot of the throne and carried out all the financial and administrative affairs (*muhimmat-i muliki wa mali*)'.[290] Some of the *wazirs* were fully devoted to their task. Nizam-ul Mulk, the *wazir* of Sultan Husain neither maintained a *hajib* nor a doorkeeper at his house so that any one could bring his grievances before him at any time.

The administration of revenue was looked after by the *wazir*. The *wazir/diwan* had an oversight of all lower revenue officials. In accordance with the old rules and practices (*dastur-i qadim*) he arranged and collected the regulations and taxes of state (*mal-i mamlakat*) and the *diwans* sent the tax collectors to the *wilayats*,[291] and for rejuvenating *mauzas* and *muzaraas*. Simnani held the charge till the accession of Sultan Husain Baiqra in 873 when Simnani was again appointed as *diwan-i mushrif*.[292] The mitigation or reduction (*takhfif*) in the *amwal-i diwani* due to the dishonesty of officials led to *arz-i daftar* (checking of accounts) as in Balkh.[293]

During the period of *wizarat* of Nematullah in Herat, the population of Qushanj which was exempted fully from taxes (*taufir-i kulli*) had to accept the payment of ten to fifteen times of the former collection (*jam-i sabiq*).[294] The order to this effect was engraved on a stone and fixed in the Jama Mosque[295] in a proper place. The order remained in force till the emperor's death. The *sahib-i diwans* and *diwan* were dismissed and overcharged and fined. After Sultan Husain's second accession in 875, the orders were issued that due to excessive demands of revenues and revenue credits and extortions (*hawalat o tahmilat*), the subjects should not suffer. In the entire *wilayats* and *bulukat* the *zarilashkar* extraordinary (taxes for raising the army) and *wujuhi kharj* which were a perennial source of trouble for the *raiyyat* should not be demanded for two years. Even an official proclamation to this effect was done by the *qazi*.[296]

Sometimes much havoc was caused by the bureaucratic proceedings of officials either erroneously or deliberately. Khwand Mir,[297] Abdurrazzaq and (more briefly) Hafiz Abru record that in 1407-8, Ghayasuddin Salar the *sahib-i diwan-i mamlakat* prepared a comprehensive list of demands upon princes and nobles. Apparently there existed a system of deliveries of various provisions in kind from the Turkish nobles' assignments (*tuyul-i atraki*). These were greatly enhanced (in case of some of the great nobles)—where an egg was previously demanded, a hen was now entered, where a maund of meat had been demanded, now a whole sheep, where a maund of barley, 10 maunds of barley; and where a tray full of grass, a full ass-load, and a dang was entered as a dinar. Moreover since high prices prevailed that year, Ghayasuddin converted the demand unto cash at current prices. The result was that the total demand upon the *tuyuls* of the Turks was enhanced from one to four times. The nobles feared that the new rates of new register would be approved and assigned for demands (*hawala*) by the king and since there would be no such payment possible, the problem would crop up. As a result of 'wickedness' and 'false' and 'imaginary fears', a number of nobles (like Hasan Jandar, Jahan, Mulk and others) thought of rebellion and even contemplated the murder of the ruler.[298] The situation became so tense that Ghayasuddin along with his officers had to take shelter elsewere. Although out of expediency, he was prepared to pay an amount of 300 *tuman*, the nobles put him to death.

Khwand Mir[299] criticizes how due to his inherent mischief, Khwaja Kalan Tarkash had extracted and used the illegal amount of the taxes on *waqf* from the mosque and *madrasas*—which should have rightly been spent on the poor and the deserving; imposed large undue sums (*tahmil*) on the poor.[300] Enquiries could be held even against the Central *diwani aala*. For example in 847 Amir Jalaluddin Firuz Shah had appointed Saiyid Imaduddin Janabadi in Balkh. Although Saiyid Janabadi tried his best, he failed to raise any profit due to the high-handedness of the *wakil*s of *amirs* and *gumashtas* of Amir Firuz. Unable to transfer his favourite to some other lucrative place, Shahrukh had ordered that the accounts for three years of that region should be placed before Mirza Jugi who intended to pass the winter there. When enquiries and investigations of the affairs of *diwani* and the riches of the *khan* were undertaken, a large sum of taxes (*mutawajjahat-i diwani*) appeared to be pending against the relatives and close associates of Amir Firuz. The *daftars* and the reports regarding expenditure and grandeur of *wakil*s of Firuz were presented before Shahrukh whose enquiries so completely sheltered Firuz that he died of shock and sorrow.[301]

There are references to the occasional enquiries ordered either prompted by the complaints of bungling or as a routine matter. On Wednesday in the end of safar 845, Khwaja Ghayasuddin Pir Ahmad and Amir Ali had informed Shahrukh about the *jama o kharj* of the wealth of Jam though Khwaja Shamsuddin Ali Balicha who had some information about the *zabt-i amwal* of that region conveyed to Shahrukh the irregularities leading to enquiry. Amir Jalaluddin Firoz Shah was appointed to investigate into the affairs of the *diwani* which displeased Ghayasuddin. But Khwaja Shamsuddin succeeded in proving the charges against Amir Ali Shiqani resulting in the latter's deposition.[302]

After the conquest of Transoxiana by the Turks, the military grants in lieu of salary became more 'widespread'.[303] Even Inam lands known as Jildu in Turko-Mongol Empire were rare earlier. Under the Seljuqids also the grant of *iqta* was a 'common occurrence which affected the interests of the class of landowners directly.

In Central Asia, the conditional military grant known as *iqta* was often, as under the Timurids, held as synonymous to *souyurghal* which was otherwise a grant given as subsistence allowance in Central Asia.

The *yirlighs* of assignment of big and small *suyurghals* specified the number of troops to be maintained by the assignee, the amount to be appropriated by him for his personal expenses and the amount to be paid to the state was also clearly mentioned. Sometimes the entire amount was to be spent on the army (*wajh-i arzaq*) without any payment made to the state. An additional grant (*zamima)* was also occasionally bestowed. The personal maintenance allowance (*alufa*) and the state share (*mal o kharaj*) was determined after an assessment of the produce.[304] The entire lands were held either by the king or by his amirs, tribal chiefs and the religious leaders. There are, however, references to *milk-i mardum* (ordinary holdings)[305] also. Calvijo saw that the inhabitants had run away due to the mistrust of the soldiers of Timur's army and that it was now about 12 days since he and his Tartar hordes had passed through this place where in truth very visibly the troops had wrought much havoc.[306] Whenever the amirs grew richer he declared that *tawachis* should enter into undertaking that the additional fixed number of the soldiers should immediately be recruited brought at *arzgah* at the appointed time.[307] Thus the increasing resources were curtailed.

Timur personally 'checked the accounts quarterly and within one hour all the ordinary and extraordinary expenses'.[308] Timur appointed his own nominees for collection of revenue from various places.[309] It seems that the regular checking of provincial revenue was also done. Once the clerks had brought to the notice of the khan the areas lying against Aidku, the matter was investigated in the *diwan-i aala*. Since Aidku was the son-in-law of Timur's cousin, he interfered and after the payment of 100 *tuman-i kebeki* to the royal treasury, *kirman* was reassigned to Aidku.[310] All the three departments of justice were supervised by him and all the decisions were certified by him.[311]

Hafiz Albru says that the *suyurghal*, *inam*, *iqta*, pensions of the deserving and grants of the members of the royal family, nobility, officers, religious groups, military servants were all fixed personally by Timur who made enquiry into the affairs and transactions. Annexation or assignment was ordered only by him and was confirmed by his signatures. Annually the *diwans* demanded the new renewed orders from each *suyurghal*.[312] Once Timur noticed that the *amirs* and *noyons* were becoming richer due to the increasing booty and surplus revenue, he decided to balance the amount by increasing the number of their army. In a big assembly which was attended by high and low military officials at Murghab when the *reaya* (peasantry) of that place complained against their *darugha* Chechaktu Abag. Immediately, Timur ordered that the culprit should be killed.[313] Timur was approached even by the petty officers of empire.[314] The nobles also saw the king to disscuss with him the problems concerning their territory.[315] On certain days, 'Timur gave secret audience for affairs of his state and advice for matters of importance which were decided daily in his presence'.[316] 'Three times a week open justice unto meanest in his Imperial majesty' was imparted. Usually Timur administered justice in public 'clad in a red robe'.[317] Ibn-i Arab, Yazdi and Khwand Mir state that during Timur's stay in Eligqan, the dignitaries (*ashraf o ayan*) of Iran and Turan visited him to congratulate him on his victory against the Ottomans. During this meeting, Timur did not want to confine his general discussions. Instead he enquired from the learned men about the situation in their respective *wilayats* and about the financial state (*kaifiyat-i maishat*) of their *hakims* and *darughas*. Consequently, each one of them told Timur about the condition of their territories. Timur immediately appointed a group of learned scholars (*ashab-i dars o fatwa*) along with honest *amins* and a set of two persons was sent to the different corners of the empire to investigate the affairs of the *hakims ummal* revenue collection from the poor and punish the tyrant and repay the victims from the treasury.[318]

Major decision like those of war and peace could be taken only by the ruler.[319] Any deviation from this or non-compliance with any royal order or alleged misadministration could result in his deposition or admonition by the king. Even a weak king like Shahrukh not only reprimanded Ulugh Beg but even temporarily withdrew from him the governorship of Transoxiana which was taken or granted to him as an act of clemency.[320]

In the *farmans* of assignment, the purpose for which the revenue of a particular region was to be spent, was specifically mentioned. Sometimes the taxes (*mal o jihat*) were to serve as subsistence allowance (*wajh-i arzaq*) for the army employed by a provincial ruler.[321] In certain other cases, the *hasilat* were to be appropriated for their treasury (*wajh-i ikhrajat-i diwan-i ishan*).[322] Sometimes the *hasil* of a particular *wilayat* was to be left at the disposal of the *nawab*.[323] The privileges and status of a Suyurghal holder differed as variously defined in the orders.[324] Sometimes the Suyurghal holder had to pay a part of the revenue to the central treasury.[325] A large Suyurghal could be assigned to the person or might even be divided and distributed among several persons. A pension (*alufa*) in addition to the land grant could also be given.[326]

The term '*suyurghal*' was not used exlusively for subsistence allowance in the sixteenth century but used as synonymous to *Iqta* covering different types of land grants as well as territorial assignments under the Seljuqs. Even provisional governorships and military grants, besides simple subsistence allowance all was designated *suyurghals*. The Timurid terminology in general seems rather vague and terms like *iqta, tuyul, milk, ushr, altamgha* and *suyurghal* are used for big and small revenue assignments often synonymously.[327] Two more specific forms of land grant were *inam* (grant in recognition of some special service) and *waqf* (grants to religious classes especially for purpose of maintenance of religious institutions). It seems that there were Crown lands (*khassa*) in the various *wilayats* from which a fixed sum was demanded by the *diwan-i aala*.[328] Sometimes, the revenue from a particular places was granted for construction, etc.[329] The communal lands also seem to have existed.[330] The governor controlled the assignment of all form of lands, *itlaq*, pensions, etc., investigated all matters, decided the additions, or reductions in assignments and even revised his own judgements on re-examination. All the *suyurghals* were to be renewed each year and the *diwan* had to seek fresh orders.[331] These *suyurghals* could be hereditary or declared to be similar to perpetual tenure (*istimrar*),[332] but renewal after a specified period had to be confirmed. During his sojourn in Shiraz in 1452-3, Abdul Qasim Babur ordered that the *farmans* of the former rulers, particularly the *nishans* of Shahrukh, should be broughı for signature (*imza*) and that such *suyurghals, hodbraiyat, mustaghallat, mussalmiyat* were to be treated as assigned and confirmed (*mussalam danistand o mujra dashtand*).[333]

The nobles and particularly, the religious personages held a large number of milk lands. Khwaja Aharar had 1,300 large tracts of lands apart from smaller ones scattered in various parts of Central Asia.

The *waqf* lands were controlled by the *sadr* and organized by the *mutawallis*. Hafiz Abru mentions that Timur never interfered in *mal-i waqf* and forbade its acquisition for the treasury allowing the poor and the students to benefit from it lawfully.[334] Abdurrazzaq echoes the same when he says that the income from the *waqf* property of Ulugh Beg's *madrasa* and *khanqah* in Samarqand exceeded their cost of maintenance and the surplus was deposited in the treasury of the same buildings.[335] Even the *milk* lands which had been converted into *waqf* were often granted immunity from the payments of taxes. Daulant Shah says that in 1417-72, a *shaikh* assigned his milk as *waqf* for the maintenance of his own tomb. The rulers, out of regard for the *shaikh* used to exempt the *mujavirs* from (taxes).[336] Often the landholders converted their lands into *waqf* just to evade taxes by appointing themselves as *mutawalli*.[337]

The *ataliqs* had defined powers though their undue interference in the affairs of state or overruling the prince assignee often gave rise to misunderstanding and quarrels. Squabbles would also arise if the *ataliq* did not allow the *suyurghal* holding prince to have 'a claim even over a single *dinar* or let the ruler *amir* have a say in the affairs of the country and finances. In such cases, the *ataliq* was to be replaced by another nominee from among the nobles already sent to that particular province.'[338] Sometimes the *ataliq* could outmanueuvre the prince as happened in the case of Ulugh Beg whose two *ataliqs* namely Muhammad Burunduq (descendant of Jaku Barlas and a favourite of Abusaid) and Jahangir Barlas came to know of 'the designs of Ulugh Beg against the two Barlas' beforehand and 'kept tight hold of him, made the tribes and hordes march, moved as far as Qunduz and when up on Hindukush they cautiously compelled Ulugh Beg to start back for Kabul' and themselves went to Sultan Hasain in Khurasan and enjoyed favours.[339] Babur also confirms the same attitude of another *ataliq*. By saying that though Qandahar was given to Muhammad Masum Mirza, he had neither power nor influence there, since if black were done, or if white were done—the act was Shah Beg Anghun's. On this account, the Mirza left Qandahar and went to Khurasan shows that provincial *ataliqs* or *nawabs* could be quite effective.[340]

Certain families monopolized the sphere of *wizarat*. Zainul Abidin was the *wazir* of Timur and Shahrukh. After his death his son Imaduddin enjoyed the favours of Shahrukh and was appointed in Balkh.[341] After the death of Shahrukh and conquest of Khurasan, Imaduddin was appointed as *wazir* and continued in office till the death of Ulugh Beg.[342] Khwaja Shamsuddin Balicha was the *wazir* of Shahrukh[343] and his brother Wajihuddin Mahmud b. Ismail Simnani was the *wazir* of Mirza Baisunghur Mirza Alauddaula for a long time. Under Mirza Abul Qasim Babur he was promoted to the rank of *diwan-i aala* and he continued to hold the rank even during the reign of Mirza Shah Mahmud (the son and successor of Abul Qasim Babur) till he deserted Mirza Shah Mahmud, during the latter's flight from fear of Mirza Ibrahim, son of Mirza Alauddaula, only to be tortured to death.[344] Similarly the post of *diwan-i aala* was held by Firuzshah and after his death by Amir Nizamuddin. Another son of Firuz Shah named Ghayasuddin Sultan Husain simultaneously served as *diwan* of Mirza Alauddaula.[345] Khwaja Alauddin Ali Quhistani was a *wazir* of Timur and his son the *khwaja*. Naimuddin Nematullah served as *diwan* once and *diwanghan* under Shahrukh and twice as the *diwan* of Ulugh Beg and Abusaid intermittently.[346]

Wazirs could be extraordinarily powerful if kings were pleased with them, Timur once ordered that Jalal-ul Islam be given the chieftainship (*sardari*) of the army of Tajiks and his fortunes and resources were not to be interfered with.[347] Khwaja Majduddin Muhammad was such a favourite of Sultan Husain that notwithstanding his *mansab* of Risalat (*wizarat*?) and his *muhur* of *parwana*, he was asked to certify and write *Atla 'alaih* near the big seal. He alone was allowed to sit at the foot of the throne and conveyed to the sultan the affairs of the country and financial matters and petitions of *dad* khwahs, and noted down the king's answers[348] notwithstanding the nobles' objections. Khwaja Shamsuddin Muhammad, a *wazir* of Sultan Abusaid in Shahur 865 had been promoted as the confidant and close associate (*harifi majlis-i khas o nadim-i bazm-i ikhtisas*)[349] and given the *muhur*. Later on he had served Amir Hasan Beg also. In 866 Hasan Beg had become so impressed by Burhan Abdul Hamid that the rulership of Iraq was given to him and even the appointments and dismissals of *darughas* of those *baldas* were given to him.[350] Khwaja Qutubuddin[351] Taus Simnani who had been appointed as *wazir* by Abul Qasim. Babur had thrown a *toi* in honour of Abul Qasim and offered him 30,000 *dinar-i kebeki* apart from a lavish entertainment. Consequently this home town Simnan was bestowed upon him as *suyurghal*. Such was his personality that he was able to win over Sultan Abusaid also who had conquered Khurasan. The considera-tion Abusaid had for Simnani excited the jealousy of people who outmanoeuvre him and got him dismissed though he was reinstated later on.[352] Similarly, Qutubuddin Taus Simnani was not only given the governorship of Iraq but also the big seal was given to him. According to Khwand Mir honesty, rectitude and moderation (*rasti wa kutah dasti*) had helped Maulana Amir Samarqandi in the prolongation of his period of *wizarat*.[353]

The Central provincial *wazir* could also create problems for the district level *wazir*. Khwand Mir[354] refers to the incident of Khwaja Abdullah Akhtab (the *wazir* of Hesar under Sultan Mahmud Mirza) who, out of sectarian bigotry, wanted to harass the *wazir* of Tirmiz by proving a discrepancy in the *jam* of Tirmiz[355] but died on his way by drowning in the flooded Amu. The misunderstanding between Khwaja Shamsuddin Muhammad and Khwaja Majduddin who held the *wizarat* under Hasan Beg is another such example. The allegations of embezzlement of *amwal-i diwani* levelled against Shamsuddin by Majduddin and others led to his dispensation never to rise again.[356] Khwand Mir woefully describes how during the 142 years of the rule of Timurid dynasty when 31 descendants of Timur had the honour of striking the coins and having the *khutba* read in their own name, the strange habit of 'quick installation and deposition of wazirs' was followed. The worthless low and ignorants (*firo mâya*) persons were raised to that high post increasing the number of *wazirs*.[357]

The righteous *wazirs* showing an inclination towards asceticism and willing to renounce the high post of *wizarat* 'not due to discontent of Turks heightened by malfunctioning but of his own sweet will' were given suitable appointments. When Shamsuddin Marwarid prompted by his honest, benevolent and peace loving nature found himself unwilling to continue as *wazir*, he was given the *shaikhi* and *tauliyat* of the *manqufat* of Abu Ismail Khwaja Abdullah Ansari. Having fulfilled the responsibility successfully for several years, the khwaja gave up that job and spent his time in writing Holy book and prepared 22 pieces till his death.[358] The high-handedness alone was not a criterion for punishment as any minor fault of manners could result in harassment.[359]

Khwaja Alauddin Ali Alsanei, the *wazir* of Herat had to suffer thirty years' inprisonment, one of the reasons of his degradation was the displeasure of Ali Shir Navoi[360] though the Khwaja utilized the time in producing good academic works.

Sometimes the members of one and the same family served in various capacities. Maulana Shahabuddin Ismail was a *qazi* of Khwaf but his son Khwaja Qiwamuddin Nizam-ul Mulk Khwafi became the *wazir* of Sultan Husain.[361] Patronage to incompetent or self-seeking nobles often led to problems. Zulnun Arghun was 'far from business like shallow petated and a bit of a fool' though he enjoyed 'chief authority in Badiuz Zaman's presence...' and was 'dominant and trusted in Heri'.[362]

Nishans were issued to the *walis* (provincial governors) according to which the provincial governors had to perform the following duties befitting to their ranks; protection of the downtrodden, artisans and peasants from exploitation; vigilance in maintaining law and order and defence of the region; regular dispatch of messengers/representatives for acquainting the king with various event, encouragement of agriculture, amelioration of the country and people; respect and rewarding of saiyids, scholars and sheikhs and care of the merchants.[363]

The tenure of an assigneee was 'at the pleasure' of the emperor and the instances of transfers, sudden recall, deposition are as numerous as the renewal of their term or their confirmation. Each provincial governor had to fulfil certain financial and military obligations, e.g. maintaining a fixed number of army personnel to be presented at appointed time and place,[364] bringing *sawurin* (presents) to the king on all special occasions like victory, etc., and entertaining the king and his entourage during his tours.[365] The rulers of the vicinity; *amirs* of various categories during the king's tours by way of *rasminisar* and *paiandaz.*[366]

Although the *appanages* tended to be hereditary, a sign of maladministration or extortion attracted prompt attention of the king. When the high-handedness and tyrannical extortions of Sultan Muhammad and his nawabs were brought to the notice of the Khan that they are not contented with the *amwal-i muqarrara* and demanded more than *dastur-i mahud*, Shahrukh ordered immediately in 847 that only Sultaniya and Qavin were to be his *suyurghals* and he was not to enter into other *mauzas.*[367] Mirza Ibrahim Sultan had also been instructed by Shahrukh to see that *nawabs* do not deviate from the established ways (*qaeda-i mahud*) in the collection of revenue and act justly.[368]

The provincial affairs were directly investigated by the kings. On hearing the defeat of Ulugh Beg and consequent plundering by the Uzbegs, Shahrukh in 831 personally came to reprimand Ulugh Beg and the prince for sometime fell into his estimation (*be etbar*) and was deprived of his territory temporarily.[369] The assignment of Kabul to Burunduq Barlas jointly with Jahangir Barlas shows that two persons could be assigned one place either as *ataliq* or governor.[370] Similarly Zulnun Arghan shared the governorship of Qandahar with his son Shah Shuja at Husain Baiqara's command.[371]

Even the appointments on *mansab* of Sheikhs in *khanqah* was made by the *diwans*. In each and every place, the *naibs* were appointed by Timur personally.[372] The headmen of the towns or villages were called *rais.*[373] *Qazis* were appointed in all big and small units of the empire. The *qazis* may or may not have the charge of *mauqufat.*[374] The post of *Shaikh-ul Islam* was usually hereditary.[375] Babur refers to Masud Umar Al Taftazani whose descendants had from Babur's time downwards served as Shaikh-ul Islams in Khurasan.[376] Starting right from the end of Shahrukh's reign, Maulana Shamsuddin Muhammad Maulana Qutubuddin Yahiya, a descendant of the above mentioned *khwaja* and a distinguished person of his time till the regime of Sultan Husain Mirza, held the *mansab* of Shaikh-ul Islam.[377]

Similarly, the family of Khwaja Abdullah Maulana Qazi had come to be the pontiff (Shaikh-ul Islam), religious guide (*muqtada*) and judge (*qazi*) in the Farghana valley.[378]

There are references to the *Bakhshian* in the sources. Beveridge has rendered the term *bakhshi* as pay master general as in India during Akbar's time.[379] In the sources of Central Asia the term *bakhshi* is applied to Uighur scribes in Turkish and in Mongolian in Mughal language, it refers to surgeons of Moghulistan.[380] Babur's referential description of the 'lord of the gate' suggests that the post was quite important.[381] The special investigating agencies (*diwan-i tafahus* and *majlis-i tajassus*) and enquiry commissions were appointed to find out the truth regarding the attempt on Shahrukh's life by Ahmad Lur.[382] There are references to the reliable groups of *echkis* (*firqa-i echkiyan-i mu'otabar*) and the *shahnas*. Apart from the spy system, night patrols (*asasan*) were also there to investigate and find out the whereabout of criminals.[383]

According to the information available in the sources, the kings exercised a direct control over finances. Timur checked ordinary— and extraordinary expenses quarterly.[384] Shahrukh reorganized the affairs of the *diwan*.[385] Even Sultan Mahmud Mirza was well versed in accounts, 'an expert in revenue matters and in the art of administration' and 'not a dinar or dirham of revenue was spent without his knowledge'.[386] He is said to have made 'new regulations and arrangements and to rate and tax on new basis'.[387]

The *diwans* were expected to learn the art of account keeping (*ilm-i siyaq*), acquired a knowledge of important transactions of exchequer (*mahamm-i diwani*).[388] Khwand Mir records an event which shows the prevalent and prescribed qualifications regarding the appointment of Diwan. Hasan Beg Turcomon is said to have appointed 'only a person well versed in accounting and knowledge of affairs of the exchequer (*istifa wa siyaq*) as *ashrf diwan* whereas the two persons who excelled in calligraphy and elegance of style or inclination towards agricultural development and construction were appointed only as wazir.'[389] Soon sometimes incompetent persons were promoted but had to be dismissed. Khwaja Muzaffaruddin Mukhtar Sabzwari who had been appointed as *wazir* (in Rabi I 865) and was allowed to put his seal above most of the *wazirs* of Abusaid was dismissed and deprived of his rank as soon as his lack of knowledge of accountancy, etc., was discovered.[390] For the joint the *wizarat* of Khwaja Ismail Khanjani and Khwaja Qutubuddin Taus, a poet had written a couplet that there was perhaps a dearth and a famine of human beings that animals and birds are being appointed as *diwans*.[391]

Seemingly a proper record of accounts and articles of royal treasures were carefully maintained as is proved by the list of the valuables said to have been provided by Abdurrazzaq and is also proved by inferences drawn from various instances.[392] After the accession of each new Sultan customarily the *muhasaba* (calculation and adjustments of accounts) followed.[393] In case of any irregularity, the *khazan* was dismissed. If suspicious, the provincial *diwan* or *wazir* could personally look after the administration of public revenue and issue *howalas* to this effect[394] as Nematullah did in Qushay 'during his *wizarat* of Herat'. Accounts were so accurately maintained that Ulugh Beg could allegedly discover a thief only by noticing an increase in the taxes due (*amwali wajibi*) and paid by the latter.[395] The embezzled amount of Tabriz by *diwan-i aala* was easily discovered with the help of the *daftar-i diwan* (registers) and could be recovered from the officials.[396] Sometimes the *diwans* like Abdullah Akhtabar and his brother were suspected of cheating (*taghallub warzida*) and forgery by not writing correctly their *jama*. Enquiry and investigations (*tafahus* and *taftish*) were ordered and they were finally exonerated from the charge after proper checking of the accounts (*hisab o muamela*). This further proves the proper maintenance of written records.[397] In 868, the *tafahus-i amwal* (checking) of the wealth of the *mamlakat* of *khurasan* and of the *khassa* of Herat and its *bulukat* was ordered by Sultan Husain which revealed that Khwaja Nematullah had spent the amount in *wajh-i barat o hawalat* and the subjects also complained of overexactions hence Sultan Husain dismissed and fined Khwaja Nematullah and ordered that he be thrown into prison.[398]

Sultan Abu Said had decreed that the amount or expenditure should not be drawn without permission from the sultan,[399] or else the *diwans* would be beheaded. The steps taken by the *diwan* or *wazir*, Khwaja Shamsuddin, for the betterment of soldiers, *sadat*, *ulama* and righteous men and the benevolence shown to them had been greatly appreciated by Khwand Mir.[400] Nevertheless the complaints against him by Khwaja Nematullah Qahistani had its effect. And Shamsuddin frankly confessed of having extracted some emoluments by way of service (*khidmatara*). He, however, assured the king that he had abstained from *mal-i diwani* and *zabtimahami* which were under his control. It was perhaps due to his deep consideration for his protégé that Sultan Abusaid, allowed Shamsuddin to retain whatever *khidmatana* he had squeezed from the people, and emphasized that he did not want that Shamsuddin should face the ordeal at his hands—the way other *wazirs* had suffered earlier. Khwaja Shamsuddin knelt before him, took off the ring, placed it on the throne and returned. 'Such a quick and easy deposition' says Khwand Mir 'had never been recorded in any history'.[401] Supposedly the revenue was also realized in three instalments.[402] Sometimes if the overexactions of *amwal-i diwani* were reported by *ummal*, the order was issued for the repayment of the excess amount from the state treasury as happened in Kossova.[403] After the murder of Ghayasuddin, his men were forced to pay 30,000 *tumans* by the next *diwan-i aala* Saiyid Fakhruddin Muhammad who was known for his pride, love for *sadat* and *ulama*, patronage to his own kith and kin, lack of kindness and mercy and continued in his callous ways for ten years till in 819, Shahrukh appointed his eldest son Baisunghar to remove the grievances and to strive to give redressal to people.[404] When investigations were made by the prince, the impropriety and the greed for the wealth of Muslims and the ill expenditure of *wajh-i diwan* was also discovered. To put matters right Khwaja Nizamuddin Ahamd was asked to be a co-*diwan* (*sharik*) and through his intelligence ultimately the truth came out. Although the extortions were stopped, the *ummal* of *diwan* due to the fear of Fakhruddin did not go against him. Finally Mirza Baisunghar's enquiries (at the complaint of Amir Ali Shiqani regarding Saiyid's embezzlement of 20,000 *tuman*) followed by an order of rechecking of the treasures revealed that the money had been drawn in the name of Saiyid and given to him by Pir Ali and others. The complications led to an intervention of Shahrukh who ordered for reimbursement and failing this Pir Ali and others were thrown into prison and Saiyid though agreed to pay the amount within an year was handed over by *amirs* and *diwans* to *muhassils*. All his appeals for mercy were rejected. On various pretexts, Saiyid took money from people to meet the demands of *muhassils* who harassed him.[405] Although the *saiyid* had to repay 200 *tuman-i kebeki* (33,333 *dinars* and 2 *dangizari* Iraqi daily) in instalments, he managed to arrange his release from prison and continued the exactions of money in cash or in the form of *qabala* till his death in Jumad I 810. Similar cases of capricious expropriation (*musadirah*) are frequently found.[406] Daulatshah denounces the Timurid *amaldars* for their excesses and relates how an *amaldar* of Sabzwar adopted coercive and extortious attitude towards an old lady and on being reminded of the day of judgement by her took a vow never to serve as an *amaldar*.[407] The demand for a loan against a draft of payment of revenue in advance (*barat bar mal-i ayenda*) during an emergency and repeated exactions of revenue during war times coupled with the high-handedness of the officers often resulted in the complete ruin of cities and districts.[408] Babur refers to 'tax gatherers' roughness' and uses it proverbially.[409] Severe punishments were given to the defaulting *wazirs*. Sultan Husain's *wazir* Alauddin Alsaric lost favour of sultan. His high turban was placed around his neck and he was brought in this condition to the sultan who threw him into prison for 30 years. It was only when another *wazir*, Saifuddin Shabankar, was imprisoned till his execution and someone reminded the sultan of the imprisoned Alsaei that their execution was ordered. Khwaja Alsaei was hanged on Taqi Chaharsuq, the market place of Herat and Khwaja Muzaffar on Darwaza-i Malik.[410] The department of finance and revenue consisting of a *diwan-i mushraf* (or *wazir*) with a number of *sahib-i diwans* (registrars or superintendents of revenue), *diwans*, *wazirs*, *munshi* (secretaries) and *navisandagan* (scribes) maintained comprehensive accounts of revenue books of receipts and disbursement and the details of the villages of the empire. Several villages were united into one fiscal unit *amal* which was supervised by one tax collector (*amaldar*) or *amil* and several *amals* constituted *sarkar*. An expert in the art of account keeping was appointed by the Khan himself for fixation, demand and acquisition of Khan's share of revenue (*mansha-i istifa-i imlak-i khassa*). The state share of revenue (*zabt-i amwal*) was to be realized by certain nominated officers of the king. They prepared the *mufarrid-i ummal* and realized the taxes.[411] The revenues of the place could be used by the *diwan-i aala* for public works independent of the ruler's permission. While Timur was busy in Rum expedition, Khwaja Ghayasuddin Salar who held the governorship of Yazd, constructed a *tim* (luxury bazaar) amidst the city market which had no parallel in the entire world as a real cloth market in richness and glamour.[412] Since the completion of the time coincided with the news of victory over Ottomans hence it was named as '*darul fath*'. Similarly Ghayasuddin Pir Ahmad Alkhwafi is said to have constructed charity houses and convents around Khurasan and *madrasa* in Khwaf apart from the building constructed on the tomb of Shaikh Zain Muhammad Alkhwafi.[413] In 810 Khwaja Ghayasuddin Pir Ahmad Khawafi had been given complete freedom in this respect.

Although Qutubuddin Simnani had been rejected for the post of *ashraf-i diwan*[414] just because of his love for amelioration of agriculture, his contributions to the sphere of agriculture had been gratefully recorded by chroniclers. Khwand Mir describes the canal 'Jui Sultani'[415] which was constructed in the north of Herat from which a thousand gardens were irrigated. It is said that when Taus discovered the inclination of Abusaid towards development of agriculture, he appointed 200 agriculturists, *barzagar* and were to work for two years. It is difficult to establish the exact rate of land revenue demand in the Timurid Empire. Equally indefinite is our knowledge of the specifics of the then prevalent several modes of assessment. But some information can be gleaned from the sources. Khwand Mir refers to certain regulations laid down by Timur for management of affairs of the *diwani* and arranging the acquisition of revenue demand in the Timurid Empire. Though he does not amplify them, Ibn-i Arab Shah quotes a revealing anecdote. Saiyid Barakat requested Timur to assign to him and his sons the province of Andkhud and suggested that the entire produce of the place be assessed and the revenue be fixed on the basis thereof.[416] This implies that assessment was done either by crop sharing (*maqasima*) or by fixing the rate in cash or kind on the measured plots (*masahat*) or in lumpsum (*muqtai*). The tax *tanabana* (fee for measurement of land by *tanab*) was also tax on produce (depending upon its quality) demanded after measurement. Usually the *kharaj* was paid in kind. It seems that the rate of demand was lowest in the first half of the fifteenth century than in the second half when Daulat Shah wrote (1487). Daulat Shah, recorded his appreciation of the rules and regulations in force under Ulugh Beg and says that the *mal o kharaj* on one *jarib* of land yielding a harvest of four *kharwars*[417] was four copper dangs which were equivalent to one unit of small money (dang in the silver dirham sale).[418] This would appear to be a rather moderate tax. From the records in *Matlab-ut talibain*, however, the share taken in revenue would seem to amount to one-third of the produce in kind. It is stated that Khwaja Ahrar paid 1,600 tonnes while 3,200 were still left with him. A number of canals were dug at the orders of Timur. Shahrukh constructed a dam on river Murghab to repopulate Merv. In the very first year the cultivation of 500 *zijiawamil* was made possible. The other known canals of the period include Ulugh Beg's *juizar* of Bukhara, Nizam Ali Shir's Chashma-i Kalat, Tus Jilan Injil at Herat and Khwaja Ahrar's Juishahr.

Clavijo states that on the land of *kesh* five crops of corn were grown yearly. There were vines and much cultivation of cotton, melon, fruit, millet and other kinds of produce due to abundant irrigation. The same author informs us that Samarqand produced wheat in abundance. There was much livestock and poultry. Clavijo was surprised at the low prices prevailing in Samarqand.[419] Timur gave orders for planting of cotton, flax and hemp.[420] Even in the last quarter of the fifteenth century, Babur refers to 'the good cheap things' at Samarqand and describes the suburban gardens and fine fruits, particularly melons and plum, pomegranates, apricots, nice almonds, grapes, apples and pears.[421]

However with the death of Timur, and the discontinuance of external campaigns and collection of booty, the main source of the prosperity of Samrqand seems to have been removed. Natural calamities like famine and drought occurred frequently and disturbed the progress of agriculture. In 813/1407-8, Samarqand was overtaken by a drought which was followed by high prices.[422] In the wake of the civil wars in the first decade of the sixteenth century there arose 'want and excessive cost of goods' in Samarqand so much so that 'nothing was cheaper among them than gold and silver'.[423] Although soon the trouble was over as there 'came plenty' of 'good supply', security, prosperity and good fortune but such civil wars were injurious to cultivators as the soldiers and army devastated agricultural field, canals, other constructions and plundered the prosperity of citizens.[424] In 875 in his letter to Amir Hasn Beg Mirza Yadgar Mohammad says that although Khurasan has been conquered, its condition was very poor due to devastation of enemy's hoofs that from the borders of Jajaram upto Murghab river there was no cultivation (Mazraa) nor was it possible to cultivate any thing.[425]

Clavijo saw at Ferrior a large town that the inhabitants in greater part had fled. This was in mistrust of soldiers of Timur's army and it was now about 12 days since he and his Tartar hordes had passed through this place where in truth very visibly the troops had wrought much havoc.[426] The effect of drought in Herat was so severe that one *sharia man* of wheat that earlier fetched only 2 silver misqal (3 *dinar-i kebeki*) could now be had for no less than 250 misqal of silver.[427] Shahrukh ordered that the royal granaries (*anbars*) should be opened and the grain be sold at the rate of one dinar i kebeki per man.[428] The situation in Transoxiana also improved gradually. But such temporary measures could not prevent the recurrence of natural calamities.[429] Excessive heat and cold caused the animals to die.[430]

Clavijo noticed how brutally the 'Tartars' treated the Persian peasants. The guides and various officers from the court sent to meet and conduct the ambassadors everywhere enforced their demands with the whip and a shower of blows.[431] Hafiz Abru gives a very bright picture of the reign of Timur by saying that even on ordinary days other than *toi*/or/*jashn*, every day about more than 10,000 persons came, even the one-tenth of it was not dressed in *kurpas*. Instead they were extremely richly clad. The army and the servants were mostly prosperous and rich and so were even the servants of nobles. It was only due to the booty from the wars as in one of the several conquests plenty of diamonds, silver, gold and other precious stones were found. Clavijo appreciated the richness of Samarqand and Ibn-i Arab also speaks highly of the rich resources of Samarqand. Ibn-i Arab, however more aptly sums up the reign of Timur in the following manner: 'the merriment that produced in the guise of seriousness and seriousness in the guise of jest, how much he build and destroyed.... How many places that were laid waste, how many he debased and honoured and made to bear changes of fortune or supported and his consultations with the learned and disputes with magnates, the raising of the lowly and debasing of the noble, the passing of the laws of state, collection of goods from far and removal of goods at hand and promulgation of edicts among all men near and distant besides other things of this sort are so many that they could scarcely be recounted'.[432] No less a person than Ibn-i Khaldun had been reported to have said that Timur 'is truly a king and knows rightly how to rule the sultanate' and 'to gain glory and honour'.[433]

Since a perfect system of checks and balances or double auditing did not exist; the *diwans* were frequently killed, punished, suspended, thrown out of service or fined[434] and even reappointed after their dismissal. The extortions often boomeranged upon the diwan and the ruler even in the provinces. Since Mirza Abu Bakr had destroyed the treasures of Mirza Umar in Sultania, Shaikh

Khuram Shahi, a former *amil* of Samarqand who received the *wizarat* under Mirza Umar, keenly wanted to recoup it through financing the *ummal* and imposing upon the wealthy men of Tabriz a large amount (tahmilat) which they could not pay. The tyranny resulted in the extermination of Mirza Umar and the *wazir* both and the latter's efforts to take shelter with Mirza Abu Bakr failed as he was executed.[435] Another *khwaja*, Ismail Khujandi, was dismissed on the allegations of embezzlement of *amwal-i diwani* and his entire savings were destroyed by the adverse circumstances.[436]

Sometimes the ambitious *zabits* wanted to over-exact. One such incident is quoted by Khwandmir who records that since the regime of Sultan Abu Said, Khwaja Nizamuddin Bakhtiyar Simnani was the *zabit* of Badghis. He was promoted to the rank of *wizarat* by Sultan Husain and entered into an engagement for the revenue based (*muta 'aa hidi 'tahqiq-i jihat-i ghaibi*) on an adhoc basis without a proper assessment after investigation. The amount thus fixed came to 3,000 *tuman*, half of which could not be possibly collected. To top it all Khwaja Nizamuddin also commented in the *diwan* that the *bagh-i safid* and the *bagh-i zaghan* and all the imperial territories come under the category of ad hoc assessment (*jihat-i ghaibi*) should be priced and commuted into cash and state share should be realized accordingly. When such reports were conveyed to Sultan Husain, he dismissed the Khwaja from his service.[437]

Usually the *sahib-i diwans* were appointed from among these *wazirs*. The *diwans* (or *wazirs*) were frequently transferred form one place to another not as a routine or after fixed number of years but anytime during the course of their career. Khwaja Nematullah was given the *wizarat* of Samarand, Herat, Astarabd, Iraq.[438]

One of the officers connected with the affairs of the *diwani* was Khazinadar who maintained the accounts of *wujuh*, *tamassukat* (bonds) etc. The checking *(arz)* of the accounts was ordered in case of suspected embezzlement and it was to be done by *khzinadar*.[439] Seemingly the *sahibi* and the *tamsassukat* were to come handy if the entries in registers (*daftarha*) were to be completed for enquiry.[440]

The civil wars gave a fatal blow to the economy, and destroyed the complex irrigational system on which local agriculture depended.[441] During war times when the resources were exhausted and even money collected as *wajh-i lashkar* no longer sufficed, certain extraordinary levies were imposed like *zar-i lashkar, nambardar jihadi* and others. Even the traders were to be approached for whatever money they could lend. But sometimes such excesses were committed in the collections that the subjects had to undergo immense troubles. Once in 866 Sultan Abusaid, during his wars against Sultan Husain Mirza, himself turned towards Astarabad appointing Khwaja Muizuddin Shirazi in Herat for collection of *zar-i lashkar* and *nambardar.* Such a large amount was imposed by him upon his own *khassa* in this *wilayat* that the subjects groaned and the traders due to exactions of loans grumbled. When Abusaid returned victorious and found the terrible devastations, Shamsuddin was sent to Herat to appease the subjects assuring that no excesses would be demanded and no such taxes would be collected from Herat *buluk*. Khwaja Muizuddin bound in hand and neck was thrown into boiling water and boiled to death. Another culprit Shaikh Ahmad's skin was flayed.[442] This exemplary punishment was given to awaken the officials to see that their job was not to grind the people but to treat them kindly.[443] But the effects were not lasting as the *diwans* hardly improved their ways. Khwaja Abdullah who had been promoted from the rank of *wazir* to that of a *diwan-i aala* showed his gratitude to the sultan by writing off 3,00,000 *dinar-i kebeki* within three times from Khwaja Qutubuddin Taus but that hardly helped the poor.

The natural calamities were no less harsh to the inhabitants. Epidemics, droughts, floods and subsequent forced exile of inhabitants causing loss of men, money, agriculture with rare possibility of regaining abandoned property. In 838 such a severe plague broke out in Herat that the death toll per day was said to be ten thousand. This epidemic was more severe in *buluks* than in the cities.[444] Such was the number of the deaths that Shahrukh had asked people not to open the report as it pained him to see his learned men and subjects thus lost.[445] In Shaban 866, a plague in Herat forced people to leave the town. Shops remained closed. Even imperial servants like *naib*, *qazi*, and *diwans* left the city. Those who could not afford to travel had to stay back to face death. The epidemic continued till 1st Muharram during which period thousands died and 'the fire of plague devoured and completely destroyed the fresh and the dry' *khushk o tar*' of that *balda*. Later on when the fury was over, the inhabitants were asked to rebuild their economy and agricultural prosperity and populousness and prosperity from a straw.[446] In Rabi II 867 such a severe snowfall occurred that movement became difficult—rather impossible. No business transactions, sale or purchase was possible. Trees and gardens remained without leaves but covered with snow. This situation continued for 50 days.[447] In 868 again a lesser epidemic in Herat and an extremely severe plague in Transoxiana spread. Again the imperial officials and people fled to mountains though casualties were considerable.[448] In 873 a drought in Qarabagh was reported. Such was the intensity that even the royal cavalcade which was in the vicinity of yilaq could not get water or eatables and even no pastures were to be seen. A maund or load of barley or wheat was not available even for 5 *tangas*. The quadrupeds died and even the rich and the affluent came at par with the needy as they were reduced to penury.[449] Famines became a common feature of the fifteenth century Central Asian economy. In 816 a famine broke out in Azerbaijan and during the drought prices soared high.[450] To add to the trouble, the rich landlords and cultivators (*reaya*) created artificial scarcity in 856 and concealed the grains and hoarded it hopeful of making profit during imminent scarcity due to famine. The *kalantars* did not leave enough for sale with the poor peasants (*raiyyat-i reza*). If the army arrived it plundered the place for provenders.[451] Although Abdussamad Khan says that the taxes under Timur and his successors were received in kind also, the royal granaries usually served for supplying good relief measures.[452]

People's unrest often took a very violent turn. Once Mirza Sultan Husain had gone to Chunaran to suppress the revolt of Yadgar Muhammad leaving Khwaja Abdullah Akhtab behind as *wazir*. In the absence of the ruler, Abdullah opened a reign of terror and started extorting from the *diwan* whatever he could in the form of cash and kind. Such a large amount was demanded that the subjects groaned under the yoke of taxes due to Khwaja Abdullah's *sar shumar* and other taxes. Consequently on such occasions, some of the common people—the mixed multitude of every class joined hands. On the morning when Khwaja Abdullah was going to the Daruladla of Mirza Shahrukh to rectify the situation, stone pelting started from both the sides of the market. With great difficulty Khwaja could hide himself in a secret corner. When Sultan Husain was informed, he ordered for exposing Khwaja to infamy and throwing him into prison. Khwaja Abdullah, however, came to know of the decision and fled to Hesar shadman.[453]

NOTES

1. Lokkegaard, *Abbasid Administration*, pp. 147-58.
2. Muhammad Asad, *Principles of State and Government in Islamic State*, pp. 1-40.
3. Ibid.
4. Ibid.
5. Saiyyid Hossein Nasr, *Sufi Essays*, London, 1972, pp. 38, 42; Montgomery Watt, *Islam and the Integration of Society*, p. 68; Gustavee von Grunebaum, *Medieval Islam*, p. 10.
6. Muhammad Asad, op. cit.
7. Lokkegaard, pp. 147-58, 173.
8. Marco Polo, *Travels of Marco Polo: the Venetian*, edited with introduction by Manuel Komroff, New York, 1930, p. 328.
9. V.V. Barthold, *Turkestan Down to the Mongol Invasion*, London, 1958, pp. 196-7.
10. Ibn-ul Abbas, *Asarul wal fi tartibul dawal*, Cairo, 1295 AH, p. 62; Philip K. Hitti, *History of the Arabs*, pp. 94, 95, 172, 217, 319, 321, 325, 335.
11. Hitti, pp. 94-5, 272-7, 318, 319, 321-5, 335.
12. Bernard Lewis, *Islam from the Prophet Muhammad to the Capture of Constantinople*, p. 303; *Siyasat Nama*, pp. 51-2; also see *Turkestan Down to . . .*, p. 229.
13. Lokkegaard, pp. 147-50.
14. Mawardi, *Ahkam*, Chapter II; Khan Haroon, *Early Muslim Political Thought*, Delhi, 1976, pp. 157-60. For the conflict between caliph and the king see p. 138.
15. Lokkegaard, pp. 147-50.
16. *Turkestan Down to . . .*, p. 230.
17. Hitti, pp. 320-5.
18. Nizam-ul Mulk Tusi, *Siyasat Nama*, Tehran, 1348, p. 56; Baihaqi, pp. 181, 393, 398.
19. Ibid., p. 20.
20. Tusi, p. 17; *Turkestan Down to . . .*, p. 232.
21. Lewis, *Islam*, p. 297; J. Schacht, *An Introduction to Islamic Law*, Oxford (Clarendon), 1964, p. 51.
22. Ibid., pp. 156-8.
23. Hitti, pp. 322 fn. 5, 326.
24. Ibid.
25. *Turkestan Down to . . .*, p. 234.
26. Ibid.; Hitti, p. 326.
27. Tusi, p. 41. Lewis, *Islam*, p. 300. For functions and details of their status see Barthold, *Turkestan Down to . . .*, pp. 227-8.
28. *Turkestan Down to . . .*, p. 306.
29. Barthold, *Tuskestan Down to . . .*, London, 1958, p. 268.
30. Ibid., p. 307.
31. Ibid., p. 25.
32. Ibid., p. 306.

33. Juvaini, *History of the World Conquerer*, Eng. tr., Vol. II, part II, p. 239; *Turkestan Down to . . .*, pp. 377-8.
34. Nasawi, pp. 102, 195, 232.
35. *Turkestan Down to . . .*, pp. 377-8.
36. Nasawi, pp. 102, 170.
37. Abul Fazl, *Akbar Nama (AN)*, Eng. tr., New Delhi, 1979, p. 194.
38. Paul Pelliot, 'Les Mongols et la Papaute', part I in Revue de le, Orient Chretien XXIII, 1922, pp. 13-23.
39. Chang Chun, *Travels*, p. 48; Juvaini, text, p. 124, Eng. tr., p. 158 fn. 14.
40. *JT*, p. 204.
41. *Works of the Peking Mission*, Vol. IV, p. 191.
42. D'Ohsen, *Histoire des Mongols*, III, p. 434.
43. *Turkestan Down to . . .*, p. 401.
44. Juvaini, pp. 87-9; Eng. tr., pp. 606-7.
45. Ibid.
46. Ibid.
47. Ibn-i Battuta, *H.A.R. Gibb Memorial Series*, p. 356.
48. Juvaini, text, p. 223; Eng. tr., p. 489.
49. Ibid., Vol. II, p. 223; Eng. tr., p. 287.
50. Ibid., pp. 228-30; Eng. tr., pp. 488, 491-3.
51. Ibid., text, pp. 229-30; Eng. tr., p. 493.
52. Ibid., pp. 85-8, Eng. tr., pp. 604-7.
53. Sharifuddin Ali Yezdi, *Zafar Nama (ZN)*, Calcutta, 1887, pp. 208-14.
    Clavijo, *Embassy to Tamerlane*, edited by Donison Ross and Eileen Power; Eng. tr. from Spanish by Guy Le Strange, London, 1928, p. 23.
    Khwand Mir, *Habib-us Siyar*, Vol. III, Tehran, 1333 AH, pp. 418-19.
54. *ZN*, Vol. I, p. 41; *Tarkikh-i Shahrukh* by Hafiz Abru, India Office, MS nos. 171, 173, 271-2.
55. Examples: *ZN*, Vol. I, pp. 30-1, 34.
56. Ibn-i Arab Shah, *Ajaib-ul Maqdur*, Eng. tr. by Sanders, London, 1936, p. 24.
57. Ibid., p. 47; Persian tr., p. 308; *Habib-us Siyar*, pp. 541-2.
58. Ibn-i Arab, pp. 24-5.
59. Ibid., Eng. tr., p. 4.
60. Ibid., pp. 299, 304.
61. Ibid., p. 49.
62. *Habib-us Siyar*, pp. 544-5.
63. Ibn-i Arab, Eng. tr., p. 91.
64. Ibid., Eng. tr., p. 119.
65. *TR*, tr., p. 31.
66. Ibid., p. 35.
67. *TR*, tr., p. 54.
68. *IA*, Eng. tr., p. 299.
69. Ibid., p. 18.
70. A.H. Lybyer insists that Ottoman state was not fully Asiatic and had European influence (Lybyer, pp. 7-13). Generally the Ottoman encounter with Western thought is said to have taken place in eighteenth century (Watt, *Islam and Integration of Society*, p. 23). But the Timurid state comparatively developed in isolation.

71. Even Prophet had allowed the use of local customs and traditions (*urf o adat*) (Levy Reuben, *Social Structure of Islam*, pp. 243, 248, 270, 295). Both Chardin (*voyages du chevalier chardin en Perse*, ed. L. Landles, Paris; *Chevalier Chardin en Perse*, ed. L. Langles, Paris, 1811, pp. 70-6); and Lybyer (*Ottoman State and Government*, pp. 7-13) had wrongly explained *urf* as the arbitrary will of the sovereign, though it was 'very much a part of civil tribunal' (see Levy, pp. 265-8).
72. *Tuzukat-i Timuri*, p. 174.
73. Ibn-i Arab, Eng. tr., pp. 198-200.
74. *Malfuzat*, p. 224.
75. Ibid., p. 228.
76. Ibid., p. 199.
77. Ibid., p. 204.
78. *Malfuzat*, pp. 217-18.
79. M. Prawdin, *The Mongol Empire: Its Rise and Legacy*, London, 1938, pp. 437-41.
80. Ibid., pp. 437-41, 448.
81. Prawdin, p. 438; *Four Studies*, Vol. II, pp. 113-19.
82. R.N. Frye, *Bukhara, the Medieval Achievement*, Norman, 1965, pp. 73-8.
83. *Matla-us Sadain*, Vol. II, I, pp. 133-4.
84. Ibn-i Arab, Eng. tr., p. 299; Pers. tr., pp. 53, 298.
85. *Tarikh-i Muhammadi*, ff. 229, 309.
86. *Matla*, pp. 739-41.
87. *Matla*, II, p. 25.
88. *TR*, Eng. tr., p. 307.
89. Ibid., pp. 69-70.
90. Ibid.
91. *BN*, pp. 298-9.
92. *Matla*, op. cit., p. 362.
93. *Dastur-ul Wuzara*, pp. 401-2.
94. *The Laws of Ceremonies and Etiquettes*, for details see Lybyer, p. 134.
95. Juvaini, pp. 20-2.
96. *ZN*, II, p. 73.
97. *Babur Nama*, pp. 20-1, also fn. 1; *The Islamic World: History of the Mongols*, California, 1972, pp. 87-8, see *Az Salajiqa ta Safaviya*, p. 278; *Sochinenija*, p. 184.
98. Hatifi, *ZN*.
99. *BN*, pp. 54, 58.
100. Ibid.
101. Ibid.
102. *BN*, Eng. tr., p. 193.
103. *BN*, text, p. 121, Eng. tr., pp. 189-90.
104. *Matla*, Vols. II, III, pp. 396-7.
105. *IA*, Persian text, p. 300.
106. Matla, *Oriental College Magazine*, 9 vols., May 1933, p. 11, for *Shura* and *Ijma* see Levy, pp. 168-82, 287-90; *Muhammedan Jurisprudence*, pp. 82-97; Asad, p. 27.
107. *ZN*, I, p. 577; *Matla*, p. 21.

108. Examples: *ZN*, I, p. 163; *Matla*, Vols. II, III, p. 457.
109. *ZN*, I, pp. 164, 223, 487.
110. Yezdi, II, pp. 520.
111. Examples: Yezdi, pp. 164, 520; Nizam-ul Mulk Tusi, *Siyar-ul Muluk*, Tehran, 1348, ed. by Jafar Shear, pp. 138-40; *Tuzukat, i Timuri*; Haji Khairullah, *Dastur-i Jahanqusha*, Aligarh MS Salam 328/98, ff. 28-32.
112. *BN*, text, p. 186; Eng. tr., pp. 298-9.
113. *ZN*, I, p. 44.
114. *Babur Name* (*BN*).
115. Ibid.
116. Mirza Rustam son of Umar Shaikh was assigned Isfahan twice and he held it till his death (*Matla*, II, p. 163).
117. *Matla*, II, III, p. 1407.
118. Ibid., p. 88.
119. As in 873, see *Matla*, II, pp. 1388-9.
120. *Matla*, II, III, pp. 795, 1369-70.
121. Ibid., pp. 14-15.
122. Ibid., II, III, p. 199.
123. *IA*, p. 250.
124. *BN*, p. 45.
125. *ZN*, II, p. 275.
126. Hafiz Abru, pp. 435-38.
127. *Matla*, II, III, pp. 374, 396.
128. Ibid.
129. Juvaini, *Tarikh-i Jahanqusha*, Leiden, 1911, pp. 30-1.
130. Ibid., pp. 30-1.
131. Ibn-i Khaldun, *The Muqaddimah*, Eng. tr. from Arabic by France Rosenthal I, New York, 1958, pp. 381-405.
132. Al-Hasan the Arab, *Purchas and his Pilgrims,* Vol. XI, p. 464.
133. Yuan Chao Pishi, *Secret History*, Aligarh, 1957, pp. 165-6. Fazlullah Ruzbehan Isfahani, pp. 22-8.
134. *Mehmannama* (*Mehn*), Tehran, 1341 AH, pp. 22-8; *Cambridge History of Islam*, vol. I, 1967, p. 252.
135. *ZN*, II, pp. 253-4; also see *Comprehensive History*, Vol. I by Habib and Nizami, p. 102.
136. *AN*, p. 449.
137. *ZN*, II, pp. 627-31.
138. *ZN*, Calcutta edn., pp. 9-10.
139. *ZN*, I, p. 192.
140. Ibid.
141. *ZN*, I, p. 73.
142. *ZN*, II, p. 279.
143. *ZN*, I, pp. 229-32, 258, 297, *ZN*, II, pp. 102, 125. Yezdi insists that through divine guidance and protection Timur was able to read the evil intentions of Shaikh Muhammad Bayan Sulduz and Adil Shah Jalair who wanted to arrest Timur in a coup de'état at Khujand.
144. *ZN*, I, Calcutta edn., pp. 5-10; *ZN*, I, Tehran edn., pp. 450-1, 459, 566, 568; *ZN*, II, Tehran edn., pp. 55, 141, 154-5, 238, 417, 419.

145. *ZN*, I, Calcutta edn., p. 16.
146. *ZN*, I, pp. 79-80; *ZN*, I, p. 385; *ZN*, II, p. 307.
147. A. Polovtsoff, *The Land of Timur*, London, 1932, p. 6; *ZN*, II, p. 383; *Tuzukat-i Timuri*, ed. Major Davy, p. 194, Oxford, 1782, p. 194.
148. Hafiz Abru, *Tarikh-i Shahrukh*, India Office Library, ff. 12, 171, 173.
149. Ibn-i Arab, Eng. tr. by Sanders, p. 295; Yezdi, *ZN*, II, pp. 170, 389.
150. Ibn-i Arab, p. 299.
151. Ibid., p. 300.
152. Ibid., p. 301.
153. Ibn-i Arab, Eng. tr., pp. 189-200.
154. Even in marriage ceremony in 807 at Kan-i Gul, the main *pandal* which could accommodate 10-12 thousand people was reserved mainly for the princes, sadat, noyon, qazis in the upper aristocracy (*akabir wayan*), whereas the provincial nobility and the gentry were to sit outside in advance stating the place of each and to ensure that none changes his station. Even the places of meat and bread sellers were fixed by Timur who personally enquired their welfare and gave them *dastmuzdi* (labour fee). *H. Siyar*, p. 528; Ibn-i Arab, Pers. tr., p. 280.
155. Beatrice Forbes Manz, 'Administration and Delegation of Authority under Timur', *Central Asiatic Journal*, pp. 203-6.
156. *IA*, Eng. tr., pp. 146, 311-13, Pers. tr., pp. 309-11; *H. Siyar*, p. 548.
157. *IA*, Pers. tr., pp. 300-1.
158. Ibid., p. 18.
159. *ZN*, I, p. 58.
160. *IA*, Pers. tr., pp. 48, 248.
161. Clavijo, p. 188.
162. Daulatshah, *Tarikh-i Daulat Shah Samarqandi*, p. 260; Petrusheveski, pp. 227-9.
163. Exmaples, *ZN*, p. 558; *H. Siyar*, p. 522.
164. Barthold, *Sochinenija*, Moscow, 1968, Vol. V, p. 8.
165. Forbes Manz, p. 197.
166. *ZN*, I, pp. 216, 326, 327, 352.
167. Manz, p. 197.
168. Nizamuddin Shami, *Zafar Nama;* Felix Tauer's edn., Vol. I, pp. 131, 145; Vol. II, p. 90.
169. Shami, II, p. 197.
170. Jean Aubin, *Deux Sayyids de Baum*, XV Siecle; Manz, 1956, p. 395.
171. *IA*, Eng. tr., p. 307.
172. Ibn-i Arab, Eng. tr., pp. 299-300.
173. *ZN*, II, pp. 546-9; *H. Siyar*, pp. 519-20.
174. *ZN*, I, p. 592.
175. Ibid., I, p. 359.
176. See *Zafar Nama* of both Shami and Yezdi and also the work of Altaftazani for significance of the tours.
177. Shami, f. 78; Altaftazani, f. 97.
178. Clavijo, pp. 178, 218.
179. Ibid.
180. Ibid.

181. *JT*, pp. 292, 307.
182. Juvaini, pp. 206-7; Eng. tr., p. 251.
183. Ibid., pp. 148, 206, 208, 219; Eng. tr., pp. 186-8, 250-3, 264.
184. Ibid., p. 148; Eng. tr., p. 188.
185. *JT*, p. 292.
186. Juvaini, text, p. 251; Eng. tr., p. 514.
187. Ibid., pp. 148, 206-8; Eng. tr., pp. 186-8.
188. Arthur Waley, *The Secret History of the Mongols*, London, 1963, Chapter III, p. 245.
189. Waley, p. 245.
190. Beveridge had wrongly translated mistaking Khwan as Khaqan. *AN*, Eng. tr., p. 974, also fn. 2.
191. *Tarkhan Nama (TN)*, pp. 21-35.
192. Haider Dughlat, pp. 300-4.
193. *AN*, III, p. 635; Eng. tr., pp. 974-5; *Ain-i Blochomann*, p. 393.
194. L.V. Chereprin, *Akti feudalnovo zemlevledeniya-e-khazyaistova*, part III, Moscow, 1961, pp. 4-44.
195. Cleaves, *Secret History*, pp. 141-2; *JT*, p. 333.
196. *Secret History*, pp. 112-6.
197. Ibid., pp. 119-21, 146-61.
198. Ibid., pp. 42, 120.
199. Ibid., pp. 83, 159.
200. Ibid., p. 208.
201. *AN*, III, text, pp. 635-7; Eng. tr., pp. 973-97; *Ain*, op. cit., p. 393.
202. Ibid.
203. Ibn-i Arab, pp. 20, 25, 48-9, 146, 150, 300, 303, 307; *AN*, III, Eng. tr., p. 973.
204. *Ain*, I, no. 42, p. 380, Badauni, *Muntakhab-ut Tawarikh*, III, p. 188.
205. *ZN*, I, p. 113.
206. *H. Siyar*, pp. 418-19.
207. *AAA*, pp. 467.
208. *ZN*, I, pp. 446-72.
209. Ibid., p. 228.
210. Ibid., p. 231.
211. Ibid., pp. 303, 471.
212. *IA*, Persian text, p. 300.
213. Shami, p. 123.
214. *ZN*, p. 560.
215. *ZN*, p. 347.
216. Ibid., p. 423.
217. *IA*, Persian text, pp. 303-7.
218. See *IA*, p. 146; *H. Siyar*, p. 519.
219. *IA*, pp. 25.
220. *IA*, Eng. tr., pp. 150-6; Persian text, p. 20.
221. *IA*, Eng. tr., pp. 48-9, 50.
222. See *ZN*, I, pp. 160, 223, 253, 264.
223. *AAA*, p. 414.
224. See *ZN*, I, pp. 160, 223, 253.

225. *ZN*, p. 264.
226. *ZN*, II, pp. 501-4; *H. Siyar*, p. 515.
227. *ZN*, II, p. 45.
228. Ibid., pp. 42, 130, 178, 133, 232-3, 277.
229. Clavijo, pp. 195-6.
230. Lybyer, *Ottoman State and Government*, pp. 114-15.
231. Juvaini, p. 8.
232. *TR*, Eng. tr., p. 41.
233. *IA*, Persian text, pp. 300-1.
234. *IA*, Eng. tr., p. 146; Persian text, p. 18.
235. Matla, *Oriental College Magazine*, Nov. 1942, pp. 840-1.
236. *BN*, p. 22; Eng. tr., p. 39.
237. Clavijo, p. 195.
238. *IA*, Persian text, p. 152; Eng. tr., p. 146
239. Juvaini, p. 598.
240. *History of Ghazan*, ed. K. John Lodo, 1940, pp. 221, 222; *Jami-ut Tawarikh*, Vol. III, Alzade Baku, 1957, p. 431.
241. J. Schacht, *An Introduction to Islamic Law*, Oxford, 1964, p. 138.
242. See Juvaini, Eng. tr., *History of the World Conquerer*, Vol. II, part II, pp. 254-7.
243. *JT*, p. 439.
244. Juvaini, text, pp. 38-9; Eng. tr., p. 53.
245. *TR*, Eng. tr., pp. 116-26.
246. *Dastur-ul Katib*, p. 366.
247. Hitti, p. 319 fn.
248. *Dastur*, p. 306.
249. Rashiduddin, *Jamiut Tawarikh*, Tehran, 1338 AH.
250. Lybyer, pp. 100-3.
251. *Matla* II, pp. 362-3, 1410-11, 1419, 1434.
252. Ibid., II, p. 363.
253. Ibid., I, p. 17.
254. Shamsuddin Muhammad Marwarid of Kirman had come to Herat where he was given the *wizarat* (*Dastur-ul Wuzara*, pp. 394-5). Another Khwaja Alauddin Ali Alsarei of Barmak dynasty came from Bakhzar and was appointed as *wazir* of Herat by Sultan Husain (*Dastur*, p. 397). Khwaja Saifuddin Muzaffar Shabankara, a *buzurgzada* of Fars and Iraq too held the rank in Herat (*Dastur*, p. 399).
255. *Matla*, II, p. 1410.
256. *Dastur*, p. 378.
257. Ibid., p. 394.
258. *IA*, Eng. tr., p. 311.
259. *Dastur*, pp. 400-41.
260. *Matla*, pp. 364, 753, 794.
261. Ibid., pp. 794, 841.
262. Ibid., pp. 294, 747, 841.
263. Ibid., pp. 841-2.
264. *Tarikh-i Daulat Shah Samarqandi*, p. 347.
265. *BN*, p. 281, Eng. tr.

266. *Matla*, pp. 539-54.
267. Ibid., II, III, pp. 376, 426, 450, 1410-11
268. *Dastur-ul Wuzara*, ff. 365-7.
269. Ibid., p. 362.
270. Amir Firuz had appointed Saiyid Imanuddin as controller of Balkh. Shahrukh wanted to shift his favourite Saiyid to some other lucrative place but failed to change Amir Firuz's opinion and had to resort to enquiry to punish Amir Firuz (*Dastur*, pp. 362-3).
271. *Dastur*, p. 377.
272. Ibid., pp. 390-2.
273. Ibid., p. 395.
274. Ibid., pp. 364, 367.
275. *Matla*, pp. 345-51.
276. Ibid., p. 753.
277. Ibid., p. 1434.
278. Ibid., p. 755.
279. The appointment of Khwaja Sidi as *shaik* with Ghayasuddin also took place in 838 though he died in 839, *Dastur-ul Wuzara*, pp. 357-8. Also see *Matla* II, p. 670.
280. *Dastur*, pp. 358-60.
281. Ibid., p. 361.
282. Amin Ahmad Razi, *Haft Aqlim* II, p. 173; Matla says thirty years (see *Matla*, pp. 364, 432, 753, 794).
283. *Dastur-ul Wuzara*, pp. 353-5.
284. Razi II, p. 326.
285. *Matla*, II, I, p. 18.
286. *BN*, text, 176-7; Eng. tr., pp. 281-2.
287. *Dastur*, pp. 401-2.
288. Ibid.
289. Ibid., p. 385.
290. Razi, II, p. 173.
291. *Matla*, II, p. 17.
292. Ibid., II, III, pp. 426, 450, 1370.
293. Ibid., pp. 794, 836, 840.
294. *Dastur*, p. 375.
295. *Matla*, II, III, pp. 370, 376.
296. Ibid., II, pp. 1430-1.
297. *Dastur-ul Wuzara*, p. 344.
298. Khwand Mir, *Habib-us Siyar*, p. 567; *Dastur-ul Wuzara*, pp. 344-5; Abdurrazzaq, II, I, p. 63; Hafiz Abru, pp. 84-5; *Dastur*, pp. 344-5.
299. *Dastur*, pp. 364-5.
300. Ibid.
301. *Dastur*, pp. 362-3.
302. Ibid., pp. 360-1.
303. Barthold, *Turkestan Down*, p. 37.
304. See *IA*, Eng. tr., pp. 14-15.
305. *IA*, Eng. tr., pp. 14-15.
306. Clavijo, p. 184.

307. *ZN*, I, p. 492.
308. Al-Hasan the Arab, *Purchas and his Pilgrims*, XD, p. 468.
309. See *ZN*, I, pp. 398, 523; *H. Siyar*, pp. 520, 574.
310. *ZN*, II pp. 560-1.
311. Clavijo, pp. 293-6.
312. Hafiz Abru, *Tarikh-i Shahrukh*, f. 17, see *ZN*, I, pp. 444-5.
313. *ZN*, II, p. 593; *H. Siyar*, p. 526.
314. Ibid., I, p. 592.
315. Ibid., I, p. 395.
316. *IA*, Eng. tr., p. 49.
317. *ZN*, I, p. 359. *IA*, Eng. tr., p. 301; *ZN*, II, pp. 546-9; *H. Siyar*, pp. 519-20, 526.
318. Ibid.
319. See Abdurrazzaq Samarqandi, *Matla-us Sadain, Oriental Colleage Magazine*, III, II, p. 210; *FS* II, p. 103.
320. Khwand Mir, p. 617.
321. Abdurrazzak, II, III, pp. 322-3.
322. Ibid., p. 283.
323. *Matla*, p. 89.
324. See *AR*, II, I, pp. 83, 98.
325. R.N. Nabiev, however says that the state had no share in the income from *suyurhghals* which went to the personal treasury of its holder, *Akhbarat, Izvestia*, 1959, III, p. 24.
326. Khwand Mir, III, p. 380.
327. *Tarikh-i Shahrukh*, ff. 17, 68; Abdurrazzak, II, I, pp. 60, 62, 85, 84, 124, 149, 150, 307.
328. See *AR*, II, III, pp. 348-9, 375, 406, 417.
329. *AR*, II, III, p. 1374.
330. Allworth, *Central Asia in Modern Times*, New York; Ghaffurov, *Tajiki*, Moscow, p. 110.
331. *Tarikh-i Shahrukh*, f. 17.
332. *AR*, II, pp. 568-9.
333. Ibid., p. 157.
334. *Tarikh-i Shahrukh*, f. 13.
335. *AR*, II, pp. 236-7.
336. *Tarikh-i Daudi* (*TD*); *Central Asia, a Century of Russian Rule*, New York, 1967, p. 49.
337. For information on the *waqf* cf. *Haft Iqlim*, II, p. 42; Ghaffurov, *Tajiki*, p. 492 says that a special tax was imposed upon *waqaf* lands by the *sadr* which was utilized for the maintenance of the office of the *waqf* land. He adds that in this way the *sadr* and his office used to take away a large share from the income of the *waqf* and even the *sadr* resorted to embezzlements. No source is however cited for these statements.
338. *Matla*, II, III, pp. 119-20, 756-7.
339. *BN*, Eng. tr., pp. 170, 270.
340. *BN*, text, p. 167, Eng. tr., p. 264.
341. *Dastur-ul Wuzara*, p. 362.
342. Ibid.

343. Ibid., p. 361.
344. Ibid., p. 364.
345. *Matla*, pp. 841-2.
346. *Dastur*, pp. 372-6.
347. *Dastur-ul Wuzara*, p. 342.
348. Ibid., pp. 401-2.
349. Ibid., pp. 368-9.
350. Ibid., pp. 379-80.
351. Ibid., pp. 382-3.
352. Ibid., pp. 383-4.
353. Ibid., p. 377.
354. Ibid., pp. 392-3.
355. Ibid., p. 393.
356. Ibid., pp. 369-70.
357. Khwaja Ghayasuddin Khwand Mir, *Dastur-ul Wuzara*, 2nd edn., Tehran, 2535 solar year.
358. *Dastur*, pp. 395-6.
359. Jalal ud Islam, the *wazir* of Timur being quite sure of Timur's regard and consideration for himself had once resorted to splendid silence resulting in fines imposed upon him and extracted from his *jihat* (duties on manufactures) and *ummal* of his *sarkar*, such was the intensity of torture and demand that Jalal was driven to stab himself but was saved as the wound was not very deep. Nevertheless, he was able to regain the lost favour of Timur thereafter. *Dastur-ul Wuzara*, p. 342.
360. *Dastur*, pp. 397-8.
361. Ibid., p. 418.
362. *BN*, text, p. 205; Eng. tr., p. 326.
363. *Matla*, Lahore, 1944, pp. 283-7, 291-6, 322-3, 376-8.
364. Khwand Mir, *Habib-us Siyar*, pp. 605-6; *Matla*, p. 1400.
365. *Tarikh-i Shahrukh*, ff. 47, 83; *Matla* III, pp. 124, 171-2, Khwand Mir.
366. *ZN*, II, pp. 154, 157, 270.
367. *Matla*, p. 795.
368. Ibid., II, I, p. 165.
369. Ibid., pp. 596-7.
370. *BN*, Eng. tr., pp. 270, 273.
371. Ibid., pp. 274, 276.
372. Samaqat b. Tariki was given the *niyabat* of Sairam.
373. *IA*, Persian text, pp. 48, 248.
374. Clavijo, p. 188.
375. *H. Siyar*, p. 548.
376. *BN*, p. 177, Eng. tr., p. 283.
377. Razi, *Haft Iqlim*, Vol. II, p. 35.
378. Ibid., pp. 89-90.
379. *BN*, Eng. tr., p. 57, also see Ibn-i Hasan, *Central Structure of the Mughal Empire*. For Mughal *bakhshis* see pp. 210-33.
380. *BN*, pp. 57, 283.
381. *BN*, p. 115.
382. *Matla* II, III, p. 389.

383. Ibid., pp. 588-9.
384. *AAA*, p. 446.
385. H. Abru, p. 187.
386. *BN*, pp. 41-5.
387. *BN*, Eng. tr., pp. 41-5; Grammont, pp. 64-5.
388. *Dastur*, pp. 372, 378-9.
389. Ibid., pp. 378-9.
390. Ibid., pp. 372, 374.
391. Ibid., p. 377.
392. When in Nov. 1542/840-1, a person informed Shahrukh about the misappropriation of treasures of fort of Ikhtiyaruddin a long checking was ordered. The stolen goods, were, somehow, found in that very place and the dishonest treasurer was thrown into prison followed by a thorough and careful rechecking of the treasuries (*Matla* I, p. 17).
393. *Dastur*, pp. 372-3.
394. Ibid., p. 375.
395. Wasifi, p. 846; Khwand Mir, pp. 630-3.
396. *ZN*, II, p. 156, also see pp. 180-1.
397. *Dastur*, pp. 390-2.
398. *Matla*, II, III, p. 406.
399. Ibid., II, III, pp. 345-55.
400. *Dastur*, pp. 367-70.
401. Ibid., pp. 368-9.
402. *Tarikh-i Qahet*, pp. 83-6.
403. *Matla*, II, III, p. 375.
404. *Dastur*, pp. 346-7.
405. Ibid., pp. 346-52.
406. *H. Siyar*, p. 631; *Matla*, pp. 345-51.
407. *Tazkira-i Daulatshah Samarqandi*, p. 70.
408. Examples, Abdurrazzaq, I, pp. 28, 85, 92, 231; II, pp. 1410-11; Khwand Mir, p. 345.
409. *BN*, Eng. tr., p. 194.
410. *Dastur*, ff. 399-400.
411. Ibid., f. 373; *ZN*, I, p. 561; II, pp. 378-9, 393-4, 397, 418, 426.
412. Ibid., f. 344.
413. Ibid., ff. 353-4.
414. Ibid., f. 379.
415. Khwand Mir, pp. 385-7.
416. *IA*, Eng. tr., p. 15.
417. According to Abul Fazl a *kharwar* was equivalent to 40 Qandhari *mans* or 10 Hindustani *mans* (*Ain* II, Jarret, p. 399).
418. *TD*, p. 158.
419. Clavijo, pp. 286-7; *BN*, pp. 3, 75.
420. Simkin, p. 170.
421. *BN*, pp. 3, 6, 7, 10, 98, 77, 82, 84.
422. *IA*, Eng. tr., p. 282.
423. *IA*, Eng. tr. pp. 281-2
424. See *Matla* II, I, p. 125.

425. Ibid., II, pp. 1417-18.
426. Clavijo, p. 184.
427. *IA*, II, I, pp. 48, 113.
428. Abdurrazzak, II, I, p. 48.
429. Ibid., II, I, pp. 55, 65, 149, 173.
430. Ibid., II, I, pp. 48, 113, 141.
431. Ibid., p. 11.
432. *IA*, Eng. tr., p. 46.
433. Ibid., p. 145.
434. *Matla*, II, III, pp. 398-9, 346-50, pp. 1410-11; *Dastur*, pp. 374-5.
435. *Dustur-ul Wuzara*, p. 343.
436. Ibid., p. 377.
437. Ibid., p. 394.
438. Ibid., pp. 341, 372-6.
439. Ibid., pp. 348-9.
440. Ibid., p. 363.
441. Azim Janova, *Babur en Transoxiana*, p. 8; *Le livre de Babur*, French tr. of *BN* by J.L. Bacquet Grammont, POF, 1980.
442. *Dastur-ul Wuzara*, pp. 370-1; *Matla*, II, III, p. 370.
443. Ibid., p. 371.
444. *Matla* II, pp. 677-8.
445. Ibid., II, pp. 678-82.
446. Ibid., II, III, pp. 379-80.
447. Ibid., II, III, pp. 387-8
448. Ibid., II, III, pp. 400-1.
449. Ibid., II, III, pp. 457-60.
450. Ibid., II, p. 149.
451. Ibid., II, III, p. 156.
452. Abdussamad Khan, *Tarikh-i Qahat*, Abdus Salam Collection, Farsiya 4272/ 42, pp. 83-6, no source has been quoted.
453. *Dastur*, pp. 391-3.

The Kurultai and the Kangash

The similarities in the Eurasian polity have seldom revealed themselves so consistently as in the institution of consultative assembly. It is difficult to determine the precise date, place and its genesis as its existence howsoever rudimentary is noticed *hic et ubrique* and ever since the beginning of monarchical form of government for assisting the king and to bridle his arrogation of power. In the Islamic world, this practice was institutionalized and the decision of the majority was considered to be 'an echo of the Divine Commandment'.[1] In every part of Asia, the counsellors may not have enjoyed an extraordinarily effective voice but their existence itself in some form or other was seemingly a semblance of sober and balanced government. In India for example, not only Manu and Brihaspaty but statesmen like Kautilya had stressed 'all kinds of administrative measures are preceded by deliberations and a well formed council'.[2] Its echoes are heard in later Persian chronicles[3] written in India. Even Babur had specifically recommended 'counselling with prudent and experienced begs', and to 'act as they say'. In his letter to Humayun, Babur has asked him to summon his younger brothers and the begs twice daily to his presence, take counsel and settle every word and 'act in agreement'. In Turkey also the counseling was especially recommended.[4]

Most of the Central Asian chroniclers had emphasized the need of consultative assembly. Nakhch-i Wani in early middle ages, had allocated one full chapter to the blessings of consultations.[5] Samundar Tirmizi[6] had endorsed the same views in eighteenth-nineteenth centuries. Mahmud bin Wali[7] described this group of counsellors as an antidote to all dangers.

After his ascendancy, the Mongol ruler Tuva had commented 'the greatest word wherever it was (said) depends upon (or was in accordance with) the consultations with relatives' (*ulugh qaul harjaki bashad bur qarar ha ba mashawarat o kangoj aqa o ini*).[8] Abdullah Khan Uzbeg too considered consultations to be a 'God's signal—a revealed truth and the safest exit from the difficulties'. He is said to have never undertaken any special assembly (*majlis-i khas*) of his own confidantes (*ahl-i ikhtesas*).[9] Although freedom of expression was granted, Abdullah could reject the opinion of the majority in favour of his own deputy's suggestion without creating any displeasure among the others.

The traditional significance attached to the consultations on all important occasions in pre- and post-Mongol Central Asia is thus very well reflected through the comments of different chroniclers and utterances of sovereigns, through the ages. It is, however interesting to note that the Timurid and Uzbeg historians like Yazdi, Samarqandi, Hafiz Tanish[10] and others feeling probably the pulse of their age always stressed that these assemblies were in pursuance of the Islamic principles. They seek to give an Islamic colour that the *Kangash* was a kind of assembly giving practical form to the concept of *ijma* and *shura*, i.e. the 'Islamic injunction of consensus'. Such comments are found even during the Mongol period. In his *Siyar-ul Muluk* (*Siyasatnama*), Tusi had praised and recommended *mushwarat* (consultations) with the wise and the aged since the 'deliberations with ten was always better than that of the two'. Tusi considered the *ijma* or *shura* institution as being 'the wisest of all the prophet's revealed directions'. Abstenance from consultations was in his opinion a clear proof of weak mind and such a person was self-willed hence each business without consultations was bound to end in utter failure.[12]

Unlike the Turkish, Persian and Arabic sources, which stress the significance of consultative assembly, the available text of the *yasa* of Chingiz Khan is bereft of a direct and specific ruling in the context of consultations. Nevertheless there is an implicit suggestion to the same effect that 'a point on which three wisemen agree can be repeated anywhere otherwise it can not be trusted. One's own words should be tallied with those of other wisemen. If in agreement they should be uttered otherwise not'.[13] It was only on the issue of Yarghu pursidan (bringing defaulting nobles to book and punishing them) that Chingiz forewarned against any wilful or arbitrary judgement in dealing with the defaulters and emphasized the need for a 'Kangameshi' (consultations) of *aqa o ini* (relatives and friends). He had, however, emphasized the need for an annual or biennial assembly of *amirs* of *tuman* and *hazara* for listening to biliks of Chingiz.[14] The custom seems to have continued even upto the very end of Mongol regime in Central Asia. Apart from the information available in Persian chronicles, even Ibn-i Battuta gives a detailed account of this annual Toi. Ibn-i Battuta says that it was the 'accepted code' among them to assemble once a year. The day is called Toi. On this occasion, the descendants of Chingiz Khan, beys, generals and the ladies arrive. Apart from the feasts and festivities, actions of kings and nobles are judged/scrutinized.[15] That a statesman of Chingiz's stature did not feel the need of consultations is not at all amazing for it reflects and confirms his love for absolute power. It should, however, be noted that in matters of war, he never hesitated in organizing the consultative assemblies. The sources are full of the details of such discussions though no particular council or specific counsellors seems to have existed. Before the campaigns, Kurultai was held to discuss the feasibility, planning and strategy of warfare, e.g. before the war against Tayauk Khan in the year of Jumad II 600 or another Kurultai in Zilqada 615 for war against Taziks. But quite in conformity with the independent outlook, the nomination of his heir apparent was accomplished in a private assembly of the princes (*dar khilwat nashista*) in Safar 613 in the year of dog.[16]

His successors also organized such assemblies. During a span of seven years (Jumad 1632—year of sheep of Shabaan 638) Ogedei organized two *Kurultai-i buzurg*, one in *mauza* Talaan Disang in the year of horse and another in the year of sheep, the purpose being that they should listen to the *Yasa* and its rules once again. All the invitees came to enjoy the Toi for a month. The tasks performed during the *kurultai* were (apart from the bestowal of *suyurghameshy* and distribution of treasure accumulated during these years) the organization of affairs of the state and army (*batartib-i maham-i mulk o lashkar*) and discussions over the proposed conquests of hitherto unconquered lands and nomination of commanders for the same.[17]

The holding of consultations was an important part of conduct of state business by the ruler in Central Asia. Different names have thus been given to this state assembly[18] such as Qurultai or Kurultai, Kengash, Janqi, Changi, Majlis-i Mashwarat-i Majlis-i Aali, and so on) in the Central Asian region.

In modern Uzbeg language the Qurultai denotes 'Congress'.[19] In the *Farhang* of Wassaf, the Mongol term Kurultai had been rendered, as a 'Turkish word denoting Majma (assembly), Kangash, Shura or Jashn'. Farhang-i Anand Raj[20] reiterates the same whereas another dictionary[21] explains the term as the Majlis-i Mushawarat of the

Mughals. Due to the lose usage of the terms by the chroniclers, the above mentioned terms have frequently been treated as synonyms notwithstanding the fact that Kurultai had a specific meaning of a 'parliament' whose members were nominated by the ruler. Similarly, even an informal discussion with one person or an entire consultative assembly are both described as 'Kangash and Kurultai, as synonyms, e.g. after the burial of Chingiz, at his real Yurt Kuluran, the princes and the nobles held Kangaj relating to settlement of affairs of state (*bab-i mulk*), unanimously highlighting the need for an immediate accession of the nominee as the throne was lying vacant for two years and there was the danger of commotion and disturbances. The messengers were sent and Kurultai was organized.[22] The Kurultai was of two kinds, the grand (*buzurg*) and the ordinary Kurultai. The word *Kurultai* had occasionally been used in the sense of consultation also.[23] The consultative assemblies were held both at the Centre and the provinces. From the account of Rashiduddin, it appears that Kangash could be anything from an ordinary, off-hand, casual discussion to a formal or special consultative meeting on any important occasion, e.g. war, peace, accession, or administrative affair, grievances pre and post war planning, etc. Any consultation by princes or nobles separately or together was thus termed as Kangaj. The Kurultai, however was a more official and formal, celebrative affair. It was attended by all the princes, members of the ruling families from every nook and corner of the empire, nobles of all categories, representatives from foreign lands (usually on accession ceremony), military aristocracy and administrative bureaucracy. The common folks, if any, were only the artisans and petty shopkeepers who had to sell their goods at less than the market rates to the participants of the assembly during the sessions of Kurultai.

Controversy surrounds Kurultai as the functions and the extent of authority vested in Kurultai have been variously interpreted. Not only, Cahun 'over evaluated' the powers of Mongol people's assembly but certain other historians also echoed the same views. Weikwei Sun more moderately underplayed the fact that Chingiz, in his later days organized it (Kurultai) on a definite basis and assigned to it the highest of all functions that of electing his successor. Only princes and the highest Government officers were admitted to the Kurultai of the Mongols. The subjects brought before it were delicate, complicated and important; and if some of its decisions, such as the final election of the Khan had to be published immediately, other decisions such as plans of the campaigns decided upon were strictly confidential.[24]

Barthold and other Central Asianists considerably deflate the position of Kurultai comparing it with a German Reichstag or describing it as a place where strength of Khaqan's power was displayed. In his opinion Kurultai was not a representative assembly (created for deciding state affairs, issues or election of a new ruler) or a mouth piece or *vox populi* in the strictest sense of the term. The Kurultai held for accession was just a formality as the task performed in this assembly was not that of election but only of proclamation followed by ceremonial and festive acclamation and accession of Khaqan. After the oath of allegiance, celebrations continued for a month or so. Barthold further contradicts Cahun's view[25] that frequent wars of succession were 'due to electoral system' or 'due to old Mongolian privileges and rights'.

In view of such contradictory opinions, a *coup de oeil* of the Persian sources seems to be only too essential. Owing to the significance of the subject and its dimensions, the detailed passages from the Persian sources have been quoted and incidents and examples pertaining to Kurultai have been generously reproduced to support the conclusions. The various duties and functions of Kurultai have been separately discussed in order to see the latent influence of Kurultai if any.

The most important function of the Kurultai was said to be the selection or election of the Khan. Almost all the Persian sources have extensively dealt with the Kurultai of accession of coronation which help us in understanding the procedure. To be precise, the Khans were not elected in these Kurultais. The decision in favour of a Khan was taken much earlier and the session of the Kurultai was conducted under the same Khan himself. These Kurultais began with oath taking by the princes and nobles expressing allegiance to the Khan. This was followed by merry-making, distribution of awards, plans for new campaigns and nomination of commanders, punishment to the defaulters, confirmation (*imza*) of old and new rules, regulations and *nishans*. The Kurultai held at *mauza* Kukanauwar, in Rabi II 643 in the spring of the year of horse for the accession of Guyuk could be cited as an example. At this assembly the participants were—the princes, nobles of the right and left wings—noyons, amirs, officials (*arbab-i ashghal*) and local governors (*ashab-i aamal*); the dignitaries and representatives from other countries (e.g. China, Lur, Iraq, Garjistan, Shervan, Rum, Azerbaijan, Helb, Mosul, Fars, Kirman, Firang, Baghdad, Armenia, Alamut, Aleppo, Georgia). There were about 2,000 *khargahs* (felt tents) erected for the participants. Due to the flood of the human beings, there remained no place vacant in the Urdu *mauza* and a sudden spurt in the prices of grains and drinks was noticed.[26] 'For one continuous month' says Juvaini 'in unison with the like minded relatives and with the assistance of kinsmen without compare, he joined dawn to dusk and morning to evening in *contrast application* to bowls and goblets and the handling round of cups by the hands of beauteous cup bearers'. After 'enjoyment of all kinds of wanton pastime' for one month, rewards were scattered upon small and great as the 'spring cloud rains upon grass and trees', so that all might have their share of the gifts of his goodness and liberality. Each of Khan in his Kurultai of accession confirmed the old and new *yasas* and ordinances of their predecessor. If the campaigns were to be undertaken, the families were nominated and dispatched. The crimes and offences of defaulters were also brought to the attention of the family and amirs and punishment was determined.[27] The details given about the other Kurultais of coronation are more or less the same. A careful study of the Persian and Arabic sources shows that the Kurultai was therefore not an 'elective' body but simply a place for public acknowledgement and acceptance of a particular candidate. This formal ceremony was as much a matter of sentiments and benefits as of politics.

Vladimirtsov and Krader confirm that Chingiz Khan was 'elected' emperor in the 'traditional manner of electing a clan chief according to Mongol custom'.[28] But the sources (including *Secret History*) do not refer to any election. Both assert that he enjoyed 'unlimited and absolute power', a fact reiterated by Barthold.[29] Since Chingiz was 'tied to a consanguineous tradition' and realized the significance of stratified society and hierarchical order of aristocracy only too well, the Kurultai was allowed to continue as a shadow of the Khan and not as a power behind the throne. The *yasa* 'affirmed . . . the duty of service in absolute terms' and there was 'no thought of a mutual set of obligations in the code'.[30] Chingiz had himself nominated Ogedei to be his successor and there was no question of his being 'elected' or 'selected' by the princess or the nobles. Thereafter the manipulation of queen mother in favour of her son Guyuk decided the issue ignoring completely the nominations of Chingiz and Ogedei.

Turakina Khatun, the queen mother continued to rule independently for three years after the death of Ogedei and thereafter as defacto ruler during her son Guyuk's regime. The sources say that during his life time, Ogedei had appointed his third son Kuchu (also from Turakia Khatun) as his heir apparent but he predeceased his father. Out of deep attachment for his lost child, Ogedei selected Kuchu's eldest son Sharamun who was, extremely popular, sagacious and then lived in his own Urdu. To formalize this decision at an assembly, the emissaries had been sent to every nook and corner for *istehzar* and Guyuk had also been invited. Long before the assembly could take place, Ogedei breathed his last and could not even see his son Guyuk who had been informed of Ogedei's illness and had by then rushed to Emil. Since the participants of the assembly had gradually assembled, the princes and the nobles discussed the issue of Khanship. It was stressed that Kutan whom Chingiz had nominated (in case of Ogedei's possible sudden death) was slightly sick and Ogedei's nominee Sheramun was yet a minor hence the candidature of Guyuk should be accepted. Apart from the fact that Guyuk was known for his strength and domineering attitude, the influential Turakina Khatun was supporting him and most of her amirs were in agreement with her. In accordance with the tradition, Guyuk showed his reluctance, naming one or the other prince and finally accepting the honour. The acceptance was however conditional demanding that the Khanship would always remain in his own *uruq*. The nobles gave an undertaking (*muchulka*) to this effect. Guyuk's accession was solemnized in the Kurultai of Rabi II 643, but he died soon after and the question of succession became more complicated as the queen mother was already sore over the attitude of her step sons and no suitable candidate from Ogedei's family seemed to be in sight. For the time being and in accordance with the Mughal custom the widow of Guyuk, Ughul Qumush was asked to look after the affairs of the state in consultation with Guyuk's *naib* Chinqai.[31] Once again the manouverings started at a large scale. Suyurquteni Begi (widow of Touloui) was keen to install her son Mongke to the throne and her efforts had the approval of Batu the mightiest of all the Chingizide princes. Mongke was the eldest son of Touloui, the Otchegin and a paragon of all requisite virtues befitting a sovereign.[32] But his accession implied the grandiose plan of shifting of Khanship from the family of Ogedei to that of Touloui for which much hobnobbing and hectic activity was needed.

After the demise of four sons of Chingiz Khan, Juji's son Sain Khan Batu enjoyed immense honour and popularity. In Kurultai no living being could transgress his verdict (*az sukhan-i oo tavawuz na namudah*) as he was 'master of all living beings' (*aqa-i hamagunan*) and all princes were subservient to him.[33] In 637, Batu had abstained from the Kurultai for the election of Guyuk due to which the appointment of Khaqan was delayed for three years. At the time of Guyuk's death, Batu was still having an aching leg but he took keen interest in furthering the interest of Mongke, the son of Touloui. He sent Yirliqs in 638 to all *aqa o ini* persuading them for *istihzar* to discuss the issue of Khanship in a Qurultai to place on the throne one who was found to be efficient and whose accession would be expedient by all considerations.

Seemingly, Batu's proposal irked the sons of Ogedei, Chaghatai and Guyuk who protested that the real yurt and capital of Chingiz was Onan o Kuluran and they would not go to Dasht-i Qipchaq for Toi. The amirs of Qaraqoram sent their representatives so as to secure a written undertaking from the princes saying that Batu happened to be the master (*aqa*) of all the princes and his *farman* was binding upon all and would not be in any way transgressed. Suyurquteni Begi also persuaded her son Mongke to visit the Aqa Batu personally along with brothers. Batu who had already 'seen the signs of greatness reflecting from his forehead',[34] further argued that Mongke was the son of youngest son of Chingiz Touloui who held the *yurt-i buzurg* of Chingiz and according to *yasa* and Mongol custom the place of father is always inherited by the youngest. Batu simultaneously sent his envoys to the ladies of the royal family (wives of Chingiz, Ogedei, Touloui) and to the princes of the left and right wings highlighting the fact that from amongst the princes one who had seen and heard the Yasaq and Yirligh of Chingiz by his own eyes and ears was Mongke and the expediency and interests of *ulus*, army, subjects and even princess demands that he should be raised to the throne. Batu instructed his own brothers—Barka, Shaiban, Orda and all the *uruq* of Juji and princes of right wing, and Qara Halaku from Chaghatais organized group, arranged a Toi and agreed upon accession of Mongke Qaan.

In accordance with the Mongol practice, Mongke showed his unwillingness to bear the burden of Khanship for sometime. It was only when his brother Mokai Ughul said that they have already submitted a written undertaking not to transgress the words of Sain

Khan Batu and that how could Mongke venure to do this, that Mongke formally accepted the offer. In conformity with the customary law and prevalent norms of the Mughals, Batu rose and all the princes and Noyons loosened their girdles and raising their caps knelt and Batu held the Kasa and Khani was thus brought to its proper claimant and all the audience paid allegiance (*baiat*). It was decided that they would arrange a large Kurultai next year. All of these went to their respective places but Batu appointed his two brothers Barka and Tuqa Timur to go with a large army with Mongke Qaan to Kuluran, the capital of Chingiz Khan and go ahead of Batu to arrange for the Toi and place Mongke on the throne in the presence of the princes.[35] Surqoteni Begi invited everyone to the Kurultai. But some of the sons of the Khan Guyuk and Yasu Mongke and Buri, as well as the sons of Chaghatai wanted (*dafai*) to float the idea that Khani should remain in the *uruq* of Khan Ogedei and Guyuk. They conveyed their dissent to any probable change and negated the agreement questioning its validity and demanding why the Khanate should not continue in their own *uruq*. Batu said that the matter had been finalized in agreement with the *aqa o ini* in view of expediency as none other could control an empire of such an extent stretching from east to west—which was obviously not a child's play. In these events, an year and a half elapsed and administration further deteriorated. Mongke and his mother used every method to please the princes—including persuasions, counselling, bestowal of favours upon, Qumush and her sons and to Yesu Mongake to convey that most of princes had already arrived at Chingiz's Kuluran and the affairs of Kurultai are still held up due to their absence. These princes nurtured and prided in the funny idea that the Kurultai can not proceed without their presence. When Barka sent messages to Batu that the sons of Ogedei, Guyuk and Yasu Mongke had not arrived though two years have elapsed and Kurultai of accession was thus delayed. Batu suggested that the accession ceremony should be solemnized in the Kurultai and those who transgress Yasa would be punished. The princes like Baraka, sons of Juji Qasar, Yusunke, Elchitai (son of Qachun), and others from the left wing and sons of Chaghtai, Qara Halaku and sons of Ogedei and others from the right wing along with reliable senior nobles, and rulers from various states attended the Kurultai.[36]

Obviously, the Kurultai of Mongke (held in Zilhij 648 at Qaraqorum, the capital of Chingiz) was unique as it had to be performed with much care and fear. A large force was stationed in the vicinity. At the time of coronation, there was fear of loss of life and property. For Yasaq and the bestowal of presents, a person was separately appointed. Barka was to sit in his own place due to pain in the leg and Qubilai was to sit at a slightly lower place. All were to be attentive to Qubilai's words. Mongke was to stand on the door so that he could prevent and control the princes and nobles. Hulaku was to stand in front of cooks and Qapuzchiyan so that none could speak or listen too much unnecessarily. There was constant alertness and two groups came and went marching. The affairs of Kurultai were thus arranged[37] and ceremonies followed. Nonetheless, some of the princes of Ogedei's *uruq* including Sheramun and Naqu (the grandsons of Ogedei) and Tuquq (son of Qarachar) joined hands for a rebellion. They appeared with a large army and war equipment stored in carts. To the good fortune of Mongke a herdsman (*janwardar*) Kishak noticed it and suspecting rebellious moves and foul play, he rushed in to inform Mongke. Since such treachery (*hil*) was not customary among the Mongols the Khasa of Chingiz and the *uruq* did not believe his words and queried but his persistence startled the princes. Finally, the princes and nobles were subjected to enquiry and investigation (*yarghu*) and subsequent punishment.[38]

Mongke ruled for eight years and after his death (in Muh. 655,[39] the Kangoj was held in 658[40] and almost the same problem arose as Ariq Buqa raised the standard of rebellion and landed himself in a *yarghu*.

Lamb's assertion that 'it is forbidden under penalty of death that anyone, whoever he be, shall be proclaimed emperor unless he has been elected previously by the princes. Khans, officers and other Mongol nobles by a general council',[41] is supported by the information available in Persian sources. There is no denying the fact that the regime of each new ruler had to be previously settled and ratified before being officially proclaimed in a Kurultai. But the procedure of selection of Khan was not through election. Either nomination, manipulation, or usurpation decided the issue and principle of might is right almost always worked. Rashiduddin records how the elders were offended and irked when the Turakina Khatun held sway without summoning a Kurultai (or a formal gathering of princes) ratifying this privilege.[42]

Since the attendance in the Kurultai of coronation was a clear indication of allegiance to a particular Khan, those princes who disliked the candidate usually abstained from such assemblies though they could hardly do anything to forestall such a move. Even a powerful prince like Batu who was displeased with the family of Ogedei and hated the idea of Guyuk's accession could not assert his view though he withheld his concurrence and did not attend the Kurultai on the pretext of sickness and pain in the legs.[43] A more glaring example of such a Kurultai is evident in the case of Mongke's accession. All the brothers and nobles who were planning a rebellion were 'leveled' by Batu.[44] In such cases where the opponents were mighty and abstained from the Kurultai, they could thereafter manage their own territory independently.[45]

Occasionally the Kangash was held to get rid of the unwanted elements and replace them by 'rightful' claimants to the royal throne, to quote an example, when Abbas Beg the son of Amir Idku Uzbeg became the ruler of the region, the heads of the Il and Ulus and princes of the house of Shaibani and Tuqa Timur assembled in a Kangash to plan his extermination. Accordingly Ghayasuddin a descendant of Ibai was placed on the throne, though after a war.[46] Similarly Tarmanshirin was deposed by the Qurultai in the annual Toi for transgressing the *yasa*.[47]

Kurultai was organized to bring about peace among the warring factions of princes[48] or to clear misunderstanding.[49] Sometimes the solution to the same grave problem or difficult situation was sought by the princes as Alghui imprisoned the emissaries of Ariq Buqa and then asked for the advice of the nobles to get out of this predicament.[50] Such clashes were to be averted through discussion.[51]

Another important task performed during the Kurultai was Yarghu purisdan, i.e. the reckoning. When the confrontation between Qubilai and his brother Ariq Buqa for Khanship resulted in the victory of the former, the Kurultai was held and Ariq Buqa along with his nobles and courtiers was brought to book[52] by Qubilai's Yarguchiyan investigating officers. All pleadings of Ariq Buqa were ignored. Qubilai even asked the Chinese scholars to give their verdict over the issue and they also insisted 'history proves that if the two brothers fight, the elder always holds sway and dominates. All such ambitious ones should be captured and thrown into prison until death'. Accordingly Ariq Buqa alongwith his ladies, children and near ones was imprisoned and a group of Turks was appointed to keep watch over him. He was only occasionally allowed to attend the function and otherwise he never came out. After an year he died.

In Yarghu pursidan (reckoning or investigation) of princes or in some such special cases during the Kurultai, the nobles were not allowed to observe or participate in the discussion. The sources confirm that the case of Otegin was 'fit to investigate carefully and examine minutely'. This examination 'was a matter of great delicacy and was impossible to confide strangers', hence only Mengu and Hordu were the examiners and no one else could have a say in the matter. When they had completed their task a group of amirs put him to death in accordance with *yasa*. Juvaini adds further, 'And in the same way they dealt with other important matters which the amirs were not allowed to discuss'.[53]

For many undesirable but expedient and important administrative decisions, the good offices and powers of Kurultai were utilized. In 1269, Qaidu held the Talas Kurultai to ensure defence of settled regions from nomadic raids. It was decided that the princes were to live in hills and steppes and they were not to allow their herds to arable and cultivated lands.[54]

The secrecy and sanctity of the decisions of the Kurultai had to be maintained religiously. If a 'confidential' decision of the Kurultai was leaked out by any person, he suffered the humiliation of exclusion from the secret assembly. When Belgutai 'revaled' or disclosed the proceedings of grand council to Yeke Cheren, Chingiz's verdict was, 'Belgutai has seen quality of the leakage of an important conference of our clan. He will be entrusted only without door administration—cases of dispute, riot, robbery, theft and the like. However, he and Daaritai will be permitted to enter the conference after the discussion of its agenda is over and all its members have drunk their cups (of Otog)'[55]

In the Kurultai or Janqi, the number, strata, class or category of the participants was determined by the significance, seriousness, nature and secrecy of the issues to be discussed. Apparently it seems that in non settled or tribal societies, the leaders of the tribes or elders of the fraternities or communes constituted this 'representative body' whereas in settled areas, the heads of military aristocracy, nobility and occasionally ecclesiastical group were included in the Kurultai. The discussions could be held with a large or a small group[56] or with the army in case of some military problem.[57] The Kurultais held before the campaigns to discuss feasibility, strategy and planning of war necessitated that the princes, *noyon-i buzurg*, amirs of *tumanat* and *hazarajat* (commanders of various ranks), *arkan-i daulat* and *avan-i hazrat* all should attend these assemblies. For Timur, the persons 'worthy of being counsellors' were such 'who steadfastly adhere to that which they say, and to that which they do'; who dare to speak with 'judgement and with firmness'. Out of the two kinds of counsel (that which proceedeth from the recesses of the heart). Timur gave the 'counsel of the heart', 'a place in the treasury of his soul'.[58]

The kings who believed in *l'etat c'etat c'est moi* (it is I who am the state) seldom added weightage to the counsels of their subordinates. Both the formulas *le roioy le veult* (the king wills it) and *le roi s'avisera* (the king will consider—the formula of rejecting a bill) were applied by such potentates. The famous work *Qabus Nama* in its chapter on 'Regulations and Conditions of Sovereignty' (*dar ain o shart-i badshahi*) categorically speaks that the 'opinions should always be subjected to and made subservient to the sovereign's wisdom and stratagem as 'the best Grand Wazir (Wazir-ul Vuzara) for a King is his own wisdom and brain'.[59] Deliberative and consultative bodies discernible in other Muslim states seem to have the same pattern, e.g. in the state of Mahmud of Ghazna the consultative body hardly played a significant role.[60]

In the early years of struggle Timur emphasized the significance of consultations in the words quoted by Yazdi that the verdict of wealthy and powerful men (*arbab-i dawal*) is the Divine Commandment (*tafsir-i qaza*) and nothing occurs except in conformity with what they say.[61] It is interesting to note that after attaining power, Timur ceased to be so enchanted by Kangash and adopted the same casual attitude towards[62] it for which he earlier criticized his rival Sultan Husain. Yazdi states this fact in the following words:

> One of the speciality of His Majesty is that though he always held discussions following the principle of Sunat-i Sunniya Mashwarat and the custom of Kurultai and Janqi which is the rule of sovereignty he never based his decisions on the opinion nor was he guided by the suggestion of any living being. In every affair of the state, he was solely directed by the revelations and also be secrets divulged to him through his own mind. According to the ideas alighted to him, he performed every work. Each contrivance or politics whether triffle or high was thus accomplished quite in conformity with the prescription of destiny and will of God and without any error. Since he was firm, all the matters of state and *millat*, affairs of administration, war and peace were, all quickly or slowly disposed of only through his own judgement.'[63]

A similar view is expressed by Ibn-i Arab Shah.[64] Timur and Abdullah Khan discarded the opinion of the majority and either accepted the opinion of their confidantes which repeated their own ideas or openly discarded majority opinion by cleverly manoeuvring the acceptance of their own views. In his *Tuzukat*, Timur had recorded his views about Kangash which are being reproduced here in view of their significance: 'I entered on every measure with counsel and advice . . .' says he.

And by experience, it is known unto me, that counsel and deliberation, and skilful measures are only to be found with the wise and the sagacious. Therefore, not withstanding, that the conclusion of every worldly event is covered by the curtain of fate. Yet according to the holy word of Muhammad (on whom be the blessings of the Almighty) in every enterprise which I undertook, I acted from counsel and deliberation.[65]

But simultaneously he adds further that:

And when my counselors and my advisers were assembled together, I demanded their opinions on the good and on the advantages and disadvantages of undertaking, or relinquishing the enterprise before us. And when I had heard their opinions thereon, I myself examined both sides of their opinions. And I duly weighed the advantages and the disadvantages; and I considered the perils thereof with the eye of attention. And every plan, in which I discovered a two fold hazard, I rejected; and I chose that in which the peril was single.[66]

At another place he specifically says:

And I asked counsel from all: but I considered the good and the evil of every opinion; and from each I selected those things which were just and expedient', that whichever of the advices 'appeared most profitable, and I preferred and approved. . . . But in every action of the actions of my life, on which I had deliberated, drew an omen from the sacred Koran and I acted according to the direction thereof. . . .[67]

Ibn-i Arab Shah confirms the above statements of Timur. In his judgement he saw openly the vicissitudes of things, as one sees with keen eye a thing perceived by the senses. 'When he has spoken his opinion or indicated his will, presently his command is counted as an oracle.'

Regarding Timur's Kurultais before campaigns, Ibn-i Arab says that:

Timur excelled in arts of leading others into error and in a profundity of actions which could scarcely be penetrated. . . . When he was making for any place or wished to descend into any plan and intended to hide his purpose and involve it in an enigma and sought to inspire error and doubt . . . he used to summon great men and leaders of his kingdom and his counsellors (*arkan-i daulat wa ayan-i mamlakat waa sahiban-i andesha*), so that none of them was left out or a son admitted in the place of the father or father instead of the son, then he expounded to them the secret of his affairs and sought from them advice about the regions against which he should move and gave them a full permission to speak, saying: By no means shall he be blamed who discusses it, whether noble or simple, observing future events from day to day and year to year, but let each one debate freely and it shall not be counted to him for a fault, whether he falls into the bottomest pit of error or climbs to the peak of right judgement; if he has missed the mark, he shall not suffer loss, but if he has put his point on the fact, he shall win reward; therefore let each one exert his strength and employ his zeal and labour and show his diligence until someone said that point which was agreeable to (Timur's) desire and so let opinions conspire to mark out place. Then he immediately dismissed that assembly. He would thereafter collect and consult his ultimate friends, such as Sulaiman Shah, (amari, Saifuddin, Allahadad, Shah Malik and Shaikh Nuruddin.

The scene does not seem to be any different in the other Kurultais held on the eve of campaigns. Similar artfulness and chicanery is noticeable in the Kurultai of 732 held by Timur at Aqyar in connection with his administrative decision of increasing the number of soldiers attached to every official in proportion to his increasing wealth. This assembly was attended by all the *amirs* and *noyons* from *tuman hazarajat*, *sadjat* and other rulers of *mauza* and *wilayat* but no one could dare to raise a voice against this new burden.

NOTES

1. The Holy Quran, *Sura* 3, 'Ali Imran', p. 159, for details regarding *Shura* see Levy Reuben, *The Social Structure of Islam*, Cambridge, 1962, pp. 168-82, 287-90; Muhammad Asad, *The Principles of State and Government in Islam*, Berkeley, Los Angeles, 1961, p. 48; *Muhammadan Jurisprudence*, pp. 82-97, Duncan B. Macdonald, *Development of Muslim Theology, Jurisprudence and Constitutional Theory*, New Delhi, 1973, pp. 101, 105; Ibn Hasan, *The Central Structure of the Mughal Empire*, New Delhi, 1970, p. 235.
2. Kautilya, *Arthasastra*, part III, ed. R.P. Kangle, Delhi, 1968, pp. 134-5; also see 5th edn. of *Arthrasastra*, ed. by Shama Shastry, Mysore, 1956, Chapters IX and XV, pp. 14-15, 26-9.

3. *Insha-i Abul Fazl*, Har Sih Daftar, Newal Kishore edn. under *Dastur-ul amal*; Haji Khairullah, *Dastur-i Jahanqusha*, Aligarh MS, Abdus Salam Collection 328/98, ff. 28-32; Ghayasuddin Ali, *Ruz Nama Ghazawat-i Hindustan*, SPB, 1915, Vol. I, p. 110; V.V. Barthold, *Four Studies*, Vol. II, pp. 23-4. Ziauddin, Barani, *Fatawa-i Jahandari*, Pers. text, Advice III, Eng. tr., *The Political Theory of the Delhi Sultanate*, Aligarh, 1957, p. 8.
   Barani categorically records:
   '. . . Even to our Prophet, inspite of his perfect wisdom and the continuity of devine relevation God gave the order, "And consult them in your affairs". How then can Kings, who receive no devine inspiration and whose judgement is vitiated by their passions, succeed in the administering the affairs of their governments without consulting their experienced officers and sincere well wishers? It has been known to all wise men, ancient and modern, that eradicating the evils of the kingdom suppressing disturbances, undertaking great enterprises, making state laws (*zawabit*) and discerning the ultimate consequences of state policies, is not possible without the advice of wise and experienced men, who are the well-wishers of the government and the chosen people of the kingdom.
4. Babur, *Babur Nama* (*BN*), Turkish text, p. 349; Eng. tr., p. 627; French tr. by Bacquet Grammont, *Livre de Babur*, POF, 1980, p. 44; Eng. tr. by Beveridge, New Delhi, 1973, S. Pasha, *The Daftardar*, Turkish text, *Nasaihul Vuzera vel Umera*, Princeton, 1935, p. 148; Eng. tr. by Walter Livington Wright, Princeton, p. 129.
   '. . . they should not refrain from consultation over every matter. Yet they should not consult with everyone. They should deliberate with those who have seen service and been present in war and battle, with well wishers of the state who hide secrets, and to those only should they disclose secrets. But to the rest of the crowd they should not divulge secret matters as they actually are; through symbols and comparisons they should explain and consult with them. For it sometimes happens that from an ignorant child or from a woman of imperfect understanding there comes fourth a correct opinion or a wise answer which brings about good results.'
5. Nakhchiwani, *Dasturul Katib fi Taiyunul Maratib*, Moscow, 1962, Chapter XI.
6. Samundar Tirmizi, *Samrat-ul Mashaikh*, MS IOST, Tashkent, pp. 1-8.
7. Mahmud bin Wali, *Bahrul Asrar fi Managibul Akhiyar*, ff. 34, 198a, 259a, 277b, 282a, 283b, 284a, 302a, 305a.
8. Wassaf, *Tarikh-i Wassaf-ul Hazrat*, Newal Kishore edn., p. 518.
9. Hafiz Tanish, *Abdullah Nama* (*Abdn*), MS, India Office Library 574; ff. 214, 235-6, 242, 262, 281-2, 392.
10. Yezdi, *Zafar Nama*, Calcutta edn., 1888, also see *Zafar Nama*, ed. Muhammad Abbasi, 1336 AH, p. 163.
11. Nizam-ul Mulk Tusi, *Siyar-ul Muluk* or *Siyasat Nama*, ed. Jafar Shear, 1348 AH, pp. 138-40.
12. Ibid.
13. Rashiduddin Fazlullah, *Jamiut Tawarikh*, Tehran, 1338 AH, pp. 435-6; also see, Riasanovsky, *Fundamental Principles of Mongol Law*, pp. 80-98. Like the Canon of Catholic truth enunciated by Vincent of Liens ('Quod Ubique quod semper, quod ab omnibus'), the Mongols also believed in *vox populi*.
14. Ibid., also see Defremery, pp. 2-43.

15. Defremery, pp. 2-43.
16. *Jamiut Tawarikh*, pp. 425-8, 432-3; *Secret History of the Mongol Dynasty*; Eng. tr. by Cleavages, pp. 164-6.
17. *Jamiut Tawarikh*, pp. 471-3.
18. See Wassaf, *Farhang*, p. 641.
19. *Al-Lughat-ul Nawait,* Paris, 1880; *Uzbegcha Ingliziha Lughat*, 1959, p. 632; also see Buronov, Akabar Khwaja Khanov et al., *Uzbeg-English Dictionary*, Tashkent, 1963, p. 178.
20. Farhang-i-Anand Raj, Lucknow edn., 1889-92, see under *Qurultai.*
21. See *Lughat-ul Nawait* under *Qurultai.*
22. *Jamiut Tawarikh*, p. 452. the Chinese chroniclers, however have given a slightly changed version as the date and place (*Kuluran*) is different.
23. *Jamiut Tawarikh*, pp. 507-8, see also pp. 455, 457, 472, 476, 547, 549, 550.
24. D'lohsson, Introduction, *la'histoire de l'Asia*, 1896.
25. Clande Cahen, *Pre-Ottoman Turkey*, p. 396.
26. W. Radlov, *Qutadgu Bilik*, Vol. III; Radlov, *A Vaprosu ob Oughurakh*, p. 69; V.V. Barthold, *Sochinenija*, Moscow edn., 1963-73, Vol. V, pp. 247, 510, 742.
27. Ata-ul Mulk Juvaini, *Tarikh-i Jahanqusha-i Juvaini*, Persian text, Leiden, 1911, pp. 154-5; Eng. tr. A.J. Boyle, pp. 196-8, 242, 248-52; *Jamiut Tawarikh*, pp. 568-70.
28. Vladimirtsov, *Feudalnistroi Mongoliski Khanstova*, p. 80; Lawrence Krader, *Peoples of Central Asia,* The Hague, 1966, pp. 85-6; Barthold, *Turkistan Down to Mongol Invasion,* 1928 edn., pp. 381-92; see *Muzzakkira-i Ahbab*, Eng. tr., p. 64.
29. Barthold, *Turkistan Down,* pp. 381-92.
30. Krader, p. 86.
31. *Jamiut Tawarikh*, pp. 480, 567-72.
32. Ibid., pp. 567-72.
33. Ibid., pp. 513, 523.
34. Ibid., pp. 581-2; Khwand Mir, *Habib-us Siyar*, Vol. III, Tehran, Khayyam, 1954 AH, and Bombay, 1857, pp. 58-60.
35. Ibid., pp. 580-93; Yezdi, *Muqaddama*, pp. 64, 148; *Habib-us Siyar*, pp. 58-60.
36. *Jamiut Tawarikh*, pp. 280-6; *Habib-us Siyar*, pp. 58-62.
37. Ibid., some Chinese sources give different dates and place.
38. *Jamiut Tawarikh*, pp. 580-96.
39. Ibid., pp. 603, 620-34.
40. Ibid., pp. 620-34.
41. Lamb, *Genghiz Khan,* Lahore, 1978, p. 214, *Jamiut Tawarikh*, p. 566.
42. Other examples; *Jamiut Tawarikh*, pp. 523-4; Yezdi, Tehran edn., Vol. I, pp. 164, 223, 487.
43 *Jamiut Tawarikh*, pp. 523-5.
44. Barthold, *Sochinenija*, Vol. I, p. 147.
45. *Bahrul Asrar*, p. 32 b.
46. Ibn-i-Battuta, *Rihla-i-Ibn Battuta*, ed. by Muhammad Ali, 3rd edn., Tehran, 1361, p. 240.
47. *Jamiut Tawarikh*, p. 528.
48. Ibid., p. 545.
49. Ibid.

50. Barthold, *Sochinenija*, Vol. II, pp. 50, 510; Vol. III, p. 1; Vol. IV, pp. 35-6, Vol. V, pp. 149, 160, Moscow, 1962-73.
51. *Habib-us Siyar*, III, pp. 63-4.
52. Juvaini, Eng. tr. by A.J. Boyle, p. 255.
53. Barthold, *Sochinenija*, Vol. V, p. 149.
54. *Secret History*, p. 83.
55. *Jamiut Tawarikh*, p. 537.
56. Ibid., pp. 547-9.
57. Ibid., pp. 546, 537-8, 547; Timur, *Tuzakat-i-Timuri*, Abu Talib Hussaini, Eng. tr. by Major Davy, Oxford, 1342 AH, pp. 1-89, Abdurrazzaq Samarkandi, *Matla-us Sadain*, II, III, p. 457; Yezdi, I, p. 163.
58. Ghulam Hussain Yusufi, *Qabus Nama*, Tehran, 1352 AH, p. 227.
59. For such examples see *Jamiut Tawarikh* and *Tarikh-i-Jahanqusha*.
60. Yezdi, Vol. I, Tehran edn., p. 94.
61. Ibid., Vol. II, Tehran edn., p. 520.
62. *Tuzakat-i-Timuri*, pp. 1-20, 24-89.
63. Ibid.
64. Ibid.
65. Ibid.
66. Ibn-i Arab Shah, *Ajaib-ul Maqdur fi Nawadir-i Timur*, Persian tr., Tehran, 1960, pp. 182, 188.
67. *Zafar Nama*, Tehran edn.; Eng. tr. by Sanders, p. 201.

Administration Under the Samanids

Despite their extraordinary attainments in the field of culture and fine arts, the Samanids are not credited with evolving a unique or novel system of administration. Their state organization was a conglomeration of several layers of polity in continuum as the region on which they were called upon to govern already had a carefully thought out and well planned state structure in which changes were not required. In his *Manaqib-ul Atrak* (Superior Qualities of the Turks) Jahiz who did not live to see the ascendancy of Samanids as he died in 869, gave a very proper assessment of the various races. In his view 'the Samanid Persians excelled all the nations in the art of governing states, as the Chinese did in handicrafts, the Greeks in science and the Turks in the art of war'. The Samanids borrowed the ideals of government as much from the Sassanids as from the Perso-Islamic traditions within the constraints of Arab imperial hegemony. The Turco-Mongols rulers succeeded in combining the qualities of a warrior-statesman with empire builders thus giving their successors, the Uzbegs a detailed and well tried scheme of administration.

It is interesting to examine as to why the Uzbegs who were the direct descendants of Mongol ruler Chingiz Khan preferred to adopt the administrative system of Samanids, discarding certain Turco-Mongol practices which had so religiously been followed by their predecessors including the Timurids. Unlike the Samanids, the Uzbegs were of Turco-Mongol or Turkish origin and did not have blood ties or kinship with the Samanid dynasty. It was perhaps the political and socio-religious circumstances as well as the rise of Safavid Empire that had compelled the Uzbegs to pick and choose whatever was similar, feasible and more pragmatic in the given situation. They had, therefore, preferred to adapt, and adopt administrative institutions, customs and traditions from the Samanids, some of which are being discussed here.

The two regimes of Tahirides and Samanids are marked by 'enlightened despotism'. The Samanid head of the state was an 'autocratic ruler who was answerable only to God'.[1] For the Caliphs who issued the investiture, these rulers could be merely *Amirs* or clients (governors or *mawalis*) or even tax gatherers, yet internally they were independent and despotic by all means. Their loyalty to the Caliph was limited to the payment of tribute, taxes, regular gifts and sending of reports though on *khutba* and coins the name of the Samanid ruler always accompanied that of Caliph. Yet the remnants of Arab hegemony (established by sword and maintained by sword) of which Samanids were originally an extension must have had its impact in deciding the civil and military authority which was unitarian.

The Samanid rulers do not seem to have adopted high sounding titles and satisfied themselves with the title *Amir* only. In their peculiar circumstances, the Uzbegs had a different outlook. Shaibani Khan the first Uzbeg ruler of Central Asia, had discarded many of the steppe traditions and in sharp deviation from the Hanafite law called himself as *Imamuzzaman* and *Khalifat-ur Rahman*. In his *Suluk-ul Mulk*, prepared at the order of Ubaidullah Khan Uzbeg (for whom it was to serve as a guide for administrative purposes), Ruzbehan Isfahani criticized this title and recommended *Amir*, *Imam* or *Khalifa* as the most suitable title for the Sultan. However, the Uzbeg rulers called themselves as *Khan* in the Turco-Mongol fashion.[2]

The rule or Custom of succession is generally amiss in the Muslim Kingdoms and so was it in both the states of Samanids and in that of Uzbegs. The Islamic injunction of consensus or *ijma* or *shura* may have had as much a casual role in the Samanid state as perhaps *Kangash* had under Timur and his successors. Amongst the Uzbegs, the *Qurultai* was seldom held and *Kangash* had perhaps only a limited role.

The bureaucratic paraphernalia inherited from Samanids continued over later centuries. Narshakhi had mentioned ten different Government offices working in environs of Registan at Bukhara. These were: *Diwan-i Wazir*; *Diwan-i Mustaufi* (treasurer); *Diwan-i Amid-ul Mulk* (head of correspondence mainstay of the state); *Diwan-i Sahib-i Barid* (*Diwan* of post master); *Diwan-i Mushrif* (*Diwan* fiscal, general and of the private domains of the ruler); *Muhtasib*; *Diwan-i Awqaf*; of Qazi.Under the Samanids, *Wazir* (also called *Khwaja-i Buzurg*) was the head of all the *ahl-i qalam* (gentlemen of pen bureaucracy) and the insignia of his office used to be an inkstand even under the Saljuqids.[3] Nizam-ul Mulk preferred that the office should be hereditary though under the Samanids it did not happen as the power went to the opponents, returning many years later to the former's descendants.

The posts could be hereditary. A closer examination, however reveals that under the Samanids, a competent *Wazir* could be the head of court (*dargah*) and chancery both and was next only to the king. There may be several other *Wazirs* or *Diwans* subservient to the central *Wazir*. It seems that the Uzbegs also had the same system of one central *Wazir* (*Wakil* or *Diwan*) with several subordinate *Wazirs*. Similarly various epithets like *Diwan-i Mushrif*, *Diwan-i-Mustaufi*, *Wazir-i Aazam*, *Diwan-i Kalan*, *Diwan-i Aala* were applied to one single *Wazir* (or *Diwan*) who held the charge of the state as deputy of the Khan. Under Abdullah Khan Uzbeg, Qulbaba Kukultash combined in himself many of these responsibilities. Several *Diwans* and *Wazirs* mentioned as *Diwanian* and *Wuzra* signify that duties were distributed among them under the Uzbegs. The *Wazir-i Kalan* (also known as the *Diwan-i Mushrif*) maintained the records of endowments, arms, robes of honour, etc.[4]

The term *Mustaufi* (synonymous to *Khazin* or *Khazinadar* (or Abbasid *Diwan-ul Kharaj*) appears under all the four designations in the Central Asian States. Tusi's dual treasury system with ordinary and extra ordinary funds existed under Timur and his successors and must have continued under the Uzbegs also. The officials like *Khatib*, *Shaikh-ul Islam*, *Qazi-ul Quzzat*, *Sadr-us Sudur*, *Mufti Qazi*, *Sadr*, *Naqib-i Ashraf* existed in both the states in the form of an Islamic norm. Similarly office of *Ihtisab* and officers called *Muhtasibs* had been highlighted by Jenkinson.[5] The turbulent military aristocracy and dynastic succession was common to both.

'Under the Samanids, as under Amr, the salary to the army and the official was paid on four days (every three months)'. Since the total sum distributed to the army was 20 million *dirhams* the issue was called *Bistgani*[6] (or in Arabic *Alashriniat*), Chroniclers like Gardizi, Ibn-i Khaliqan Sallami and Tusi describe in detail the method of distribution. In Khurasan, the army received its pay every three months with 'solemn ceremonial'.[7]

The distribution was done by a special official, the *Ariz* who took his seat in the place appointed for the ceremony and on hearing the sound of the two large drums the whole army assembled there. In front of the *Ariz* lay sacks with money. The *Ariz's* assistant had before him a list of the soldiers with their names. The first called was

Amr himself. The *Ariz* made a close inspection of his horse and equipment, then expressed his approval and gave him 3,000 *dirhams*, Amr placed the money in boot. After this he took his seat and watched the horsemen and infantry in turn present themselves before the *Ariz*, undergo the same close secutiny, and receive the money. Ibn-i Khaliqan rightly points out the resemblance between this custom of Amr's and the picture of the review of the armies in Sassanid Persia under Khusru Anushirwan. It is doubtful whether this resemblance was accidental. *Ariz* was perhaps subordinate to the *Sahib-i Shurat*. It was the duty of the *Ariz* to distribute pay to the army and to ensure that the army was maintained in good condition. Under the Uzbegs also, a separate department of *Ariz* seems to have existed. The inspection of the army had been described by Masud Kuhistani Hafiz Tanish and others. The registration of the army was done and a roll was prepared. The army received its pay likewise and the practice was called *atiya dadan*.[8] Nevertheless in most of the military arrangements and organization the Uzbegs prepared to follow Turco-Mongol practices as the Turks were better warriors than the Persians.

Ever since the reign of Samanids, provincial rulers and officials were generally appointed by the Central Ruler when the power of bureaucracy outmanoeuvred the king. The Central Officials themselves appointed their subordinates in provincial towns.[9] Almost a similar situation is noticed in the Uzbeg provinces under Abdullah Khan Uzbeg. Prior to the unification of Khanates, however, the appanages were governed by the Sultans (hereditary rulers of the provinces) who alone could appoint the officers and administer the province.

Under the Samanids the espionage system and postal services for the Government were carried on by the officials like *Sahib-i Barid*, *Sahib-i Khabar*, *Munhi* (pl. *Munhiyan*). For a veracious transmission of news even against the most powerful provincial potentate, these officials sent reports to the king independently. Disguised couriers were also dispatched separately if the provincial governor bullied the informer into sending a partisan report.[10] Under the Uzbegs the intelligence system worked on the same lines and the offices carried the same names.

Another sphere in which the Uzbegs seem to have been influenced by the Samanids was the ecclesiastical sphere. Under the Samanids, the religious groups and priests particularly enjoyed special status and the chosen one from among the men of jurisprudence and scholars of Hanafite school of thought was particularly closer to the State, serving as adviser to the king. Such was the respect for him that 'important matters were settled on his advice, his requests were fulfilled, and office were filled according to his instructions'. Similarly, the exemption from *Paibosi* (Kissing of ground before rulers) to scholars, the patronage to *Muftis* and *Shaikhs* and higher places allotted to the clergly were common expressions of formal respect shown to the learned and the clergly. Several reasons may be put forward for this extraordinary respect for the ecclesiasts. The sources indicate that the Samanids were greatly helped by the ecclesiastical groups in augmenting their influence over Central Asia. The role of clergy as a connecting link between the ruler and the ruled may have made them indispensable. It is surmised that the urge for breaking the chains of orthodoxy or removing the shackles of Caliphal authority may have necessitated this holy alliance. It is also possible that Samanids inherited a very strong clergy from the preceding dynasty of Sassanids who evolved a novel tradition of eliminating the *tug* of war between temporal and spiritual power by introducing the concept of *Mobadan-i Mobad*. It seems more plausible that the Samanids felt threatened due to the various movements (like that of Saped Jamagan, Dayalama raging in Central Asia and men like Mugannoy)[11] and wanted to use the Hanafite religious groups as a counter poise to them. Under the successors of the Samanids and particularly under the Qarakhanids this harmony gradually faded away, but with the arrival of Turco-Mongols, the scenario totally changed.

In his *Yasa*, Chingiz had categorically decreed that in his empire, 'all religions were to be respected and that no preference was to be shown to any of them'. Yet Juwaini confirms that Chingiz 'honoured and respected the learned and pious of every sect recognizing such conduct the way to the court of God'.

Both Ibn-i Arab Shah and Al Hasan the Arab had depicted Timur as a person far from orthodoxy. Almost all other sources more or less confirm this fact.

Although both Chingiz and Timur were at best believers in eclecticism or pantheism and respect for saints was one of the important precept of their code of conduct, they never agreed to accord a higher or even equal status to the 'Men of Turban'. Due to jealousy of power, Chingiz killed Qoqchu Shaman and Timur continued to adopt an attitude of deference mixed with indifference towards the religious groups.

Like Chingiz who invited Changchun to guide him in administrative affairs, Timur also invited the Mullas only once to assist him in dealing with the dishonest officials. But this amiability of Chingiz and Timur both was entirely transformed whenever they noticed even the slightest high handedness or suspected an encroachment upon their absolute rights of sovereignty. The religious groups of all religions were exempted from taxes. Timur and Timurids each had their own 'spiritual guide'. Although the Naqshbandi saints had decided to come closer to the State in the beginning of fifteenth century and their influence over the subject population was indeed tremendous, they got a chance to dominate the political scenario only in the sixteenth century when Uzbegs came to power. Jenkinson who visited Central Asia in 1556-8 reports that this 'metropolitan in Boghar was more respected than the king'. The *Malfuzat* literature show how these Juibari *Shaikhs* became the real power behind the throne, whether it was Khwaja Juibari, Khwaja Kalan, Khwaja Sad, Khwaja Mushtari or any other Naqshbandi saint, they had a great say in administrative matters. Khwaja Juibari was highly displeased when Abdullah Khan Uzbeg II exchanged certain territories without his knowledge. The royal princes clustered around the *Khwaja* of Juibar, seeking justice against each other or even complaining against the Central Ruler. The Rulers walked several miles on foot to received the *Khwajas* and paid them real allegiance. The Plenitudo[12] Potestatis was the hallmark of the Qarakhanid dynasty is very well reflected through the statements found in Rawandi and Iman Ghazali. The conflict between the temporal power and the ecclesiasts, however, never occurred under the Uzbegs who, like the Samanids coexisted in the political and socio-religious environs in the most harmonious way.

Certain factors were all along alive in the socio-religious milieu of Transoxiana, as much under the Samanids as under the Uzbegs. The existence of Shias in Khurasan and its vicinity was felt in more than one sphere. The reading of the *khutba* in the name of Abul Husain Muhammad—an *Alid* at Nishapur and granting of State pension by Nasr to such a political rival proves well that the Shia influence in the region was sufficiently strong. Besides, political conflagrations often led to expedient alliances with the discontented elements of the states who were only too ready to rise in opposition at the slightest pretext. The rebellion of Samanid Ruler Nasr's three imprisoned brothers, namely Yahya, Ibrahim and Mansur, in which the Daylamites, Shias and Ghazis equally collaborated in 930 is an example in question.[13] The ascendancy of Fatimides of Egypt further strengthened the Shia sector as Fatimide nominees spread over Khurasan and even managed to win over Husain B. Ali Marwazi to the Shia precepts. Subsequently, his successor Muhammad B. Ahmad Nakhshabi extended his activities to Transoxiana. From Nasaf, the Shia impact engulfed the capital and its surrounding regions and not only important nobles like Aytash, Abu Bakr and Abu Mansur but even the ruler Ilaq Husain Malik was carried away by the new zealots—a factor which finally resulted in the deposition of the ruler and Massacre of Qaramatians. Not only Nakhshabi but all his aristocratic converts were slaughtered so mercilessly that the very sect of Shiites felt so threatened that they decided to exist in Transoxiana as a secret sect only.[14] Nevertheless the fact that important artisans like the father and brother of famous Avicenna belonged to this sect shows that the faith continued to be popular among the elite also. Barthold blames the Samanids that they 'never tried to acquire the confidence of the masses, and to make them a mainstay of their throne, as is witnessed by their persecution of the Shiite movement, launch undoubtedly bore a democratic character'.

Towards the end of the Samanid rule, the tax on inheritance had been introduced. Accordingly the death of an officer of the *Diwan* was to be followed by a share of his property passing to the king. This law of escheat was, thereafter, gradually applied even to those inhabitants who died without leaving an heir in Bayhaq and other places and later on imposed even upon those who had direct male [15] heirs. The practice was followed in a different style by the Ottomans who confiscated the entire property of their nobles—a custom known as *ankari*. The Mongols, however, detested the practice. Not only Chingiz Khan's *Yasa* undermined this practice of the law of escheat but even Kebek is said to have abstained from it. The Timurids also considered it to be unlawful. The Uzbeg rulers, however, seem to have followed this Samanid practice. *Abdullah Nama* gives several instances where Abdullah Khan visited the house of a deceased noble and the surviving son brought before him the valuables, etc., for the first pick.

The tradition of a personal guard of the sovereign 'composed of slaves purchased for the purpose and mainly Turkish' is first noticed only in the Samanid period. In this view the concept of *Bandaidargah* did not attain such importance (during Ismail's period) as in later times. Seemingly, a highly developed system of bodyguards must have existed under the Sassanids from whom Indian Turkish ruler Balban is said to have borrowed the idea—a fact emphasized by Barani at length in his *Tarikh*. Under Mongol Khans, the bodyguards were introduced by Chingiz Khan. Apparently the Uzbegs in Central Asia behaved more like nomad democrats who did not feel the need of imperial bodyguards. The slaves serving as the pillars of the states who gradually grew powerful or even into usurpers (e.g. the Janissaries under the Ottomans, the Jani Qurbani under the Ilkhans, the slave Mamluks or the modified form found in slave dynasty of India, e.g. Turkani Chihilgani) were nowhere to be seen in the Uzbeg Empire. In the early years of Uzbeg rule, the formation of an Uzbeg detachment was the only sign of their racial or imperial identity. During the Samanid rule, the brisk export of slaves earned toll at Oxus crossing which amounted to 70 to 100 *dirham* for each Turkish *ghulam*. The fortified points on the frontiers facing steppes and manned by volunteer warriors—the *ghazis* were called *ribats* from where the raids into the nomadic territories for catching Turkish slaves and organizing defence of their own borders was made possible.[16] Thanks to the constant sectarian wars between the Uzbegs and the Persians, a large number of prisoners of war were sold as slaves in the markets of Samarqand and Bukhara. It was only a fraction of the proceeds of this amount that the Madrasa-i Mir-i Arab was constructed in Bukhara. Like the Samanids, the Uzbegs too were very found of constructing *ribats* on the frontiers of the empire. Abdullah Khan Uzbeg alone is said to have built 11,000 *sardabahs* and *ribats*.

NOTES

1. Qatifi's *Tarikh-ul Hukma*, p. 416; Thalibi's autobiography.
2. Philip K. Hitti, *History of the Arabs*, pp. 414-15, V.V. Bathold, *Turkestan Down to Mongol Invasion*, London, 1958, pp. 236-7.
3. Narshakhi, *History of Bukhara*, Eng., tr. by R.N. Frye, 1954, pp. 80-95; Khwand Mir, *Rauzat-us Safa*, Vol. IV, Tehran, 1339 AH, pp. 30-5.
4. Nizam-ul Mulk Tusi, *Siyasat Nama*, Tehran, 1348, p. 9.
5. Ruzbihan Isfahani, *Suluk-ul Muluk*, MS, Tashkent, pp. 15, 105.

6. Tusi suggested that the funds for extra ordinary expenses should be treated as inviolable and were to be used only under very compulsive circumstances and that too as a loan. Tusi, op. cit., p. 205.
7. Mirza Badi Diwan, *Majma-ul Araqam*, Moscow, 1981, pp. 1-60.
8. Barthold, p. 230.
9. Ibid.
10. *Miftahululum*, p. 65.
11. Mirza Badi Diwan, p. 40.
12. Baihaqi, *Tarikh-i Baihaqi*, MS British Museum 3587, pp. 165-6, Barthold, p. 232.
13. Baihaqi, pp. 395, 398; Gardizi, p. 98; Barthold, pp. 230-1.
14. Narshakhi, pp. 65-76.
15. Hafiz Tanish, *Abdullah Nama*, MS British Museum, ff 118-28; *Rauzat-ur Rizwan*, f. 250.
16. Ibn-al Asir, VIII, f. 155, also see Barthold, pp. 242-6.

The Administrative Structure Under the Uzbegs

It may be said that the Uzbegs had a Turco-Mongol state structure with a considerable influence of Perso-Islamic traditions. In the Golden Horde (the ancestral domain of the Uzbegs), Batu's strict orders were that 'anyone who violates *Yasa* must lose his head'. Frequent references were made to the *Yasa* in the *Yirlighs* (orders) Khans of the Golden Horde issued to the Russian Church;[1] and the frequent references in our texts too suggest a continuing adherence to Turco-Mongol traditions. But in course of time, with the increasing influence of Islam, the shariat tended to overshadow the *Yasa*.[2]

In Central Asia a similar process of assimilation of Mongol with Islamic tradition took place perhaps even earlier. The already existing Central Asian traditions too passed on to the Uzbegs when they moved over to Central Asia as it was not easy to resist the effects of the social structure and organizational apparatus of the conquered lands. In addition, the Shaibanids had their own steppe traditions originating in their manner of life which again reflected a complicated picture of the conflict between Islamic principles and their own steppe traditions.[3] The Uzbeg Empire thus combined such discrepant elements within its polity as royal absolutism, clan organization and divisions and distinctions according to wealth and status; and it also bore the deep imprint of the shariat and the mystic influence of Naqshbandi saints. It was not a new phenomenon even in Yuan Chwang's time (AD 629-45), all the 'Hu' (Muslim) States regarded Samarkand as their Centre and made its social institutions their model (Walters: 94).

Concerning the ideals of sovereignty and royal authority, the Uzbegs believed in a kind of divine theory of kingship. As a ruler of the steppes tribal aristocracy, Abulkhair enjoyed immense despotic power and his autocratic instinct was never moderated. The *Qurultai* or Consultative Assembly lost its significance owing to the ruler's direct appeal to Islamic law and the assertion of his own complete authority.[4] Although the Mongols too had some notions of divine kingship,[5] this disregard of the clansmen was perhaps one of the important reasons for the overthrow of Abulkhair's empire and the ejection of his descendants from Central Asia. Later on, the Manghit Chiefs refused to accept Shaibani as their ruler simply because they were afraid of losing their privileges due to the latter's autocratic behaviour and his inclination towards absolute sovereignty.[6]

In Central Asia the traditions of absolute despotism were discernible much earlier as in accordance with Islamic traditions, Ghazali, Tusi, Rawandi and Ali Sher Navoi[7] had equally emphasized a 'divine theory of sovereignty'. When the Uzbegs conquered Central Asia, they continued their traditions of absolute sovereignty. Since Shaibani had himself been a witness to the destructive role not only of the steppe aristocracy but also of later Timurid nobility he took special care to revive the prestige of the sovereign by declaring himself as *Imamuzzaman* and *Khalifat-ur Rahman* ('*Imam* of the age' and '*Agent* of God'). The court historian puts his claims in the following terms; 'Now the *Imam* of the Muslims in our times is *Hazarat Imamuzzaman* and *Khalifat-ur Rahman* Shaibani Khan and all Muslims have promised fealty (*baiat*) to him.'[8] According to Wasifi Shaibani considered three qualities essential for a Sultan, namely knowledge to the extent of taking legal or theological decisions, wisdom and justice.[9] Isfahani refers to a discussion held by Shaibani Khan in 914/1508 at Kan-i Gil on the divine right and theory of the sovereignty. Shaibani claimed that the king was a shadow of God on earth under whose protection the oppressed from amongst the subjects find shelter. The king earns a rightful remuneration (*Cast Muzd*) only if he imparts justice. Shaibani argued that the epithet *zilullah* should not be taken to denote the unlimited powers of a Khan against whose words and actions no one could raise his voice, for a ruler with such powers could become a tyrant also; instead the term should only signify that the king is the real shadow of God in that through his dignity and power he exterminates evil, suppresses the tyrants, manages the affairs of state and was the redresser of people's grievances (*dafa' aziat*) in the same way as God is the protector of mankind. A king was not supposed to be oblivious of the affairs of his subjects and the excuses of an ignorant (*ghafil*) sovereign are not accepted by God.[10] Shaibani's short regime of less than a decade is characterized by large scale stringent administrative reforms, plunder and destruction of large bodies of his conquered subjects. Like Timur, Shaibani too was jealous of power, which is best reflected in his comments on the death of his younger brother Mahmud Sultan 'The death of Mahmud is a good thing: men have been wont to say that the power of Shahi Beg Khan was upheld by Mahmud: let it now be known that Shahi Beg Khan was in no way whatever dependent upon Mahumd. Carry him away now and bury him.'[11]

Shaibani inscribed the title *Imamuzzaman* and *Khalifat-ur Rahman* on his coins too. After Shaibani Khan, the only other Khan who adopted this title was Iskandar Khan. Clande Cahen's assertion that 'The earlier Turkish Mongol idea that 'all members of the family had a certain right to a share of the inheritance, pre-eminence being given to the oldest of the family in the wide sense'[12] is traceable in the Uzbeg Empire also though only in the context of accession of the oldest.'[13] Hafiz Tanish emphasized that 'after shariat and *tariqat* there was no rank higher than that of the king and no magnificence greater than rulership and that God had himself appointed Sovereigns to be his Caliph and deputy and His shadow on earth.[14] Abdullah Khan is said to have believed that the greatness of a sovereign depended upon his excellence attained through five important qualities—benevolence and mercy towards subjects; keeping an eye over the affairs of the empire; imposing terror of a kind that would prevent tyranny; recognizing the significance of vicegerency and absolute monarchy bestowed upon kings by God, by gratefully opening the gates of justice and equality to all the needy; wisdom and farsightedness in anticipating the enemy's moves; and finally, the prudence to value and utilize the time and opportunity.[15] Abdullah Khan is reported to have once told Shighai Khan that no empire could last long if it suffered from two evils, i.e. excessive pleasure seeking and the wasting of precious time.[16] These were not shallow pronouncements, as Abdullah Khan was particularly keen to establish a centralized state based on enlightened despotism.

The Turco-Mongol custom of succession of the oldest member of the family became rampant which led to the accession of weak rulers. Under such weak Khans the theory of absolute power with all its obligations was at times faced with a tendency towards the erosion of the authority of the king. After Shaibani's death, Khans like Souyunch, Kuchum and Abu Said could only maintain Uzbeg power because of the authority passing de facto to Ubaidullah. But the death of Ubaidullah (1539) heralded the disintegration, his own son Abdul Aziz declared himself as an independent ruler in 1545 even though the reigning Khan happened to be alive. Though somewhat exaggerated Jenkinson's assessment of the situation in 1558 depicts the picture well, 'Civil war chanceth in the countries (Turan) once in two or three years. For it is a marvel if a king reigned there above three or four years to the great destruction of the country and merchants "and very often" he be either slain or driven away.'[17]

The laws of Chingiz Khan are said to have included a clause that 'It is forbidden under penalty of death that anyone, whoever he be, shall be proclaimed Emperor, unless he has been elected previously by the princes, Khans, officers and other Mongol nobles in a general council.'[18]

It was Abdullah Khan who at last managed to revive the prestige of the Uzbeg sovereign and unified the Khanates, though during his regime the Naqshbandi saints served as the power behind the throne.

Custom of Succession

Shaibani did not invoke the formalities of any *Qurultai* (assembly of chiefs) for his own accession.[19] Presumably, Shaibani's discussion at Kan-i Gil regarding inheritance and the right of a grandson to inherit his grandfather's property and demand for an injunction from the *Mullas* over this issue (see *Mehn*, pp. 220-8) aimed at setting at rest any controversy involving his accession to the throne, and his nomination of his own son as successor. Departing from the steppe traditions, he nominated his own son Timur Sultan as his *Qa 'Algha*[20] (heir-apparent) while he styled himself as *Khaqan*. But soon after his death, the steppe custom of succession seems to have been asserted and his own nomination was not respected. This sudden change was mainly necessitated by circumstances.

In 1512 the Uzbegs were able to recover the territories lost to the Timurids after the death of Shaibani, with the help of the steppe population. Since this section became the mainstay of their power now, and also because the hangover of the steppe archaism was not yet over, it was necessary to revive the steppe traditions, by which the succession went to the oldest member of the family. This tradition has been described in certain Uzbeg sources as being in conformity with the *Yasa,* though Haider Dughlat and Wasifi say that this was 'an old and nomadic' custom of the Shaibanids.[21]

Wasifi says 'As the prevalent traditions and the fixed law of succession amongst the Shaibanid Sultans demands, the younger ones do not step on the throne till the older brothers and other older members of the family are alive.'[22] Haider Dughlat also tells us that 'the dignity of the Khan, according to the custom was vested in the eldest Sultan'.[23] While the oldest member of the dynasty was selected as the *Khaqan*, the second oldest was nominated as the *Qa 'Algha*[24] (heir apparent).

The same system continued till the ascendancy of Abdullah Khan who at first arranged the enthronement of his father in 1560 and then occupied the throne himself after the death of Iskander Khan in 1583. In the *Kangash* (consultative assembly) convened before his own accession, Abdullah Khan emphasized that though the 'Chingizi laws and customs demanded the enthronement of the oldest, the divine law (*Shari' Nabi*) and true religion (*Mazhab-i Haqiqi*) required the accession of a sultan whose forehead reflected the rays of justice and who was a defender of the faith (*Dinparwar*); whose inner self bore the stamp of benevolence (*Nekkhwahi*) and who through the wholesome water of his sword refreshes the plant of benevolence and rectitude'. Khwaja Juibari elaborated this point by saying that 'at this time the *Khal'at* for spreading Islam and for strengthening its principles have been placed over one of the servants and the diadem suits the head of Khan Abdullah; hence it seems only proper that he should be enthroned'.[25] All this was done to ensure an easy accession of Abdullah even during the lifetime of his older uncle and the old steppe system was disregarded by expressly asserting the custom of the Islamic states.

It seems that the ceremonies for the coronation of *Khaqan* had remained unchanged throughout the Mongolian period[26] (i.e. thirteenth-seventeenth centuries). During this ceremony, which was known as *Khan Kutardilar* (lit. the raising of the Khan) all the four corners of the white felt were raised by the leader of the tribal chiefs, dignitaries of military aristocracy and important nobles. Almost all the chroniclers and travellers give the same details of the ceremonies:

> all their Barons being assembled placed a golden seat in the midst whereon they caused him (the Khan) to sit, and set a sword before him saying, we wish and desire, and demand thee to rule over us. He demanded if they

were contended to do, come, go, stay as he should command. They answered yes. Then said he 'the word of my mouth shall henceforth be my sword'; and they all consented. After this they spread a felt on the ground and sat him thereon saying, look upwards and acknowledge God and look down on the felt whereon thou sittest. If thou shall govern well, will be liberal, just and honor thy princes according to their dignities, thou shall reign magnificent and the whole world shall be subject to thy dominion and God will give thee all thy heart desire, if otherwise, thy shall be miserable, and so popper that the flat shall not be left to thee whereon thou sittest. This done they sit his wife with him on the felt and lifted them up both so sitting and proclaimed them Emperor and Empresses of the Tartars. After which they brought before him infinite store of gold and silver and gems-who distributed what he pleased and reserved the rest. Then began they to drink until night.

At the time of Abdullah Khan's accession, however, a *Khwaja* of *Naqshband-i Qutubulatabi* and a *Khwajazada* Yusuf Khwaja had held the corners while the remaining two were lifted by nobles and tribal chiefs like Tursun Bi, Tardike Khan and Nazar Bi Noyon.[27]

Like the Timurids, the Uzbegs too continued certain Turco-Mongol ceremonies, and customs, e.g. *Zanu Zadan* (kneeling down) before the Khan, *Kasa Dashtan* (offering wine), *Rasm-i Uljameshi* (offering presents), e.g. the gift of horse (*Asp Kashidan*) by the *Ataliq* at the time of his appointment. Shaibani's feigned adherence to orthodox Islamic practices was made real by Ubaidullah's solemn vow (on the eve of decisive battle against the Timurids) to organize the empire and its administration in conformity with the *sharia*. Isfahani was ordered to prepare a book on jurisprudence.[28] Accordingly a treatise on Hanafite form of an ideal government entitled *Suluk-ul Mulk* was made available. Thereafter the Uzbeg Khans began to invoke Islamic traditions much more heavily than their Mongol inheritance.

THE CAPITAL CITY

Shaibani used to say that 'the saddle of his horse' was his capital (*Paya-i ma pushtizin*).[29] However, Samarqand, was chosen as his usual seat. Undoubtedly, the administrative set up of his Uzbeg Empire was somewhat peculiar and in certain respects new to the Central Asian polity and existing norms, structure, forms and patterns. In accordance with *Tura-i Chingizi* to which the Uzbegs still adhered in many ways during the years of the tribal hegemony (i.e. 1439-65 and 1510-12). The Turco-Mongol tribal traditions favoured the accession of the oldest member of the ruling dynasty as *Khaqan* or *Khan* and the second oldest as the *Qaalgha* or heir apparent 'who was to succeed the Khan after his death. The provincial rulers called 'Sultans' were hereditary rulers of their appanages or *Khanates*. The provincial capital was converted into the central capital as soon as the prince of that particular appanage emerged as *Khaqan*. Thus the capital shifted by turn to each provincial capital. Lenepoole points out the 'dual character' of Shaibani's dynasty saying that though Samarqand was the capital there was generally a powerful and sometimes an independent government at Bukhara.[30] In fact from 1510 onwards, the capital shifted with the each new *Khaqan* whose headquarter was treated as the central capital. Thus, within a period of a century the following places served as capitals: Samarqand (1505-33/and 1539-91); Tashkent (1551-5); Balkh (1555-9); Bukhara (1533-9 and 1559-99).

Central Administration

THE KHAN AND STATE BUSINESS

The Khan was the pivot of administration. He traditionally enjoyed numerous rights and was expected to fulfil a variety of obligations. He had to look after the distribution of principalities and jurisdictions with their limits, the assignment of various forms of land grants (including even *Ulufa*), appointment of various officers in the centre and the provinces, appointment of custodians of various tombs and Waqf lands, issuing administrative decrees, regulations, etc.

The Khan could intervene in feuds between the subordinate rulers or sultans. While the sultan (provincial rulers) could maintain diplomatic relations with external powers through embassies, certain major decisions like waging war or making treaties were vested exclusively in the Khan.

In accordance with the laws prescribed by Chingiz Khan, frequent tours had to be undertaken by the Khan to acquaint himself personally with the affairs of each province.[31] Thus the Khans considered it obligatory to make a general inspection of the country. For this purpose hunting excursions were organized regularly so that the Khan could appear incognito and inspect the administrative condition without prior information. Furthermore, these hunting excursions provided an opportunity to the army also to practice archery and carry out other activities connected with warfare. During such tours, the Khan punished and rewarded officials.[32] Sometimes when necessary, the Khan announced exemptions from certain taxes for the relief of his subjects.[33]

The Khan himself appointed and fixed the maintenance allowance and place of stay of foreign dignitaries.[34] Enquiries were made[35] by the Khan regarding the performance of various sultans and officials not only through his tours but also during his stay at the capital.[36] Transfers were sometimes ordered on the basis of these complaints.

On all important occasions (e.g. selection or election of a new Khan), a *Qurultai*[37] was organized, attended by the sultans, *oughlans*, a large number of nobles and tribal chiefs of various grades.[38] Other routine matters were discussed in consultation with high officials in smaller consultative assemblies called *Kangash, Janqi, Majlis-i Mashwrat.* Both Yazdi and Hafiz Tanish seek to give an Islamic colour that the *Kangash* was a kind of assembly giving practical form to the concept of *Ijma* and *Shura*,[39] i.e. the Islamic injunction of consensus. Yet Timur and Abdullah discarded the opinion of the majority and either accepted the opinion of their confidantes which repeated their own ideas or openly discarded majority opinion by cleverly manouvering the acceptance of their own views.[40]

There is no special mention of the *Mullas* sitting separately in such assemblies, probably because they were an integral part of the court. The Uzbeg rulers demanded their opinion. An important role is attributed to the consultative assembly and the significance of consultations is stressed in almost all the medieval Central Asian sources. However, Shaibani is reported to have often discussed administrative affairs with the *Mullas* separately and the court chronicler Mullah Muhammad Shahi stresses the fact that 'the orders issued by the Khan Shaibani could never be changed even one word' and justified this firmness as 'variable attitude of a sultan was sure to create dissensions and lack of faith in his words',[41] and demanded their opinion, *Nass* (injunction). The *Mullas* could sometimes display independence. When an obliging Mulla Mir Ahu tried to please Shaibani, he was snubbed by the others who charged him with behaving 'like those *Ulama* of Isreal who strengthened the claims of rulers by inverting the word of God (*Tahrif-i Ahkam*)'.[42] During

.Ubaidullah's time, Isfahani criticized the adoption of the title *Khalifat-ur Rahman* by Shaibani saying that a ruler may be called *Khalifa*, *Imam*, *Amir-ul Mominin* or even *Khalifa-i Rasul* but not *Khalifatullah* which is not legal (*jaez*).[43] Even the declaration of holy war against the Qazaqas was not considered justified by him. Isfahani clearly stated that 'the Sovereign is the one who strengthened his hold over the Muslims by way of his magnificence and strength of his army. Obedience to his orders was, therefore, binding upon all (provided they did not contradict the sharia)'. But he emphasized that 'sultans ought to abide by the advices of the *Mujtahid*' and that 'imparting counsel to him was justified'.[44] Although neither Shaibani nor Ubaidullah conducted themselves solely by the guidance of the *Mullas*, they certainly sought their counsel. Even if the advice given was not accepted, *Mullahs* were permitted to express their opinions freely.[45]

Abdullah Khan too considered consultations to be a 'God's signal—a revealed truth and the safest exit from the difficulties'.[46] He is said to 'have never undertaken any special task or campaign without proper consultation in the special assembly (*Majlis-i Khas*) of his own confidantes *(Ahl-i Ikhtesas*)'.[47] Although freedom of expression was granted, Abdullah could reject the opinion of the majority in favour of his own deputy's suggestion without creating any displeasure among the others.[48] Nonetheless, the holding of consultations was an important part of conduct of state business by him.[49]

CENTRAL OFFICIALS

Before discussing the functions of various central officers in Uzbeg *Khanates*, it is necessary to mention that though each post had its own usual and fixed functions, the duties of each officer was determined by the exigencies of the situation and personal decisions of the Khan. Sometimes one confidante of Khan held the charge of *Shaikh-ul Islam*, *Naqib* and *Mufti* simultaneously or of *Diwan-i Mushrif* and *Sadarat*.[50] A *Muhdar* could be asked to perform *Qarauli*[51] (sentinel) and a *Qazi* could be ordered to supply fodder to the army.[52] Nevertheless some order and organization is noticeable in different spheres though not to the extent found in the Ottoman Empire. Another extremely valuable source for this purpose is the *Ruznama-i Qazi* (IOST No. 2277)—an administrative manual prepared by Mirza Muhammad Sharif Sadr Zia for illustrating various principles and aspects of existing Uzbeg polity. Sadr Zia categorically asserts that posts and the institutions of the Uzbeg Sultans (*Mansab o Amalhai Salatin-i Uzbegiya*) had continued on the same pattern at least from the reign of Chingiz Khan up to their own extinction.

Although no contemporary administrative manual on officers or their functions are available here, two works, the *Majma-ul Arqam* of Mirza Badi (comp. 1798) and a collection of later documents (MS. No. 2374 of state library AN uz SSR) by Qazi Kalan Sharif Jan Makhdum furnish information on the functions of various officials. The information is confirmed by earlier accounts like *Nama-i Nami* or the meagre evidence scattered in the contemporary and later sources. Since glimpses of Mongol body politics are visible in Uzbeg administration, the work *Dastur-ul Katib Fitaiyyun-ul Maratib* is also important for the study.

The Khan appointed a number of officers to assist him in state business. Apart from the army personnel, there were three broad categories of officers: religious, administrative and general.

Religious Officers

Both Mirza Badi Sadr Zia and Sharif Jan affirm that in accordance with the *sharia*, the kings of Transoxiana appointed four main religious officers.

The first were the judges (*Mansab-i Quzzat*) in which category the highest place was held by *Shaikh-ul Islam*, who happened to be the court of first instance (*Murafa-i Ula*), a binding force (*Aqid*) and higher in position than the *Qazi-ul Qazzat*.[51] The *Khwajas* of Naqshbandi and Jahria silsilah were appointed to the office of *Shaikh-ul Islam* and the post was usually hereditary.[52] In one of his *farmans*, Abdullah had called its incumbents 'the steadfast pillars of the religious affairs the arrangement of the affairs of people and the disposal of affairs of the people and the disposal of matters concerning those who offer prayers and are obedient to God'.[53] Sometimes the *Sajjada Nashin* (rank of an *Imam*) of a tomb also accompanied the post of *Shaikh-ul Islam* both being hereditary privilege.[54] Ubaidullah's *Shaikh-ul Islam* weiged himself in bread and *halwa* and often organized public feasts (*suhbat-i Amma*).[55] Abdullah's *Shaikh-ul Islams* often came from amongst the *Khwajas* of *Naqshband*[56] whose open kitchens (*langar*) and other acts of charity were well known. Members of the same family could hold various posts. Hasan Nisari says that the *Shaikh-ul Islam* of Bukhara was very closely related to Qazi.[57]

The *Qazi-ul quzzat* or the chief *Qazi* at the capital was inferior to the *Shaikh-ul Islam* at the centre and superior to dignitaries like *Wali-i Askar* and *Qazi-i Askar*. The chief *Qazi* was appointed by the king and entrusted mainly with the management of the affairs of the common people which included justice in accordance with sharia (to settle civil disputes, the trial of the cases, sit in judgement over disputes of marriage, divorce, inheritance, *auqaf*, etc.) Abdullah once even entrusted the administration of Bukhara to Qazi Nur Muhammad during his absence from the capital.[58]

As in other Muslim states, the *Qazi-i Askar* were sultan's most influential assistants and advisors. In the large towns, there would be a *Darogha* or road governor, with absolute authority in his district. With him would be a clerk, to write down the names of the personages who called at the station, and the merchandise that went by.[59] Sometimes the posts of the *Gazi* and *Sadr* were held by one person.[60] The *Qazis* could hold charge for long periods,[61] and the post could also be hereditary.[62]

The *Qazi* who was entrusted with dispensing justice among the soldiery was known as *Qazi-i Askar*[63] somewhat lower in rank than the *Wali-i Askar*. In each town there were a *Qazi* and *Darogha* both of whom seemed to have been engaged in maintaining law and order. Cases of murder, etc., were often investigated by the *Darogha*.[64] The *Qazi* was also expected to organize charity, look after the stay and entertainments of the envoys and even at times supervise the construction of bridges and other public works,[65] and oversee the mint. Sometimes the chief *Qazi* was quite an influential person. The *Qazi-ul Quzzat* Nuruddin Muhammad who not only held this post but enjoyed 'the charge of the affairs of the country and all the important and trivial matters'.[66] *Qazis* could also be removed.[67]

The highest place in the second office of *Mufti* was enjoyed by the *Alim* (most learned man) who issued *fatwa* (opinion on legal matters) to the common and the poor people. The *Mufti-i Askar* issued *fatwas* for the army particularly when the Khan travelled from one region to another or during army's march.[68] Abdullah described the *Muftis* in one of his *farmans* as persons 'whose tip of the pen was equivalent to the report (decisions) of an assembly'.[69] The Islamic polity generally needed analogical deductions and expert advice. The view that in Islamic States the 'spiritual weapons' were used to arrive at 'understanding between theologians and the kings based on the mutual recognition of their sphere of interests'[70] took place in Central Asia also. Since most of the Uzbeg Sultans were highly educated and particularly Shaibani Khan and Ubaidullah were themselves well-versed in jurisprudence, the Naqshbandi saints were supporting the rulers. In central Asia, the *Ghazawat* (holy wars) were declared against any hostile power by the obliging *Muftis* justifying it through far fetched arguments,[71] thus the holy war against the Qazaqs was sanctioned on the plea that 'they were Muslims in name only'.[72]

In the third office of *Ihtisab, Muhtasibs* were performing almost the same duties as in other Islamic states,[73] i.e. the supervision of public morals, prevention of fraud, fraudulent sales, payment of debts, illegal deeds, checking of weights and measures, enforcement of religious and moral precepts of Islam; supervision over traders and artisans,[74] the task of *Ihtisab* and the power of command and prohibition and orders and counter orders.[75] If a Siyid was not available for the post of *Muhtasib* a non-*Sadat* was usually not appointed though exceptions were always there. Once the *Mansab* of *Ihtisab* of Merv is said to have been given by Keldi Muhammad to a poet in reward for a eulogy he wrote for the ruler.[76] Dealings with non Muslims and prohibition of wine was also included in the *Muhtasibs'* duties. The verdict of the *Muhtasib* was to be respected even by the dignitaries; and all defaulters were to be punished.[77]

The fourth in the religious sphere was the *Mansab-i Tadrisi*, i.e. the category of teachers who devoted their time to educating students.[78] They were appointed by the Khan himself[79] in the *Madrasa*. Some other posts were merely and presumably decorative and for purposes of obliging certain important segments of society. In this category were four other posts exclusively allocated and held by *Saadats*. One of these was *Masnad/Nashin* who 'looked after international, internal and external affairs'. This rank was usually assigned even without an area to govern.[80]

Another important officer in this category was the *Naqib*. He held charge of army organization before and during war and on marches seeing to discipline and proper accoutrement of soldiers logistics and other arrangements.[81] According to Barthold, the *Naqib* was expected to attend to law suite of soldiers in the absence of an *Amir* and also enjoyed greater powers than the *Qazi-i Askar*.[82] Abdullah's Naqib Hasan Khwaja seems to have exercised considerable influence in matters of civil administration and at the court also. The *Sadr-us Sudur* or the chief *Sadr* has been described by Hafiz Tanish as 'the accounts officer dealing with matters concerning the lands and the affairs of country and property'.[83] 'He was also the controller of *waqf* lands'.[84] His high status is shown by the dictum that all the ministers of the Khan (*Wuzra-i Uzzam*) were to regard him as their rendezvous and asylum'.[85] He was responsible for the supervision and distribution of religious grants and endowments. In these matters he was supposed to follow the mandates (*Misalat*) of the *Diwan-i Aala*.[86] Shaibani's *Sadr*, Khwaja Ali, was highly respected though he is said to have lacked competence and intelligence.[87] Maulana Abdur Rahim Turkestani and another *Sadr* of Shaibani, enjoyed extraordinary powers.[88] There were often more than one *Sadr*. Under Ubaidullah Khan, each one of the two *Sadrs* is reported to have received a salary of about 30,000 *khani* annually.[89] Sometimes the mutual rivalries of these *Sadrs* created problems for the ruler. Wasifi reports how the nobles and officers of Ubaidullah were divided into two groups each supporting one of the *Sadrs*.[90]

Syed Hasan Askari described the two terms separately as *Mushrif-i diwan,* explaining that *Mushrif* stood for 'the official who studied the accounts' and *Diwani* denoted 'the tribunal of revenue and justice'.[91]

The post of *Sadr* could be hereditary, though always subject to the Khan's pleasure. Qulbaba's father had the *Sadarat-i Khani* of all the *Wilayats* under Abdullah Khan. After his death, Qulbaba himself received this post in addition to his existing post of *Diwan-i Mushrif*.[92] The third officer was *Oraq-i Kalan* who held the charge of *Ihtisab* of the *Saadats* of the army. The fourth post was that of *Amal-i Naqshbandi* under whose stewardship was the superintendence and command of the management of holy tombs (*Mazar-i Sharif*) in the area.

The other four posts were not fixed for any specific group and the rulers could select any one from amongst the *Ulama* and *Saadat* of the Uzbegs. These included the ranks of the class of Faizi and *Sadr-us Sudur*. If Faizi was an *Alim* or *Saiyid* his jurisdiction of *Ihtisab* extended inside and outside the city upto a distance of one *farsakh* only whereas the audit accounts and management of the endowments (*quqaf*) outside the towns was conducted by the *Mutassadis* and the *Sadrs*.[93]

Administrative and Revenue Officers

The chancery or the bureaucracy (*Amala-i Ahl-i Qalam* or *Arbab-i Qalam*) had four main officers, the highest being the chief minister styled the *Diwan-i Kalan* or *Wazir-i Azam* who also happened to be the supervisor (*Amin-i daftar-i ali*) of all the registers, salaries, records and orders (*Bilku*). The second dignitary was the *Diwan-i Mushrif* who 'maintained the records of gifts royal awards (e.g. *Alam*, endowments, armour, *Jiba, Joshan* account, horse, *Yaraq*, etc.). In the sixteenth century these two posts seemed to have been combined and held by one person known under various titles (e.g. *Mustauf-i Diwan, Diwan-i Mushrif, Wazir-i Azam, Naib-i Mamlakat, Diwan Begi, Diwan-i Kalan* or *Diwan-i Aala*) and he accomplished his duties with the help of other *Wazirs* or *Diwans*. In the *Suluk-ul Muluk*, Isfahani describes the *Wazir* as the *Naib* (deputy) of the ruler.[94] Two categories of *Wazirs* have been mentioned by him. *Wazir-i Tafvizi* who reported the affairs to the emperor and took action according to the emperor's suggestions. He was, authorized to appoint and dismiss nobles of the provinces, *Qazis* and other post holders and could perform other acts delegated to him by the ruler. Three things were forbidden to him, i.e. the *Imamat* itself (rulership), appointment of his successor in office and dismissal of an officer appointed by the ruler himself. The second type of *Wizarat*, i.e. *Wazir-i Tanfizi* did not involve the enjoyment of any delegated powers. The ministers' duties merely comprised compliance of administrative orders of the ruler, conveying these to the officers concerned and ensuring their enforcement.[95] The *Mehman Nama* only once refers to the existence of these two kinds of *Wazirs* under Shaibani Khan. In later sources, there are references to a number of *Wazirs* without any specification of titles. Several passages in the *Abdullah Nama* also refer to the *Wizarat* as synonymous with the *Diwani*,[96] the word *Diwan* would seem to have indifferently been used for the *Wazir*.

The *Diwan-i Mushrif* exercised overall control over finances and verified petitions to be submitted before the Khan. Abdullah's *Diwan* Walijan Jalair was deposed owing to his incompetence and a 'high-born person' Qazi Nuruddin Muhammad, who could 'appreciate the difficulties of high and low', was appointed in his place.[97]

The post of *Diwan* could be hereditary though always subject to the approval of the sovereign. In 1586 Khwaja Mirzam (the son of Mirza Beg Diwan) was removed from the post due to certain mistakes and errors on his part after two years service though he was well versed in rules and regulations (of *Wizarat*), arithmatic and correspondence.[98]

The *Diwans* were required to supervise the assessment and collection of revenue,[99] to make arrangements of battle, arrange for the supply of food, arms and equipment during war, [100] and to suppress unruly elements.[101] Besides, the assessment of taxes on agriculture and artisans, the supervision or division of booty, collection of *Mal-i Amani* after war, transactions with traders were part of his duties.[102]

With such varied and excessive powers, the *Diwans* sometimes became dishonest even under such strong rulers as Abdullah. Both Abdussalam and Hafiz Tanish have given instances of certain *Diwans* being dismissed, transferred or fined for the embezzlement[103] or for practising revenue. When Khwaja Muhammad Qasim, who held the *Diwani* of Balkh failed to deposit the fine for embezzlement he was tortured to death by the *Qalamqs*, appointed for the purpose by Qulbaba.[104] Nevertheless the *Diwans*, if efficient, could hold the charge for long periods. Abdullah's *Diwan* Khwaja Kamaluddin held the *Diwani* of Bukhara and its vicinity for quite a long time.[105] Abdullah Khan's *Diwan-i Mushrif* was Qulbaba Kukultash who held independent charge of affairs. The dignitaries of the state and all the *Wazirs* visited him every day and consulted him in all the important affairs. His advice was taken and his orders were obeyed in all matters concerning the *Diwani*.[106] Qulbaba used to sit in the office of *Diwan* every day. Suits and plaintiffs were settled by him since he held the charge of *Sadarat* as well.[109] Another *Diwan-i Mushrif* of Abdullah, Abdur Rahim Bi Husain Bi Durman held the charge for quite a long time and was entirely independent (*Mutlaq-ul 'inan*).[108]

The political intrigues often pursued such influential officers. Ubaidulah's *Wazir* Khwaja Nizam is said to have been an honest and just official. Nevertheless his enemies maligned him and though the latter could regain his position through the intercession of Mir-i Arab, the opposition did not subside. Khwaja Nizam was ultimately put to death on the pretext of being a Shia.[109] Under the chief *Diwan*, there were *Wuzra-i Uzzam* and other *Diwans* of lower ranks and of various categories at the centre as well as in the provinces to assist the *Diwan-i Aala*.[110] The *Kharaj-i Muazzaf* was collected twice, in the spring and the autumn from *Muazzaf* lands (*Araz-i Kharaj-i Muazzaf*), its income and expenditure being settled in accordance with the government's directions. The *Daftardars* maintained complete and up to date records of revenue deductions and enhancements.

There were other officers in the chancery, namely, the *Munshi*, who wrote down official grants (*Inayat Nama*), directives (*Khwadhish Nama*), and the orders (*Yirligh-i Amiat*)[111] of the *Amils*. The *Munshis* also wrote victory proclamations or *Fath Namas*. Abdullah's *Munshi*, Maulana Haider Muhammad, is said to have created a 'spell of eloquence'.[112]

The *Shighawul* was incharge of the maintenance of envoys, etc. Aban *Shighawul* was asked by Abdullah to look after the Indian envoys. Shahna, or the *Mir-i Shab*, was required to maintain peace at nights. The *Qarawut Begi* along with the *Qarawuls* looked after watch and ward on the roads. The *Kutwal* was incharge of all construction and the supply of bricklayers and labourers, etc., for the Khan's buildings and corvee.[115] The *Uragi Khurd* fulfilled the task of *Muhtasibs* among servants of the *Amirs* and other highly placed officials with Mir, *Hakims* or *Qushbegi*, etc.[114] The *Khwaja Kalan* was the head of all the eunuchs who supplied the harem of the sultan with food, dress and other necessaries and also arranged for the distribution of charity. The *Kitabadaars* looked after the maintenances of the imperial library, the *Parwanchi* conveyed the *Yirliqs* to the nobles at the orders of the Khan, and *Dadkhwah* submitted the petitions seeking justice and conveyed orders thereon.

According to Mirza Badi, there existed mainly 'four supporting amirs' of the Khan, one of which was the *Ataliq*. The term *Ataliq* (lit., 'like a father' or father designate) denotes a tutor, but came to mean the deputy or vicegerent of the sovereign. The *Ataliqs* existed both at the centre and in the provinces. In accordance with old tradition, the *Ataliq* at centre was accorded a high status and his functions included the supervision, equal distribution and administration of the water resources, river, etc., control of lower Bukhara from Samarqand to Qarakul and all *tumanat* organization of distribution and supply of water to the *Tumans*, *Hazaras* and in the four corners of Saghraj, Miyankalat and Tumanat of Bukhara upto canal of Qarakul. On him depended the superintendence of the *Rud-i Shahr* (canal from Zarafshan) and of the caravanserais *(rabat)* of Bukhara. The *Ataliq* was to ensure that each member of the community whether high or low and the village communes received their fair share of water (*Haqqaba*) in accordance with the availability of water.[115]

The third post in order of importance was that of *Daftardar* who was entrusted with *Daftar-i Kalan* (Big Registers) which included and continued all laws and covenants, administrative directions, records and accounts, affirmation and annulment of the sultan's court. The fourth was the *Diwan-i Tanabana* holding the charge of *Mahsulat* (collection of taxes), *Kharaj-i Muazzaf* (regular poll tax) and the royal lands. The *Kharaj-i Muazzaf* was collected twice, in the spring and the autumn from *Muazzaf* lands (*Araz-i Kharji Muazzaj*), its income had expenditure being settled in accordance with the government's directions. The *Daftardars* maintained complete and upto date records of revenue deductions and enhancements.

Another set of four officers included in the same category of 'men of pen' *(Ahl-i Qalam)* were: *Munshi* who drafted *Manshurs* and *Mubarak Namas* (royal orders and congratulatory letters). He wrote down official grants *(Inayat Nama)* directives *(Khwahish Nama)* and orders (*Yirligh-i Amilat*)[116] of the Amils. They *Munshis* also wrote victory proclamations or *Fath Namas*. Abdullah's *Munshi* Maulana Haider Muhammad is said to have created a 'spell of eloquence'.[117] The *Diwan-i Darun-i Shahr* (*Diwan* of interior of the city) who belonged to the tribe of the group dealing with assignment of taxes and carried and transmitted the *farmans* of the Sultan as soon as he got it; *Diwan-i Arab Khana* who dealt with the affairs of *Arab Khana*, concerning appointments and nominations, etc., the last and perhaps the most active and frequently mentioned was the *Diwan-i Tanfih* (*Diwan* of assessment and adjustment) whose importance is visible in that it deals with putting together and comparing (*Tatbiq*) of the accounts of *Diwan-i Daftardar* and *Diwan-i Tanabana*.[118]

Another set of four officials of 'men of pen' category was involved in the management of general affairs. One of these was the *Kitabdar* who looked after the maintenance of the scholars and the poets. The *Diwan Bakhshi* was the superintending officer of all income and expenditure the *Kutwal* spent on all imperial buildings. The *Diwan-i Shishkhana* (the incharge of baggage horses employed in war) was the overseer of all the matters conserving *Shishkhana*. The *Diwan-i Tuskhakhana* (incharge of wardrobe) was the steward of *Balas* (haircloth, sack cloth, mattresses), its acquisition, distribution, registration records were all planned and maintained by him. Inferior in the rank of above four were the four posts namely *Mushrif-i Khurd, Pagir Navis, Diwan-i Mahram* and *Diwan-i Yasawul*.

There were four kinds of *Muharirs* (scribes, accountants) namely *Munharrir-i Diwan-i Sarkar, Muharrir-i Imlak, Muharrir-i Ikhbar* and *Muharrir-i Kitabkhana.*

The *Daroghas* were appointed by the Khan in each town to maintain law and order[119] as well as for the general superintendence of the towns.[120] He collected a cess known as *Daroghai.* In certain *Yirliqs,* written in the old Uzbeg language even the powers of a ruler have been assigned to a *Darogha.* From one of these *Yirliqs*, we learn that the people in the region of Andijan were ordered to consider the *Darogha* as their governor.[121] It seems that these *Daroghas* also maintained troops and supplied forces to the Khan whenever needed.[122] In the big cities, however, they were appointed only to help the governor.

The *Diwan-i Maharim* was the incharge of *Mahrams* the court or palace 'confidantes'—for carrying out errands. The *Diwan-i Yasawul* were officers concerned with records and copying or correspondence of the affairs of the *Yasawuls*. The *Yasawuls* were rather low level officials placed under the ruler and the high central officials like the *Qazi-i Kalan*, etc., for carrying out assigned tasks.[123] Their importance varied with their tasks. Apart from submission of presents and petitions from princes and nobles,[124] they helped in army organization and served as emissaries.[125] There were several categories of *Yasawuls* such as *Boroniji, Mahram*, etc. Unlike the Indian *Yasawuls* who were only used for implementing orders, these *Yasawuls* sometimes held important positions as Sulaiman Yasawul who was once appointed *Hakim* of Merv Shahijan, Sari Yasawul held the *Mansab* of *Ataliqi* of Souyunj Muhammad.[126] Nevertheless later records describe *Yasawuls* as 'local police, striking right and left with sticks and shouting reproaches against the sightseers for their violent breach of decorum'.[127]

During war *Yasawuls* separated servants from soldiers at the advice of the *Naqib*. The posts of *Yasawuls* and their *Avedachi* were reserved for the Qirat and the Oughlans.[128]

Another of the same category was *Diwan Begi-i Kalan* who was the controller of *Kharaj* from the *Wilayat* and the *Kharaj-i Muazzaf* etc. The cash from a *Wilayat* was sent by him to *Mihtar* (superintendent) of *Tushakkana* whereas the corn and grains were consigned/dispatched and deposited to the *Imlakdar* according to the reckoning of *Diwan-i Kalan* and the *Daftar-i Tanabana*. The *Diwan-i Kalan* happened to hold the charge of *Mir-i Abi* of Qarakul. The

Parwanchis dealt with the *Manshurs* and other presents to be sent to the *Amirs* and the *Ulama* and the others. Similarly the administration concerning the *taefa* of Arabs was also under surveillance of the *Parwanchis*. The fourth officer was *Dad Khwah* who brought the petitions of the downtrodden to the notice of the king and brought back the answers to the petitioner.[129]

There were four posts reserved only for the *Muqarraban* (kindred or close associates of the King) one of them was *Kukultash* who was the officer dealing with news agencies, spy system and intelligence. The reports and the information from the friend and foe alike in the *Wilayats* were to be collected and necessary presents and reparations were to be taken by him. The second in this category was the *Qush Beg-i Kul* who was incharge of hunters, fowlers, falconers, fishermen and all kinds of their instruments and tools. The third officer was *Inaq-i Kalan* who carried the orders of the king issued those not belonging to the emirate or elite but to Shagird Pesha (retinue or menial). The fourth officer was *Khwaja Kalan* (the head of *Khwajasaras* (eunuchs) of the kingdom), who was superintendent of victuals, viands and wearing apparels of the royal harem. These above mentioned officers, however belong to the category of men of pen. From amongst the 'men of pen' only *Diwan-i Kalan* could ride to his destination from the court.

The other four officers who by virtue of their being related to *Khaqan* (*Muqarri-ul Khaqan*) ride from the court by king's order (though they are inferior to *Kukultash*, *Qushbegi* and *Khwaja-i Kalan*) are: *Inaq-i Khurd*, *Mihtar-i Kalan* whose duties include the collection of *Zakat* and *Rabai Ushr* 4/10 from the Momins and *Ulsb Ushr* from the *Zimmis*.

Apparently it seems that there were certain posts which were merely and presumably decorative and meant for obliging important and sensitive segments of society. In this category there were four posts exclusively allocated for the sadats. One of these was *Masnad Nashin* who 'looked after internal and external affairs'. This rank was usually assigned ever without an area to govern.[130]

If the seating arrangement in the court is any indication of position of office holders, the *Ataliq* and the *Naqib* held the highest position sitting left to the Khan. The post of *Naqib* was hereditary and was held only by the Saiyids. He was highly respected by the members of the ruling family. In Abdullah Khan's court, the *Naqib* always occupied a higher place than even Qulbaba Kukultash in all the state assemblies. In *Abdullah Nama*, the name of *Naqib* almost always appears next to Abdullah Khan preceding the names of all other higher nobles and officials.[131]

The *Yasawul Ikhania* was always an Oughlan whose duty was to bring to the Emperor the gifts, offerings and reports of sultans and men of ruling classes in the court.[132] The post of chief *Yasawul Ouidachi* or *Oudaji* (lit. household) was usually held by two *Wairat Tuqsaba* (officer for serving eatables) and *Dadkhwah* (for conveying the petitions and their answers).[133] The post of *Yasawul* could be hereditary or for longer periods.[134] They carried out their appointed tasks in the general audience or pleasure assemblies and court ceremonials and during army marches. Some of the *Chehras* (pages) were promoted as *Yasawuls* on performing any acts of bravery and courage.[135]

JUDICIARY AND LAW

The rulers of Transoxiana were said to be the followers of Abu Hanifa[136] and disputes in the Uzbeg *Khanate* seem to have been usually decided according to the Hanafite school of law.[137]

The *Diwani-i Mazalim*[138] was the court of justice where the king personally or his *Wazir* presided. Usually cases such as extortion, discontinuation of stipends and restoration of wrongfully seized property were decided by the Diwan. Justice (*Baz Khwast*) in case of rebels or the criminals was done by *Gazis.*[139] The princes and the nobles were brought to book and interrogated (*Yarghu Pursidan*) by Khan or his nominees. The Qazi also decided matters of indiscipline.[140] The *Shahnai Qahr* punished, executed, tortured and dealt with criminals in accordance with imperial orders.

Punishments were of various kinds ranging from blinding, mutilation, flaying of skin,[141] fine or blood with compensation *(Khunbah)* for murder,[142] Wasifi refers to the strange punishments[143] like culprits being tied hand and feet and thrown into stables.[144] Rebel princes were given special punishments. Tahir Sultan was imprisoned in a well, though special windows were provided for the supply of food and clothes.[145] Capital punishment, like severing of heads was also common.

As might be evident from the above discussion, the Uzbeg rulers do not seem to have introduced any elaborate departmentalization or clear-cut delimitation of various administrative spheres. There is no mention of any department or office except that of *Diwani* or the revenue department or the *Diwan-i Mazalim* or judiciary. The detailed descriptions of duties of various officers in our sources are, however, quite impressive, though we have selected a few only.

THE COURT

No contemporary account of the court is available but one may legitimately refer not only to Ibn-i Battuta (for Uzbeg Khan's court) and more specifically to Mahmud bin Wali to fill the gap.[146] The latter had given a vivid description of the Uzbeg court and its ceremonials under Nazar Muhammad in his *Bahr-ul Asrar fi Manaqib ul Akhiyar* (compiled in 1634-41). The Central Asian sources, always refer to the fixed places (*Jai Muaiyan*) of various officers and tribal magnates in accordance with a hierarchical ranking and are available only in the above mentioned sources which indicates not only the significance of 'ranks and posts related to highly placed group of the nobles styled by them (Uzbegs) as *Bis*'[147] but also names and functions of various other grades of officials associated with the court. Conforming to the *Yasa* and *Yasun* of Uzbegs, the court had three different sections, right, left and centre, each of which had two rows.

Mahmud bin Wali's description indicates that the left side consisted mainly of the highest echeleon of the tribal magnates irrespective of their ranks. Here the highest place nearest to the throne was occupied by the *Naqibs*—the 'representatives of the descendants of Ali'. Even the princes and the heir apparent held lower position than the *Naqib*. Next to *Naqib* were the seats (*Urunat*) of the leaders (*Qart*) of Durman, Qushchi, Naiman and lastly the Qunghrats. Then the *Ataliq* of the Khan—also a tribal dignitary and a little lower than him were the seats of *Oughlans*. Near the *Oughlans* were the places of *Nana* (*Nankana*) of Durman, Qushchi and Naimans followed by Qarluqs, Buiraks and other important officers of various *Ulus* and *Aimaqs*.

The left side was reserved for administrative officers—the highest place being always occupied by *Shaikh-ul Islam* except when a foreign ruler or refugee was given an audience and a carpet was laid especially for him on a higher place in front of the *Shaikh-ul Islam*.[148] Behind the *Shaikh-ul Islam* sat the *Qazi-ul Quzzat* (though this place could often be taken over by Saiyids as well). Then came the places of Naqshbandi saints who were also included in administrative circle; along with the *Sadr* and behind them the *Qazi-i Askar.* A little farther sat the *Allama* (chief or elder *Mufti*). Next to them were the seats assigned to any tribe (like Qarat, Qiyat or Keneges) at the ruler's will. The next seats were held by the Middle strata (*Ara*) of Durman, Qushchi and Naiman. Farther away sat those who had distinguished themselves in bravery and competence. In Mahmud bin Wali's time, in the centre, the highest place in front of throne was held by the Manghits opposite them were the Qara Qiyats and then the *Chaharyar* of Durman tribe. Under the Uzbegs in sixteenth century the centre must have consisted of the Shaibanids, being replaced by the Manghits under the Ashtarakhanids.

The second row of both the right and left consisted of the places of *Yasawul-i Khani* behind whom sat *Eishik Aqa Bashi* (chief of the porters)—then *Mir Akhur* (chief of stable)—if the *Aimaqs* belonged to the *Ulus* of left side; *Shighawul* (master of ceremonies), *Mirza Bashi* (chief of writers), *Khazanchi* (treasurer) and others. The Diwan Begi occupied the place near these three wings. Behind the throne were the places of *Qurchis* (body guards) and *Ichkis* (the servants of inner circle) who organized the assemblies; the right place was held by *Qurch Bashi* (chief of the bodyguards); behind them sat *Qush Begi* (chief of hunting), *Chehra Aqasi* (chief of pages), *Hajibs* (servants of the palace), *Yasawuls* and their chief *Yasawul Oudachi, Dadkhwah* and *Chobdar*. Whenever the general assembly (*Kornish-i Aamma*) was organised for the pleasure of the ruler and the army and for giving out rewards, convention (*Yusun-i Humayuni*) prescribed drinking of *Qumiz* served by *Sauchis* (wine servers) and *Sabadars* (wine skin carriers). In this also the hierarchy was always respected as the *Oudachis* first served the ruler then the circles of *Amirs* followed by *Eishik Aqayan* (lord of gatekeepers), *Qurchi* (bodyguards), *Qurq* (?) *Chehra* and *Kubchehra* (pageboys). Later on the feast for the army started and in groups of four the soldiery came and drank. Anyone violating the rule or order had to drink 13 cups (including the one cup of excuse) at the doorstep and was subjected to punishment (except death).

According to Mahmud bin Wali the custom and ceremonials regarding the reception and audience given to the envoys of other rulers or emissaries from the rulers of *Tumans* or heads of *Ulus* were as follows: the *Shighawul* first conveyed the envoy's respects, request and presents. Thereafter if the envoy belonged to the category of important nobles, two persons (from both the sides) of the rank of *Parwanchi* and *Tuqsaba* brought him to the throne. When the hand of the Khan touched the shoulders of the envoy, he was brought back to his place at a hint from the ruler to the right or left side and he did not speak till he was asked to do so. He sat opposite to the throne till his gradation and class was fixed by the Khan personally. When the feasts started then he got up and the supervisor of the table (*Khwan Nawal* or *Khwansalar*) prepared the eatables for him till the end of Khan's feast.[149] A Somewhat similar account is found in *Abdullah Nama.*[150]

Provincial Government

The ruler was given the title of Khan while the princes usually placed over provinces, were called sultans.[151] The *Khutba* was read and the coins were struck in the name of the Khan throughout the Empire.

The empire was divided into various large and small provinces called *Yurts* in earlier days. The Uzbegs had brought with them the old Mongolian concept of *Yurt* and therefore in the first few years, Uzbeg princes and nobles were assigned as their *Yurts* various territories with their settled populations. Under the Mongols the word *Yurt* had been widely used and it also occurs in the sources of the reign of Timur. Lambton renders the term as tribal pastures.[152] In the Uzbeg language, however, the term had come to denote simply 'country' or 'place' which suits the sense better when the term is read in the *Matla-us Sadain* or in *Zafar Nama.*[153] Under the Mongols, the term had specifically meant the 'appanage of a Mongol prince'. In the sixteenth-seventeenth centuries the term seems to have acquired much fluidity. It has been used in the sense of a territory or military post or land grant or camps and tents. Frequent references have been made to this term in the *Mehman Nama.*[154] At one place one hears of 'noted Uzbeg nobles' whose *Yurt* was near the territories (*Mamalik*) of Hazarat Sultan Timur (son of Shaibani).[155] Soviet historians tend to take *Yurt* in the sense of appanages assigned to the members of the ruling family or the leaders of the tribes.[156] For landgrant, the term seems to have fallen out of use only after the first two dècades of Uzbeg rule. References to it in this sense are rarely found in later sources. The appanages were called *Wilayat Mamlakat* or *Mulk* which were assigned to various sultans by the *Khaqan*.

The holders of each *Wilayat* used to govern the territories and distribute *Iqtas* and other forms of assignments to his relatives and nobles in his own appanage. The portion of the land which belonged to the Khan personally was known as *Khassa* or *Khas* and it was probably selected by the Khan himself. Abdullah had done so in Balkh.[157] Portions of the *Khassa* lands of the sixteenth century were in turn assigned as *Iqta* or *Waqf* or alienated in some other form by the king. Apart from these lands the Khan also possessed palaces, workshops, shops, water mills, pastures, flocks of sheep, herds of livestock, etc., in the form of *Khassa*.[158] The *Wilayats* were divided into *Tumans* or *Buluks* (districts). The *Tuman* was not a military unit only, though there is some controversy surrounding the term *Tuman* (lit. 10,000) as a territorial division both in the context of extent and expression. Ibn-i Arab Shah explains that *Tuman* was an area providing for the upkeep of 10,000 soldiers.[159] But Arab Shah's own information that Andijan in its vicinity had nine *Tumans* shows that a *Tuman* as a territorial division could not have maintained 10,000 men.[160] Babur categorically says that 'if people do justly, only three or four thousand men may be maintained by the revenues of Farghana'.[161] According to Mirza Badi, the Uzbeg Empire was divided into different agro-fiscal units of *Tuman, Hazara, Nimhazara, Abkhwar, Qariya* and *Mazra'a:* 'Such has been the customary practice (*Qaida Wazabita*) in Bukhara', says he 'that the region where high officials were appointed and maintained along with their army by the revenue of that place by the king's command was known as *Wilayat*'. If a canal was extracted from a river and that water irrigated 1,00,000 *tanabs* of land, that area was called *Tuman*.[162] The controversy regarding *Tuman* is set at rest when one correlates the statements in these sources with the following explanations given in *Ain-i Akbari.* Abul Fazl the court historian of Emperor Akbar says that in Samarqand and Bukhara, a *Pargana* (a territorial subdivision in India) comprising towns and villages is called a *Tuman*.[163] Nevertheless the extent is nowhere given. Radloff's explanation of the term tuman 'as a measure of area equal to 40,000 *tanabs* in Bukhara'; the Persian connotation of the term *Tuman* that it was 'a district consisting of 100 villages', are also there. Barthold's view that *Tuman* denoted a fief seems to be more appropriately applicable.

The sultans were bound to act in accordance with the regulations, *Nishans* and orders of Khans, and owed their status to the sweet will of the Khan. Although the system of dynastic Khanates had come into vogue under the Uzbegs and later on for sometime anarchy prevailed (1540-65), the position of the Khan and the provincial rulers did not undergo a permanent change. Abdullah Khan re-established the centralized system. The distinctive positions of the Khan and the sultans are aptly described in one of the *farmans* of Abdullah Khan where the Khan is styled *Zilullah* (the shadow of God) and the sultans as the visible canopy of the shadow of God (*Namudar-i Sayabani Zilullah*).[164] The sultans were not permitted to decide issues independently. The sultans as well as their *Ataliqs* (advisers) were appointed by Abdullah Khan himself. These *Ataliqs* helped in the collection of revenue[165] and other such matters and served as Khan's agents in the provinces. At the time of appointment of the sultans, the Khan not only nominated the *Ataliq* but also certain *Amirs* and a detachment to accompany the sultans to his territory. The Khan used to exercise his authority over certain important appointments also and thereby limited the autonomy of the principalities. The failure of a Sultan to comply with the orders of the Khan to fulfil his military obligations laid himself open to punishment, which could amount to deposition or simply a warning for the future.[166]

Apart from supplying the fixed number of soldiers demanded, the sultans owed the Khan a number of financial obligations besides, the Khan's share of the forms of gifts (*Peshkash*) for his benefit. During hunting excursions and other tours of the Khan, the entire expenditure for the feasts with lavish entertainments and festivities of the royal party had to be borne by the sultan of the principality concerned. Besides, the sultan was also expected to offer the Khan large sums of money, valuables and rarities of the region. All the *Reis*, *Oghlans* and other big and small rulers of the vicinity also brought presents. This had become such a common practice that the Khan used to prolong his stay at a place only to receive gifts.[167]

On all important occasions (e.g. accession or victory) the sultans were expected to convey their greetings to the Khan and offer *Sawuri* (presents) either personally or through embassies. [168]

In *Nishans* of the Khan, a large number of general duties of the sultans are prescribed; but the texts are stereotyped and sufficiently revealing. The duties of the sultans as enumerated in the *Nishans* issued at the time of assignment of *Wilayat* consisted of the following:

'Enforcement of the laws of Empire and accomplishment of the regulations of monarchy; upholding of the principles of religion; extension of justice from east to west, maintenance of regard for the *Ulama* philosophers, grandees and nobles; reverence and reward for the divines and the mystics; dutiful consideration to the men of swords and lanes; proper maintenance of cavalry and a retinue of servants, tribes and slaves, with suitable provision for their comforts and rewards.'

In another *Nishan* the duties are described in the following words 'To enforce justice so strictly that tyranny is eliminated completely and not to be inconsiderate and improvident to the starving and the destitute; to light the candles of mercy in lances and corners, to be prompt in erecting the pillars of sovereignty so that the conflicts and disputes do not disturb him even in dreams; to be considerate and thoughtful towards the soldiers who were the helpers and defenders of the country; to look after and favour the *Sadat, Ulama* and *Mashaikh-ul Islam—so* that radiance of this important group would be reflected from the face of his principality.' The sole exception is the *farman* issued to Abdulmomin which puts him as a *Wali*, concedes him despotic power and directs that the taxes (*Mutawajjahat-i Diwani*) should be paid to the princes, *Amils* and *Qusmhtas* without any delay and that his servants should be respected.[169]

The assignments to the princes and nobles seem to have been of different kinds. Some were hereditary (*Mamlakat-i Maurusi, Arsa, Watan*)[170] like Andijan or Shahr-i Sabz though it may or may not always have been free from resumption. Hafiz Tanish reports an exchange of Andijan *(Muaweza)* for Shahr-i Sabz; in 1583 Andijan was given to Isfandyar as *Suyurghal*[171] and the hereditary concept of *Watan*, if any, was ignored.

The military grant *Iqta* or *Wajh-i Iqta* meant territory or part of revenues of an area granted for maintenance of its holder and the army. The *Iqta* could sometimes carry (*Zamima*) additinal assignments as well, e.g. Kulab had once been added as *Zamima* to the *Iqta* of Uzbeg Sultan.[172]

The size of *Iqta* and therefore emoluments were decreased or increased at the pleasure of the Khan. An addition (*Izafa*) could be made by assigning other territory, though the Momin Sultan held Andijan in 1579-1580, he was given *Ayalat* (rulership) of Tashkent, Khujand and its dependencies were added as *Zamima* in 1580-1.[173]

On another occasion, Momin Sultan was given a large monthly

sum from the *Amwai-i Wajibi* of Bukhara even though he happened to hold Andijan.[174]

It was only under special circumstances that the state share of revenue from a place was given as an additional grant to a particular person. This additional grant is mentioned in the sources as *Alufa*. Nobiev explains the term *Alufa* as an annual grant and *Ratiba* as daily allowance.[175] Either the entire revenue or only a part of it could be granted as *Alufa*. Abdullah Khan granted both the *Iqta* and *Alufa* to Hasan Khwaja Nagib.[176] Khan Pir Muhammad assigned the *Wilayat* of Shibarghan to Padshah Muhammad as an *Iqta* along with its revenues *(Hasilat)* which were treated as *Alufa*.[177] At times, the *Amirs* were also given territory in *Wajh-i Alufa* thus Rustam Bakawal was granted Kulab in 1585. Kulab was included in the *Iqta* of Uzbeg Sultan but Rustam Bakawal was sent there to put down rebellious elements.[178] In such cases, presumably the holder of the *Iqta* paid the *Alufa* out of the revenue collected by him.

An *Iqta* was sometimes granted to one person and the *Alufa* to another. After the death of Ibdullah, Abdullah assigned the *Wilayat* of Samarqand to Hasan Khwaja with a cosharer Nizamuddin Haji Bi, while granting the *Alufa* and customary cesses (*Marsumat*) to the minor son of Ibaduallh Yadgar Sultan.[179] At times the *Iqta* did not carry any *alufa* with it. In this category one finds the great Noyon, Qambar Bi as the *Iqta* holder of Shahr-i Sabz, who had entertained the Khan lavishly, hoping that the *Alufa* (the remaining *Alufa*) would additionally be granted to him. When he failed to attain his objectives, Qambar Bi fled to Samarqand. Hence the Khan assigned the *Iqta* of Shahr-i Sabz to another Noyon, Abdussamad Bi. Although Qambar Bi failed to acquire the *Zamima* or *Alufa,* his successor, Abdussamad Bi, not only enjoyed the rulership of Shahr-i Sabz but was granted 1,50,000 *khani* additionally from the revenue of Shahr-i Sabz.[180] Khwajam Quli Qush Begi was given Chechaktu as a *Wajh-i Iqta* on 1586-7. These instances not only indicate that Uzbeg rulers had full control over the revenue of each province but also signify that the grant of an *Iqta* for the maintenance of the army had a personal maintenance allowance of *Wajh, Alufa, Zamima* or *Marsum* over and above the military grant. These additional grants must have been a strong weapon in the hands of the sovereign in keeping assignees under this control.[181]

By the first half of the sixteenth century, the bigger *Iqtas* had almost been converted into the dynastic principalities of Uzbeg princes. Since the appanages were usually dynastic, the custom of the oldest son of the deceased sultan succeeding him became prevalent. The oldest son in the principality usually succeeded, but sometimes he was superseded by a nominee of the Khan. At least twice in the Uzbeg Empire, dual authority is noticed in the provinces. Gadai Sultan and Baba Sultan once became the rulers simultaneously in Samarqand; and in Bukhara on another occasion Burhan Sultan and Yar Muhammad Sultan ruled together.[182] But these instances are only found during the period of weak central government (1540-60). Otherwise, fairly strong control over the provincial governments continued throughout the sixteenth century. After the formation of a centralized empire by Abdullah, the *Iqtas* or appanages were assigned by him personally.

After the dynastic appanages ceased to exist, the transfer of provincial rulers was also common during the reign of Abdullah Khan. Any resistance from a provincial ruler invited the wrath of the Khan. When Momin Sultan was not agreeable to changing his *Iqta* from the border province of Farghana to Shahr-i Sabz, Abdullah decided to march against him.[183] Even transfers from hereditary home towns are recorded, for example, Rustam Sultan the hereditary ruler (*Abai Hakim*) of Tashkent was sent to Karmina, away from his real centre and natural homeland; and Tashkent was granted as *Wajh-i Iqta* to Uzbeg Sultan.[184]

The transfers from border province were usually more frequent. Tashkent Khujand and its dependencies were given to Momin Sultan in 1579-80 and a new arrangement followed in 1580, when Tashkent and Uratiba were given to Abdul Quddus, Isfandyar was assigned Khujand, Aush and Andijan in 1583.[185] We have already seen that the *Iqta* of Shahr-i Sabz, which was once held by Abdulkhair Sultan, was later given to Amir Qambar and then assigned to Abdussamad Bi.[186] From Bukhara the Khan assigned three *Tumans* to Ibadullah and simultaneously added (*Izafa*) Qarshi to Shahr-i Sabz and assigned it to Khusru Sultan.[187] Then in 1568 he bestowed it upon Uzbeg Sultan.[188] The Khan retained his share in the *Iqta* grant as *Khassa*. The *Iqta* and *Suyurghal* are often referred to by chroniclers as synonymous. Hafiz Tanish refers to Khujand being assigned to Tawakkul Sultan as *Wajh-i Iqta* and elsewhere calls it his *Suyurghal*.[189]

Iqtas were assigned by the Sultans in their respective territories to princes and nobles. Although there are instances of the Khan sub-assigning the smaller *Iqtas* in the provinces to his own nominees, these territories were either newly conquered or belonged to the *Khassa* category or the region itself had its limits altered.[190] The *Ataliqs* at sub-provincial level were nominated by the sultans or provincial governors.[191]

As mentioned earlier the *Ataliqs* in the provinces were the highest officers and usually nominated by the Khan at his discretion. It was rare for a prince to be allowed to have an *Ataliq* of his own choice. There are, however, two such examples: Sultan Ibadullah successfully sought the appointment of Yar Ali Bi Durman as his *Ataliq*.[192] Darvesh Sultan of Tashkent also selected his own *Ataliq*, Ali Saiyyid Bi Qushji, a distinguished *Amir* of his times.[193] All administrative and financial affairs (*Ikhtiyar Mulk o Mal*) and their control were entrusted to him.[194] The *Ataliq* was responsible for the collection of the royal share of the revenue.[195] The post was usually reserved for members of three tribes (*Ulusat*) namely, the Durman, Qushchi and Naiman. Among the duties of an *Ataliq* were the supervision of administration, satisfaction of the needs of subjects, the development of agriculture and building,[196] the realization of *Khassa* (the Khan's revenue), the supply of *Mard-i Kars* (labourers), and compliance with any other demands of the centre. In accordance with the Chingizide custom, an *Ataliq* was expected to bring a swift horse (besides a number of other presents) for his sultan at the time of appointment.[197]

With his extensive privileges, the *Ataliq* could at times become a threat to the sultan's authority. In a letter, Mahmud Sultan complains to Khwaja Kalan about the high handedness and insubordination of his *Ataliq* and his helplessness in the matter.[198] Referring to the appointment of Khaqani Khushi as *Ataliq* and the imperial *Yirliq* demanding 30,000 *khani* for the treasury, Mahmud Sultan complains that the *Ataliq* 'managed the affairs of the *Wilayat* all by himself and had even appropriated the authority of the ruler'. Within four years the entire money acquired from *Muqarrari, Mal, Ikhrajat, Ghallat* and everything pertaining to the sultan's *Sarkar* had been devoured by the *Ataliq* without the provinces knowledge. While the *Ataliq* had been doing this, the sultan had not interfered in any of his affairs.[199]

The provincial government was in many ways a miniature replica of the central government. Officers like *Shaikh-ul Islam, Naqib, Sadr, Diwans*, etc., had the same functions as at the centre.

The province was divided into *Tumans,* and each *Tuman* was further subdivided into *Hazara, Mauza, Qasba, Qariya, Dehat* and *Mazraa.* Certain places like Khulm have been described in the sources as *Hazara.* According to Mirza Badi, if the water from a canal irrigated only 50,000 *Tanabs* of land, the area was called *Hazara,* as it could maintain a *Ghazi* (military grant holder). If the water from a canal irrigated 25,000 *Tanabs* of land, it was called *Nimhazara.* If irrigated only 10,000 or 15,000 *Tanabs* of a *Deh* the portion of the land was called the *Abkhwar* of such and such canal. If the irrigated lands in a village (*Deh*) comprised 400 *tanabs* of land they were, if inhabited, called *Qariya.* Irrigated land of 300 *Tanabs* or less were called *Mazraa* whether it was populated or not. The populated areas were called *Balda* and *Qariay,* hence they did not include vineyards.[200]

In all the various units, the same pattern of administration seems to have prevailed. The heads of these units consisted of the *Hakim, Darogha, Qazi, Reis, Ketkhuda, Aqsaqals (Rish Sfedan-Muisafedan* elders), etc. Although the *Ketkhudas* are often described as cultivators or proprietors.[201] Barthold shows that they were city patriarchs or chiefs of different quarters of a town.[202] The *Reis* were also chiefs of army detachments and used to hold small territories.[203]

NOTES

1. Riasanovsky, *Fundamental Principles of Mongol Law*, p. 300.
2. Ibn-i Arab Shah, *Ajaib-ul Maqdur*, Eng. tr. by Sanders, London, 1936, pp. 73-9.
3. V.V. Barthold, *Sochinenija*, Vol. V, p. 465. For details see Mansura Haidar, 'Mongol Traditions and their Survival in Central Asia', *Central Asiatic Journal*, Vol. 28, nos. 1-2, 1984.
4. *Tarikh-i Abulkhair*, unpaginated.
5. Vincentius Beluacensis, *Al Alimul Islami Series*, Eng. tr. by B. Spuler, pp. 169-70.
6. *Futuhat*, pp. 54-62; *Shaibani Nama*, pp. 122-42.
7. Nizam-ul Mulk Tusi, *Siyasat Nama*, Tehran, 1348, pp. 5-27; Lambton Holt et al., *Cambridge History of Islam*; Navoi, *Izbraniya Sochinenija*, 1948; also see, *Istorya poiticheskikh Oocheniy*, edited by S.F. Kechekyan and G.E. Fedkina, 2nd edn., Moscow, 1960, pp. 150-2.
8. *Mehmannama* (*Mehn*), p. 140.
9. Wasifi, *Badaiul Waqai*, 2 vols., Moscow, 1961, p. 1301.
10. *Mehn*, pp. 7-22, 33-7.
11. *Tarikh-a Rashidi* (*TR*), Eng. tr., p. 179.

12. Clande Cahen, *Pre-Ottoman Turkey*, pp. 36-7.
13. *Abdullah Nama* (*Abdn*).
14. Ibid., p. 402.
15. Ibid., pp. 90, 331.
16. Ibid., p. 331.
17. Jenkinson, Hakluyt Society Series, 1456-7, p. 460.
18. Lamb, *Genghis Khan*, Lahorc, 1978, p. 214.
19. For interesting reference to Islamic concept of inheritance see Schacht, pp. 168-74.
20. The term denoting heir apparent, was used by Crimean Tartars from the time of Mangli Gerai (last accession 1478-1515). The origin of this title is unknown. Smirnov suggests that it was a Mongol word. Barthold describes it as being synonymous with Q'alkhan, the ruler of Balkh whereas the Khan was used for the ruler of Bukhara (*Sochinenija* V, p. 537).
21. *Mehn*, p. 42; *Abdn*, pp. 391-3. According to Juvaini (Eng. tr. I, pp. 178-90) 'in accordance with the Mongol custom, it is the youngest son from the eldest house that is the heir of his father though Chingiz had nominated his second son Ogedei as his successor'.
22. *Badai-ul Waqai*, pp. 46-7.
23. *TR*, p. 173; Eng. tr., pp. 282-3; *Tarikh-i Shaibani*, p. 45, also see H.H. Howorth, *History of the Mongols*, Vol. II seems to have continued intermittently till 1888 as Bonvalot refers to it (pp. 230-1). In the Chaghati's Empire also, Kebek had placed his elder brother on the throne.
24. *Abdn*, pp. 29-30; *Silsilat-us Salatin*, p. 204.
25. *Abdn*, pp. 391-3. Timur had also put forward the same arguments.
26. Vincentus Beluacensis (1246). *Purchas and his Pilgrims*, XI, p. 168; Carpini (1245-7), MS Oriental Institute, Tashkent, no. 835, f. 1092; *Babur Nama* (*BN*), pp. 10-11; *Abdn*, pp. 370-1; Bertold Spuler, *Islamic World*, pp. 87-8.
27. *Abdn*, pp. 392-8; *Rauzat*, p. 240; *Soch*. V, p. 184 for Chingiz, however, a black belt was used (Prawdin, p. 84).
28. *Suluklul Muluk*, pp. 1-7.
29. *Mehn*, pp. 53-5.
30. Lanepool, *Catalogue of Oriental Coins in British Museum*, Vol. VII, p. xiv.
31. *Tarikh-i Jahankusha*, tr., pp. 27-8; *Tarkhan Nama* (*TN*), pp. 19-20.
32. *Mehn*, pp. 306-8; *Abdn*, pp. 270-3, 445.
33. Ibid.
34. *Abdn*, pp. 207.
35. Ibid., p. 445.
36. Ibid., p. 445.
37. The word *qurultai* is still being used in Central Asia and Turkey for a general meeting or conference (for details about *qurultai* refer to *Secret History*, p. 107 fn. 1.
38. Ibn-i Battuta says that it is the accepted code among them to assemble once a year. The day is called *Toi*. On this occasion the descendants of Chingiz Khan, beys, ladies and generals arrive. Apart from feasts and festivities actions of king and nobles are judged (Defremery, pp. 2-43).
39. For *ijma* and *shura* cf. Muhammad Asad, p. 48.
40. *ZN*.

41. Mullah Shadi, *Fathnama-i Khani*, IOST 5369, 855/1451, pp. 18-24.
42. *Mehn*, pp. 7-40, 22-8.
43. *Suluk*, pp. 1-7.
44. Ibid., p. 4.
45. *Mehn*, pp. 7-40.
46. *Abdn*, pp. 242, 262, 281-2.
47. Ibid., p. 392.
48. Ibid., p. 262.
49. Ibid., pp. 235-6, 241.
50. Ibid., p. 310.
51. Sadr Zia, *Ruznama-i Qazi Jami Majmua-i Sharif Jan-Makhdum*, MS, IOST 2193, f. 231.
52. *Abdn*, pp. 114, 275; *Muzzakkira-i Ahbab*, pp. 352, 373-4, 379.
53. *Abdn*, pp. 46, 275; *Badai-ul Waqai*, pp. 1185-6.
54. *Abdn*, p. 275.
55. Wasifi, p. 325.
56. *Abdn*, p. 114.
57. *Muzzakkira*, pp. 379-80.
58. *Abdn*, pp. 160, 376, 384; *Badai-ul Waqai*, pp. 925-7; *Nama-i Nami*, ff. 91-2; Zia, f. 231.
59. *Cambridge History of Islam*, I, pp. 301; Lamb, *Genghiz Khan*, p. 173.
60. *Muzzakkira*, p. 409.
61. Ibid., p. 210.
62. Ibid., pp. 354, 380, 407.
63. Mirza Badi, *Majma-ul Arqam*, p. 37; Zia, f. 231; *Soch.*, II, p. 394; Hanikov, *Apisaniya Bukharaskovo Khanstova*, p. 190.
64. *Badai*, pp. 1045-8.
65. *Abdn*, pp. 376, 396, 485; *Mehn*, p. 263; *Tarikh-i Raqim*, p. 188.
66. *Abdn*, p. 376.
67. *Muzzakkira*, pp. 193, 197.
68. Badi, p. 87.
69. *Abdn*, pp. 370-2.
70. Snouck Hurgrounji, *Selected Works*, pp. 264-95.
71. Examples: *Abdn*, pp. 499-503; *Mehn*, pp. 42-57, 171-6; *TR*, p. 104.
72. Ibid.
73. See *Suluk-ul Muluk*, pp. 53-65 for the duties of *Muhtasibs* in Islamic States, also cf. Levy, pp. 335-9.
74. A.A. Semenov, *Bukharski Traktat*, pp. 40-55; Mirza Badi, p. 87.
75. Ziya, f. 231.
76. Wasifi, p. 1223.
77. *Suluk*, pp. 44-63.
78. Badi, p. 87.
79. See Wasifi, pp. 47-9, 72, 74, 76.
80. Zia, f. 231.
81. Badi, p. 87; Zia, f. 231.
82. *Soch.*, p. 11396.
83. *Abdn*, p. 310.

84. Badi, p. 87
85. *Abdn*, p. 310; also see *Nama-i Nami*, ff. 85-8.
86. *Mehn*, pp. 306-8; Wasifi, pp. 822.
87. Wasifi, pp. 947-57.
88. *Tarikh-i Shaibani*, pp. 24-5.
89. Wasifi, pp. 956-7.
90. Ibid., pp. 369-70.
91. S.H. Askari, *Zain Kahn's Tabaqat-i Baburi*, Delhi, 1982-3, p. 183 fns. 9a and 9b.
92. *Abdn*, pp. 202, 275; Zia, f. 231.
93. Ibid., pp. 231-2.
94. *Suluk*, p. 18.
95. *Suluk*, p. 18.
96. *Abdn*, pp. 310-11, 443-5.
97. Ibid., pp. 16-161, 443; *Istorija Balkha*, p. 147.
98. Ibid., pp. 443-4.
99. *Abdn*, pp. 160-1, 443, 465-6.
100. Ibid., pp. 201, 226, 346, 352, 381, 443, 471-2; Wasifi, pp. 57-8; *Mehn*, p. 132.
101. *Mehn*, pp. 91-2, 132, 140.
102. Ibid., pp. 91, 132-40, 306-7; *Tarikh-i Shaibani*, pp. 24-5.
103. *Abdn* pp. 346, 443.
104. Ibid., p. 381.
105. Ibid., p. 346.
106. Ibid., pp. 220, 310-11, 346.
107. Ibid., pp. 202, 275.
108. Ibid., p. 459.
109. Wasifi, pp. 355-60, 370-7.
110. For details of various *diwans* see Glossary.
111. Badi, pp. 88-9.
112. *Abdn*, p. 152.
113. *Rauzat*, p. 296.
114. Dobson, however, says that in 1888 Inaq was the Chief Treasurer and Minister of Commerce who collected the tax (*Railways Advance*, p. 259).
115. *Bukharski Traktat*, pp. 144-7; Zia, p. 232.
116. Badi, pp. 88-9.
117. *Abdn*, p. 152; Badi, pp. 88-9.
118. Zia, ff. 231-2.
119. *Abdn*, p. 356.
120. Example: *Mehn*, p. 263; Wasifi, pp. 1043-5.
121. MS 210, ff. 122, 151.
122. *Mehn*, p. 125.
123. Badi, pp. 88-90; *Bukharski Traktat*, pp. 142-5.
124. *Bahr-ul Asrar* (*BA*), pp. 387-9.
125. *Tarikh-i Abulfaiz Khan*, pp. 162, 257; *Abdn*, pp. 257, 434; Bori Ahmedov, *Gasudarstova Kochevikh Uzbekov*, Tashkent edn., p. 102.
126. *Silsilat*, pp. 302-3, 315.

127. *Abdn*, p. 250.
128. O. Danovan, *Reconnoitring Central Asia*, O. Danovan's dash to Merv, pp. 330-3.
129. Zia, ff. 231-3.
130. Ibid., f. 231.
131. *Abdn*, pp. 243, 245-60, *BA*, pp. 185, 287; *Tarikh-i Abulfaiz Khan*, p. 41.
132. *BA*, pp. 387-9.
133. Ibid.
134. *Abdn*, p. 434.
135. Ibid., p. 266.
136. *Suluk*, p. 13.
137. For Hanafite law see *Suluk* or Schacht, *An Introduction to Islamic Law*, Oxford, 1964, pp. 28-57.
138. It seems to be a continuation of Islamic institution of *nazar fil mazalim*. See Schacht, pp. 51, 54, 84, 189, 208.
139. *Abdn*, p. 351.
140. Wasifi, p. 420.
141. *Abdn*, pp. 351-63.
142. Ibid., pp. 185, 248; Wasifi, pp. 1211-12; *Majgharaib*, p. 248.
143. Wasifi, p. 1046.
144. Ibid., p. 420.
145. *Abdn*, p. 345.
146. Mahmud b. Wali, pp. 387-9; also see Barthold, *Sochinenija*.
147. Ibid. Mahmud b. Wali, pp. 387-9. An interesting account of the camp court of Tarmashirin is, however, available in Ibn-i Battuta.
(After Ibn-i Battuta, *Voyages*, ed. and trans. Charles Deffremery and Benjam in R. Sanguinetti, Vols. II, III, 2nd edn., Paris, 1877, pp. 2-43).
148. The same practice seems to have continued down to the first half of eighteenth century for Muhammad Wafa Karmingi refers to it. *Tuhfat-ul Khani*, MS Asiatic Museum, f. 170, also see *Sochinenija*.
149. *BA*, pp. 387-9.
150. *Abdn*, pp. 484-5.
151. *AAA*, p. 375, old edn.
152. *Landlord and Peasants*, glossary and also see p. 100.
153. *ZN*, p. 733; *Matla*, pp. 14, 15, 353, 383.
154. *Mehn*, pp. 46, 60, 91.
155. Ibid., pp. 46, 60, 91.
156. Ibid., 46, 60, 91.
157. Ibid., p. 454.
158. *Istorija*, pp. 525-6.
159. Arab Shah, Eng. tr., p. 17.
160. Ibid.
161. *BN*, text, p. 5, Eng. tr., p. 13.
162. Badi, Persian text, pp. 12-15; Russian tr., pp. 35-7.
163. *Ain*, Vol. II, Eng. tr. by Jarret, p. 409.
164. *Abdn*, p. 90.
165. *Soch.* II, pp. 58-60; *Four Studies*, Vol. I, pp. 43-5.

166. *Abdn*, pp. 128, 156-9, 204, 268, 410, 412, 453; *Mehn*, pp. 198, 262, 281, 290, 301, 302, 304, 307, 308.
167. *Abdn*, pp. 77, 204, 268, 370, 410, 412, 453; *Mehn*, pp. 198, 262, 281, 290, 301, 302, 304, 307-8; *Rauzat*, p. 213.
168. *Tarikh-i Abulkhair*, p. 245; *Abdn*, pp. 90, 116, 121, 197-8, 370-2.
169. *Abdn*, p. 373.
170. Ibid., pp. 229, 232, 270, 273.
171. Ibid., p. 385.
172. Ibid., p. 445.
173. Ibid., pp. 270, 285, 453-5.
174. Ibid., p. 270
175. *Izvestia*, pp. 26, 30.
176. Ibid., p. 189.
177. Ibid., p. 158.
178. Ibid., p. 445.
179. Ibid., pp. 433-4.
180. Ibid., pp. 453-4.
181. Ibid., p. 471.
182. Ibid., pp. 70-91.
183. Ibid., p. 378.
184. Ibid., p. 462.
185. Ibid., pp. 270, 285, 385, 453-5.
186. Ibid. 164, 433, 454.
187. Ibid. 105.
188. Ibid. 144.
189. Ibid., pp. 313, 315.
190. Ibid., pp. 156, 197.
191. Ibid., pp. 56-8.
192. Ibid., p. 104.
193. *Tarikh-i Shaibani*, p. 62.
194. *Abdn*, pp. 197-290.
195. *Rauzat*, p. 325.
196. *Abdn*, pp. 166, 230, 252
197. Ibid., p. 374.
198. *Rauzat*, p. 325.
199. Ibid., p. 352.
200. Badi, text, pp. 11-14; Russian tr., pp. 33-6.
201. D'Ohsen, *Histoire de l'Mongols et des Tartars*, IV, pp. 387, 470.
202. *Sochinenija*, Vol. IV, Moscow, 1966, p. 337.
203. *Abdn*, p. 343.

The Uzbeg State and Nobility in the Sixteenth-Seventeenth Centuries

The Chroniclers of the neighbouring regions have criticized the Uzbeg nobility for a variety of reasons. Abul Fazl the celebrated sixteenth-century chronicler of Akbar's reign, condemns the unitary composition of the Uzbeg nobility, saying that 'one class of people if employed to the exclusion of others would cause rebellion as in the case of the Uzbegs and Qizilbash who used to dethrone their kings'.[1] Elsewhere, Abul Fazl wonders how wise sovereigns could make *Tarkhani* grants to nobles, according such open offers of forgiveness for up to nine offence—a fact which 'does not appear to be consonant with propriety'.[2] The alleged 'opportunism' and 'faithlessness' of Uzbeg nobles have also been commented upon by the Persian chronicler Iskandar Munshi. He quotes the Safavid noble Durmesh Khan as refusing to betray his masters (the Persians) because he was not a noble capable of such unholy alliances.[3]

Abul Fazl's opinion echoes Tusi's ideas. Centuries earlier he had warned emperors against employing 'one class (*yakjins*) of people' in an army as it was a sure signal for danger (*khatarha khezand*), for they stop working hard and indulge in conspiracies (*takhlit*)'.[4] But it is doubtful that the shifting loyalties of the Uzbeg nobility at various times were the simple consequence of their homogeneity. In the Uzbeg Empire, too, the same Turco-Mongol nobility behaved in different ways at different times, Shaibani Khan and Ubaidullah Khan controlled the same nobility with a stern hand, while its weak allegiance created problems for rulers like Burhan, Sultan, Souyunch Khan and Abu Said. Abdullah Khan exiled and executed large number of nobles, and converted other nobles into effective tools of administration and conquest. But members of the same nobility hesitated to put up with Abdul Momin for more than six months and murdered him afterwards.

Moreover, the Uzbeg nobility comprised not only the 'Pure Uzbegs' but heterogeneous tribes adopting the name of their conquerors in the age-old fashion. Thus the tribal elements like Jalair, Manghits Keneges, Uishun, Qunghrat, Khitai, Kerait, Naiman Qarluq and Qipchaq could hardly be deemed to belong to one distinct group or class, though they no doubt had some common features like pastoralism or certain nomadic customs. Other than the settled Muslim and some tribal populations, the ethnic communities and groups (like Jews, Christian and others) residing in Central Asia had no warrior classes like the Rajputs of India; thus the questions of recruiting them into the nobility did not arise. The chief of the Turco-Mongol tribes pressed into a single nobility by the Uzbegs had a political and social base in the conquered region, and so were a welcome reinforcement for the Uzbegs. The purely Uzbeg element in the early years of the sixteenth century had been retained only in the first two decades, after which they disappeared.

Notwithstanding the increasing influence of these tribal elements in the Uzbeg social structure, the absolutist traditions of the Turco-Mongols and their inherent discipline and self control sustained the Uzbeg Empire for more than two centuries.

The nobility not only existed at the centre but also in the provinces and played an active role in politics, serving either as officials of the Emperor or occasionally turning against him. Thus, general features of the nobility were somewhat peculiar and slightly different from those under preceding dynasties.

In the political structure of the Uzbegs, like that of the Ottomans, a member of the nobility not belonging to the Uzbeg dynasty, could not aspire to the Sceptre, though a commoner through sheer merit could acquire the highest rank possible among nobles. The examples of hereditary nobility, however, outnumber those of self made nobles. A *Chehraaqasi* (head of page boys), Dust Mirza, was raised to the rank of *Amir* for bringing the head of Momin Sultan from Kashgahr, and was also given *Tauq*.[5] Another person, Rustam, who held the rank of *Bakawal* (steward), was admitted to the class of *Amirs* and given Kulab as *Alufa* in 1585.[6] Amir Sotilghan became an *Amir* thanks to his *Alufa*, excellent generalship and gallantry and Abdussamad Bi acquired promotions in rank and closeness to the Khan through his good services (*Husn-i Ubudiat*). Khwajam Quli Qush Begi reached the status of *Amir* from a 'whirlpool of service' (*Warta-i Ubudiyat*).

The concept of the nobility of birth was not altogether absent, though rarely noticed in the sources. Burhan Sultan, the ruler of

Bukhara became unpopular and was ultimately overthrown, one of the reasons being the patronage extended by him to the class of people dubbed as *Qizilayaq* and *Jamukha* (vagabonds and commoners).

Certain families seem to have dominated the political arena and its member held various posts for a long time. Some administrative posts were also monopolized by particular families, Dust Hasan was a *Khazindar* (treasurer) of Shibani and his brother Shahak happened to be the *Muhrdar* of Shaibani.[8] The family of Amir Janwafa and his brother Fazil Tarkhan comes in the same category.[9] Hereditary tribal *Amirs* (*pidar bar pidar*) have also been mentioned;[10] and a number of important *Amirs* belonged often to the same family. Under Abdullah Khan Uzbeg, Abdulwasey was the *Mirakhur*, and his brother Abdussamad Bi held various posts. Muhammad Baqi Bi Durman, son of Amir Rustum Durman, and brothers like Jan Daulat Bi Naiman and Mirza Ali Bi Naiman[11] were nobles of high category. Amir Tinkari Quli Bi Qushji was the *Amir-ul umara* of Samarqand and an *Ataliq* of Khan 'Abdul Latif. His son Rustam Bi was appointed *Ataliq* of Isfand Yar Khan.[12]

Nobles were often lavishly rewarded for rendering good service. Shaibani generously rewarded the loyalists, and Abdullah Khan distributed handsome awards. On being informed of Baba Khan's capture by Abdussamad Bi, Abdullah conferred upon him the *Wilayat* of Tirmiz (*Darubast*) along with 10,000 *Khani*, camps, cap, belt, camels, etc.

The privileges of the nobles were exclusively specified and their status was defined by varied expressions. Some of them were *Togh Begi*,[13] holders of the standard, *Naqqara* (trumpet), etc., all granted by the Khan. Certain nobles are described as close associates *(Bandagani Hazarat* or *Muqarraban-i Hazrat)*, or as grand nobles *(Umardi Sahab-i Jah)* and nobles of the *Tauq* (*Tauqbegi*—recipient of Tauq).[14] There were *Amirs* mentioned as high nobles '*Uzma-i Umara*,[15] *Umra-i Buzurg*,[16] *Umra-i ba Igtidar*,[17] according to their status.

Generally the nobility and the officers were selected from amongst six tribes, namely, the Durman, Qushchi, Naiman, Qarluq, Barlas and Qunghrat. While referring to the Court audience, Hafiz Tanish always mentions two groups *Arkan-i Daulat* (pillars of the empire—the nobles) and *Ayan-i Hazrat*[18] (eyes of the emperor—the ministers). Of the next two categories nobles in the higher strata, the first was that of the *Amir-ul Umara,* equivalent to the Ottoman and Mongolian *Belglarbegi.* The *Amir-ul Marl*—entrusted with administrative control of the area in his jurisdiction enjoyed an important position as a deputy (*naib*) of the Ataliq Khan or the Sultan. The title was usually added to or used synonymously by those who performed the same duties, as the Saljuqid *Ataliqs*. The same nobles are mentioned as *Noyon-i a zam, Umra-i uzzam, Uzma-i Amir-ul, Umra-i Kabbar, Umra-i Umara* and held large land assignments and were usually included in the consultative assembly (*Jangi* or *Kangash*).[19]

The next category was much wider, consisting of those with the title *Bi* (*Be* or *Bai*) included in their proper names. As additional title was also attached sometimes, denoting a rise in status. The *Mehman Nama* explains the term *Bai* or *Baikalan* as 'rich reliable Mughals'.[20] A modern Uzbeg dictionary defines the term as head or chief of a tribe or union of tribes.[21] Elsewhere, *Bi* is explained as the commanders of various ranks in the army in all Turkish, near and Middle-Eastern countries, in the Crimean and amongst other Tartars.[22] The term *Bi* was popular even in the Golden Horde and could be a hereditary title or a name conferred through a state grant. Among the Uzbegs, Qirghiz and Qaraqalpaqs, the *Bi* were tribal chiefs as well whose influence and strength was drawn not from their tribal status but basically from their privileges of control over lands, numerous servants and cattle. The Qazaqs, however, used the term to denote elders and especially 'privileged and kindred group' of wealth and influence. The title was hereditary and continuing over generations.[23] Some Soviet scholars render the term *Bi* or *Biatir* as 'one of the patriarchal tribal class of Qazaq society, having its origin in the primitive communal structure'. The *Bai* or *Bi* could even be someone without any hereditary property and could be one emerging from a peasant group.[24] The entire military aristocracy, the tribal element and the higher strata of the bureaucracy seems to have carried this title under the Uzbegs. Mahmud Bin Wali points out that each dignitary of the Uzbeg state enjoyed this title.[25]

Shahnawaz Khan says that the term *Oghal* in Turkish means a son, and *Oghlan* is its plural. 'In the Kingdom of Bokhara it is the title of Saiyids and Sharif; and they have a right to its use in the assembly of the ruler of the territory', *Maasir-ul Umara*, Eng. tr. Beveridge.

A class of nobles or other privileged groups enjoyed the title *Tarkh"an.* The term *Tarkhan* is elaborately explained by medieval historians. The *Tarkhan Nama* gives a literal meaning as 'blood thirsty' and the technical sense as free *mutlaqul-inan*, one who does what he pleases, is exempt from service and is forgiven for nine generations till nine offences.[26] The *Tarikh-i Rashidi* refers to the seven ceremonial and other privileges bestowed upon nobles as *Tarkhas*.[27] and an exemption from nine offences, but to be followed by severe punishments after the tenth offence.

Noyon or *Noyan* was usually the commander of a *Tuman* or division of a thousand. The term sometimes denoted merely a noble. A rather uncommon term *Orkhan* or *Ur-Khan* is rendered as the commander of an army.[28]

Abul Fazl also gives almost the same details regarding *Tarkhans*.[29] The privileges thus granted could be apparently hereditary, though subject to renewal by every new Khan.[30] The custom of *Tarkhan* seems to have continued even in the seventeenth-eighteenth centuries, for Abulghazi and other chroniclers also refer to it. The only difference presumably was that the system of *Tarkhani* grants was now extended from the military sphere to the agricultural and commercial domain. The *Tarkhani* came increasingly to imply the privilege of not paying any taxes. From the sixteenth century onwards the lands were assigned to various persons attached to the ruling class in any capacity. To those who did something praise-worthy or who had to be pacified with some concession or were politically or socially significant were given exemption from taxes in land, trade, workshop, etc. Abulghazi categorically says that the *Tarkhans* were exempted from all taxes, apart from enjoying other privileges mentioned above, including free entry and exit to and from the court.[31] Some of the Uzbeg nobles carried the title *Bahadur* also. Haider Dughlat defines *Bahadur* as 'the class of men, who had no following but were quite alone; yet they had distinguished themselves above the rest by their courage in many battles', hence the name.

In essence, individual members of the nobility were in power with their patrons; they then obtained certain privileges which they hoped to make permanent. This sometimes made sections of the tribal nobility prone to resist any wilful exercise of absolutism. But they could succeed in deposing the Khan only if other Sultans cooperated and the Khan himself was inefficient.

The autocratic and despotic behaviour of Abulkhair had somewhat alienated the Qazaq Sultans and the nobility in the steppes, and his incompetent successor, Shaikh Haider, was assassinated and the dynasty overthrown. Even Shaibani Khan was rejected by the Manghit nobles despite his nomination by their leader, Musa Mirza, for they were opposed to Shaibani's despotic and autocratic ways. But the nobles mainstay was their capacity and strength and their utility for the Khan; they had no private ownership of land. All their privileges were held during the pleasure of the Khan. A number of examples may be cited. Arba Bi Qushji, whose ancestors and family had long been associated with the court and enjoyed royal favour lost his position and was 'squeezed out like a drop of tear' by Abdullah Khan thanks to his rebellious ways. When Arab Bi took shelter with Hashim Sultan of Hesar, the latter was instructed to confiscate his property and expel him. Non-compliance led to the downfall of Hashim Sultan.[32] Similarly, notable *Amirs* like Tardike Khan, Sarkhun *Ataliq* and Nazar Bi, who had earlier enjoyed the confidence of Abdullah Khan and were even participants in the *Khan Kutardilar* (coronation ceremony) fell in the estimation of Khan and suffered. Nazar Bi had held the governorship of Balkh for ten years but was exiled along with his three sons for 'committing certain improper acts'. He was once 'sent to Mecca', even if later forgiven through the intercession of Khwaja Kalan.[33] Subsequently he was exiled to India where he served Akbar; but here too he met his end thanks to rebellious activities.[34] Sarkhun *Ataliq,* formerly one of the reliable nobles (*umra-ī E'itbar*) of Abdullah, was 'dragged down from the horse of greatness and left in the wilderness of no-confidence' for instigating prince Abulkhair.[35] Maulana Husain was flayed in 1544 and certain other noble were also expelled.[36] The sons of important *Amirs*, Turum Bi Durman and Dust Mirza also lost favour and with it their positions.[37] Another noble, Mirza Khan Andkhui was expelled from Balkh.[38] After his conquest of Central Asia, Shaibani Khan attempted to create a strong nobility by assigning them large *Iqtas*,[39] but the failure of Muhammad Saleh at Bukhara, and that of Janwafa at Samarqand seems to have shaken his confidence in the capabilities of the nobility. The provincial rulerships were, thereafter, assigned to members of the ruling family and each province almost became a hereditary appanage, the sons of Sultans succeeding to them. This situation continued till the rise of 'Abdullah Khan, who created his own nobility, assigned them large *Wilayats* and granted favours. Since members of the ruling family had already been eliminated by Abdullah Khan in the process of centralization and unification of the Empire, the *Iqtas* were now granted to the nobility after the fashion of the Saljukids. As discussed earlier, a group of loyal nobles and a detachments of the army, accompanied the *Ataliq* and the provincial governor on his new assignment nominated by the Khan.

A careful study of the sources shows that Abdullah respected paternal claims only in certain appanages and that too only till 1580 were other territories held by the princes. The hereditary (*Arsā*) appanages included Shahr-i Sabz, Andijān, Tāshkent, Aush, Khujand, etc.[40]

We have already seen that the Uzbegs inherited from their predecessors—the late Timurids—a class of turbulent, intriguing, affluent and influential nobles amongst whom Shaibani Khan had cleverly made his way to acquire their help to overthrow the Timurid dynasty. But Shaibani's attitude towards the former Timurid nobility was one of guile and ruthlessness. Immediately after his conquest of Samarqand, Shaibani was advised by his officers (*Arkani Daulat*) that the reason for the nobles' (*Akabir*) treason (*sarkashi wa 'inad*) was their wealth and property, which was the main cause of their disobedience and mischief (*fiftna wa fasad* and *adm ingiyad*). Consequently, Shaibani ordered that all the riches of such an *Akabir* who interfered with the affairs of the country be confiscated and converted into *Diwani* (state possessions). Large-scale confiscations were undertaken, though this led to the temporary overthrow of Uzbeg rule in Samarqand. The Timurid nobles who were willing to join Shaibani's services had to pass through a test of loyalty, after which alone they were either given posts or destroyed in myriad ways. Shaibani even used their talent for intrigue and machination to his own advantage. The incidents of Jafar Khwaja and Mir Khawand are examples of this.

Under the weaker Shaibani Khans, particularly from 1540 to 1560, the nobility became more powerful. With frequent civil wars the fortunes of the nobles continued to improve as each Sultan tried to win over as many tribal chiefs and nobles as possible. In the process, the nobles often received large land grants, *Tarkhani* and other privileges. As the nobles could change their patrons easily, they tended to exploit the existing mutual rivalries amongst the Sultans for their own benefit. The provincial nobles had better prospects of such expedient alliances whenever the centre was weak. During the Khanship of Iskandar Khan, some of the expelled nobles *(randai dargah)* of the court of Balkh went to Muzaffar—the ruler of

Samarqand—where they were appointed *Chehras* (page boys). When Samarqand was besieged by prince Abdullah Khan, they opened negotiations with the latter, promising to blast one of the towers of the fort to facilitate the entry of his army.[41] Abdussamad Bi, a noble of Jawanmard Khan, was included amongst *Amirs* of Abdullah Khan.[42] The nobles of Burhan Sultan joined Abdullah at a crucial moment for their master. When Abdullah refused to grant an additional *Alufa* to Qambar Bi, the latter rushed to Samarqand in protest and received a high rank among the nobility there.[43]

Provincial rulers at times punished rebellious *Amirs* with a heavy hand; the repercussions varied according to their relations with the centre. Mirza Ali Bi Naiman who happened to be one of the great *Amirs* of Balkh was plundered and exiled from Balkh along with his brothers and had to seek shelter in the territory of his brother Jan Daulat Bi at Andkhud. Abdullah Khan exploited the situation and occupied the territory with Jan Daulat's collusion.[44] After the disturbances in Tarkent, Rustam Bi, the son of Boltorok Bi who had sought shelter with the Khan received some post in the palace.[45]

The provincial *Amirs* apparently maintained their own armies. Tandurust Bi Durman is said to have belonged to the *Umara-i E'itbar* (truste nobles) of Tashkent and surpassed all others in the size of his army and the number of weapons.[46] Amir Jan Daulat Bi Naiman of Andkhud in 1579-80 is said to have numerous weapons and servants.[47]

The nobility and the bureaucracy naturally enjoyed considerable wealth. Like the *Khwajas*, they held a number of *milk* lands, immovable property (*Sukuniyat*), etc. Besides, the nobles had a share in trade and owned workshops as well. Even a high official like Qulbaba indulged in usury. The verdict of the *Qazi* in 1590 and legal documents in this connection amply prove that this dignitary of the state charged interest at high rates.[48] The sale deeds often refer to the excessive wealth of nobles. Abdullah Khan ordered large-scale confiscations of the nobles' properties with apparent impunity. But the attempts of Nazar Muhammad to act in the footsteps of Abdullah Khan brought about his downfall. Lahori gives a detailed description of the nobles displeasure at Nazar Muhammad's high-handedness and their combined efforts to overthrow him.[49]

It is debatable if the law of escheat existed in the Uzbeg Empire. According to the *Yasa* of Chingiz Khan, the property of a deceased subject was not to be touched by the state, as this was considered to be inauspicious. It was to be kept for relatives or the nearest acquaintance, or, failing any heirs, distributed among the poor.[50] Allworth observes that the property of the deceased was acquired by Central Asian rulers, though he does not cite any source or evidence.[51] The Mongol *Qirat* regulations, however, included the law of escheat.[52] A somewhat similar system known as *Ankari* seems to have existed in the Ottoman Empire where, as a rule, the property of deceased nobles was confiscated by the state treasury—a fact explicitly criticized by Akbar in one of his *farmans* warning the officers against such practice.[53]

Under the Timurids the law of escheat does not seem to have been practiced. Umar Shaikh is said to have refused to take over the property of deceased strangers and summoned their heirs from Khurasan and Samarqand to state their claims.[54] Abandoned property was, however, often appropriated by the state.[55]

In the case of the Uzbegs there is no specific mention of the law of escheat. The *Suluk-ul Mulk* devotes a separate section for detailed treatment about the use of abandoned and inherited (*Lugtat* and *Turkat*) property which, according to the Hanafite law (followed by the Uzbeg rulers) was to be spent in various welfare works by the state under the Timurids. Such instances are found but neither here nor in our chronicles do we hear of the escheating of dead nobles' properties. Usually, only the property of rebellious nobles was confiscated. In *Abdullah Nama* and other sources there are some instances of the property of a deceased officer being recorded, though the reason for this is nowhere stated. Once, when Abdullah visited the son of Hasan Khwaja Naqib to offer his condolences, the son is said to have informed Abdullah that the entire wealth and property of his father had been listed by him and that the Khan might take whatever he wished. Hafiz Tanish boasts that the Khan graciously bestowed the entire wealth and property upon the dead nobles, son and did not accept anything from him.[56]

NOTES

1. *Ain-i Akbari*, Vol. I; Eng. tr. by Blochmann, 1965, p. 221.
2. *Akbar Nama* (*AN*), text, pp. 635-6; Eng. tr., pp. 973-5.
3. *Alam Ara-i Abbasi*.

4. *Siyasat Nama*, Tehran edn., p. 154; Ibn-i Hauqal, however, holds a different opinion.
5. *Abdullah Nama* (*Abdn*), p. 465.
6. Ibid., p. 445.
7. *Tarikh-i Shaibani* (*T.Sh*), p. 32; *Abdn*, p. 374.
8. *Lataif Nama-i Fakhri*, p. 305.
9. *T.Sh*, pp. 4-5.
10. *Abdn*, p. 99.
11. Ibid., pp. 179, 210, 307, 322.
12. Ibid., p. 374.
13. Ibid., p. 377. The *tugh* were of varied kinds like *Tuman tugh*, *Qushun tugh* or *Chapar tugh* and so on. *Tarikh-i Rashidi* (*TR*), Eng. tr., pp. 54-7; for *tugh* see *Abdn*, p. 248.
14. *Abdn*, pp. 93, 381, 465.
15. Ibid., p. 220.
16. Ibid., p. 81.
17. Ibid., p. 93.
18. *Abdn*, pp. 139, 142.
19. Ibid., p. 81.
20. *Mehmannama* (*Mehn*), p. 149.
21. Akabirova, Maghrufova and Khwaja Khanov, *Uzbegski Russki Slavar*, Moscow, 1959, p. 71.
22. Evliya Chelebi, *Kneega Puteshestviya*, Vol. I, Moscow, 1961, p. 274.
23. M.P. Vyatkin, *Batir Srim*, Leningrad, 1947, pp. 107-13, 128.
24. For a detailed and interesting account of Bek cf. E. Bek Makhov, 'Baiskoi Khazyaistova va kazakhstane e ivo osobennosti va aftaroi palavine', XIXE nachale XX; *Vaprosi istori selskovo khazyaistova e revalutsennovo dwisheniya va Rassiye*, Moscow, 1961, pp. 338-47; M.P. Vyatkin, *Ocherki pa istori kazakhskoj*, SSR, 1941, p. 298; S. Zimanov, *Obshestvenni Stroi Kazakhov Pervoi Palavina*, XIX Vek, Alma Ata, 1958, p. 214.
25. Mahmud Wali, *Bahr-ul Asrar*, Vol. II, II, ff. 387-9.
26. *Tarkhan Nama* (*TN*), f. 3.
27. *TR*, Eng. tr., pp. 54-7; *Maasir-ul Umara*, Vol. III, text, pp. 302-14; Eng. tr., Vol. I, p. 743.
28. See Abbott, p. 106 fns.
29. *AN*, tr., pp. 973-5.
30. *TR*, pp. 55-6.
31. *Shajratul Atrak*, Russian tr. G. Sablukova, *Biblioteka Vastochinikh Istorikov*, III, Kazan, 1854, p. 53, *TR*, Eng. tr., p. 309.
32. *Abdn*, pp. 190-9.
33. Ibid., pp. 197, 204, 390-1, 464; Badauni, Eng., tr. Vol. II, pp. 362-3.
34. Ibid; Badauni, pp. 362-3.
35. *Abdn*, p. 204.
36. Balkhi, *Majmaul Gharaib*, p. 248.
37. *Abdn*, p. 165.
38. *Rauzat*, p. 218.
39. *T.Sh.*, pp. 30-1; *Habib-us Siyar* (*H. Siyar*), p. 338.

40. The assignments during 1579-84 were:

Memna, Gharjistan	987/1579	Tahhur Ali Mardan Bahadur (*Abdn*, pp. 196-7, 238)
Balkh	995/1584	Nazar Bi. Abdulmomin
Samarqand	985-71/ 1584-6	held by Abulkhair Ibadullah & others (*Abdn*, pp. 207, 232, 260, 385, 459, 460, 469-470)
	994 onwards	assigned to nobles
Tashkent, Uratiba	987/1579-83	held by princes *Abdn*, pp. 232, 285, 230, 270, 267, 370, 380, 385, 363, 483.
Khujand, Andijan Sabran	987/1579	Abulkhair later on by nobles like Aisankeldi and Jankeldi
	988/1580	Utarchi (*Abdn*, pp. 230, 363, 483)
Aibak	987/1579	Shah Said Bi, Qarluq (*Abdn*, pp. 196-7, 260, 274).
Shibarghan	987/1579	Jan Daulat Bi. Amir Junaid (*Abdn*, pp. 238, 374).

41. *Abdn*, p. 219.
42. Ibid., p. 189.
43. Ibid., pp. 453-4, 460-1.
44. The expelled noble, quite aware of Abdullah's ambitions informed him that Din Muhammad of Balkh had confiscated his property and deprived him of his wealth without any cause and in this way ignited Abdullah to wrest it from Din Muhammad (*Abdn*, p. 179).
45. *Abdn.*, p. 269.
46. Ibid., p. 90.
47. Ibid., p. 156.
48. *Maktubat wa Asnad*, p. 76.
49. Lahori, *Badshahnama*, pp. 14, 498.
50. *Secret History*, p. 89; Juvaini, *Tarikh-i Jahanqusha*, Leiden, 1911, pp. 18-24.
51. Allworth, *Central Asia under the Russian rule*, p. 277.
52. Riasanovsky, p. 238.
53. *Insha-i Abul Fazl*, p. 90. This system of law of escheat, however, is said to have existed in Mughal India also, Athar Ali, *The Mugal Nobility*, pp. 63-8.
54. *BN*, text, p. 7; Eng. tr., p. 15.
55. *Matla*, II, III, pp. 379-80.
56. *Abdn*, p. 391.

State and Religion Under Timur and His Successors

A prologue on Timur's attitude towards religion and *yasa* seems essential in view of its impact on his administrative and state policies and also as a clue to many of his unusual actions (i.e. behaving like a pious Muslim and adhering to the laws of *yasa*, nurturing ideals of an absolute despotism and appointing nominal Khans and so on), each of which had a peculiar reason and a particular background. Such a discussion becomes all the more necessary because conflicting accounts have been given by the medieval chroniclers about Timur's religious attitudes. Some like Yazdi depicted him as a Muslim monarch par excellence.[1] Others denounce him as an 'irreligious, faithless' person, who acted upon the principles of *yasa* disregarding the *sharia* completely.[2] Even in Timur's lifetime, this controversy must have existed as Ibni Khaldun refers to this enigma in the following words: 'Some attribute to him knowledge (of Islam?), others attribute to him heresy because they note his preference for the members of the House (of Ali). Still others attribute to him the employment of magic and sorcery, but in all this there is nothing.'[3]

This controversy about Timur's personal beliefs involves his State policies as well. The religion of Timur is presented in some sources as the one bearing the stamp of *sharia*—in others it is depicted as being entirely based on the principles of *yasa*. Except Barthold, Hilda Hookham and Sinor, who observed that Timur made use of both *sharia* and *yasa* alternately, most of the modern historians have usually accepted one or the other hypothesis (branding Timur either as an orthodox Muslim or as a complete stranger to Islam) thereby prolonging the confusion created by historical raw material. Since no detailed explanation of the vacillating attitude of Timur in religious and political affairs is available anywhere and since the sources supply both kinds of information to suit every probable conclusions, the existing confusion can only be removed if the problem is studied in its true perspective.

This confusion mainly stems from two facts. In the first place, while discussing Timur's religious attitudes, the socio-religious milieu from which Timur had acqired his inclinations and prejudices and which left an indelible stamp on Timur's ideological attitudes forming his state policies is altogether ignored. Even the political circumstances which necessitated a dual policy on the part of Timur, resulting in peculiar anomalies like the coexistence of *sharia* and *yasa* in Timurid polity are not taken into account. Secondly Timur's personal beliefs and religious attitudes are mixed up with his state policies and social and political decisions and behaviour. Such a generalized overview camouflages the perspective and blurs the judgement.

An attempts is, therefore, being made here to discuss at length the socio-religious atmosphere before and on the eve of Timur's ascendency mainly in the context of the formation of Timur's religious attitudes and policy.

The factors which forced Timur to show due regard both to *sharia* and *yasa* are briefly highlighted presupposing the simultaneous co-existence of *sharia* and *yasa* in the polity of Timur's time. Subsequently Timur's personal views about religion, his attitude towards Islamic laws, the observance of its tenets and the impact of these notions on his state policies with particular reference to the relations with the mullas and the non-Muslims are discussed as existed on the eve of Timur's rise.

The socio-religious atmosphere on the eve of Timur's ascendancy is characterized by three main features, namely, the not so pronounced ideological conflicts between the Muslim divines supporting the *sharia* and the Mongols trying to uphold the law of Chingiz Khan, the *yasa*; secondly the much publicized struggle between the normadic and settled elements trying to live upon each other and maintain their respective way of life; and the third point emerging from the first two is the resultant anarchy, maladministration due to apathy of the Mongols, and the discontent of the Central Asian population which in turn further strengthened the hold of religion and aggravated the conflict between the followers[4] of *yasa* and *sharia*. All the three aspects will be dealt with separately here in the same order to appreciate the dilemma in which Timur was placed owing to his own emergence from a purely military circle with a Turko-Mongol heritage in an age surrounded by ecclesiastical magnates and humming with their activities.

Socio-religious Atmosphere of Central Asia (Ninth–Fourteenth Century)

Central Asia had become a stronghold of *sharia* and a spiritual centre from the ninth century when Balkh, Bukhara, Samarqand and Farghana became Arab colonies. The Arab conquest, however 'imperialistic', 'non-cooperative' and 'oppressive',[5] had left its impact upon the socio-religious arena notwithstanding Barthold's assumption that though mosques were being built 'religion was of as little importance to the Arabs as to the defenders of the land'.[6] Barthold says that under the Omayyads the attempts of conversions, the exemption of converts from the taxation, the two dirham gift for offering prayers, the purnishment for shirking from prayers, the Persian translation of Koran[7] were the measures aiming at introducing the new philosophy. In the beginning, the people converted thrice in Bukhara resumed their religion in a jiffy the next morning. Nevertheless in the following centuries, Central Asia developed as the leading resort of Muslim culture with all the progress of Muslim jurisprudence having it's theological centers at Tirmiz, Bukhara and Balkh ensuring emergence of various religious orders, large scale production of canonical works and widespread religious schools dotted[8] its environs. The revolutionary idealism of Islam and presumably/probably the similarities with Zoroastrianism (monotheism, five times prayers) hastened the process of amalgamation. The Islamisation of Central Asia was a slow and gradual but steady process. Nevertheless, the commercial prospects, agricultural prosperity and benefits of weaving and other industries of Transoxiana hopefully compensated for the hazards of conquest. In the Omayyid province of Transoxiana, however, the principle of *cujus regio ejus religio* was far to seek. It is surmised that conversion was in this conquest 'a secondary factor' and though mosques were being constructed 'religion was of as little importance to the Arabs as to the defenders of the land'. The loss of revenue received through capitation had once even compelled Ashras the reneged to go back on the promise of remitting *jaziay*, its reimposition on the newly converts provoked them to call for help from the Turks.

Islam had come to stay in a stable and enduring manner. In Barthold's view, the first Saljuqids and Qarakhainds were 'better Muslims' than Mahmud and Masud. He further says that for Qarakhanids religion was 'not only a weapon for the maintenance of their rule', but the 'precepts of the faith were recognized as binding on the sovereign also who abstained from the use of wine'.[9]

With Islam gaining a permanent foothold after the Arab conquest the initial opposition towards the new conquerors gradually diminished and sporadic uprisings during the subsequent decades died down.

The onset of Islam suffered a setback when taking advantage of the fall of western Turkish Empire, the Chinese took *suyab* and devastated it. Subsequently, they executed the ruler of Shagh for 'non- fulfilment of obligations of a vassal' presumably in response to invitations sent by Ikhshids of Ferghana. The Arabs took up the cause of the liquidated ruler and a battle ensued between the Arabs and the Chinese in July 751. The Chinese Commander Kao Hsien-Chih was badly routed along with his 30,000 soldiers. Although the Chinese are said to have achieved some success in the extreme south-eastern side of Transoxiana, they desisted from assisting the ruler of Ushrusana in 752—thus leaving the territory entirely to the Muslims. Barthold had rightly asserted that the decisive battle of 751 'undoubtedly of great importance in the history of Turkestan as it determined the question which of the two civilizations, the Chinese or the Muslims should predominate in the land'.[10]

During Umayyads no religious revolts broke out in Khurasan or Transoxiana. Under Abbasids there were many uprisings—the reason being a 'synthesis of Islamic ideas and local belief' which did not manifest itself until the end of Umayyads or beginning of the Abbasid era. Cities in Transoxiana like Bukhara, Balkh, Merv and other places were once again shaken with revolts everywhere against Abu Muslim. The uprising under Ishaq lasted in Transoxiana for three years, i.e. 755-7, Ostad Sis's revolt of Al Barm Badghis, revolt of Yusuf in Bukhara, revolt of Al Muqanna in Merv, Alakhshi Kish, uprising of Babak 816-38.[11]

On the eve of the Arab and Mongol invasion, Central Asia was a cockpit of various religions having in its fold for example Buddhism, Nestorianism, Christanity, Manichaenism, local Zoroastrianism (religion of Magi) even small colonies of Jews and Hindus. The advent of Islam had much less of a 'disturbing impact in the order of society than elsewhere since Islam was more concerned with orthodoxy than Zoroastrianism's orthopraxy. There were said to be 'many similarities between Zoroastrianism and Islam both monolithic with five prayers daily hence identification of the two religions was not only possible but made it easy to convert from an orthopraxy oriented religion to one more concerned with orthodoxy'.[12] There was rise of Ismaili influnce at the court of Bukhara in the tenth century.

Al-Biruni says that Arab conquerors especially, Qutayba Ibn-i Muslim in the beginning of eight AD in Persia Sughdiana and Khwarazmia tried to exterminate the priests. Barthold asserts that earlier Arab accounts have no mention of such extermination. 'In accounts of Arab conquests—no facts are quoted which would point to the existence of the influential local priesthood inciting the people to oppose the Arabs.' Neverthleless Abdullah al Bayya, an Naysaburi (1041) mentions in his famous work 'history of the Ulama of the town of Nishapur' (in eight thick volumes that the Simjurids when they came into open conflict with the Samanid dynasty enjoyed the undisguised sympathy of the priesthood, who in the struggle between bureaucratic administration and military aristocracy generally espoused the cause of the latter.

In the first half of the twelfth century, the dynasty of Khatibs and with raises is their hereditary privileges and the title of *Sadr-i Jahan* must have had regular points of discord with the Qarakhitays which led to the 'martyrdom' of 'People of the turbans' (*ahl-i dastar*), i.e. priests, but they were powerful enough to extend protection even to the men of sceptor and crown.[13] Occasionally the extraordinary influence enjoyed by them in temporal matters must have aroused the jealousy of both the Khans of Samarqand and the Qarakhitays. Ibn-al Asir had recounted the story of the *rais* of the Hanafite of Bukhara, Burhanuddin Muhammad b. Ahmad Abdal Aziz who had gone to perform the *hajj*. He was a nominee of the Qarakhitays for collecting the tribute in Baghdad where he acted as the real authority and roused so much of general ill will that his surname *Sadr-i Jahan* was changed to *Sadr-i Jahannum*. The *sadr* performed the *hajj* with fanfare sitting in a litter and followed by a large terrain of *ulama*, baggage and hundred camels. The account of the luxuries enjoyed by these *sadrs* as found in Awfi, Nasawi and Ibn-al Asir confirm that these *Khatibs* and *rais* lived with regal pomp. With the immense resources of Burhanuddin 6,000 *faqirs* could be maintained at his expense easily. The democratic movement which broke out in Bukhara on the eve of Khwarazm Shah's campaign was directed against the *sadrs* also. The leader of the rebels was Sanjar, the son of a shield seller who behaved like master of the town and held the important persons of the town in utter contempt.[14]

The Mongol conquest of Central Asia did not break the stronghold of ecclesiastical power and the special status enjoyed by the divines and Shaikhs further strengthened due to the increasing difficulties created by Mongol maladministration.[15]

It is also surmised that the 'use of spiritual weapons'[16] by the representatives of religious and judicial ideals are said to have been age old and prevalent in all Islamic countries probably because of 'insufficient Islamic principles of polity and subsequent need for frequent interpretations of a definite constitution and the separation of spiritual and temporal power under the Umayyads. Moreover it is also emphasized that the Islamic jurisprudence with its theoretical side being dependent for its practical importance on analogical deductions and the common sense application resultant or dependent upon Kalam, the all-pervasive organ, the Ummah and necessity for *ijma* (consensus) and ijtihad were also other restrictive factors.

The fact that in the longer run the earlier opponent groups of theologians came to terms with kings and the 'two powers (temporal and spiritual) arrived at an understanding based on the mutual recognition of their sphere of interests was said to be an Islamic world characteristic'.[17]

It was inevitable, therefore, that the hereditary dynasties of the ecclesiastical supremos would dominate the political field. Exponents of Hanafite, Mutazalite, Hanbatite, Shafaite and other sects as well as the Dervish, Shaikhs with their cloisters in Chaghaniyan, Khwarazm, Syr darya region, Tirmiz, Balkh and Bukhara and with its theological centers at Tirmiz, Bukhara and Balkh will also have their share in the glory of Central Asian culture with a deep impact upon the rulers and the ruled alike.[18]

Essentially the role of these *mullas* in Central Asian politics provide the clue to appreciate the dilemma in which Timur was placed owing to his emergence from a military circle with a Mongol heritage in an atmosphere humming with the political activities of ecclesiastical divines, in a Muslim world.

The existence of mullas as interpreters of Muslim law and the position of these very religions divines in various administrative capacities like Mufti, Shaikh-ul Islam, Naqib-i Ashraf and so on was essential in Islamic polity. They were to be consulted in political and state affairs from the very beginning throughout the Muslim world and gradually became very influential.[19]

In Central Asia, the Samanids rose to powers with the help of these *mullas* in Bukhara who enjoyed so much honour in Samanid court that they were not only exempted from *paibso* (kissing of the ground) but were consulted on all important affairs and even appointments were made in consultation with them.[20]

Similarly, Qarakhands were also 'Clients of the Commander of the faithful' who coined the money bearing the Caliph's name and recognized religion not only as a 'weapon for maintaining their rule'[21] but as a true duty 'binding upon the sovereign. Incidentally, the struggle between the religious divines and the kings often sharpened due to such trivial affairs in the beginning as the *mulla* exhorting the Khan to carry out the ordinances of religion and to restrain themselves from forbidden things.[22] In due course the grievances increased and the anxious measures taken by the kings to defend his authority and the reaction of religious groups in asserting *sharia* tempts one to presume that '*plenitudo potestatis*' which was so prominent in Europe was not altogether missing from Inner Asia. Contrary to Pope's position, however, the limited power of an ordinary *mulla* could easily be curbed by a powerful king through various means or pretexts though often at the risk of his personal popularity and strength. But there was another dimension also. The assessment of Rawandi[23]regarding this tussle between caliph and the king not only shows the feelings of bitter cold war nurtured by the two parties but 'also brings to the fore the increasing influence and interference of caliphs in state affairs. 'If the caliph is the Imam', says Rawandi, 'then his constant occupation must be the performance of *namaz*—his preeminence in this respect and the fact that he serves as an example for the caliph in the affairs of temporal rule is senseless; they must be entrusted to the sultans'.

The mutual struggle sharpened during the later years and the Saljuqid Sultan Tughril lost the good will of the ecclesiastical groups. The politics of the caliph must have made the going difficult for the divines as well whose interference was thought to be an encroachment upon the prerogatives of the king. The elements of divine rights of kingship continued and Timur appears as a worldly sovereign and a politician first and a Muslim monarch afterwards.

In the next few decades, the increasing influence of religious and spiritual leaders often led to disputes between them and the rulers of Samarqand. The movement which broke out in Bukhara on the eve of Khwarazm Shah's campaign was partly directed against these *sadrs*[24] also due to their worldly pursuits.

The only rulers of Central Asia who had no inclination towards Islam were the Qarakhitays who followed Buddhism but they introduced little change in the social and economic order of Transoxiana.[25] During the regime of the Khwarazm Shahs, the situation of a confrontation between the ruling group and ecclesiasts occurred with such an intensity that even Caliph Abdul Nasir had to invite Chingiz Khan to invade Transoxiana and the 'Mutazaliite' views of Muhammad b. Khwarazm Shah and the murder of Majduddin Baghdadi antogonised the religious groups to an extent that they are said to have bonds of sympathies and the links with the leaders of the military rebellion which broke out against Khwarazm Shah,[26] a version yet to be confirmed through researches. The view that since no particular harsh measures against the rebel Khwarazmian division were taken except that the 'dangerous elements' from among the rebels were exiled is not a very convincing argument. Nevertheless the murder of Majduddin was one of the several reasons for the fall of Khwarazm Shah and for the successful entry of Mongols in Central Asia.[27] The divines of Samarqand quite contrary to those of Bukhara, showed no opposition to the Mongol conquerors taking them as their 'saviours' from heretic tyrants—the Qarakhitays and the reckless Khwarazm Shahs. Reciprocally, more than 50,000 persons including *Qazis*, *Shaikh-ul Islams* and other former dignitaries were exempted by Chingiz from leaving the town and were given royal protection.[28]

Chang Chun's eyewitness account shows that the invasion of Chingiz Khan had no particular effect upon the Muslims at least apparently as there were usual regular prayers, 'night feasts' of Ramazan, Id celebrations, etc. The Muslim divines enjoyed the respect and consideration commonly shown by the Mongols to the clergy of every religion.[29] Juwaini categorically speaks of the fact that 'being the adherent of no religion and the follower of no creed, Chingiz eschewed bigotry and the preference of one faith to another—though they (succesors of Chingiz Khan) adopted some religion they still for the most part avoided all show of fanaticism and do not swerve from the *yasa* of Chingiz, namely to consider all sects as one and not to distinguish them from one another'.[30]

In accordance with the clause tenth of *yasa* of Chingiz Khan 'no taxes or duties should be imposed upon the descendants of Ali Beg Abu Talib without exception as well as upon fakirs, readers of Koran, lawyers, physicians, scholars, people who devote themselves to prayers and asceticism muezzins and those who wash the bodies of the dead'.[31] Documentary evidence confirms this fact for Chingiz had issued a *yirliq* to this effect. Vartang also says that Chingiz ordered 'to free from taxes temples consecrated to God'.[32] Apart from other sources, the first *yirliq* of Mongke Timur (though a *yasa* follower) in 1279 contains the following information: 'as former kings protected priests and monks and all paupers and he do not mean to change their charters we also protect them and who would nab them—be he *basqaq* or prince's scribe or tax gatherer or custom officer will not be forgiven but in accordance with great *yasa* be punished with death'.

SHARIA AND THE *YASA*

During the regime of Ogedei, also Islam spread far and wide and notwithstanding the *hiped* expedient prejudices of his own elder brother Chaghatai against Islam power and the special status enjoyed by the divines and Shaikhs further strengthened presumably due to the increasing difficulties created by subsequent mal-administration. Unlike Khaqan Ogedei, Chaghatai—the ruler of Transoxiana and guardian of *yasa*—was 'fierce' and particularly 'hostile' towards the Muslims who undertook the task of imposition of *yasa* upon people. A declaration was made that none might slaughter meat in the Muslim fashion nor sit by day in the running water. Besides, the Muslims were allegedly being forced to eat carion and so on. Juvaini boasts that Ogedei was kind by temperament and tried to save every one whom Chaghatai wanted to punish for so-called violation and transgression of *yasa*. Nevertheless, in some other context the same author mentions that in Chingiz Khan's time 'the Mongols regarded the Muslims with an eye of respect and for their dignity and comfort would erect for them clean tents of winter felt but today on account of their calumny one or another defects in their morals they have rendered themselves thus abject and ragged'.[33] The other sources also confirm that the condition of Muslims had temporarily deteriorated partly because of favours shown by the Mongols to Buddhists and partly because of the degeneration—a byproduct of demoralization due to fall of Caliphate and other Muslim states and such other events in the Muslim world. Apart from this, there were several other points of discord between the conquerors and the conquered as the philosophies of their lives also differed. The Mongol conquerors clung to their peculiar pattern of life prescribed by their ancestor Oghuz 'to wander and never to settle down'. Whereas the Muslims of a highly urbanized and Islamized Central Asia adhered to their settled ways at least in certain regions. Thus continuous uprisings of the Mongols in favour of *yasa's* laws which had started creeping gradually in central Asian superstructure made the unchallenged supremacy of *sharia* a bit shaky in the ruling echeleon of the society. While the inherent liberalism prevented Mongols from religious persecution (thousands could otherwise be killed in wars), initially the Mongol 'cataclysm' had certainly played havoc to an extent with the agrarian economy of Central Asia. The strife between the settled and the nomadic population would have come to an end much earlier but for the Chaghatai *ulus's* eastern part of Moghulistan expedient penchant for *yasa*—obviously for self-preservation as in the absence of any common Holy Book, apostle or spiritual bonds, the code of laws prepared by Chingiz Khan the *Ssuto Bogdo* of the Mongols could serve as the only effective binding and cementing force among the Mongols. It was through this common law that comradeship in arms could be turned into a community or brotherhood of devoted followers of Chingiz Khan who could unitedly check the re-emergence of the former displaced ruling families whose imminent possible rise due to Mongol maladministration often seemed to threaten their supremacy and could keep at bay the Mongols of Moghulistan thwarting their attempts to convert highly urbanized Chaghatai *ulus* into a nomadic ownership with pastures and pastoral economy. For some reason, the name, 'Chaghatai' (which rightfully, belonged only to the Chaghatai's descendants) called 'Chaghatai Nizadan and to the Mongol ruling family now residing in western part was applied to those Turko-Mongol tribes who had arrived in Central Asia in three different phases.[34] These immigrants were conscious of their of own failings and afraid of threat of imminent overthrow of unpopular Mongol rule of Mongolistan. These new entrant gradually learnt the ways of Central Asian urbanized and Islamised polity and culture but kept alive their right to Central Asian sovereignty through their 'unflinching' though usually outward adherence to *yasa*. The view that the arrival of the Mongols 'drove Islam for a while on the defensive'[26] may not be true but the rules of *yasa* of Chingiz Khan, almost continuously flickered through the thick screen of *sharia* reminding the conquered of the existence of Mongol rulers and their *yasa* which, however, could never engulf the Islamic laws though occasionally may have tried to overshadow it. However the need to transform the new 'heathen' rulers (i.e. Mongol) and their attitudes and way of life was never felt by the Central Asians. Being exposed to foreign invasions and subsequent large-scale amalgamation of various races, and due to its crises, cross-cultural shades and multiplicity of religions, Central Asia had deep-rooted traditions of liberalism pervading in the veins of its essence. The Islamic *sharia* and the Mongol traditions, therefore coexisted simultaneously in Central Asia though *sharia* with all its antiquity and reasonable cultural freedom flourished more than *yasa*. Ibn-i Battuta who happened to be in Central Asia a few years before the birth of Timur clearly describes that not only the ecclesiastical divines, the *Khudavandzadas* of Tirmiz held the entire power of Transoxiana but the Mongol aristocracy also knew how to hold to ransom their Khan who was inclined towards Islam. Only a single example of Tarmashirin's experiences as described by Ibn-i Battuta would illustrate the point. The account proves beyond doubt that on the eve of Timur's birth there was conflict still going on between *sharia* and *yasa* and between the semi-settled and settled populations. Ibn-i Battuta says the Mongol ruler, that Tarmashirin of the steppes, was a pious Muslim who offered regular prayers and it was no wonder that the *mullas* in his regions were free to assert their authority. Once when Tarmashirin sent words to the *mulla* of the Central mosque to wait for him for a few moments for noon prayers as he was pre-occupied with state matters, the *mulla* ignored his request and started prayers. Tarmashirin had to join the congregation in the middle. As there was no space, he was seen kneeling just where the people had left their shoes. Instead of expressing any kind words after the prayers, the *mulla* reprimanded the Khan saying that prayers are offered to God and not to the king and that they are not in any way bound to a ruler's orders or convenience in matters of faith. The strong influence of *yasa* as emphasized by Ibn-i Battuta is also simultaneously well proved by Tarmashirin's exile from Central Asia. His exile was probably not so much due to his conversion to Islam as out of Mongol hatred for him due to his attempts to establish a settled pattern of living which was contrary to the principles of *yasa*. Ibn-i Battuta says that

> the reason why they (Mongol inhabitants of Transoxiana) paid homage to Buzum Oghly and turned away from Tarmashirin was that the latter no

longer kept the laws of their 'accursed' ancestor Chingiz Khan. He had produced a book containing his laws called *yasag*. It is the accepted code among these people that anybody who contravenes this law must be deposed. One of these laws requires them to assemble once a year. That day is called *toi* which means the day of festival gathering. On this occasion, the descendants of Chingiz Khan and the boys arrive from all regions of the Empire, the 'ladies' and the generals were also present. If any of the 'Khans has changed anything with regard to the precepts of this law, the notables go upto him and say: You have changed this and that, and done this and that they take him by the hand and lead him down from the throne, and put some other descendants of Chingiz Khan in his place. If one of the grand Amirs had been guilty of an offence in his district, they judge him according to his deeds.[35]

TIMUR'S DILEMMA

Even when Timur and his ally Amir Husain hunted for power and frequently appointed and deposed Khans, the danger from the Mongol lobby on the one hand and the displaced Central Asian ruling families on the other continued. The *mullas* in Central Asia were still holding much political authority as is proved by the frequent intercessions of the *mullas* and the *mashaikhs* of Khujand and Tashkent on behalf of Amir Husain to bring about peace with Timur. It was infact a vicious circle since the Moghulistan rulers like Iliyas Khwaja (1365), still prompted purportedly by nostalgic love for ancestral Chaghatai *ulus* of Central Asia invaded it to enjoy the benefits of settled economy by plundering. While such raids always reverberated the Chaghatais to cling more vigorously to Mongol lineage and *yasa* to safeguard their military privileges as a Mongol against their eastern counter parts the *jetah*, these raids further strengthened the hold of the *mullas* by uniting the Central Asian people against the Mongols and provoking a stiff resistance on the part of the conquered people; awakening the defenders of Islam, the *ghazis*, the *mullas* and the medieval champions of human rights, i.e. the *sarbadars* against the encroachment of the Mongols. Neither the Mongol traditions nor the Mongols, who were so firmly saddled in Central Asia and Mongolistan, could be exterminated from the soil which they had conquered by force and since then held it lawfully, nor the Islamized and urbanized Central Asia could be converted into a pasture for the Mongols and its people into herdsmen. The only workable solution could be to get the support of each of the two militant groups to whatever extent it was possible.

Such was the land in which Timur was called upon to play his role, realizing fully well that the surrender to or complete identification with any of the two groups could sound the death knell of his ambitions or even existence. Simultaneously none of the two groups was indispensable since both were strong in their own peculiar way and a balance between the two was essential at least for one who aspired for their leadership.

The Mongols as a warrior clan were extremely obedient to their ruler. Being devoted to Chingiz Khan's blood and loyal to *yasa*, they were less prone to be attracted towards sovereign power or nurture the royal ambitions. They could easily be won over merely by small favours like share in booty and minimal needs of life though they were a source of greater strength as a trustworthy military group. Timur could claim over Central Asian territory (and even the places once under Chingiz's rule) easily through his matrimonial connections with the Mongol ruling dynasty, howsoever, flimsy the ground may be. But the Mongols alone could not have succeeded in elevating him to rulership in a place where a purely military rule supported by semi-nomadic traditions could never work its way particularly after the terrible experience of complete anarchy in the past under the Mongols for more than a century.[36] The Central Asian displaced hereditary dynasties still flaming with the ambition of recovering lost suzerainty, the *sarbadars* and the divines were not going to give their wholehearted support to a person whose association with Mongols was a harbinger of devastation of a settled state unless there was a definite hope of salvation from Mongol military rule, semi-nomadic influence and a sure promise of establishment of peace and prosperity through trade, agriculture and stable government. During his hunt for power, Timur had to compromise almost continuously with several groups for neither Mongols were repressible nor Central Asians could altogether be ignored.

Thus, Timur belonged to an age of transition when religious orthodoxy was in a state of gradual revival. The Perso-Turkish lands where a long struggle for the restoration of the supremacy of settled Turks over Mongol nomadic rule had been going on offered to Timur a society and a political arena in which the well-entrenched religious groups played an active role offering the umbrella of *sharia* to the king and protecting the masses against the royal tyranny if any through recommendations and in which the fast waning glory of

Mongol was offering Timur a safe bet. To attain power, therefore, it was necessary to develop friendship with these religious personages in order to gain the confidence of the subjects and an authority over their state. Timur fully realized the significance of their support from the very beginning. Being in close contact with the subjects and enjoying their immense affection, these mystics and ecclesiastical leaders could serve as a link between Timur and the people. From the outset, therefore, Timur adopted several ways to appease and please the various influential groups of Central Asia. There were *sarbadars* and the Mongols on the one hand and the religious divines, the Muslims potentates and displaced ruling families on the other. To keep the wheels of his aspirations moving towards his goal much in the same way as Berke had done earlier, Timur tried to win over these groups in a subtle way gradually. It was Timur's good fortune that the 'interests of the Mongols seeking an Empire and looking for scope for' booty and the political magnates, traders and merchants aspiring for a centralized government which could guarantee urban, agrarian and commercial development coincided. They found in Timur a person who could fulfil the needs of every class of society and the common people—guaranteeing them peace, commercial and agricultural prosperity, strong rule on the one and through his vigilant and strict administration and ensuring an inflow of booty and newly conquered regions on the other through continuous conquests.

Timur's Personal Faith: An Arab traveller of the fourteenth century related the views of Timur about religion at length. According to him Timur believed in one God but he respected all the religions alike.[37] A careful study of the development of Timur's career as described in the sources, therefore, shows that Timur was neither a bigot nor a stranger to the tenets of Islam. In Central Asia, where Islam had clouded Christianity, Shamanism, Judaism and Buddhism and was trying to engulf *yasa*, the survival of any ruler seemed easy only within its fold. It was no wonder then that Timur's piety, faith and devotion to Islam were highlighted by court historians to present him as the ideal Muslim sovereign far excellence.

Shami, Yazdi and Hafiz Abru stress that Timur 'removed the rust of heresy (*bidat*), respected *sharia*; and held the Holy Household (*ahl-i bait*) dear. The medieval Indian sources provide contradictory information but some of the Mughal sources confirm that he was a Muslim extraordinarily devoted to the *ahl-i bait* (Prophet's household).[38] He was devoted to *sadat*, *ulama*, pious *ahl-i dastar* (lit. men of turban, i.e. the *mullas*), *muftis*, recluses, saints; visited the holy tombs, gave away charities, spent his time in prayers (*nawafil o tilawat-i Quran*) and avoided pleasure seeking; offered regular prayers, attended Friday congregational prayers and visited tombs of saints before every campaign. Fasting during Ramzan days were also observed by his courtiers. Timur is presented as the one 'busy in the elevation of the signs of faith and *sharia* rules, under whose reign, Islam was so exalted that nowhere a hundredth part of it was visible' while examining Timur's personal faith, the fact that he belonged to a place and an age in which heresy of any kind or atheism was neither trendy nor permissible. In that orbit Timur and his successors had to follow the precepts and practices suggested by the religion. In this context also Timur was suspected of trickery as is well proved by the Comments from several European scholars. Hilda Hookham observed that 'traditions of Islam were exploited only to consolidate his power and to justify his actions' and that 'Muslim faith was used to support the despotic form of Timur's state power'. Witteck concludes that 'Timur cared much for public opinion of Islam and exerted to win the approbation of the entire muslim world'. Prawdin thinks that Timur's dream was to be a 'new Moslem Chingiz Khan' that his personal attitude towards Islam 'remained throughout one of Mongol tolerance and indifference' and that 'the great calculator established his realm upon two different and most utility based hostile elements and upon two conflicting law books'. Barthold sums up that 'more often than not, religion was for Timur a means for attaining some political aim rather than a cause determining his actions though he cleverly exploited the tradition of Islam to justify his actions and to enhance the splendour of his throne'. Peter Brent called him 'a man of agreed piety who used religion like the most cynical of modern propagandists'.

There seems to be an element of truth in both kinds of these remarks. While discussing Timur's religious policy one finds less of conviction and more of expediency though a bit of both. Religious sentiments attributed to Timur were conditioned by and should be reviewed in the same perspective—that religious factor was a social product of that particular form of society which prevailed at a particular period. Although personally Timur was a believer in monotheism and sought the blessings of saints, he never allowed religion or the saints to share in his authority. Timur's accession to the throne had been justified by the saints on the ground that he was distinguished amongst all contemporary rulers in that he busied himself in strengthening of religion and in promoting Islam. Accordingly Timur did everything to present himself as an ideal Muslim fulfilling the demands of his time to win over his hitherto suspicious Muslim subjects. In these sources, Timur is called as the 'protector of Islam' (*Islam panah*) a title never claimed by Timur himself. The army of Timur is described as (*lashkar-i Islam*) and his court as *dargah-i-Islam panah*. Timur cannot be branded as a faithless irreligious person for he conformed to all the existing norms of religion and demands of his age but certainly religion was not the guiding factor in his scheme of things. In his personal and political life he was motivated not so much by religious dogmas or *yasa* but by his political interests. He appears to be a worldly sovereign and a politician first and a Muslim or Mongol monarch afterwards.

The most favourite device of Timur was to give the colour of *jihad, ghazawa* or holy wars to his ambitious imperialistic wars claiming to spreading the path of *din-i Muhammadi* and replacing the cross by *azan*. Strangely enough these so called holy wars were fought against a staunch and orthodox sunni rulers like the Ottomans and the Arabs who were themselves muslims and champions of holy wars. In Amul, Timur brought the charges that there were no mosques, no Friday prayers, no following of *sharia* and that the men of piety were being tortured. He invaded Khurasan because it belonged to the shia faction; he swooped on Syria and took up the cause of the shias—condemning Yazid and Muawiya and appreciating Imam Husain's stand so vehemently that the theologians there took him for being a shia.[39] The Christian states of Caucasus were attacked because they were 'infidels' and 'not Muslims' the Orthodox crusading Ottomans were attacked 'to deliver the Empire of Greece from the bondage of the Ottomans'. Here Timur did not hesitate coming to terms with Axalla and Emperor Paleologus against a Muslim king. Surprisingly Timur managed to extract a *fatwa* also justifying the expediency of war against Muslim countries in the light of 'doctrinal dispute, hostility of the sects' and 'defence of religious heritage' and fighting for 'justice'.

Yazdi proudly boasts that in Moscow the people were massacred and their houses were to be destroyed and put to fire. In Amul, Sari and Mahana Sar all the *sadats* whether among the army or civilian population were to be picked up and put to death because 'they had only the name of Siyadat and Timur reprimanded them for their ill beliefs and advised them to follow sunnism and *sharia*. In India, holy war against Muslims was fought because they failed in putting down the idolatory. The ecclesiastical dignitaries of the army of Timur who had not the slightest acquaintance with the sword were asked to put all those Hindustani Muslims to death.[40]

Even these 'holy wars' of Timur were not without mundane motives of gain. During the expedition to Siwalik hills, Timur himself stressed that there were two benefits accruing from *jihad*: one was the hoarding of recompense for the next world and the other acquisition of booty and conquests of territory and that Timur aspired for himself the eternal bliss and everlasting luxuries as well as benefits and wealth for the army.

Timur is said to have demanded *mal-i amani* (security deposits) from the Muslims after war and *jaziya* from the non-Muslim population. In Turtum 200 paganas were assured of safety provided they paid *jaziya*. In Garjistan also Timur demanded an annual payment of *jaziya* and safety and good treatment to the non-Muslims. Muslims, however, were granted 'safety after payment of *mal-i amani*'.

After holy wars, Timur reprimanded the Qipchaqis over their strange reversion after accepting Islam. Timur is reported to have persuaded Buqrat Tiflisi after the holy war in Garaagh to accept the religion of Islam and *sharia* of Muhammad. If Yazdi is to be believed, not only Buqrat but several others were attracted towards Islam and Hanafite sect. Another example is that of the Rai of Jammu who became a Muslim through Timur's *Taklif*.[41] Nevertheless, Timur is never reported to have indulged in large-scale conversions. No attempt on his part is ever noticeable equally in the spread of Islam by any means. Seemingly the above mentioned two examples were also literary flourished to boost the image of Timur.

Relations with the Religious Divines

In the entire game of religious politics, the only measure in which Timur remained consistent was his immense and continued patronage to the *ulama* of his age to guarantee 'celestial insurance'. Like Chingiz Khan, who 'honoured and respected the learned and pious of every sect, regarding such conduct as the way to the court of God', Timur also showed every kindness to the *ulama* of his times.

Ibn-i Arab Shah makes us believe that the grandeur which surrounded Timur was actually due to the blessings of these saints. Early in his career, when Timur was 'poor and weak and between his imagined greatness and actual wretchedness' he came to the famous saint of Kesh named Shamsuddin Fahuri with a she-goat (which he had bought from the money acquired by selling his shirt) and 'entrusted his plan to the Shaikh's honour'. In fact Shamsuddin Fahuri was the most influential saint, 'the greatest authority in those parts consulted by all in affairs of state and religion'. Incidentally, he happened to be a spiritual guide of Timur's father Targhi as well. The Shaikh seems to have supported Timur in his ventures, 'assisted him with prayers—aided his desire' that he (Timur), continues Arab Shah, 'then gradually climbed, lame though he was, to his desired eminence'. Similarly, another saint, Baraka, who happened to be 'among the great magnates of the provinces of Transoxiana and Khurasan' also aided Timur so actively and snatched him from that danger—his cunning coinciding with destiny and providence. Baraka remained as a spiritual guide of Timur throughout his reign 'supporting with his prayers what Timur did with his sword'. It was no wonder then that 'Timur conferred great authority in his court on Saiyid Baraka and made him governor throughout his domain and kingdom'. Timur also approached Shaikh Zainuddin Abu Bakr Tayabadi of Khwaf to take a lesson from him 'concerning justice and equity'. Ibn-i Arab Shah[42] quotes Timur as acknowledging that: 'Whatever Empire, I have gained and whatever forts I have stormed are due to the intercession of Shaikh Shamsuddin Fahuri and the zeal of Shaikh Zainuddin. Khwafi and I have not won success except by the aid of Saiyid Baraka'. Timur had been buried in the same Mausoleam near the feet of Shaikh Baraka in a position that his face was turned towards Shaikh Baraka.

In Sabzwar, Sharif Muhammad Sarbadar suggested to Timur to come to terms with Khwaja Ali Ibn-i Muid Tusi, the ecclesiastical leader of the region, described by Sharif as the 'hub of the wheel of these realms, on whose allegiance hinges the allegiance of the rest, by whose counsel, the acts of all are bound, who do what he does; stand if he stand; and go if he goes. Timur did as he was told and consequently there remained in Khurasan no *amir* of city, governor of a fortress or counsellor, but came to Timur and joined his side'.[43]

Timur had been seeking power so desperately that even odd and cynical activities of saints filled him with hope. Before his Khurasan campaign, Timur visited the famous saints Wali and Sahib-i Jazba of the region for his blessings and the piece of flesh thrown by Baba Sanku gave him the impression that he was destined to conquer Khurasan. Throughout his reign, Timur kept contact with various members of the clergy whether they were from Kash, Samarqand, Tirmiz or any other place. Hafiz Abru appreciates that one of the wisest policies of Timur was that he tried his best to accord respect to *sadat*, *ulama* and *sulha*. Even in India he saw Shaikh Farid Ganj-i Shakar.[44] The practice was continued by Indian Timurids who maintained the 'army of prayers' (*lashkar-i dua*).

These saints were rich and possessed numerous gifts and land grants. Timur is reported to have asked Saiyid Baraka as to what services he could render to him and on the latter's request assigned to him the revenues, estates and hereditary land grants and property which remained with his successors till the middle of the fifteenth century.[45] Another Saiyid Raza Kiya was granted 1/3 of the revenue of Gilan and *muhassils* were ordered not to demand the *wajh* from him.[46] A number of other charitable acts are also attributed to Timur.

Barthold expresses his surprise over the complete silence of the sources over Timur's relations with Naqshbandi saints.[47] Notwithstanding the fact that Khwaja Bahauddin was a contemporary of Timur and also a student of the latter's teacher Amir Kulal,[48] the relations between them could not develop probably because of the policy of isolation on the part of the Naqshbandi saints. It was only in the fifteenth century that a Naqshbandi mystic Khwaja Ahrar for the first time decided to come closer to the state 'in order to protect the Muslims'.[49]

While describing Timur's visit to the tombs for prayers and subsequent payment of 10,000 *dinar-i kepeki* at each *mazar* for construction of domes as well as for benefits of the dervishes and deserving, Yazdi explains that 'the definite hope which goads the just and religious sovereigns continuously for charitable deeds was that charity assists them in bringing good fortune, grandeur and magnificence in this world and be source of forgiveness of sins and a sure way to heaven[50] in the world hereafter'. Nevertheless, these expressions of honour and consideration never exceeded their limits, Ibn-i Arab says 'Timur loved learned men and admitted to his inner reception nobles of the family of Muhammad, gave the highest honour to the learned and doctors and preferred them to all others. In his arguments with them he mingled moderation with splendour, clemency with rigour and covered his severity with kindness'.[51]

Timur loved the company of learned men. He equally loved to hear the historical and religious discourses. Ibn-i Khaldun a contemporary historian commented that 'it is simply that Timur is highly intelligent and very perspicacious, addicted to debate and argumentation about what he knows and also about what he does not know'.[52] Every day after administrative business was over, the learned men and *ashraf* assembled and religious discussions over issues of *sharia* were held.[53] In Damascus, Timur himself told the *ulama* 'I am intimate with learned men, to whom I am greatly devoted and in whose company I delight and I have the ancient zeal for learning'. During a journey to various places on administrative purposes or for military campaigns, *sadat,* and *fuqaha* always accompanied Timur. In this respect Timur seems to have followed Chingiz's dictum that: 'to cross a river we need a boat and rudder. Likewise we invite sages and choose assistants to keep the Empire in good order'. During Timur's tours and sojourn at various places, the *ulama* and *aimma* of the vicinity rushed to see him, so sure were they of his generosity. In Tabriz, learned men of the vicinity came and twice Timur had an inclination towards the expert explanation of the religions and faith and thoroughly researched problems of *sharia* were taken up and learned discussions were held. Through such discussions, Timur, who was not highly educated could increase his knowledge about various aspects of Islamic law and also history so much that his knowledge surprised even Ibn-i Khaldun.[54] The debate in Aleppo also proves that Timur gained much by these discussions.[55] Equipped with this knowledge, Timur not only created embarrassment for those *mullas* with shallow knowledge but also used this knowledge to encourage and guide his men during war by quoting instances and examples from history, and also enabled himself to justify his military actions and political activities and to thwart the plans of others to outwit him.[56]

While it cannot be denied that either due to his Mongol heritage[57] or owing to an impact of the age in which Timur was born, his attitude towards *sadats*, *ulama* and theologians was of kindness and respect, yet it is also true that Timur (though sometimes conceded to the wishes of the *mullas*) he was never guided by them. He accepted only such requests which seemed plausible even otherwise. Timur's appreciation of intelligent men of varied walks of life and professions reflected in case of *mullas* also. When prisoners of Indian campaign were being carried to Transoxiana, one Shaikh Ahmad Khattu, an Indian saint came to Timur to intercede on their behalf. Having made apparent to Timur his condition as a dervish and his surpassing knowledge, arguing with and confuting over and over again with the learned doctors' who accompanied Timur's force, Shaikh Khattu greatly impressed the conqueror who 'conceived such a strong liking for him that acceding to his request immediately, he liberated all his (Indian) prisoners.[58] The boldness of *ulama*, though a rare phenomenon under Timur's harsh rule was often appreciated by Timur.[59] Ibn-i Khaldun's intelligence and learning, wit and diplomacy not only won for him his freedom but also Timur's admiration.[60] Shami also secured protection and service in Timur's court. In Baghdad, the *ulama* and *mashaikh* who approached Timur were all awarded robes and taken to a safe place.[61] After the conquest of Iraq, Timur himself asked his governors to show deference and request to *sadat* and *ulama*.[62] In Jalan special officers were appointed by Timur to ensure safety for *ulamas* and religious divines just because they were 'the descendants and devotee of prophets' heritage' and for whom Timur had a 'special regard'.[63] During Haleb expedition, Timur Tash, the *malik-ul umara* of Haleb, advised that only *sadat*, *aimma* and *ulama* should intercede on their behalf 'since none except that *taefa* (group) had any say and value before Timur. The key of the fort was also sent to Timur through, *sadat, aimma Quzzat*.[64] *Sadats* were exempted from the payment of *mal-i amani* near Multan,[65] but Timur never objected when his soldiers went to collect *taghar* (provisions during the march) and did not spare even the *sadats*,[66] before these refinements of cruelty on the part of a Muslim conqueror.' Such accounts which contain Timur's cruelty towards religious groups are usually followed by the court historians' apologetics and vindicating commentary. The massacre of Muslims in India allegedly at the order of Timur was explained away in the same way. Exonerating Timur and saying that his word had been misunderstood since Timur had simply asked for 'the heads of the slain' to build towers of victory and not for 'heads of Muslims'.[67] Similarly, if the religious groups were punished by Timur for political reasons, they were dubbed by Yazdi as '*ghul-i biyabani*' or '*Shaikhan-i zahiri*' (specious Shaikhs) having no acquaintance with '*sair o suluk*' and '*maarifat*'; who had decorated themselves with '*zuhd o salah*' only apparently and make the students of right path wander in wilderness.[68] By such comments, Yazdi justified Timur's actions against religious groups and tried to save his patron's image as the defender and protector of Islam and the Muslims. When in Ajodhan, Shaikh Musawwar and Shaikh Saad kidnapped the population to Delhi after the invasion of Timur, they were criticized for 'misguiding' the people.[69]

Timur never hesitated in giving due punishment even to the religious groups. When Khanzada Ali Abullais Samarqandi, Saiyid Abulmaali of Tirmiz with other *amirs* rebelled against him in 1371, Khanzada was asked to leave the *wilayat* as his life was spared only due to his connections with the family of the prophet. Saiyid was, however, exiled and Khwaja Abdullais was sent to Mecca. Yazdi mentions how the 'heretical' Saiyids in Gurgan and Mazanderan were put to death 'delivering those regions from the mischievous influence of these people'.[70]

The same author refers to the 'harassment' of *ulama* by Timur and describes how the *ulama* were 'silent because of fear'.[71] In fact the theologians' always feared 'some snare' in their conversation with Timur.[72] Timur himself claimed while talking to Hafiz Abru that 'whenever he had met ascetics they had shown signs of fear and only in his interview with Tayabadi it was he (Timur) and not the hermit who was overawed.[73] This could be the reason why the name of this Shaikh, to whom Timur confessedly owed his success, is nowhere mentioned in Timur's history after 1381 though the Shaikh was alive till 1388. If Timur spared certain ecclesiastical groups of *ulamas* and theologians,[74] he also tortured, maltreated and killed them if the occasion demanded, e.g. Muhiuddin of Damascus, a Hanafite theologian of eminence, Shamsuddin Hanbalite, Sadruddin Shafaite and Shahabuddin Ahmad (a 90 year old theologian).[75] Qazi Sadruddin Maulavi was dragged to the ground and smitten excessively with feet and fists and tortured.[76] In Isfizar and Siwas people were buried alive.[77] Maulana Abdullah Sadr was beheaded.[78] The treatment meted out to Muslims of Islamic lands and the tortures hardly differ from the reign of terror unleashed by Timur in the holy war holocaust in non-Muslim countries.[79] Barthold, therefore writes that 'in India the mass extermination committed in Muslim countries pale into insignificance before these refinements of cruelly on the part of a Muslim conqueror'. There were other ways to harrass them. Timur never hesitated in creating embarrassing situations for the religious groups for their liking for worldly pleasures. Khwand Mir refers to the incident of Maulana Sadat who was ridiculed for taking illegitimate morsel by Maulana Muhammad and others. Later on when Maulana Muhammad visited Timur he asked the diwan to write a *barat* for collection of *tamgha* to Maulana which was readily accepted by the latter. Now it was Timur's turn to make fun of him for accepting an unlawful *wajh*.

Timur was not very keen to absorb the religious divines in administration. As they were already to some extent an integral part of every Islamic State and their participation in the capacity of judicial and financial officials and interpreters of Islamic law in state matters was essential, Timur had no option but to allow them to exist. Nevertheless, their independent opinion was never accepted by Timur unless he himself thought that way. Even Shaikh Baraka, his spiritual guide, is nowhere found to be advising Timur on political affairs as one finds the Naqshbandi saints dominating the political scene during fifteenth-sixteenth centuries in Central Asia. Although Yazdi and Shami continually speak of Timur holding consultative assemblies purportedly 'in accordance with the *shura* or Islamic *nass* injunction', the religious leaders were seldom mentioned in the list of participants attending the *majlis-i mashawarat* and offering advices. Usually the *amirs*, *noyons* and the princes are described as participating in the discussions much in the manner of Mongol *janqi*, Turkish *kangash* or *qurultai*. Even in such assemblies the freedom of speech was given to all but the final decision rested with Timur.

Timur took along with him certain selected learned men and theologians, lawyers, physicians from newly conquered lands much in the same manner as he took artisans and other men of skill and art. The friendly attitude of Timur towards these religious groups was altered completely whenever Timur sensed any possible hostile activity on their part. Even the slight suspicion of an encroachment on his rights could enrage Timur and lead him to take action against the theologians.

Clavijo says that during construction of the market place, all the houses were brought down and the property holders had to quit. But those whose houses had been demolished had a right to complain. They, therefore, turned to Saiyids. But when the Saiyids told Timur, he waxed declaring that all the land of Samarqand was his private property for he had bought the same with his own money, further that he had the title deeds in his possession and would produce them for inspection tomorrow. Nobody could demand the proofs.

There are just two instances where *mullas* seem to have advised

Timur directly. Once in 780 AH when Timur, mourning the death of his wife Dilshad Agha and Timur's younger sister Qutlugh Turkan Agha had lost interest in worldly affairs, the *ulama* and *mashaikh* at that time arrived to console him. They quoted the divine words and *hadis* on the laws of religion and nature, inevitability of death and on the mortality of this temporal world in order to persuade Timur to return to normal life and worldly responsibilities.[80] But this incident is obviously of no consequence. Timur had just once asked the *ulama* for their cooperation and advice. Both Shami and Yazdi proudly refer to the fact that in 1403 during his Sojourn at Yilqan, Timur held discussions in the *bari aam* on the problems of the faith and religion in his usual way. During one such discussions, when the reputed *mullas* were present, the discussion on the significance and excellence of justice and benevolence started. Timur did not want it to be just a verbal exercise without any concrete results. He, therefore, asked the learned men and the pious to point out to him the lawful and unlawful acts, saying that in every age the *ulama* did impart sage counsels to the kings invoking them for good deeds and preventing him from the improper things whereas now the *ulama* in his times abstain from it. The learned men present there unanimously replied that Timur was able to do even without their advices as his words and deeds were such that they could be a real beacon light—a direction for others and Timur was (*mustaqhni*) not in any need of instructions from such as they. Timur thereupon retorted by saying that such pleasing comments do not satisfy him for he is not insisting upon this point just to win over the faith and loyalty of people to facilitate financial or political benefits for he had acquired much of it already. The purpose of this query was that since each one of them was coming from a province (*mamlakat*), they must be aware of the state of affairs and the condition (*ahwal o auza*) of their respective regions and also the manners and subsistence of *darughas* and *gumashtas* of the *diwan*. Whatever they think to be contrary to *sharia* or principle of justice should be brought to his notice for consideration and rectification so that the weak and helpless may be saved from tyranny. The *ulama* having made sure that the word had been spoken sincerely, started appreciating Timur and ventured to tell him whatever they knew about the good and bad (*ghassu samin*) of their area. Timur, thereupon selected a group of pious learned men (*ahl-i ilm o taqwa*) who were renowned for their integrity, each to go with an honest *amin* nominated by the *diwan-i aala* so as to go to various places to consider and attend to the affairs of subject people and if harm is caused to any helpless person proper recompense should be given. If any extortions are noticed, the money should be given back from the treasury. The tyrants should be executed or be given exemplary punishment. The ulama were to return after the investigations to inform the Emperor so that the practice of cruelty and tyranny (*rusum-i jaur o bidat*) is altogether exterminated and subjects may repose in peace and prosperity.[81]

Timur is said to have confessed there that till now (*ta ghayat*) his attention was fixed upon the royal affairs and conquests (*masalah-i jahangiri o Kishwar Kushai*). 'But now (1403) his entire ambition is directed towards the welfare of the people should, from now onwards, bring to his notice all the events and do whatever was right for the Muslims and extermination of the wicked should be accomplished.'[82] The passage suggests very clearly that till then Timur had not received any suggestions or advices from the *mullas* and that he wanted their cooperation and advice not to transform the empire into an Islamic country but only to enforce rules and exterminate evil for establishment of justice, peace and prosperity and to bring to Timur's notice not just 'whatever they think contrary to *sharia* or principle of justice.[83]

Timur utilized the services of the *mullas* only when the exigencies of the situation demanded. In Ajodhan, when a group of *mullas* stood in defence of the people and carried them away to save them from the onslaught of Timur, the latter counteracted by appointing another group of *mullas* like Jamal Siddiq and Nasiruddin Umar in that very city professedly to ensure that no injustice or tyranny is caused to the people by his own army. The measure was obviously directed towards eliminating any ill will amongst the *mullas* which may have been created due to the activities of the other groups for Timur never wanted to besmirch his image.

Similarly, Timur does not seem to be very anxious to seek assistance of religious groups for intercession of mediation (a common practice in those days) except in one instance where Maulana Jalal himself wanted to intercede and Timur allowed it. No other example is cited by the historians. Nevertheless the *mullas* sent to him as intermediaries by other kings were, however, honourably received by him though they could never persuade or outwit Timur who did what he thought best. When Shaikh Ibrahim of Shirwan pleaded for peace with Georgians, he obliged him only after the agreement on the payment of a large sum. When Shaikh-ul Islam Nuruddin Abdurrahman Isfahani a highly placed Shaikh came as an envoy from Sultan Ahmad Jalair of Baghdad, he was given lots of presents and shown much regard. Nevertheless, Baghdad was invaded as per schedule. It would not be very fair with Timur to presume that the intercession of *ulama* and *mashaikh*, sought by Amir Husain and accepted by Timur was due to 'common bond of religion'. It was neither the sanctity of the holy book nor the *mullas*' mediation but Timur made peace with Amir Husain with full knowledge of his devious ways only 'out of expediency and due to unanimous advice of his *amirs*'.

Timur often appointed *mullas* as informers or spies not because of his own faith in them but because the *mullas* were respected and trusted by the people who confided in them more easily.[84] Similarly, the view that *ulamas* were entitled to a share in the booty is also erroneous. The distribution of booty even by Islamic theory was clearly laid down. Nomadic pragmatism confirmed that booty was the exclusive privilege of the ruler who was entitled to dispose it of in whichever manner he deemed fit. Usually, Timur gave a share of booty to the soldiers. It was only once (on the death anniversary of his beloved grandson) that *mullas* benefited from this generosity.[85] They were, however, entitled to many other financial benefits, e.g. the exemption from taxes, *barat* for money and so on.

Not only the group of *ulama* but also a large number of astrologers accompanied Timur during war and peace. Yazdi justified Timur's orders to astrologers to prepare Prince Ibrahim's horoscope (clearly an un-Islamic practice) explaining that 'though Timur knew that God is the doer of everything and one's fortune is determined by his adherence to religious precepts, the astrology as a lower science was deemed sacred because it is based upon the movement of the sun, the moon and other zodiac signs which also determines the arrangement of timings of prayers, *haj* and *zakat*'. Sometimes Timur asked the astrologers to study the movement of stars and give their verdict though it was not accepted by Timur except when it supported Timur's own farsighted and well thought-out plans. Contrary to the astrologer's advices regarding Indian campaign, Timur went ahead with his plans purportedly after divining in the Koran. The decision was taken mainly because the preparations seemed to him to be satisfactory though Yazdi boasts that Timur preferred word of God to that of astrologers due to his deep faith in Islam like Chingiz.

Timur's 'superstitious reverence for omens and prophecies' is well proved through sources as he even divined from white falcon. Whenever it suited him Timur divined in the Koran also. Timur certainly could be blamed for negligence if not of deliberate destruction and demolition of holy places. On another occasion, when Timur constructed a mosque after his Indian expedition, a madraas constructed by his wife opposite to that mosque was better planned, high lofty more beautiful. Timur who believed as Ibn-i Arab Shah says 'no head was ever raised above him but he brought it low and no back grew stronger than his but he broke it' ordered it to be demolished. Yazdi gives the account of this demolition in a vague manner but both Yazdi and Ibn-i Arab say that Timur planned to get it reconstructed but it could never be completed. Ibn-i Arab[86] complains that mullas were compelled by Timur to offer prayer in that dilapidated mosque and they were all the time afraid of being crushed under the building tottering to its fall.

In the light of the above discussion, it would be erroneous to see in Timur a conscious promoter of Islam or Islamic civilization or the one who accelerated the process of Islamization of Central Asia as Central Asia was already considered 'an advanced Islamic state, politically, economically and culturally' which led the other Islamic countries ahead even long before the rise of Timur. It would be just as hazardous to suggest that the conquests of other Islamic countries like Persia, Iraq and Syria may have inculcated any genuine interest in and commitment to Islamic civilization or religion in Timur who was himself a product of a highly Islamised and urbanized land. Chronology does not seem to have any impact on Timur's religious ideas and if at all, it had any impact it was on the wrong side for he showed clemency to the *mulla* rebels in 1370, had active contacts with the *ulama* in the beginning of his reign when he needed their help. With the passage of time and after an increase in his power, the active contacts with some were discontinued while with a few some kind of relations were maintained till the end of his reign though with lot of circumspection.

There was no particular steps taken by Timur which could in any way indicate that the conquests of Islamic countries had brought any change in his attitudes. The political exigencies, the demand of the existing strings of power and a longstanding custom had compelled Timur to adopt an extremely diplomatic and apparently favourable attitude towards religious groups. No changes occurred after the conquest of Islamic lands for Timur himself emerged to power in an Islamic land and possessed the same 'inherent susceptibilities'. Neither the transportation of people from Islamic countries nor the conquest of Syria and Persia helped in the diffusion of Islamic culture or made Timur's interest in Islamic civilization and his commitment to Islamic religion in any way genuine. Central Asia itself surpassed other Islamic lands as a centre of Islamic learning and culture. It was only in the sphere of secular sciences and arts that Timur and his successors to some extent could depend upon the outside world. The cultural renaissance which followed Timur's conquests was not purely Islamic in its basic spirit as the artisans from non Muslim countries equally contributed to it. The cities of Persia attracted Timur's attention not so much because of their being Islamic lands but because of their being centres of civilization of silk and carpets with all their natural resources and industries. It was not only the muslim artisan group which was brought by Timur but the craftsmen from India and Christian states were also equally picked up in the same manner hence there does not seem to be any particular zest for artisans from peculiarly Islamic countries.

The construction of the mausoleum of Qussam bin Abbas and the establishment of villages with the names of famous Islamic towns was, however, an attempt to make his empire a centre of Muslim culture at the global level with grandeur and pomp of sovereignty of Muslims then badly needed by Timur. He also ordered for construction of a mausoleum over the tomb of the famous saint Shaikh Ahmad Yasawi alongwith *jamaat khanas* and *hujras*. In the fort of Airab the construction of Jami Masjid and other mosque is also recorded, these religious constructions were built alongside with secular architecture in 799 which is a fair proof that constructions were done not because Timur received any inspiration from Islamic lands to build mosques but becaue he had surplus money only in the later years of his reign. The fact that Timur spent 1,500 *tuman-i kepeki* from the treasury for constructing a mosque seems in significant when one looks at the immense treasures spent on a secular architecture.

The destruction of mosque is noticed twice in Timur's reign. Ibn-i Arab Shah says that when Damascus was set on fire by Timur, among the army of Timur there were Rafzis of Khurasan who set on fire the mosque of Omayyads and it clung by its own heat. Yazdi, however, explains that a sudden fire engulfed the city after peace had been established after the war. Since people were worried, they did not take care to put it off in time. As Timur was keen to save holy places, he sent Shah Mulk to save the mosque of Bani Umayya but the attempts failed as the entire eastern part of the mosque was reduced to ashes.[87] It was a strange thing that only the stone portion was burnt and the wooden part remained in tact. Whatever be the truth, if strict discipline could have been enforced it would have saved the situation.

According to Al Hasan Arab, Timur believed in one God, but he respected all the religions alike and though he still preferred that people worshipped only one God, he permitted and granted 'the use of all religions within the countries of his obedience' saying that the 'greatness of Divinities consisted in the sundry kinds of people which are under the cape of Heaven who served the same diversely nourishing itself with adversities as the nature was diverse where it had printed His image, God remaining notwithstanding one in Essence, not receiving therein any diversity'.

Timur's attitude to his non-Muslim subjects does not reflect fanaticism. It seems that Timur had adopted a liberal attitude towards non-Muslims. Even Ibn-i Arab Shah writes that the idol worshippers carried their idols with them during the march. The Christians formed the fourth part of Timur's army. There were 'Persian magis in his army who worshiped fire and Turks that worshipped idols'[88] Axalla a Genoise by birth was much favoured by Timur and given the post of captain general' of infantry.

Timur himself avoided drinking. In Baghdad all the wine was poured out in Dajla. Nevertheless, in banquets, the 'goblets of wine' were served' in the manner of the Mongols'. Timur is said to have closed the places of entertainment in Baghdad, Tabriz, Shiraz, Sultania, Kirman and Khwarazm even by incurring a loss to the treasury. Another deed of religious merit ascribed to Timur was his decision to refrain from the realization of *mal-i-waqf* for royal treasury. Timur allocated the money from the waqf (*mal-i-waqf*) for the benefit of poor and the students of *madrasas* in accordance with the conditions laid down by the *waqf* and never intermeddled (*muta'arriz*) with the *mal-i waqf* and ordered that it should never be brought to the royal treasury. In the Damishq fort there were grains acquired from *mal-i waqf* which at the order of Timur was sold at 3 *dinar i kepeki* a maund at the end of the year and lot of money was acquired and given to '*Khuddam-i harmain al Sharifain*. Since none was allowed to touch it Hari Mulk who had taken hundred maunds of barley was lashed. Nevertheless, a scanty glance at the sources would reveal the fact that Timur rarely bothered about illegal or legal taxation.[89] Moreover, in this case of *mal-i waqf*, he was not only missing a negligible amount but was also winning over the sympathy of the most sensitive and powerful section of the population. Hafiz Abru's comments that Timur did his best to strive and to strengthen the religion of the prophet can only be accepted partially. Another fact which indicates the nature of Timur's interest in religion is his discussions over the problems of *sharia*.[90] It is quite likely that Timur like his predecessors Chingiz and others was anxious to know about Islam. Besides, it seems that he wanted to equip himself with the knowledge of Islamic traditions so as to guard against any pilfalls. It seems that Timur had adopted a liberal attitude towards non-Muslims. Sometimes he ordered the massacre of the Christians or other non-Muslim population of the conquered area but so he did with the Muslims.[91] Notwithstanding these, his motives behind every campaign were other than religious. He was a medieval king anxious for expansion of his frontiers, keen to control the trade routes and eager to increase his power. The fact that he had to abide by certain rules of the *sharia* in the sphere of administration was a matter mainly of expediency.

Religion and Central Asia States under the Timurids

A significant feature of the socio-religious atmosphere of Central Asia during the fifteenth and sixteenth centuries was the predominance of religious, groups. Horgronje says that through 'spiritual weapons,[92] their influence increased and that the temporal and spiritual leaders—the king and the *mullas*—seem to have 'arrived at an understanding based on the mutual recognition of their exclusive spheres of interests[93] throughout the Muslim world', and Central Asia was no exception.

The mutual conflicts and points of discords between the *ulama* and the sufis the former being the law-givers regulating only the 'externals' and the latter being 'the guardian of the inner tribunal of conscience in man',[94] do not seem to be so prominent in Central Asian socio-religions millieu as in that of Iran mainly because the Naqshbandi saints combined in themselves both the roles. Like early medieval India, Central Asia too seems to have had two types of religious groups both professing and clinging to sufi principles and *sharia* (in their own peculiar fashion) and had large following and a hold over the masses in their own regions. They both had only one point of difference that the dervish group shunned association with the court and regal fanfare and avoided political involvement. This group whether of wandering sufis or silsilah sufis stationed in their respective poverty stricken surroundings refused to accept royal favours, jobs and grants, and avoided any contact with the ruling groups. Since this group did not play any significant role in the state, an accounting of it is beyond the purview of this discussion. The other group which was closely connected with the state and left an imprint on the history of its times is being discussed here.

From early fifteenth century, the Naqshbandi saints had decided to come closer to the ruling classes as they thought that by being nearer to the throne, they could have better control, guide and show the path of righteous governance streamline administrative structure on the lines of *sharia* and serve as the light house for the rulers and ruled alike. Writing in the sixteenth century, Hasan Nisari Bukhari had rightly pointed out that the Naqshbandi saints believed in the dictum 'Khidmat-ul Mulk Nisf-ul Suluk'[95] (i.e. the service to the king is half the path to mysticism). The religious groups were already well entrenched in the Timurid Central Asia when the Uzbegs had further strengthened their influence to an extent that the Naqshbandi Khwajas became the power behind the throne. Shaibani visited the shrine of Khwaja Bahauddin Naqshbandi (1317-89) who was attached to Nizamuddin Mir Muhammad Naqshbandi the maternal grandson of Bahauddin.[96] Although Suluk-ul Mulk recommended that a group of learned men and *ulamas* ought to be attached to the Court to warn the ruler, it is interesting to note that *Suluk-ul Mulk*—the work prepared by Ruzbehan Isfahani at the order of Ubaidullah for guiding him unto Hanafite silsilah asserts that the one appointed as the Shaikh-ul Islam should not be kept engaged in the service and company of the king as the companionship and continuous attendance upon the king takes away the elegance and splendour of the *ulama* and distracts and disturbs him.[97] Ubaidullah's spiritual guide Amir Abdullah Yemini of the Naqshbandi order was regarded as 'Ashob-i Turk o sher-i Ajam fitna-i Arab'.[98] He tried to enforce centralized administration in an appanage system though failed but his influence was indeed extraordinary over the rulers and the ruled alike.

Apart from the silsilah-i Khwajagan-i Naqshbandi, there were two other popular sufi groups mentioned in the sources namely, Jahriya and Kubrawiah *silsilah*. To Jahria group belonged the most influential saints of the time who patronized Timurid and mainly Uzbeg rulers, as spiritual guides. The name Jahriya is usually not found in the medieval works on *sufism*. Even in *Kitabul Milal wa'l-Nihal*[99] which deals at length with almost all sects and divisions, their *silsilah* has not been described. The Jahriya group is totally different from the commonly known Jabriya, the follower of Jabr, the doctrine of predeterminism clearly write the spelling with a *du chashmih* but also because the *silsilah* Jahriya has been discussed in *Samrat-ul mashaikh* as a separate *silsilah*.[100] The word 'Jahr' in Chaghatai Turkish denotes sufi ecstasy and exultations. Similarly, there are two other names of Zikr-i khafi and Zikr-i jahr. It is more plausible that ecstasy and exultations and open recitation and dances of whirling dervishes might have given the name Jahriya to a group of Naqshbandis.

As in the Ottoman Empire, the Khwaja or the Chief of the learned men used to be the adviser of the king. In every town and province, a certain family attained the position of spiritual guide and exercised much authority and influence as Shaikh-ul Islam *Muqtada* (exemplar of). Thus in Samarqand Khwaja Ahrar and his family monopolized this post, in Herat Jami and in Farghana the family of Babur's spiritual guide Maulana Qazi[101] reigned supreme. Haider Dughlat categorically states that it was customary for every sultan in those days to have one of Maulana Muhammad bin Burhanuddin's disciples as spiritual guide.[102] One of the disciples of Khwaja Hazrat Maulana (see of Khwaja Isamuddin Shaikh-ul Islam) was usually employed by the princes as a 'medium of communication'[103] among themselves.

Abdurrazzaq Samarqandi depicted the reign of Shahrukh as the beginning of an era of strengthening of the faith and *sharia* when respect for *sadat*, *ulama* and *mashaikh* had increased and charitable deeds and justice were at its zenith.[104] It is said that Timurid rulers used to hold consultations in conformity with the *nas amr hum shura bainahum wa shwarahum fil amr*. In 826, Shahrukh visited the tomb of Sh. Abusaid b. Abulkhair and offered gifts and distributed charity.[105] In 829 the construction of the tomb of Khwaja Abdullah Ansari comprising two *jamaat khanas*, several houses and cells was ordered by Shahrukh. The entire building was of stone tiles (*ajur*), glazed plaster (*kashi*), *zarhall* (a solution of gold used for painting), azure (*lajawardi)*. Immense property and goods (*imlak o asbab*) was given in *waqf*.[106] The tomb in Meshed attracted Shahrukh so much that apart from the usual charities distributed and gifts, [including a *qandil* (chandelier) of 3,000 golden *misqals* especially meant for this place], a *chaharbagh* and a sarai was also built there for a pleasant stay of Shahrukh and his paraphernalia.[107] Frequent visits to the tombs of various saints like Sh. Abu Ishaq, Qusam b. Abbas and several others have been recorded in the sources.[108]

When Shahrukh visited the tomb of Sh. Abusaid b. Abulkhair, the son of the Shaikh not only entertained the entire army but also gave them sheep, suitable presents and necessaries.[109] Ulugh Beg had a great liking for constructing charity houses and welfare centres (*baqai khair*)[110]. In 823 he had constructed a *madrasa* and a *khanqah* near *ark-i aali,* encircled on all sides by papulous markets and residential quarters for choicest families (of pious saints) such was the extent of these buildings, farms, and movable and immovable property (*muzar, 'musta ghallt*) and canals given to it as *waqf* that it exceeded the necessary expenditure of the two buildings (*buq*) though several (*mashaikh* and *mubashirs)* were maintained by it and the surplus was entered into the treasury of the *waqf*.

Abul Qasim Babur constructed a building over the tomb of Maulana Shaikh Umar of whom he was an ardent devotee.[111] The excessive respect offered to Khwaja Maulana Samarqandi by Sultan Abusaid and Abul Qasim Babur[112] is fully brought out by the sources. Sultan Abusaid had a deep regard for saints and *ulama*[113] and sought enlightenment from dervishes and ascetics from the very beginning of his career. He was a devotee of Khwaja Nasiruddin Ubaidûllah Ahrar and never went against his wishes even if he could do so.[114] He entertained Maulana Qasim also. Sultan Abusaid always consulted Khwaja Nasiruddin Ubaidullah in all administrative and financial affairs of the country and never deviated from orders.[115] Similarly, the forty years' reign of Ulugh Beg is said to have been succeeded by the forty years' domination of Khwaja Ahrar of the Naqshbandi order. Sultan Abusaid is said to have entirely remitted the *tamgha* tax of Samarqand and Bukhara in 865 (though losing a very large sum) just at the instance of Khwaja Ubaidullah. Similarly, Sultan Ahmad Mirza, an ardent follower of Khwaja Ahrar, remitted the *tamgha* of Samarqand at the instance of Khwaja Ahrar.[116] Even in the financial workings of the state, the religions groups interfered if they noted unfair dealings.[117]

Sultan Husain Mirza is said to have had leanings towards *shiism*. He thought of even reciting the names of the twelve *imams* in the *khutba* but Ali Sher Beg and others prevented him from doing so.[118] Babur stresses that 'thereafter all his important acts were done in accordance with orthodox law,' though he 'could not perform the prayers on account of trouble in the joints and he kept no fasts'.[119] He is reported to have shown great respect for the law (*sharia*) in several weighty maters; he once surrendered to the avengers of blood a son of his own who had killed man, and had him taken to the judgement gate (*dar-ul qazai)*[120] nevertheless, Muhammad Husain Mirza—a son of Sultan Husain was a 'rank heretic' and died while 'at the same wrong road' and with the 'same absurd opinions because he was shut up with Shah Ismail at some place in Iraq and had become his disciple. Sultan Husain Baiqra had an immense faith and devotion for Jami[121] and preferred him than others. Nevertheless Sultan Husain was a devotee of Shaikh Sadruddin also and visited the tombs of shaikhs and auliyas also.[122]

Sultan Ahmad Mirza, Mahmud Mirza and Babur were formally the disciples of Khwaja Ahrar and showed all respect to his sons and dervishes in general.[123] Sultan Ahmad Mirza is described by Babur as a true believer pure in faith and regularly offering prayers. Disciple of Khwaja Ahrar who was his instructor in religion and strengthening of faith.[124] Babur believes that Sultan Ahmad was 'just' because the 'Khwaja (Ahrar) was there, accompanying him step by step—most of his affairs found lawful settlement'.[125] It was only Sultan Mahmud Mirza who 'was not firm in faith and held his Highness Khwaja Ubaidullah Ahrar in slight esteem.[126] Usman Shaikh was a Hanafite 'pure in faith not neglecting five prayers and even making up omissions, read Koran frequently and was a disciple of Khwaja Ubaidullah Ahrar'.[127] He had an inclination towards the society of religious personages.[128] Khwajagi Khwaja has been appointed as the keeper of seal by Umar Shaikh. Babur refers to enmity existing between the sons of Khwaja Ahrar, the elder son Khwajagi Khwaja supporting Baisunqur Mirza as his spiritual guide and the younger son Khwaja Yahya giving shelter to their rival prince Sultan Ali Mirza. Ikbal's view that Babur tried to persuade or 'seduce' Khwaja Yahya[129]from his allegiance to Sultan Ali is not proved as the overtures were made by Babur against the Uzbegs not against Sultan Ali. Khwaja Yahya's desertion of Sultan Ali and tardy submission to Shaibanids betrayed his suspected alliance with Babur and led to his murder. Some of the nobles also had their religious and spiritual guides. Mir Ali Sher is said to have apparently renounced worldly luxuries after his initiation into the Naqshbandi order.[130] Darwesh Ali Tarkhan and Arghun were orthodox and deeply religious and even transcribed Koran. Another noble Darwesh Beg was a disciple of Khwaja Ubaidullah Ahrar. Not only the kings but the nobles and the commoners used to have their spiritual guides. Amir Abdul Ali was also a devotee of Khwaja Maulana Badruddin Sarraf was a *murid* of Khwaja Alauddin (*Rashhat* 78). Such was the devotion that Maulana Ahmad Misgar even asked for permission of the Khwaja to allow him to meet his own relatives.[131]

The wealth of the religious groups increased with their political power. The gifts and the riches received from the kings multiplied and the Khwajas engaged themselves in commerce and agriculture. Khwaja Ahrar is said to have possessed 1,300 land holdings some of which were equivalent to 300 *juftgao* each.[132] From the *Manaqib-i Ahrar* and *Rashhat*, it is learnt that very high rents were collected by Khwaja Ahrar. The Khwaja maintained a stronghold over external and internal trade, employed merchants for carrying on trade with various places and even owned a number of workshops for manufacturing paper. With such vast resources, he could naturally be extremely powerful. Another rich person Shahabuddin Shashi engaged himself in agriculture and occasionally in trade also. The Khwajas were exempted often from high taxes.[133] Similarly the rulers of surrounding counties like Iran, Kashgar, India, etc., seem to be enchanted by the Khwajas and showered Padnashini on them. Juibar Shaikhs were given expensive cloths (*aqmashia*), dresses, precious gifts (*amtiya)* and 20,000 *tangas* of one *misqal* from Yarqand Khan Abdur Rashid Khan (1533-68). These Ishans received Chinese handicrafts pieces, kalmik horses, etc., from Aiyuk Khan and Abdul Karim Khan (1560-91). Even Jahangir sent twice a large number of pieces of clothes, mink coat, ivory horses, hunting birds and 50,000 *khanis*.[134]

The matrimonial relations between the families of Naqshbandi saints and the rulers further enriched the Khwajas and strengthened their influence. Not only did Khwaja Muhammad Islam and his son have such ties with Timurid Amir Muhammad Tuman by marrying his daughter and granddaughter. In 1588 after the conquest of Herat, Abdullah Khan had given vast possessions of Amir Tuman at the disposal of Khwaja Sad.

There were a number of pious Khwajas who never accepted any gifts or offerings from anyone. Khwaja Bahauddin Shaikh-ul Islam refused to accept any, offering and spent the life as a dervish.[135] Hazrat Maulana Kalan, the respected figure of his times, was offered an office by Shahrukh but he did not accept it.[136] Haider Dughlat also refers to Khwaja Tajuddin who avoided taking 'unlawful food' and gifts from the rich and the poor alike. As the Khwaja engaged himself in commerce and agriculture and gathered together much wealth through these means he could himself oblige the Khans and the *amirs* and the poor alike with his riches.[137] Since 'all profitted'—for this reason no one denied him any thing'.[138]

Some Khwajas never accepted any gift from their *murids*. On the contrary they themselves helped and provided their disciples with financial support. One Farah Tabrizi—a *sahib-i 'iyâr* (assayer of weights and measures) and *mihtar* of *sarafs* and *zargar* of Herat—though, poor, had once invited the Khwaja for dinner. After his devotee's death, the Khwaja had given his son, 10,000 *dinar-i kebeki.*[139] Both Sultan Ahmad Khan and Mansur Khan were among the disciples of Khwaja Tajuddin and 'all the affairs of the kingdom were laid before him in delail'.[140]

The amount of unflinching faith and obedience demanded from the princes by their spiritual guides is well expressed by Hazrat Maulana about Mahmud Khan in the following words: 'Sultan Mahmud was indeed a capable young man but he had one fault which was a hindrance to his advancement. A pupil with such an instructor ought to do all that his instructor told him and not rely on his own judgement; but like a hawk should pounce down upon whatever prey he is sent againt whether or not he has strength sufficient and should not hesitate and doubt as the Khan did. It was this that prevented him from rising to that elevation which his people had expected of him.'[141] Sultan Mahmud Khan had as his guide Maulana Muhammad Burhanuddin.[142] If, however, the advices of Khwajas of Naqshband were ignored either deliberately or inadvertently, they expressed their utmost resentment.

Ahrar fought for peaceful coexistence. He understood the significance of his new role only too well. He is reported to have said that 'until our times shaikhs did not turn towards amirs and padishahs with request for common people's cause but we consider it to be essential. Now God had selected me to be the one to intercede for Muslims.'[143] This was understood by his contemporary Jami as well.

Ahrar's role is important even in organizing Samarqand's defence in 1454 and repulsion of destructive elements of Chaghatais of Khurasan under Abul Qasim Babur. Mir Abulaliya, the son-in-law of Ahrar, wrote *Masmuat*.[144] Mir-i Arab wanted political centralization in a period of appanage system but failed in this mission though his personal influence continued.

In discipleship some kind of strict discipline and an unquestioning obedience and complete submission with voluntary compliance; extreme desire to please the Khwaja through good deeds and persistence in loyalty and submissiveness were the prerequisites to ensure blessings[145] of Khwaja. Even the students (*talib-i ilm*) were to comply with Khwajas' orders. One Maulana Shamsuddin lost the favour of Khwaja just because he felt weak and lethargic to carry out the order of Khwaja.[146]

Not every ruler appreciated the interference of Khwajas of Naqshband in the affairs of people even where 'the interest and welfare' of the latter was concerned. One of the Khwajas of Bukhara frequently wrote to Shahrukh recommending and pleading for the case of the Muslims. When he tried to adopt the same attitude towards Khalil Sultan, the latter reacted sharply by ordering the Khwaja to leave for Dasht so as to spread Islam there. The Khwaja pretended to leave though he remained in Samarqand. The author of *Rashhat* says that it was this behaviour of Khalil Sultan which brought his downfall.[147] Babur condemns Sultan Mahmud for imposing oppressive exactions over Khwaja Ubaidullah Ahrar's family and says that this was one of the reasons of alienating high and low, soldiers and peasants from him. 'The dependants of Khwaja Ubaidullah under whose protection formerly many poor, destitute persons had lived free from the burden of dues and imposts were now themselves treated with harshness and oppression. On what ground should hardship have touched them? Nevertheless opressive exactions were made from them—indeed from Khwaja's very children.'[148]

The basis of the strength of the Khwaja's power lay in his influence over the masses. The population, already torn by internal and external invasions and wars and harassed by plunder, over-exaction and extortions found solace in the *khanqahs* of the Khwajas who stood up to defend alternately the king and the subjects alike in the name of religion.

The economic discontent facing the ordinary man in Central Asia in the fifteenth century also contributed to the strengthening of the hold of the Khwajas over the subjects and the kings alike. The Khwajas extended hospitality and financial assistance to the needy, pressurized the kings to reduce burdensome taxes and also recommended posts and grants for their protégés. Although Timur patronized religions groups, he never allowed himself to be overruled or to be out manoeuvred by them.[149] Under weaker kings, however, the interference of the Khwajas became frequent and more effective. For example, Sultan Ali's desperate attempts to punish Mazid Tarkhan were foiled when the Khwaja took his family and property to his house. The affair ultimately ended in Sultan Ali's annihilation.[150] The Juibari Shaiks particularly Muhammad Islam, Sad and Tajuddin did their best to acquire, increase and to protect their assets. It was with this purpose that Muhammad Islam had deprived his two younger sons, Khwaja Bahauddin Umar and Khwaja Muhammad Kasim, of inheritance and bequeathed every thing to his elder son Khwaja Sad in a proper legal way, written and certified by the Khan. Within 20 days after the death of Muhammad Islam both Khwaja Umar and Kasim also died and all their wealth was inherited by Khwaja Sad. Ahmedov's suggestion that cross-marriages within the family and between cousins were arranged to ensure that property did not go out of family seems to be too sharp as the custom was prevalent among Muslims generally.

During war or in other difficult situations, the intercession of the Khwajas was frequently sought to bring about peace.[151] The Khwajas led peace missions and embassies and even actively participated in the defence of a town against an undesirable ruler.[152] In Shiraz, Amir Nizamuddin Saiyid Niamatullah of Kirman mediated to bring peace among the rulers.[153] Amir Nizamuddin and Abdul Karim were leaders in Amul and Sari.[154] Religious personages were often asked to mediate.[155]

The Khwajas frequently interfered in state matters by pleading for the reduction of taxes (*matalibat-i Sultani wa diwani*). Sometimes the people approached the Khwajas for help against cruel *amils*.[156]

Khwaja Ubaidullah Aharar and Khwaja Abdur Rahman Jami who dominated the political arena of Transoxiana and Herat respectively were in touch with each other as the correspondence between them shows. Sometimes the Khwajas themselves wrote to each other regarding internal affairs. Once Ubaidullah Ahrar wrote a letter to Jami pleading the case of a group of nobles who had fled from

Samarqand leaving their relatives behind in Khurasan. Jami had been asked to overlook their faults.[157] Sultan Husain, therefore, was also bound to Jami. The mutual appreciation of both Jami and Ubaidullah Ahrar is very well reflected through the appreciation of Ubaidullah Ahrar's activities in Transoxiana. Jami is said to have written a *masnavi* in praise of the *mazra'as* of Khwaja Ahrar.[158]

One of Jami's letter to Ubaidullah speaks of the influence of Ubaidullah and Jami in their respective territories. Jami compared the kingdom (sultanate) to a camp whose pillars were only justice and truthfulness *(rasti wa adl)* without which an empire cannot last long and appreciates the acts of justice and suppression of oppressors by Ubaidullah Ahrar's just rule.[159]

Since Soviet scholars have not studied *Risalaye Walidia, Risala-i Sharh-i Khaipaiya* and *Faqrat ul Arifain Khwaja Ahrar*, they do not know even about Ahrars's conceptions and sufi ideas and ideals. His language and thoughts reveal his depth of knowledge and sense of Arabic language and his son Khwaja Yahiya (killed by Shaibani in 1500) was highly educated which also gives credence to Ahrar's wisdom. The dependants of Khwaja Ahrar were spread in three *madrasas*, namely, in Kabul, Tashkent and Samarqand (in *bazar-i attaran*), his *murids* and students were educated people like Jami, Navoi, Babur, Umar Shaikh and others. Ahrar did not like exact sciences including astronomy. It is also erroneous to say that he was an enemy of culture. The observatory of Ulugh Beg and philosophical researches of Ali Qushiji, who stayed in Samarkand till 1470, are a fair proof of the fact that Ahrar was not a lover of culture and his riches did not disturb cultural development as in the case of Jami, Navoi, and Ulugh Beg.[160]

Both Jami and Navoi were members of the Silsilah Naqshband and could not possibly be a party to the reactionary elements.

It should be noted that these aristocratic theologians connected with the ruling family were being constantly opposed by the dervishes who charged them with deviation from the truth and declared themselves to be the real upholders of the *sharia*. Simultaneously the sunni orthodoxy remained to be strong. Jenkinson saw how the 'metropolitan in Boghar' was more powerful than the kings.[161]

He further describes the enforcement of prohibition. Similarly Bente De Goes also confirms his account that sectarian bigotry must also have existed. Babur was not the only one to criticize Baisunghar for holding favourable views on shiism. Abdurrazzaq too had earlier alleged Sultan Husain also for having shii views and earning the displeasure of people. Haider Dughlat categorically speaks of the disappointment of the people on seeing Babur in a Persian dress and says that his associations with shiism led to his eviction from Central Asia as people wanted a 'saviour of Islam' and not a representative of heretics.[162]

One of pseudo shaikhs of Tashkent known for his love for worldly things was a scholar of external sciences and had a such large number of *murids* that fifty of his several hundred *ashabs* were appointed by him for *irshad* (directing people).[163]

Another disciple of Khwaja Ahrar with almost the same name, i.e. Hazrat Maulana Muhammad Qazi (d. 1516), author of *Silsilat-ul Arifin*, honoured by title of 'Ishan' by no less a person than 'Hazrat Ishan' thought he was not attached to any prince. Khwaja Abdullah popularly known as Khwaja Maulana Qazi—a disciple of Khwaja Ahrar—was executed by Babur's enemies in 1498 for his favourable attitude towards Babur notwithstanding his spiritual status.

Mulla Saiyid Qasim Tabrizi for whom Mirza Baisunghar is said to have had a deep regard was exiled (*ikhraj*) for joining hands with the rebels who were the conspirators in the stabbing of Shahrukh.[164]

The cases of confiscation of these Khwajas' property notwithstanding their influence, were not very rare, e.g. the village of Khwaja Ahrar was confiscated by Muhammad Husain Gurgan, an uncle of Babur, and confiscation of hereditary village of Makhdum-i Azam Kashane by Barak Khan of Tashkent (1551-61). There were shaikhs and shaikhzadas also who tended the *murids* and usually had a large following. Occasionally there were rivalries existing between such shaikhs which were accentuated by the overzealous glorification done by their respective *murids*. Once the *murids* of Shaikhzada Iliyas who were Turks of Kash wanted to kill Shaikh Muhammad the rival shaikh of their spiritual guide. When Khwaja tried to intervene to save the life of Shaikh Muhammad, he had to face the bitter criticism by Shaikhzada Iliyas who wrote to Amir Darvesh Muhammad Tarkhan 'referring to the deteriorating conditions of religion caused by such Shaikhs who engaged themselves in agriculture and transactions'.[165]

Khwaja Ahrar's grandson Khwaja Nura or Hazrat Makhdumi Nura (named as Mahmud from his father's side and Shahabuddin from his grandfather), received the title of Khwaja Khawand

Mahmud. It also said that Humayun's favours shown to Shaikh Bahlol bypassig Nura's claims to veneration led to Humayun's downfall.[166]

Devotion to Khwajas was said to be a source of prosperity and greatness. Shaibani ardently doted in Khwaja Bahauddin Naqshbandi and turned towards his tomb with every prayer and desire. During his stay in Bukhara when some misunderstanding occurred between Shaibani and the Timurid governor of Bukhara Amir Abdul Ali Tarkhan, the former visited the tomb of the Khwaja and took service with Khwaja's nephew Khwaja Nizamuddin Mir Muhammad Naqshbandi. It is recorded by Hasan Nisari that Shaibani had expressed a desire to leave the place but the Mir declined to give him permission to leave. Shaibani thereafter, stayed on for a long time in the vicinity of the tomb offering prayers. It was then that the Khwaja gave him the assurance that he would acquire the rulership though it should start from Turkestan and that Shaibani should leave for that particular place. Another significant dimension of sixteenth century was the sudden upsurge of Christian missionaries whose activities seem to have started in the second half of the sixteenth century.

After the occupation of Siberia in 1570, the Qazaq Khan Kucham is said to have allowed the missionaries to convert as many people as possible and summoned missionaries from Bukhara, one of whom left his account which Radloff had discussed in detail.[167] After the Russian conquest of Qazan, the attempts to convert people to Christianity are said to have continued though Arnold stresses that these failed miserably as *mullas* succeeded in converting people from that region also.[168]

NOTES

1. Yezdi, *Zafar Nama* (*ZN*), Calcutta, 1888, I, pp. 5-10, 574, 577; Hafiz Abru, *Tarikh-i Shahrukh*, MS. India Office Library, nos. 171, 173, ff. 12, 13, 16, 19.
2. Ibn-i Arab Shah, *Ajaib-ul Maqdur fi nawadir-i Timur*, Pers. tr. *Zindgani-i Shaguft Awur-i Timur*, Tehran, 1960, pp. 68-9; Eng. tr. by Sanders, *The Life of Timur*, London, 1936.
3. Ibn-i Khaldun quoted by Hilda Hookham, *Tamburlaine the Conqueror*, London, 1962, pp. 7-8.
4. Even during the reign of Chingiz Yeh lu Chutsai always insisted that 'Mongol Empire had been won from the saddle it cannot be ruled from the saddle' and

argued against destruction that 'a razed city paid no taxes—a depopulated land bring neither tribute nor trade, a decimated people were no help in war' (Peter Brent, p. 60).

5. S.A.A. Rizvi, *History of Sufism in India*, Vol. I, 1978, p. 109. V.V. Barthold, *Turkestan Down to Mongol Invasion*, pp. 180-6. H.A.R. Gibb, *The Arab Conquests in Central Asia*, p. 67.
6. *Turkestan Down*, pp. 180-6.
7. S.A. Hasan, 'A survey of expansion of Islam into Central Asia during the Umayyad Caliphat', *Islamic Culture*, Vol. XLV, no. 2, April 1971, pp. 95-113; *Turkestan Down*, p. 188. William Ambrose, *Islam and the Oriental Churches*, New York, 1908, pp. 150-5, 178.
8. Rizvi, *A History of Sufism*, p. 66; Khurshid Ahmad Fariq, *Tarikh-i Islam*, Delhi, pp. 395-9, 494-509.
9. Barthold, *Turkestan Down to . . .*
10. Ibid., pp. 195-7; R.N. Frye, *Bukhara: the Medieval Achievement*, pp. 100-10, 127-8.
11. Ibid.
12. Frye, p. 144.
13. *Turkestan Down*, pp. 16-17.
14. Nasawi, pp. 23-4; Ibn-ul Asir, XII, pp. 170-1; *Kitab-i Mullazada*, p. 169; *Turkestan Down*, pp. 326, 353, 354.
15. Juvaini, Vol. II, p. 74, Khwand Mir, *Khwarazm*, p. 54.
16. Snouck Hurgronje, *Selected Works*, pp. 264-7, 268-95. Reuben Levy, *Social Structure*.
17. Hurgronje, p. 276.
18. Barthold, *Four Studies*, pp. 4-10; Hookham, pp. 25-9.
19. Unlike Indian *Shaikh-ul Islam* who were usually merely religious dignitaries with no active role in political affairs (Rizvi, *History of Sufism*, Vol. I, p. 192). Central Asia had quite influential religious officials.
20. Barthold, *Turkestan Down*, pp. 232, 255.
21. Ibid., pp. 305-6.
22. Ibid., pp. 315-16.
23. Rawandi, *Rahat-us Sudur*, MS As. Mus. 590 b, pp. 116-17.
24. Barthold, *Turkestan Down*, pp. 326, 353-4, 346-76.
25. Hookham, p. 28.
26. Barthold, op. cit., pp. 346-7; Hookham, pp. 25-30.
27. Barthold, op. cit., pp. 346-85.
28. Juvaini, *Tarikh-i Jahanqusha*, text, Vol. I, p. 120; Peter Brent, *The Mongol Empire*, London, 1976, pp. 63-6, also p. 10.
29. Breteschneider, *Medieval Researches*, p. 220.
30. Juvaini, I, Eng. tr., pp. 271-2.
31. Ibid.
32. Ibid., pp. 205, 208, 223-5.
33. Ibid., p. 78.
34. Peter Brent, p. 245.
35. Ibn-i Battuta, p. 440
36. For details see Mansura Haidar, 'Sovereign in the Tumurid Empire', *Turcica*, Vol. VIII, 1976.

37. Al-Hasan the Arab, *Purchas and his Pilgrims*, Vol. XI, Glasgow, 1906, p. 407.
38. Khafi Khan, *Muntakhab-ul Lubab*, Vol. I, ed. Kabiruddin Ahmad, Calcutta, 1868, p. 1.
39. *ZN*, II, pp. 71-5, 97-9, 102-5; Ibn-i Arab Shah, Eng. tr., pp. 2-5, 14-15, 25-7, 121, 183-218, 224.
40. Ibid., pp. 14-15; *ZN*, pp. 145-6.
41. Ibid., pp. 121-6.
42. Ibn-i Arab Shah, Eng. tr., pp. 2-5, 14-15; *ZN*, I, pp. 145-6; Polovtsoff, *The Land of Timur*, London, 1932, p. 10.
43. Ibn-i Arab Shah, Eng. tr., pp. 24-7.
44. Ibid., pp. 25-7, *ZN*, Calcutta edn., I, p. 310, II, p. 563; *Habib-us Siyar*, p. 543; *T. Shahrukh*, pp. 12-13; Farishta, p. 156.
45. Ibn-i Arab Shah, pp. 14-15.
46. *ZN*, II, Calcutta edn., p. 563.
47. *Four Studies*, Vol. I, p. 59.
48. *Ain-i-Akbari*, Vol. III, p. 401; *Rashhat-i-Ain-ul Hayat*, Bodleian Library, no. 176, ff. 8-9.
49. Rizvi, *Muslim Revivalist Movements in Northern India*, Agra, 1965, pp. 176-8; *Shorter Encyclopaedia of Islam*, 1953, pp. 436-7.
50. *ZN*, I, p. 470.
51. Ibn-i Arab Shah, pp. 211, 298.
52. Ibid., p. 298; Hookham, p. 209.
53. Hafiz Abru, *Tarikh-i Hafiz Abru*, pp. 13, 19, 173; Abul Fazl, *Ain-i Akbari*, p. 155.
54. Ibn-i Arab Shah, Eng. tr., pp. 127, 144, 296-8.
55. *ZN*, I, p. 19; II, p. 79; *IA*, pp. 143-51.
56. *Four Studies*, II, p. 39.
57. *Tabaqat-i-Nasiri* of Minhaj Siraj, Eng. tr. by Raverty, Vol. II, Delhi, 1970, p. 1040; Vladimirtsov, *Life of Chingiz Khan*, p. 98.
58. Badauni, *Muntakhab-ut Tawarikh*, Vol. I, Patna, 1973; Eng. tr., pp. 357-8, text, p. 27.
59. *IA*, Eng. tr., pp. 143-9.
60. Ibid., pp. 143-5, 295-8.
61. Ibid.; *ZN*, II, pp. 265-6.
62. *ZN*, I, p. 469; Farishta, pp. 156-60.
63. *ZN*, II, pp. 64-5.
64. Ibid. pp. 209-21.
65. Ibid., p. 46.
66. Ibid.
67. *IA*, p. 131.
68. *ZN*, II, p. 54.
69. Ibid.
70. *IA*, pp. 128, 143-9.
71. Ibid.
72. Shami, f. 210b; *ZN*, II, pp. 387-9.
73. *Four Studies*, Vol. II, p. 21.
74. Occasionally Timur followed the example of Chingiz. Since Chingiz had a deep regard for religious groups he spared them in Samarqand and Khwarazm. Even

the famous saint Najmuddin Kubra had been requested by Chingiz to leave the town as he (Chingiz) was going to order a general massacre. The saint did not come out and preferred to die with his fellow countrymen when amnesty was not granted. T. Banakiti, p. 367.

75. *IA*, Eng. tr., pp. 160-3.
76. Ibid., p. 145.
77. *ZN*, Calcutta edn., p. 360; ibid., II, p. 269; *IA*, p. 88; Clavijo, p. 143.
78. Farishta, p. 159; *Four Studies*, II, p. 40.
79. *IA*, pp. 129-32.
80. *ZN*, II, pp. 262-5.
81. Ibid., pp. 245, 387-90.
82. Ibid.
83. Ibid.
84. Ibid.
85. Ibid.
86. Ibn-i Arab, pp. 323, 360.
87. *ZN*, II, pp. 235-48.
88. *Tarikh-i-Shahrukh*, pp. 12-13, 16.
89. *Ajaib-ul Maqdur*, p. 323.
90. *ZN*, II, pp. 362-5.
91. See *ZN*, Vol. I, pp. 527, 570-3.
92. Hurgronje, pp. 264-7, 276, 295.
93. Ibid.
94. Fazlur Rahman, *Islamic Methodology in History*, Karachi, 1965, pp. 112-13.
95. *Muzzakkira*, text, pp. 15-20; Eng. tr., p. 15.
96. Ibid., pp. 15-22; Eng. tr., p. 15.
97. *Suluk-ul Muluk*, text, pp. 20-2.
98. Ibid., p. 19.
99. Muhammad b. Abdul Karim Shahristani, *Kitabal mila wal Nihal*, Eng. tr. by A.K. Kazi and J.G. Flynn, *Muslim Sects and Divisions*, Kegan Paul International, 1984, p. 72.
100. According to Muhammad b. Abdul Karim Shahristani (d. 1153) Jabr is a doctrine which denies that a deed is in reality to be attributed to man and ascribes it to God.
101. *Matla*, II, I, pp. 40-4, 88; *BN*, pp. 89, 98; *Four Studies*, Vol. III, p. 34.
102. *TR*, p. 213, also see introduction, pp. 116-18.
103. *TR*, p. 114.
104. *Matla*, II, I, ed. by Muhammad Shafi, 1946, pp. 6-7.
105. Ibid., pp. 532-3.
106. Ibid., pp. 562-6.
107. Ibid., II, pp. 378-9, 465.
108. Ibid., II, I, pp. 260, 324-5, 329, 596, 602.
109. Ibid., pp. 532, 533.
110. Ibid., pp. 420-1.
111. Ibid., II, III, p. 166.
112. Ibid., II, III, pp. 166, 167, 172-3, 178, 212-25.

113. Ibid., II, III, pp. 406-8.
114. Ibid., II, III, pp. 352-3.
115. Ibid., II, III, pp. 441-3; Razi, *Haft Iqlim*, III, p. 469.
116. *Matla*, II, III, pp. 183, 214, 353-4; *Tarikh-i Abulkhair*, pp. 251, 260, 264.
117. *Nama-i Nami*, ff. 16-18.
118. *BN*, pp. 164-6; Eng. tr., pp. 258-9, 262.
119. Ibid.
120. *BN*, pp. 164-5; Eng. tr., pp. 258-9.
121. *Matla*, II, I, p. 1392.
122. Ibid., II, III, pp. 407-8.
123. *Muzzakkira*, p. 91; *Abdn*, pp. 43-4.
124. *BN*, p. 33.
125. *BN*, p. 34.
126. *BN*, p. 46.
127. *BN*, p. 15.
128. *BN*, p. 15; *Akbar Nama*, Eng. tr., p. 218.
129. Ikbal, p. 7. Of Khwaja Yahya's four sons, Zakaria and Abdulbaqi were murdered by Uzbegs in 1500 while the remaining two, Muhammad Amin and Yaqub are said to have continued the *silsilah*.
130. *Four Studies*, Vol. III, p. 41.
131. *Rashhat-i ainul hayat*, Bodleian Library, MS no. 360, ff. 78, 107, 355.
132. Ibid., f. 84.
133. Ibid., f. 249, tr., p. 127.
134. *Matla*, pp. 47a, 131b-132a, 133a, 140, 212b; also see Ahmedov, p. 20.
135. *Matla*, p. 743, see also *Matla* II, III, p. 166.
136. *Muzzakkira*, p. 72.
137. *TR*, p. 127.
138. Ibid.
139. *Rashhat*, pp. 259-60.
140. *TR*, p. 127.
141. Ibid., p. 213.
142. Ibid., p. 213, also see introduction, pp. 116-18.
143. Mohd. Qazi, *Silsilat-ul Arifain*, p. 10; *AN*, uz SSR, no. 4452/1, f. 74a.
144. Baldirov, pp. 59-60.
145. *Rashhat*, p. 86.
146. Ibid., p. 85.
147. Ibid., pp. 66-7.
148. *BN*, pp. 41-2.
149. *IA*, p. 14b.
150. *Rauzat*, p. 83b, 180, 186; *Matlab*, pp. 67, 73; Bori Ahmedov, *Gasudarstova Kochevikh Uzbekova*, Moscow, 1965, p. 21.
151. See *Matla* II, III, pp. 175, 329-30, 350-1, 370, 385, 394, 418; *Mujam-i al akhbar*, p. 290.
152. *ZN*, I, pp. 448-9.
153. *Matla*, II, I, p. 19.
154. Ibid., II, III, p. 171.
155. See *BN*, p. 53.

156. *Rashhat*, p. 141.
157. *Insha-i Jami*, Newal Kishore edn., p. 6, for other examples see *Matla*, II, III, pp. 352, 1398.
158. *Abdn*, pp. 51-2.
159. *Insha-i Jami*, Newal Kishore edn., pp. 6-7; *Samarkandski documenti*, p. 37.
160. Baldirov, p. 49.
161. Jenkinson, pp. 20-6.
162. Haidar Dughlat, p. 295.
163. *Rashhat*, pp. 354-5.
164. *Matla*, pp. 591-2.
165. *Rashhat*, pp. 353-4.
166. *TR*, pp. 212, 398-9; Ikbal, pp. 106-7.
167. Radloff, *Sredni Zarafshanskaja Dalina*, Vol. I, 1968, p. 147; Arnold, *Preaching of Islam*, pp. 254-5, Missionaries also came from Kazan.
168. Arnold, *Preaching of Islam*, pp. 249-52.

State and Religion Under the Uzbegs

Central Asia has been a stronghold of Islam since its advent in the region. Orthodoxy in Central Asia, however, gradually revived from fifteenth century onwards after a lapse of two centuries of Mongol hegemony. Chroniclers betray popular prevalent opinion when they praise a ruler for his religious zeal and depict him as a holy warrior for the faith, emphasizing the need for the imposition of the *jaziya*. Traveller's accounts also confirm that Central Asians were ardent Muslims, tolerant fanatics if not always fanatical.[1]

After Timur, non Muslims may not have enjoyed high posts or positions in the governing cadres as extra territorial contacts and conquests, aspirations and ambitions no longer excited their cupidity, yet the Jews, Christians, Shamanists and Buddhists of Central Asia rarely suffered from large-scale religious persecution[2] and, by and large, enjoyed freedom of worship. But the situation was less favourable for the Persians in the sixteenth century, when imperial ambitions in the garb of sectarian bigotry assumed grave proportions not only in central Asia but in Persia and Turkey as well.[3] Expansionist wars were given sectarian colours[4] and when fugitives from these countries brought tales of tyranny against their coreligionists, the fervour for retaliation heightened expansionist ambitions against each other. Although it is alleged that the safe extermination of personal enemies was never so easy as in the sixteenth century, when anyone could be brought to the gallows or deprived of his belongings on the basis of an alleged allegiance to an opposite sect,[5] only a few stray cases of this nature are found in the sources. This genocide is said to have taken a different form in Turkey, where they did away with Shias on the alleged charges of misconduct, robbery or brigandage.[6]

Another significant feature of the sixteenth century was the increasing predominance of religious groups. It is surmised that in a socio-religious atmosphere charged with hyper-orthodoxy, the, *Mullas* were destined to become influential by using 'spiritual weapons'[7] and that the temporal and spiritual leaders—the king and the *Mullas* seem to have 'arrived at an understanding based on the mutual recognition of their exclusive spheres of interests'[8] throughout the Muslims world, and Central Asia was no exception. The Shaibanid Sultans inherited a strong religious group from the Timurids—the Naqshbandi saints who exercised considerable influence on the state not only in the sphere of religion but also in the realm of politics. Like early medieval India, Central Asia too seems to have had two types of religious groups—both professing and clinging to the *sharia*, with large followings and a hold over the masses, but differing only in one respect—that a group shunned political involvements. This group refused to accept royal favours, jobs and grants, and avoided association with the ruling groups. Since it did not play any significant role in the state, an account of it is beyond the purview of this discussion.[9] The other group was closely connected with the state and left an imprint on the history of its times.[10]

Either due to the exigencies of the situation or through personal faith, most of the Shaibanid Khans and Sultans fell under the spell of one or other *Khwaja* or *Mulla* of the times. Shaibani Khan is said to be a staunch believer who offered prayers regularly, possessed a fair knowledge of the works of jurisprudence visited the tombs of *Khwajas*, and was also an ardent devotee of Nizamuddin Khwaja Mir Muhammad (a grandson of Khwaja Bahauddin Naqshbandi) and other saints who had helped and guided him in his early ventures.[11] While describing many of Shaibani's deeds as 'absurd, impudent' and 'heathenish', even his arch enemy Babur confirms Shaibani's 'early rising, his not neglecting the Five Prayers, and his fair knowledge of the art of reciting the Koran'.[12] But Shaibani was personally neither a bigot nor a puppet in the hands of the *Mullas*. In most matters he was guided by his own interests, tactfully giving the colour of *Ghazawat* (holy war) to his campaigns of plunder against the Qazaqs and Persians. Having declared himself as *Imamuzzaman* and *Khalifat-ur Rahman* (the *Imam* of the people and a *Khalifa* of God), he sought to claim spiritual authority and to prevent the *Mullas* from having an undue influence. Shaibani's religious discussions have been recorded at length by Isfahani who says that Shaibani demanded *nass* on various aspects of administration (e.g. the imposition of *jaziya,* the theory of kingship, the law of inheritance, etc.), from *Qazis, Muftis* and the *Ulama*. An incident which took place during one such discussion proves that Shaibani adopted *sharia* principles mostly out of expediency. While the Chingizide and Islamic laws of inheritance were being discussed and compared, a certain *Mulla*, Mir Ahu, obliged Shaibani by supplying a desired injunction in the face of stiff opposition by other *Mullas* who charged Mir Ahu with 'strengthening the claims of rulers by subverting the rules (of Islam) like the *Ulama* of Israel'.[13] Although Shaibani accepted Mir Ahu's interpretation and even ordered the *Qazi* to send a *Nishan* to that effect, the *Ulama* continued to oppose it till another discussion was organized on the same subject; finally Mulla Isfahani's verdict was accepted.[14] Isfahani further records that there were *Ulama* from Rum and Khurasan (beside Transoxiana) also in Shaibani's service.[15] In his earlier years Khwaja Hasan had supported Shaibani, and later served as a major prop to his power.

Shaibani's attempts to improve the condition of Waqf grants, *Khanqahs,* tombs, etc., have been appreciated by Isfahani who says that Shaibani instituted an inquiry into Waqf establishments after which heretic customs (*rusum-i bida'ati*) were removed and scholarships, charities, *zakat,* offerings, etc., were ordered to be renewed.[16]

While Shaibani was personally a practicing Muslim he did not hesitate in using religion for his political ends. His successors not only proved to be deeply religious people but also exhibited a keenness to enforce the laws of religion. Kuchum spent most of his time in *Zikr-i qalbi* and also chanted the *Sura-i Ikhlas* a thousand times daily.[17] Abu Said, an ardent devotee of Shaikh Khudaidad, used to visit the Shaikh every day[18] and was also strongly attached to Shaikh Husain Khwarazmi.[19]

Apart from such devout though weak Khans, even a strong ruler like Ubaidullah was an ardent follower of Mir-i Arab, Shaikh Jalal and Maulana Khwajagi Kashani[20] and ordered the compilation of a book, *Suluk-ul Mulk,* on Islamic jurisprudence to enable himself to establish an ideal Islamic state. His campaigns against Persia were also allegedly motivated by his love for Iraq.[21] Wasifi's accounts prove that Mir-i Arab played an important role in the political adventures of Ubaidullah.[22] His son and successor, Abdul Aziz, was deeply religious and was a devotee of Hazrat Shah Nakshbandi and Shaikh Jalal. He is said to have consulted holy men (*auliya-i karam*) on administrative affairs and spent much of his time in prayers. As these Sultans took a keen interest in constructing mosques, *sardabahs, madrasas, khanqahs,* etc.[23] In this respect the greatest act of devotion was performed by Abdul Aziz who not only built *madrasas, khanqahs, juibars* (canals), etc., in the vicinity of Bukhara but also allocated lands in Waqf and *Altamgha* for their maintenance. The entire Juibar region was offered to the Naqshbandi saints who from then on became associated closely with the Uzbeg court and came to be known as the *Khwajas* of Juibar. This continued down to the eighteenth century as the authors of *silsilat—ussalatin* and *Majma-ul Argam* refer to these influential dignitaries of the Uzbeg court.[24]

Abdul Aziz received religious instruction from Maulana Nasir and others.[25] Iskandar Khan and Pir Muhammad[26] also belonged to the same category of Sultans. Iskandar Khan, particularly, relished the company of learned men, dervishes and Shaikhs and was an ardent devotee of several *Khwajas* like Khwaja Juibari, Khwajagi Kashani and others. Even the chronogram of his death was *badshah-i dervishan* (king of dervishes).[27]

The influence of these saints attained such a degree that the *Khwajas* of Naqshband, like the *Sadr-i Jahans* of Bukhara previously, enjoyed immense privileges in return for extending support to the Khan and were richer and more powerful than the Khans. Jenkinson's statement, though somewhat exaggerated, depicts the position in 1558: 'There is a metropolitaine in Boghar (Bukhara) which is more obeyed than the kings and will depose the king and place another at his will and pleasure as he did by this king that reigned at our being there and his predecessor by the means of the said Metropolitan for he betrayed him and in the night slew him in his chamber.'[28]

Such a situation compelled even a powerful Khan like Abdullah to show special consideration to the *Mullas*, was initially tried to tide over such influences. Although Khwaja Juibari had helped Abdullah in his first military ventures, the latter did not consult him in his political decisions, which led to the Khwaja's displeasure.[29] Later, Abdullah's devotion to the *Khwaja* was shown to increase; he not only expressed his complete submission to Khwaja Juibari but also stressed that 'his own life as well as the territories conquered by him were a present (*niyaz*) to the *Khwaja* and the distribution, appointments and dismissals were within the jurisdiction of *Khwaja*'.[30]

Abdullah's devotion did not remain confined to the Juibari Shaikhs.[31] He realized the significance of the entire class of theologians and called them 'the source of pleasure of God and a way of good fortune in both the worlds'.[32] In those days, Abdullah was particularly devoted to the shaikhs of the Jahria order; there are references to his consulting Darvesh Alia Bari and Qasim Shaikh.[33] Later, on his regard for the Naqshbandi saints also increased.[34] He not only heeded the advice of shaikhs but even of their disciples.[35] Any deviation from this usual path, however genuine, met with resistance. Abdullah's attempts to punish Shaikh Khalil for rebellious activities ignited the resentment of Khwaja Kalan, who pleaded Shaikh Khalil's case in the following words: 'The foundation of justice and the amelioration of subjects cannot be achieved except with the help and consideration of holy men and shaikhs whose shadow of kindness and assistance is in fact an asylum—a refuge and a shelter for the kings—hence the reverence of this group and patronage of all their desires is binding (upon the sovereigns)'.[36] Hafiz Tanish described Khwaja Kalan as the shelter for the group of elders and gentry of the time.[37] These comments amply prove the significance of religious groups in the sixteenth century.

Abdullah is said to have personally dedicated himself to the strengthening of religion and extending patronage to theologians.[38] He often attended religious assemblies (*majlis-i suflyana*) in saintly dresses.[39] He not only liked the company of the saints but discussed with them matters concerning the welfare of the people. He was called *Padshah-i Islam* and visited the tombs of saints before every campaign or during royal tours.[40] Special consideration was shown to the Saiyids and even war captives were released if they were found to be Saiyyid.[41] Abdulllah used to walk on foot to receive the *Khwaja* while the latter remained on horseback; he also arranged for grand feasts (*Toi Ziafat*) in honour of the *Khwaja* and offered him the choicest gifts.[42]

Unlike Abdullah Khan, the fantasies of Abdul Momin never allowed him to have close contacts with the religious groups, and this was perhaps the only significant feature of his short reign.

The high position enjoyed by the Juibari shaikhs and *Khwajas* in the socio-political arena of Central Asia was acknowledged even by the neighbouring rulers.[43] The Czar of Russia gave an extremely warm welcome to the *Khwaja's* trade mission.[44] The Ottoman Sultan also sent friendly messages.[45] Even Mirza Hakim of Kabul[46] and Mirza Shahrukh of Badakhshan,[47] the rulers of Kashghar and Khwarazam as well as Shah Ismail II of Persia maintained diplomatic relations with Khwaja Juibari and discussed political matters in letters addressed to the Khwajas.[48]

The basis of the strength of the Khwaja's power lay in his influences over the common man. The population, already torn by internal and external invasions and wars and harassed by plunder, over exaction and extortions, found solace in the *khanqahs* of the *Khwajas* who stood up to defend alternately the king and the subjects alike in the name of religion. Often the *Khwajas* tried to gain popularity through charitable deeds. Their philanthropic acts are gratefully recorded in the sources, e.g. the laying of canals in deserts and the building of *madrasas,* mosques, *khanqahs* and *sardabahs.*[49] Hafiz Tanish says that Shaikh Azizan constantly worked for the welfare of the *wilayat* and the prosperity of the artisans, and that he made unceasing efforts to obtain the reduction or repeal of taxes like *matalibat-i sultani* or *amwal-i diwani.*[50] Khwaja Lutfullah's father opened a permanent kitchen for the people coming to him with families during a famine.[51] Khwaja Mushtari is reported to have arranged the distribution of 1,001 *naans* (large breadcakes) daily among the poor and students of the *madrasas* of Juibar.[52] Similarly, 16,000 maunds of wheat were once distributed among the poor and besides,[53] 10,000 silver *tangas* were given. Even in the financial affairs of the state, the *Khwajas* often intervened to serve the interests of the poor. The *Rauzat-ur Rizwan* contains letters of such a nature. A letter from Sulaiman Sultan to *Khwaja* refers to the difficulties faced by a certain Mirak who had earlier given his arable lands in *mauza* Naubahar to some *barzgars* (peasants) and was then harassed by Sultan Ali Arab with constant demands. The letter requested the *Khwaja* to issue a letter of authority to Mirak exempting him from all demands and assuring him that no one would bother him.[54] Even land-holders, whose peasants had fled on account of civil wars asked a *Khwaja* to negotiate and persuade them to come back.[55]

If Shahnawaz Khan is to be believed Khwaja Muin the grandson of Khwaja Kalan 'acquired great influence' with Abdullah Khan and 'obtained the grant of the produce of the Jade river'. As the Khwajazada was a shrewd man he 'so arranged that no one could see any zade even in a dream, and so had to buy it from him at high price. In this way, he acquired much wealth but he was a great miser'.[56]

The Khwajas frequently advised the Khan about the appointment of Sultans and *Ataliqs.* If, however, their advice was ignored either deliberately or inadvertently they expressed their utmost resentment.[57] The extent of the *Khwajas'* active participation in administrative affairs can well be seen from a number of *farmans* and in correspondence about political matters which was exchanged between the *Khaqan,* Sultans and *Khwajas*. Evidence of this kind is preserved especially in the letters contained in *Rauzat-ur Rizwan*.[58] Hafiz Tanish categorically speaks of the fact that during the early years of Abdullahs's career the 'management of people's hopes and the organization of mankind' were connected with Qasim Shaikh Azizan.[59] Some instances gleaned from the sources throw light on the fact that kings had to comply with the demands of *Khwajas*. Amir Arab is said to have instructed Ubaidullah that 'in the relations of love and faith, it is binding that whatever is agreeable to us should be agreeable to you and whatever is rejected by us should be rejected by you'.[60] Consequently at Amir Arab's recommendation, Ubaidullah's *Wazir* Khwaja Nizam regained his lost status.[61] Similarly, Abdullah's decision to exchange Bukhara for Balkh without consulting Khwaja Juibari was greatly resented by the latter. His anger subsided only when the decision was revoked.[62] From then onwards, Abdullah always consulted the *Khwajas* on important affairs and invariably[63] abided by their decisions. Even princes and nobles who had lost favour with the Khans were able to regain their position through the recommendations of the *Khwajas*.[64] The victories and political successes attained by Abdullah Khan Uzbeg are attributed directly to the faith and sincerity of the ruler for Khwaja Kalan (Khwaja Abu Bakr), and the patronage extended by the latter to the former.[65] The Khwaja's disciples also constantly received patronage from him.[66]

The verdict of these *Khwajas* had to be respected by nobles and kings alike. It was only after the recommendation of Khwaja Kalan that the *Amirs* released Abdul Baqi Bi Durman[67] whom they were determined to destroy; and Khwaja Saad was requested to recommend that a *Tarkhani* is made for Sultan[68] Sulaiman. The *Rauzat-ur Rizwan* includes a petition from Mahmud Sultan to Khwaja Juibari in connection with the renewal of his mother's *milk* grant of two *Kariz* and her right of one-fifth (*malikan deh dui*)[69] which had been suspended by Abdullah. During the conflict with Baba, Abdullah wrote to Khwaja Kalan for his advice and acted upon it. When Din Muhammad of Balkh sent Khwaja Muhammad Tahir to Abdullah, the *Khwaja's* intercession seeking forgiveness for Din Muhammad was accepted by Abdullah.[70] During the Balkh expedition, Din Muhammad used Maulana Muhammad Zahid of the Kubrawiah order to win over Abdullah.[71] Similarly, even Baba Sultan approached Khwaja Saiyid Atai Naqshband[72] to establish peace with Abdullah. One of the shaikhs is said to have compelled the besiegers of a fort to raise a siege when he lay on the parapets of the fort.[73] On different occasions, the *Khwajas* brought down rulers and officers who were arrogant enough to displease them. The forecasts of the degradation and extermination of Sultan Burhan (the ruler of Bukhara) and Abdullah Khan (the ruler of Samarqand) by the *Khwajas*, and the subsequent accomplishment of their prophecy exhibits merely the acute faith of the chroniclers in the miraculous powers and revealed verdicts of the *Khwajas*. Jenkinson's statement that the *Khwajas* murdered the kings or at least were privy to such plans has no basis nor evidence. The innumerable letters of courtesy contained in the *Rauzat-ur Rizwan* and calculated to seek the *Khwaja's* cooperation against rival princes, and mode of addressing him as '*pir, pehswa, wali-i ni'amat, pushtpanah*, or as *nasah-i zumara-i muluk* (leader, guide, benefactor, supporter, advisers of the ruling classes) involved in contemporary politics'.[74] A letter of Abul Ghazi Ali, Sultan to Ghaus-i Jahan reveals that even the 'holy wars' against Persia were encouraged by Ghaus-i Jahan.[75]

A sixteenth century work, the *Siraj-us Salikain wa Lataif-ul Arifain* of Ubaidullah Naqshbandi Samarqandi, throws light on the activities of the highly placed *Khwajas* and their circles as the author was a close disciple of the famous saint Maulana Lutfullah. According to Ubaidullah, there were two main dervish orders, namely, the Naqshbandia (commonly known as *silsila-i khwajagani)* and Kubrawia[76] (with Shia leanings). Uzbeg sources mention the most influential group of the Jahria.[77] The rivalry between the Naqshbandia and Kubrawia orders is said to have flowed from the number of *Murids* (followers) who enriched them through offerings and gifts. On the number and status of *Murids* depended the position of the *Khwajas*. These *Murids* came from all classes[78] and from different parts of the country.[79] Not only the Sultans and their family, but the entire ruling class, the merchants, artisans, warriors and cooks sought the *Khwajas*' protection. The *Khwajas* demanded complete obedience. Any defiance on the part of *Murids* brought upon them the *Khwaja's* wrath. Somenov concludes that in the regions of Hesar, Samarqand, Akhsi, Ahangaran and Tashkent, the struggle between the Kubrawia and Naqshbandia[80] orders was usually followed by a political upheaval, indicating participation of these groups in political matters also.[81] The *Khwajas* were so powerful that they discarded or accepted a *Murid* at their own sweet will. Shaikh Azizan is reported to have refused to include prince Abulkhair in his circle of disciples (*halga-i iradat*), and only after recommendations from Maulana Ismatullah did he agree to accept him 'in order to prevent him (Abulkhair) from causing harm to the people as he was mischievous'. The same *Khwaja* patronized and assisted Abdullah in his rise to power.[82] Only a few instances are given in the sources of a *Khwaja* bearing the brunt of the wrath of the sovereign. Wasifi refers to the plundering and devastation of the house of Mir-i Arab at the infuriated Souyunch Khan's order because a forged letter of Mir-i Arab promising support to Ubaidullah against his elders (including Souyunch) had been produced by a certain Mir Ibrahim.[83] The ruthless treatment meted out to Shaikh Khalil at the order of Abdullah[84] provides another example. But such cases were rare.

Apart from enjoying considerable political power, the *Khwajas* also possessed much wealth. They held large properties and engaged in external and internal trade not only by providing capital for investment but also by sending their representatives as merchants to far-off places.[85] Khwaja Qutub-ul Islam sent Maulana Jan Muhammad to Moscow, from where he returned after concluding profitable transactions (*sud o sauda*).[86] The Khwaja's landed property was scattered all over the country in the form of large rent-free estates, immovable property (*Sukniyat*) like caravansarais, bath-houses, and canals. Khwaja Saad is said to have boasted once that from Darband in Turkestan up to the borders of Khurasan, there was not a single city or plain where he did not own some *Imlak*.[87] Once Khwaja Qutubuzzaman even purchased Khan Iskandar Khan's *milk* from him for 40,000 silver *tangas*.[88] Another *Khwaja*, Mushtari, ordered that wherever *milk* land was being sold by its owners, the Khwaja's servants should seize the opportunity to buy it.[89] Khwaja Juibari is said to have possessed more than a thousand green and prosperous farms (*mazaraa*).[90] Surviving sale deeds also confirm large-scale purchase of lands and *milks* by the *Khwajas*. Waqf documents show how extensively the *Khwajas* received fertile revenue-yielding lands as gifts. In 1570-1 Ibadullah Sar Khwaja Muhammad Islam Khwaja Juibari was given three *Chaharbaghs* with fruit trees, and three gardens in Aush, one piece of *milk* land consisting of 40 *tanab* of melon fields. Another order of Rabi II 980 assigns the villages, canals and arable lands (*arazi-i zeraat*) as *milk* and *suyurghal* to the Khwaja's *Wakil*, with exemptions from *mal o jihat, muqarrari, ikhrajat, mirabana, gaozakhira, tarh-i sabun and tanabana.*[91] The *Rauzat-ur Rizwan* contains a number of such *farmans* granting complete *Tarkhani* (exemption) from all taxes. Most of the lands thus held by the *Khwajas* of Naqshband were hereditary (*ba tariq-i ars*).[92] Even a ruler like Abdullah, who had confiscated all other kinds of personal property of people had allowed the *Khwajas* to hold hereditary landed property exempted from all the taxes.[93]

In another *Nishan* issued in July 1583 Abdullah ordered that 'owing to his deep regard' for the *Khwaja*, all the villages, canals, arable lands *milk* and *suyurghalat* mentioned should be considered exclusively held for the *Khwaja's Wakils* and the *mal o jihat, muqarrari, ikhrajat, mirabana, gaozakhira, tarh-i sabun* and such other demands should be imposed upon them.[94]

Not only the Khans, but also the Sultans too gave away lands, which were usually exempted from state obligations, to the *Khwajas*. In one of the *Souzomiz* Abdul Quddus Bahadur declares in 1583 that 250 *zauj-i awamil* (measures of land), water, and the lands from Juizagh from the *Juibarhai Khasa* (which was described in detail) had been presented (*batariqi niyaz*) to the Khwaja in entirety (*muqarrar wa mussallam*) so that he could cultivate it or give it to a *Karinda* and realize the *Hasilat* (revenue). The document further warns all concerned to consider the *Yabisat, Imlak* and *Zimn* as *Darubast,* entirely in the possession of the *Khwaja*. In accordance with the order, no one was to disturb his *Wakils* by demanding *mal o jihat* and *awarizat* and should not interfere with them for any reason whatsoever. No *Hashr* (corvee) or *Mardikar* (labourer) was to be demanded. *Mirabana, Haqqabana* was to be given to him without any altercation and none should violate the imperial order. A renewal of the *Nishan* and *Parwana* was not to be demanded.[95]

The sale documents also show the enormous size of landed property held by the *Khwajas*. One such sale deed of 12 February 1606 was prepared when Oui Begum, the daughter of Khwaja Hashim Ahrar had sold some of her property in Yalintugh at Samarqand *Tuman* of Afrinkent for 4,300 *tangas* to Yilingtush Bahadur. The same land was declared by Imam Quli as *Milk-i Khas* (exempted from all sorts of taxes like *mal o jihat, awarizat,* etc.) in 1611.[96]

The *Matlab-ut Talibain* also records certain possessions under the Juibari Shaikhs, e.g. *Imlak Chaharbagh* and shops. We learn that the *Hasil* realized by Khwaja Mushtari amounted to 16,00,000 *tangas* per annum, besides a considerable quantity of grain. The Diwans of Khwaj Mushtari's father once calculated the revenues of the *Khwaja* and found that these were equivalent to those of the whole of Samarqand.[97] The same author boastfully records that once Abdullah sent 300 *tangas* to the *Khwaja*, to which the latter himself added another 1000 *tangas*, and continued to distribute this amount among his people for twenty days.

Abdurrahim Khwaja's annual income form land tax (*Hasilat*) was 10,000 *mans* of grain in addition to 40,000 *khanis* per annum.[98] He is said to have held 800 pieces of cultivable lands, 40 *chaharbagh,* market places, seven fountainheads, *timchas,* two caravansarais, *haramsarais, havelis* and 500 *milk* lands. According to Abul Abbas, the wealth possessed by Khwaja Tajuddin was 3,000 *juftgao* lands in Bukhara, Nasaf, Merv and Qarakul and in cattle: 10,000 sheep, 700 horses, 500 camels, besides birds, etc. Khwaja Mushtari held 2,000 *juftgao* lands and maintained a full *Daftar-i Buyutat.* In the Bukhara region alone he possessed four stacks *(anbars)* of grain at Juibar, Sarvfan, Paimir and Simatan, each consisting of 1,00,000 *mans* of grain.[99] Wheat was stored in several underground wells, each of which contained 1,000 *mans* of grain.[100]

Muqminova's view that these highly placed *Khwajas* often worked as usurers, lending at a high rate of interest, is however not credible, since the usury is not permitted in Islam and since this is not supported by any documents, though she argues that the *Khwajas* collaborated with the rich secretly in the exploitation of peasants and artisans in both rural and urban areas.[101]

It seems that the Shaikh acquired a very high education from other Shaikhs and learned men at different places. Apart from the Koran and *hadis,* they studied jurisprudence and also learnt how to draft *fatwas.* Maulana Lutfullah Naqshbandi completed his training only after studying in Khwaja Kafshar's *Muhalla* in Samarqand, Marghilan and Farghana. Amongst his teachers were Shaikh Husamuddin, Shaikh Muhammad Qazi (with whom he travelled) and, finally, Shaikh Darvesh Naqshbandi (commonly known as Khwajagi Kashani). The latter appointed him as his deputy (*khalifa*) and gave an *Irshad Nama* containing thirteen principles to serve as guidelines for the population of Akhsikat, Pishkant and Tashkent who were particularly instructed to be obedient to the orders of Lutfullah.[102]

It is said that the *Khwajas* regularly[103] received (offerings) from their devotees. The *khalifas* (their agents) also paid a sum to the *Khwaja* at the time of appointment and, even later, shared their *padnashini* (disciple's gifts) with the *Khwaja*. When Lutfullah offered 250 sheep and goats, 200 *tangas,* dishes of gold and a carpet to Khwajagi Kashani on the eve of his own appointment as *khalifa,* Khwajagi Kashani is reported to have remarked 'you are willing to give me all so as to receive more' and, later on appointed him a full-fledged *Pir* in Farghana.[104]

The *Khwajas* were accorded grand receptions which lasted for several days whenever they went to a particular place. Not only did the rulers receive them graciously but the ordinary population of the vicinity also waited upon the *Khwaja* continuously.[105] During the *Khwaja's* visits to tombs, etc. the Khans arranged for the sites to be repaired, distributed charity,[106] organized open kitchens.[107] The *Khwajas* rode on horse-back when the Khan went out on foot to receive them.[108]

Along with their financial strength, these *Khwajas* were also supported by a large following of devotees,[109] such as those who resided in the states of these *Khwajas* at Juibar, Gujduwan and other places. Complete faith in God and the *Khwajas* of Naqshband (*tawakkul bar'aun-i Khudawand o takiya bar taiyid-i khwaja Naqshaband*)[110] was the order of the day. *Nishans* issued to provincial governors frequently asked them to be particularly respectful to the *Khwajas.*[111]

Although the ruling classes, the nobility and the middle and lower ranking officials still seemed to lean on the *Khwajas* to protect their interests, a section of the population of the sixteenth-seventeenth centuries managed to articulate some protest against the power of *Khwajas*. Even the court poet Binai Harwi refers to the moral decay of the religious notables, *Qazi,* judges or *Mufti* who were allegedly only interested in amassing more property, and oppressed and deceived the people. Hilali's view that a 'good infidel is better than a bad Muslim finds' an echo in poems of the seventeenth century poets like Maghrab Namanghani and Fitrat Zarduzi Samarqandi who sharply criticized the religious groups as stumbling blocks.[112] Imperialist travellers were keen to create a wedge between the various nationalities. Nevertheless, the power of the divines remained substantially unaffected. Burnes, who was in Central Asia in 1831 says that the capitation tax (*jaziya*) was levied on Jews and Hindus and the revenues of the country were spent in maintaining *Mullas* and mosques.[113] The same traveller noted that a 'pleasant toleration' was practiced in Central Asia.[114] A similar picture is given by Obruchev and other travellers of a later period.[115]

NOTES

1. A.S. Kent, *The Call of Tartary*, Shanghai, 1919, pp. 7-12, 54.
2. There are instances quoted by the traveller like Bento De Goes and Bailey that in medieval Central Asia, the Bukharan fanatics sometimes harassed and even at times killed all European unbelievers. Bento De Goes, *Early Jesuit Travellers in Central Asia*; Bailey, *Mission to Tashkent*, p. 245.
3. Ahmad Rafiq, *Altinsi asirdar afzilik va Bektasilik*, 1932, pp. 19, 29, 33, 47 ff.; also see C.H. Imber, *The Persecution of the Shiite according to Muhimme defterleri, 1565-1585*, Der Islam, 1979, Ban 56, Heft 2, pp. 244-73; Wasifi, *Badaiul Wakai*, 2 vols., Moscow, 1961, pp. 2-4, 19-41, 72, 376, 1014-25, 1056-70.
4. Wasifi, *Badaiul Waqai*, 2 Vols., Moscow, 1961, pp. 2-4, 19-41, 72, 376, 1014-25, 1056-70.
5. *Habib-us Siyar*.
6. Ahmad Rafiq, p. 29.
7. Snouck Hurgronje, *Selected Works*, p. 29.
8. Ibid.
9. For their account see infra chapter on Urban Classes.
10. There were three important groups of saints called Khwajagan, Jahria and Kubrawiah who associated themselves with the court.
11. *Futuhat-i Khani*, pp. 49-50; *Abdn*, p. 32, *Mehn*, pp. 5-40; *Silsilat*, pp. 110-14; *BN*, p. 206; Eng. tr., p. 329.
12. *BN*, text, p. 206; Eng. tr., p. 329.
13. *Mehn*, pp. 22-30.
14. Ibid., pp. 22-8.
15. Ibid., p. 77.
16. Ibid., pp. 306-8.
17. *Tarikh-i Abulkhair*, pp. 265-6.
18. *Silsilat*, pp. 116-18.
19. *Muzzakkira*, p. 25.
20. *Silsilat*, pp. 117-18; *Muzzakkira*, p. 21.
21. *Abdn*, pp. 32-3; *Silsilat*, pp. 120-1; *Suluk*, pp. 1-9.
22. Wasifi, pp. 362-8.
23. *Silsilat*, pp. 121-3; *Tarikh-i Raqimi*, pp. 134, 145, 240.
24. *Silsilat*, pp. 121-3; Mirza Badi, *Majma-ul Arqam*, Persian text, pp. 87-8.
25. *Silsilat*, pp. 121-3; *Tarikh-i Raqimi*, pp. 24, 134, 145.

26. Ibid., *Abdn*, p. 88.
27. *Tarikh-i Raqimi*, pp. 176-7; *Muzzakkira*, pp. 2-3; *Abdn*, p. 115; *Rauzat*, pp. 70-1; *Soch*. II, part 2, p. 521.
28. Jenkinson, Hakluyt Society Series 456.
29. *Abdn*, pp. 114-15. Khwaja Juibari was a descendant of Khwaja Saduddin Abu Bakr Saad. For a full genealogy of Khwaja Juibari see *Abdn*, pp. 47-8.
30. *Rauzat*, pp. 245, 269.
31. Apart form the Juibari Shaikhs who were called also as Khwajagan, the saints of Jahria and Kubrawiah orders also were very popular.
32. *Abdn*, p. 395; *Rauzat*, p. 316.
33. *Abdn*, p. 60.
34. Ibid., p. 62.
35. Ibid., p. 290.
36. Ibid., p. 430.
37. Ibid., p. 50.
38. Ibid., pp. 328, 357.
39. *Silsilat*, pp. 124-5.
40. Ibid., p. 198.
41. *Abdn*, pp. 317, 367.
42. Ibid., p. 185.
43. The sons of Khwaja Juibari (namely Hasan and Abdur Rahim) have continued to enjoy the position of 'leading holy men of Transoxiana'. Jahangir, Eng. tr., Vol. II, p. 166; *Maasir-ul Umara*, Vol. II, pp. 379-96; Eng. tr., p. 895.
44. *Rauzat*, p. 90.
45. *Munshaat*.
46. *Rauzat*, p. 333.
47. Ibid., pp. 336-7.
48. Ibid., pp. 338-41.
49. *Rauzat*, pp. 253, 286, 290-5, 356, 436, e.g. Khwaja Juibari is said to have constructed eleven bath-houses in various parts of Transoxiana. Ten deep reservoirs made of stone and bricks covered with a net were built for supplying drinking water to the people (*Rauzat*, pp. 294-5).
50. *Abdn*, p. 237.
51. *Siraj-us Salikain*, p. 884.
52. *Matlab*, p. 173.
53. *Rauzat*, p. 442.
54. Ibid., p. 319.
55. *Maasir-ul Umara*, Vol. III, text, pp. 232-8; Eng. tr., pp. 808-9.
56. Ibid., p. 46.
57. *Abdn*, pp. 114-15, 195, 236; *Rauzat*, pp. 274-5, 307, 311-12, 326-8, 332-48.
58. *Rauzat*, pp. 201-11, 274-6, 285, 319-20, 322-36, 342-6, 350-68.
59. *Abdn*, pp. 153, 155.
60. *Rauzat*, pp. 245, 269.
61. Wasifi, p. 370 (Moscow edn.).
62. *Rauzat*, pp. 178-83; *Abdn*, pp. 114-15.
63. See *Abdn*, pp. 214, 235, 298.
64. Ibid., pp. 165, 197, 204, 323, 390-3, 464.
65. *Abdn*, p. 358; Lahori, *Badshahnama*, Vol. I, Calcutta, 1867, pp. 194-5.

66. *Abdn*, p. 88.
67. Ibid., p. 430.
68. *Rauzat*, p. 320.
69. Ibid., pp. 115, 319, 320.
70. *Abdn*, pp. 152, 195, 298, 316, 323.
71. Ibid., pp. 159-65, 166.
72. Ibid., pp. 152, 316, 323.
73. *Siraj-us Salikain*, p. 92; Semenov, *Istoria Shaibanidov*, p. 59.
74. *Rauzat*, pp. 109-13. The view that the 'theory of two powers' existing in medieval Christianity was missing in Islam (*Cambridge History of Islam*, Vol. 2, 1970, p. 531) does not seem to be applicable at least to Central Asia of fifteenth-seventeenth centuries.
75. Ibid., p. 156.
76. *Muzzakkira*, pp. 55, 410.
77. Ibid.
78. Even a Nankash (baker) Darvesh Babai had been described as *Murid-i Khas* of Qutubul Abrar (*Rauzat*, p. 85).
79. *Muzzakkira*, p. 25.
80. The term *Naqshband* denoted the weavers of *kimkhwab* (velvet) and the founder of this *silsilah*. Khwaja Bahauddin had this same profession hence the name. *Ain* III, Eng. tr., p. 399.
81. For a very interesting and detailed account of such events and political role of these saints of the three orders, see Saiyid Zinda Ali Mufti's famous work *Samrat-ul mashaikh,* IOST MS no. 1336, also see A.A. Rizvi, *History of Sufism*, Vol. I, part 1, pp. 92, 248, 289, 296, 299, 320, 350, 394.
82. *Silsilat*, pp. 116-26.
83. Wasifi, pp. 375-9.
84. *Abdn*, pp. 430-1.
85. *Rashhat*, f. 249.
86. *Rauzat*, p. 90.
87. Ibid., p. 447.
88. Ibid., pp. 71-2.
89. *Matlab*, p. 263.
90. *Abdn*, pp. 51-2.
91. Ibid., pp. 312-17, 355-6.
92. Ibid., p. 316.
93. Abdullah Khan's *Nishan* issued in 8 January 1590, refers to all the *imlak* and the excessive wealth of Khwaja Saad conferred and confirmed upon his sons in *darubast* and enjoins all the *mustaufis* of the diwans, arbab *ketkhudas* of the *wilayats* of Bukhara, Qarakul, and charjui to consider (in accordance with the enclosure (*zimn*) *imlak* and *suyurghals* as belonging to the above mentioned *makhdumzadas*. The 'umal and *arbabs* of the said *wilayat* should not demand from the *balda* (town) and *tumans* (districts), the *mal-i muqarrari, ikhrajat, amilat,* and *taklifat* or taxes on any other pretexts (as *bahar ism o rasm* and *az henh mamr*). The amount fixed should be considered as remitted (*marful qalam*). No demands (*hawala wa mataliba*) be made and due regard of the *wakils* and *gumasthas* of the *makhdumzadas* should be binding upon them. They should refrain from paying less provisions. No renewals or new *Nishans* be demanded

annually. The *makhdumzadas* were also instructed to divide the *imlak* in accordance with the *shar,* i.e. two thirds (*sulsan*) for the elder son and one third (*suls*) for the younger out of all *suyurghalat.* The diwans of the *wilayat* were ordered not to allow any change in the royal orders. Similarly another *Nishan* issued by Nur Muhammad Khan of Merv in Rabi II 998/8 February 1590 informs the *amirs, wazirs,* officers, *hukkam, darguhas, arbabs* and *kalantars, riaya* inhabitants that out of gratitude for bestowal of 'rulership upon himself by God, he (Nur Muhammad) expressed his regard for the great *taefa* (group) and that the entire *imlak,* property, establishments and cultivations of Khwaja Kalan Saad in the *balda* of Chacha, now belongs to Hasan Khwaja. All the *amirs, wazirs, ummal, mubashir* and others should consider these as exempted from all *taklif-i diwani* and *hashr band-i sultani.* The orders should not be violated and no deviation, delay, change in the rules be allowed to occur and every year no renewal order be demanded (*Rauzat,* pp. 477-9, 480-4).

94. *Rauzat,* p. 355.
95. Ibid., pp. 305, 355-6.
96. *Documenti k istorii agrarnikh atnashenya va Bukharaskom Khanstave,* Tashkent, 1954, pp. 3-12.
97. *Matlab-ut Talibain,* MS Oriental Institute Library, Tashkent, no. 60, ff 170-5.
98. *Matlab,* pp. 531-2, Lahori (*Badshahnama,* Vol. I, Calcutta, 1867, p. 79) says that 4 crores of *khanis* were equivalent to 100 crores of Indian rupees and 3 lakhs 33 thousands of Iraqi *tumans.*
99. *Muzzakkira,* pp. 84, 174-8, 283-4; Wasifi, p. 379.
100. *Matlab,* pp. 104, 486.
101. *Istorya remeslai,* pp. 39-40.
102. *Siraj-us Salikain,* pp. 82-8.
103. The system seems to have continued till the nineteenth century as Joshua Kunitz refers to this custom (*The Dawn over Samarqand,* p. 269).
104. *Siraj-us Salikain,* pp. 82-7.
105. *Rauzat,* p. 171; *Abdn,* p. 198.
106. *Abdn,* pp. 197-8, 234, 238, 257, 276, 317-18, 367, 454.
107. Ibid., pp. 230, 234, 238, 268, 317-18, 454.
108. *Abdn,* p. 268.
109. *Matlab,* pp. 104, 486.
110. *Abdn,* p. 335.
111. Ibid., p. 373.
112. Jan Rypka, *History of Persian Literature,* pp. 496, 499-502, 506-7.
113. Burnes, pp. 292-3.
114. Ibid., p. 285.
115. Not only Obruchev but also Bailey (1918-19) says that both Hindus and Jews were forbidden to wear *sash.* No Jew or Hindu could carry arms. Jews were not allowed to ride or drive in the streets of a town (Bailey, *Mission to Tashkent,* London, 1946, pp. 242-4.

Military Organization Under Chingiz Khan

During the middle ages, war was developed as an art since it was considered to be one source of worldly glory and a precursor of heavenly blessings. Under the cover of holy wars, imperialist ambitions were fulfilled and chivalrous impulses were satiated. Concern for the tax payers' safety often provided a fair justification for maintenance of a large army and also for defensive fighting whereas the offensive onslaught was often impelled by an urge for immense booty. In such areas where booty formed the main source of surplus revenue as in Central Asia, the military ventures acquired an added importance. External inroads were a regular feature supplementing economy. The army was therefore, an important instrument for acquiring wealth and grandeur and thus had to be and was invariably well maintained. Ambitious sovereigns like Chingiz, Timur and others whose age was fraught with battles recognized the army's significance only too well.

Indeed the Mongols had rightly claimed that 'they had no country; their homes were their horse's back' a dictum which the descendants of the Mongols followed even in the sixteenth century. Timur dreamt 'reduction of kingdoms' obtainment of Empire, defeating armies, circumventing enemies, maming friends of foes' believed that 'the dignity of Empire is supported by extensive territories, by a rich treasury and by numerous armies', because 'there was naught more worthy the valour of princes than conquering of kingdoms and empires, waging holy wars with infidels'.[1] The Uzbegs also strove to follow the traditions of their medieval predecessor. The Uzbeg ruler, Shaibani Khan declared 'the saddle of his horse to be his capital'.[2] Abdullah Khan also considered 'excellent generalship to be the prop of magnificence and one of the two emblems of the greatness of a ruler', and even reminded the *Mardikars* that 'our livelihood lies beneath the shadow of our lances'.

In medieval Central Asia, therefore, the required accomplishment in the war game, necessitated continuous effort for improving tactics and strategic methods in order to surpass the rivals. The emphasis on the compilation of treatises and exclusive works on the art of warfare with detailed description of weapons as well as generous patronage extended to the armourers workshop and acquisition of imported techniques, arms and ammunitions by the kings (and sometimes by the higher (nobles) shows how keenly the need for advancement of this art was felt all over the world. A number of treatises were written on the art of war in various corners of Islamic world. Apart from works like *Nihayatal sul wal ummiyya fi tahim a Malal Furusiya* (complete instructions in the practice of the military art) compiled in Damascus in the early part of fourteenth century by Isa Ibn-i Ismail Al Hanafi, there were a number of other exclusive productions on the firearms, naphtha and incendiary warfare. Ibn-i Sabir Al Manjaniqi is also said to have 'left an unfinished book which treats the art of warfare in all its details'.[3] In Transoxiana, Razi's Encyclopaedic work *Jamiul Ulum* comprised one full section on firearms. Although *Adabul Harb wa Shujaat* was compiled by Fakhri Mudabbir—(a Central Asian by birth) and dedicated to an Indian ruler Iltutmish, its contents give a fairly comprehensive description of Turco-Mongol weaponery, art and method of warfare. Continuous exchange of ideas and technology in the sphere of warfare and new creations in the armourer's workshop (*Zarrad Khana*) further confirm the inclination of the elite towards this medieval adventurous engagement. In India several works were prepared on the art of warfare during the reign of Akbar in whose court also a galaxy of such artisans flourished.

As a hardy mountainous people, the Turks were renowned for being 'men of sword' and excelled in martial skill. In his *Manaqib-ul Atrak* (Superior Qualities of the Turks), Jahiz (d. 869) had given a correct assessment of the superiority of Turks in military affairs. In his view 'the Sassanid Persians excelled all the nations in the art of governing states, as the Chinese did in handicrafts, the Greeks in science and the Turks in the art of war'.[4]

Masudi also describes how the new Turkish division raised by Caliph al Mutasum from amongst his slaves in Farghana and other regions of Central Asia 'became the terror of the whole capital'.[5] With the advent of the Mongols and the worldwide conquest of Chingiz Khan, the emphasis on formation and excellence of army was natural. To the valour and courage of these Turks was added the adventurous spirit and steadfast gallantry of Mongols whose combination resulted in an army which proved to be a marvel in the East and West alike.

Even before the arrival of the Mongols, the army of Samarqand was 'celebrated and famous for its organization'. Yuan Chwang had described it as 'splendid army' since most of its soldiers were Chei-Kre who were 'men of ardent valour, who looked on death as a going back to their kindered and against whom no foe could stand in combat'.[6] Both Juvaini and Wassaf had praised the army of Turks/Tartars and the Mongols. Chingiz too always assured his comrades that 'as a merchant trusts in his stuff for profit, the Mongol puts his only hope of fortune in his bravery'.[7]

For the Mongols chivalry, adventure and resolute gallantry were real expressions of glory. The author of *Secret History* asserts[8] that for the Mongols 'it was good to be dead with his quiver and his bow in one place with his bones', i.e. to die fighting bravely in the battlefield. To this spirit of dedicated and courageous hardihood and fortitude was added Chingiz's personal valour, ability in the art of physiognomy, administrative genius and resoluteness. The seven clauses relating to military organization and administrative reforms (see nos 9, 17, 18, 22, 24, 27) amply confirm the point. The Turco-Mongol army, therefore, was carefully planned and ably organized. Like a shrewd general and a capable administrator, Chingiz had planned that a regular inflow of money through booty should be ensured. War was going to form a regular feature of his activities and improvement in the organization and functioning of army was, therefore, essential. Undoubtedly, Chingiz had studied thoroughly the evils which had crept into the military system and had to be particularly careful not to allow these characteristics to recur and infect the army created by him.

Juvaini had very carefully pointed out these evils and had summed up the situation prevailing in the army in pre-Mongolian era in the following words:

Whenever these kings prepare to attack an enemy or are themselves attacked by an enemy, months and years are required to equip an army and it takes a brimful treasury to meet the expense of salaries and allotment of land. When they draw their pay and allowances, the soldiers' numbers increase by hundreds and thousands but on the day of combat their ranks are everywhere vague and uncertain and none presents himself on the battlefield. A shepherd was once called upon to render an account of his

> office. Said the accountant 'How many sheep remain?' 'where?' asked the shepherd 'in the register'. 'That' replied the shepherded 'is why I asked: there are none in the flock'. This is a parable to be applied to their armies; wherein each commander, in order to increase the appropriation for his men's pay, declares 'I have so and so many men' and at the time of inspection they impersonate one another in order to make up their full strength.[9]

Since in Central Asia, the army played a pivotal role in strengthening king's position, adding to his glory and stood by him in thick and thin, its importance could often threaten the authority of the Sultan. Each king in his own way tried to please and assuage the military as no parallel or counterpoise to their power could ever be created. There were kings like Arslan II the successor of Atsiz (the founder of the Khwarazmian dynasty) whose enthronement after the cruelty of fratricide on 22 August 1156 was 'inaugurated by increasing the pay and territorial grants of the army.[10] Such was the intensity of the power of Qarluq division that in its struggle against the Khans the Qarluqs managed to kill Tamghach Khan Ibrahim, ruler of Samarqand and threw his body on the Steppes.[11] The revolt of the army for non payment of salaries or arrears was not an uncommon feature. In pre-Mongol Central Asia, the conflict between the throne and the military class was customary. One such rebellion which shook the Empire of Saljuqids led to the subjugation of Transoxiana (including Bukhara) in 1142 after the overthrow of Saljuqids.

Chingiz, therefore, wanted to create an army which was subservient to him—entirely appointed, maintained and sustained by him. Disobedience, impersonation, greediness and rebellious tendencies were firmly controlled through direct personal supervision of each and every detail pertaining to military. To ensure efficiency and promptitude Chingiz had 'promoted Touloui to the command and organization of troops and the equipment of armies'[12] (Juvaini, text 29; tr. 40). Unlike the 'migratory mass' of Huns, Chingiz's army was more disciplined and well equipped. Chingiz Khan was deified by his country men as well as by his army as a hero who raised a backward nation to the highest pinnacle of glory hence he was called as *Ssuto Bogdo*. As early as 1206, the title 'Chingiz' had been bestowed upon Temuchin by the highly respected Teb Tengri Kokchu Shaman which confirms people's faith in Chingiz's gallantry as the title Chingiz (which is the plural of Chin which means strong and hard like iron steel.[13] This personal image of Chingiz Khan considerably added to his army's adoration for their leader which went a long way in ensuring his army's sense of dedication, self sacrifice, unquestioning loyalty and service. Chroniclers and travellers from the thirteenth to the seventeenth centuries have lavished high praises on the Central Asian armies for their chivalry, sense of service, steadfastness, perseverance and faithfulness.[14]

Juvaini records:

with regard to the organization of these army from Adam down to the present day, when the greater part of the Climes are at the disposition and command of the seed of Chingiz Khan, it can be read in no history and is recorded in no book that any of the kings that were lords of the nations ever attainted an army like the army of the Tartars, so patient of hardship, so grateful for comforts, so obedient to its commanders both in prosperity and adversity; and this not in the hope of wages and fiefs nor in expectation of income or promotion. . . . What army in the whole world can equal the Mongol army? In time of action, when attacking and assaulting they are like trained wild beasts out after game and in the days of peace and security, they are like sheep, yielding milk and wool and many other useful things. In misfortune and adversity, they are free from dissension and opposition. It is an army after the fashion of a peasantry, being liable to all manner of contributions (*Muan*) and rendering without complaint, whatever is enjoined upon it, whether *Qupchur*, occasional taxes (*Avarizat*), the maintenance (Ikhrajat) of travellers or the upkeep of post-stations (*Yam*). With the provision of mounts (*Ulagh*) and food (*Ulufat*), therefore, it is also a peasantry in the guise of an army, all of them great and small, noble and base, in time of battle becoming swordsmen, archers and lancers and advancing in whatever manner, the occasion requires.[15]

Similarly Mir Khond adds that these soldiers were like ants or locsts:

gallant and capable of measuring the vistas from ground upto the sky. In wars they were jubilant and in pleasure assemblies morose. With their unquestioning obedience and loyalty, they were keen to sacrifice themselves for the pleasure of the ruler. They preferred arrows than robes of brocade; sword and lances were more dear to them than valuables, gold, silver and precious stones. During wars, they were more patient and powerful than others, were negligent of comforts and ease and defeat was an experience unknown to them. They used to manufacture their own arms, weave their own clothes, and never needed anything from outside during the march. They had their sheep, cow and camels with them and could live on *Qurut* and *Dogh* (dishes prepared from almost soured milk) continuously. Their quadrupeds are also expert in digging the ground with their hoofs and finding the roots to eat and subsist—never needing any hay or barley. Although they knelt down at dawn and dusk, they were not bound by the concept of unlawful or lawful food. They eat the meat of dog, pig, cock and could even drink blood to satiate their hunger by opening the veins of their quadrupeds. If they reach a big river while marching, they do not look or wait for boats. They tailor the skin of the animals together in order to preserve the valuables and eatables and tie it with the tail of a horse. They themselves hold the mane of the horse and plunge into river safely crossing it to reach in time for the war.[16]

The words of Eastern chroniclers find an echo in the comments of Western travellers and observers. Similarly the Mongols had been highly praised by Spalato for their personal valour and advanced knowledge of method of warfare.[17] Emperor Fredrick II's letter to England also shows his fear and awe of the 'high strung, valiant and daring' Mongol soldiers who were always ready to throw themselves into peril at the slightest sign from their commander.[18]

Carpini asserts that 'no single kingdom of province can resist the Tartars' and that the 'Tartars fight more by strategem then by sheer force'.

Carpini's description of Mongol weapons and his suggestions to European soldiery to improve their arms confirms that the Mongol weapons were also dreaded everywhere.[19]

The organization of the army was planned by the medieval rulers of Transoxiana mainly on the basis of the time honoured decimal system. It should, however, be borne in mind that the decimal system being most manageable, found its way into all the nomadic states with slight variations. Incidentally the military ranks, gradations and decimal divisions are also traced in the Arabic *Irafa*[20] system and in the Mongol,[21] Uigher and Turkic[22] military system. In ancient India also traces of decimal system are noticed and Kautilya[23] too refers to these units.

Similarly, the militia was not an innovation of Chingiz Khan. He had only reinforced an age old decimal and militia system more vigorously and with an iron discipline which was carried still further by Timur. The Turkish and Arab military terms seem to have been replaced by Turco-Mongol nomenclature and terminology. Thus the usual Turkish terms of *Sari Khail, Sipahsalar, Malik, Amir*, etc., and the Arab and Perso Islamic terms like *Pai* (ten) and *Paitsitou* (ten thousand) were replaced purely by the Turco-Mongol terms; thus the detachment of *Dehhazar* or ten thousand was called *Tuman* and its chief as *Tuman Begi* or *Tuman Bashi*. Similarly the *Hazaras* or detachment of thousands were called *Ming* and its chief was called

Ming Bashi (*Mir-i-Hazara*). The centurion or a hundred or *Sadah* was called *Yuz* and its chief as *Yuz Bashi* or *Yuz Begi*. The *Deh* or ten was the *Un* or *Unter* and its chief as *Un Bashi*. The *Rauzat-us Safa* mentions the lowest rank as *Panja* (five), though all the other sources (thirteenth-seventeenth centuries) speak of the ranks ranging from ten to ten thousand only—a system borrowed by the Timurids.

As was customary, there were five Tabias (divisions) namely *Qaul*, *Qalb*, *Jinah*, Baranghar, Jaranghar centre right or left rear and avant-garde Mir Khond says that these five tabias were 'united together like five fingers in one hand and their different detachments served like a protective and defensive bulwork'.[24] The ambuscade was not an essential part of Chingiz's army and its presence was need based and not a regular feature. There were *Ghacharchians* also.

Presumably the princes of the right, left and middle wings were fixed by Chingiz Khan. In the account of 1228, the *Secret History* refers to Chaghatai and Batu as the head of the right wing, Odeigin Noyon, Yesu and Yesunge at the head of left and the prince of the middle being headed by Tolui.[25] It seems that the division of the army's right and left wing was done on a permanent basis. This custom of permanence in military division is traced back to the time of Oghuz—the ancestor of Turco-Mongols. As the legend goes (or has it) the six sons of Oghuz namely Guyuk (sky), Gun (sun), Dagh (mountain), Denghiz (sea), Yilduz (star), Oiy (moon) once went on a hunting spree and found only three sets of golden bows and arrows. Unable to divide it among themselves, they brought it to father Oghuz whose discretion was as follows: the elder sons were given the bows, the title of *Buduq* (lit. piecing) and the command of right wing of the army and their *Urugh* whereas the three younger sons were the recipients of three arrows, title of *Ujuq* (or *Uojuq*, i.e. three arrows) and the command of the left wing. This allocation was hereditary. It was also made clear that since the right hand was higher in status as bows were an insignia of royalty (*ba masabat-i badshahi*) the privilege of the crown, throne and the succession. The right wing is said to have included: Jalair, Qiyat Barlas, Ormankqit, Suniyat, Barin. Despite his professed (feigned) ignorance, Rashiduddin also supplies some meagre and scattered information about the *Tabias* (centre, right and left). The divisions existing in the forces inherited by Touloui the youngest son of Chingiz Khan. The eight *Sadah* (*Yuz*) or centurious of Chingiz's army received by Touloui were said to have hailed from Soniyal, Durman, Jalair, Karait, Merkit, Tatar Qiyachi.

The centre, left and right wings of Chingiz's army inherited by Touloui alone included hundred thousand soldiers out of whom only thirty eight thousand belonged to the right wing which was led by three *Muqaddams* namely Borchi Noyon, Sungar Subdei and Borghul Noyon.[26]

Thus the three elder sons of Oghuz (namely Gun, Oiy, Yilduz) held the reins of the right wing. Each of these three had four sons (namely Qai, Bayat, Yavuz, Dukar, Aoshar, Qariq, Alqarawali, Qarawali, Dudurgha, Yayerli, Bekdili, Qarqin) who were also included as the warriors of right wing. The left wing was entrusted to the command of three younger sons (namely: Guyuk, Taq Khan or Dagh Khan and Dingiz) with their four sons each (namely Bayandar, Biejna, Sutur, Aimur, Bekdir, Bukdur, Jawuldur, Chibni, Alayuntali, Urghuz, Biwa, Qutiq.)[27]

There is some discrepancy in the list of the tribes included in various sources though most of them are unanimous in recording that the tribal personnel in the *Hazaras* of the centre, right and left wings were determined on permanent basis. The list of the tribal divisions found in *Muizzul Ansab* places the following tribes in the left wing: Chuman, Qunghrat, Urmankiqat, Mashub, Jalair, Ahtai; Mama, Sun.

Rashiduddin Fazlullah says that the army of Juji was divided between his sons, one half (*Yak Nima*) falling to Orda and another to Batu who along with his own army and that of his four brothers (namely Dur, Tuqa Timur, Shink Qur and Shank Kum) formed the left wing of the army. They were called as princess of the left wing (*shahzadagan-i dastichap*)[28].

It is interesting to note that the rank stated did not always signify the actual number or numerical strength of the detachment, e.g. the *Hazaras* of Qirat comprised four thousand and the *Hazaras* of Barin led by Qurchi Noyon was a conglomeration of ten thousand diverse elements and was therefore known as *Tuman*.[30]

The *Secret History* refers to the three Toyuraud, five Taryud with the cook, Onggir (son of Mongetu Kiyan) with the Cangsiud and the Bayand forming one *Gureen* for him.[31] The number, too was nominal in many instances, since there were two *Hazaras* of 10,000 men each, and several others of a higher number than a thousand. The Baranghar contained 30,000 men in 22 *Hazaras*. Out of these, there was one of Qirat Mughals 4,000; one of Barin Mughals 2,000; another of Ungkut Turks 4,000; and one of various Kalat tribes

10,000. The Nu Yin Burji or Burjin of Arlat tribe was its head. The Jaranghar comprised 25 *Hazaras*, among which was the Urut Gazarah, 4,000 men; the Angiras Qunghrats 3,000; the Qunghrats, 5,000; the Barins, 3,000; and another of Qunghrat, of 4,000. Besides, the other Mughal *Hazaras*, there was one *Hazara* of Karakhitais of 10,000 men, and another called the Khurjah *Hazara* of 10,000 men. Its head was Nuiyan Mukali the Jalair surnamed the Ko-yang (Chinese the Great Khan).[32]

Earlier the Mongols and the Keraits were divided into detachments on the basis of clans with its chief as the commander. The same style was adopted by Chingiz, it was only the Keshikten or the Battallion of bodyguards which was picked and chosen from different clans. Thus a tribe is said to have comprised an *Ulus Tuman* (10,000), a large clan represented by thousand and smaller ones by hundred.[33]

Chingiz maintained his own trustworthy and efficient personal guards for his movable headquarters and a chosen corps of selected soldiers. Chingiz had his own personal liaison with each guard, settled their suits personally.[34] The Keshikten were given certain special privileges and distinctions. In the army of Chingiz, centre was headed by Naya, left wing by Mukali and right wing by Baglurchi.

The *Secret History* refers to two categories of the military aristocracy namely *Hula'an* (lit. Red coats, i.e. the high grade) and *Degelen Chungen* (blackheads, i.e. the commoners).[35] It seems that like the Turkish and Ottoman soldiers, Chingiz's military personnel could rise to the highest post (irrespective of his birth or descent) by sheer dint of merit. Burghuchin Noyon of Arlat tribe was only *Amir-i Kuzik* from where he rose to the rank of *Amir-i Tuman* and then held the charge of the right wing.[36]

The military aristocracy could enjoy its ranks continuously generations after generations though not on the basis of hereditary claims but as a privilege accruing to the family through personal valour and merit of its descendants, e.g. Jaddi Noyon and his grandson Monkqumai and Amir Bulghanshah Noyon; Borghul Noyon, Hashim and his son Jubur Kur Qubilai. Several members of one family often joined Chingiz's army simultaneously in various capacities due to their personal valour. Thus Taichu Gurgan was the *Myriarch* of *Hazara* of Oriyankqat, his father looked after Kasulan and his younger brother Yasu Buqai was himself a Qurchi and an *Amir* of the *Hazara* of Qurchis.[37] Marco Polo confirms that those who distinguished themselves in acts of bravery were generously rewarded whereas the cowards were punished. Rashiduddin and other chroniclers refer to twelve (or thirteen) Korans. A council of twelve barons is said to have been appointed by Kubilai Khan for dealing with the affairs of the army and a committee of twelve was also appointed for supervision of administration and general welfare of the Empire.[38]

The appointments of captains of *Pai* (ten) to *Paitsitou* (ten thousand) was done by Chingiz Khan personally during his own pleasure and discretion. The sources confirm that Chingiz Khan had his own criterion for appointing his generals. The *Secret History* categorically quotes Chingiz Khan's verdict 'for those who are gone with me together, setting up a nation, I shall be making bands of thousands and appointing captains of thousands—speak words of favour'.[39] The same source describes at length[40] allocation of privileges proportionate to their services. The chiefs selected by Chingiz Khan were personally known to him. They were reliable and usually the kinsmen of the known warriors under him. This policy is said to have 'preserved the clan constitution from decomposition' giving it a 'regular (if rudimentary) military skeleton'. In certain cases, however, this privilege was delegated. Qutuqu Begi, the chief of *Hazara* of Qirat tribe in the right wing was entitled to appoint the *Hazara Amirs* in his own detachment—a privilege later on enjoyed by his two sons namely Anda and Quda.[41] The Qarakhatai *Tuman Bashi* (*daishi* or *taishi*) was allowed to appoint his own *Amirs* of the army.

Chingiz, therefore, distributed the rank of thousands to those who 'worked' with him in 'the making of the Khanate and appointing Noyons to command the thousands'.[42] Chingiz had never forsaken his old friends. Borghul Noyon of Hoshin tribe rose from the humble position of *Borchi* (*Bawarchi*) and *Bakawul* to the post of highest officer in the right wing and thereafter became an *Amir-i Tuman*.[43] The status of *Gurgan* was also bestowed upon him through his marriage with the niece of Hulaku. Notwithstanding such favours, these high officials were 'bound by their service to the Khan and by military discipline'.

The norms for allotment of posts and ranks were prescribed. If the sons of military aristocrats and of ordinary persons (*Ming Bashis* to *Yuz Begis*) were to be considered for appointment to such posts, their 'ability' and 'good physical appearance' was to be a prerequisite.[44] They were to be 'apparently apt for serving' in Chingiz's presence. Another precondition was that the sons of *Ming Bashis* (commander of thousands) were to bring with them a younger brother in addition to his ten companions. The sons of *Yuz Begis* (commanders of 100) if recruited were to bring with them five companions and a younger brother. In case of sons of *Un Begis* (commanders of ten) and ordinary folks, the recruited one had to come with three companions and a younger brother. The horses were also to be made available. The part and portion of goods, men and geldings which came to them by way of inheritance or acquired by them through personal efforts were to levy men and horses accordingly to their immediate superiors. Any transgression was to be punished. If those employed in Chingiz's service avoided their turn, shirking from service or were not 'fit', looked upon the job as too difficult', they were to be 'warned consecutively by giving three seven and thirty seven lashes', If still they persist, they were to be exiled to a distant place out of sight and replaced. The captains of thousands were those 'who had set up the nation with him and who had suffered with him. The rank of ten thousands and thousands was given to those who deserved 'and whom it seemed to be fit that they be given favour', to be favoured.[45] Chingiz had following generals namely: Jelme, Jebei, Subdei, Boghurchi, Sorghunshira, Borokuta and Muqali who were called *Orloks* (eagles) as they distinguished themselves in boldness and loyalty.[46] Four generals of Chingiz Khan namely Boorcu, Muqali, Boroyul and Citaun were declared to be the *Kuluud* (a plural of *Kulud* by adding ud means heroes).[47] Since Boorcu and Muqali had made Chingiz Khan 'to attain unto his throne, both were favored to (sit on seats overall and not to be punished until nine transgressions. While Boorcu was to govern the ten thousand of those of the right hand of Altai people, Muqali was to govern the ten thousand of those of the left hand of the inhabitants of mountain front of Qaraun Jidun. Additionally, Muqali was given the privilege of sitting on a higher seat on a hereditary basis (unto the seed of the seed). And the title of Gui Ong (prince of the Realm)'.[48] Chingiz once commented that if on the day of a battle these four *Kuluud* were at his side, and the two generals Jurcedei and Quyildar stood in front of him with their *Uru'ud* and *Mangyud*, Chingiz was 'at ease as to all thoughts' and had no more worries.[49]

The generals were chosen from amongst those whose individual characteristics were personally known to the Emperor whose extraordinary skill in physiognomy is highly appreciated by chronicles After numbering his numbers' and dividing the army into *Ming* (thousands), Chingiz appointed captains of thousands, captains of hundreds and captains of ten. In addition to these, six stewards (namely Dodai Cerbi, Doqalqui Cerbi, Tolun Cerbi, Thin Cerbi, Bucaran Cerbi and Sojiketu Cerbi) were appointed. Out of his ninety five thousand soldiers ten thousand guards were selected as 'private servants who watched Chingiz's golden life'.[50] The decree of the guards as recorded in *Secret History*[51] shows that Chingiz selected and enrolled eighty nightguards and seventy day guards headed by Ogeli Cerbi. The night guards were replaced by the dayguards. These guards were to stand at the door *Aishik Aqasi Bashi Qishikten Aishik Aqasi* against and to be round the tents by shifts usually of three days and three nights. In appointments preference was given to those who 'had ability and whose body and appearance were good' though the selection was made both from the circle of relatives of (sons and brothers of) rank holding captains and those 'commoners' outside the government circle. It was to be ensured that the selected ones were 'apparently apt for serving in' Khan's presence. The sons of the thousands of selected, had to furnish ten men and a younger brother, with son of a *Yuz Bashi* had to bring five companions and younger brother. The sons or younger brother of Daha were to bring with them only three companions, a horse to ride on and a horse to side on. Although the translation of the passage is rather confusing it seems that the levy of men could be arranged through the thousands and hundred. Imperial guards were made superior to all the outward guards of thousand to him by a decree.[52] They were forbidden to equate themselves or quarrel with the imperial guards. The night guards, quiver bearers, day guards, cooks sit at the *Kirue* (place where one assembles the horses) until Chingiz had finished his meal. The quiver bearers were to depart earlier than the night guards. The changing guards of day and night of the company of relief were to remit their tablets and then come in. They were to check the person, gelding, saddle and bird of any one walking between or coming to them.[53] If a messenger comes with an urgent message for Chingiz Khan, he was to convey it to night guards. There were *Cherig* (irregular forces) also.[54]

In 1203, office of six ranks of Cerbi was also introduced to look after the supplies.[55] Earlier there were merely eighty nightguards and seventy dayguards of Chingiz Khan. Their number was first raised to eight hundred and twenty thousands after Chingiz Khan's ascendancy.[56] Chingiz Khan expected his successors to consider the night bodyguards (*Kebtent*) as 'good genii' through whom he had attained 'supreme rank'. Yeke Neurin was the captain of the nightguards commanding a thousand.[57] Juji (Joci) being the oldest of Chingiz's sons enjoyed respect and was to be at the head of his *Geniges* and be a captain of ten thousand under Juji.[58] Customarily, the prisoners of war (particularly the brave ones) were given the option to join Chingiz's army. The practice of lodging these prisoners of war in the tents of private persons in rotation was common among the Mongols.[59]

There were four hundred chosen quiverbearers headed by a captain Yesun Te'e, son of Jelme. In this task he was to take counsel with Bugidai, son of Tuge. There were diverse companies of quiverbearers who were to be headed by Bugidai, Horquday and Lablaga.[60] There were eight thousand day guards, one thousand each selected from amongst the family of Boorcu (headed by Ogele Cerbi), Muqali (headed by Buqa), Ilugei (head Alcidai), Jur Cedier (Canai), Alci (Aqutai). In addition to the *Mings* headed by Dodai Cerbi, Doqalqn, Araqi Qasar. These were to stand in front of the army on the day of battle and be *ba'atud*. Another two thousand with nightguards and quiver bearers increased the number to ten thousand. The ten thousand guards who remained in the presence of Chingiz Khan were to become the great middle of army.[61] Ogedei had confirmed the same rules and regulations for the day and nightguards as prescribed by his father.[62]

Being aware of the need for the organization of Steppe aristocracy and disciplining of 'disorderly militia' Chingiz Khan recruited *Keshikten* (guard corps) from young agile and well-shaped men selected from the *Noyons, Yuz Begis* and *Ming Bashis* and *Tarkat* (free man) for serving as Khan's personal guards as well as military elite. This detachment of chosen braves called *Bagaturs* (heroes) of *Ming* (thousand) was placed in the front during war times while they mounted guard during peacetimes.[63]

Chingiz Khan's diplomacy required that the tribal structure should not be disturbed. The old tribal groups were retained perhaps to ensure discipline and loyalty of the mass of military. The safety valve to their undue pressure was provided by one practical step that their leader was to be nominated by Chingiz himself. Those segments of non Turco-Mongol detachments which were subjugated by Chingiz through conquests or those who voluntarily surrendered (*il shudah*) were given some extra privilege of having some freedom in the management and appointment of subordinate chiefs, e.g. the Qarakhitai detachment led by Adiyar Daishi comprised several thousands soldiers, ten thousand since the term *Daishi* signifies *Amiri tuman*) and its chiefs and *Hazara Amirs* were trustworthy high class *Amirs* (*umarai buzurg*) of Chingiz Khan.[64]

The Turco-Mongol elements in the army structure had their own separate places attached to their own tribes. The incident of the husband of Chingiz's wife's sister who had stealthily entered the court of Chingiz Khan and could easily be discovered through a curious method (of asking the audience present therein the court to stand together with their own tribesmen to isolate the intruder) confirms that tribal arrangement continued to exist and detachments were also tribally divided. The *Hazara* of Oirat which consisted of four thousand men was bestowed upon their Amir Qutuqu Begi and later on inherited by his two sons namely Anda and Quda. Qutuqi Begi was entitled to chose his own *Amirs* of *Hazaras*. The ten thousand strong group '*Tuman* of Barin' was led by Qurchi Noyon and was perhaps a conglomeration of many diverse elements. Its left wing was led by a *Muqaddam*, Muqali Kyyank, and its *Sunkusun* was Naya Noyan. The left wing of Barin tribe comprised 60,000 men. Muqali had been given the rank of *Gui Ong* (prince of the Realm) in Ziqada 614[65] and was also assigned the entire army of Lalaurs which according to the review report consisted of 3,000 men. In the ancient times, Barin tribe happened to be a powerful entity as most of the soldiers in those days hailed from this tribe. Later on, these off shoots from Barin tribe assimilated with others. The *Hazara* of Ongut comprising four thousand soldiers was led by Aibuqa, Alaqush Tegin and Sankui . The Qiyat tribe at that time consisted of ten thousand soldiers and was led by Kui Noyon and Mokbu Qatan. Most of the later Qiyat traced their lineage from them as they were the subjects of Tuqta in the twelfth century.

Although no specific reason had been mentioned in the sources for assignment of higher ranks to certain tribes, it seems that a few of such tribes superseded others in monopolizing higher ranks. Thus there were ten *Myriarchs* each in the right from the Barin and Qiyat tribe; four each from Ongut, Qirat, three each from Jalair and Qunkqotan; two each from Sulduz, Alqunt and two in the Khass from Tankqut; and one each from Arlat, Hoshin, Oryankqat, Durban, Tartar. Similarly the *Amir-i-Sadah* or *Yuz Begi* of the right had one each from Soniyat, Durban, Jalair, Kerait Merkit and Tartar. Amongst the *Myriarchs* of left, seven chiefs are mentioned from Tankqut and three from Oryankqat.[66]

The art of warfare and battle tactics had further received an impetus with the arrival of the Mongols on the Central Asian arena. Although in Central Asia, many remnants of earlier military system continued to linger on particularly those of Abbasids and the Ghaznavids which was bequeathed as a legacy by the Turco-Mongols, Chingiz's knowledge about the tactics and stratagem of warfare was further increased during his campaigns in various corners of the world.

Chingiz's army was heterogeneous in composition, comprising numerically less Mongols and more Turks who joined him on his way to Turan. There were mountainous warriors of Caucasus, the Cherkesses, the Lesginen and the Alauns later on joined by the semi-nomads of the plains. The ever ready warlike Turkish population wandering between Mongolia and Central Asia came forward to join Chingiz Khan swelling his rank and serving as guides, soldiers or spies in accordance with the requirements. For example in 615 Arslan Khan came with his tribes from Qunaliq, Aidiqut and Uighurs of Besh Baligh, Sighnaq and Tengiz joined him.[67] The Turks had considerably influenced the Mongolian pattern of warfare. The bulk of Chingiz's army comprised primarily the two clans of Uruts and Mankquts perhaps because they were adept in retaining their position and arrayed in the most difficult situation in a disturbing melee. From their earliest childhood, they learnt and mastered the use of spears and swords. Their banners were usually coloured or black. Yaqubovski is of the view that basically the army of Chingiz Khan was nomadic and settled people had a very nominal role to play.

There are references to the formation of a new army known as *Tamma* (or Tammachi or Tangmachi Chung).[68] The scholars had variously interpreted the term.[69] Some have considered it to be identical with *Qaraunahs* while others have confused it with 'tribal' militia.[70] Presumably, they were different from *Qaraunahs* and the *Jetas*, the two splinter groups which emerged after the break up of Chaghatai horde. It should be noted here that the word *Tamma* should not be confused with the *Altoma* grants of the Muslim land grant system. *Secret History*[71] specifically refers to this particular word explaining that the post was organized in compliance with Ogedei's decree. The *Tammachis* were 'to make one to bring unto us (Ogedei) in each year yellow gold, naqud, brocades, damasks having all three yellow gold, little big pearls, tipuchaq (tobi chaud—western horses) of long neck and high leg; *guring eloud, da usi kicidud* (mules of burden and mules to ride upon camels and so on'. Elsewhere the *Secret History* records about the appointment of *Darughchian* and *Tammachis* in diverse quarters and in each city.[72] The section dedicated to the army by Rashiduddin does not include any reference to the *Tamma*. In the account of the tribe of Suniyat, however, he records that Chormaghun, the *Qurchi* of Chingiz, had been sent towards Jaunpur (then conquered by Subedei and Jebe) alongwith the *Tamma* army comprising four *Tumans*. A detailed description of this *Tamma* army and a short definition of the term available in the same continuation is being reproduced here.

'The *lashkar-i tamma,* was the one which is distinguished as peculiar and special corps having supremacy over other armies (*bar lashkarha takhsis karda*) by selecting experts from amongst *Myriarchs* (*Hazara*) and *Sadah* (centurions). This army is sent to the *Wilayats* (provinces) to settle down there. Some of the elite *Amirs* (*Umara-i Buzurg*) of *Hazara* and *Tuman* accompany them though they all belong to different stocks.'

The *Amirs* who were included in this particular detachment hailed from the tribes (*Qaum*) of Yesut, Qurlas, Uighir, Qarluq, Turcoman, Kashghar, Kucha. Rashiduddin again refers to *Tamma* army released in connection with the defence of Qurtghan. After the death of Chingiz Khan the princes and the nobles who were in the *Urdu* of Chingiz Khan held a *Kangaj* and sent Elchidai Noyon (the nephew of Chingiz Khan) and Guyuk Khan (son of Ogedei) to Qurtghan. They devastated the place. After its conquest a certain Amir Tankqut Bahadur was appointed along with a *Tamma* army released for its defence.[73] It may be argued that the term *Tamma* was perhaps a Mongol version of the word *Altamgha.*

Since the Mongols did not have an alphabet with phonetic sound of 'hg' (e.g. the name Chaghatai was always written and pronounced by them as *Jaadai*) hence the term *Tamgha* may have been written *Tamma*, Akbar's complaints in a letter to Abdullah Khan Uzbeg that the tribal population on the frontiers plundered the people and the traders alike and called this booty as *Tamgha* and not *Yaghma* may indirect clarify the issue. It is quite likely that the force sent at Emperor or Khan's order to accompany the *Ataliq* and to reside in a town was authorized to realize the *Khassa* revenue of Khan and *Khalsa* (the state share) from that particular place hence the name. The realization of *Mal-i Amani* from the rich magnates of the town and the plunder spree which followed every conquest was a routine affair for the Mongols. Seemingly, it was for this purpose that this chosen army was employed to fulfil the task as discreetly and honestly as possible.

The numerical strength of Chingiz's army had been variously estimated by the chroniclers and the modern historians. Rashiduddin expresses his ignorance about the exact number of Chingiz's army owing to the long distances existing between the two states of Turan and Iran where he was stationed writing the book. The other sources also contradict each other in assessing the numerical details of Mongol army. There is Rashiduddin Fazlullah's somewhat confusing account. At one place he gives the total number of Chingiz's forces as 1,00,000. Elsewhere he records that only the right and left wings of the army comprised 1,00,000. The number of forces allocated to be given to Mother Hoelun 'who assembling the nation hath suffered' and to royal princes, *Noyons* and nobles had also been variously described in the *Secret History* and *Jamiut Tawarikh*. Raverty's analysis that the entire forces of Chingiz Khan amounted to 1,29,000 (*Khas Ming* or *Hazara* 1,000; *Ming* or *Hazara* of Noyon Burji—also called *Qaul* 8,000; the right or *Baranghar* 30,000; the left or *Jaranghar* 62,000; the *Ming* or *Hazaras* of the sons 16,000; the king or Hazaras of the brothers, nephews and mother 12,000) is also not corroborated by other sources. Although there is no discrepancy in the forces assigned to Juji, i.e. 900, other details given are different, e.g. the number of soldiers assigned to the mother Ulun Ikka were 3,000; to Chaghatai 8,000; in *Secret History* and 4,000 in *Jamiut Tawarikh*, Ogedei: 5,000 in *Secret History* and 400 in *Jamiut Tawarikh* and to Otcegin (Touli 1,000 with Mother Hoelun and 5,000 in *Secret History*. Besides, Qasar received 4,000, Belgutei 1,500, nephews 12,000. It seems that the numbers mentioned in *Secret History* are more correct and the number was presumably determined by the seniority of a person. During the lifetime of his father Otchegin, Toulou had received 5,000 only, though after the death of his father, he inherited 10,000 forces. If Rashiduddin is to be believed, it was the tradition/customary (*Mahud*) in those days that the *Hazara-i Khass* (special *Myriarch*—the personal guards) of the *Khaqan* did not exceed one thousand.[74] This special *Myriarch* consisted of all the Oughlans and of those who had belonged to Chingiz Khan's *Urdu* led by Chaghan Noyon of Tanghut *Qaum*. The *Amir* of this *Myriarch* was Chaghan Tankqut who was 'like an eagle in sagacity and wisdom' and also held the charge of *Sadah-i-Buzurg* of Chingiz. The *Ulugh* was banished from this *Hazara* at the order of aforementioned *Amir*. After Chingiz Khan's death, he was sent away to China as the *Muqaddam* of princes and *Amirs*. Apart from this *Sadah-i Buzurg*, there were seven more *Sadahs* or *Yuz* out of which only six names of the tribes comprising each *Sadah* were known to the author. These were: Sunyat, Durman, Jalair, Kerait, Merkit and Tartar. According to Rashiduddin the seventh of the *Urdu-i-Buzurg* of Yesulun Khatun belonged to *Urdu* of Borte Qurchin and Qulan Khatun. A *Sadah* seems to be superior to *Urdu*.

Modern historians also differ on the question of exact number of Chingiz Khan's army. Some have placed its number as quarter of a million with a heavy artillery, [75] whereas others have mentioned its strength as merely 1,50,000 cavalry and 1,000 siege engines. On the eve of war against Khwarazm Shah, the numerical strength of the army of Chingiz Khan as given by Howorth and accepted by Lamb amounted to 2,30,000.[76] To this number were further added 10,000 Cathayans and Uighurs under Idikut, the chroniclers supply only answers to the question whether the Mongols used guns at all. One version attributes 10,000 siege engines from China, equipped with catapaults, mangonels, ballistas for hurling heavy blocks of stone. There is said to be have been a primitive cannon charged with gunpowder for firing, iron or stone balls, flame throwers; another Chinese invention was a undershirt of raw silk which an arrow would not penetrate.[77]

The artillery unit from Cathay fashioned a weapon to deal with the barges. Balistas were built to throw fire pots at the boats and jars or kegs filled with flaming sulphur or another concoction prepared by the Cathay units. As a matter of policy, Chingiz did not rely upon the Tajiks though he enrolled them in the army and each of the Tajik squadron of ten was to be governed by a Mongol commander.

In the early years of his rivalry against Altun Khan, Chingiz had nominated a force of 3,00,000 horse in order to guard the route.[78] At the time of his march against Khwarazm Shah, there were six hundred banners—under each banner there were one thousand horsemen and six hundred thousand horses assigned to the Bahadurs.[79] Chingiz's army is generally supposed to have consisted primarily of a cavalry only as most of the territories where he lived or waged wars were mountainous. Although the Saljuqids too are said to have 'had nearly all mounted men'.[80] The Mongols had perhaps more valid reasons for their dependence upon cavalry. The geographical condition of the area where the Mongols were brought up and carried their wars far and wide necessitated utility of cavalry more than infantry which was rarely used. The regional village created by Chingiz Khan through his large scale conquest was connected by *Yams* (post stations) where the mounts for change were always available. Commenting upon Barthold's assumption, Levy however says that the 'Saracenic tactic' of 'speed and mobility' must have necessitated the riding by infantry behind the cavalry.[81]

The swift moving cavalry with additional four to six remounts was a great asset for the Mongols. The Turco-Mongol soldiers were usually provided with clothes suitable for the area of their campaign, thus having fur caps, warm leather boots and coats for the Steppe cold and summer dress for a hot country. While on march for proposed campaign, each soldier carried his 'iron, ration, a camp kettle and a water proof pouch with a change of clothing for crossing swamps and rivers. At the time of inspection, the kit of the troopers was rigorously examined[82] and the deficiency discovered was punished. These soldiers used to wear a special undershirt of raw silk to serve as Cuirasses. Care was taken to increase the efficiency of cavalry through the use of Crupper (a strap of leather fastened to the saddle and passing under the horse's tail to keep the saddle in its place).[83]

In the front of the army, 'there were two ranks of heavy armed cavalry with three ranks of armour less mounted archers behind'[84] which moved forward through intervals of front rank. This cavalry was light with bow and javelin. The most 'accurate' and 'deadliest' weapon of the Mongols, the Bow (and arrow) was extremely heavy with a pull of 160 pounds and having a range of 200 to 300 yards. The arrow head could pierce the armour when dipped in red-hot brine. Initially this light cavalry 'poured forth fire' and withdrew after which the heavy cavalry 'charged and demoralized the army of enemy'. There were archers each of whose arrows could 'make Sagittarius, the bane of Mercury and turn the sons of the saddle and Rankhsh into "Daughters of the Bier" that by the shooting of an arrow, they could bring down a hawk from the hollow of the ether and on dark nights with thrust of their spear heads would cast out fish from the bottom of the sea'.[85]

Saunders records that each archer carried with him two to three bows, three quivers, files for sharpening the arrow heads. Marco Polo, however categorically says that 'when they go to war each is obliged to carry with him sixty arrows, thirty of which are of a smaller size intended for shooting at a distance but the other thirty are larger and have a broad blade. Those they use near at hand, and strike their enemies in the faces and arms, and cut the strings of their bows, and do great damage with them. And when they discharged all their arrows, they take their swords and maces, and give one another heavy blows with them.'[96]

Their saddles made in Mexican style were good for the horses as even during very long journeys they seldom caused a sore back.[87] 'Both the horses and the men were hardy, equally inured to short rations, and long journeys, equally adaptable to almost any climate' and so closely accustomed to each other that anyone contesting with them was 'at a decided disadvantage'. In one of the paintings[88] the Mongol horses have been shown wearing Cuirasses after the Chinese fashion.[89] The life figure of a horseman painted on the uncoloured walls of scanty remains in Nishapur under the Samanids shows that 'the costume of the rider is that of the Steppe long boots decorated with a flower pattern, and a leopard skin saddle cloth; and he uses stirrups, a Central Asian invention. Three straps hang from the leather waist belt which is a Turkish fashion found again in the costume of most important composition surviving from the medieval wall painting of the Eastern caliphate.'[90]

As prescribed by *Yasa*,[91] hunting was an essential part of military discipline and a regular feature of army routine. The hunting excursion was not merely a major source of recreation for the army but a customary device essentially evolved for military training, reconnaissance of administrative units and collection of provisions for the winter. Ibn-i Tiqtiqa had criticized Chingiz Khan for this love for hunting saying his (Chingiz's) army wasted three months in sheer pleasure of hunting and such excursions were unbecoming of a sovereign .of Chingiz's stature. Hunting was, in fact, a source for creating courage and fearlessness in the army personnel as well as a contributory factor in facilitating regular physical exercise. *Secret History* confirms that hunting was to be limited to a given period of time and had to be brought to an end long before the horses and the provisions were completely exhausted.[92]

The importance attached to hunting by Chingiz Khan and the curious method of *Nerge* is described in detail by Juvaini who draws a parallel between the *Nerge* and the war. 'Now war' says Juvaini 'with its killing, counting of the slain and sparing of the survivors is after the same fashion (of hunting *Nerge*) and indeed analogus in every detail, because all that is left in the neighborhood of the battlefield are a few broken down wretches.' The pattern of *Nerge* resembles the tactics of circular movement of the army so frequently applied to corner the enemy. Due to the importance of this *Nerge* method, the passage is being reproduced here.

Chingiz paid extraordinary attention to the chase and used to say that the hunting of wild beasts was a proper occupation for the commanders of armies; and that instruction and training therein was incumbent on warriors and men at arms who should learn how the huntsmen come up with the quarry, how they hunt it in what manner they array themselves and after what fashion they surround it according as the party is great or small. And when they are not engaged in warfare, they are even eager for the chase and encourage their armies thus to occupy themselves, not for the sake of game alone but also in order that they may become accustomed and inured to hunting and familiarized with the handling of the bow and the endurance of hardships. For a month or two they form a hunting ring and drive the game slowly and gradually before them taking care lest any escape from the ring. And if unexpectedly, any game should break through, a minute inquiry is made into the cause and reason, and the commanders of thousands, hundreds and tens are clubbed, therefore, and often even put to death. And if a man does not keep to the line (which they call *Nerge*) but takes a step forward or backwards, severe punishment is dealt out to him and is never remitted. For two or three months, by day and by night, they drive the game in this manner, like a flock of sheep, and dispatch messages to the Khan to inform him of the condition of the quarry, its scarcity or plenty, whither it has come and from whence it has been started. Finally, when the ring had been contracted to a diameter of two or three pharsangs, they bind ropes together and cast felts over them; while the troops come to a halt all around the ring, standing shoulder to shoulder. The ring is now filled with the cries and commotion of every manner of game and the roaring and tumult of every kind of ferocious beast; lions becoming familiar with wild asses, hyenas friendly with foxes, wolves intimate with hares, when the ring has been so much contracted that the wild beasts are unable to stir, first the Khan sides in together with some of his retinue, then after he has wearied of the spot, they dismount upon high ground in the center of the nerge to watch the princes likewise entering the ring, and after them in due order, the noyons, the commanders and the troops. Several days pass in this manner, then when nothing is left of the game but a few wounded and emaciated stragglers, old men and grey beards approach the Khan offer up prayers for his well being and intercede for the lives of the remaining animals asking that they be suffered to depart to some place nearer to grass and water. Thereupon they collect together all the game that they have gagged; and if the enumeration for every species of animal proves impracticable they count only the beasts of pray and the wild asses.[93]

Chingiz Khan's army had a tremendous capacity to bear all sorts of hardships. While sending troops to Turan, every contingent of ten received merely three heads of *Tukli* sheep with orders to dry them. The soldiers carried with them an iron cauldron and a skin bag of water. Although the *Nuzul* or *Qunuigha* was allowed, nothing could be demanded on the way since the journey of Chingiz Khan's army from Mongolian frontiers to Khwarazmia Shah's territory of Otrar necessitated long march through 'wild and uncultivated tracts'. It was commanded that during the three months march, the soldiers were to subsist upon negligible provision and to eke it out with *Kumiz* and with the milk of their mares and a bag of millet.[94] During the march, soldiers had to perform multifarious duties. The soldiers were employed in constructing roads and bridges. A road was constructed at the order of Ogedei in the mountainous region of Tien Shan. Similarly, during the western campaigns of Chingiz Khan, a road was constructed through the defiles by piercing rocks. Simultaneously forty-eight timber bridges were raised and their width was such that two carts could easily pass over it side by side.[95] In Samarqand 3,000 men built the bridge on river Amu.[96] During the siege of Khujand, Temur Malik had fortified a tall stronghold into the middle of the river where the stream was divided into two parts so that the Mongols found it impossible to capture the place immediately since it could be reached neither by arrows nor by mangonels. The Tajik soldiers had to carry stones a distance of three *Pharsangs* on foot and the Mongols on horseback dropped these stones into the river.[97]

Secret History describes the custom of sprinkling the standard with mare's milk.[98] Before organizing his march to a new direction, Chingiz Khan offered sacrifices to his banner in which remained concealed the spirit and genius of the army (*Sulde*).[99] A painting in *Babur Nama* shows how the custom was performed. The war cry or the *Uran* was the 'common property of a political group' usually named after a hero of the same clan, e.g. the Jalairs and the Dughlats used an *Uran* named Bakhtiar—after a Qazaq hero and Qanghli too had Bayterek. Sometimes the name of the clan was also adopted as its battle cry, e.g. Seykym clan of Qazaqs had the same name as their *Uran.*[100]

The three types of war tactics which continued to govern Mongol military system throughout the vast realm and over a period of several centuries have been discussed in detail in various sources including the *Secret History*.

These three tactics were the following:

1. *Qarayana* March: in which the troops marched massed in close order in the manner of the *Qarayana*, a thorny shrub which grows in thick clumps on the steppe.
2. Lake array: to array in the lake array means to deploy with the troops widely scattered in the manner of the water of a lake which spreads over a large area.
3. Chisel fight: to fight and engage the enemy with a thrust at his centre in the manner of a chisel which is thrust into a piece of wood.[101] The other tactics mentioned in the source include: Single Combat (*Yakkatazi*), skirmishes (dog fights), etc.

The custom of *Yakkatazi* is said to have 'psychological influence' when the champions from each side come into actual contact (e.g. Caliph Ali and Muawiya in 657).[102] In some of the Turanian paintings a scene of single combat is depicted.

In the battlefield during the offence and defense, they never broke their formation. Juvaini describes how the Mongol army had cut off Sultan Jalauddin's front and rear wings of army and 'encompassed him on every side; they stood behind one another in several rings in the shape of a bow and made the Indus like a bowstring. Mongol army advanced little by little leaving Sultan less space to manoeuvre and less room to do battle.[103] During the siege warfare, the army of Hulegu 'numerous as ants had snake like formed seven coils around the castle (of Maimun Diz). As in *Panja* dance, they had joined rank to rank and laid hand in hand. In the day time as far as their right could reach, the people of Maimun Diz could see nothing but men and standard, and at night, because of the great quantity of fires, they thought the earth to be like a sky full of stars and a world full of swords and daggers whereof neither middle nor edge was visible'.[104] The *Amirs* and *Noyons* were stationed round the castle at a distance like a belt round the waist of a wasp.

The tribal elements usually performed *'amal-i sang-i yadah* (the act of stone *yadah*) which caused hailstorm, snowfall, excessive rains, chill and lighting to discourage the enemy from marching forward and fighting.[105] *Arais-ul Jawahir* (comp. 700) refers to a stone called *Yadah* (*yat*) which, if placed in a water pond creates such an effect.[106] According to Abul Qasim Abdullah Kashani Uighurs and Turks were adept in this art.[107]

In the wake of Mongol conquest, the traditional local armour factories were enriched further by newly introduced equipments, e.g. metal greaves and mail thigh guards, Mongol lamellar or laminated armour (*khuyagh*) of two different types, the cuirass (with attached shoulder guards and tassets) and coat (with shoulder guards), some armour having metal discs on front and back. Mongol helmets with their remarkable pointed tops and the round shield with a metal boss surrounded by concentric cane work decorated with wool or silk overlay were other novelties, with a pyramidal spike on the crown. The helmet (*kotah*) was usually hemispherical in shape with three plumeholders and a movable noseguard set by a small screw. On the basis of Central Asian and near eastern style the metal bands 'shaped to the body and joined to form one piece were prepared with handbraces, metal gauntlets and folding graves, oval shaped kneeguards and metal boots and armraces (*bazuband*) Mongols introduced a round shield with "a metal boss surrounded by concentric cane work decorated with wool or silk overlay"'.[108] A number of other weapons were also brought into use by the Mongols.

Apart from the wooden bows the *Secret History* refers to a number of varied kinds of arrows namely: *Gonkhua* (piercing 10-20 men), *Keibur* (from a long distance piercing through armour of enemy, *Odora* (arrows of a near bow shot), *Qoocay* (arrows of a far bow shot), *Yadoli* (with a tip of cypress wood and without a point which does not hurt, *Angylla* (arrow with a forked tip), arrows garnished with peach bark; the sounding *Yor* with the tip of a sounding bone arrow (made of the horns after gluing together the four halves of two horns of a two year old calf and boring holes) in them.[109]

Other weapons mentioned in the sources included steel lances, square shields, brass knucklebones, breast plates with slender thongs (which held together the various parts of breast plates of leather) or of three layers, breast plates with three layers, roebuck. Copper helmets, square shields. There were axes, saws, chisel, awls, whips for various use, a pole with a noose at the end called lasso and used to catch horsemen and draw them nearer to kill or capture had been depicted in medieval Mughal paintings. The fire sickle (a sickle shaped piece of steel enveloped in leather used for striking a spark to ignite tinder).[110]

Ibn-i Khaldun refers to the shooting style: 'we hear that fighting technique of contemporary Turkish nation is the shooting of arrow. They dismount from their horses, empty their quivers on the ground in front of them and then shoot from a squatting or kneeling position'.[111] The same scholar further records: 'Their (Turkish) battle order consists of a 'line formation'. They divide their army into three lines, one placed behind the other. Each line protects the one ahead of it against being overrun by the enemy until victory is assured for one party. This is a very good and remarkable battle order'.

The *Kang, Konj,* or *Conge* (or yoke—Persian *Doshakha*) continued to be commonly used as a punitive weapon. The *Doshakha* was 'a sort of portable pillory, described as a block of wood with two horns, hence the term. In those days it may have been formed out of two pieces of crooked wood, but what was used in after years and continues to be used still, consists of two flat boards with a hollow for the neck to be fashioned round the neck of the captive'.

The *Qurultai* which assembled in the year of Tiger (1206) is credited with setting up a white standard (*Tuqi*) having nine feet. There were various kinds of tents and carts, e.g. *Corqan* (tents with locks), *Coory Yatai Tergeni Terme* (a type of spread tents), iron carts, and *Qa atai carts.*

The age-old and widely practiced system of *Arz* is said to have originated from the Greeks or Sassanids from whom it was adopted by the Umayyads, gradually emerging from ordinary checking and assessment of strength and equipment into a sophisticated organ for ancillary purposes.[112] In *Siyasat Nama*, the numbering of the army was described as *ba sar-i taziyana shumurdan.*[113] In Turkish, the word used was *Dim Kurmak.* Nobody was to leave the unit of a thousand, hundred or ten to which he was assigned. Otherwise he was to be severely punished.[114]

In order to ensure that evils of impersonation are removed, Chingiz had abolished the registry of inspection (*Daftar-i Arz*) and dismissed the officials and clerks. The reviewing and mustering of the army was accomplished through the division of all the people into companies of ten, hundred, thousand and ten thousand with a commander selected from amongst that very detachment. In accordance with this arrangement if in an emergency any man or thing be required, they used to apply to the commanders of *Tuman*; who in turn used to apply to the commanders of thousands and so on down to the commanders of tens. Juvaini says that 'there is a true equality in this; each man toils as much as the next, and no difference is made between them, no attention being paid to wealth or power. If there is a sudden call for soldiers, an order is issued that so many thousands men must present themselves in such and such a place at such and such an hour of that day or night.'

In the Islamic world mode of payment to the army kept on changing with the holders of the throne. Caliph Umar is credited with the innovation of the *Divan* or register in which names of warriors were recorded. An officer called *Arif* maintained the list of troopers in his unit and paid the actual cash to each soldier of his unit. The status in religious sphere determining the amount as higher sums were given to earlier converts.[115] In Central Asia, we hear of this custom only under the Samanids and the Uzbegs under the name *Atiya Dadan*. The custom of soldiers receiving land grants in lieu of cash salary was probably introduced by Buwayhids and certainly developed by the Saljuqids into a 'feudal military system' in which the generals ruling over provinces paid annual tribute and supplied the stipulated number of soldiers if and when demanded.

The age old and universally acclaimed custom of division of spoil among *Myriarchs*, *Chiharchs* and centurions and even the common soldiers in hierarchic order for serving as an incentive was followed by Chingiz also. Chingiz verdict on the division of troops is recorded in the *Secret History*.[116] In December 1255 the Khan is reported to have distributed all the spoils that had been collected, amongst the great and small Turks and Tajiks.[117]

For each peculiar situation, specific regulations were framed, e.g. for spoils of war,[118] the 'Great principle' in Mongolia was that 'everything—the booty belongs to the possessions of the Atlan Qaan which continued to guide the Mongol warrior community. Chingiz issued an "ordinance" saying that "if we overcome the enemy let us not tarry for spoil. When we have made an end of overcoming that spoil shall be ours. We shall part it with one another."' In case of retreat, the principle was laid down that: 'if we be made to withdraw ourselves by an enemy, let us return unto our place from whence we first rushed (forward). We shall make one to behead the man which shall not have returned into the (palace of) the first rushing (forward).'[119]

Before a campaign, the inhabitants of the state were expected to share the burden of war by supplying provisions and the mounts (*Ghalla-i taghar; Ulagh*). Whenever the beasts belonging to the *Diwan* seemed to be 'insufficient', for the purposes of war, the order was given that the animals of any person whatsoever, whether noble or base, Turk and Tajik, should be seized as *Ulagh*. For collection of provisions for the army, two methods were adopted. Either *Elchis* were dispatched beforehand to procure flour, etc., or the army collected it on its way to the place of war, if the route was not barren.[120] Rashiduddin refers to the fact that the soldiers demanded the food, fodder and the dress (*Khurusho Poshish*) wherever they went and acquired it.[121]

Unlike the Ottoman Janissaries who were exempted from taxes, the Mongol army had to pay numerous taxes over and above the Corvee (*hashr-i bigar-i qala*) and a number of odd jobs and errands which they had to perform.

Juvianis' elaborate account is available to prove that the army had to pay taxes also 'since all countries and people have come under their (Mongol) domination they have established a census after their accustomed fashion and classified everyone into tens, hundreds and thousands; and required military service and the equipment of *Yams* together with the expenses entailed and the provision of fodder—this in addition to ordinary taxes—and over and above all this, they have fixed the *Qupchur* charges also'.[122] Even when the soldiers were engaged in fighting, various taxes were demanded from their wives and those of them that remained behind. Thus if work be a foot in which a man had his share of forced labour (*begar*) and if the man himself be absent, his wife goes forth in person and performs that duty in his stead. Unlike the Ottoman Janissaries who were exempted from taxes, the Mongol army had to pay numerous taxes over and above the Corvee and a number of odd jobs and errands which they had to perform.

Chingiz had his own code of conduct prescribed for his military and nobility. In principle, Chingiz was harsh towards those who deserted their masters. He always asserted 'Is it possible to leave alive men who have betrayed their own lord? Let them be put to death, with their sons and grandsons'.[123] He therefore always appreciated the quality of loyalty in servants and punished those who betrayed their lords even though the latter be Chingiz's bitterest enemy. The attitude towards the vassals of Taichut leader Targutai Kiriunk is an example in question.[124] Chingiz's insistence that the brave fleeing prince Jalaluddin should not be shot at but brought alive shows his attitude towards bravery. Even during his early career, the story of Jebe's arrival from the Tayiciud (Taichut) and his becoming a companion of Chingiz confirms the same (Cleaves).[125]

It is surmised that Chingiz was aristocratic by principle upholding the feudal worlds' authority over his vassal and the master over his slave. While the loyal and the brave soldiers even in enemy's camp earned the admiration and rank from Chingiz Khan, the treacherous and the coward, whatever be their designation or calling failed to please him. Generally, it was considered to be an obligation for the Mongols 'to be dead with his quiver and his bow in one place with his bones',[126] i.e. to die as a brave man.

For each and every corps of troops new rules and regulations were laid down. The soldiers and the messengers were to abstain from 'wounding or making to suffer men or geldings in the land' in which they were called upon to serve.[127] The hierarchy was properly defined and enforced. For example imperial guards were made superior to outward guards by a decree.[128] The latter were forbidden to equate themselves or quarrel with them. Nevertheless the 'comradeship in extremity' was the key note of norms and obligations prescribed by Chingiz to his armed nation.[129]

'If in a battle, during attack or a retreat any one let fall his pack, or bow, or any luggage, the man behind him must alight and return the thing fallen to its owner, if he does not do so he is to be put to death'. The *Yasa* contains seven clauses relating to military organization and administration. None could abandon the wounded.[130]

Such was the discipline prevailing in the army that Chingiz's mandate had religious sanctity. Juvaini says that the unquestioning obedience and loyalty of his army towards Chingiz Khan was so strong that 'if there be a commander of a hundred thousand between whom and the Khan there is a distance of sunrise and sunset, and if he but commit some fault, the Khan dispatches a single horseman to punish him after the manner prescribed. If his head had been demanded he cuts it off and if gold be required, he takes it from them.[131] Juvaini wondered how difficult it was with other kings who must speak cautiously to their own slave, bought with their own money, as soon as he has ten horses in his stable, to say nothing of when they place an army under his command and he attains to wealth and power, then they cannot displace him and more often than not he actually rises in rebellion and insurrection'.[132] Chingiz had once ordered his soldiers not to pick any ingots of silver and gold which were being discharged in place of stones and bricks from the catapults of Altun Khan's army. After his victory, the whole lot of ingots the discharged were recovered as they tallied with the records later on supplied by the auditors (*mushrifs*) of Altun Khan.[133]

Another method to enforce strict discipline in the army was the *Yasa* framed under Chingiz Khan that: 'no man was allowed to join another unit than the hundred, thousand or ten to which he has been assigned nor could he seek refuge elsewhere. And if this order was transgressed the man who transferred was executed in the presence of the troops, while he that had received him was severely punished. For this reason no man could give refuge to another, if (for example) the commander be a prince, he does not permit the meanest person to take refuge in his company and so avoided a breach of *Yasa*. Due to this, no man could take liberties with his commander or leader, nor could another commander entice him.'[134]

Chingiz had conquered numerous countries and fought many wars without facing a defeat, merely because of a fixed and highly elaborate plan of action. In the first place, a three tier discussion programme always preceded the war. In a general council of military aristocracy and higher officials the feasibility of campaign was discussed and minutest details were to be pondered over. Thereafter, a special assembly of selected and reliable officials followed by the meeting of chosen group of closest and most shrewed confidants was summoned. The issues were discussed elaborately regarding choice and details of selected route, divisions of army to be summoned, ways and means to be devised to win over border allies or discontented elements to facilitate penetration stratagem and tactics to be evolved to outmanoeuvre the enemy. The planning was finalized in the third and the last meeting. If any one ever dared to disclose their plans (especially about a campaign) he was to be pursued by a hundred strokes on his back as hard as a peasant can give them with a big stick.[135]

When the military affairs were discussed in the *Qurultai* strict secrecy had to be maintained. The episode of Belgutai who was debarred from the privilege of attending the *Qurultai* due to his having leaked the deliberations of the counsel shows how strongly these norms were followed. He was thereafter asked to judge quarrel and question theft and lies for the people. He was to enter the counsel after it had come to an end and after the *atog* had been drunk.[136]

Even campaign was thoroughly organized. To ensure a victory, care was taken to misguide the target country, and even the soldiers were kept uninformed about their destination for fear of leaking the news of invasion though each and every information was acquired about the country to be invaded.

The choice or nomination of a particular army depended upon the importance of the campaign. At the time of sending a detachment on a war, Chingiz was most careful and selective, e.g. while sending Touli to invade Khurasan, Chingiz Khan 'detached men from the army of all his sons in proportionate number, and from each ten he designated one to accompany Touli'.[137] Juvaini says that whenever the 'slaying of foes and the attacking of rebels is purposed, they specify all that will be of service for that business, from the various arms and implements down to banners, needles, ropes, mounts and pack-animals such as donkeys and camels; and every man must provide his share according to his ten or hundred. On the day of review and in the eve of a campaign, the inspection of the army was done by *Dim* (or counting) by a whip. As the army stood in a battle array, the Khan visited each detachment where the chief knelt before him and presented him with a horse. Afterwards, the armour weapons and equipment of the detachment were inspected. If only a little was missing, those responsible were severely punished though distribution of bows, arrows and weapons is also mentioned in the sources. If the army had to be summoned from the far off regions *Tuvachis* were sent to the particular areas. He gave them a *Jar* (ultimatum) to reach at an appointed time and place. Every detachment confirmed their proposed presence by submitting to *Tuvachis* a *Muchulka* (guarantee). Any defaulter was severely punished. Even before the ascendancy of Chingiz Khan, the allied army always reached at the appointed place without being late notwithstanding snow, hailstorm, etc.[138] An unquestioning sub-mission was the order of the day and one who hesitated was to be expelled from the ranks. The logistics were similarly pre-planned and acquired beforehand.

Chingiz evolved his own methods to take every advantage over his enemies. In his view his campaigns were 'divine mission' and he himself was *Azab-i Khuda*, the scourge of God, i.e. 'sent to punish the people for their sins. Every resistance to surrender was, therefore, a sin against God' Chingiz resorted to what Saunders had termed as 'Psychological warfare of horrid kind' which he mixed with expedient leniency and strategies. The merchants bridged the gulf between the Mongols and the population of target country and acquainted the invaders before hand with the geographical conditions, shortest routes, socio-economic factors responsible for the discontent of the people and most likely to be exploited. Attempts were made successfully to establish contacts with the discontented elements and to use them against the enemy. The information regarding the weaknesses of Sultan's army and the bid on his life was brought to Chingiz Khan by a section of the Qara Khatais and Ataul Mulk Alaudin the ruler of Qunduz who had only recently deserted the Sultan.[139] In Otrar Chingiz won over Badruddin Amid whose father and uncles had earlier been executed by the Sultan and burning with vendetta Amid supplied him with intricate complexities of Khwarazm Shah's empire and latter's problems including the enmity of the Sultan with Turakina Khatun and a section of the army.

It is interesting to note that the Mongols tried to turn over the semi nomadic but formidable Kumans who were savage and pugnacious people of the Qipchaq region. Subtai had lured them into obedience saying that they were his own kith and kin, men of the same stock and should stand by them against an alien race. After they (Mongols) won the war against their enemy with the help of Kumans, they (Mongols) snatched away all gifts bestowed upon them (Kumans) earlier and countercharged them for being traitors.[140] Similarly when the treacherous captain of the guard in Otrar (who had earlier suggested the surrender of Bukhara) being eager for his own safety deserted the ruler along with his 1,000 soldiers. Yet he failed to win the favour of Chingiz Khan and was finally killed also.[141] Methods were devised to outmanoeuvre the enemy. To quote an example: In Juji's army an engineer built and kept ready the ladders and bridges. Through feigned night attack, the Mongols attracted the attention of the besieged and lured them—calling off all the soldiers to repel the attackers while the ambuscade boldly mounted these ladders and entered the fort.[142]

Spies and informers were sent beforehand to prepare maps and acquire relevant information. Usually the country was attacked simultaneously from several corners. Surprise or sudden attacks to take the enemy unawares, *Tulughma* or standard sweep; feigned flight; sandwitching the enemy's forces from two sides after deceptive retreat; spreading false rumours to deliberately misguide the enemy, cutting off supplies of the besieged towns were the usual tactics of the Mongols. During Central Asian campaigns, Jebe Noyon had 'stolen up' on the Turkish contingent and Muhammad was 'in a fair way to be cut off from his second and main line of defence'. The bewildered Sultan divided his forces. Simultaneously, a second Mongol army took Tashkent and a third detachment 'scoured the northern end of Syr storming the smaller towns'. To add to the discomfiture Chingiz also quietly crossed red sand deserts (*Qizil Qum*) and marched towards Bukhara from the west.[143] In order to deprive the besieged of water supplies during Khwarazm expedition, the waters of Amu going to the town were diverted by Chingiz Khan's 3,000 men.

Surreptitious methods to unnerve the enemy were also used. A former servant of the Sultan who, in 'connivance with' Chingiz drafted several unsigned letters using the details of events in the court to add to their authenticity and revealing a 'pretended conspiracy' against the Sultan which naturally bewildered the latter.[144] There were hydraulic engineers to divert the course of rivers and cause floods that might help in siege operations.[145] In order to make his army look larger during Ghazni and Afghanistan campaign at the Wani, Shizi Khutukus ordered scarecrows in human forms prepared of felt and straw and got them sewn and fixed to the spare horses.[146]

A number of tactics were applied to frighten away the enemy. Usually the stratagem of lighting fire at several far off places to create the illusion of excessive numbers or to prepare scarecrows of the male figures stuffed with felt, sewn and bound upon spare horses in several rows at the end of the army (as was done by Shigi Khudku in Ghazni and Afghanistan campaign) for the same purpose was not so rare. The jade stone (*Amal-i Yadah*) was often applied to bring hail storm or rain to create difficulties for the army. The scorched earth policy frequently deterred the enemy from fast advance and Mongols easily got time to prepare for war. Besides, supplies too were cut off to deprive the enemy of provisions or reinforcements. Chingiz kept himself informed of the details of enemy's plans so that the last minute changes could be made to suit his strategy.[147]

In the orient the two tactics *Albayt wal kamin* (night attacks, ambush) or *Adab-ul harb wal khud* were frequently used to outmanoeuvre the enemy. The choicest force lay in ambush and the other detachments engaged the enemy till they were exhausted. By the feigned retreat, they lured the enemy to pursue them to some extent till the ambuscade followed the enemy and the fleeing army also turned back to attack the enemy's pursuing army, which was thus sandwitched between the two groups of army of the enemy only to meet its doom.

Forms may differ but the Mongols always made people submit through threats and the dictum that 'surrender is safety' often won the day. An example may be quoted: In Khurasan, *Yeme* admonished the people saying that they should eschew opposition and hostility and whenever a Mongol envoy arrived they should welcome him and not rely upon the strength of their walls and multitude of their forces; so that their horses and property might go unscathed. By way of a token they gave the envoys an *Altamgha* in the Uighur script and a copy of a *Yirligh* of Chingiz Khan, whereof the gist was as follows: Let the *Amirs* and great ones and the numerous common people know this that. . . . All the face of the earth from the going up of the sun to his going down I have given into thee. Whosoever therefore, shall submit, mercy shall be shown unto him and into his tribes and children and household; but whosoever shall not submit shall perish together with all his wives and children and kinsmen.'[148]

Haider Dughlat had rightly pointed out that during 'twelve years (908-920) the Mongols had been continually engaged in warfare and contests and disputes subject to many vicissitudes and changes of fortune and had endured incumbently reverses and trials, so that each one of them had gained great experiences and was acquainted with all the details of the art of war, such as marches and counter marches and forced marches. Nor was the knowledge peculiar to the *Amirs*—nay rather in every tribe of the Mughals many men were to be found in whose judgement and advice everyone placed reliance.'

The army of Chingiz Khan had an immense capacity for removing or overcoming the hurdles in their path during the march. Both Ibn-ul Asir and Caspini describe that as soon as the soldiers discovered that river Amu was not frozen, they, instead of being unnerved, swiftly prepared the wooden light circular troughs covered by oxhide to make them water tight in which they placed their armaments and fastening it to themselves, they grasped the tails of their horses and crossed Amu.[149] During the siege of Jend fort, Mongols found that there were trenches which served as protective barriers for the besieged. They built the bridges over the trenches and easily managed to climb the walls of the fort to take the besieged soldiers unawares.[150]

Even when stones were not available as in Khwarazm the undeterring army of Chingiz quickly cut down the mulberry trees, dried and used it in the mangonels.[151]

NOTES

1. *Tuzakat-i Timuri*, Introduction, pp. XXXI, 3, 141, 259.
2. *Mehmannama* (*Mehn*), pp. 54, 55; *Abdullahnama* (*Abdn*), p. 281.
3. *Ibn-i Khaliqan*, Vol. III, p. 397; Hitti, *History of the Arabs*, p. 328.
4. *Risala fi Fazailul Atrak*, ed. by Van Vloten, Eng. tr. by Harley Walker, *JRAS*, 1915, pp. 631-97, see also p. 682.
5. Masudi, Vol. VII, p. 118; Hitti, p. 328.
6. Watters, p. 94.
7. Wassaf, *Tarikh-i Wassaf-ul Hazrat*, Vol. II, pp. 203-4.
8. Cleaves, *Secret History of the Mongol Dynasity*, pp. 118-19.
9. Juvaini, *Tarikh-i-Jahankusha*, Leiden, 1911; text, pp. 23-4; Eng. tr., p. 32.
10. V.V. Barthold, *Turkestan Down to Mongol Invasion*, London, 1958, p. 332.
11. Juvaini, text, p. 34; Ibnal Asir XI 205; *Turkestan Down*, p. 333.
12. Juvaini, text, p. 29; Eng. tr., p. 40.
13. *Jamiut Tawarikh*, text, p. 307.
14. Juvaini, Persian text, pp. 21-4, 29; Eng. tr., p. 40. Rashiduddin Fazlullah, *Jamiut Tawarikh*, Tehran, 1338 AH, pp. 338-409, 440; *Secret History of the Mongol Dynasty*, Eng. tr. by Cleaves, Arthur Waley, London, 1963, pp. 141-9; Marco Polo, *The Travels of Marco Polo*, New York, 1930, pp. 117-19; also see Ibn-i Hauqal, *Surat-ul Arz*, Iran, 1345 AH, pp. 196-7; Abul Ghazi, *Shajratul Atrak*, Ms. British Museum Add 26190, ff. 57-8; Khwand Mir, *Rauzat-us Safa*, Vol. V, pp. 66-7; Hafiz Tanish, *Abdullah Nama*, Ms. India Office Library, Ethe 14, ff. 233, 333, 343. Bejins, *Letters and Historical Documents*, Ms. India Office Library, Ethe 12067-70, f. 379.
15. Juvaini, text, 22; Eng. tr., p. 30.
16. *Rauzat*, pp. 82-3; Prawdin, pp. 157, 160.
17. Lamb, *Gingiz Khan*, Lahore, 1478, p. 236.
18. Ibid., p. 238.
19. Ibid., pp. 223-7, 237.
20. The Islamic *Irafas* (squads of 10-15 men) led by an *Arif*, 49 soldiers led by a *Khalifa* and 99 soldiers by a *Qaid* and so on. For details on *Irafa* system see, Levy Reuben, *The Social Structure of Islam*, Cambridge, 1962, pp. 412, 426, 445.
21. For Mongol military system cf. Juvaini, op. cit., pp. 20-5; *Secret History* pp. 141-9; Marco Polo, pp. 117-19; Khwand Mir, V, pp. 66-7; *Abdn*, pp. 233-43.
22. For Turkic Military organization cf. *Shajratul Atrak*, Ms. British Museum, 26190, ff. 57-8; Bosworth, *The Ghaznavides*, Edinburgh, 1963, pp. 98-129; Barthold, *Turkestan Down to . . .*, p. 386.

23. Kautilya, *Arthashastra*, quoted by J.N. Sarkar, pp. 75-6.
24. *Rauzat*; 82-3; Prawdin, 1657, p. 160.
25. Cleaves, pp. 209, 223.
26. *JT*, pp. 399-400.
27. *JT*, pp. 25, 399; *Muizz-ul ansab*, pp. 30-3; *Secret History*, p. 209.
28. *JT*, p. 506.
29. *JT*, p. 455.
30. *JT*, pp. 399-408.
31. Cleaves, pp. 153-4.
32. *Tabaqat-i Nasiri*, Eng. tr. by Raverty, p. 1093 fn.
33. Riasanovsky, *Fundamental Principles of Mongol Law*, p. 210.
34. Vladimirtsov, *Life of Chingiz Khan*, pp. 65-7.
35. Cleaves, p. 187.
36. *JT*, p. 401.
37. *JT*, p. 403.
38. Saunders, p. 161.
39. Cleaves, pp. 4, 134, 144.
40. Ibid., pp. 113-16.
41. *JT*, pp. 402-6.
42. Vladimirtsov, pp. 53-64.
43. *JT*, p. 401.
44. *Secret History*, pp. 162-7.
45. Cf. *Secret History*, pp. 141, 161.
46. *Cambridge History of Islam*, p. 162; Lamb, pp. 133-5; *Turkestan Down*, pp. 430-43.
47. Cleaves, p. 87.
48. Ibid., p. 147.
49. Ibid., p. 151.
50. Ibid., p. 170.
51. Ibid., pp. 19-21.
52. Ibid., pp. 166, 170.
53. Ibid., pp. 119-22, 162-3, 166-70.
54. Juvaini, Eng. tr., p. 97 fn. 4.
55. Weikwei Sun, *Secret History*, p. 132.
56. Cleaves, pp. 162-3.
57. Ibid.
58. Cleaves, p. 152.
59. Ibid., pp. 26 and 27.
60. Ibid., p. 164.
61. Ibid., pp. 164-5.
62. Ibid., p. 219.
63. Vladimirtsov, pp. 58-9.
64. *JT*, p. 402.
65. *JT*, pp. 141-2, 333, 339-403.
66. *JT*, pp. 399-410.
67. *Rauzat*, p. 28.
68. Cleaves, pp. 214-15.
69. Aubin, 'L'ethnogenesa des Qaraunas Turks', *Turcica*, Vol. I, 1969, pp. 65-94; Morgan, pp. 94-6; Weikwei Sun, p. 132 fn. 4.

70. Weikwei Sun, p. 132, fn.14.
71. Cleaves, pp. 214-21.
72. Ibid., pp. 214-15, 227.
73. *JT*, p. 455.
74. *JT*, pp. 399-408.
75. Prawdin, pp. 79, 157.
76. These 2,30,000 forces comprised: Imperial guards 1,000; Centre under Touli 1,01,000; Right wing 47,000; Left wing 52,000; Other contingents 29,000. For interesting details on army see Abbot, pp. 241-2; Lamb, pp. 218-20.
77. Philip, pp. 60-1; Lamb, *Gingiz Khan*, pp. 133-5, 221-7, *Turkestan Down*, p. 430.
78. Levy, p. 433.
79. *Minhaj*, Vol. 2, pp. 953-4.
80. Levy, p. 433.
81. Ibid., pp. 433-6.
82. Saunders, p. 4.
83. Cleaves, p. 134.
84. Juvaini, text, p. 118; tr., p. 625.
85. Ibid., text, p. 63; tr., p. 82.
86. *Travels of Marco Polo*, ed. with introduction by Manuel Komraff, New York, 1930, p. 328.
87. Kent, pp. 40-1.
88. Plate *XCIV*, E. Blochet, tr. from French by C.M. Binyon, *Musulman Painting*, XII-XVII, London, 1929, pp. 60-1.
89. *History of Mongols*, Juvaini, Tabriz 1438, Bib., Nation, Parıs.
90. *Persian Painting Sikra*, Switzerland, 1977, p. 15.
91. *JT*, pp. 8, 13, 21-4.
92. Cleaves, p. 134.
93. Juvaini, text, pp. 19-21; tr., pp. 27-9.
94. *Minhaj*, II, pp. 968-9.
95. Chang Chun, *The Travels of an Alchemist* recorded by his disciple Li Chih Chang, tr. with an introduction by Arthur Waley, London, 1931, pp. 76, 85.
96. Wassaf, p. 568.
97. Juvaini, text, pp. 70-1; tr., pp. 91-2.
98. Cleaves, pp. 42-120.
99. Vladimirtsov, p. 159.
100. Czaplicka, *The Turks of Central Asia in History and at the Present Day*, Oxford, 1918, p. 44.
101. *The Secret History*, Eng. tr. by Cleaves, p. 124, also see fn. 49.
102. Bernard Lewis, *World of Islam*, London, 1976, pp. 203-4.
103. Juvaini, text, p. 106; Eng. tr., p. 134.
104. *Secret History*, pp. 119, 120-2, 161; Juvaini, pp. 117, 24; Eng. tr., pp. 624-8.
105. *Abdn*, pp. 282, 312.
106. *Arais-ul Jawahir* by Abdullah Kashani, Tehran, 1345, pp. 170-2.
107. Ibid.
108. Mongol armour is said to be a product of Central Asian and Far East. Geoffrey Tantum, *Muslim Warfare*.
109. Cleaves, pp. 42, 47, 49, 57, 70.

110. Ibid., pp. 16, 29, 142, 47-9, 57, 70, 123, 127, 133, 174.
111. Quoted by Lewis, *The World of Islam*, London, 1976, pp. 205-6.
112. Elgood, pp. 188-98.
113. Tusi, *Siyasat Nama*, Persian text, p. 151.
114. Juvaini, text, pp. 21-5.
115. Lewis, *The World of Islam*, London, 1976, p. 203.
116. Cleaves, p. 81.
117. Juvaini, text, p. 138; tr., p. 638.
118. Cleaves, pp. 81-4.
119. Ibid.
120. Juvaini, text, p. 112; tr., p. 621.
121. *JT*, pp. 364-9.
122. Juvaini, text, pp. 22-5; Eng. tr., pp. 30-1, 33-4.
123. Vladimirtsov, p. 62.
124. Ibid., p. 56.
125. Ibid., pp. 73-6.
126. Ibid., pp. 118-19.
127. Ibid., p. 173.
128. Ibid., pp. 162-70.
129. Prawdin, p. 69.
130. Juvaini, pp. 21-30; Riasanovsky, *Fundamental Principles of Mongol Law*, Clauses 8, 9, 17, 18, 19, 22, 24, 27.
131. Juvaini, text, p. 23; Eng. tr., pp. 131-2.
132. Ibid.
133. Minhaj, Eng. tr., pp. 962-3.
134. Juvaini, Eng. tr., p. 32.
135. Riasanovsky, Clause 37.
136. Cleaves, pp. 82-3.
137. Juvaini, text, p. 117; Eng. tr., pp. 150-1.
138. Cleaves, pp. 43-4.
139. Juvaini, pp. 11, 18, 197; Minhaj, 1023.
140. Lamb, pp. 133-5, 221-36; Prawdin, pp. 102-8, 112-24.
141. Abbot, pp. 234-7.
142. Abdal, pp. 241-5.
143. Lamb, pp. 122-40.
144. Abbot, pp. 225-6.
145. Prawdin, p. 38.
146. Ibid., pp. 195-6; for military starategem see Abbot, pp. 241-5.
147. See *Rauzat*, p. 93; Cleaves, pp. 120-2, 161; Abbot, pp. 241-5.
148. Juvaini, text, p. 114; tr., p. 145.
149. Carpini, Hakluyt Society Series, Vol. XII, pp. 81, 113, 156.
150. Khwand Mir, p. 89.
151. *JT*, pp. 361, 363, 373.

Military Organization Under Timur and His Successors

The army was one of the important instruments of wealth and grandeur in medieval times and an ambitious sovereign like Timur realized its significance only too well.

Almost all the contemporary accounts indicate that Timur's army was 'extremely large', 'like a surging sea', 'numerous like rain and atoms', and that such a vast number of troops were never seen after Chingiz Khan's time. In grandeur and decor 'Timur's army is said to have resembled the legendary magnificence of the army of the Great Emperors of Persia'.[1] Whether or not such comments exaggerate the size of Timur's army, the strength and organization of his army which shook the world certainly deserves to be examined by scholars in detail.

It is generally accepted that Timur's army retained the Chingizide pattern, since it consisted of militia and was based upon the decimal system.[2] Nevertheless, the main point of difference was that, whereas nomadic elements formed the core of Chingiz's army, and settled elements were recruited mainly as *Hashr* (labour force), a considerable number of settled people together (with nomads) constituted the core of Timur's forces.[3] With the arrival of Shaibanids, a significant role was played by nomadic elements which formed the kernel of the army comprising cavalry.

Although a detailed administrative manual on the method of assignments and the working of military grants (*Iqta*) is not available, important information can still be gathered from incidental statements found in various chronicles.

In Central Asia, the division of the army rested on ranks of ten (*Deh* or *Un*), hundred (*Yuz* or *Sadah*), thousand (*Hazara* or *Ming*), and ten thousand (*Tuman* or *Deh Hazara*) with their respective leaders namely *Un Bashi, Deh Bashi, Yuz Begi* or *Sad Begi, Ming Bashi* or *Hazari* and *Tuman Begi* or *Deh Hazari*. The highest military rank and division was the *tuman* which literally meant ten thousand.

A permanent army with a suitably trained and disciplined reserve force and bodyguards existed at the Centre. The military orientation of the state was reflected in the association of this military division with territory. The *tuman* simultaneously signified the largest military detachment as well as a district, and a *hazara* also carried with it the same double meaning. This duality of meaning could not but modify the rigour of the arithmetical division. *A tuman* was supposed to consist of 10,000 soldiers, but this was seldom the actual military strength of a *tuman*. Both Ibn-i Arab Shah and Abdurrazzaq state that a *tuman* was an area from which 10,000 men (or the revenue for the maintenance of 10,000 soldiers) was raised.[4] But the very fact that Samarqand consisted of seven *tumans* and Andijan and its vicinities of nine *tumans*[5] seems to suggest that there was no uniformity in the size of a *tuman*. These districts could hardly be expected to yield the necessary amount to raise such a large number of *tumans*, if each *tuman* meant 10,000 troops. Regarding the revenues of Farghana, Babur comments that, 'if people do justly, three or four thousand persons may be maintained by the revenues of Farghana.[6] This is a far cry from the 90,000 soldiers supposedly constituting *tumans*. Radloff's explanation of the word *tuman* as 'a measure of surface equal to 40,000 *tanabs* in Bukhara'[7] and Barthold's statement that 'as in Persia the division must have been connected with distribution of fiefs' both bring out more or less the territorial basis of the division into *tumans*. Hookham says that *tuman* is used frequently in the sense of a large tribal group or an army division of a considerable size and not ten thousand as these figures did not always correspond with the effectives provided by these regions, and eighteenth century sources indeed describe these territorial denominations as agrarian and fiscal divisions. *Tuman Begs* were 'headmen of a horde subdivision normally numbering 10,000 and paying their dues direct to the Supreme Khan.[9] Barthold held the view that 'the significance of 10,000 is evident only during the Mongol era and that the Turkish word *tuman ming* denoted only 1,000 × 1,000 = 1 million and not 10,000 = 10 millions,[10] meaning thereby that a *tuman* now meant 1,000 only. Ultimately, we get the Persian connotation of the term *tuman* i.e. a district consisting of a hundred villages. The *Nuzghat-ul Gulub* and *Babur Nama* both use the term in the sense of an administrative unit or a district. Various types of *tumans* like *tuman-i sansiz*,[11] *tuman-i kalan* and *tuman-i tusqal* have been mentioned by Yazdi.[12] According to Ghayasuddin, *tuman-i sansiz* was the detachment of 10,000 representing the ruler's personal brave royal bodyguards selected from amongst the chosen slaves bought against gold.[13] It seems to be the *corps d'elite* and was perhaps not subjected to *san* hence the name. It appears the *tuman-i kalan* (big *tuman*) was usually held by princes and major nobles, and its general was called *tuman begi*. The *Qushun* was headed by a leader (*sar*) who was under the charge of a third category of nobles, though it could often serve as a part of one or the other *tuman*[14] and also as a separate unit. The *tuman-i tusqal* seems to have been held by nobles of a lower category and its number seems to vary. Marco Palo explains the term *toscal* in the context of Qubila's hunting excursion in the following words: 'other ten thousand men also go with the king who in that hawking, runne hither and thither by two and two and marke whiter the fadcons nd Hawkes flie, that are cast from the first, that (if need be) they may helpe them. And these, in the Tartar language, are called *toscal,* that is to says, watch men or Markes men, being skilfull in a certain kind of whistle, wherewith they call in the Hawkes that are flowen'.[15] Beveridge renders the term as a 'kind of hunting analogous to driving'. It seems that these *Tumans* must have been the forces which were reserved to be used in the hour of need either during the war or hunting excursions

Amongst the Tartars, the word *koc* denoted two thirds of the main force which formed an encampment. Remaining third now forming two groups set out from *koc*. When they had travelled a certain distance from the main encampment these two groups would subdivide into raiding parties (*cambuli*) usually about 100 men strong. These raiding parties attacked villages situated within eighty miles of Tartar *kocs*.

Almost a similar situation exists in the case of *hazaras*. Yazdi designates the district of Khulm as yielding a *hazara*,[16] suggesting a territorial connotation only. The numerical names of various military units thus do not denote actual numbers. Long marches and on deserts, they may still denote hierarchical levels however, i.e. a *tuman* being above a *hazara*.

Another controversial term is *qushun*. The context in which the term appears in the *Zafar Nama* or *Matla-us Sadain*[17] yields different meanings, i.e. fluctuating from 50 to 500 men or even simply signifying a squadron or detachment of any strength between 50 to 500. In the *Tarikh-i Rashidi, qushun is* said to denote a force of 1,000 in Moghulistan.[18] Since the *qushun* has nowhere been mentioned as a rank, it can only be deduced that the term was simply used in the sense of a squadron irrespective of strength. Soviet scholars stress that in the decimal system an important role was played by the *qushun* which consisted of several hundreds though no evidence is cited for this.[19] One soldier from each unit of ten was appointed as its commander. It is more likely that the term *koshun* or *khoshun* was a remnant of Mongol *khoshun* or *koshun* which was a feudal principality in pre-revolutionary Mongolia and was also an administrative unit in the MPR until 1931.

The Central Asian rulers certainly believed in a set military hierarchy. The difference between upper, middle and lower strata of the military aristocracy was more sharp and noticeable though even a commander of hundred enjoyed the title of *begi* or *amir*.[20]

Haider Dughlat refers to various categories of soldiers in Kashghar and explains their status in military hierarchy. Apart from the *amirs* and commanders of regiments and detachments, *mirs* or *mirzadas* there were men who, Haider says, had their own tribes or following, e.g. *sarkhil, sirdar, kalantars*, etc., each of whom were chief or a tribe and had a retinue. There was another class of men who had no following but were quite alone, yet they had distinguished themselves over the rest by their courage in many battles and engagements and thus they had acquired the name of heroes or *bahadurs*.[21]

Among the army personnel, the post of *tawajis* (prefect, chief commander) was considered to be a high post among the Turks.[22] Since the *tawajis* were the chief organizers, only reliable persons could be appointed to the position. They acted as messengers, conveying the orders for the assembling or collection of the army at an appointed time and place before the battle, supervised the battle array and were also required to assign various responsibilities to the army personnel.[23] There were separate *tawajis* for infantry and cavalry.[24] Yazdi mentions that *amirs* like Haji Saifuddin. Amir Jahnashah Jaku and Amir Shamsuddin Abbas were appointed as *tawajian-i buzurg* during the *qurultai* at Aqyar to ensure the maintenance of the required number of soldiers.

Clavijo says that Jahanshah was 'the commander in chief of the imperial army and except Timur in person, none had a higher command'.[25] Al Hasan the Arab informs us that as a reward for his services in the (Chinese) wars,[26] Axalla (a Genoese by birth) had been appointed as the 'captain general' of all his 'footman' which was one of the 'principal honours' of the army and later on he was given the whole charge of the army.[27] The entire horde was divided clanwise and there were in all about 20,000 camps.[28] Timur had a number of spies employed in the army to keep him informed of minutest details regarding his enemy's territory and his (enemy's) army's movements.[29]

Varying accounts are given regarding the strength of the army under Timur. Ibn-i Arab Shah says on the evidence of Ibn-i Shahna that Hafiz Khwarazmi had once entered in the *diwan-i lashkar* some 8,00,000 men in *shumar* (counting).[30] Khwand Mir[31] also stresses that Timur's army amounted to 8,00,000 cavalry and infantry as registered in the *Daftar-i san* apart from 3,82,612 personal servants. In the *Tuzukat-i Timuri,* the number of cavalry in Timur's army is said to have been 92,000 which was considered by Timur as a good omen, since the number was equal to that yielded by the alphabets in the name of the Prophet.[32]

Apart from permanent army, often the need based additional recruitments were done and fresh army was raised before campaigns. The significance of the expedition determined the number and the formation of military forces. In various campaigns therefore, different numbers of the strength of Timur's army are given. Al Hasan says that during the Russian expedition, Timur's army was about 'six scores of thousand horses and a hundred and fifty thousand men on foot'. During the Chinese campaign the army comprised 50,000 horses and 1,00,000 foot men. During the Ottoman wars, Timur's forces reportedly 'consisted of 3,00,000 horses and 5,00,000 foot men from all nations'. During the battle of Angora, Timur 'received four scores of thousand horses and a hundred thousand footmen, a similar number from Changhatais and some 50,000 from various other lords'.[33] Alexandrescu-Dersca's analysis of the information regarding the strength of the army of Timur during the Ottoman campaign (as found in Timurid and Ottoman sources) best exemplifies the confusion created by the contradictory statements.[34] Apart from the main mass of the army Timur had his personal army (*Bandagan-i Khassa*).[35] There was a standing force at the court of Chingiz Khan prepared to serve him day and night, similarly Timur too had 'kept ready' a force, whenever 'he was in extremity'. This force left his side neither abroad nor at home, but guarded him in every vicissitude, fortunate or adverse'. Occasionally, the prisoners of war were added to the existing soldiers. It is, therefore, difficult to ascertain the exact number of Timur's army at any point of time partly because of the numerous categories involved. Yazdi mentions that at the time of the return of army from the Steppes the army had swelled to such an extent that 'if someone lost his *wisaq* (camp), he did not recover it for a month or two'.[36] Since general and vague statements regarding the strength of Timur's army as found in the sources do not solve the problem, one has to be content with information of the kind given by Ibn-i Arab Shah and Khwand Mir which is confirmed by later sources also. While writing to Mirza Iskandar in 816 Shahrukh boasted of having 1,00,000 cavalry at his command.[37] During Iraq and Azerbaijan campaigns in 823 counting (*san*) of the stipulated fixed stipulated number of the provincial army (*Lashkar-i Muqarrari-i Wilayat*) by *tawajis* showed 2,00,000 cavalry[38] though elsewhere the same number is presented as 1,00,000 men.[39] From Transoxoiana and Turkestan alone, there were 10,000 fixed cavalry. Like Chingiz, Timur also had introduced an army of *keshekten* (personal body guards). Since in the hour of need usually an additional force over and above the already existing provincial army was recruited by way of *nambardar* (presumably from civil population) with Tajik chiefs from all over the country (excluding Transoxiana), the *nambardar* forces in 823 amounted to another 15,000 cavalry and infantry who were to serve the emperor.[40] In the overall counting (*ihtiyat-i san*), however, 22,00,000 cavalry was said to have been recorded.[41] Mirza Sultan Abu said had given subsistence allowance (*ulufa*) to 1,80,000 cavalry which in sultan's own assertions was a number 'unheard of since the time of Chingiz and even afterwards'.[42] The decreasing number of the forces under later Timurids was obviously a result of their declining interest in conquests. Similar doubts prevail regarding the number of provincial armies also. Mirza Umar's provincial army is said to have comprised 47 *qushuns*, each consisting of 500 cavalry besides 5,000 *ughruq* in the *qaul*[43] (centre). The retainers of Abdul Ali Tarkhan, the governor of Bukhara were reckoned at 3,000 whom he 'kept well and handsomely'[44] whereas his son had 5,000 to 6,000 retainers. Khusru Shah's retainers under Mahmud Mirza were also 5,000 or 6,000 which under Mahmud Miraz's son increased to 20,000.[45]

Manz, however, observes that the personal armies of the princes were not very large as princes did not have command over all the troops levied in their provinces and had only partial control over the armies of the provinces they governed.[46] From a careful study of the sources, the inference can be drawn that 'appointment of nobles and officials was done by Timur himself and the recruitment of soldiers was left to the respective officers.

In accordance with the *Yasa*, the soldiers once enrolled were not allowed to change their squadron and had to furnish a written *muchulka* in this regard. In case of violation, each person was put to death.

The old army (*kuhna sipahiyan* or *lashkar-i qadim*) of the former ruler and the newly recruited ones (*lashkar-i jadid*) were both entered on the muster rolls (*daftar-i san*) and were granted stipends (*mursum* or *wajh*). For the maintenance of the revenue of the territory concerned *mal* and *mutswajjahat* and the taxes like *kharj-i lashkar* was appropriated.[47]

The armies of the king were registered in the central muster roll and were given salaries by the king.[48] For celebrating a victory or for purposes of meeting additional expense (e.g. warm clothes during an expedition to a cold place), the soldiers were granted extra allowances. Or sometimes their pay was doubled.[49] On certain occasion, even an ordinary soldier was given an *ulka*.

Unlike the Ottoman soldiers the Mongol army was not entitled to any salary in the initial stages and lived only on their flocks and herds, *qupchur* tax (cattle tax) trade and booty[50] though they always paid taxes of various kinds to the ruler. When the system of payment was introduced by later Mongol Khans, the *barat* (draft) was issued to the soldiers much to the chagrin of the peasants and artisans as the *barat* could be misused for squeezing maximum benefit from them. Although Ghazan's reforms including elimination of *barat* system was much appreciated in Persia and its surrounding regions, the system of *barat* could not be altogether eliminated. It seems to have continued even though partially in Central Asia as the sources refer to them during the reign of Timur and his successors. It was no wonder then that Abdurrazzaq, the traveller from Central Asia was so surprised to see that the soldiers in Calicut used to get stipend every fourth month and none of them was given any draft for a *wilayat*[51]—a practice common in Central Asia. Although no source has been cited, some interesting information is available in *Ancient Art of Warfare*. It is categorically mentioned that

> Timur's army had been paid in six months. Chiefs were paid in accordance to their rank but a soldier's pay was a sum equal to the market value of his best horse. Specialized or crack troops received higher wages equaling the price of two to four horses. The *Un Bashi* leaders of ten men earned ten

times the pay of the common soldiers they commanded and a third as much as their superiors, the *Un Bashi* who each commanded one hundred men. The *Gin Bashi* who approximated today's colonels and left one thousand men earned three times the wages of the *Yuz Bashi* and were in addition granted land fiefs within the Empire. Amirs who held the highest positions in the army or on Timur's[52] staff owned vast fiefs on the borders of the Empire.

It is stated in the sources that at the time of assignment of each new province (called *iqta* or *suyurghal*), each prince was allotted certain reliable officers (*amiran-i khassa*) along with a large army receiving an annual pay (*tushmal saliyana*).[53] The troops accompanied the prince much in the same way as when Chingiz had distributed territories along with a definite number of forces to his sons.[54] The provincial army was separately raised and was given its maintenance allowance from the revenues of the respective *wilayats* and the detachments sent by the central ruler only served as an additional reserve force to provincial army. Each *suyurghal* was expected to furnish contingents of main force (*asl*) and an additional detachment (*izafa*), if the *suyurghal* included an additional (*ulufa*) grant also. There are references to the old army (*kuhna sipahiyan or lashkar-i qadim*) and the newly recruited ones (*lashkar-i jadid*) both of whom received stipends (*marsum* or *wajh*).[55] The payment to the army was made through military grants (*iqta, ulka, ukalka*), from local revenues and even out of the booty gained in campaigns. The central troops receiving subsistence money and supplies (*arzaq*) either at the centre or in provinces formed the nucleus of the army. During the campaigns all the forces joining the Emperor were paid directly by Timur's treasury and a general muster was also undertaken.[56] Besides, taxes like *kharj-i lashkar* (levy for maintenance of the army), *taghar* (provisions, a levy in kind) and *nimari* (extra ordinary levies) also were realized from the people to lessen the burden on the state. Even under the later Timurids the practice continued. In 858 Abul Qasim Babur who was planning a campaign against Transoxiana had ordered the collection of *mal-i nan; zabt-i lashkar* and *zar-i lashkar.* Khwaja Wajihuddin Ismail Simnani along with the *amirs* had realized 'whatever was possible' and the large amount thus accumulated as *wajh* was brought to Abul Qasim Babur who distributed it among his *amirs* and soldiers.[57] Additional stipendiary money (*mawajib o marsumat*) were also given to the soldiers in Turkish fashion to serve as an incentive. The provider to the army was supplied before hand by the state in case the places around the region were deserted, otherwise they raised provisions on the route by means of *taghar* tax.[58] On certain occasions, the soldier was given an *ulka* or *ukalka* (region for pasturing) allowing the soldiers to roam around in the assigned place.[59] During Iraq and Azerbaijan campaign in 823, Shahrukh is reported to have ordered that excessive wealth and immense cash should be given to the soldiers by way of *ukalka, inam mawajib* and *marsumat*.[60] In difficult days the pay of the soldiers must have depended upon irregular income received by the patron. Babur's *begs* of all ranks, retainers and the household (*tabinan*) were given the money received from the plunder of treasure of the Arghuns which served as their own subsistence and also for the pay of their soldiers.[61] Money received as indemnity of war, charges of the army and even the expenses of the army (*nal*) were demanded from the defeated.[62] For celebrating a victory or for purpose of meeting additional expenses the soldiers were granted extra allowances or some times their pay was doubled.[63] For this purpose large sum was allocated by the ruler. The armies of the central ruler were registered in the central treasury.[64]

Timur demanded a great deal from his soldiers in order to support his ambitions. To attract soldiers, he acted upon the age-old tactics of allowing them to share the spoils of war. In the distribution of money, however, Timur was far more generous than Chingiz who is said to have believed that 'lions do not hunt unless they are hungry' 'starve thy dog that it may follow thee'.[65] Manucci's[66] comments that 'none could recount property, the courage or vigour or wealth of the conqueror Timur who paid his soldiers and generals at one time for eight years in advance relying on the fidelity of his vassals' may or may not be correct but the entire booty received by Timur was frequently, though not always, distributed amongst the soldiers.[67] If, however, the amount of booty was not sufficient for all the soldiers, compensation was sometimes granted from the royal treasury.[68] On certain occasions, even the *peshkash* (magnificent presents offered to superiors) brought to Timur was given away to the soldiers and the *amirs*. Although the tribute of security (*mal-i amani*) imposed upon the subjects of the newly conquered territory in the form of cash or kind was basically a source of income to the state treasury, Timur and his successors often permitted nobles and soldiers to share in this also.[69] Nevertheless, Timur was alert enough to restrain his largesse as soon as the evil effects of wealth were noticed 'since affluence created an attitude of indifference, particularly among the lower circles of *amirs*', who were not directly responsible to the ruler. Timur was once informed that the income from such resources had enriched the officers and the soldiers considerably and this in turn had led them to contemplate treachery and indifference to military obligations deeming that the entire responsibility would fall on their superiors. Timur thereupon summoned a *qurultai* in the village of Aqyar in 1389-90: he immediately increased the number of soldiers in each squadron without increasing the salary of its officers so that the money accumulated had to be spent and could no longer distract the attention of soldiers from their primary duty. To ensure an immediate compliance of the order, a written assurance was taken by the *amirs* from their chiefs for providing the required number of troops at the appointed place and time.[70]

Promotions and Punishments

Timur had a great liking for brave and courageous soldiers.[71] A person was immediately rewarded for his gallantry according to services rendered. Thus a *Yuz Begi* was to be promoted to the rank of *Hazari*.[72] Certain others were favoured with land grants in the form of *jildu* (*inam*) or *suyurghal*.[73] If an *Un Bashi* vanquished the forces of an enemy, he was to receive the government of a city in reward (*jildu*) whereas a *Yuz Bashi* was to get the command of a province. The *amirs* received the vicegerency of the place they conquered for a period of three years as a reward. An additional honour of *Tarkhani* was sometimes conferred upon the high *begs*.[74] While Chingiz used to give posthumous awards, Timur is reported to have been exceptionally considerate towards the relatives of those killed in war. The wounded also received Timur's personal attention. To cite an instance: Amir 'Usman' Abbas who was injured during the Baghdad campaigns, was granted a daily allowance of 1,000 *dinar-i kebeki* for ointment.[75]

The punishment for shirking military responsibility or for showing timidity was equally severe. Either the person was put to death, fined or physically tortured.[76] Certain curious ways of humiliating such defaulters were resorted to.[77]

Tarkhani was granted by Timur to those who distinguished themselves in the art of warfare. It is, however, significant to note that such a *tarkhani* carried with it three clauses, i.e. the group of the *yasawuls* should not demand wages (*dast-i radd*) from them, should not detain them from coming directly to the Emperor and should not bring them to book till nine faults have been committed by them or their sons.[78]

Under the Uzbegs also the army was rewarded or reprimanded before and after a battle.[79] The wounded soldiers were given medical aid.[80] Emperor personally visited them and sent physicians[81] and even granted extra money for ointment, etc. Those who showed bravery were handsomely rewarded and promoted by Abdullah and given horses, saddles and money. There was invariably an increase in the fixed stipend (*marsum*) of the victorious army.[82] After the victory in Balkh, Abdullah had awarded 20,000 *khanis* to Nazar Bi Naiman and 10,000 *khanis* to Aqum Chehra.[83]

The matrimonial relations were also established with *tarkhan amirs*.[84]

The defaulting nobles were frequently lashed, fined, hanged, killed, put under house arrest and exiled.[85]

Either conforming to the age old universal method of incentive to the army in the form of booty or adhering to the Islamic principle of division of spoils[86] (*alanfal*), the Central Asian rulers laid down rules for a sharing of the spoils. After a victory, plundering was done only when the permission to do so had been granted and it was stopped as soon as the *mal-i amani* (money to ensure peace) was determined. The defaulters in this regard were severely punished.

The rules and regulations and an iron discipline were enforced strictly everywhere. Even at the time of plunder which followed a victory, certain decorum had to be maintained by the soldiers, though each was entitled to booty.[87] In this respect there was no difference between a general and a soldier 'as the general and the rank and file of the army were made equal' as soon as Timur 'had given reign to general plunder'.[88] Even a slave or a foreigner could enjoy this right. The only condition was that plunder should start only after royal permission. If anyone committed such an act 'before the granting of license, though he might be to Timur in the position of father or son, he punished him with loss of goods and life and violated his dignity. Neither prayers of penitence nor excuse of ignorance could save him and his family'; this rule was an inviolable custom'.[89] Similarly, no plundering was allowed after a proclamation of peace.[90] For misbehavior to village elders or for similar small offences, the offending soldiers were cut to pieces. Al Hasan boasts that 'justice reigns so amongst us, in so much as if a soldier had taken but an apple he was put to death and this was severely observed over all'.[91]

The discipline and the strict regulations of the army hardly changed even in days of adversity. Babur's description of how the crowd of Muslim traders (who had come for buying and selling in the bazaar) were plundered by Babur's needy forces at the *Yam* near Qara Bulaq and how his disciplined army restored everything just after an order by Babur proves it well, he affirms that: 'the first watch of the next day had not passed before nothing not a tag of cotton, not a broken needle's point remained in the possession of any man of the force, all was back with its owners'.[92]

COMPOSITION OF THE ARMY

Both Yazdi and Ibn-i Arab Shah give interesting details of the composition of Timur's army which consisted of persons from various races.[93] The liquid resources of not only tax and trade but also booty helped Timur to raise professional, tribal, feudal as well as personal standing army. In all the newly conquered regions, Timur granted permission to soldiers to join his service. Those who were willing to come under his banner were given passes for safe conduct and other facilities for joining their regiments.[94] If, however, any soldier resisted, he was hanged or punished. Consequently, the army of Timur was not confined only to Central Asian soldiers, i.e. Chaghatai, Jetah, Turkestani, etc. According to Ibn-i Arab Shah,

> To many of the citizens the Tartar army seemed like the nightmare, advance of hordes pouring from the jungles of hell: there were men of Turan, warriors of Iran, leopards of Turkestan, tigers of Badakhshan, hawks of Dasht and Khata, Mongols, vultures of Jetta, eagles, vipers of Khujand, Basilisks of Andakan, reptiles of Khwarazm, wild beasts of Jurjan, eagles of Zaghanian and hounds of Hisar Shadman, horsemen of Fars, lions of Khurasan, hyenas of Ghildu, lions of Mazendarana, wild beast of the mountains, crocodiles of Rustamdar and Taliban, vipers of the tribe of Ghuzz and Kirman, wolves of Isfahan, wolves of Kaiff and Ghazni and Hamadan, elephants of Hindustan, Sind and Multan, rams of the province of Lur, bulls of the high mountains of Ghor, scorpions of Shahrizor (capital of Kurdish state), serpents of Askar Makram (Samarra in Iraq) and Jandisabur. To these were added hyena cubs of slaves and whales of

Turkmans and rabble and followers and ravening dogs of base Arabs and gnats of Persians and crowds of idolators and profane Magi; people whom no list could cover and no roll include. In a word he was a false prophet and with him Gog and Magog and barren rushing winds.[95]

Khwand Mir records that there were '1,00,000 Indians who fell into captivity during the Indian expedition and are still there in his army'. Nevertheless Badauni speaks of the killing of the captives or their release.[96] The soldiers from various races who were fully trained by Timur stood by him in difficult situations, later on, they rallied around Khalil Sultan who is said to have recruited Arabs also in his army.[97] Al Hasan adds that Timur had many Christians from Georgia and Pont Euxin.[98]

According to Ibn-i Arab Shah Timur had in his army 'Turks that worsipped idols and men who worshipped fire, Persians, Magi soothsayers and wicked enchanters and the idolators carried their idols, soothsayers spoke in verses and devoured that which had died'[99] and that 'there were many women also in Timur's army who mingled in the mellee of battle and overcame mighty heroes in battle'.[100] Yazdi refers to a squadron of the Qipchaq tribe. Al Hasan the Arab records his appreciation of the military knowledge of Timur's army though he considered Muscovites to be superior to them as the Timurid soldiers 'were indeed trained up in the discipline of wares but not in the practice there of'.[101] A careful study of the sources shows that Timur's army was dominated by Turkicized Mongol tribes namely Qauchin, Barlas, Arlat and Sulduz.

Amongst the soldiers of various races, Timur shared the Turkish feelings[102] and considered the Khurasanis (Persians) to be the most efficient and trustworthy. Although Timur liked them, their leader Bahlul was burnt alive when his squadron revolted. Nevertheless the Turks were considered to be faithful. They 'took pride in their excellent warfare and denounced the Tajiks for being ignorant of the art and tactics of battle'.[103] Juvaini appreciates Turkish archers who 'sew up the eyes of the heavens with the discharge of an arrow'. The Chaghatai soldiers formed the most favoured group which enjoyed complete freedom in Timur's Empire.[104] Babur considered Mughal army being 'of no use in fighting. This is always the way with those ill omened Mughals. If they win, they grab at booty, if they lose they unhorse and pilfer their own side.'[105]

According to Al Hasan, footmen of Timur were 'armed after the

Christian manner and all were commanded by sundry captains, but all obeyed Axalla who commanded them as a general'.[106]

In his *Tuzukat,* Timur had laid down some regulations of promotions and rewards to his soldiers. If anyone of his select soldiers distinguished himself in battle he was to be given rapid promotions, i.e. in recompense for the first exploit, he was to be made an *Un Bashi* and for the second exploit an *Yuz Bashi* and for the third exploit a Ming Bashi. The *tabinan* of the *Un Bashis* were to be raised to the rank of *Un Bashi.* Similarly a *Ming Bashi*, was in case of his victory was to be promoted to the rank of first *Amir*, the first army to the rank of second and his 'every amir who signalized his valour and abilities, and overthrew the forces of his enemy, should be promoted from his own to a superior station and that the private soldiers who distinguished themselves in battle, should be rewarded by an increase of pay'.[107]

Timur believed that the rights of the warrior were to be protected 'for those men who sell their permanent happiness for perishable honours, merit compensation'.[108] And that every chief had a claim on Timur's fortune by sheer dint of his services.

The old soldiers were not to be deprived of their *ulufa* and *rank* and his rights were not to be suspended. Instead they and their counsels which emanated from experience were to be respected. They were to be considered as 'the ingredients of the workshop of Empire' and after them their sons should succeed.'[109] Similarly it would amount to 'an act of injustice' if the good deeds of a soldier are concealed. Instead he should be amply rewarded. The wounded soldier after a resolute fighting was to receive awards and *jildu*.

Timur ordered that 'the right of the warrior should not be injured. The soldiers grown in years should not be deprived of his station or wages. The actions of the soldier should not be suppressed. For those men who sell their permanent happiness for perishable horror are worthy of reward.'[110] The rights of the civil population were not always protected. During his campaigns, Timur, did not shirk from destruction of buildings, fields, etc., to strike terror.[111] A runaway soldier was to be deprived of *Kornish,* if he fled from 'absolute necessity' or of 'panic', he should be considered as 'invalid' (*mazur*) and 'mad' (*bawle*).[112] The captive were to be given an option. If they had shown bravery coupled with loyalty to the masters and later on after defeat were willing to surrender, Timur received them with honour and gave them befitting ranks, e.g. Sher Bahrain and Mangli

Khwaja are examples in question. Sher Bahrain was a general of Amir Husain with whom he fought bravely against Timur. Later on he joined Timur. Mangli Bugha in Balkh turned down Timur's offer and fought loyally for his master Tughlaq Timur. When after latter's defeat he joined Timur's services, he fought bravely and always won Timur's appreciation.

Sinor, however, says that Timur's army was predominantly Turkish but he emulated Mongol traditions.[113] In many ways, Timur adhered to the Turco-Mongol traditions. During the march towards east and north, the left wing proceeded first in accordance with the tradition of Turkish armies.[114] Besides, the custom of *surudguftan* (to play a musical instrument), *rasm-i uljameshi* (act of submission by bending the knees and kissing the hands), *kasadaashtan, asp kashidan, zanu zadan* (a present of horse offered to the king in kneeling position) were also continued by Timur.[115]

Barthold says that Timur's army mainly consisted of cavalry,[116] though the sources indicate that in almost every campaign the infantry outnumbered the cavalry.[117] Usually, the infantry like the Ottoman *azabs* and *akinjis* stood in front of the cavalry (often *qaul*) and the former were the 'shock troops' first to countercharge.[118] They were protected by the shield and the *tura* (screen). The infantry thus played an important role in defence. Ghayasuddin Ali highlights the exclusive role played by the infantry in the Indian and Qipchaq campaigns. Timur's knowledge about 'the good and bad stock of horses' was highly admired by Ibn-i Arab Shah,[119] though no definite information is available regarding remounts. There are references to the presence of *yakaspa* (one horse) troops[120] though as a rule one spare horse was maintained by every two horsemen. Once when the horses of the troopers became weak and tired after a long journey, an order was issued that three persons from each squadron of ten should be sent back to the capital and their horses be distributed amongst the remaining seven so as to make them *doaspas*[121] (a soldier with two horses). This would imply that four out of ten were already *doaspas*. Morgan's view that the Mongol armies in Persia carried with them a string of horses for remounts and the number of Mongol troops must be multiplied several times to arrive at a likely estimate of the number of horses accompanying which might have had five horses per head, seems applicable to Timur's army as well, even if partially. When the horses in Mirza Pir Muhammad

Jahangir's army died during the rainy season in India his soldiers appeared before Timur either on foot or riding oxen. Timur immediately granted them, 3,000 horses and each one of them was made a rider (*sawar*) [122] which shows that Timur had some extra horses.

In the age-old pattern, the army was divided into five *tabiya* (arrangement of the five main divisions of the centre, right, left wings, vanguard and rearguard *janah qalb muqaddama* and *saqa*. A special detachment for ambuscade called *kamingah* was to be used for a sudden surprise attack, to sandwich the fleeing army or simply for reinforcement. The centre in battle was usually led by the ruler or one of the princes. Originally, the *aq orda* (white horde) supplied the soldiers for the left wing (*ong*) and the *altun orda* (golden horde), those for the right wing (*sol*). Babur comments at the turn of the sixteenth century that 'each right right, left left, centre centre. The most reliable men go to the extreme points of the right and left. The Chiras and Begchik clans always demand to go to the point in the right[123] and even fought among themselves[124] for that'.

Such a hard and fast rule was neither feasible nor advisable for a cautious statesman like Timur who 'preferred change to permanence'. Manz rightly concludes that 'the right and left wings of the army were probably reorganized for each major campaign though theoretically the *amirs* served permanently in either the right or left wings, a step directly taken by Timur to prevent his *amirs* from creating too strong a power base'.[125] A study of various campaigns in the sources prove the point well. Both Rustam, Taghai Bugha and Ghayasuddin Tarkhan have been described by Yazdi as *Umara-i gaul*[126] (commanders of the centre) though they served in the left wing during the Haruk, Angora and Egyptian campaigns. Even Amir Jahan Shah who had been described by Yazdi[127] as an *amir* of the left wing (*jaranghar*) who had efficiently served in the same wing during the Indian, Egyptian and Halb campaigns had to fight at the battle of Angora in the right wing. The other notable generals also usually served alternately in the right or left wing depending upon the sovereign's will.[128] The system appears to have continued during the fifteenth century. Babur says that there were fixed places for each of the men, decided beforehand while forming up right, lefts, centre and vanguard. Babur even refers to the names of those in the left wing as 'inscribed' which led Beveridge to presume that Babur used a written record.[129]

REVIEW OF THE ARMY

Timur's consultative assemblies had also a diplomatic pattern. Before every campaign, Timur summoned great men and leaders of his kingdom and his counsellors, 'so that none of them was left out or a son admitted in the place of the father or father instead of the son'; then he expounded to them the secrets of his affairs and demanded frank fearless advice.[130]

Babur's observation that 'precisely as Chingiz Khan laid down his rules so the Mughals still observe them' is confirmed by the accounts of army organization prevalent in all the Mongol states.[131]

Dismissing this large assembly, Timur would invite all his intimate friends such as Sulaiman Shah, Qamari, Saifuddin, Allahadad, Shah Malik and Shaikh Nuruddin who would discuss that question zealously and dispute subtly thereon.[132]

Babur records:[133] 'Precisely as Chingiz Khan laid down his rules, so the Mughals still observe them. Each man has his place just where his ancestor had it; right, right, left, left—centre, centre. The most reliable men go to the extreme points of the right and left. The Chiras and Begchik clans always demand to go to the point in the right. At that time, the *beg* of the Chiras *tuman* was a very bold brave, Qashka Mahmud and the *beg* of the renowned Beghchik *tuman* was Ayub Begchik. These two disputing which should go out to the point, drew swords on one another. At last it seems to have been settled, that one should take the highest place in the hunting circle, the other in the battle array.'

The feasibility, plans and strategy of war discussed by Khan, *Noyons*, Sultans and the remaining ruling group in various assemblies (*kangash*) were finalized by the Khan himself in his special assembly (*majlis-i khas*). Having decided upon a war, *tawajis* were sent to inform the nominated army (*namzad*) and to collect (*zabt-i sipah*) the required number of soldiers alongwith their arms (*silah*). The proposed duration of campaign (one year or more and other details were given to them to enable them to prepare accordingly. [134] The soldiers could be informed at a very short notice to join the imperial army immediately. The *tawajis* conveyed the *jar* to the army taking a *muchulka* for *istihzar* (attendance) from the army to the effect that the required number would be reaching at the appointed place (*miadgah, mahal-i ijtimaa*) within the given period (*miad-i muqarrara*).[135]

It is not certain whether a separate department of *arz* existed for the inspection of the army and its recruitment or a simple verification was sufficient. The registration of the soldiers was done as under before every march where a roll list was prepared by the Khan's officers. Masud Kuhistani refers to the *tahqiq* of the army by Abulkhair before a campaign.[136] Hafiz Tanish records that Qulbaba and Haider Munshi had been appointed for the verification (*tahqiq*) of the army of Abdullah Khan which was in addition to the armies maintained by the sultans and receiving subsistence allowance from the latter.[137] For three days the soldiers constantly came and got themselves enrolled. In this way, about 30,000 people were checked (*ba arz dar amad*).[138] On another occasion, Muhammad Baqi Bi Durman was ordered to prepare a roll of the army and to submit it before the Khan,[139] such roll lists included even the names of the *amirs*, *eshik aqasi* and other officers also. On the eve of the battle, the *jibs didan* (the inspection of arms and armaments) and the *arz-i lashkar* (checking) was done personally by the Khan in accordance with Chingizid custom of *dim*. The fully equipped army stood in a battle array in divisions of right, left, centre and rear. The Khan rode through each of the detachment and carefully examined its equipment and arms. The chief of each detachment, whether prince or a noble, knelt and offered the Khan a horse and *tansuq* (presents). In return the Khan also rewarded them and encouraged them with promises. The *arz* continued from morning till evening.[140]

Since a full-fledged department of *arz* and system of registration existed under the Abbasids and all its provinces had more or less the same administrative structure it may be presumed that the traditions continued. Although there are references in the sources to the registration of soldiers (*dakhil-i daftar*)[141] and to the registers (*daftar-i san*), the actual procedure of recruitment has not been described. When the *tawajis* organized the army before every campaign, registers were brought to the emperor.[142] The *bakhshis* are said to have arranged the *san* and registered the name *huliya* (descriptive roll, the external form or bearing) of the soldiers.[143] The armies seem to have been centrally recruited (though these conclusions are by no means final).

Before every campaign, the review[144] of the army (*izhar-i lashkar* or *arz*) and armaments (*jeha didan* or *namudan-i jiba*) was done by Timur and his successors personally. The proposed place (*arzgah*) and the time for arrival of the troops were conveyed to the officers through *ajar* (news) sent by *tawajis* who in turn demanded a receipt (*khattaha* or *muchulka*) as a token of acceptance from the officers for reaching at appointed time and place. During the *arz* (inspection), various regiments were arranged in battle array (in the right, left, centre and rear) and came fully equipped to the *murchal* (site of inspection, intrenchment). Each *tuman* was divided into *hazara, sadah* and *un* and fully equipped they marched in groups in front of the soevereign who personally visited each regiments on a horseback and checked the arms. The *muqaddams* (chiefs) of each *tuman* or regiment got down from the horse and kneeling down in 'Turco-Mongol fashion', presented to the emperor a saddled horse—a custom known as *asp kashidan*.[145] The continuous checking and rechecking was done to assess whether any increase (*izafa*) in the number or any reorganization was needed.[146] Often the review continued for two days from morning till evening. There is no separate department of *arz* mentioned in the sources. Apparently, the checking was done through the Mongol method of *dim* (counting). If Tusi is to be believed counting (*dim*) was done with the help of a whip or bow which was used in the count presumably held by the teller to keep his place in the marchpast. The *Siyasat Nama* refers to the whip in the context of numbering an army.[147] The *arz* of the army was done presumably by counting which was called *san-i lashkar*, once counting was completed the soldiers crossed the river. It was in 698 that a large army amounting to 3,00,000 was to be counted in *arz* but owing to mild winter, the water of the river was not yet properly thawed and the soldiers, therefore could not walk over the river or even cross it (*Jt* 530). Once Ahmad Tambal had disappeared from the rank and file of Babur's army longwith his detachment.

When a few days later, the Khan heard that Tambol had gone up into Aura-tipa, he got his army to horse in the battle array and rode out from Tashkent. Between Pishkent and Sam-Sirak he formed up into array of right and left saw the count of his men (*dim*). This done, the standards were acclaimed in Mughal fashion. The Khan dismounted and nine standards were set up in front of him. A Mughal tied a long strip of white cloth to the thigh bone (*aurtailik*) of a cow and took the other end in his hand. Three other strips of white cloth were tied to the staves of three of the (nine) standards, just below the Yaktails, and their other ends were brought for the Khan to stand on one and for me and Sultan Muhammad Khan to stand each on one of the two others.[148]

Haider Dughlat describes the procedure of *dim* (counting) during the Kashghar campaign. According to Haider Dughlat the *tawajis* were ordered to take up their stand in a narrow passage and the troops passed through the files, regiment by regiment, the *tawajis* counting them and the scribes (*bakhshis*) writing down the numbers. Even the count of women, children, the baggage and the roadguards were all noted down. Incidentally, Haider Dughlat's account further conveys implicitly that only the numbers were recorded against the name of the commanders and that the order of the reckoning was determined by the importance or nobility of the family (*tabeqa*). In certain cases the affairs were entrusted by the father to son. Sometimes the entire family was included in the army.[149] Yazdi refers to some sort of *dagh* (branding) and *tamgha* of the army though in a rather confusing manner. He says, for instance, that while the *amirs* of Qamruddin stayed in one of the forests during the Jetah campaign, each one of them passed through the Irtish river one after another so that their *dagh* and *tamgha* could be stamped on *sanobar* (any conebearing tree, a fir) trees.[150] This is difficult to understand and since the reference to such *dagh* and *tamgha is* not found anywhere Yazdi's meagre information cannot be of much use. No other information regarding the scrutiny of physical features of the soldiers and the marks on their mounts is available at the moment. Several sale documents, however refer to various horses branded with a variety of stamps. But they could also be tribal totems; individual or communal mark.

In a *qurultai,* Timur is said to have declared that the conditions of the cavalry and infantry needed to be examined by him thoroughly and that care for the equipment which were needed in the war was necessary as they were the instruments of victory. Before the Chinese campaign, the *amirs* of tawajis were to demand a bond (*muchulka*) by the commanders (*mirs*) of *hazaras* and *sadahs* mentioning their arms and order in which they were going to appear in the battlefield.[151] Such an elaborate investigation followed by a ready supply of arms and necessaries was a common feature of Timur's military system. During the Mazandaran expedition (786), Timur asked for a similar *muchulka* even from the *amirs* of *sadah* and *hazara* that they would not leave their squadron without permission, otherwise they would be killed.[152] Clavijo wondered how the great horde of Timur was so well organized that from the greatest to the humblest, each man knew his allocated position, each clan taking up its appointed place and without confusion in most orderly fashion with twenty thousand tents with family and children, every craft and art needful for supply was to be found throughout the camp'.[153] Ibn-i Arab Shah also appreciated Timur's military discipline saying that 'Timur's army was not wanting in these things, since what each one had to do was decided and explored and where to fight and where to stand was inscribed on the front of its standards'.[154] The same discipline prevailed during the Timurids also. Babur gives a very graphic description of the first rate plan and method of the organization of his small army in 1507 on the eve of battle of Qandahar. For Babur's 'immediate command (*Khasa tabinan*), he had selected braves from whose hands comes work and had inscribed them by tens and fifties, each ten and each fifty under a leader who knew the post in the right or of the centre for his ten or his fifty, knew the work of each in the battle and was there on the observant watch, so that, after mounting the right and left, right and left, hands, right and left sides charged right and left without the trouble of arranging them or the need of a *tawaji*.'

On the eve of each campaign, a thorough rechecking was also done to investigate whether any change or addition seemed essential in the army. Before the Chinese campaign, Timur ordered that the *tawajis*, should count the *hazaras* of each army, make proper investigations and increase their number. Accordingly, the *amirs* increased *san* (number) wherever there was some possibilities and need for *izafa* (addition) and got the new recruits registered. Subsequently, the commanders (*amirs* of *uluses* and governors (*hakims*) of *wilayats* engaged themselves in the collection and organization of troops. The leading men (*kalantars*) or an *ulus* and the heads of the villages were to take the *nuskha-i tunqal* (passport of transporting arms from one place to another) from the great *tawajis* regarding the details of the required number of arms (*yaraq*) and the regulations (*dastur*) under which they were to be supplied. Amir Burunduq was appointed to go through the list of the army to find out how many additional soldiers would be employed for the campaign. In accordance with the *san* fixed at Kan-i Gil, Timur was informed that there would be 2,00,000 cavalary and infantry from Transoxiana, Turkestan, Khwarazm, Balkh, Badakhshan, Khurasan, Sistan, Mazandaran and Tartar from Azerbaijan and Iraq. Such a large army was bound to have detachments coming from various sides trained in different ways. Al Hasan says that Timur's thirty thousand horsemen were 'all Scythians, who observe not the same order the Parthians do', but the clever supervision of Timur, must have made all the different regiments to act uniformly.

According to Abdurrazzaq each soldier was to bring with him provisions for a specific time (depending upon the period of a campaign), a bow with 30 arrows, quiver, shells, shields, an additional horse between each of two horsemen, ten for each *un* (ten), 2 spades, 1 hoe, 1 sickle, 1 axe, 1 awl, 100 needles, rope for binding, half a maund wheat, one thick piece of skin and 1 boiler.[155] A very strict organization (*murchal*) was maintained during the march. The vanguard (*manghalay*) consisting of several *tumans* was sent as the first main force, through a group of scouts or *qarawuls* was sent ahead of them.[156] The intelligence officials (*khabargir*) could be from any group but the service secret consisted of the choicest warriors. During the march, an important role was played by the conductors (*ghacharchi*) whom Timur himself appointed and sent to different detachments.

It seems that usually the two words were settled on beforehand as pass words 'for the use of the whole army so that of two men meeting in the fight, one may give the one, the other give back the second in order to distinguish friends from foes, own men form strangers'.[157] Sometimes confusion was created leading to unnecessary destruction as during the Andijan struggle when the passwords given by the Mughals was not replied back through the proper countersign and the Mughals taking Babur's men for enemy fell upon them.[158]

There was a royal armourer's workshop or depot of arms *zarrad Khana-i Khas* or *jeba Khana-i Humayun* where varied kinds of war equipments were kept to be supplied to the soldiers.[159] Clavijo refers to the innumerable workshops with thousands of captive artisans who prepared the various armaments[160] during the reign of Timur, 'These upward of a thousand workmen' says Clavijo 'labour at making plate armour and helms with bows and arrows and to this business they are kept at work throughout the whole of their time in the service of His Highness'.[161] Elsewhere Clavijo refers to the bow makers brought from Damascus who produced cross bow which are so famous.[162] All the nobles from the *tuman* down to the hundred and the soldiers were provided horse and *jeba*.[163] Even the horse shoes were supplied form the royal stables. The same practice continued during the fifteenth century. Before the Iraq and Azarbaijan campaigns in 823 Shahrukh is reported to have ordered that lances, spears, swords, daggers, bows and arrows should be bought from every nook and corner of the Empire at current market prices and an additional 1,000 armours should be deposited with the royal treasure and store inhabitants of Chigil a city in Turkestan were exceedingly beautiful and unequalled in archery.[164]

The quality of the arms depended upon the status of its owner. Ibn-i Arab Shah says that the equipments and the weapons of Timur were 'adorned with gems and gold and embroidered and decked with so much art that even the meanest of them equalled the income of a country and one grain from the heap of those gems was beyond price'. Even the governor of Mazandaran Pir Badshaḥ in 809 was said to have worn a golden helmet (*khudizar*). The 'typiçal' Bukḥara sword with a good quality damascened blade which were worn on the hips and not hung on the back in the Arab fashion, Bukharan sheaths and scabbard with a wooden core covered with leather, velvet or metal.[165]

The paintings provide a great deal of information regarding the Military system under Chingiz, Timur and the Uzbeg rulers. Interesting depiction of battle scenes, night attacks and sieges is available in the Turkish paintings of *Rauzat-us Safa*, *Timur Nama* of Hatifi, *Tazkira-i Salatin-i Chaghatai* and others. The painting 'Timur Attacks on Balkh' shows soldiers with brass helmets, conical camps and others wearing helmets which were like those of the Tartars. The two types of trumpets (one straight and one curved), horse with saddles, *kajim,* stirrups and long lances with sharp edged blades, some more with peculiar Turco-Mongol *yurts* and soldiers are presented in the most aggressive posture. Another painting depicting a battle between Timur and Toqtamish Khan of the Golden Horde presents the impressive sight of lancers, standard bearers, etc. Elsewhere Timur is shown holding a flanged mace. The archers are aiming their arrows in a kneeling position. Timur's standard is also painted which carried an imprint of a 'dragons's head and elaborate trident finial'.

In *Babur Nama*, numerous other kinds of arrows have been mentioned. There are references to *goshawks* which had been translated by Elphinston as playing (*ba bazi*) with falcons. In fact the word, is *piazi bila*, i.e. 'arrows having sharp points'. They were elsewhere called as *sanglakh*. Beveridge had explained the Persian word *goshagir* which appears frequently in almost all the Persian sources known as *chapras*, brooch or buckle and the *kardang* and is said to bead these names because it fastens in the string, it serves to make good a warped bow, without the use of fire and it should be kept upon the bow tip till this has reverted to its original state.[166]

During the period of actual fighting, the food and fodder was to be supplied by the government which constantly received its supplies from various towns. The depots in the rear of the army with trains of provisions having a supply base nearby discouraged 'a scorehed earth policy'. Although Chingiz had continued Chirbi (a department for collecting provisions).[167] A reference to this is not available in the *Timurid Uzbeg* sources. It seems that provisions (*aliq-i ulaghan* or *yurtawal*) for soldiers were collected by the soldiers themselves from the population on their way in the form of *taghar* tax;[168] or the same was supplied to them, if necessary, by the State.[169] During the Qazaq campaigns in 1509, Shaibani's soldiers collected *azuqa* (provisions) in Turkistan. During the Herat campaign Abdullah wrote to Khwaja Juibari to supply 1,000 camel loads of barley which amounted to 10,000 *mans* from Andkhud or Merv since the entire stocks available in the royal establishment had already been distributed.[170] Once when the traders sent eatables and large quantities of grains with the *diwan* of Bukhara, Khwaja Kamaluddin Husain, it was directly distributed among the army. On the other hand from lack of supplies, famine could strike the army so that one maund of flour (*arad*) was once (in 1581-2 near Dasht-i Qipchaq) sold for hundred *tanga-i Iskandar Khan* and even then was rarely found.[171]

The maintenance of the army was not exclusively a state affair. Much of its burden fell upon the subjects who had to supply the food, fodder and other necessities in addition to military taxes. During a march, the army collected provisions in the form of *taghar* tax which was later on distributed among the soldiers.[172] To Timur the needs of his army were allegedly far more important than the interests of the settled subjects population. If the supplies were insufficient, the standing crop could be swiftly cut down. Clavijo records the attitude of these soldiers who used to demand supplies from town people at odd hours even during peace times and off the battleground. If there was even the slightest delay, merciless beatings would follow. In case, a proper reception was not given to the soldiers, the defaulter had to pay through the loss of their lives and goods. These soldiers boasted that 'they could even take away the lives of the people without any resistance on their part'. Clavijo saw the depopulated towns and was surprised that everyone lived in terror of these messengers.[173] Like the Jelalis of the Ottoman Empire, the nomadic Turco-Mongol soldiers, the so called 'Chaghatays'[174] enjoyed a special status and Clavijo confirms that 'they go where they will with their flock, graze them, sow and live where they wish, summer and winter; they are free and pay no tribute to the king, because they serve him in times of war when he calls them'.[175]

Apart from grains and eatables, other necessaries were also required to be supplied by the artisans. They prepared various articles and placed them before the tents of Timur's court behind which they had their market places.[176] If, however, the prices in this market were found to be too high, punishments were accorded to the traders. The penalties varied from death to a mere fine. Clavijo says that butchers and shoemakers were punished for over-charging.[177] On special occasions these 'trading folks of the town were under obligation to sell their product'.[178] In accordance with the longstanding practice the regular market always accompanied the army. Timur had gathered together the artisans from each and every corner of his subjugated lands for this purpose.[179] When the sellers were asked to bring their goods for sale to the military market outside the city, they thought it to be a 'measure threatening their livelihood'[180] for they had to sell at much less than the market price and no pains were taken to protect the interest of this trading community and peasantry.[181]

Both Ibn-i Arab Shah and Al Hasan, the Arab speak of he extreme devotion which the soldiers of Timur had for their ruler as a 'Patron beside God—that if he claimed either the rank of a prophet or divinity, they put faith in him and approached God relying on his merits, made vows to him and honoured these vows and persisted in their vain and impious religion . . . .' and that the 'soldiers considered Timur to be an intermediary for their access to God. In difficulty, they brought him presents (*nazr*) during his lifetime and after his death.'[182] The reason for this is explained by the remarks of Al Hasan that 'Timur had no other care than preserving the good will of his most famous soldiers' and that he 'maintained a general muster book' where daily entries were made and the names of the renowned soldiers were recorded and they were in turn rewarded'.[183] This however does not mean that the condition of the soldiers was quite satisfactory.

While the military aristocracy lived luxurious lives,[184] a soldier was not in such a fortunate position. According to Ibn-i Arab Shah, the army of Timur consisted of inhuman, hard and cruel men as well as generous, God fearing good men who followed Timur 'under compulsion'. To support his point, Arab Shah gives details of a dialogue which took place between the soldiers of Timur and a certain Maulana Jamaluddin, an *imam* of Muhammad Sultan (a grandson of Timur). On being reminded of the day of judgement and their own cruel deeds, the soldiers retorted that they were forcibly carried off and were enrolled and registered in the army against their wishes. Since the rules were strict, they could not dare to ignore the summons for war and refuse or delay by an hour even on festival days. By violating this order, one could only pay by his life. Even a migration from one's own place was difficult. Before the start of the expedition they had to enquire about the proposed period of campaign and made preparations accordingly.

> Each of them has his own bag in which he had his barley and ration with him and his horse and fodder, for the most part hungry and content with what suffices the needs of life and clad in torn garments, which suffice to cover nakedness and all this comes from the sowing of our own hands and our labour and from the sweat of our brow and our great zeal is lawful in waging holy war. We attack the goods and wealth of none, we do not demand them with impunity; none of us has immovable estate; we have no relationship with any important men nor link of kinship.[185]

The lot of soldiers is said to have been really bad due to the excessive endurance and little food no doubt that the soldiers were 'weak like timber, rotted with age, lean unkempt, pallid, clothed in torn rags, and dusty'.

Apart from the usual military duties, the army was required to do some extra work. During the march, they were expected to make their way by cutting down trees in the forests, constructing bridges over rivers, digging wells and canals, fixing poles and performing many other odd jobs.[186] During the Chinese campaigns in 806-7 the army was asked to build an asylum in a harbour and 'to fill the country with crop' and 'to omit regular prayers than tillage'.[187] The construction and repairs of new and old forts and palaces was assigned to the *amirs* and the soldiers who were required to complete the task within a specified period.[188] The digging of the canals was also a part of the duty of the soldiers. They were often appointed by the *amirs* for the collection of security and other taxes.[189] After such hard work, soldiers were not sure to get even the required food. During long journey and routes, when provisions were exhausted and scarcity caused the prices to shoot up, a written undertaking was demanded from all the units that none would be cooking any bread or dishes and that soldiers would be provided with only 'iron ration', i.e. one cup of soup. The majority of soldiers, however, had to live even without this small quantity of soup.[190] Unpleasant duties were sometimes assigned to the soldiers. Once, the soldiers were ordered to bring a specified number of heads of persons killed by them and to present them to the *tawajis* for constructing towers. The soldiers who wished to avoid this butchery had to purchase heads at a high price and presented them to *tawajis*.[191]

Soldiers even had to execute such orders of Timur as 'to erect a tower of two thousand live men laid one upon the other smothered with clay and fragments of brick' after the conquest of Isfizar or the burying alive of 4,000 captive soldiers after the taking of Siwas.[192] Ibn-i Arab Shah gives a very impressive account of these soldiers who were

> sharpened by experience, knew changes of fortune, and had endured calamities, sustained ambushes struggled with adversity, dealt with affairs, explored men and the world and knew the approach of every field of battle and the way from it and had passed through all its vicissitudes; no evil affrighted them too much nor did insolence lead them into error—and in their time they had marvelous cunning and wonderful acuteness which struck the mark. They put loads upon cattle and rode upon them and fitted asses with saddles and bits and with them outstripped those who rode on Arab horses going to depart the towns, and they took the sports; they fed their camels on the flesh of dogs and rains, instead of barley, they gave their horses wheat, rice, millet, dry grapes and beans and if perchance those were lacking on the march they fed their beasts with the bark of trees. To them every difficult thing was easy and each of them following the example of his king reached the highest peak in his own kind. There were men without religion base, savage—but also men of intellect, learning and ability, poets and excellent doctors, defenders of the truth, students of science and subtle explorers thereof and men who in every sort of science and its full investigation, combined the double path of enquiry, logic and perception approving the principles of Sufism—and by their deeds wounded more vehemently than the blows of the sharpest sword'.[193]

The same author however, gives the stories of their cruelty as well. Under the Timurids, however, the army was not always so submissive and like the Ottoman janissaries tried to resolve the issue of succession. Ibn-i Arab Shah reports the mutiny of the army of Iraq led by Haji Basha in favour of Alauddaula against Khalil Sultan.[194]

The Uzbeg troops were generally patient and forbearing, fighting in starvation, subsisting on hunt or even on their horse's meat.[195] Manucci records how he saw an Uzbeg soldier 'laying hold of a small knife bleed his horses on the neck with great dexterity. Having drawn forty ounces of blood, he closed the wound with one finger and drank the blood with great gusto. Others followed him. Afterwards the wound was tied up with a cloth and the horse left to get well of it self. On question, the soldier replied that they were accustomed to it because in their country, when plundering within an enemy's boundary, if provisions failed, their soldiers sustained life with the blood of their horses; nor from this bloodletting did the horse lapse their vigour'. He adds 'when these soldiers captured any camel, horse or sheep in any enemy's country and if they were unable to carry it off (it was their practice), to decapitate it, cut into pieces and place some piece between their saddle and their horse's back, for consumption on the march whenever they were hungry'.[196] Even when the provisions could be collected they would not search for or buy them but subsisted on whatever they had, lest the enemy discovered about their poor state of supplies and take advantage of that in overpowering them.[197] Timur always stressed that the most desirable quality for a ruler was his keen interest in three things namely; the holy war against the infidels, the world conquest and a nice administration'.[198] Timur had tried to live up to that standard. Al Hasan speaks highly of Timur's courage, valour, popularity among his soldiers and the endurance and perseverance due to which there was 'no alteration in his countenance adversities and prosperities were so indifferent into him'.[199] After success Timur's magnanimity is said to have prevented him from 'vaunting or boasting'[200] and that Timur was considerate towards the fallen foe 'making them to take all their losses with patience' by 'being most friendly' to the defeated kings and the prisoners.[201] Ibn-i Arab Shah, however, gives another version that though Timur gave a very warm welcome to Bayazid in his court during festivities after the latter's defeat, he arranged that Bayazid's own wives and servants should be present in the court as Timur's attendants which certainly tortured Bayazid more than anything.[202] The soldiers of the defeated army were also buried alive if they resisted joining Timur's army.[203]

While describing Timur's campaigns, Ibn-i Arab Shah asserts that the army of Timur received no harm in the whole period of his rule in all his battles, fights and expeditions except from three men namely Abu Bakr of Shasban, Ali Kurd and Almma Turcoman.[204] Timur's amazing and extensive conquests were achieved by his 'extraordinary, obsessive inner drive, his dynamism and his recklessness rather than by his military qualities'.[205] There were circumstantial factors also which weakened his enemies in various ways and facilitated Timur's task, e.g., the discord among the *amirs* of Toqtamish[206] or the internal troubles in the Ottoman Empire. Timur's principal delight is said to be wars for he was 'called of God to punish the pride of Tyrants',[207] and that 'nothing withheld him where there was either glory or means to increase his reputation, and profit the common wealth'.[208]

Notwithstanding such lofty claims of generalship Timur is once reported to have emphasized that 'I should not so much trust into the lion's skin wherein I wrap my arm that I should not serve myself with the foxes, to wrap herewith my head', which indicates that Timur believed in the favourable end whatever be the means—and attitude well confirmed by his actions.[209]

MILITARY TACTICS, TECHNIQUES AND STRATEGY

It is possible that Timur owed much of his success to his undiminished concern for improvement in his military technique and forms of strategy. Since 'war was an art in the east', a gradual and continuous development in military organization of Timur is therefore, noticed. In his war with Iliyas Khwaja (1365), the army followed the traditional style of organization, i.e. there were right and left wings each of which had reserves (*gambit*) and vanguard. Out of seven detachments, three were assigned an independent position while the fourth (having two vanguards and two *qambil*) was a subordinate one. The Centre had no reserve or vanguard. Gradually, however, more emphasis was laid on a strong centre as in the war against Toqtamish in 1391.

Yazdi says that Timur was an innovator in the art of military organization as he had employed a new technique of forming seven centers (*qaul*) which were unheard of till that time (Rajab 793). One of these centres was named after Mahmud Khan and consisted of experienced soldiers. A grand centre (*qaul-i buzurg*) comprising 20 *qushuns* supported by a rear, right, left, and centre and flanked by two detachments of right and left must have proved to be a strong bulwark against the enemy.[216] Another new feature was that Timur had himself devised a felt cap with a peculiar design so that these caps should be the sign to them where to proceed for he usually conveyed to them army destinations and expected them to follow blindly.[210] One of the princes Muhammad Sultan is reported to have arranged his army in such a way that each of the regiments could have one distinct colour for all its articles like banners, arms, bows, arrow, belts saddles, etc. One of his detachments was assigned the red colour, another was given white and still another yellow colour. One of these detachments had engraved equipment and so on.[211]

Some of the choicest squadrons were distinguished by popular titles, for example the regiment of Allahdad was known as *wafadar* and consisted of *qushuns* only. The squadron of Shaikh Nuruddin was famous as *pai mulk* (foothold of the state), another squadron was called *qauchin*.[212] Sometimes the regiments were known by their regional associations, when Sultan Abusaid first started to arrange the government of Samarqand and Khurasan, he had formed two special cadet corps of serviceable youngmen called presumably by him as Khurasan corps and Samarqand corps.[213]

Under the Uzbegs also certain innovation in the army arrangement could always be made by the *khaqan*. Sometimes a large centre was arranged on one side (*qaul-i buzurg*) where certain princes and *amirs* were placed in the vanguard (*manghalay*). The *khaqan* personally organized another *qaul* (centre). The *qaul-i buzurg* usually had well armed extra reserve forces at its disposal. Usually the oldest sultan or the *khaqan* led the centre of an army in conformity with the laws of Chingiz Khan.[214] The princes and provincial rulers, each one alongwith his army stayed in his own intrenchment (*baljar murcahl*).[215]

The use of elephants in the army was also started by Timur who brought from India 95 elephants, quite a surprise for Central Asians who had 'never seen the elephants before'. These elephants were used as a front bulwark in the Damascus, Halb and Angora campaigns by Timur and also for carrying the luggage. They wore *kajim* (armour) on their back and carried archers and cannoneers also on their backs.[216] In 824, a few lines (*zanjirs*) of huge elephants were used by Shahrukh to terrorize the Turcoman horses which had not seen the elephants before. Earthen horses were prepared and elephants were trained before had for this assault.[217]

Before the abortive Chinese campaign, Timur ordered special coverings tents to be prepared and tunics to be kept ready covered on both sides with thick, cloth, shirts, double breast plates and cloaks for shields to protect against the injuries of winter.[218] Since there were frequent raids on Jetah and Mongol territory, special military outposts and stations were established as in Ashbara where troops alongwith a tried commander were placed to keep watch on the border and to facilitate plundering incursions.[219] Another border fortress was ordered to be built at Dermiro to strengthen frontiers towards China as well.[220]

Timur developed highly sophisticated methods of siege warfare and is, renowned for his siege craft and devices for capturing forts (*qalagiri*). The techniques of reducing forts had also improved considerably in the wake of every new conquest. Timur applied the age old methods of Maljur Sarkobs, *damdama* scaling ladders, lassoes and ropes with nooses[221] along with the then prevalent latest method of mining, sapping, tunnelling and blasting.

NOTES

1. Yezdi, *Zafar Nama* (*ZN*), Tehran edn., Vol. I, p. 527; Ibn-i Arab Shah, *Ajaib-ul Maqdur fi nawadir-i Timur,* Eng. tran. by Sanders, *Life of Timur,* London, 1936, pp. 215, 221; Persian tr. *Zindgani-i Shaguft Awar-i Timur,* Tehran, 1960, Ch. 4.
2. *Istorya Uzbegskoj SSR I,* Tashkent, 1955, pp. 328-30 (hereafter *Istorija Uzbegskoj*); Denis Sinor, *Inner Asia—A Syllabus,* Bloomington, 1969, p. 188.
3. V.V. Barthold, *Four Studies on the History of Central Asia* (*FS*), Leiden, 1962, Vol. II, p. 38; *Istorija Uzbegskoj,* pp. 328-30; Hilda Hookham (*Tamburlaine the Conqueror,* London, 1962, pp. 53, 61) says they were primarily nomadic.
4. Ibn-i Arab Shah, Eng. tr., p. 17. The Chaghatai Khan Kebek (1318-26) is said to have introduced *tuman* as the unit of administration of an area charged with providing and supporting 10,000 soldiers. Hilda Hookham, p. 391; *Istorija Uzbegskoj,* pp. 309, 327.
5. *Babur Nama,* Eng. tr. Beveridge, New Delhi, 1979, p. 12 (hereafter *BN*).
6. *BN*, p. 12.
7. *Slovar Terminologij*, Moscow, 1950, p. 157; V.V. Radloff, *Dictionary*, III, op. cit.; *Slavar Turkish Turkskikh Narechi*, 1893-1911, p. 1218; Barthold, *FS*, Vol. II, pp. 9, 27-8; Hilda Hookham, p. 58.
8. *Majma-ul Arqam*, f. 28.
9. *BN*, pp. 17, 47; *TR*, p. 301.
10. *FS*, Vol. II, pp. 3-9, 27-8; Barthold, *Sochinenija*, Vol. V, Moscow, 1968, p. 570.
11. Ghayasuddin Ali, *Safarnama-i Ghazawat-i Hindustan,* Russian translation *Dnevnik Pakhoda Timura va Indiu,* Moscow, 1958, p. 110; Calcutta, 1888.
12. Yezdi, *ZN*, Vol. I, Calcutta, 1888, pp. 463, 475; *ZN*, Vol. II, pp. 66, 80. Qazvini, *Nuzhat-ul qulub,* Bombay edn., 1311 AH, p. 90.

13. Ghaysasuddin Ali, op. cit., p. 110; Yezdi, *ZN*, Tehran edn., Shamsi 1336 AH, Vol. I, edited by Muhammad Abbasi, pp. 462-3.
14. *ZN*, Vol. I, Tehran edn. While describing the *tuman* in Alauddin's army, Amir Khusrau says that each *tuman* was assigned 1,200 yards of land.
15. Marco Polo, *Purchas*, Vol. XI, p. 246. Beveridge's Eng. tr. of Abul Fazl's *Akbar Nama*, Vol. I, pp. 590-1 fn. 3.
16. *ZN*, Calcutta edn., Vol. I, pp. 154, 384, 458; *ZN*, Calcutta edn., Vol. II, p. 426; Abdurrazaq Samarqandi, *Matla-us Sadain*, Lahore, 1946, Vol. I, part I, p. 15 (hereater *Matla*).
17. Haidar Dughlat, *Tarikh-i Rashidi*, Eng. tr. by Denison Ross, Patna, 1973, p. 55; *FS*, Vol. II, p. 27.
18. *Istorija Uzbegskoj*, pp. 328-30.
19. See *Perspectives on Mongolia*, p. 121 fn. 3.
20. *ZN*, Vol. II, Calcutta edn., p. 365; *Matla*, p. 42.
21. *TR*, Eng. tr., p. 3098; Aljuzzani also says that among the Mongols, the term *bahadur* denoted warriors (Minhaj ur Siraj Aljuzzani, *Tabaqat-i Nasiri*, Vol. II; Eng. tr. by Ravery, New Delhi, 1970, p. 968; also see *War, Technology and Society in Middle East*, p. 260.
22. *ZN*, Vol. I, Calcutta edn., p. 216; Barthold, *FS*, Vol. II, p. 27; Hilda Hookham, p. 130; De Courteille renders the term *tawaji* as 'Haut Commissre', *Dictionary*, p. 219.
23. *ZN*, Vol. I, Calcutta edn., p. 564; Vol. II, pp. 207, 394-5.
24. Ibid.
25. Clavijo, *Embassy to Tamerlane*, ed. by Ross and Power, tr. from Spanish by Guy Le Strange, London, 1928, p. 213.
26. There seems to be an error as Chinese campaign was undertaken by Timur in 1905 on the eve of his death.
27. Al-Hasan the Arab, *Purchas and his Pilgrims*, Vol. XI, Glasgow MCM VI, pp. 425, 442, 445.
28. Ibid.; also see Clavijo, pp. 233-4.
29. Ibn-i Arab Shah, Pers. tr., pp. 229-30; Al-Hasan the Arab, pp. 421-3.
30. *IA*, Eng. tr., p. 125; Pers. tr., p. 131.
31. Khwand Mir, *Habib-us Siyar*, Tehran edn., 1333 AH, Vol. III, part III, p. 530 (hereafter *H. Siyar)*.
32. *Tuzukat-i Timuri*, Eng. tr. by Major Davy, Tehran, 1942, pp. 134-5, also introduction 'View of the Work'.
33. Al-Hasan, the Arab, pp. 404-11, 425-50.
34. Dersce, *Le Campagne de Timur en Anatolia (1402)*, London, 1977, pp. 122-3.
35. *ZN*, Vol. II, p. 107.
36. *ZN*, Vol. I, p. 398.
37. *Matla*, pp. 144, 401.
38. Ibid., p. 1453.
39. Ibid., p. 23.
40. Ibid., p. 398.
41. Ibid., pp. 394-400.
42. Ibid., pp. 378, 440; *H. Siyar*.
43. *Matla*, p. 23.
44. *BN*, pp. 39-40.

45. *BN*, p. 50.
46. Forbes Manz, 'Administration and the Delegation of Authority in Timur's Domirtions', *Central Asiatic Journal*, Vol. II, pp. 204-5.
47. *IA*, Persian text, p. 50; MS. II, part ii, pp. 17-18, 322; *BN*, p. 55.
48. *AAA*, pp. 419, 446.
49. Ibid., pp. 417-18, 460, 463; MS. 42.
50. The *muta tawwali* (volunteers who were entitled to a share in booty but received no pay) and the soldiers formally enrolled in the registers, both.
51. *Matla*, p. 802.
52. *Ancient Art of Warfare I*, London, 1966, p. 292 from Ramses to Vauban.
53. *ZN*, Vol. I, pp. 558, 618.
54. Juvaini, *Tarikh-i Jahanqusha*, pp. 10-30.
55. *Matla*, II, pp. 17, 198, 332.
56. *ZN*, Vol. II, p. 273; Al-Hasan the Arab, pp. 419, 446; Ibn-i Arab, Pers. tr., p. 50; *Matla*, II, pp. 17-18, 42, 322; *BN*, p. 55.
57. *Matla*, II, pp. 173-5.
58. *TR*, pp. 53, 155; *Matla*, II, pp. 42, 224-5; Al-Hasan the Arab, pp. 417-18, 460, 463.
59. *ZN*, Vol. II, p. 273.
60. *Matla*, pp. 394-400.
61. *BN*, p. 212.
62. Al-Hasan the Arab, p. 440.
63. Ibid., pp. 417-18, 463; *Matla*, p. 42.
64. *AAA*, pp. 419, 446.
65. *Tarikh-i Jahanqusha*, p. 30.
66. Juvaini, text, pp. 21-2; also see Manucci, *Storia De Mogor*, Eng. tr. by W. Irvine, Vol. I, Calcutta, 1965, pp. 100-14.
67. Examples in *ZN*, I, Calcutta edn., pp. 475, 483, 576, 591, 614; *ZN*, II, Calcutta edn., pp. 61-2, 66-7, 305-7; *Tuzukat-i Timuri*, Tehran, 1942, p. 64; *ZN*, II, pp. 323-4, 347; also see *Tuzukat-i Timuri*, pp. 161, 207.
68. *ZN*, II, Calcutta edn., p. 159.
69. *ZN*, I, Calcutta edn., pp. 614, 645; *ZN*, II, Calcutta edn., pp. 131, 273; also see *Tuzukat-i Timuri*, p. 65.
70. *ZN*, I, Calcutta edn., p. 492.
71. Ibn-i Arab Shah, Pers. tr., p. 295; Eng. tr. p. 295.
72. Ibid.
73. *ZN*, I, Calcutta edn., pp. 382, 447, 529; Daulatshah Samarqandi, *Tazkiratush-shuara*, Lahore, 1939, pp. 225-6; *Tuzukat*, pp. 288-92.
74. *ZN*, I, Calcutta edn., pp. 530, 538; Al-Hasan, pp. 424-5; *AN*, III, Eng. tr., p. 937.
75. *ZN*, Calcutta edn., p. 645; Al-Hasan the Arab, p. 435.
76. *ZN*, II, Calcutta edn., p. 228.
77. *ZN*, I, Calcutta edn., p. 446. One such person, Barat Khwaja Kukultash was given a peculiar punishment. Having reprimanded him for a fault, Timur ordered that his beard should be shaved off and his face should be painted and veiled like a woman and that he be paraded in the city. Even the opponents in the defeated army were very ruthlessly dealt with. After the Siwas campaign, 4,000 soldiers were buried alive in a wall to serve as a lesson for other

recalcitrant soldiers (*ZN*, II, p. 196). Even during the reign of Shahrukh in the recklessness or negligence during war was equally punished. Even an *amir-i azam* like Amir Nur Saidin was thrown into prison and all his *amwalojihat* were destroyed for the same fault though he was later on forgiven and reinstated after the reprimand (*Matla* II, iii, pp. 432-3).

78. *ZN*, pp. 529-30.
79. *Abdn*, pp. 129, 188; *Mehn*, p. 214; *Tarikh Qipchaqi* unpaginated.
80. *Abdn*, p. 252.
81. Ibid., pp. 129, 241, 252.
82. Ibid., pp. 229, 241, 266, 334.
83. Ibid.
84. *ZN*, p. 560.
85. *ZN*, p. 1231.
86. M. Querry, *Droit Mussulman*, Paris, 1871; Kautilya, Vol. I, p. 335; Ameer Ali, *The Spirit of Islam*, Delhi, 1978, p. 63; A. Ben Shemesh, *Taxation in Islam*, Leiden, 1967, pp. 23-6. The principle of *alanfal* meant reserving 1/5 for public treasury leaving the rest to the discretion of commander in chief; what remained after the deduction of the fifth belonged to the Muslims who captured it and was to be divided among them.
87. Ibn-i Arab Shah gives a really horrible picture of Timur's army plundering in Rum where they unleashed a reign of terror (Ibn-i Arab, Eng. tr., pp. 191-2).
88. Ibn-i Arab, Pers. tr., p. 162; *ZN*, II, Calcutta edn., p. 334.
89. Ibid., p. 162; *ZN*, II, Calcutta edn., p. 334. Farishta (*Gulshan-i Ibrahimi*, I, Newal Kishore edn., p. 158.) nevertheless records that in Delhi devastation took place and the army of Timur which had entered the city to enquire about the rebels hidden in the city indulged in plundering so much that each one of them acquired more than a hundred captives and immense unaccountable gold, silver, precious stones and wealth. Since Timur had been engaged in a five days pleasure spree, none could dare to approach him. When ultimately Timur was informed, it was already too late. The subjugated people, however, took revenge by killing a few *muhassils* who had come to collect *mal-i amani* which infuriated Timur so much that he ordered the general massacre of the populations sparing only *sadat, ulama* and *shaikh*, sayyids, learned men and theologians.
90. Ibn-i Arab Shah informs us that when certain Chaghatais even 'after hearing the edict of proclamation of peace and security, put forth their hands to plunder. Timur, as soon as he learnt it, ordered them to be fixed to the cross in a public place. Therefore, they crucified them in the Silk Market' (Ibn-i Arab, Eng. tr., p. 146).
91. Al-Hasan the Arab, *Purchas and his Pilgrims*, p. 447.
92. *BN*, text, p. 40; Eng. tr. p. 67.
93. Tusi advised the rulers to maintain a multiracial army so as to prevent any danger of concerned and joint rebellion. Nizam-ul Mulk Tusi, *Siyasat Nama*, Tehran, 1348 AH, p. 154 (hereafter Tusi).
94. *ZN*, I, Calcutta edn., p. 547.
95. Ibn-i Arab, Eng. tr., pp. 117-18; Hilda Hookham, p. 228.
96. Khwand Mir, p. 474; Badauni, *Muntakhab ut Tawarikh*, p. 74.
97. *ZN*, I, 655, 658; II, p. 260, Calcutta edn.; *ZN*, I, Tehran edn., pp. 462-3.
98. Al-Hasan the Arab, p. 413.

99. Ibn-i Arab, Pers. tr., p. 269.
100. Ibid., pp. 321-4.
101. Al-Hasan the Arab, pp. 434-5, 448.
102. Juvaini, text, p. 151, Eng. tr., p. 192; Tusi, p. 154; V.V. Barthold, *Sochinenija*, Vol. II, p. 187.
103. *ZN*, p. 34. For military virtues of Turks see *War, Technology and Society in the Middle East*, edited by Parry and Yapp, London, 1975, p. 64.
104. Clavijo, *Embassy to Tamerlane,* pp. 38-9; Barthold, *FS*, II, pp. 26-7. The Chaghatais here refer to Turco-Mongol tribes and should not be confused with '*chaghatai nazadan*' (the successors of Chaghatai).
105. *BN*, text, p. 90; Eng. tr., p. 140.
106. Al-Hasan the Arab, pp. 430-1.
107. *Tuzukat*, book II, pp. 274-5.
108. Ibid., p. 277.
109. Ibid., pp. 278-9.
110. Ibid., p. 277, also introduction, p. xliv.
111. *ZN*, II, pp. 172-3.
112. *Tuzukat*, II, p. 277.
113. *Inner Asia*, p. 188, Ottoman Turkish military tactics were both appreciated and feared by the Franks also in the Middle Ages; R.C. Smail, *Crusading Warfare (1097-1193)*, Cambridge, 1956, pp. 75-83.
114. *ZN*, I, p. 523.
115. *ZN*, I, pp. 362-72, 437; Hatifi, pp. 85, 108, 207.
116. Barthold, *Sochinenija*, Vol. II, part I, p. 18.
117. Al-Hasan the Arab, pp. 404-11, 425-50.
118. *ZN*, II, Tehran edn., p. 47. This was probably in accordance with the chingizide pattern of light armed *qarauls* followed by quick shooting archers who then retired to allow heavy cavalry to pass through them (Philip, *The Mongols*, London, 1965, p. 50).
119. Ibn-i Arab, Pers. tr., p. 93.
120. *ZN*, I, Calcutta edn., p. 606.
121. Ibid., p. 470; Tehran edn., I, p. 338.
122. *ZN*, II, pp. 51-2; Farishta, p. 156.
123. *Babur Nama,* text, p. 100; Eng. tr., p. 155.
124. *TR*, Eng. tr., pp. 308-9.
125. Beatrice Forbes Manz, 'Administration and the Delegation of Authority in Timur's Dominions', *Central Asiatic Journal*, pp. 204, 205.
126. *ZN*, I, p. 467.
127. *ZN*, II, p. 114.
128. Each of the renowned generals of Timur had the same record: Sulaiman Shah: left wing, Rum, right wing, Egypt, Halb, India; Amirshah Mulk: centre Angora, Egypt, left wing India; Amir Shaikh Nuruddin: right wing, Rum, India, centre: India. There were, however, certain generals who had served only in one wing, e.g. Amir Haji Saifuddin: right wing, Sistan, India; Shaikh Arslan: left wing, Egypt, India. For these details see Yezdi's *Zafar Nama*, Tehran edn., pp. 449-51, 524-42. For definite code for *filing* his army on a battleground see *Tuzukat-i Timuri,* Tehran, 1942, pp. 191-210; also see

Sahabuddin, 'Conduct of Stretegy and Tactics of War During the Muslim Rule in India', *Islamic Culture*, Vol. XX, nos. 1-4 (1946), pp. 158-9.

129. *BN*, p. 113, also fn. 1; Eng. tr., p. 139.
130. Sanders, p. 301.
131. *BN*, text, p. 100.
132. Sanders, p. 302.
133. *BN*, text, p. 100.
134. *Abdn*, pp. 133, 162, 167, 200, 236, 274, 310, 328, 377, 409.
135. Ibid., pp. 71, 133, 136, 137, 167, 172, 200, 236, 274, 310, 328, 377, 409.
136. *T. Abulkhair*, pp. 257-8.
137. *Abdn*, p. 223.
138. Mirza Badi, pp. 14-16.
139. *T. Abulkhair*, pp. 257-8.
140. *Abdn*, p. 223.
141. *ZN*, Vol. I, p. 383; Vol. II, p. 370.
142. *ZN*, Vol. I, pp. 383, 543; *ZN*, II, p. 370; *Matla* II, pp. 17, 42, 198, 332, 649.
143. Examples: *Matla*, II, iii, p. 374; *Matla* II, i, pp. 17, 198, 332; *H. Siyar*, III, iii, pp. 529-30.
144. *BN*, p. 113, also Eng. tr., p. 139.
145. *ZN*, pp. 293-6, 362, 506-16, 528-9; *ZN*, II, pp. 409-12; Hatifi, *Timur Nama*, Madras, 1958, pp. 84-90, 207; *Tarikh-i Shahrukh*, pp. 55, 63-4, 99; Hafiz Abru, pp. 474-5; *Matla*, II, pp. 40-1, 179, 445-7, 600-6.
146. *ZN*, II, Tehran edn., p. 448.
147. *BN*, pp. 154-5 fn. 3, pp. 183, 264.
148. See *Babur Nama*, Turkish text; Persian tr., pp. 154-5; Eng. tr., pp. 183, 264 fn. 3. For a depiction of the *dim* mentioned here see Miniatures of *Babur Nama*, copy by Hamid Sulaiman, Tashkent, 1970, see Illustration No. 20.
149. *Tarikh-i Rashidi*, Eng. tr., pp. 304-7.
150. *ZN*, I, pp. 355, 363.
151. Khwand Mir, p. 529; *ZN*, II, pp. 447-50.
152. *ZN*, I, p. 279.
153. Clavijo, pp. 233-5.
154. *Babur Nama*, Pers. text, pp. 209-10; Eng. tr., pp. 334-5.
155. *Istorija Uzbegskoj*, pp. 328-30.
156. Hatifi, pp. 205-14.
157. *Babur Nama*, p. 80.
158. Ibid.
159. *ZN*, p. 145; *Matla*, II, pp. 224-5, 396-7.
160. Clavijo, p. 290; G.N. Pant, *Studies in Indian Weapons and Warfare*, New Delhi, 1970, pp. 46-7.
161. Ibid., p. 287.
162. Ibid.
163. Velvet coat of mail studded with small studs or knobs all over were called *jaibah* (G.N. Pant, p. 167).
164. *ZN*, I, pp. 496, 522; *ZN*, II, pp. 184-5, 409-12. also Badauni, I, Eng. tr., p. 158 fn. 6.
165. Elgood, pp. 22-5. *IA*, Eng. tr., p. 244. *Matla*, p. 45.

166. *Paintings from Islamic Lands*, edited by R. Pindev Wilson, Glasgow, 1969, pp. 112-13 (plate 74), 113-18.
167. *Secret History*, pp. 132-3 fn. 15.
168. *Mehn*, pp. 179-99.
169. *Abdn*, p. 352; *Mehn*, pp. 132, 140.
170. *Rauzat*, pp. 260-2; *Abdn*, p. 306.
171. *Abdn*, pp. 331-3.
172. *ZN*, I, pp. 281, 359; *ZN*, II, pp. 572, 583. Even in a foreign land the same practice was followed. Farishta records the devastations caused by Timur's army in collecting food and fodder in India (*Tarikh-i Farishta*, Vol. I, p. 156; *ZN*, I, Tehran edn., p. 410).
173. Clavijo, p. 36; *ZN*, I, Tehran edn., pp. 312-15.
174. They were Turco-Mongol tribes and should not be confused with successors of Chaghatai who were called as '*chaghatai nazadan*'.
175. Clavijo, pp. 195-6, 220.
176. *IA*, Pers. text, p. 225.
177. Clavijo, pp. 250-3.
178. Ibid., p. 248. When Clavijo reached Ferrior, he found that 'inhabitants in greater part had fled. This was in mistrust of soldiers of Timur's army and it was now about 12 days since he and his Tartar bands had passed through this place where in truth very visibly the troops had wrought much havoc' Clavijo, p. 184.
179. *ZN*, I, Calcutta edn., pp. 398, 641; ibid II, pp. 124, 335.
180. Clavijo, pp. 39, 251.
181. *Shajratul Atrak* (pp. 64-5) gives a somewhat similar example of Chingiz's attitude towards the trading community.
182. *IA*, Persian text, p. 322, *AAA*, p. 404.
183. *AAA*, pp. 459, 467.
184. Haft Abru says that the army was rolling in affluence due to excessive booty.
185. *IA*, Persian text, p. 329, Eng. tr., p. 168. Carpini also gives a similar account about earlier Mongol army.
186. See *ZN*, I (Calcutta edn.), pp. 301, 383, 470, 572, 621, 660; *ZN*, p. 338; *ZN*, II (Calcutta edn.), pp. 46, 394-418, 486, 544.

     During the Mongol period a road was constructed for military purposes in the mountainous regions of Tienshan at the order of Ogedei. Another road was built during the western campaign of Chingiz Khan. Chaghatai's constructed a road through the defile piercing the rocks. They built no less than forty-eight timber bridges of such width that two carts could drive over them side by side. Chang Chun, *The Travels of an Alchemist Recorded by his Disciple Chih-Chang*, tr. with an introduction by Arthur Waltey, London, 1931, pp. 76, 85, for such examples under Timur and Uzbegs see infra.
187. *ZN*, Eng. tr., pp. 224-5. During Qipchaq campaigns the same orders were issued.
188. *ZN*, I, pp. 217, 301, 343, 503-504; II, pp. 20, 38, 544 (Calcutta edn.); *AAA*, p. 447.
189. *ZN*, I, p. 432, Calcutta edn.; *ZN*, II, p. 330; *BN*, p. 55.
190. *ZN*, p. 504, Calcutta edn. During eastern campaigns the soldiers were supplied with seven years provisions. As the country between Transoxiana

and Khata was a little uncultivated and thinly populated. Timur ordered each man to take two milch cows and ten goats so as to subsist on milk when the supplies were exhausted. When the milk should come to an end they were to convert the animals themselves into provisions. During Jetah expedition, the soldiers had to subsist for six months only on meat acquired from hunting the wild animals (*ZN*, pp. 355, 361; *AAA*, p. 425; *Tarikh-i Rashidi*, p. 53; *ZN*, I, p. 282; *ZN*, II, pp. 572-83; Clavijo, p. 191).

191. *ZN*, I, 313-14, 434, Calcutta edn. Yezdi says that separate *tawajis* had been appointed to collect these heads. In the beginning the heads were sold at 20 *dinar-i kebeki*, one head could be bought for half a *dinar* and even then there was none to buy it. Whoever was caught was bound to lose his head. In this about 70,000 heads were collected in Isfahan and several minarets were erected there. Other examples *ZN*, II, pp. 254-65; Prawdin, *History of the Mongol Conqueror*, p. 448, says that soldiers did not hesitate even in killing friend or brother if there were no enemies for they 'could not fall in obedience'.
192. *ZN*, I, p. 360, ibid., II, p. 296; *IA*, 88; Clavijo, p. 143.
193. *IA*, pp. 316-19, 322-3.
194. Ibn-i Arab Shah, Eng. tr., pp. 269-70.
195. Manucci, p. 42. It was generally believed that one Uzbeg soldier was equal to hundred others. See Begin, p. 14; *Abdn*, p. 6.
196. Manucci, p. 42.
197. *Abdn*, p. 343.
198. *Tuzukat-i Timuri*, p. 140.
199. *AAA*, p. 433.
200. Ibid., p. 435.
201. Ibid., pp. 437, 439.
202. *IA*, Eng. tr., p. 188.
203. *ZN*, II, p. 196.
204. *IA*, Eng. tr., p. 34, 118.
205. Sinor, *Inner Asia*, pp. 188-9.
206. *IA*, pp. 80-1, 140-1, 146-7; Hookham, p. 230.
207. *AAA*, p. 445.
208. Ibid.
209. For similar interesting references see Hookham, pp. 62-6.
210. *IA*, Eng. tr., p. 56.
211. *ZN*, II, Calcutta edn., pp. 400-12.
212. *ZN*, I, Calcutta edn., pp. 611-12; II, p. 130.
213. *BN*, p. 28.
214. *Abdn*, pp. 143, 225, 226, 285.
215. Ibid., p. 352.
216. *ZN*, II, pp. 143-4, 213, 235; Yahya Sirhindi, *Tarikh-i Mubarak Shahi*, Calcutta, 1931, pp. 162-8.
217. *Matla*, II, pp. 143, 453.
218. *IA*, Eng. tr., pp. 226-7; *AAA*, p. 417.
219. Ibid., pp. 193-4.
220. *AAA*, p. 441.
221. Either *siba* high (siegetowers), *maijurs* (raised platforms of wooden pieces

place alongwith the earth and stone through which the besiegers could easily reach the parapets of the fort), or ropes with running nooses (*kamand o tanab*) and scaling ladder of rope and raw silk flung on to turrets enabled the besiegers to climb and penetrate into the fort and open the gates. Usually these tactics were used at night, e.g. in Garjistan and Abkhaz campaigns (*ZN*, I, pp. 493-7; *ZN*, II, pp. 55-60, 289, 375). *Maljurs* were later on employed only where tunnelling was not possible. This happened for example in Siwas fort which was surrounded by big deep ditches (*khundaq*) filled with water and where the excavation to a depth of even one yard brought up water. Sometimes holes were made in the trenches to left out water by *kharaks* (an instrument for pecking) though it was not always possible (*ZN*, I, pp. 493-7; *ZN*, II, pp. 194, 239; *ZN*, II, Calcutta edn., p. 346). *Sabats* (an open trench or a covered passage) was used. For interesting detail about *sabat* see Sarkar, p. 169. *Sarkobs* and *Damdama* were constructed opposite to and at an equal height of the besieged for to continue warfare (*Farhang-i Anand Raj*, II, p. 408; also see Ahmad Yadgar, *Tarikh-i Shahi* or *Tarikh-i Salatins Afaghana*, Calcutta, 1939, p. 149).

Military Organization Under the Uzbegs

Chroniclers and travellers from the thirteenth to seventeenth centuries[1] have lavished high praises on the Central Asian armies for their chivalry, sense of service, steadfastness. For an area like Central Asia, which largely depended upon booty for its surplus revenue and resources, the army was a particularly important instrument and was thus well maintained. The Uzbegs sought to follow the traditions of their medieval predecessors. Shaibani Khan 'declared the saddle of his horse to be his capital'.[2] Abdullah Khan considered 'excellent generalship' to be 'the prop of magnificence and one of the two emblems of the greatness of a ruler',[3] and even reminded the *mard-i kars* that 'our livelihood lies beneath the shadow of our lances'.[4] In almost all his *nishans,* the provincial rulers are instructed to be particularly kind, humane and generous towards the soldiers as they were 'pilgrims of the sacred wealth and defenders and protectors of the country and its people'.[5]

The organization of the army was planned by the Uzbegs on the basis of the time-honoured Uighur and Mongol decimal system.[6] Babur's observation that 'precisely as Chingiz Khan laid down his rules, so the Mughals still observe them', is confirmed by accounts of army organization prevalent in Turco-Mongol Central Asia from thirteenth-seventeenth centuries.[8] The *Rauzat-us Safa* mentions the lowest rank as *panja* (five),[9] though all our other sources speak of the following groups ranging from ten to ten thousand: the *unbashi* (or *unter, dehbashi, sarikhail dehchaha*), *uzbegi* (*sad chaha, sad-bashi*) commander of hundred, *qushun* (any detachment above 100 and below 1,000, *mingbashi*-commander of 1,000) and *tumanbegi* (or *dehhazari*-commander of 10,000).[10]

Apart from the military ranks of ten to ten thousand, there were a large number of officials with military and administrative functions, like the *aishik aqasis* (lord of the gate) of the right and left wings, *chehra aqasis, tuwachis, zarchis, chehras ichkis, yasawuls,*[11] cuirassiers, keeper of the armour, *qurchis, jebajis rekhtagar* (for casting guns), *mard-i kars*, etc. Such officers looked after the arrangement of the army before and after a war organized hunting excursion, collection of taxes (supply of provisions for the army), and so on.[12] Theologians and *mullas* also usually accompanied the army.[13] Ubaidullah is reported to have brought with him 'forty *mullas* to pray for his success in the Herat campaign, all of whom were said to have been beheaded after his defeat'.[14] There were the infantry (*piyadagan*) and auxiliary force (*aitam*)[15] as well as cavalry. It seems that a cavalry soldiers was called *duaspa* (soldier with two horses), though there is sufficient ground for concluding that the number of horses could increase six fold in military expeditions.[16] Isfahani says that during the Qazaq campaigns Ubaidullah's army consisted of more than ten thousand cavalry and more than 1,00,000 animals.[17] The chronicles also refer to *sih asea* and *chaharaspa*, we hear of *chaharaspa* or *duaspa* being made *yakaspa* or vice versa.[18] Sometimes, even camels were used not only for carrying loads but also in warfare in the steppes, or when horses could not be used.[19] The Khan stayed in along with the princes, and *chehragan-i khassa* (special pageboys). The general army (*amma-i lashkar*) along with the *amirs* stayed separately. As prescribed by Chingiz, hunting was not only a major recreation for the army but a customary device essential for military training.[21] Abdullah Khan spent part of each day in hunting.[22]

According to Haider Dughlat, the numerical strength of Shaibani's troops in 1502 was 50,000-60,000. When he captured and released Khan Mahmud, he took from him as many of the Mughals as possible. Thus to his Uzbeg army there were added 30,000 Mughals.[23] During the Qazaq campaigns in 1509, Shaibani's personal army alone is said to have consisted of about 30,000 cavalry.[24] The numerical strength of the provincial army as given by Isfahani in 1509 (on the eve of the Qazaq campaigns) is fairly impressive. The Sultans who came to help Shaibani brought their forces with them. Kuchum, the ruler of Turkestan, came with 10,000 cavalry (*jangi*) and more than 20,000 infantry (*sipahi*); Souyunch Khan of Tashkent came with more than 10,000 Uzbeg cavalry and 30,000 mixed forces.[25] In 1528 the total force of the Uzbegs was estimated by the Persians at about 1,20,000, out of which 80,000 were said to be special troops and 40,000 predatory auxiliaries (*almanchis*), and messengers (*parwanas*).[26] Hafiz Tanish does not give the number of provincial armies but he points out that once the total force that Abdullah Khan collected from all sides was said to have amounted to 1,00,000 cavalry.[27] Besides, Abdullah Khan had his own personal army which constantly remained with him and even sat in special assemblies.[28] In areas where there was large scale recruitment of nomadic element, the army swelled considerably. In 1576 the force which came from Tashkent to suppress the rebellion in Samarqand was said to be 30,000.[29] Prisoners of war taken after battle were either included in the victorious armies or executed and plundered.[30]

The Uzbeg army was not as varied in its composition as that of Timur. Nevertheless, racial diversity was still prominent in all its ranks. The ranks of Shaibani's army was swelled by adventurers out of every race between the Volga and Kashghar.[31] In the early sixteenth century, Shaibani is said to have released the Mughal Khans after their defeat, though 'the greater part of the Mughal *ulus*' was not allowed to depart.[32] Moreover, Shaibani had probably no confidence in the Uzbeg army since 'in the Uzbeg Empire it was well known that the obedience and fidelity of the Uzbeg army was not like that of the Chaghatais.[33] On the contrary, the Uzbegs under Souyunch Khan tried to raise an army consisting 'exclusively of pure Uzbegs' who could sustain and support them in an alien land. Isfahani says that this special racial feature was so strictly maintained that no person other than a 'pure Uzbeg' (*ghair Uzbeg-i khalis*), whose ancestral blood was mixed with that of the Mughals or Chaghatais could be enrolled in that detachment.[34] Another detachment consisting of Mughals and Chaghatai *sardars* and the Uzbegis of Tashkent totalled 30,000. In other Uzbeg armies one found Turks, Chaghatais, Mughals, Turcomans, Qipchaqis, Khurasanis, Qirghiz and others. The Uzbegs condemned the Arabs and 'Turks' for lacking in generalship and gallantry. Once, when a detachment of Abdullah's army retreated, Kuchuk Ughlan explained this retreat to Abdullah by saying that 'the retreating army comprised Arabs and Turks who are not adept in warfare and shun bloodshed'.[35]

With the arrival of the Shaibanids a singnificant role was played by nomadic elements, which formed the kernel of the cavalry. During a siege Chingiz's formula, that each living being was a soldier was often applied and the civilian population, artisans, Sayyids, and merchants were all brought within the fort and contributed to its defence. Even peasants were not spared. In the *Mukhtubat wa Asnad,* a *Nishan* issued to Sultan Muhammad of the Yasawi family instructed the latter to send 200 peasants (*reaya*) to serve in the royal army twice an year in exchange for his relief. They were freed from all other obligations.[36]

Babur refers to the Mongol practice of dividing the right and left wings of the army on a permanent basis.[37] This is discernible in the Uzbeg military system as well. The right wing was considered to be superior, as is implied in Babur's statement and reflected in Mirza Badi's comments and the practice of placing ruling groups in the right wing.[38] The nobles could belong to either wing and registered accordingly. They could however, serve in the other wing if the ruler so nominated. The right wing comprised the Uzbegs and tribes like the Manghit, Keneges, Kerait, Durman, Qunghrat, Khitai, Qipchaq, Utarchi, Trucoman, Arlat, Kail, Kirghiz Qulan, Ushun, Chubachi, Qari, Mongol, Hafizi, Ughlan, and Tilad. In the left wing were tribes like the Qataghan, Sarai, Yabu, Bahrin, Jalair, Qanghli, Yuz, Ming, Naima, Qarluq, Barqut, Arghu, Qushchi, Ughlan, Kalmik, Fuladchi, Kiriku, Alchin, Major, Oshimbai, Badaias, Jebergen, Kilchi, Tinai, Misit, Tarta, Uighur, Baghaln, Ilaji, Tanghut, and Shagird Pishi. The Biyat and Qiyats were occasionally given right and left wings by their chief. Mirza Badi stresses that this division of tribes was not a commonplace affair but indicated the political and racial standing of a particular tribe.[39]

It is not certain whether a separate department existed for the inspection of the army or whether a simple verification was sufficient. The registration of soldiers was done before every march and a roll list was prepared by the Khan's officers. Masud refers to the verification (*tahqiq*) of the army by Abulkhair before a campaign. [40] Hafiz Tanish records that Qulbaba and Haider Munshi had been appointed for the *tahqiq* of the royal army of Abdullah Khan.[41] For three days soldiers were constantly being enrolled.

No wages were paid in Chingiz's realm, on the contrary, a little of every man's possessions belonged to the *khaqan*.[42]

In this way, about 30,000 people were checked (*ba arz dar amad*).[43] On another occasion, Muhammad Baqi Bi Durman was ordered to prepare a roll of the army and to submit it before the Khan.[44] Such roll lists even included the names of the *amirs*, *eshik aqasi* and other officers. On the eve of battle, the *jiba didan* (the inspection of arms and armaments) and *arz-i lashkar* (checking) was done personally by the Khan in accordance with Chingizid custom. The fully equipped army stood in battle array in divisions of right, left, centre and rear. The Khan rode through each of detachment and carefully examined its equipment and arms. The chief of each detachment, whether prince or noble, knelt and offered the Khan a horse and *tansuq* (presents). In return, the Khan rewarded him and encouraged him with promises. The *arz* continued from morning till evening.[45]

It seems that the army was usually assigned *iqtas* or territories for its maintenance. *Nishans* were issued to provincial rulers entitling them to utilize the revenue of the assigned regions for the maintenance of troops. The troops too were sometimes assigned villages as their salary. Tanish refers to the villages of Nasaf assigned to the royal army as *tankhwah,* and also to an *iqta* being given to the army in the region of Badakhshan.[46] The allocation of the daily allowance was done by the *diwan-i ata* (office for distribution of gifts and salaries). Isfahani describes how in 914 during the Qazaq expedition of Dashi-i Qipchaq, Shaibani halted in Turkestan to deliver *ata* to the army and fix their income and allowance, livelihood and provisions (*qut o azuq*). Shaibani is said to have asked the *ulama* to describe the order and references given by Caliph Umar in the distribution of *ata.* On being told that close associates of the Prophet were preferred in the allocation, Shaibani decided that the *ulama*, being successors of the Prophet's associates, should enjoy precedence in receiving the *ata.* Hence *khatib* of the *diwan-i ata* was instructed to write down Isfahani's name as the *sadr* of the *diwan-i ata,* with other learned men coming next. Preference was similarly given in the distribution of provisions, allowances (*qismat-i azuq o ghalla-i tughar*), accutrements and arms (*yaraq*). The remaining warriors were to be considered later, 'in accordance with customs prevalent among the Uzbegs'.[47] The same system seems to have continued in later years, since Mirza Badi Diwan in his *Majma-ul Arqam* (com. 1798) describes at length the registration of soldiers for the payment of salaries (*atiya dadan*). The Sultans in *atiya dadan*, therefore, usually started with officers of inner circle (*mahrams*) and *ulama* of the army. Later on the payment was made to the Uzbeg *amirs* (in the right wing), then to *amirs* of the left wing (*sol urun*) and, finally, to the warriors (*mubarizan*). Under the name of each *muazzaf-i ata* (stipend holder) the name of the assigned *qariya* alongwith the details of *wazifa* was written. The *awarijas* and *tujih* had full details of the army assignments. In the *tujih* the names of *muazzafin* (stipend holder) were written down according to hierarchy, with his *amal* and *urugh*, rank, category and name of the grant and place; *matbu*, if he was *a tabi* (subordinate of someone); and the *jama* from the village (*qariya*) in cash and kind.[48] The only information regarding the exact amount of salary comes down to us from the nineteenth century. During the regime of Bukhara *amir*, Nasrullah (1827-60), the regular and irregular troops of the Khan are said to have received payments of one *tilla* (gold coin) per head,[49] irrespective of his office or duties. Besides, the soldiers received during each campaign food allowances in the following manner: the *sarbaz* detachment and artillery received one *tanga* each for 3 days, *unter* or *dehbashi* (commander of ten) one *tanga* for two days, *penjaqbashi-i khurd* (sub in charge of artillery) one *tanga* for one day, the *penjaqbashi* (inchagre of artillery) one and a half *tangas*, *qaraulbegi* (chief of *sipahis*) two tangas per day and *yuzbashi* (commander of 100) four *tangas* a day. The musicians received the same amount as *sarbaz*. During the march the *sarbaz* and *topchi* also received from the imperial treasury one camp for 10 persons, one *araba* for baggage. Each army carried its own labourers and servants for errands and corvee.[50]

Either conforming to the age old universal method of incentive to the army in the form of booty or adhering to the Islamic principle of division of spoils[51] (*alanfal*), the Uzbeg rulers laid down rules for a sharing of the spoils. After a victory, plundering was stopped as soon as the *mal-i amani* (security depositor money to ensure peace) was determined. The defaulters in this regard were severely punished.[52] To prevent undue harassment of the conquered population, sometimes even the possessions of the soldiers were checked (*tahqiq-i amwal*) in order to ensure that plunder had not been illicitly indulged in. Once Kuchuk Ughlan, an *amir*, was sent to investigate, by checking the soldiers possessions, whether they had laid hands upon the wealth of the people.[53]

Otherwise, the booty acquired by the soldiers was enjoyed by them without any royal interference. Once a soldier complained to Abdullah Khan that during the plunder of Kistan Qara's treasures, each participant took five *seers* of red and white gold (*zar-i surkh o safed*) but the complainant was given only one *seer*. Abdullah asked him to be forbearing and did not demand any explanation.[54] Even when Abdullah's position had strengthened considerably, the distribution of booty continued to be the privilege of the soldiers[55] though in its division, the hierarchy was always respected. In *Nasfain ata*, the *amirs* requested Abdullah to allow the army 'pleasure by pillaging' which could be an act of goodwill (*bais-i khushnudi*) for the army.[56]

The army was rewarded or reprimanded before and after a battle.[57] The wounded soldiers were given medical aid.[58] The emperor personally visited them and sent physicians[59] and even granted extra money for ointment, etc. Those who showed bravery were handsomely rewarded and promoted by Abdullah and given horse, saddles and money. There was invariably an increase in the fixed stripend (*marsum*) of the victorious army.[60] After the victory in Balkh, Abdullah had awarded 20,000 *khanis* to Nazar Bi Naiman and 10,000 *khanis* to Aqum Chehra.[61]

Although Chingiz had continued Chirbi (a department for collecting provisions), a reference to this is not available in the Uzbeg sources. It seems that provisions (*aliq-i ulaghan* or *yurtawal*) for soldiers were collected by the soldiers themselves from the population on their way in the form of *taghar* tax;[62] or the same was supplied to them, if necessary, by the State.[63] During Qazaq campaigns in 1509, Shaibani's soldiers collected *azuqa* (provisions) in Turkistan. During the Herat campaign Abdullah wrote to Khwaja Juibari to supply 1,000 camel loads of barley which amounted to 10,000 *mans* from Andkhud or Merv since the entire stocks available in the royal establishment had already been distributed.[64] Once when the traders sent eatables and large quantitites of grains with the *diwan* of Bukhara, Khwaja Kamaluddin Husain, it was directly distributed among the army. On the other hand from lack of supplies, famine could strike the army so that one maund of flour (*arad*) was once (in 1581-2 near Dasht-i Qipchaq) sold for 100 *tanga-i Iskandar Khan* and even then was rarely found.[65]

The Uzbeg troops were generally patient and forbearing, fighting in starvation, subsisting on hunt or even on their horse's meat.[66] Manucci records how he saw a soldier stab his horse on the neck with great dexterity. Having drawn 40 ounces of blood, he closed the wound with one finger and drank the blood with great gusto. Others followed him. Afterwards the wound was tied up with a cloth and the horse left to recuperate. On being questioned, the soldier replied that they were accustomed to it because in their country, when plundering within an enemy's boundary, if provisions failed, their soldiers sustained life with the blood of their horses; nor from his bloodletting did the horse lapse their vigour. He adds 'when these soldiers captured any camel, horse or sheep in any enemy's country and if they were unable to carry it off (it was their practice) to decapitate it, into pieces and place some piece between their saddle and their horse's back, for consumption on the march whenever they were hungry'. Even when the provisions could be collected they would not search for or buy them but subsisted on whatever they had, lest the enemy discovered about their poor state of supplies and take advantage of that in overpowering them.[67]

The feasibility, plans and strategy of war discussed by Khan, Noyons, Sultans and the remaining ruling group in various assemblies (*kangash*) were finalized by the Khan himself in his special assembly (*majlis-i khas*). Having decided upon a war, *tawajis* were sent to inform the nominated army (*namzad*) and to collect (*zabt-i sipah*) the required number of soldiers alongwith their arms (*silah*). The proposed duration of campaign (one year or more) and other such details were given to them to enable them to prepare accordingly.[68] The soldiers could be informed at a very short notice to join the imperial army immediately. The *tawajis* conveyed the *jar* to the army taking a *muchulka* for *istihzar* (attendance) from the army to the effect that the required number would be reaching at the appointed place (*miadgah, mahal-i ijtimaa*) within the given period (*miad-i muqarrara*).[69]

The arms and equipment (*yaraq*) were brought by the *khails* (detachments) themselves.[70] Sometimes the army was supplied with the *jeba* (armour), instruments and armaments (*alat-i karzar* and *asbab-i razm*) before the campaign. The cash and arms were distributed among the soldiers.[71] Once Ahmad Jebaji (armourer) brought *silah* and *yaraq* from Bukhara. Abdullah Khan examined it and distributed about 2,000 lances (*neza*), spears (*sinan*), 1,000 suits of armour, *opker* (*gav sar*), shield, headgear (*khud mighfar*), sword, cuirass and other things among the soldiers of his army.[72]

The previously arrived army selected the place for war.[73] The parties of informers (*ghacharchi*) were sent ahead by Uzbegs to enquire about the plans and whereabouts of the enemy.[74] The venue for war was carefully determined. Before the Herat campaign, an attempt was made to control the only water resource available in the vicinity thus depriving the enemy of the water.[75] Before the march or attack all sorts of drums like Arabian drums (*jalajil*), kettledrums (*kos*), war tambourine (*tabla*) were beaten. The blowing of trumpets (*damama, kurka*) and ringing of globular bells to announce battle was very common.[76] The watch was kept (*pas dashtan* or *talabadari*) throughout the night by armed soldiers[77] with torches (*mashal o gandil*) before and during battle; and the dispatch of an advance guard for checking the enemy's army were routine part of military measures.

Fighting was an art for the Mongols which was transmitted from the one generation to another. Before battle, therefore, the most effective tactics of warfare were recounted by a veteran general—a custom continuing from the thirteenth century onwards. Hafiz Tanish affirms that before battle, 'in conformity with the *tura* and *yasaq* of earlier sultans',[78] a ninety year old Amir-i Azam Sari Khwaja Be Qushji described in detail the intensity of warfare (*ghamart-i hurub*), tactics, rules and regulations of fighting (*qawaid o rusum-i razm azmai*), safe exit from the whirlpool of combat (*gardab-i haija*) and other such methods.[79] During the battle, Abdullah usually stayed in the battlefield under a *chatr* (parasol) alongwith his associate and directed action from that position.

In accordance with the chingizide custom, the army was divided into six parts namely *maimna* (right wing), *maisra* (left wing), *qalb* (centre), *janah* (advance gurad), *saqa* (the rearguard) and *kamingah* (an ambush). Certain innovations in the army arrangement could always be made by the *khaqan*. Sometimes a large centre was arranged on one side (*qaul-i buzurg*) where certain princes and *amirs* were placed in the vanguard (*manghalay*). The *khaqan* personally organized another *qalb* (centre). The *qaul-i buzurg* usually had well armed extra reserve forces at its disposal. Usually the oldest sultan or the *khaqan* led the centre (*qalb*) of an army in conformity with the law of Chingiz Khan.[80] The princes and provincial rulers, each one alongwith his army stayed in his own intrenchment (*baljur murcha*).[81]

There was risk involved in allowing fully armed soldiers to wander over a million square miles.

The weapons like heavy armour, shields, lances, etc., of the horde were kept in the arsenal by certain officers and were cared for and cleaned until the warriors were summoned for a campaign, when they were issued weapons, mustered and inspected by *gurkhans*.

The soldiers had a tiny serviceable kit of leather, contaning a nose-bag for the pony, wax and files for sharpening the arrow heads, spare bowstrings and necessary utensils for (soldier's) use. They brought with them emergency ration (smoke cured meat, dry milk curds, etc.).[82]

The various weapons and armour used by the Uzbeg in various campaigns as mentioned by Hafiz Tanish and others may be listed as follows. Bow and arrow of different sizes and forms *takhsh, khadang-i kharaguzar* (marble piercing bow and arrow made of poplar) *sah choba tir, do choba tir,* short bow[83] (*kaman-i kutah*), *silah o joshan* (arms, sword mace, stringless bow, coat of mail), *joshan-i firangi* (European coat of mail, *zirih* (cuirass), fire lances (*sinan-i atishbari*), *khudi-zarrin* (golden helmet), *khaftan* (*a* vest worn under armour), hard bow (*kaman-i sakht*), *mighfar* (mail or network of steel worn under the cap or hat and also a protection for the face), *jiba o joshan, paikan* (javellin), *teghahai Hindi* and *Misri* (Egyptian and Indian sword), *gav sar* (pokers), *kajim* (armour for men and horse), *bargustuwan* (horse armour), *chamaq* (iron mace), Chinese armour (*joshan-i khitaii*), steel head gear (*khud-i pulad*), *nezahi khiti* (Chinese lances), *chirkas* (circassian) sword.[84] Later on hand guns were also introduced.

The quality of the arms depended upon the status of its owner. The armours of rich magnates and kings were naturally very expensive. Abdullah used golden shield, golden belt and golden head gear.[85] The poor soldiers had ordinary wooden shields and covered their body with felt instead of armour (*jeba siz kizbita chalghandi*).[86]

It is generally assumed that the Uzbegs earlier lacked the incendiary methods of warfare which even led to their defeat in the battle of Tahirabad and Herat (1510) and that they took heed of fire weapons only in the second half of the sixteenth century. Muhammad Saleh however, refers to the use of hand fire weapons[87] during Uzbeg-Timurid conflict (1510-40). Burhan Khan and other rulers of Bukhara were also reported to have used handguns with copper balls and later on with iron balls of Rumi style.[88] Sidi Ali Reis says that Khan Nauroz Ahmad had received Turkish guns, cannons and firearms sent by the Ottoman Sultan along with the Ottoman Janissaries, Ketkhudas and archers.[89] During Abdullah Khan's reign also 2000 Rumi *tufungandaz* (gunbearers and musketeers) riding on gold saddled horses have been mentioned.[90] The firearms occupied a strong place in the Uzbeg army in the second half of the sixteenth century, though a description of artillery is found earlier also.[91] Ali Sher Navoi described the artillery of Iskandar as having wheels, standing on metal stand, shooting grenades of bronze and alloy, ignited by matches through two openings. The art was learnt from Osmani Turks and Europeans. Abdullah was to be so excited over the 'hand guns' that he had 'caused' Jenkinson 'to shoot in handguns before him and did himself practise the use thereof'.[92]

The secrets of flaming naphtha and the terrible Greek fire were known to the caliphs of Baghdad even in early thirteenth century.[93]

The gunners were subject to the head of *qurkhana* who controlled them and looked after their welfare. By the end of the sixteenth century, artillery was usually made locally as we hear of *farangi* artillery very rarely. During Abdullah Khan's regime the *deg-i Qara Bughra* were said to have been founded by Ustad Ruhi.[94] Some of the *degs* (cannons) cast by Mir Qasim and Qurban were so huge as to throw away a stone ball of about three Bukhara *mans*.[95] After the death of Ustad Ruhi, Mirak *topbashi* had been given the charge of artillery.[96] The other *degs* (large cannons or mortars) mentioned by Tanish were *deg-i Qara Bahadur* and *deg-i Jahangir*.[97] The Russian envoy Gregory Vasilovich informed Shah Abbas of Persia about the use of firearms and during the Herat campaign (1588) Uzbegs fought with artillery and arquebuses.[98] Hafiz Tanish confirms that during this campaign Miran *rekhtagar* was ordered to cast a number of guns (*degs*) and Diwan Khwaja Raziuddin Ahmad was asked to supply copper (*mis*) and *khaula*; and in a short time seven large guns, each of which could carry 2½ Bukhara *mans* of stone, were cast.[99] At the end of the sixteenth century the size of the artillery was reported to be almost uniform, each having seven cannons, cast at the order of Abdullah and shooting cannon balls of 2-3 *mans* each.[100] Similarly the technical use of naphtha is described both by Muhammad Saleh and Hafiz Tanish.[101] not only arrows were filled with naphtha but hot cloth soaked in naphtha were thrown at the time of the fall of boundary wall. Sometimes *Shatu* (lit. Turkish staircase), *narduban* (a scaling ladder), noose or slip knots (*kamand*), tent rope (*tanab*) were placed on the prarapets of the fort to open an outlet.[102] The doors of the fort were also forced open by striking hatchet and *tabarzan* (wood cutter).[103]

When besieged, a group of people were appointed on various towers and turrets and lances, stones and cups of ashes were kept handy.[104] During the Sabran campaign, there were boxes fixed at every step in the fort where bowmen and archers sat. In each tower *tufakchis* stood and as soon as any one was sighted he was made the target of *fir-i partap*. On each parapet people sat along with goblets of oil (*kadu roghan*), pots of ashes (*kuza-i khakistar*), lances, bricks and stones.[105] The cannons were also used for defence. Tanish refers to the guns, *deg-i Jahangiri* and *Qara Bughra* that were fixed on the gates (*darwaza-i chaharraha* and *darwaza-i suzangaran*) as being manipulated by Ustad Ruhi.[106] Hand mortars were also common.

The siege warfare already well developed under Timur and his successors futher improved under the Uzbegs. During the siege of Andkhud in (1570-1) use was made of the *zarbuzan* (a piece of artillery, field guns[107]). Tanish describes how Ustad Ruhi threw stones by *arrada* and *manjaniq* (ballista, catapault) and made breaches in the walls. Through the spark of a flame of *tufang* (a musket or a tube for shooting clay balls through the force of a breath) they caused fire at the base of the fort. The *zarbuzan* shot from its mouth stones of the weight of one Bukhara man with such force that through constant bombardment, the towers and turrets crumbled down and its walls became full of holes.[108] Similarly during the Tirmiz expendition, there were fifty *naftbaz* and *tufakandaz* (naphtha-throwers and musketeers) lying in ambush.[109] The *Qara Bughra deg* is said to have exuded fire. The *ra 'adandazan* and *manjaniq sazan* turned the *degs* towards the fort for hunting stones. The *atishbazan* and *tufakandazan* fixed *arrada* and *manjaniq*.[110] The miners ran mines by digging under towers and turrets with pokers (*kulank metin*) and axes and placed the beams (*sutun*) inside so that whenever there was need, it should be filled with naphtha and fuel (*hima*) and set on fire. Sometimes during the excavation of mines, water had to be first taken out of the ditches and then the mines laid.[111]

During the campaign near turrets of the fort were razed to the ground by the constant shower of stones.[112] The *amirs* and supervisors of the *degs* including Mirak Yasawul *topchibashi* alongwith a group of excellent musketeers opened fire from the 'python like *degs*' (which must mean guns and not containers for *manjaniq*-balls). Through a shower of stones, the parapet and fortifications fell to the ground.[113] The use of naptha and gunpowder was very common.[114]

The *Kamanaha-i raad,* fire throwing lances in the *tufaks* and *tir-i partap* are mentioned in 1588 in the description of the Herat campaigns.[115] Each of the arrow of *degahi Qara Bughara* was of 3 *mans* (Bukhara[116]). *Kaman-i raad* is said to be manufactured by Amir Rekhtagar; the *degs* cast by him reportedly carried stones of 3 Bukhara maunds.[117] During the Ghauriyan expedition *zamburak* was also used.[118]

In open battle, the artillery and musketeers usually stood in front of the army and the *amirs* to provide a bulwark against the enemy. Sometimes *tufakandaz* stood on foot in front of right wing.[119] During the Herat campaign, all the *tufakchis* were summoned by Ustad Ruhi at the order of the Khan. The carts (*arabas*) collected from all over Bukhara were brought to the battlefield, chained together and placed before the army to protect the musketeers, gunbearer and the engineers of Turkish, Tajik, Arab and Persian descent.[120] In his campaign against Baba Sultan, Ustad Ruhi ordered *tufakandazan* to fire the many *zamburaks* all of a sudden and himself aimed at Baba and his friends so efficiently that as soon as they ignited the *deg*, the stone hurled by them hit an enemy warrior to death instantly.[121] On another occasion even Ustad Ruhi was unhorsed when a fire lance hit him.[122] Other *tufakchis* were also wounded.

During the Khurasan exedition 964 wooden palisades (*chaparha*) and *tura* (mantelets—a kind of screen behind which warriors used to send their missiles) were arranged to provide a fortified place to the soldiers. Abdullah's men also prepared *sarkobaha* (battering machines erected to overtop a wall) and *murchal* (an intrenchment for besieging a fortified place) so as to shoot at those who were clinging to fort walls. The trees were cut down and the ditch was filled up to the height of the fort. The army then rushed with the *sipars* (shields) on their heads and crossed the ditch. Notwithstanding the shower of stones from the parapets killing a few of them, the army managed to cause holes and breaches in the wall through shovels (*kuland*) and spade (*mitin*).

A popular tactic in battle was the *tulughma*.[123] Babur records how in the battle of Sar-i Pul, he drove the Uzbegs who 'attacked our front by several vigorous assaults but who had wheeled to our rear came up and rained arrows on our standard. Falling on us in this way, from the front and from the rear, they made our men hurry off'. According to Babur 'this same turning movement is one of the great merits of Uzbeg fighting; no battle of theirs is ever without it. Another merit is that they, all begs and retainers from their front to their rear, ride, loose rein at the gallop, shouting as they come and in retiring do not scatter but ride off, at the gallop in a body'.[124]

In many of their battles, the Timurids and Uzbegs resorted to the age old method of *albayt wal kamin* (night attacks and ambush) and *alharb-i khad* (deceiving war tactics) by leaving almost always a force in ambush which fell upon the enemy's army which pursued the Uzbeg army after a feigned retreat. The treatise written probably in Damascus by Isa Ibn-i Ismail ul Hanafi and entitled *Nihayatal Sul wa-i Umniya fi Tahim Amalat Furusiyya* (complete instructions in the practice of the military art) gives a detailed account of this type of warfare. The sources refer even to the *kamingah sakhtan* (allocation of ambuscade). The Uzbegs often resorted to a night attack (*shabkhun*[125]). In an open battle *tauq* and *tauqdar* is often found which was apparently a mode of enticing the enemy in a circle[126] which is very well depicted in a painting with scene of army. If an individual charged the foe alone in one sweep, it may be called *yakka tazi* (individual combat) which was also common.[127]

An interesting belief surrounded the methods of fighting of the tribal elements who were supposed to resort to the *amal-i sang-i yadah* (the act of stone *yadah*) for causing hail storm, snowfall, excessive rains, chill and lightning to discourage the enemy from marching forward.[128] The *Arais-ul Jwahir* (comp. 700) refers to a stone called *yadah* (*vat*) which, if placed in a water pond created such an effect.[129] According to Abul Qasim Abdullah Kashani the Uighurs and Turks were adept in this craft.[130] Abul Fazl says that Abul Turk Yafis Bin Noah had begged his father to teach him a prayer by which he might have rain whenever he wanted it. Noah gave him stone which had the property of bringing rain. There were many of these stones available with these Turks which they called *yedatash*. The Persians called it *sangiyada* and the Arabs *hajara almatar* (rain stone).

In Samarqand in Yuan Chang's time there were fire worshippers and Buddhists though the latter were often persecuted (94 wolters). Balkh alone had more than 3,000 Brethren—all adherents of the 'small vehicle' system and above 100 Buddhist monasteries (ibid., 108).

Khwaja Kalan Juibari was the 'thirty removes from Saiyid Ali Ariz's the Great Imam Jafar-i Sadiq'—and was one of the 'glorious Saiyids'[131] of Turan and an 'object of faith and reverence' with the Uzbeg Khans who are entirely devoted to this family. Abdullah Khan then 'wore in this mental ear the discipleship' to Khawaja Kalan.

In the combat process speed, mobility and strategy were the keynote to success. The sweeping movement of the right flank called *tulughma* (a standard sweep)[132] was indeed very effective. Babur seems to be fairly impressed by the Uzbeg methods and tactics of warfare as his following reprimand to Darwesh Muhammad

Tarkhan proves 'Are you likening him (Ibrahim Lodi) to the Uzbeg Khans and sultans. In what of movement under arms or of planned operations is he to be compared with them'.

The *dastur-i rumi* (called by Ottomans as *tabur-i chingi*) by the Turks as *chapar, cheper, sauran andakhatan*, and by the Mongols as *kuriyan* or *kuren*, frequently found in the sixteenth century sources was also an order of battle.[133]

NOTES

1. Juvaini, *History of the World Conquerer*, text, pp. 21-4; *JT*, pp. 338-409, 440; Cleaves, *Secret History*, pp. 141-9; Marco Polo, *Travels*, pp. 117-19; *H. Siyar*, p. 24; *Rauzat-us Safa* V, pp. 66-7; *Abdullah Nama*, pp. 233, 333, 343; *Shajratul Atrak*, MS British Museum Add 26190, ff. 57-8; Begin, p. 14; Ibn-i Hauqal, pp. 196-7.
2. *Mehn*, pp. 54-5.
3. *Abdn*, p. 281.
4. Ibid., p. 245.
5. Ibid., p. 372.
6. For Mongol decimal system cf. Juvaini, pp. 20-5; *Secret History*, pp. 141-9.
7. *BN*, p. 100.
8. For the description of army organization of the original Mongols see Marco Polo, p. 118.
9. *Rauzat-us Safa*, V, pp. 66-7.
10. A nineteenth century Persian work gives a somewhat different system of military organization consisting of a battalion of 700 *sarbaz* divided into seven detachments (*dasta*) each of which had two wings (*nimdasta*), four artillery, *rasad* (provisions) and eight *bar'aa*; each *dasta* having a commander *yuzbashi* or *yuzbegi* with a helper *qaraulbegi*. The incharge of the artillery *penjabashi* had a subordinate *penjabashikhurd*. Each *dasta* had ten officers and ten *unter*. Under the *sarbaz* and *topchis* worked the musicians of the army (A.A. Troitskaya, *Vainnovai dela va Bukhare va pervi palavine* XIX vek, p. 215.
11. For their functions and other details cf. chapter on administration.
12. *Abdn*, pp. 248, 262-3, 351, 377, 385.
13. Ibid., p. 218.
14. *AAA*, pp. 40-2; *Afzalt*, pp. 34-5; *Ahsant*, pp. 205-25.
15. *Abdn*, pp. 217-18.
16. D.O. Morgan, 'The Mongol Armies in Persia', *Der Islam*, Band 56, Heft I, 1979, pp. 81-96.
17. *Mehn*, pp. 72-3; *Abdn*, p. 325.
18. *Abdn*, pp. 309, 325.
19. Ibid., pp. 239, 259.
20. *Mehn*, p. 108.
21. *JT*, pp. 8, 13, 21-4.

22. *Kashkul-i Salimi*, p. 24.
23. *TR*, Eng. tr., pp. 120, 123.
24. *Mehn*, p. 108.
25. Ibid., pp. 93-7.
26. *AAA*, pp. 40-2; *Afzalt*, pp. 34-5; *Ahsant*, pp. 205-25.
27. *Abdn*, p. 279; Erskin, p. 38.
28. Ibid., p. 333.
29. *Abdn*, p. 279.
30. Ibid., pp. 252-3, 257, 285, 422.
31. *TR*, Eng. tr., p. 123; also see *Central Asia in the Sixteenth Century*, New Delhi, 2002, chapter on Shaibani Khan.
32. *TR*, Eng. tr., p. 12; also see chapter on Shaibani Khan, ibid.
33. *T. Shaibani*, p. 75, Institute Vastoka Vegeniya, No. 1505 f. 4; *Abdn*, pp. 251, 218.
34. *Mehn*, pp. 122-3.
35. *Abdn*, pp. 252-3, 257, 258, 422.
36. *Maktubat wa asnad*, p. 181.
37. *BN*, Eng. tr., pp. 100, 155; also see *Abdn*, p. 111; Lamb, *Gengiz Khan*, p. 79.
38. *BN*, Eng. tr., pp. 100, 155; *TR*, p. 308; Mirza Badi, pp. 14-16.
39. Badi, pp. 14-16.
40. *T. Abulkhair*, pp. 257-8.
41. *Abdn*, p. 223.
42. Prawdin, p. 94.
43. Ibid.
44. *Abdn*, p. 380.
45. Ibid., pp. 61, 137-40, 204, 246, 328-9.
46. Ibid., pp. 67, 444. The payment of the army was introduced by Ghazan Khan (in 1303), for details cf. Morgan, pp. 91-6; *T. Ghazani*, p. 71.
47. *Suluk*, p. 97; *Mehn*, pp. 43, 61, 132.
48. *Majma-ul Arqam*, pp. 14-16.
49. Troitskaya, pp. 215-16; *Sbornik statiya pa istori e filologi narodov Sredni Azi*. Obruchev however says that the ordinary soldier received a monthly stipend of 5 *tangas* only. Obruchev, *Pa goram e pustiniyam Sredni Azi*, p. 66.
50. Ibid.
51. M. Querry, *Droit Mussulman*, Paris, 1871, Vol. I, p. 335; Amir Ali, *The Spirit of Islam*, Delhi, 1978, p. 63; A. Ben Shemesh, *Taxation in Islam*, Leiden, 1967, pp. 23-6.
52. Chingiz had not spared even his son-in-law Toguchar who was ordered to lay down his commission and to 'serve as a private' just because he (Toguchar) plundered the town which had already surrendered to Jebc (Prawdin, p. 173).
53. *Abdn*, p. 252.
54. Ibid., p. 70.
55. Ibid., pp. 70, 129, 438.
56. Ibid., p. 145.
57. Ibid., pp. 129, 188; *Mehn*, p. 214; *T. Qipchaqi* unpaginated.
58. *Abdn*, p. 252.
59. Ibid., pp. 129, 241, 252.
60. Ibid., pp. 229, 241, 266, 334.

61. Ibid.
62. *Mehn*, pp. 179-199.
63. *Abdn*, p. 352; *Mehn*, pp. 132, 140.
64. *Rauzat*, pp. 260-2; *Abdn*, p. 306.
65. *Abdn*, pp. 331-3.
66. *Manucci*, p. 42; also see Lamb, pp. 128-38. It was generally believed the one Uzbeg soldier was equal to hundred others. See Begin, p. 14; *Abdn*, p. 6.
67. *Abdn*, p. 343.
68. Ibid., pp. 133, 162, 167, 200, 236, 310, 328, 377, 409.
69. Ibid., pp. 71, 133, 136, 137, 167, 172, 200, 236, 274, 310, 328, 377, 409.
70. *Mehn*, pp. 91-2, 132, 140, 191.
71. *Abdn*, p. 133.
72. Ibid., pp. 244-6.
73. Ibid., p. 295.
74. Ibid., p. 244.
75. Ibid., p. 224.
76. Ibid., pp. 139-42.
77. Ibid., pp. 205, 427, 328.
78. This custom should not be confused with Arab custom of denunciation and praise.
79. *Abdn*, p. 93.
80. Ibid., pp. 143, 225, 226, 285.
81. Ibid., p. 352.
82. Lamb, pp. 79, 125.
83. Shah Tahmasp's letter to Sulaiman of Turkey praises the Uzbeg archers 'who could shoot an arrow in the dark night and hit the target even though it be the eye of an ant'.
84. *Abdn*, pp. 71, 86, 89, 137, 148-9, 169, 174, 183-4, 188, 204, 205, 216-17, 224, 239, 265, 279, 380, 421; Muhammad Saleh, pp. 52-3; *BN*, Eng. tr., pp. 31, 65. For design and manufacture of arms cf. infra chapter on Markets and Workshops.
85. *Abdn*, pp. 464, 490.
86. *Shaibani Nama* (*Sh. N.*), p. 168, also see *Abdn*, p. 455. Among the Mongol arms, Babur refers to *shash par* (six flanged mace), the *piyazi* (rugged mace), *kistin, tabarzin* (saddle gatchet) and *battu* (battle axe). *BN*, Eng. tr., p. 160.
87. *Sh. N.*, p. 56.
88. Sidi Ali Reis, *Miratul Mamalik*, Tashkent, 1963, p. 100.
89. Sidi Ali Reis, *Travels*, Eng. tr. by Vambery, pp. 69, 73-6.
90. *Abdn.*, pp. 97, 184.
91. *ZN*, pp. 478-9; Clavijo, p. 168.
92. Jenkinson, Hakluyt Society Series, p. 457, for Egyptian and Ottoman contribution to Central Asian artillery cf. Mansura Haidar, 'Military Organization under Timur', *CAJ*.
93. Lamb, p. 119.
94. *Abdn*, p. 345.
95. Ibid., p. 299.
96. Ibid., p. 345.
97. Ibid., p. 215.

98. V.A. Ulyanitski, *Otnoshenija Russia sa Sredni Azi e Indiva*, XVI-XVII, p. 11.
99. *Abdn*, pp. 475-7; *Istorija Samarqanda*, p. 270. Babur says that the artillery of Ali Quli were of varied sizes, comprised two parts—*tashooe* (the stone chamber) and *darukhana* (powder compartment). This could kill eight persons in one shot. *Rekhtagars* were helped by auxiliary in the task (*BN*, pp. 302-69).
100. *Abdn*, p. 469.
101. *Sh. N.*, p. 52; *Abdn*, p. 163.
102. *Abdn*, pp. 89, 203, 245.
103. Ibid., p. 203.
104. Ibid., p. 215.
105. Ibid., pp. 215, 338, 354, 365.
106. Ibid., p. 215.
107. For earlier reference to *zarbuzan* cf. *BN*, pp. 266-7; Eng. tr., pp. 473-4.
108. *Abdn*, p. 157, see also pp. 13, 164-5, 190-3, 200-3, 215, 492-4.
109. *Abdn*, p. 164.
110. Ibid., p. 345.
111. Ibid., pp. 105, 346, 352-353, 486, 488.
112. Ibid., p. 301.
113. Ibid., p.189.
114. Ibid., pp. 201, 301-4, 365.
115. *Abdn*, pp. 475-7, 487.
116. Ibid., p. 437.
117. Ibid., pp. 479, 487.
118. Ibid., p. 486.
119. Ibid., pp. 173, 263.
120. Ibid., pp. 224-8, 263.
121. Ibid., p. 228.
122. Ibid., p. 264.
123. Lamb says it was 'the favorite manouevre of the Mongols, the standard sweep, that turns an enemy's flank and takes him in the rear' (pp. 63-4).
124. *BN*, text, p. 90; Eng. tr., p. 140.
125. *BN*, Eng. tr., p. 139.
126. *Abdn*, pp. 81, 250.
127. Ibid., p. 218.
128. Ibid., pp. 282, 312.
129. Abul Fazl, I, Eng. tr., pp. 167-8 also fn. 3. Abdullah Kashani, *Araisul Jwahar*, 1345 AH, pp. 170-2.
130. Ibid.
131. *Maasir-ul Umara*, Vol. I, Patna, 1979, p. 101.
132. *The Ancient Art of Warfare*, Vol. I, London, 1966, p. 289; Irvine, *Army of the Mughals*, p. 43.
133. *BN*, text, p. 265; Eng. tr., pp. 470-1. Halil Inalcik, 'The Social and Political Effects of the Diffusions of Firearms in the Middle East', in Parry and Yapp, eds., *War, Technology and Society*, pp. 204-6.

Incendiary Warfare and the Use of Firearms in Central Asia

The Mongols rightly claimed that 'they had no country, their homes were their horse's back' a dictum which the descendants of the Mongols followed even in the sixteenth century. Timur 'dreamt of reduction of kingdoms, obtainment of empire, defeating armies, circumventing enemies, making friends of foes as he believed that the dignity of empire is supported by extensive territories, by a rich treasury and by numerous armies', because 'there was naught more worthy the valour of princes than conquering of kingdoms and empires waging holy wars with infidels'.[1] The Uzbegs also strove to follow in the traditions of their medieval predecessor. The Uzbeg ruler, Shaibani Khan declared 'the saddle of his horse to be his capital'.[2] Abdullah Khan also considered 'excellent generalship' to be the prop of magnificence and one of the two emblems of the greatness of a ruler'[3] and even reminded the *mardikars* that 'our livelihood lies beneath the shadow of our lances'.[4] In almost all his *nishans*, the provincial rulers are instructed to be particularly kind, humane and generous towards the soldiers as they were 'pilgrims of the sacred wealth and defenders and protectors of the country and its people.[5] In medieval Central Asia, this requisite nuisance necessitated continuous effort for improving tactics and strategy methods in order to surpass the rivals.

In medieval Central Asia, therefore, the required accomplishment in the war game necessitated continuous effort for improving tactics and strategic methods in order to surpass the rivals. The emphasis on the compilation of treatises and exclusive works on the art of warfare with detailed description of weapons as well as generous patronage extended to the armourer's workshop and acquisition of imported techniques, arms and armaments by the kings (and sometimes by the higher nobles shows how keenly the need for advancement of this art was felt all over the world. *A Wal Umiyya fi Talim-i Mal al Furusiyya* (Complete Instructions in the Practice of the Military Art) compiled in Damascus in the early fourteenth century by Isa Ibn-i Ismail al-Hanafi, there were a number of other exclusive treatises on firearms, naphtha and incendiary warfare. Ibn-i Sabir Al Manjaniqi is also said to have 'left an unfinished book which treats the art of warfare in all its details.[6] In Transoxiana, Razi's Encyclopaedic work *Jamiul Ulum* comprised one full section on the use of firearms. Although *Adabul Harb wa Shujaat* was compiled by Fakhri Mudabbir (a Central Asian by birth) and dedicated to an Indian ruler Iltutmish, its contents give a fairly comprehensive description of Turco-Mongol weaponery, art and method of warfare. Continuous exchange of ideas and technology in the sphere of warfare and new creations in the armourer's workshop (*zarrad khana*) further confirm the inclination of the elite towards this medieval adventurous engagement. In India several works were prepared on the art of warfare during the reign of Akbar, in whose court also a galaxy of such artisans flourished. In the medieval warfare[7] the use of firearm played an important role. Polemical points provoking discussions on its place of origin, extent of expansion, process of evolution is being carried further here. The controversy, whether the credit of introduction of firearms and artillery should go to Asia or Europe however continues. The lack of sufficient evidence further complicates the matter.

It is indeed very surprising that the *Secret History of the Mongol Dynasty* does not refer to any kind of firearms (though there are frequent references to several equipments of warfare) except fire sickles (sickle shaped piece of steel enveloped in leather used for striking a spark to ignite tinder).[8] While describing the organization of Chingizd army, Marco Polo does not describe any firearms used by the Chinese armies. Both Carpini and Marco Polo however, speak of leather arms and breast plate of Mongols which were replaced by iron and metal armours after their contacts with the foreigners.[9] Although it can not be established with certainty who had actually introduced gunpowder to Europe, the fact that the Mongols learnt the art of siege artillery from their Chinese subjects is proved beyond doubt. 'Khitayan mangonel men (who with a stone missile would convert the eye of a needle into a passage for a camel, having fastened the poles of the mangonels so firmly with sinews (*pai*) and glue that when they aimed from the nadir to the zenith the missile did not return)', Juvaini records that Mangu Qaan sent (his men) to Khitai to fetch mangonel experts and naphtha throwers and they brought from Khitai 1,000 household of Khitayan mangonel men'.[10] Prawdin asserts that the Mongols learnt form the Chinese, about the fighting engines, instruments for hurling explosive fire, mangonel, catapult.[11] Many years before its introduction in Europe, where Barthold Schwarz 'discovered' the gunpowder, flame throwers and cannons to ignite wooden towers and to overwhelm the defenders of fortresses with a hail of stones and iron were being used. The same writer further informs us that the Mongols and Chinese 'learned from the chemists of the West how to use flame throwers which squirted burning naphtha against the enemy'.[12]

To be fair to the Turani technology, siege engines were very common in Central Asia even before the Mongols. In 1201 Sultan Muhammad had used the mangonel 'until the walls were humbled like the earth'.[13] In 1204 the mangonels were aimed at razing the towers to the ground for which the stones rained down like hail upon the bazaars and streets.[14] The people of Nishapur are reported to have employed 3,000 crossbows on the walls, 300 mangonels and ballistas and corresponding quantity of missiles and naphtha against Mongol besiegers under Toului in 1221.[15] The fact that the best Muslim engineers were picked up by Chingiz to manufacture new catapults, mangonels and battering rams indicates that the practice was already old enough to facilitate their manufacture. In the Islamic countries in the initial stages, the expert gunners not only knew about casting of cannons and its manufacture but also served in the army, supplied the powder and showered shot.[16] Even testing of guns and the composition of gunpowder was their duty.[17]

In the beginning, the Mongols knew only fast moving mounted warfare having no idea of sandbags, wickershields, scaling ladders and battering rams. The only reliable weapon was their science of *Yaior Yada,*[18] i.e. the use of rain and hailstorm through trickery with which they could often create trouble for the enemy. It is reported that Mongols faced a terrible setback only during the Volo Hai siege realizing for the first time the significance of the art of siege warfare. The problem was somehow, solved by Chingiz Khan[19] but Mongol siege craft remained to be unsophisticated till 1211-12. It was only after the second siege of Tatung Fu and Peking that Mongols learnt from their Chinese captives the art of siege warfare. In the second decade of the thirteenth century, Chinese engineers were hired for imparting their knowledge of the fire, explosives, catapults and siege engines. Soon a variety of engines and weapons which flung fire and threw rocks, flame throwers, the tools for mining of saps, hurling of pots of flaming naphtha from catapults, filling of moats and the thunderous ramming of the Mongol gates were an inseparable part of Chingiz Khan's equipage of war.[20] The Mongols are reported to have used mangonel, fire, naphtha and stone during Chingiz Khan's Khujand and Samarqand campaigns.[21] They filled the moat by setting up battering rams, catapults and scaling ladders upon the Jand fort in 1219.[22] During the Khawarazm expedition 'even instruments of warlike wood mangonels and missiles' were repaired by them and since there were no stones in the neighbourhood of Khwarazm they manufactured these missiles from the wood of mulberry trees.[23] They set fire to horses with pots of naphtha 'sewing the people to one another with arrows and mangonels'. In 1221 Tirmiz was reduced by the new large siege engines perfected by Ogedei, with flaming pots of naphtha. In Urganj siege, it was the barrage of blazing naphtha which decided in favour of Mongols. After the Nishapur siege, Mongols used threes thousand ballistas, three thousand catapults and seven hundred war engines for hurling naphtha.[25] During the Russian campaign Batu's mangonels opposite the walls are said to have destroyed the city within a few days.[26]

While describing the Bukhara campaign of Chingiz, Juvaini records, 'And on either side the furnace of the battle was heated. On the outside, mangonels were erected, bows bent and stones and arrows discharged; and on the inside, ballistas and pots of naphtha were set in motion. It was like a red hot furnace fed from without by hard sticks thrust into the recesses, while from the belly of the furnace sparks shoot into the air'.[27]

As early as Chaghatai's reign, Abu Yusuf Al Sakkaki is said to have created 'an army of firearms'. Instead of being pleased with the new innovation, Chaghatai (being instigated by Habash Amid), ordered for his (Sakkaki's) killing as he feared that Sakkaki could with the help of his firearms murder or overthrow him (Chaghatai) Sakkaki was, therefore, imprisoned and died after 3 years.[28]

Ogedei's arsenal of new siege machines, the strong thunder weight stone missiles, pots filled with burning naphtha 'falling upon roofs and seeing them breaking into pieces and buildings burning into flames provided quite an enjoyable sight for Chingiz Khan'.[29] Where there were no rocks or blocks of stone, trees were felled and cut into blocks of suitable size which were soaked in water till they became heavy enough to be used as missiles. But they proved ineffective in storming the walls.[30]

During Hulegu's war against Rukunddin in September-December 1256, there was such a heavy use of incendiary warfare that 'because of the great quantity of fires, they thought the earth a sky full of stars', the description categorically refers to the use of firearms 'from the towers, bows sent up swift feathered shafts, and a *kaman* I gave which had been constructed by Khitayan craftsmen and had a range of 2,500 paces, was brought to bear on those fools, when no other remedy remained; and of the devil-like heretics many soldiers were burnt by those meteoric shafts'. Further 'A great fear of the arrows from the crossbows overcame them so that they were utterly distraught. Some were left wounded and source lifeless.'[31]

Although Mongols did not possess guns they frequently used fire-arms. The firearms adopted by the Mongols were further improved by Timur.

It is possible that Timur owed much of his success to his undiminished concern for improvement in his military technique, strategy and form of army organization. In his war with Iliyas Khwaja (1365), the army followed the traditional style of organization, i.e. there were right and left wings, each of which had reserves (*qambil*) and vanguard. Out of seven detachments, three were assigned an independent position while the fourth (having two vanguard and two *qambil*) was a subordinate one. The centre had no reserve, parallel or vanguard. Gradually, however, more emphasis was laid on a strong centre as in the war against Toqtamish in 1391. Similarly, technique of reducing forts had also improved considerably.

Timur is renowned for his devices in capturing forts (*qalagiri*). In the early years, he used only *maliyur* (raised platforms) and the various siege engines (catapults), such as *manjaniqs* (in Shiraz and Khwarazim),[32] and *arrad* (in Tirshiz)[33] and *raad*[34] (as in Onk). Usually breaches in the walls were achieved only by the constant bombardment of stones. It seems that mining was rare in the early stages. It was only during the siege of Takrit that we hear of the setting of fire in connection with mining.[35] Timur developed highly sophisticated methods of reaching the top of the walls. Wooden pieces were placed along with the earth and stone and formed these raised platforms (*maljurs*) the besiegers could easily reach the parapets of the fort.[36] The *maljurs* were usually employed where tunnelling was not possible (e.g. in Siwas fort which was surrounded by big deep ditches (*khundaq*) filled with water and where the excavation to a depth of even one yard brought up water.[37] Sometimes holes were made in the trenches to let out water by *kharaks* (an instrument for pecking)[38] but it was not always possible. Ropes with running nooses (*kamand otanab*) and scaling ladders of rope and raw silk were flung on to turrets to enable climbers to penetrate into the fort and open the gates.[39] The smaller engines (*arrad*) loaded on to a barge or boat were moved to any suitable place along the walls and the wheels, crossbows, *zambur* or *zamburuk* were used for firing large arrows. The siege engines threw stones. The pick axe (*kulang*) and the stone mason's chisel *metin* were also used to make breaches in the walls.[40] During the Egyptian campaign, the *amirs* of Tuman were required to stand in their own *siba* (enclosed quarter or a place surrounded by walls) and arranged the *manjaniq* and *arrad*, *raad* and *tir-i charkh*, etc. While the stones thrown by *manjaniqs* hit the besieged fortifications and razed part of them to the ground, the already constructed pavilions (*kharrah*) helped the soldiers to reach the top which was 3,000 yards in height from the bottom.[41]

Mining or tunnelling was used to reduce stubborn garrisons. The digging or pecking *naqabzadan* either through *manjaniqs* or by men manually was followed by conflagration *aatishzadan* thus blasting the parapets and the walls. Yazdi gives a detailed description of mining or tunnelling during the siege of Takrit fort. According to him, *tuwajis* were instructed by Timur to allocate various stretches of the fort to several persons for digging through the fort walls, *naqab-zadan* while using catapults and starting from the left. Each portion was dug by two or three persons and there were forty such groups. Some of them pierced through the stone up to 35 *gaz*, others cut through the stones and in a short time, the whole area was like a 'netted sieve'.[42] The breaching (*hafri khundaq* or *kundani*) was either caused through managing or by arrow shots? The walls of the Takrit fort were undermined by tunnelling *naqab* and the hollowed places were filled in with the fuel and the firewood (*hema*) and sprinkled with *naft* and set on fire. The walls of the fort fell to the ground and a tower was entirely demolished.[43] During the siege of Meerut, Timur's men were able to dig a tunnel of 10 to 15 yards under each tower and turret and the mines were set on fire.[44] The question arises whether *naft* here means Greek fire or naphtha? In the earlier stages of gun processing even 'the hollowed out logs were used as mortars'.

On the next occasion of its use, it was almost certainly gunpowder.

During the siege of Damascus, Yazdi says that due to *kaman raad*, people were aghast and due to the accuracy of the pots of naphtha *qarurahai naft*, there was lot of smoke. Nazabchis miners set on fire the large stones and sprinkled vinegar, *sirka baban mi rekhtand*. Stones and towers and parapets were filled with bamboo tubes held on logs. Orders were given for setting them on fire. Suddenly a tower of such a strength and height fell down so that a vast passage was created through which 70 to 80 persons could enter the fort. In the meantime another portion of the wall fell and dust arose, that some were buried others alive though besieged soon repaired the breach. Nevertheless when there was conflagration in other mines, one side of the fort all of a sudden fell down.[45] Here, it is very probable that we have the use of gunpowder proper for breaching purposes: only gunpowder could perhaps have created such a shattering explosion. One could argue that whether guns or mortars had come in use as it still remains uncertain because the evidence does not directly indicate anything more than siege engines on the catapault principle and the use of naphtha.

Although the actual date of the invention of gunpowder is controversial, we know for certain that the black powder was the sole but commonly known explosive material from thirteenth to the nineteenth century. The first guns to utilize the gunpowder as a propellants are said to have had already been invented in the early years of the fourteenth century.[46] These were small and crude with ill assorted projectiles and incapable of causing large scale destruction.[47] The ignited gun powder rapidly burns evolving a whitish gas. In a confined space, this pent up gas could be used for blasting or for propelling missiles. Black powder is a slow explosive and is widely used for blank fire charges in military ammunitions. The instrument employing gunpowder to project missiles dates from early fourteenth century and these first ordnance projectiles were obviously adaptations of those already used in contemporary weapons like crossbow and longbow. Being nothing more nor less than iron darts 'feathered with brass, their shafts wrapped with stuffing of leather to lessen leakage of powder gases'.[48]

The gunpowder and individual firearms were 'first used successfully on a large scale within what looks very much like the old pattern of military skills acquired through immersion in the total cultural environment. New weapons are at first almost invariably used within the conceptual framework established by their predecessors'.[49] A sudden and complete drift from the already existing pattern of the use of siege engines was neither possible nor feasible. It is possible, therefore, that the early siege artillery still carried certain remnants of the pre-gunpowder weaponry.

Although modern writers often hold the view that the proper employment and development of gunpowder technology and fire-arms took place only in the sixteenth centry,[50] the field and siege artillery and even gunpowder weapons were already in vogue much before the fourteenth century and huge cast-bronze siege pedreros were already known to the Ottomans in the fifteenth century.[51] By sixteenth century the artillery designs and all the cannons fell into one of the following three categories according to designs; the culverins, the cannons and the pedreros. Nevertheless gunnery even in sixteenth century was 'an uncertain business with a grim glamour and a tangible aura of mystery about it'.[52]

During Timur's time, the sources, refer to the use of *naft* (naphtha), *naft siyah* (black naphtha), *atashi naft* and no frequent mention of any other inflammable material like *barud* is found. The references to *kamani raad*, *sangi raad* and *raad andazan* found so frequently in Timur's sources[53] suggest an extensive use of incendiary warfare. There are references to *narduban stair casee*, the gun carriages or engines for hurling missiles (*arrad*), catapult (*manjaniq*), naphtha cannoneers (*raad andazan*) cross bow (*tir-i charkh*), *arsenal zeba*, *karbatugaha*, *qarabughra*.[54] It seems that Timur had started the use of firearms on a large-scale for the first time in the near east as the souces refer to blasting and powder explosions.[55]

Al Hasan, the Arab mentions specifically the use of artilleries, engines and munitions and says that during the Chinese campaign Axalla was the incharge of artillery which was set upon the chariots,[56] Yazdi, Shami and Abdurrazzaq, however, refer to *qarabugha* war engines only.[57] Muinuddin Natanzi categorically says that the firearms were used by Timur's forces in 1379 at the siege of Urganj and Shami compared the primitive projectiles of the Indians at the battle of Delhi in 1399 unfavourably with the siege engines of Timur. The description given by Shami tempts one to presume that 'these machines may have been the thunder carriages of the Chinese annals, mangonels which could cast stones (weighing half a ton or more or incendiaries'.[58] Clavijo better acquainted with latest equipment says that 'Timur had gathered to settle here in Samarqand, artillery men both engineers and bombardiers, besides those who make the rope by which these engines work'.[59] This again suggests the traditional pre-gunpowder artillery. The ballistas had to be worked by ropes and even the *arrad* (a medieval siege in which a projectile was propelled by a shaft) was also driven forward by the release of a rope.[60] But there is still the possibility that we have here a reference to the 'early wrought iron guns' known as 'bombards' which were already in vogue in Europe from 1313 to 1520 and were different from their predecessors the catapults, trebuchet or ballista as it depended for its propulsive power upon expansion of gas due to combustion of an explosive material.[61]

Shami refers to the *amal' chakhurghan* (thunder, uproar) which had been ordered to arrange for the mining of the Helb fort.[62] During the same expedition an effective display of *naft bazan* and *raad andazan* is recorded.[63] Yazdi notes with appreciation the use of missiles of naphtha and ballistas for throwing large stones (*kaman-i raad* and *raad asmai*).[64] During the siege of the fort of Bhisti, a stone was thrown by the hostile forces from a revolving catapult (*manjaniq-i gardan*) which went inside the camp of Timur. In a rage, Timur ordered twenty catapults to surround the fort and the very first stone by chance broke the offending catapult of the enemy into pieces. These *manjaniqs* threw stones and miners (*naqabchiyan*) were employed to make breaches in the walls (*mujawwuf sakhta*). Those mines and concaves were set on fire and the towers started falling (*uftadan grift*).[65] In the siege of Uzmer when the mines were dug out and the stones were removed, the hollow cylinders of bamboo or the bamboo tubes filled with powder were placed in the towers and the parapets of the fort. It was ordered that mines should be filled with fuel (*hema*) smeared with naphtha and set on fire. Many persons fell alongwith the walls of the fort.[66] Such an effect again presupposes the use of gunpowder or some other combustible material for blasting or exploding the walls. The combustible material was apparently filled in bamboo tubes or placed on some wooden instrument in preparation for the explosion.

If we accept, therefore, that Clavijo's bombards and arquqbus were a reality, two questions immediately follow this hypothesis: What was the source through which Timur received these 'bombards' and whether gunpowder technology or wrought iron guns were even in use in Timur's Kingdom?

Although no definite information regarding the supply of arms and artillery from European countries to Timur is available, the vital contacts and exchange of embassies between Timur and European rulers tempts one to presume that some assistance might have been received by Timur the 'saviour' of the crusade ridden Europen kings from the much hated 'common enemy' the Ottomans. The possibility of an alliance or a rapprochement between Timur and Europe against Ottomans certainly existed.[67] Some sort of communication between Timur on the one side and Charles VI of France and Henry III of Castile on the other is recorded through the exchange of embassies. The ambassador Payato Sotomayor and Harman Sanchez sent by Henry III of Castile and Leon were accomponied by Haji Muhammad an envoy of Timur on their return. Timur's envoy returned in 1403 accompanied by Spanish embassy consisting of Fray Alfonso Reazde Santa Maria a master theologian, Gomezde Salzar a royal guard and Clavijo, Archbishop John II of Sultaniya who had gone to Tartar court with Friar Francis and Alexander returned to Charies VI of France. Hookham thinks that these embassies were simply 'probing missions' to discover the strength of the Ottomans and Tartar Emperors and as 'mutually hostile and feeble warriors, these European princes could be of little help to Timur at a time when the neutrality or help of Western kings was desirable'.[68] What then could be the motivating factor to compel Timur to incur such expenses on sending and receiving embassies? Commercial enterprises emphasized in these letters were only of a parallel if not of secondary importance. The congratulatory embassies received by Timur on his victory against the 'common enemy', i.e. the Ottomans and the hurried return of Manuel Palaeologus from the West to his throne in Constantinople suggests the deep concern with which Timur's activities were watched by the crusaders. In retrospect the much needed respite acquired through the defeat of the Ottomans at Angora was certainly well earned. The possibility, therefore, arises of a transmission, either in the material articles or in that of skill through migration of artisans, of the gunpowder weaponry of the West to Central Asia under Timur. Even if we discard the view altogether that European princess supplied artillery to Timur, the existence and use of pyrotechnic devices may be regarded as fairly certain. The gun running practiced by Western merchants (particularly in Venice and Genoa) and the presence of Axalla (a Genoese by birth) as the chief of artillery in the army of Timur further confirms the hypothesis. The controversy, however, remains unsolved as to who were the real innovators introducing pyrotechnic devices and small firearms in Central Asia. The problem is further aggravated as the dictionaries and the paintings belong to the later period and often presume and project late innovation to fit into a former frame. Similarly the loose usage of terms like *tir-i charkh, tir-i hawai*, etc., also create some confusion.

The sources of Timur's reign refer to the *naft* (which in Persian denotes gunpowder as well), *naft siyah* (black naphtha), *atash-i naft*, etc., as the sole agent for exploding or blasting. Shirani also says that there was no other combustible material found in medieval firearms except, naphtha and oil from Mahmud of Ghazni down to Timur.[69]

Although the actual date and place of the use of gunpowder is controversial, it is certain that black powder was the sole but commonly known explosive material from thirteenth to nineteenth century. Modern writers generally support the view that the proper employment and development of gunpowder technology and firearms took place only in the sixteenth century.[70] The field and siege artillery and even gunpowder were also described to be already in vogue from end of fourth to the early fourteenth century. The earliest use of cannons in England is said to be in 1327 and in Italy in 1326, whereas giant guns were being constructed in 1375. In early fifteenth century cannons had five different categories.[71] The infantry of Crimean Tartars was armed with arquebus as early as 1493. The first guns to utilize the gunpowder's volatile properties of naphtha as a propellant had already been invented in the early years of the fourteenth century. These were small and crude with illassorted projectiles and incapable of causing large scale destruction. In the earliest processes these were combined by simple mortar and pestle methods often with improvised equipment to the point of using hollowed out logs as mortars. Lugs also concluded that gunpowder was discovered in about 1300 though it did not possess the blasting effect of oriental powders, it did burn more slowly and regularly overcoming the resistance of the ball in a barrel. The first firearms i.e. big guns and small arms dated from the fourteenth century.[72] The use of petroleum, naphtha, silver and quick lime, bituminous products were in vogue even in early middle ages and a crude type of firearm (*madfa*) is said to be derived in 1304.[73]

During the Khurasan expedition 964 wooden palisades (*chaparha*) and *tura* (mantelets, a kind of screen from behind which warriors used to send their missiles) were arranged to provide a fortified place to the soldiers. Abdullah's men also prepared *sarkobaha* (battering machines erected to overtop a wall) and *murchal* (an intrenchement for besieging a fortified place) so as to shoot at those who were clinging to fort walls. The trees were cut down and the ditch was filled up to the height of the fort. The army then rushed with the *sipars* (shields) on their heads and crossed the ditch. Notwithstanding the shower of stones from the parapets, killing quite a few of them, the army managed to cause holes and breaches in the wall through shovels (*kuland*) and spade (*mitin*).

Notwithstanding Levy's assertion that the West preceded eastern Islamic countries in the use of gunpowder, Ibn-i Khaldun insists that Arabs can be given the credit of modern use of gunpowder for offence and defence purposes. Hilda Hookham asserts that though the incendiary naphtha was used by the Arabs from the seventeenth century, it was through Central Asia that the gunpowder was introduced to the near east and from the near east to Europe in the thirteenth and fourteenth centuries and that the Mongols learnt form the Chinese the explosive qualities of gunpowder which they used for sapping and mining.[74] Hall on the other hand argues that the gunpowder first appeared in Europe and that the Mongols made little use of pyrotechnical inventions of their Chinese subjects. The use of gunpowder in firearms again is said to have occurred in the early years of the fourteenth century.[75] Carman too disagrees with the view that gunpowder was known to Arabs, Chinese, Greeks or Hindus even in ancient times.[76] As would be proved by subsequent discussion, the principle of propulsion and explosion as described by Yazdi and Shami apparently suggests the existence and use of gun powder in Timur's artillery and incendiary warfare as simply naphtha and that can not explode.

During the siege of Damascus, Yazdi says that due to *kaman-i raad* (a balista for throwing large stones) people were against and due to the sharpness of the pots of naphtha there was lot of smoke. The miners and sappers (*naqabchis*) set on fire the large stones and sprinkled vinegar (*sirka rekhtand*) and by stone mason's chisel brought out the stones. Wooden beams were placed to support the walls (*bar sari chob*). Orders were given for setting them on fire (*atash daran zadnad*). Suddenly a tower of such a strength and height fell down that a vast passage was created through which 70 to 80 persons rushed to enter the fort. In the meantime another portion of the wall fell and dust arose that thousands were buried alive though besieged soon repaired the breach. In other mines one side of the fort all of a sudden fell down.[77] Here it is very probable that we have the use of gunpowder proper for breaching purposes. Only gunpowder could perhaps have created such a shattering explosion though 'there can be an explosion without gunpowder'[78] as well. During the Egyptian campaign the *amirs* of *tumans* were protected by their own *siba* (enclosed quarter or a place surrounded by walls) and arranged the *manjaniq, arrad, raad* and *tir-i charkh*. While the stones thrown by *manjaniq* hit the fortification and razed part of it to the ground, the already constructed pavilion (*khargah*) helped the soldiers to reach the top which was 300 yards in height from the bottom.[79] Similarly *tawajis* were instructed by Timur to allocate various stretches of the fort to several persons for digging through the walls (during the sieges of Takrit) while using catapult and starting from the left. Each portion was dug by two or three persons and there were forty such groups. Some of them pierced through the stone up to 35 *gaz*, others cut through the stones and in a short time, the while was like a 'netted sieve'.[80] The breaching (*hafri khundaq* or *kundani*) was neither caused through the usual *manjaniq* nor by arrow shot. When the walls of the Takrit fort were undermined by tunnelling (*naqab*), the hollowed places were filled in by the fuel and firewood (*hema*) and sprinkled with naphtha and set on fire. The walls of the fort fell to the ground and a tower was entirely demolished.[81] During the siege of Meerut, Timur's men were able to dig a tunnel of 10 to 15 yards under each tower and a turret and the mines were set on fire, *manjaniqs* in Shiraz and Khwarazm campaigns, *arrad* (in Tirshiz) and *raad* (as in Onk campaign). The art of blasting (which implies the use of gunpowder) was successfully used by Timur in the war against Sultan Mahmud (1399), in Damascus campaign (1400-1), in Ottoman campaign (1402) and even before 1399.[82] The mining of the fort was carefully done. The assault on the fort of Smyrna in December 1402 had been depicted by Bihzad in one of his illustrious paintings in *Zafar Nama*.[83] At the top of the picture, some workmen are engaged in digging a pit in order to undermine the fortress. The drawbridge is seen pulled up to close the main entrance into the castle, but the soldiers of Timur seem to have broken into a side entrance, from which one of the defenders had fallen headlong. In the foreground of the picture, Timur, is seated on a horse superintending the operations.[84]

Numerous sieges of Timur could be narrated in similar terms stressing the significant part played by mechanical art of mining and blasting. According to Hall the catapult type of siege engines had passed into disuse in Europe before the end of fourteenth century and guns of a primitive kind and metal barrel cannons have appeared before 1356. Hall considers the hollow cylinders of bamboo tubes filled with gun powder as being the 'precursors of more effective grenades' and refers to barrels of metal flowing naturally from compression of explosive compositions into hollow cylinders of bamboo. A similar view is expressed by Damas and Saunders.[85] Carman's discussion on XX tronckes charged with wild fire or 'trombes' (which again were 'hollow wooden cylinders as big as a man's thigh and the length of...and filled with a mixture of sulphur, charcoal, pitch, turpentine, bay salt and saltpetre') further echoes the same view. Carman is more explicit when he says that 'it is this saltpetre that made a revolution in the many experiments of the early days, for it was its use in a purified form in the various fire compounds that led to the discovery of gunpowder'.[86] Nevertheless the same author as well as Oman criticized 'the anonymous ignorant Arab wrote on hearsay' about *madfa* though his account with corrections could apply to mortars and chambered cannons. According to the chronicler *madfa* was in the shape of a hollow cylindrical log of wood, short like a mortar and wider at the top than the bottom. Its bore was to be filled half way up with primitive gun powder of the proportions three of sulphar, four of charcoal and twenty of saltpeter. It was to be tamped down with a wad. The manuscript mentioned here as anonymous was presumably Razi's *Jamiul Ulum*.

Whether these European innovations had extended upto the Asian borders and particularly to Central Asia or not is yet to be established. Apparently the evidence does not directly indicate anything more than siege engines on the catapult principle and the use of naphtha. The extensive use of incendiary warfare and pyrotechniques is, however, confirmed by the frequent references to *kaman-i raad, sang-i raad andazan*[87] fire arrows (prepared by coating slow burning naphtha to arrow heads) to set light to any flame throwing machines, sophisticated missiles, naphtha bombs, metal tipped rockets, etc., which were presumably already learnt from the mongols.[88] Besides, the Muslim countries being in close contacts with Byzantium and due to their control of petroleum technology were already familiar with fire arrows, fire lances and fire pots (thrown by some form of projectile engines) for breaking down gates, palisades, wooden constructions and houses or even for causing a breach in the walls.[89] Timur's contacts with the outside world and the experiences gained through various campaigns must have contributed immensely towards, perfection. After his conquest of Syria, its skilled workmen were employed in the factories established at Ispahar, Khurasan and Samarqand. Damascus lost its importance and Persia became the great supplier of swords. Even then the Indian blade was used but known as 'Damascus steel'.[90] Stray references to the use of incendiary warfare, ammunitions are therefore, also found in contemporary sources. Yazdi says that when Timur sent his second envoy to Haleb on the eve of his expedition to convey the message to hand over refugees, the ruler of Haleb received the envoys honourably. To please the emperor he sent a group of artillery men to Timur. Yazdi records:

Since in those areas (Haleb) *atashbazi* (fireplay) and *raad andazi* (throwing of thunder bolts ordance) are much practiced (*bisyar mi warzand*) and it had its significance before them (Timur), the majority of that groups of *atashbazan, radandazan, charkh kashayan; nawakzanan* (fire workers, cannoneers, crossbowmen, arches respectively) were collected, described and showed to the envoy taking it for and considering it a show of valour. They did not know that more than 10,000 experienced men of this sort and flock (*qabib, qimash*) do exist in the royal army (of Timur).[91] Presumably the *atashbazi* here refers to firearms since Egypt and Syria were already well acquainted with these firearms through Morocco and Spain the birth place of firearms.[92] Thus the presence of such firearms in Timur's army even before his Halb expedition is amply borne out by the above passage. Inspite of the distinction between fire works and firearms, the context and contents apparently suggest the definite existence of pyrotechny based on gun powder technology if not field artillery.

Although the date and source of introduction of firearms in Central Asia as elsewhere remains to be a controversial issue, presumably Timur was the first ruler who had introduced the use of firearms in near east. Not only the Timurid sources refer to blasting tand powder explosions,[93] but Al Hasan, the Arab mentions specifically the use of artilleries, engines and munitions and says that during the Chinese campaign, Axalla was the incharge of artillery which was set upon the chariots.[94] Muinuddin Natazi mentions that firearms were used by Timur's forces in 1379 at the siege of Urganj and Shami compared the primitive projectiles of the Indians at the battle of Delhi in 1399 in unfavourable light with the siege engines of Timur. The description given by Shami tempts one to presume that 'these machines may have been the 'Thunder carriages' of the Chinese annals, mangonel which could cast stones (weighing half a ton or more) or incendiaries'.[95] Clavijo better acquainted with latest equipment informs us that Timur had also brought 'the gunsmiths who make arquebus from Turkey'[96] The same traveller explains that 'Timur had gathered to settle here in Samarqand artillery men, both engineers and bombardiers, besides those who make the rope by which these engines work'.[97] This apparently suggests not only the traditional pre-gunpowder artillery but also the ballistas which had to be worked. The very fact that Serbia a vassal state of Ottomans since 1389 supplied arsenal to Bayazid I though the guns of fourteenth century were different from those of fifteenth century, smaller in number, dimensions, preference and appearance. Both Inclik and Petrovic have conclusively proved that the guns were used by Bayazid in the battle of Ankara also.[98] by ropes and even the *arrad* (a medieval siege weapon in which a projectile was propelled by a shaft) was also driven forward by the release of a rope.[99] There is still a greater possibility that we have a reference to the 'early wrought iron guns' known as 'Bombards' which were already in vogue in Europe from 1313 to 1520 and were different from their predecessors the catapult, trebuchet or ballista as it depended for its propulsive powder upon expansion of gas due to combustion of an explosive material.[100] Incidentally, sometimes the crossbows were also called an arquebus as they had a similar butt and trigger arrangement for releasing the projectile. Some of these could even fire leaden bullets. Thus if a metal barrel replaced the bow on a crossbow it was converted into firearms. The Hempen rope was also used till replaced by pyrites in seventeenth century.[101] On the basis of Alqashqandi and Ibn-i Khaldun, Parry goes to the extent of asserting that cannons existed at Alexandria and Cairo in 1365-76.[102] It is generally accepted that firearms or metal guns were being used in Europe from the second quarter of fourteenth century in western Balkan from 1378 and in Hungry from 1354. In Europe they may have 'made more din than damage' in earlier stages though by the eighth decade of the same century, their effective performance is noticed. In the Ottoman Empire the existence of firearms is confirmed not only by the account of Schitberger but by the use of cannons in the battle of Ankara (1402) as well. The use of siege engines, with an explosive material (consisting of a refined saltpetre with a blending of adequate proportions of sulphur and charcoal or carbon which the Europeans called 'powder' developed in Europe gradually from 1314 onwards, passing through various stages of trebuchetsm fleets, caulverins and ribandequins still the 'huge bombardes'[103] (which were made up of wrought iron staves, could throw large cut stone balls and were helpful as a siege weapon came into vogue. The first English 'bombard' in l346 was quite amazing for the French, till a century later in 1447, Milan fell into the hands of French through the blessings of the 'battery of artillery'. Louis XI and Charles of Temeraine organized their bands of artillery in 1467. Apparently manufacture of bombards did help in the exploitation of mining to reduce the strong obstinate garrisons, the immobility of this system was more noxious than useful for the swift moving cavalry and infantry or at least so did the Europeans believed.[104] No clear cut technical superiority in making of siege artillery subsequent to 'hoped bombard' is noticed till the invention of gun carriages towards the end of fifteenth century though the large wrought iron cannons were becoming obsolete at the dawn of sixteenth century.[105]

In the early fifteenth century Europe, therefore, the use of the built up iron gun or bombard' was common for siege work[95] and the large cannons presumably of cupreous metal were already being cast soon after mid-fourteenth century though the art of handling masses of molten metal only developed in the fifteenth and sixteenth centuries.[106] The Ottoman and Portuguese guns of the early 1500 designed to shoot iron projectiles or stone cannon balls[107] were as good as the French cannons throwing cast iron balls. Nevertheless extensive use of explosive projectiles ensued in the form of hand grenades and mortar bombs which were a major innovation of the next few centuries.[108] The hand guns, field and siege artillery played a vital role.[109] Ustad Farah Rekhtagar constructed *kaman-i raad* which threw stones of 400 maunds.[110] As proved by the above discussion it would not be very correct to credit Timur for being the ruler 'who introduced firearms for the first time in the near east'. The only important thing about Timur's reign is that, as in other spheres, there was a definite technical improvement and considerably extensive use of incendiary warfare as is confirmed by the references to *kaman-i raad, sang-i raad, raad andazan* found so frequently in Timur's sources. There were fire-arrows, flame throwing machines, sophisticated missiles, naphtha bombs, metal tipped rockets, etc., learnt from the Mongols.

Side by side with the gunpowder devices, there existed the traditional style of warfare Shami refers to the *amal-i chakhurgan* (lit. thunderbolt, uproar) which had been ordered to arrange for the mining of Halb fort. During the same expedition an effective display of *naftabaza* and *raad andazan* is recorded. Yazdi notes with appreciation the use of missiles of naphtha and ballistas for throwing large stones (*kaman-i raad* and *raad azami*). The crossbow,[111] a crude weapon earlier had improved into a steel bow during the fourteenth century Europe (1370) with an elaborate pulley and windlass system and reigned supreme until the first practical firearms began to appear about the third quarter of the fifteenth century, when the crossbow was replaced by arquebus. Nevertheless since the heavy steel cross-bow was unsuitable for use on horseback and outclassed by the composite recurved bow, 'the traditional weapons of antiquity dominated in Central Asian plains' and in other Islamic lands.[112] The composite recurved bows were more common among the nomads of the steppes and were in many ways 'superior even to gunpowder weapons'.[113]

Introduction and Spread of Firearms in Central Asia

Long before the invention of gunpowder, the destructive power of the fire was utilized for military purposes as fire-arrows, fire lances, fire balls, fire pots, flaming missiles, liquid fire, Greek fire, volatile properties of naphtha and petroleum were fully exploited. Zygulsk, had given a very detailed account of such pyrotechnic devices. An arrow carrying below its barb, a paper or fabric bag filled with gunpowder with an ignited match and shot from a bow was called *feikho*. There were tubes to project incendiary discuss and arrows as well as grenades made of baked clay fitted with gunpowder and ignited by a match through a touch hole. Another type of grenade, called Khopao, projected from catapults or thrown by hand was constructed from several layers of terred paper fastened together with hemp cord. Besides, another 'prototype 22' was called 'lightning fire-balls' (flame projectors) which was similar to Byzantine projectors of Greek fire. In China, they took the form of bamboo joints filled with powder tied to the end of long lances called *khotasian*[114] (which were probably the much emphasized *ho-chiang*) with a series of charges of powder and projectiles, which were fired off successively by means of a row of touch holes. This stage occurred in China about the middle of thirteenth century, soon afterwards the first reference to metal barrels, guns of a primitive kind were brought into use and its oldest surviving example came from 1356.[115] The four Yuan weapons namely *huo pao*, *huo chiang tu huo chiang* and *pao chang* described in Iqtidar Alam Khan's article published in *Journal of Asian History* in 1996 have already been described at length by Lamb decades earlier.

Generally a number of other methods were also used to hurl incendiary substance, e.g. Siphon (*zarraqa, mizraq, nafata*), a bronze piston pump from whose nozzle a jet of burning liquid was projected or a jet of fire (*shihab*) to burn the enemy.

Rockets with incendiary material or gunpowder were used frequently. Firearms and *amdara tir*, *tir-i parran*, *shami tuli* and *shami sai* have also been mentioned in the sources. There were ballistas and sharpened mallots eyes. 'The most common method was perhaps to fill naphtha and other inflammable mixture into containers of different sizes and fix them to arrows or pour them into grenades or pots and either throw them on the enemy by hand or shoot them as rockets. The fire pot grenades or containers of glass or clay were of various sizes. The most common size was *karaz* (*karraz*) whereas the larger fire pots were called *gidr*.[116] For effective long distance throwing of fire pots, some kind of machines were to be evolved.

In earlier stages, there were bamboo tubes filled with gunpowder. Invention of firearms with barrebay metals followed naturally from compression of explosive material into hollow cylinders of bamboo or rolled paper along with stones, broken porcelain and bullets. From this, a more devilish version of the Roman candle was the next step, the filling of a tube with a series of charges of poser of projectiles fired off successively by means of a row of touch holes. This stage occurred in China about middle of thirteenth century. Soon afterwards the first reference to metal barrel, gun of a primitive kind is followed and oldest surviving example came from 1356. Gunpowder is thus a direct Chinese transmission to Europe.[117]

The catapults of classical age were replaced by many beam operated siege engines, the resilient wooden or twisted fibres were required to serve as propellant for the missiles. According to Hill these missile throwers 'the powerful tactiontrebuchet' were introduced from China by way of Central Asia towards the close of seventh century to the Islamic world. It comprised a 'wooden spar provided with an axle which was supported on bearings at the top of two wooden towers. At the end of the short arm was a special attachment to which a number of ropes were fixed. In some types, this attachment consisted of a single piece of hardwood. Sometimes it was made of iron and divided into two legs, each of which terminated in a ring. At the other end was a sling with a pouch for the missiles. One end of this sling was attached to the underside of the spar and the other which was made into a loop was slipped over a projection at the end of the spar. A team of men was stationed on the ropes while the artillery men held the missiles in its pouch when be gave the signal, the men pulled on the rapes and he released the pouch at the critical moment.'[118]

Although the catapults were too 'slow and immobile for work in the field' they proved to be an 'efficient artillery' in the siege warfare. There is a very detailed description given by Zygulski about the various types of guns. The 'primitive hand gun' called *madfa* was in the form of a 'wooden cylinder attached to a pole. Loaded one third with gunpowder and discharging arrows or bullets. Traditionally barrels of primitive cannons were made of bamboo, strengthened on the inside with clay and iron disc; a cord coiled round the outside and touch hole pierced in the side, capable of withstanding a pressure of explosive gasses. A further stage was metal barrel made of iron or copper.[119]

With the discovery and use of gunpowder, the emergence of a new class of military, e.g. artillery engineers, artisans, smiths, carpenters, bronze founders, *naft* craftsmen and others are noticed. Zygulski had given the instruction for the manufacture of gunpowder which was a proportionate combination of sulphur saltpetre, charcoal, colaphony, sealing fax, bamboo core, hemp oil, wax paper and land oxide, ignition of missile was followed by a whirring noise and the belching of poisonous fumes. By eleventh century the production of gunpowder and incendiary missiles in China was taken over by special state manufacturing plants.

The invention of gunpowder is variously dated by different scholars. Some have placed it in the ninth century and beginning of firearms as an 'Asiatic achievement' following traditional theory, others assert that it was an invention of Europe. It is not certain which of the hypothesis (i.e. its invention in China, India and spain) is more acceptable. Barthold Schwartz, a monk of Mentz in 1320 is said to have discovered the use of gunpowder by accident, though the fact of its application to firearms is yet to be confirmed as medieval travellers Carpini and Marco Polo make only a cursory mention of such adventures.[120] It is interesting to note that even while underevaluating the achievements of Chinese and taking pride in the Quahti and Excellencies of Europe (where the *qualite* exceeds her *quantite*), the credit of all achievements is being given to Europe and China is being despicably set aside as incapable of such ventures:

> And what hath Mars in the world elsewhere to parallel with our ordnances and all sorts of Gunnes ... ? alas, China yields babes and babes in both compared with us and ours; the rest of the world have them borrowed of us or not at all. And for the art, military, discipline exactest science, weapons, stratagems, engines, resolution, successes herein leave honored Europe with the Macedonian and Roman spoiles of the world, and even still the Turkish puissance is here seated; the English Dutch French Italian Spanish courages have not degenerated from those ancestors, which tamed and shooke in pieces that Tamer and Terror of the world, the Roman Monarchy.[121]

Another passage in *Purchas and his Pilgrims*, Vol. II, contradicts this version and throws some light on this polemic issue where Chinese and Muslims are credited with this honour. The full passage is being quoted here 'Others therefore, look further into the East, whence the light of the Sune and Arts have seemed first to arise to our world; and will have Marco Polo the venetian above three hundred years since to have brought it of Mangi (which we now call China) into Italy. True it is that most magnified Arts have there first been borne, Printing Gunnies and perhaps this also of a compasse, which the Portugals at their first entry of the Indian seas found amongst the Moors'.[122] In the account of Vasco da Gama, the definition of Moors is given in the following words: 'Moors or Turkes (usually all Mahumetans of Africa, Arabia and the Indian coasts are called Moors from which name, the greatness of the Turke, Tartars, Persian and Mogull which I know not what differences of sect have in ordinary appellation exempted them' and further that 'they came out of the remotest west; that they used such armour as he saw, with such ordnance able to ruin castles.'[123]

Seemingly, the Persians and Indians, having been blessed with all natural, agricultural and mineral wealth were least interested in the development of firearms yet sometimes. Persians are described to be one of the earliest users of such devices. Procopius had recorded in sixth century AD that 'Persians filled vessels with naphtha, lighting them, they hurled them against framework of battering rams and soon set them ablaze, for this fire consumes the objects which it touches unless withdrawn'.[124] Similarly it is said that the Safavids had all along detested the use of firearms as they thought it to be below the dignity, valour and chivalry of dedicated fighters though the firearms with Turcomans were available even with long before their ascendancy in the region. Nevertheless, the lessons in Chaldiran could not be easily forgotten as they must have led them willy nilly to resort to acquisition of firearms. If Halil Inalcik is to be believed, the Safavids received firearms from their allies the Portuguese as early as 1548 when Shah Tahmasp received twenty pieces of artillery to be used against Sultan Sulaiman. With the Russian occupation of Astarakhan and Terek in 1556, another route for acquiring firearms was opened for the Safavids.[125] Although it can not be denied that Shah Abbas had improvised his army, introduced the institution of Ghulam forces and provided his soldiers with better equipments of warfare, the claims of Shirley brothers that they gave a new lease to the life of Persian army, reorganized and remodeled it however, should be accepted with care particularly in the context of firearms as later information negates their assertion.

Criticizing the Persian ignorance of the art of warfare, Edward Monoxe categorically mentions in 1621 that: 'The Persians are ignorant of the art of ware, for they entered without feare or wit and lost with shame what they might have maintained with honour.'

Elaborating on the same point he says that

> other defects I observed in the very sinews of warre, such that I cannot but wonder that one of the wonders of age Shah Abbas should send over an Army so weakly provided of money, arms, munition, ships and all necessarie furniture. For the first, I think the Dukes' treasure was consumed in one months pay unto our ships, and I feare we shall stay for the rest till money be made of the spoil. For armes and munition they have no other then small pieces, bowes and arrowes, swords by their sides, and some of their chiefs have coates of mails. Powder so scarce that after blowing up the castle they had scarcely powder to pile their small shot to enter the breach, and yet were furnished with twenty or five and twenty barrels from our ships. They had not one scaling ladder to help their entrance.[126]

Mclagan concludes that 'there appears to be a good evidence in support of the idea that Asia had a knowledge of gunpowder and used firearms before Europe. There are plain indications that the knowledge of the most improved weapons of war both before and since the introduction gunpowder and the skill to make and use them came from Europe to India and other Asiatic countries.' The same writer further opines that 'there is no good evidence to support the belief that the Arabs were the first to use powder' and that the European nations 'were the first to discover its most important form and applications'.[127] There are, however, references to the 'house size of the guns' used in *Indica One* at Bijapur was 4 feet 8 inches in diameter at the muzzle and had a caliber of 2 feet 4 inches. It was cast at Ahmad Nagar in 1549.[128]

Tavernier records certain interesting though contradictory facts in this regard. While referring to Aurangzeb's decisions to conquer Assam, where no wars were fought for 500 or 600 yeas (AD 1150 or thereabouts) and 'the people being without experience in arms'. He stresses further that 'it is believed that there people in ancient time, first discovered gunpowder and guns, which passed from Assam to Pegu and from Pegu to China; this is the reason why the discovery is generally ascribed to the Chinese'. Mir Jumla brought back from this war numerous iron guns and the gunpowder made in that country is excellent. Its grain is not long as in the kingdom of Bhutan, but is round and small like ours, and is much more effective than the other powder. He further adds that the king of Assam had come in the field (against Mir Jumla) 'with a larger force than had been expected; that he had many guns, and an abundance of fireworks somewhat like our grenades which are fixed at the end of a stick as long as a short pike and carry more than 500 paces,'[129] like rockets described by Tavernier earlier.[130] In this context, Iqtidar Alam's view that 'gunpowder had originally come to the valley of the Brahmputra from south China through overland contacts'[131] and that 'it points to close interaction' needs reconsideration. The fact is that Qubilai Khan had conquered Burma and the region had maintained and retained Mongol and Chinese traditions of warfare till its conquest by the British.

According to Prawdin gunpowder was first used on 11 April 1241 in the battle fought beside the Sajo by the Mongols under Batu and King Bela's forces. While admitting that the question of the origin of the cannon 'may never be answered satisfactorily', Prawdin, however asserts that the firecrackers and other allied fireworks are of Chinese origin.[132] Laufer also places rational development of gunpowder from humble firecrackers (known in sixth century AD) originally employed in fiery religious ceremonies to the launching of projectiles in warfare as early as twelfth century and full development of fire weapons under Mongols in the thirteenth-fourteenth century.[133]

Needham categorically says that the gunpowder 'was a direct Chinese transmission to Europe' and the gun barrel sighting tube is mentioned in fifth century AD in China. According to him the bamboo tubes were filled with gunpowder, though invention of firearms with barrels of metals followed naturally from compression of explosive compositions into hollow cylinders of bamboo or rolled paper along with stones or broken porcelain and bullets.[134] From this crude method of Roman candle sprung up the more effective way of filling up a tube with powder. Blackpowder was known to Chinese much before than the Europeans as Wu Ching Trung Yao had recorded its preparation in AD 1044. According to certain other Chinese historians, explosive powder was first used in the warfare in 1161-2 when the Jarchen army tried to cross Yangtze near Nanking. The Sung army is said to have flung thunderbolt projectiles which were made of papers filled with lime and sulphur. When these fell into the water fire leapt out from them, the paper burst and lime diffused itself in a dense vapour which blinded both men and horses, thus causing defeat to the enemy. In 1232 again in a 'desperate defence' offered by Jarchen against Mongols in Kaifeng, 'offered by Jarchen against Mongol in Kai feng', apparently bombs or hand grenades were used. It is also stressed that cannons were used at the siege of Hsiang Yang with the help of engineers hired by the Mongols in Java in 1293. Similarly, a thousand engineers from China had to serve the catapults in the campaigns waged by Halaku in Western Asia (1235-58).[135]

The gunpowder was a 'generic name applied originally to a mechanical mixture of saltpetre (potassium nitrate) charcoal (cartoon) and sulphur, that black powder was the sole explosive material for 600 years from its discovery to mid nineteenth century; Chinese knew about it; the first guns to utilize gun powder as a propellant were invented in early fourteenth century; in the earliest processes, these were combined by simple mortar and pestle methods often with improvised equipment even to the point of using hollowed out logs as mortars'.[136] There were three phases of guns, first were 'early wrought iron guns (1313-1520) known as Bombards'. These guns were different from that of its predecessors, i.e. the catapults, trebuchet or ballistas depending for its propulsive power upon expansion of gas due to combustion of an explosive material. The wheeled carriages were introduced towards the latter end of fifteenth century.[137]

Hall says that the gunpowder 'first appeared' in Western Europe and Mongols 'made little use of pyrotechnical inventions of their Chinese subjects'.[138] And that the manufacture of fireworks was well-known in Europe before the end of thirteenth century, whereas the use of gunpowder in firearms occurred in the early years of fourteenth century. Lamb's conclusion is therefore, more convincing. He said that after 1211 gunpowder was frequently used particularly in the *huo-pao* or fire projectors which destroyed the wooden towers. The discharge of the powder in the fire projectors made 'a noise like thunder heard at a distance of 100 to 230 miles. Another machine called *chin-tien-tei* was also a kind of fire projector. The discharge of 'fire guns' is noticed during Kubilai's reign. Nevertheless the firearms and cannons both began to appear in Germany about the time of monk Schwartz.[139] Thus the Chinese may have 'made gun powder and understood its explosive qualities long before Francis Bacon and Schwartz but put it to little (or limited) use in warfare whether the Europeans learnt about it from them or discovered it on their own account is an open question but Europeans certainly made the first serviceable guns'.

Commenting opon the important question of when and where the gunpowder was first used, Al Hassan stresses the 'Muslim superiority in arms'.[140] According to him the new era of military pyrotechnics began in 1139; Shawar had put to use 2,000 pots of naphtha in Karazshami in 1168 which had traces of gunpowder and that the same was the deciding factor in the battle of al-Mansura in 1249 when Louis IX of France was imprisoned.[141]

While accepting that the Chinese (who were renowned for their expertise in handicrafts since time immemorial), may have been the original experts in the sphere of military fire devices and firearms, the role of Muslims who were men of sword cannot be ignored. It is probable that the Muslims generally excelled in their mastery of the art of distillation which coupled together with their control of sources of petroleum invariably enabled them to better develop the incendiary technique.[142] Since the Muslim State had a very active and close contact with Byzantium and had thoroughly studied Greek technological texts, they could better comprehend and prepare such technical devices.[143] Since the Arabs already knew about the heavy artillery represented by the ballistas (*arrada*), the mangonel (*manjaniq*) and the battering ram (*dabbabah*, *kabash*). These heavy engines and siege machines must have already been known to the Central Asians before Mongol invasion. The Abbasids had an archer's corps having a separate body of naphtha throwers (*naffatun*) who used to wear fire proof suits and hurled incendiary material at their enemy.[144] Cannons were said to have been used in 1204 by Caliph Al Nasir in his siege of al Mahdiya in the North Africa, in servile in 1248, in Baghdad in 1258, in Ayn Jalut in Gali in 1260, in Marjal Suffar in 1303. During the siege of Acre (1291), Sultan's trebuchets and catapults flung their pottery containers filled with an explosive mixture at the walls of the city or over them into town. Egyptians had a large detachment of cavalry which carried such cannons (*madfa*) and with crackers (*sawarikh*). Thus cannons were already in vogue long before the battle of Ayn Jalut. Ibn-i Khaldun who compiled his history in 1377 had described the cannons used in the battle of Sijil Mas. The gunpowder engines (*hindamulnaft*) projecting small balls of iron which were ejected from a chamber (*khazna*) were placed in from of a kindling fire of the gunpowder.[145]

In his famous work *Altarif bil Mu Stalah al Sharif* Shihabuddin's, Fazlullah Alamara had written a chapter on siege engines in action during the reign of Sultan Al Nasir (1309-40). There were six kinds of siege engines in use at that time namely: *manjaniq* (trebuchet); the *ziyarat* (mechanical cross-bow); the *satair* (protective coverings) *khitai* (arrows); the *makhail-ul barud* (gunpowder cannon) and the *qarurah-i naft* (pots of naphtha). The last three were described as 'the gunpowder weapons', since there are references to red balls breaking arches and damaging structures. It is difficult to determine who had preceded in this adventure. Presumably it is evident from the above description that the Muslims had acquired the knowledge of incendiary fighting almost simultaneously as in China.

NOTES

1. Cleaves, *Secret History*, p. 29; Timur, *Tuzukat-i Tamuri*, Introduction, XXXI, II, pp. 3, 141, 259.
2. *Mehmannama* (*Mehn*), pp. 54-5.
3. *Abdullahnama* (*Abdn*), p. 281.

4. Ibid., p. 245.
5. Ibid., p. 372.
6. Denis Sinor, *Inner Asia—A Syllabus*, 190.
7. Mansura Haidar, *Indo-Central Asian Relations*, Introduction, New Delhi, 2004.
8. Cleaves, p. 29.
9. Marco Polo's *Asia*, an introduction to his Description of the 'world' by Leanardo Olschki, 1960, pp. 138 fn. 31, 137-8, 171, 361. Howorth, *History of the Mongols,* pp. 81-2, Vol. 3. Rubruquis conclude that the only arms indigeneous with the Mongols were quivers, bows, arrows and pellicine (skin or felt as). Among the recent offered to them were iron plates or scales and iron helmets from Persia.
10. Juvaini, *Tarikh-i Jahanqusha-i Juvaini*, Vol. II, text, pp. 91-3; Eng. tr., Vol. II, p. 608.
11. Prawdin, *The Mongol Empire*, pp. 130, 156-8.
12. Ibid., p. 179.
13. Juvaini, Eng. tr. by A.J. Boyle, Vol. I, p. 317.
14. Ibid., p. 320.
15. Ibid., p. 176, text, p. 139.
16. *History of Technology*, Vol. III, pp. 360-1.
17. Ibid.
18. Cf. Juvaini, Eng. tr., pp. 193-4.
19. Chingiz promised the besieger chief to return immediately if the payment of a tribute of 1,000 cats and 1,000 swallows was made to him, when the cusions payment was made, cotton, wool was tied to their tails and set on fire. The stampede through air and overland by these in search of their nests and haunts caused a terrible fire in the garrison which was then reduce easily (Peter Brent, p. 48).
20. For development of Mongol siege warfare, cf. Peter Brent, *The Mongol Empire*, pp. 48-51, 56, 59, 62, 71-2; Webb, *Genghiz Khan Conqueror of the Medieval World*, New York, 1967-84; E.D. Philip, *The Mongols*, London, 1965, p. 50.
21. Juvaini, I, Eng. tr., pp. 92, 119, 129, 132, 176, 282.
22. Ibid., p. 89.
23. Ibid., pp. 126-7.
24. Ibid., p. 129.
25. Webb, p. 84.
26. Juvaini, text, pp. 282-3, see also pp. 129, 132, 176.
27. Ibid., text, pp. 82-3; Eng. tr., p. 106.
28. *Habib-us Siyar*, pp. 77-98.
29. Prawdin, p. 183.
30. Ibid., p. 186.
31. Juvaini, Vol. II, text, pp. 107-20, 618-25.
32. *ZN*, Vol. II, pp. 219, 460.
33. Ibid., p. 254.
34. Ibid., pp. 493-5.
35. Ibid., pp. 465-7.
36. Ibid., pp. 493-7.
37. Ibid., p. 194.
38. Ibid., p. 239, Calcutta edn., p. 346.

39. *ZN*, Vol. II, pp. 55-60, 289. Timur used them at night also in Garijistan and Abkhaz Campaigns.
40. *ZN*, Vol. II, p. 496; Farishta, Vol. I, p. 159.
41. *ZN*, Vol. II, pp. 493-4.
42. Ibid., pp. 458-64.
43. Ibid., pp. 100-2, 464-6; Hatifi, *Timur Nama*, p. 176; Farishta, p. 159.
44. A.R. Hall, *Military Technology: A History of Technology*, pp. 374-82; *Encyclopaedia Britannica*, Vol. X, 1966, pp. 1038-40.
45. *ZN*, I, pp. 473-93; *ZN*, II, p. 206; Shami, pp. 46, 47, 48, 234-7.
46. Hall, pp. 374-82; *Encyclopaedia Britannica*, Vol. X, 1966, pp. 1038-40. In the earliest processes, these were combined by simple mortar and pestle methods often with improvised equipment to the point of using hollowed out logs as mortars.
47. *Gunpowder and Galleys*, pp. 157-9.
48. Ibid., also see *Encyclopaedia Britannica*, Vol. I under Ammunition, Artillery, pp. 799-801; Napoleon, III 'Etudes surl'artillerie', *Encyclopaedia Britannica*, Vol. II under Artillery, p. 529.
49. *Gunpowder and Galleys, Changing Technology and Mediterranean Warfare at Sea in the Sixteenth Century*, ed. by J.H. Elite and H.G. Koenig Sheryer, Cambridge, 1974, p. 139.
50. C.W.C. Oman, *The Art of War in the Middle Ages,* pp. 162-3; Oman, *A History of the Art of War in the Sixteenth Century*, pp. 71-211, 288; Hall, *The History of Technology*, II, pp. 374-82, also Vol. III, pp. 361-75; *Gunpowder and Galleys*, pp. 86-8, 137, 156-60, 255-66, 273-84; Peter Brent, *Mongol Empire*, p. 250.
51. *Gunpowder and Galleys*, pp. 158, 255, 263, 295; *The Art of Warfare*, pp. 28-30, 223-5.
52. *Gunpowder and Galleys*, p. 174.
53. Yezdi, *ZN*, I, pp. 239-40; Shami, pp. 155, 234; *IA*, pp. 164-5; *AAA*, pp. 425-33; Hatifi, pp. 62, 176-7, 202.
54. *ZN*, Vol. I, pp. 159, 219, 231, 339, 275, 412, 493 for details and some interesting information about various firearms cf. Hafiz Muhammad Shirazi, '*Atashin Aslaha*', *Oriental College Magazine*, Vol. 14, part 4, August 1938, pp. 38-52.
55. *ZN*, Vol. I, pp. 465-7, 473-93; *ZN*, Vol. II, pp. 194-5, 204-8, 219, 239, 262, 290, 339-40.
56. *AAA*, pp. 425-33.
57. *ZN*, Vol. II, p. 374.
58. Hilda Hookham, pp. 61-2.
59. Clavjijo, p. 288.
60. Bernard Lewis, *Islam*, UK, 1976, Glossary, p. 289.
61. Chamber's *Encyclopaedia*, VI, 1967, p. 655. For 'Bombards' see *Encyclopaedia Britannica*, Vol. III, p. 893.
62. Shami, 1938, pp. 34, 227, 237.
63. *ZN*, Vol. I, p. 219.
64. *ZN*, Vol. II, p. 239; *IA*, Eng. tr., pp. 151, 164.
65. Ibid., pp. 204-8, other examples: pp. 194-5, 239, 262-90, 339; *Tarikh-i Farishta*, p. 159.
66. Ibid., pp. 339-40.

67. *The Mongol Empire*, pp. 250. By the sixteenth century, the artillery designs and all the cannons fell into one of the three categories according to designs, i.e. the culverins, the cannons and the pedreros.
68. Ibid.
69. Shirazi, '*Atashin Aslaha*', *Oriental College Magazine*, Vol. 14, part 4, August 1938, pp. 3-35. Shirazi perceptibly proved that black naphtha, *manjaniq*, *dabbaba* (called *kharak* in Persian), *arrada*, *charkh* and *aad* were very commonly used equipments since 73 AH, *manjaniq* for throwing balls, threw pots of naphtha, fire balls, etc. Wassaf even mentions the mining and Shirazi, '*Atashin Aslaha*', pp. 351-2. Firdausi in *Shah Nama*, Vol. I, p. 56; II, pp. 197, 225, 227; III, p. 67; IV, pp. 7, 41. Ababul harb wa Shujaat describes four types of *manjaniq* namely: *Manjaniq-i urus, Manjaniq-i dev, Ghauriwar, Manjaniq-i rawan.* Abadul harb wa Shujaat, p. 181. All of these were mentioned in Timurid source.
70. Ibid.
71. For details see W.Y. Carman, *A History of Firearms from Earliest Times to 1914*, London, 1970, pp. 1-3, 80-100, 180-200; also see Frederick Wilkinsen, *Arms and Armours*, London, 1971, pp. 94-5.
72. Jaroshtav Lugs, *Firearms Past and Present*, Vol. I, London, 1975, pp. 12-18.
73. Sarkar, p. 127.
74. Hilda Hookham, pp. 258-61.
75. Hall, Vol. II, pp. 374-82; *Encyclopaedia Britannica*, Vol. X, pp. 1038-40.
76. Carman, *A History of Firearms from earliest Times to 1914*, London, 1970.
77. Hall, 'A Note on Military Pyrotechnics', in *A History of Technology*, Vol. II, pp. 374, 382, 701. Hall says that the knowledge of black powder was noticed in China much earlier than in Europe as Wu Ching Tsung mentions its preparation in Hall, op. cit., III, p. 377, AD 1044. *Ustandani*, *manjaniniqi* and *naftandazan* were ordered by Alghu Qaan an Ghazan also received 699 *manjaniqs* (*ustads*) from Mosul (Shirazi, pp. 12-18). Elsewhere gunpowder is said to be a 'direct Chinese' transmission to Europe through Arabs in fourteenth century (*The Columbia Encyclopaedia*, 2nd edn., New York, 1956, p. 836).

    Oman, *The Art of War in the Middle Ages*, pp. 162-3; Oman, *A History of the Art of War in the Sixteenth Century*, pp. 71, 211, 228; Hall, *The History of Technology*, Vol. II, pp. 374-82, ibid., Vol. III, pp. 361-75; *Gunpowder and Galleys*, pp. 86-8, 137, 156-60, 255, 266, 273-84, 303; Peter Brent, *War, Technology*, p. 260. Hall, 'A Note on Military Pyrotechnics', in *A History of Technology* edited by Singer et al., Vol. II, Oxford, 1967, pp. 374-82, also see *Technology*, edited by Singer Holmyard, Hall and William, Vol. II, Oxford, 1967, p. 727. *Encyclopaedia Britannica*, Vol. X, 1966, pp. 1038-40. The references to the use of *aradah, tiricharkh, naft, sahchobatir* are found in the Mongol campaigns of Fanakat and Khugand (*Jamiut Tawarikh*, Vol. I, p. 375). *ZN*, Vol. I, pp. 473-93, *ZN*, Vol. II, p. 206; Shami, pp. 234-7.
78. Sarkar, p. 127. While criticizing Iqtidar Alam's views Sarkar in his valuable work has tried to prove that explosion by gunpowder was well known (Sarkar), pp. 130-1 also fn. 3.
79. *ZN*, Vol. I, pp. 493-4.
80. Ibid., pp. 485-6. Hall says that in the earlier stages of gun processing hollowed out logs were used as mortars.

81. *ZN*, Vol. I, pp. 464-6; *ZN*, Tehran edn., pp. 100-2; Hatifi, *Timur Nama*, pp. 176-7.
82. M.M. Alexandre Derssca, *Le campagne de Timur en Anatali*, London, 1977, pp. 43-4; *Istorya Uzbegskoj*, pp. 328-33.
83. *ZN*, pp. 449-50.
84. Thomas W. Arnold, *Bihzad and his Paintings in the Zafar Nama*, MS, London, 1930, p. 8, Illustrations XI-XII.
85. Dumas describes the long and thin cannons called 'veuglaires' being, in vogue in fourteenth century though he concedes that the progress in the use of firearms was slow from mid-fourteenth to mid-fifteenth century and that trebuchets were used even at the end of fourteenth century while pointing out that the gunpowder is one thing and firearms quite another. Saunders refers to 'thunder bomb' being used in 1232 and firelances (gunpowder exploded in a bamboo tube to discharge a cluster of pellets) and fire barrels in 1273-4 and 1281. Both Saunders and Hall refer to the appearance of the metal barrel cannon. Saunders places their appearance between 1280 and 1320, first among Arabs or the Latins and then to Chinese iron bombard in 1377. Maurice Dumas, *A History of Technology and Invention*, English tr. by Eileen B. Hennery, Vol. II, USA, 1969, p. 103. J.J. Saunders, *The History of the Mongol Conquests*, London, 1971, pp. 196-9.
86. Carman, p. 10.
87. Shami, pp. 155, 234; *ZN*, II, pp. 239-40; *IA*, pp. 164-5; *AAA*, pp. 425-33; Hatifi, pp. 62, 176-7, 202.
88. Hookham, pp. 61-2; Peter Brent, *The Mongol Empire*, London, 1976, p. 233. The naphtha arrows were known to the Arabs even perhaps much earlier (in eighth century), see G.N. Pant, *Studies in Indian Weapons and Warfare*, New Delhi, 1970, pp. 47-8.
89. Hall says that the fire pots were in use since sixth century AD. Hall 'A Note on Military Pyrotechnics', in *A History of Technology*, edited by Charles Singer et al., Vol. II, Oxford, 1957, pp. 374-82, 701.
90. Pant, p. 128.
91. Yezdi II, p. 229; Shami, p. 231; *Matla*, p. 784.
92. Shirazi, pp. 46-8. The guns are said to be one of the chief items of export from Bengal in 1406 (Sarkar, p. 131). The gunnery in Nujaynagar Empire was known in 1316, and by 1420 Indians were acquainted with cannons, ballistas, bombards and other implements (Sarkar, p. 132).
93. *ZN* I, pp. 465-7; *ZN* II pp. 194-5, 204-8, 219, 239, 262, 290, 339-40; *Istorija Uzbegskoj*, old edn. Sarkar considers Turks to be the first Asian power to muster new 'Rumi mode' and to introduce into Asia field artillery and infantry with muskets. Turks are otherwise described as Eurasian (Sarkar), p. 134.
94. Al-Hasan the Arab, *Purchas and his Pilgrims*.
95. Hilda Hookham, pp. 61-2.
96. Clavijo, p. 288, also see Pant, p. 170. Surprisingly Oman places the date of invention of Arquebus later than Timur. Oman, *The Art of War in the Sixteenth Century*, London, 1937, pp. 80-2. Though Parry places them slightly earlier saying that Arquebus was used first in 1440 by the Ottomans during the reign of Sultan Murad in Hungarian campaigns (*Cambridge History of Islam*, II, p. 834).

97. Clavijo, p. 288. The tailors were engaged for making ropes to envelop guns and of covering them with hides to protect them from rain and corrosion (*War, Technology and Society*, pp. 171-4).
98. Djurdijica Petrovic, 'Firearms in the Balkans on the eve of and after the Ottoman conquests of the fourteenth and fifteenth centuries', in Parsy and Yapp, *War, Technology and Society in the Middle East*, London, 1975, pp. 173-9.
99. Lewis, *Islam*, UK, 1976, Glossary, p. 289.
100. Chamber's *Encyclopaedia*, VI, 1967, p. 655; see *Encylopaedia Britannica*, Vol. II, p. 893 for 'Bombard'.
101. For details see Carman, pp. 94, 98.
102. Parry, p. 836; Djurdijica Petrovic, 'Firearms in the Balkans on the eve of and after the Ottoman conquests of the fourteenth and fifteenth centuries', op. cit., pp. 165-74.
103. *Less Temps Difficiles Le Moyen Age*, Vol. III, edited by Edward Perry, Claude Cahen et al., Paris, 1975, p. 463 (74: 6 per cent salt petre, 13.5 per cent, charcoal, 11.9 per cent sulphur), canon balls were helpful as a siege weapon. They came into vogue around middle of fourteenth century rapidly burns evolving a whitish gas. In a confined space, this pent up gas can be used for blasting or for propelling missiles. Black powder is a slow explosive and is widely used for blank fire charges in military ammunitions. The instrument employing gunpowder to project missiles dates from early fourteenth century and these first ordance projectiles were obviously adaptations for those already used in contemporary weapons like cross bow and long bow being nothing more nor less than iron darts 'feathered' with brass, their shafts wrapped with stuffings of leather to lessen leakage of powder gases.
    Gunpowder and Galleys, pp. 157-9, also see *Encyclopaedia Britannica*, Vol. I, under Ammunition, Artillery, pp. 799-801; Napoleon, III, 'Etudes sur l'artillerie'; *Encyclopaedia Britannica*, Vol. II under Artillery.
104. *Le Moyen Age*, p. 463.
105. *Gunpowder and Galleys*, p. 174.
106. Hall, *Military Technology: A History of Technology*, Vol. III, Oxford, 1957, pp. 361, 363; *Gunpowder*, p. 271.
108. Hall, *Military Technology*, op. cit., p. 347.
109. Ibid.
110. *Matla* II, p. 645.
111. The cross bows, effective in the hands of archers were used by the first crusader in 1192, one-fifth of the infantry was armed with cross bows (*Crusading Warfare*, pp. 116-17 also fn. 2.
112. *Gunpowder and Galleys*, pp. 141-7 also fn.
113. Ibid., pp. 151, 156.
114. Zygluski, *Oriental and Levantine Firearms*; Pollards, op. cit., pp. 425-30.
115. Needham, p. 378.
116. *Journal of Asian History*, 30 (1996) Ibn-i Arab Shah, Eng. tr., pp. 164-5.
    Ahmad Al-Hassan and Donald R. Hill, *Islamic Technology*, pp. 107-9; also see Charles Singer, *A History of Technology*, Vol. II, Oxford, 1957; Hall, 'A Note on Military Pyrotechnics', pp. 374-82; Alberuni, pp. 114-19.

117. *Science and Civilisation in China*, Vol. 3, 1975; Needham, 1975, p. 378.
118. Ahmad Al-Hassan and Donald R. Hill, *Islamic Technology*, UNESCO, 1986, p. 99.
119. See *IA*, pp. 164-5, Zygluski, *Oriental and Levantine Firearms*, Chapter 15 of Claude work; also see Needham, p. 378; Hall, p. 701.
120. Jaroshtav Lugs, *Firearms Past and Present*, Vol. I, London, 1975, pp. 11-20; Caraman, *A History of Firearms from Earliest Times to 1914*, London, 1970, pp. 1-30, 80-100, 180-200; also see Fredrick Wilkinson, *Arms and Armour*, London, 1971, pp. 94-5.
121. *Purchas and his Pilgrims*, pp. 258-61.
122. Ibid., Vol. II, pp. 4-5.
123. Ibid., pp. 86-9.
124. Hall, 'A Note on Military Pyrotechnics', in Charles Singer, ed., *A History of Technology*, Vol. II, Oxford, 1957, pp. 374-5, 701.
125. Halil Inalcik, *War, Technology*, pp. 200-10.
126. Master Edward Monoxe, *The Agent of the East Indian Merchants Trading in Persia; Purchas and his Pilgrims*, Vol. X, Glassgow, MCMV, p. 348.
127. Machagan, 'Early Asiatic Fire Weapons', *Journal of Asiatic Society of Bengal*, Vol. XIV, pp. 64-70; *Encyclopaedia Britannica*, Vol. XII, p. 723; *Cambridge History of India*, Vol. I, p. 271.
128. *Asiatic Journal*, 1827, p. 65; *Bombay Gazetteer*, Vol. XXIII, p. 638.
129. Jean-Baptiste Tavernier, *Travels in India*, tr. by Ball.
130. W. Crooke, Vol. II, Delhi, 1977, pp. 217-18.
131. I.A. Khan, 'Coming of Gunpowder of the Islamic World', *Journal of Asian History*, 30 (1996) I, p. 44.
132. Prawdin, *History*, 1940, pp. 259-60.
133. Lanferr, quoted by L. Carrington Goodrich, *A Short History of Chinese People*, 1943, p. 148.
134. *Science and Civilisation in China*, Vol. 3, 1975, p. 352.
135. Hall, 'A Note on Military Pyrotechnics', in *A History of Technology*, edited by Charles Singer, Vol. II, Oxford, 1957, pp. 374-82. L. Carrington Goodrich, *A Short History of the Chinese People*, 1943, pp. 148-9, 169.
136. *Encyclopaedia Britannica*, Vol. X, 1966, pp. 1038-40.
137. Chamber's *Encyclopaedia*, Vol. VI, 1967, pp. 655-58.
138. Hall, op. cit., p. 377.
139. Lamb, *Gengiz Khan*, pp. 223-4, 227.
140. Al-Hassan, *Islamic Technology*, p. 111.
141. Ibid.
142. *Islamic Technology*, pp. 106-11.
143. Hall, 'A Note on Military Pyrotechnics', op. cit., p. 377.
144. Hitti, pp. 226, 327.
145. Al-Hassan, *Islamic Technology*, pp. 112-14.

The Tribes of the Central Asia Steppes (Fourteeth-Sixteenth Centuries)

Sociologically speaking the general population of Central Asia was broadly categorized in internal terms into three groups—the settled (*shahr nashin*), people in the process of settlement the (*dehnashin*) and nomadic (*sahra nashin*), the latter mainly comprising the tribes. The Central Asian tribal system has received considerable attention from scholars like Czaplica, Barthold, Spuler, Radloff, Ivanov, Krader and others, whose studies throw much light on various ethnographic and sociological aspects.[1]

The study of tribal system, however, has its limitations in that our medieval Persian sources are not sufficiently precise and often fail to give adequate details. For example, the terms Mongolo-Tarar, Turco-Mongol, Turco-Tajika or simply *Atrak Turk* or *Tarakuma* are applied to all the tribal populations without much discrimination. The names and locales of the different tribes living in eastern and western Central Asia are sometimes not properly described. The confusion is aggravated when the names of the tribes change with the transformation of States and a set of new tribal names replace the old without any explanation. There are tribes (or tribal federations) which continue to appear in the historical narratives though their constituents changed radically. The factors leading to rearrangement of various tribal groups and its ethnic effects are altogether ignored.

Almost all the medieval sources in Turkish and Persian touch on the history of various tribes, but most dwell upon a legendary geneology and fictitious history, which do not help much except by way of nomenclature. The Turkish tribes were described as the followers of Oghuz, from whom each Turkish tribe seems to have derived its origin. The Uighurs (lit. those who join and help) were so called because they were the first to support *ghuz*. From among them the best were called Qanghli, and then the remainder were called Khalj and Taijut. A posthumous child born to a soldier's wife and adopted by Oghuz; was given the name *Qipchaq*; certain Turks, reluctant to march in snowfall, stayed back and were therefore called *Qarlugs* (Lord of snow); another group in Iran established its *yurt* in the forests and were therefore called *aghaj airi* (lit., the people of forests). Turks who were assimilated with the Tajiks of Iran after Oghuz's conquest lost their original features and became an admixture of both, though still resembling the Turks in many ways. They were designated *Turk Manad* (lit. like Turks), later on abbreviated to *Turkman.* The Dughlats were said to be descended from the sixth son of Tumna Khan; the *Qiyat* were said to be the descendants of Qil Khan, the sixth son of Alongova, and so on.[2]

According to the sources, not only the Mongols but the Timurids and the Uzbegs were originally Turks, though known by various names. In one of his letters to Ottoman ruler Ibn-i Usman, Timur categorically stressed, 'we have the same ancestors, we are all shoots and branches of the same tree; our forefathers long ago in the past grew up in one nest and gradually occupied countless others'.[3] Notwithstanding certain minor variations, the genealogical tables and legendary details about the origin and historical evolution of various tribes in Persian and Turkish sources mostly agree, first, that the Turks and Chingizide Mongols are the same people,[4] and secondly, that they were descended from the common ancestors Oghuz and Alongova.[5] Rashiduddin categorically says that the Mongols were 'one of the kindred groups (*qaum*) from amongst the Turks' who were in his days called 'Mughul' but in ancient times each one of whom individually had a different name, speech, separate *amirs* and descending Tubal divisions (*shuba-o qabail*), *yurts.* Since in those days the Mughal tribal division was one of the branches of Turkish people (*dar in zaman shubai-i mughul qawmi az aqwam-i atrak budand*); these days due to their own (Mughal's) wealth, grandeur and might they had distinguished themselves from the other peoples (*aqwam*) by giving them their own names and that 'the entire Turkish people like Jalair, Tartar, Qiyat, Onk, Karait, Naiman, Tankqut, etc., each of whom had a separate fixed name and title called themselves Mughals to add to their own prestige'. It is not the same as in the past when the nomadic Mughal (*shahr nashin*) were only one of the *qaum* or tribe of the total Turkish population. Indeed by Rashiduddin's time, the tribes of the Khitai, Jurja, Nankiyas, Uighur, Qipchaq, Turcomans, Qanuqs, Qulich and the captives and even the Tajiks who had been brought up among

Mughals were also called Mughals and (they too) out of expediency willingly considered it a source of honour to be called Mughul. That is why the Turks were called Tartar everywhere. It was also an honour thereafter for them to take brides from Tartars. These Tartars had six clans. Similarly Juwaini Ibn-ul Asir and all others use the term Tartar for the Mongols. It is interesting to note that the Mongols were not of the same race as the Chinese proper. They were descended from the Tungusor aboriginal stock with a strong mixture of Iranian and Turkish blood—a race now called Ural-Altaic,[6] Chingiz had however, his own notion or idea of a Mongol: 'These men who will share with me the good and bad of the future, whose loyalty will be like the clear rock crystal—I wish them to be called Mongols.' Hence Uighurs Karaits, Yakka, Mongols, Tartars, Merkits, Tundra hunters and high Asian raiders were all included into 'a single gigantic clan', i.e. the Mongols. This means that the term Mongol came into vogue at the time of ascendancy of Chingiz Khan.[7]

It is also said that the Turks (including Ottoman Turks) and the Mongols drew their lineage respectively from Turk and Munsuk the two sons of Alongova. The other theory refers to sons of Yafis b. Nuh. (Also referred Kiumars or Abubija). Since Nuh is perhaps Noah, this tradition could only have developed once some of the Mongols became Muslims. The fact is confirmed by a twelfth century chronicle *Sharaf al Zaman Tahir Marwazi*. The Uighur, Tibetan and Turkish scholars unanimously assert that Noah had dispatched his son Yafis towards eastern regions. It was Oghuz the grandson of Yafis who killed his Gurkhan, organized the Turkish people into tribes, conquered new lands and sent his men to the region nowadays known as Moghulistan. Munsuk's grandson Oghuz established his[8] way over Iran, Transoxiana and other places. The Turkish followers of Oghuz were called *Alghuz*. Oghuz's six sons namely, Gun, Oiy, Yilduz, Guyuk, Tugh, Tingiz (lit. sun, moon, sky, star, sea, mountains) had four sons each from whom descended the 24 *shubas* of Turkish tribes which are so frequently mentioned in Persian Ottoman and Uzbeg sources. During the holy wars of Oghuz against his father, the *atrak* rallied round him. After Oghuz's death, a severe battle between Turks and Mongols resulted in the flight of the two last surviving persons from whom descended two types of Mongols, internal and external. It was from a damsel of *Durlikin* and *Nerun* the last being the real Mongols of special importance who were also known as Qiyat. Mongols named Alongova as the ancestress of Murun Mongols from whom the Turks also draw their lineage. Both views, however, indicate that the Central Asian population mainly consisted of Turks of varied composition, spread far and wide in the early Christian era and described by chroniclers in equally varied colours. Mahmud Kashghari calls all the Turkish-speaking people Turks and divides the entire group into two elements northern and southern Turks.[9] According to him, the pure Turks comprised the following: Kirghiz, Qipchaq, Oghuz, Tukhsi, Yaghma, Chighit, Igrak and Charuk, whereas the others, like Jumal, Basmil, Kai, Yabaku and Tartar were not considered to be Turkish speaking.[10]

Rashiduddin divided the tribes of his times into three groups, first, the Oghuz Turks and their kindred of purely Turkic blood; second the tribes which were considered to be Mongols but were in fact Mongolized Turks; and thirdly, the tribes of purely Mongol blood who lived on the eastern and northern borders of the Turkic lands.[11]

According to this classification, the Ottomans and the Uzbegs would be descendants of the first group and the Chingizide Mongols those of the second, while the Mongols in purely racial terms formed the third category. Similar statements, though not so elaborate, occur in other sources, with certain modifications. Historical narratives amply show that Turks had politically and linguistically dominated the entire region of Transoxiana for several centuries. Mahmud Kashghari says that there were people who spoke Turkish and Sughdi (Soghdanian),[12] others who spoke only Turkish, but none who knew only Sughdi. During Babur's time the people were still bilingual, though speaking Tajik rather than Sughdi, besides Turkish. 'Andijanis are all Turks' says Babur; not a man in town or bazaar but knows Turki, the speech of the people is correct for the pen'.[13] Nevertheless, the people of Asfara were described by Babur as 'Persian speaking Sarts'.[14] Although the Central Asian literature of the fourteenth-sixteenth centuries was produced in both the Persian and Turkish languages, royal *farmans* were conveyed either in Turkish or Persian, according to the region for which they were issued.[15] Turkish titles and words[16] were inscribed on the coins (thirteenth-sixteenth centuries). In administrative spheres Turkish terminology equally prevailed.[17] Even after their conversion to Islam and the introduction of Arabic language, the rulers and the chancellory in Golden Horde continued to use Uighur language in which all the important documents and internal and official work was carried out. In the personal collection of Qazi Jan Khwaja there are a number of documents, e.g. the *Qazi* documents of Uzgand and Marghinan and also a grant order of *milk* land issued by Umar Shaikh Mirza in Uighur alphabets and Chaghatai Turkish language. The Uzbeg ruler Sultan Said Khan was well versed both in Turkish and in Persian. The Uzbeg Khan Kuchum is described by the chroniclers as a 'Turk who does not know Persian at all,[18] thereby suggesting that, in the ruling classes at least, such a person was an exception and the Turkish language seems to have been employed more frequently than before'.

Our sources of the fourteenth to eighteenth centuries introduce us to an apparent medley of peoples and tribes: Tajiks, Mongols, Sarts, Turcomans, Uzbegs, Chaghatai's, Qazaqs, Mughals, Qirghiz, Arabs Uighurs, etc. Grunebaum says that Arabs have been absorbed by older ethnic groups in Central Asia but the sources refer to them as a separate group, however insignificant.[19] Ibn-i Khaldun had categorically stated that 'when the Tartars and the Mongols, who were not Muslims, became the rulers in the East, this element in favour of the Arabic language disappeared, and the Arabic language was absolutely doomed. No trace of it has remained in these Muslim provinces: the Iraq, Khanrasan, Jars, Transoxiana, India and Anatatia.[20] It seems that the different designations were based on linguistic if not racial differences. Some of these tribes were Turks, who spoke one Turkish dialect or another; or those who were bilingual, as we have seen; or finally, those who spoke non-Turkic tongues. Apart from the lingual classification we find the definition provided by Haider Dughlat who had divided the people *Khatan-i-Kashghar* into four classes. 'One is called Tuman which means peasantry, they are dependant upon the Khan, and pay their taxes to him yearly. Another class is Kuchin, which means soldiery, who are all dependant upon my relations. A third is called *imak* or *aimak* all of whom receive a fixed revenue (*mukataa*) of grain cloth and the like. These people are also dependant upon my relations. The fourth class are the controllers of legal jurisdiction and the custodians of religious houses and pious foundations; most of these are of my family.[21]

Writers like Shami, Yazdi, Abdurrazzaq, Babur, Haider Dughlat and Abul Ghazi point out distinctly the weaknesses, qualities and characteristics of each tribal or territorial population. Even Abul

Ghazi, who uses the term Turk for all steppe dwelling nomadic tribes, is careful to distinguish their particular racial, descent, language and cultural characteristics.

The sources generally refer to the following tribal units; *qaum, qabila, taefa, shuba, il, ulus, orda, yurts, aimaq, eshligh.* Although the first four terms are found in the pre-Chingizide period, the last six came into vogue only after the Mongol conquests. *Tarikh-i Guzida* says that each tribe consisted of several divisions (*sho'b*)—further ramifications in descending order being *qabila, fasilah, imarah, batn* and *fakhiz.* No details about these groups are available anywhere though the divisions of each tribe are given by the author, e.g. that Jalair comprised 12 divisions like Kuskin, Qunghrat, Barlas, Markit, Quilaut; Tartars had 8 divisions; Soniyat consisted of 5 divisions; Naiman, Qirghiz and Qiyat each had four divisions. A long list of the names of these divisions follow. Elsewhere the same author describes the tribal divisions as being the *khanawars, deh, taefa, qabila* and *orda* or even, as *aqwam, qaum, sho'b* and *qabila.*[22]

The tribal population usually lived in *yurts* (nomadic camps) which formed the basis of the smallest unit of the tribal structure, i.e. the *khanawar.* Marco Polo, Ibn-i Battuta and Jenkinson all described the *yurts;* and they evoked admiration from eighteenth century travellers as well. During his sojourn in Central Asia; Friar William of Rubruquis in 1253 made a drawing of typical comical Mongol tents which served as fragile abode of these nomads. The term Aghacheri so frequently mentioned in the Uzbeg sources denotes. The term has been explained by Cahen as (lit. men of trees) 'not the name of a traditional Oghuz tribe but they were an ancient people from Russia transplanted into Asia minor. They are only recorded in the thirteenth 'century and for the most part in the central and eastern Tains regions.' These *yurts*[23] were usually round, made of wattled rods and covered with felt which could be put together into a bundle or package and carried on a wagon with four wheels. When they had to set them up again the entrance was always placed towards the south. There were also some superior carts with two wheels, covered, likewise with black felt and so effective as to remain waterproof during a whole day of rain. Drawn by oxen and camels, these carts carried the nomads' wives, children, utensils and provisions.[24] John Smith was surprised to see the carts of the Manghit (Nogai) Tartars which were fifteen to sixteenth feet broad, covered with small rods, which 'rattled like a birds' nest', tempered with oil and clay, and camel's hair; 'they loom so well still they are very light'.[25] The Uzbegs appeared to have lived in *yurts* only during their campaigns, but the Manghits, Qazaqs, Turcomans, Chaghatais, Mongol and Qirghiz usually lived in *yurts*. Obruchev and Berg, who visited Central Asia in the second half of the nineteenth century found the *yurts* stuffed with people and cattle, with little place for fresh air; but the residents hospitably invited the foreign guests to stay inside.[26]

The tribal organization of the Uzbegs was largely a stereotype of the nomadic Turkish tribal system. Several families were united together to form a *khanewar* and several *khanewars* (a cluster of tents or *yurts*) were combined into *a firga* (group), a number of *firgas* collected together to make a *taefa* (kindred groups—also called *taipa* and a nomadic group as *aul*). The small territory assigned to each *taefa* was called *a mahal*. The *mahals* were usually assigned to tribal nobles. A collection of *taefas* formed an *urchki* which further constituted a *boi* then several *bois* formed an *aimaq* (with its head as *kalantar*). Then it and *ashligh* (tribal groups were constituted from several *aimaqs* ascending order ultimately constituted an *ulus*.[27] In the construction of society of the Mongols and the Turco-Mongols, a family or household meant not one household but a large conglomeration of households, including all those that were of known relationship to each other. Each of these terms was, however, fluid; thus the *ulus* could be used in the sense of a tribe as well as a group of tribes, or even in the sense of an empire or territory, e.g. the *ulus* of Chaghatai or of Juji. The same was the case with *yurt*, or *aimaqs*. Elsewhere an *aimaq* is described as 'a division of persons and not of territory. In Mongolia under the Chinese government it answers to Khanate. A Khan is at the head of an *aimaq*. *Aimaqs* are divided into *koshung*, i.e. banners.'[28]

The office of the *ulus begi* (chief of *ulus*) could be hereditary, but it was subject to royal appointment.[29] Under Sultan Ahmad Khan, this office in the 'Dughlat tribe belonged to the family of Muhammad Amir Mirza Dughlat'.[30] In the sources, persons bearing the designation of *kalantar, sarikhail, amil baj* (lit. in Turkish rich chief of a tribe) or *bi*, *beg* (lit. ruler of a region or city) are mentioned as chiefs of various tribal units. The most commonly used term, *Beg* carried three different connotations from the eighth century onwards:

1. A man of some rank but not belonging to the royal family.

2. The leader of a small tribe, kin or kindred group.
3. The head of an army detachment of big and small units, e.g. *unbegi* (commander of ten), *uzbegi* (commander of one hundred). In the Golden Horde the term was applied to a village elder or to a governor also. Early inscriptions refer to the aristocracy as *begiar*.[31] The term *beki* had been defined by the another of the Secret History 'As to the way of Chief, there is a custom whereby one may become a *beki* . . . from among and above us'. A *Beki* was to wear 'white rainment, to ride upon a white gelding'. 'The *beki* was to determine what action it might be appropriate to take. Abul Fazl says that '*be is* the abbreviation of *Beg*.'[32]

The *el* or *il* found even in old *Uighur* documents was a smaller social unit than the tribe; it has been compared by a Soviet scholar to the European commune.[33] In the Uzbeg Empire these 'communes' were headed by *aqsaqal* (lit. white beards, also called *rish-safedan* or *muisafedan,* elders) or *elikbashi* (the elder of society) with helpers both men (*paikar*) and women (*kaivan-ikhadim*). Like the *el,* the *aimaqs* in the eastern Turkish or Mongolian languages also denoted tribes as well as a political union of tribes. Blood relations[34] were called *urugh aimaqs*. The term *aimaqesh*[35] (*aimaq,* tribe, *esh,* companion) referred to the chieftain of the tribe. In Uzbeg sources the term *qushchi* or *qushbegi* is also frequently found. Barthold's identification of *qushbegi* with the falconer is showed by Beveridge. Nevertheless, there seems to be a difference between *qushchi* and *qushbegi* for the former was a tribal chief of a kindred patriarchal blood group (*koshe* or *qush,* lit. small patriarchal blood group and *bi* or *chi,* head of kin group also known as *ketkhuda*) and the latter was the incharge of hunting.[36]

The tribal aristocracy enjoyed the right to distribute pastures and agricultural lands and controlled tribal armies which strengthened the influence of a tribal leader over the tribesmen. Through matrimonial relations on political alliances, the tribes cooperated with each other to extend their influence at the expense of others. Incidentally the strengthening of connection between the ruling group became paramount only in the seventeenth century. Abul Ghazi is said to have consolidated four Uzbeg groups and divided them into (1) Uighur and Naiman (2) Qunghrat, Qiyat (3) Manghit and Nukuz (4) Qanghli Qipchaq. Marriage among these groups could be concluded more easily. To them were added 14 kin-groups called *unturt urugh* (lit. 14 kindred groups). The property of the conquered tribe was divided among the victors, and the captives sold as slaves, strengthening one tribal 'federation' and disintegrating another.[37] A union of tribes could invite any Chingizide sultan to sanctify their regime. The tribal leader had to depend upon the support of his tribesmen for all minor and major actions though the final decision still rested with him. The unwritten tribal norms and traditions were strictly followed, e.g. installed totems, guarded the ownership rights of tribes even when they were away on hunting. Similarly, the shift from one tribe to another as a new entrant or member was discouraged in the interest of maintaining harmony and discipline, people who attempted such a change forfeited the privileges of their own clan and were not immediately entitled to the privileges of the newly adopted clan.[389] An outsider could be admitted to a clan either through marriage or by adoption. Abdul Quddus, who helped Yunus Khan, was given the title of *Gurgani* (son-in-law) and all the privileges of the clan of Dughlat were bestowed upon him.[39]

Retainers (*nukar, hashm*) depending solely upon the martial profession formed the second core of the structure of power, and received horses, gifts, cattle and other booty in times of successful wars.

In Central Asia the tribal population seems to have been like a commodity which could be transferred, exchanged, sold and destroyed by its lord or claimant or even used as a pawn.[40] The tribal populations' *Khana Kuch, Koran* or *Kuchanidan* (emigration or forced settlement) and *Surgun* (compulsory shifting) either willingly or through pressure, also resulted in the assimilation of the immigrants with the local population. After the conquests, new populations were often sent to live in the newly conquered areas; thus Uzbegs and Turcomans were sent to live in Khwarazm in 1538 to strengthen the Uzbeg hold in the newly conquered region. There were also economic exigencies which forced temporary, long tremor permanent alliances among the tribes, leading sometimes to submersion. In certain cases the division of the tribes occurs and the same people are found in various tribes as a different entity without fusion. The war captives distributed among various tribes increased the number of soldiers losing their identity. Certain Qazaqs who had joined the banner of Shaibani also came under the Uzbeg tribes though their kindred and kin-groups living in the Dasht and

Moghulistan also retained their separate identity as Qazaqs. The Uzbegs apparently swelled from 24 tribal groups to 32 and later on to 92 much in the same manner. The tribal names attached to various tribal unions do indicate that some of the Turco Mongolian tribes living in Transoxiana and Khurasan had their kindred groups in the Dasht-i Qipchaq too. Among such tribal groups found in Central Asia and the Qipchaq steppes were the Jalair, Khitai, Ijan, Qiyat, Tuman, Tunghut, Naiman and so on. The Khitais are found among the Uzbegs, Qarluqs and other tribal peoples. If Banakati's version that the tribe of Jalair originated from the Jata, who had also supported Abulkhair, is correct then the presence of Jalairs throughout Central Asia and Qipchaq plains is clearly explained. Aristov says that the Qanghli and Qipchaq belonged to the south western Turks who played a significant role in the formation of the Uzbeg, Sart, Kirghiz, and Qazaq tribal peoples, so that two-thirds of all the existing turks are from Qanghli and Qipchaq; the designations are indeed synonymously used by historians in twelfth-thirteenth century. Rashiduddin even says that the Saljuqs came from the Qanghli.

There are certain tribes of the Dasht who are not found among Central Asian population. The Manghits never entered the Central Asian heartland though they retained their independent identity at least till the seventeenth century. Some of their leading men participated in the Central Asian history. The Qushchi, Durman Shinkarli, Shadbakl and certain other tribes have never been mentioned in earlier history and they must have come from the Dasht. Some tribes, of course, simply disappeared.

The tribes could be a political hazard for a sovereign seeking to establish stable power, but militarily and financially they were an asset—low paid, half-starved, hardy warriors 'born' and 'dying' during the march—spending their whole lives horseback; supplying the king with the required number of soldiers and serving as a civil tax paying population in times of peace. The settled and the nomadic population supplemented each other's economy by exchanging their respective special commodities. It was the tribal chief on whom a Central government relied as an agent for the maintenance of order, tax collection from his region (*nahiya*) or grazing territory as well as for ensuring the safety of travellers and traders. The tribes had to pay the land tax, *kharaj*, *jaziya* (and a number of other taxes, namely, *qupchur, sarshumari, amwal-i-taqabbul, ghan, sav* (tribute esp. of oxen), *amwal-i-muqarrari* (stipulated money), *iasaghi, ashligh, tughar, qunulgha, kazu, saan, soghum, sachi, zakat, shibaghu, quozakhira, qupchur iasaghi* and so on.[41] These taxes were realized by the *basqaqs, uimaqush mukuz* and *muhassils* explain who they were and deposited in the state treasury. If the taxes could not be realized in time, the arrears were raised later. Non payment or any resistance invited armed action against the defaulting tribe (*kari aimaq takhtan*) on behalf of or by the Khans and Sultans.

The tribes which grew very strong or lived in the mountains or border areas 'had a fashion of not paying tribute'. Babur refers to a five or six thousand *khanawars* (households) of the Jigrak tribes in the wilds of Andijan living between Kashghar and Farghana who had horses, sheep and yaks. Babur sent Qasim Beg with an army to realize the taxes. This tribute of about 20,000 sheep and 1,000-1,500 horses was distributed among his soldiers.[42]

Although no definite information about the rate of demand is available, Abul Ghazi says that from *uch el* the Khwarazm Uzbegs demanded one tenth of the produce and from others they realized an additional tax on their cattle. Sometimes forced labour or payment in the form of *nukars* were also demanded.[43]

The *sawai'm zakat* tax was also realized on heads of pasturing animals (like goats, sheep, cows, camels, horses, etc. The rate of demand was as follows: one sheep for every herd of 40-120 sheep; two for 121-200; three for any herd comprising the numbers ranging from 201-400; one sheep for every herd of 100 over and above 400. For the goats also the same rate prevailed. For every string of five camels upto a number of 26 camels; four years old camel for 46 camels and five years old camel one sheep was demanded. A two year camel was demanded for each string of 26 camels; two four year old camels for 91 camels. The option for payment in cash was also given and such payers in cash were called *mukhayyers* (free to choose). According to Babur, the demand in kind on each herd of 40 horses was one horse and in cash one gold *misqal*. Tribes were to be counted not per head of persons, for men die and others are born—but by tents, the summer and winter quarters were allotted to each tribe according to their size by a permanent general staff.[44]

During the reign of Pir Muhammad Uzbeg the *muqarrari* tax alone brought an annual payment of 12,000 sheep; *ashligh* and other taxes were received additionally.[45] The new conquests and the forced or willing emigration of the tribes was followed by a registration of *khanawars* (households) for tax purposes.[46] After the conquest of Khurasan by Shaibani, 1,70,000 *khanawars* were registered in Sarkhas alone.[47] Sometimes the term *aimaqesh mukuz* appears in the sources, which seems to refer to the person entrusted with the task of tax collection from a particular tribe as the name itself suggests (lit. *aimaqesh* chief of tribe: *Mukuz* incidental taxes).[48]

Whenever the tribal groups felt that their life or property was endangered, they moved from one place to another.[49] In the absence of any agricultural ties with the land, such population movements were not difficult and the rulers, in need of taxes, militia and labour, happily welcomed such immigrants.[50] Conversely, the flight of tribes from his dominions, was a disturbing event for a ruler. When the *aimaqs* of Badakhshan fled to India, thanks to the tyranny of Abdul Momin, the latter wrote a number of letters to the emperor Akbar asking for their return.[51]

But there was not a significant tribal counterweight to the despotism of Central Asian rulers. Krader's view seems sound when he says that 'Central Asian monarchy was typical of the orient in its despotic character, if the despot could enforce his rule it was absolute. If he could not then the regime fell apart into smaller centralized units.[52] Even the consultative assembly was a formality, for such absolute Khans as they followed what appealed to them most.[53] The tribes within an empire could individually be crushed by the centralized power.[54] Nomads at the borders and particularly outside the empire, like the Qazaqs, Mongols, etc., posed a danger, but they were external to the system.

In general, the Sultans or Khans exercised their control over the tribes through the chiefs. The tribal chiefs (*kalantars, muqaddams, bis, begs*) were appointed by the Sultans from amongst loyalist population and held office during the pleasure of the Khan.[55] They could be deposed, punished and deprived of their wealth. The recalcitrant tribes were severely dealt with and subjected to forced migrations, disbanding, massacre, imprisonment and so on. The Shaibanid Khans had undertaken various campaigns against the Qazaqs whose constant incursions destroyed their peace and prosperity of the empire. The war was declared to be a *ghazawa* (holy war) and the obliging *mullas* came forward to issue a *fatwa* pronouncing the Qazaqs infidels. The tribes, whether great or small, could easily be put down as they were mutually divided and hostile towards each other. They often had a wide region at their disposal, but they could not turn it into a State. Thus the Qirghiz,[56] the Qara Qirghiz and Qazaqs held the entire Semiriche region throughout the sixteenth century but could not create an empire thanks to mutual differences. There was always a group of dissident tribes who sabotaged and subverted such plans. The civil wars further weakened them, Jenkinson says that the area controlled by the Manghits 'at my being there (in 1558) was destroyed through civil wars, accompanied with famine, pestilence and such plagues in such sort that in the said year there were consumed of the people in one sort and another above one hundred thousand so that the country of Nogai being a country of great pastures remained now unreplenished'.[57]

Like his predecessors, Shaibani Khan and Ubaidullah, Abdullah was also extremely ruthless towards the turbulent chiefs. Along with other *sardars* of that tribe, servants and soldiers, Abulqasim Baluch was suppressed with a heavy hand and put to death at the order of Abdullah Khan.[58] Although Mirza Walijan Jalair held an extremely important administrative position for an extended period he was deprived of this responsibility[59] partly because of his conspiracy with Burhan sultan and partly because Abdullah Khan wanted to curtail tribal influence. 'Arab Bi Qushji', whose forefathers held a distinguished position in the court earlier, lost his balance after seeing such an honour for himself; gave up obedience and behaved in a rebellious manner. He fell in Abdullah's estimation 'like a tear drop' and was removed from the court.[60] The tribes of a newly conquered district were transplanted to a far off place to circumvent the possibility of any rebellion. They were deprived of their cattle and wealth except in such cases where flight was apprehended. Like Timur, Abdullah too used diplomatic means to win over rebellious chiefs, since these tribal chiefs were the intermediaries through whom the nomads were controlled. Ahan Pulad was appointed as the chief of the Qipchaq and was also given the *toq* due to exigencies of the situation.[61] The defaulting chiefs were often replaced by the central ruler in order to ensure peace and security in the region. Qazi Nuruddin Muhammad was appointed to replace Wali Jan Jalair to look after the administration and finances.[62] Much care was, however, taken to let sleeping dogs lie. An Amir, Jankeldi bi, was given the *qaziship* of Sabran when Maulana Idi was deposed because the latter was inciting Muslims and the region mostly had a tribal population.[63] Shaibani was not acceptable as ruler in the Manghit *ulus* because the Manghits nobles were used to certain extra privileges and were co-sharers in administration and these rights, they feared, were going to be lost since Shaibani was a non-Manghit.[64] In the second decade of sixteenth century there was a reversion to the old nomadic Turkish traditions for a short time in the Uzbeg Empire under weak Khans. Nevertheless, strong rulers like Shaibani Khan, Ubaidullah Khan and Abdullah Khan tried to eliminate such steppe traditions as the accession to power of the oldest member of the family. During the coronation ceremony of Abdullah Khan the tribal chiefs and religious leaders equally held the four corners of the felt carpet on which he was sitting, which shows that power was not entirely in the hands of tribal chiefs.

The tribal association or following ceased to be the only criteria for appointment under Abdullah Khan who appointed Rustam Bi qushchi as the *ataliq* of Din Muhammad in Qunduz because he was 'a devotee of men of God and religion' (*ahlu'l-ilahi o arbab-i intibah*).[65] Amir Jan Ali Bi Naiman was given the rank of *ataliq* at the recommendation of Khwaja Juibari.[66] The Khwajas (Naqshbandi saints) often pleaded the case of the tribesmen and served as a link between them and the Khans. During fifteenth to sixteenth centuries, the increasing influence of *mullas* reduced influence of the tribal chiefs considerably. Everything was measured through the yardstick of the *sharia*. The contrast presented by the prevalent settled traditions in Central Asia on the one hand and the continuing semi-nomadic Uzbeg traditions on the other, though sharp initially got gradually blurred as both the requirements of a settled economy and the increasing pretensions of the religious leaders asserted themselves.

A short account of important tribes living in Central Asia during the fifteenth to sixteenth centuries is necessary here to clarify the development of Uzbeg power in Central Asia.

The Mughals

Haider Dughlat, a Mughal himself, is sometimes as critical of the Mughals as the other contemporary chroniclers who denounce them as being completely unfamiliar with the ways of settled life, and 'as wild as the beasts of the mountains' who never possessed or even lived in a village and had never even seen cultivation.[67] The Mughals rebelled whenever any of their Khans showed too marked an inclination towards settled agricultural life. Even Khan Yunus of Moghulistan was dethroned on this score, and was later reinstated only when he took a vow never to attempt to make the Mughals dwell in cities of cultivated countries. The resentment of settled population against the Mughals who were half way through civilization was understandable as their constant incursions disturbed the peace and prosperity of the country.

Although the Mughals are said to have 'avoided all the towns and the cultivated countries with great repugnance',[68] they obtained the produce of settled life through plunder. The only advantage accruing to the other side from such warfare was that, when captured, Mughals were carried away and sold as slaves in the markets of Transoxiana and Khurasan 'like other infidels'. The conflict lessened in its intensity during the regime of Yunus Khan, when Khwaja Nasiruddin Ubaidullah converted the Mughals to Islam.[69] Babur compares the Mughals with the Hazaras and Afghans of Kabul because they all lived in 'open country[70] like nomads. They were described as 'plunderers'[71] from whom only mischief and devastation' should be expected. By 1527 they had rebelled five times against Babur not because they were not getting along well with him but because they were accustomed to revolting frequently against all non-mongol Khans.[72] In Haider Dughlat's time the Mughals had become the most 'remote and insignificant of tribes notwithstanding their former grandeur as "Lords of the world" under Chingiz Khan'.[73] Although there were still about 30,000 Mughals in the neighborhood of Turfan and Kashghar, the main reason for their being 'most isolated and paltry' was probably their diffidence and rigidity and failure to adapt to new circumstances.

As a fighting force, the only sphere in which they excelled, their utility was limited. Although cheaply maintained, they were 'unworthy of any trust'.[74] The Timurids frequently recruited them for their army as they were accustomed to hardship. But while the prospect of grain or food could lure them to fight in the army, the same desire for booty could tempt them to change sides.[75] Even matrimonial alliances had no permanent effect.[76] Babur holds them responsible for many a defeat—'this is always the way with those ill-omened Mughals. If they win, they grab at booty; if they lose, they unhorse and pilfer their own side'.[77] For Babur, any treacherous action was the clear product of Mughal nature.[78] They were numerous and strong but disunited and nomadic. Haider Dughlat[79] refers to Mughal *ulus* frequently quarrelling among themselves over pastures, for the wide grazing grounds of Kashghar had become too confined for them as both men and beast greatly increased in number.[80] The chief Mughal clans mentioned by Babur were the Chiras, Begchik reliable in the right of the army, Barin, Urdu Beg Utarji, Jalair, Urban, Kunchi, Qalmaq Manghits Barki and others.[81] The Chiras and Begchik clans regularly quarrelled over positions.[82] Juvaini describes Rat as one of the 'best known of the Mongol tribes, and to that tribe belonged most of the maternal uncles of the children and grand children of Chingiz Khan, the reason being that at the time of the first rise to power the Qirat came forward to support and assist him and vied with one another in their alacrity to tender allegiance and in recognition of their services an edict was issued concerning that tribe to the effect that the daughters of their *amirs* should be married to the descendants of Chingiz Khan and he bestowed upon the chief of the tribe a daughter of his own called Checheken Beki. This is the reason why all the princes take their wives from the Qirat'.[83] The system however must have irritated the Qirat as Rashiduddin refers to a discord over the issue during Ogedie's reign followed by a forced seizure of even married ones at Ogedei's order.[84] The three other tribes of Mongols namely Orasut, Tilankut and Kustami called 'forest people' (*aqwami besha*) were distinguished for their capacity and ability to cure the Mongols.[85] It was ultimately settled that a representation of one day should take the highest place in the hunting circle, and thus of the other in battle array.[86] Some of the Mughal chiefs were able to rise to the highest position particularly among the Chiras and Barin Tuman Begs, but such cases were rare. Their deep attachment to their own blood and race often provoked them to revolt against non-Mughals or to conspire against the Timurids. Haider Dughlat observes 'The Mughals, more especially, who are distinguished above all other tribes by their numbers and their strength, and whose amirs have been the most eminent of amirs, have always devoted their energies to the advancement of the work of their own (racial) colleagues (*ibnijins*)'.[87] As rulers too they were exceptionally tyrannical. Not only Juvaini and Fazlullah, but Haider Dughlat, too, describe their extortions and high-handedness:

> The whole province of Hesar except the fort, fell into the hands of the Mughals. The Mughals have a proverb which runs: 'when a place is left unoccupied, the pigs will mount to the top of the hillock'. They withdrew

the hand of tyranny and oppression from the sleeve of violence and enmity, and seized upon the households, families, possessions and cattle of all the people. One of the most distinguished of those Mughals, who was in my service at one time used to relate: they once (by way of paying my allowance) gave me an assignment (*barat*) for obtaining provisions; which was addressed to one of the inferior officials at Vakhsh. I alighted at his house and showed him my assignment. He pondered for a while; then he came out and displayed before my view about 200 horses, and a proportionate number of sheep, camels, slaves, household furniture, clothes and (various) materials, saying: 'I entreat you to let me and my children and wives go with the clothes we have on, while you take possession of all that is here, and release me from the balance of the sum that is mentioned in the order. When I had reckoned up the value of the cattle and property, though it came to a considerable sum, it was only half of that entered in the assignment.' This story shows what degree of tyranny, violence and oppression they had begun to practice. Whatever property or flocks they found among the people of Hesar, they extorted from the owners, whom they ruined with waste and extravagance. There ensued a terrible famine among the usulman and in the whole town of Hesar only sixty persons survived. The living eat the dead and when these had died in the such a condition that no nourishment was left in their flesh, the living fell upon one another.[88]

Since the Mughals still followed the *tura* ardently,[89] the only way of living known to them was nomadism supported by booty. Throughout the fifteenth and sixteenth centuries the Mughals were the most dreaded and detested people: they were imprisoned, scattered, dispersed over the country, killed on a large scale through organized massacres [90] and then disbanded. Sometimes forced migrations were inflicted upon them as after the defeat of Sultan Mahmud and Ahmad Khan in Akhsi in 1406, when the Mughals were compelled to migrate into Khurasan and areas remote from Moghulistan.[91] Many of them were sold as slaves, a practice discontinued under Yunus Khan.[92] The lot of the Mughals hardly improved under the Uzbegs, though they had helped Shaibani Khan in the crucial battle of Syr against the Timurids. Like Babur, Shaibani also suspected the Mughals, 30,000 of whom served in his army. Two Uzbeg Sultans namely Mahmud (brother of Shaibani) and his son 'Ubaidullah, were kind to the Mughals, the latter had even married Haider Dughlat's sister. Yet massacres of the Mughals were twice organized by the Uzbegs'.[93] It seems that in the second half of sixteenth century the Mughals ceased to play an important role in the Central Asian history. Then power was re-established under Sultan Abdur Rashid (1533-70) who allied himself with the Uzbegs in opposing the common enemy, the Qazaqs, whom they defeated in 1537-8. The alliance between the Mughals and the Uzbegs continued, for Sultan Rashid is said to have been friendly with Nauruz Ahmad and a meeting took place between the two on the shores of the Issyk Kul in 1544-5. But as the Qazaqs and Kirghiz became stronger, Mongol power again started declining. After the death of Sultan Rashid in 1570, his son Sultan Abdul Latif was killed in a war against the joint forces of the Qazaq and Kirghiz.[94] The continuous wars and devastation must have told heavily upon the commercial and agricultural conditions of the tribal region of semireche, forcing the nomads to compensate themselves with predatory raids over neighbouring, settled regions in Central Asia, which naturally further embittered their relations with the Uzbegs.

THE CHAGHATAI'S

If Haider Dughlat is to be believed, Mirza Ulugh Beg in his *Tarikh-i Ulus-i-Arbaa*[95] describes the four sons of Chingiz Khan as holding charge of four different hordes: one of these was 'that of the Mughal, who are divided into two branches, the Mughal and the Chaghatai'. The same author further says that, these two branches, referred to each other by special derogatory names thanks to mutual enmity. Thus, the Chaghatai called the Mughal *Jetah,* while the Mughal called the Chaghatai *Qarawnas.*[96] Babur clearly distinguishes between the Chaghatais and the Mughals and[97] other sources also echo this.[98]

Although the distinguishing features of the two groups have not been highlighted in our sources, it is certain that the term Chaghatai did not stand for the successors of Chaghatai, for whom an exclusive epithet *Chaghatai-nizadan*[99] i.e. born in Chaghatai family is used in the sources of fourteenth to fifteenth centuries. It seems that the term Chaghatai came to be applied to the entire nomadic Turkish population of the dominions inherited by Chaghatai, e.g. for tribes such as the Arlat, Jalair, Qauchin and Barlas. The term also signified the successors of Timur. In this connection, it is interesting to examine the statements of sixteenth century chroniclers like Hasan Nisari Bukhari and Isfahani.[100] Even Haider Dughlat categorically says 'at the present time, there are no Chaghatais left excepting the kings who are the sons of Babur Padishah and the place of Chaghatai is now occupied by some other civilized people'.[101] In a letter to Abdul Momin, Shah Abbas also described Sultan Husain Mirza as a Chaghatai ruler[102] as his mother came from the Arlat tribe. While the struggle between the nomads and the nomads in transition was in progress, the tribes favouring nomadism and living in Moghulistan in eastern Central Asia were called Mughal. Those who preferred settled ways, shifted to western Central Asia to rule over the region in Chaghatai's name and preserve Mughal domination. They continued to call themselves Chaghatais, even after the descendants of Chaghatai ceased to rule over the region. The eastern Transoxiana or Moghulistan, where the Chaghatai dynasty also ruled, was called Moghulistan. Even in Transoxiana proper, the leading tribes of the Chaghatai horde preserved their nomadic ways for quite some time. Clavijo[103] calls these Chaghatais a 'nomad folk', living in the open throughout winter and summer, though they passed on to the plains by summer where they sowed corn, cotton, melons and millet. On the eve of Timur's ascendancy and labour these four tribes were, in the words of Ibn-i Arab, as 'the hinge of evil and good', 'the eyes of the kingdom with whose advice affairs were directed'.[104] But Timur's harsh measures had considerably reduced tribal independence[105] and his successors were equally harsh towards the tribes. The chief tribes of the Chaghatai state, namely the Arlat, Jalair, Qauchin and Barlas, lived in nomadic fashion in different regions. It should be noted that the Qauchin did not form a tribe in the strictest sense of the term, but a privileged personal force of the Khan to the number of 1,000, as Yazdi and Haider Dughlat tell us. The other three had their definite territory in the Chaghatai Empire. The Arlat lived in northern Afghanistan; the Jalair near Khujand on the Syr river, and the Barlas near the Qashqa river.[106] Haider Dughlat calls the Chaghatais rude, uncultured and not refined.[107] In Timur's Empire, however, the Chaghatai tribes held a very important position as Timur owed his throne to the military support of these tribes. Clavijo therefore says that this particular tribe of Chaghatai is privileged as it, enjoys the special favour of Timur, is allowed to herd their flocks wheresoever they wish and sow their crops in all districts, wandering summer and winter without hindrance. The clansmen are free of all burdens and pay no government taxes but serve Timur constantly in his armies and act as his guard and are never separated on a march from their women folk or children or herds and flock.[108] Elsewhere, however, Clavijo mentions about the registration of Chaghatais for tax purposes.

Since most of the tribal chiefs, military aristocracy and nobility emerged from these four tribes even under the Timurids, their domination continued, though with the slight difference that now religious divines also became important in the management of affairs. During the encounter of the Timurids with the Uzbegs, the Chaghatais were 'defeated; a great number of them were slain and those who escaped became so scattered that they were never united again'.[109] The deteriorating condition of Chaghatais in the first decade of sixteenth century is well depicted by Muhammad Saleh in the following words: 'the poor Chaghatais are being kicked about day and night—their days are black and their condition deplorable. Being intoxicated with pride, their golden ten thousand were kicked out like a mouse by a united hundred'.[110] Under the Uzbegs, the Chaghatais (except the Jalairs) do not seem to have occupied an important place. A Chaghatai *amirzada,* Mirza Qubuli, is said to have held the mansab of *ugta* (mufti) and another, Pahelwan Yari, is reported to have 'enjoyed the rank of emirate of Chaghatai' under the Uzbegs in the sixteenth century.[111] The Chaghatais do not thus seem to have lost their identity at least till the eighteenth century: they are mentioned as an independent, separate group by Mirza Badi[112] in 1789 and by Shergul Afghan[113] and others even later. The term Chaghatai also came to be applied to the Timurids in India from the sixteenth century onwards.

Shahnawaz Khan renders the word Barlas as 'courageous and of gentle birth'.[114] A serious dispute as to the precedence between Dukhtu and Barlas tribe was settled establishing the former's right over the latter (*TR*, tr.: 306-9). Juvaini describes Qirat as one of the 'best known of the Mongol tribes', and to that tribe belong most of the maternal uncles of the children and grand children of Chingiz Khan, the reason being that at the time of the first rise to power the Qirat came forward to support and assist him and vied with one another in their alacrity to tender allegiance and in recognition of their services an edict was issued concerning that trip to the effect that the daughters of their *amirs* should be married to the descendants of Chingiz Khan and he bestowed upon the chief of the tribe a daughter of his own called Checkeken Beki. This is the reason why all the princes take their wives from the Qirat.[115] The system however must have irritated the Qirat as Rashiduddin refers to a discord over the issue during Ogedei's reign, followed by a forced seizure of even married ones at Ogedei's orders.[116] The three other tribes of Mongolis namely Orasut, Tilankut and Kustami called as 'first people' (*aqwami besha*) were distinguished for their capacity and ability to cure the Mongols.[117]

The Chaghatai clans comprised Toqbai, Sildoz.[118] The whole clan of Barlas is derived from Iradamci who was the first person who bore the title of Barlas. He was son of Qachruli Bahadur the eighth ancestor of Amir Timur. Barlas is said to be also the name of a province near Samarqand.[119] Wassaf says that the tribes subjugated by the ancestors of Chingiz Khan and *intima-i-qarabat dashtand* were: Urut, Mauqut Qadashan, Seljut, Sughalut, Lutat, Barin, Hunus, Budat, Juhut Arulas, Urqin, Dughlat. The tribes of Uirat, Qunghrat, Qaranans, Tartar, Kirait Jalair, Bayashut, Sulduz, Tubat, Liunkut and Artat who were sons and sons-in-law. There were some others like Akirs Mulan, Kubin,[120] Saqat Burutasim Budaqin, Jirghan, Nauman, Andakat. In the tribal assignment done by Chingiz Khan, the tribe of Dughlat 'fell to the lot of Chaghatai'.[121]

Ibn-i Khaldun had placed the Turcomans in the list of 'savage' people who are 'better able to achieve superiority and full control and to subdue other groups'. The members of such a nation says he, 'have the strength to fight other nations, and they are among human beings what beasts of prey are among dumb animals'.[122]

Ever since Tatatungo the Uighur prime minister of Baibuka Tayan (ruler of eastern part of Altai range) became the keeper of Chingiz's seal, higher writing became the official script of the Mongols and remained so when Temuchin later came into close contacts with Chinese and with Islamic culture (Prawdin: 80). Chingiz rejected both Chinese and Mohammedan civilization as 'unduly urban' whereas to him the Uighurs were a kin, being themselves archetypal nomads'.

THE TURCOMANS

The Turcomans of Khwarazm, the Caspian Sea area, Turkestan and the Syr darya region were said to be the descendants of Oghuz and ancestors of the Saljuqid Turks and Ottomans; they spoke a Turkish akin to that of 'Osmanlis'. They were Muslims 'without prejudices' and Marco Polo further found them 'rude, dull of intellect and living entirely upon animal food', quite in contrast with the Greeks and Armenians in Turcomania who gained their living by commerce and manufacture as the best carpets and silk of crimson and other colours are made here.[123] Nevertheless, Ibn-i Battuta noticed a brisk trade in horses carried on by these Turcomans, each of whom possessed numerous horses which were very cheap in the region. The livelihood of the Turcomans depended on the horses which were exported to India in droves of six thousand or so.[124] Yazdi says that foolishness and ignorance were the inevitable traits of the Turcoman temperament.[125]

The Turcomans played an important role in the history of the Uzbeg Khanates. There were many battles fought between the Kgwarai Mian Uzbegs and the Turcomans as the former considered them to be their subjects.[126] The Turcomans had to pay a tenth part of their crops to the Khan of Khwarazm. When Ubaidullah occupied Khwarazm in 1538, Sarts and Turcomans were left there as *Riaya* (subjects—sedentary agriculturists). The Turcomans also find mention, as allies or enemies, in the accounts of the Uzbegs campaigns in Merv, Iran and Khwarazm.

The Turcomans were a numerous people. Abul Ghazi's father, Timur Sultan who was one of the several chiefs, alone exercised authority over 5,000 to 6,000 families.[127] The Turcomans had a number of clans, important among whom were the Yazir, the Solor or Salir, the Sain Khani Turcomans, the *Qizil ayaqs,* Issu, and Yakka Turcomans.[128] Babur refers to the Bayandari, Talal, Bharlu and Qajar as amongst the chief Turcoman clans.[129] Like every other tribe they too had the same broad division of *Aq* and *Qara,* the black and white Quyunlu (sheep) Turcomans. Since these Turcomans occupied the entire western border of the Uzbeg Empire, their allegiance or hostility were of great importance for the Uzbegs.

The Turcomans had once helped Din Muhammad Uzbeg against Ubaidullah Khan and, as a reward had asked for Tarkhani for themselves and also equality with the Uzbegs. It is not certain whether these were granted, but they paid taxes to Ali Sultan Uzbeg in 1565.[130]

During the Persian campaigns of Ubaidullah and Abdullah Khan, the Turcomans often played an important role.

The Qirghiz

In Haider Dughlat's opinion, the Qirghiz were of the same stock as Mughals or Mongols. They separated from them on account of their repeated rebellions against the Mughal *Khaqans*. All the Mughals became Musulmans, but the Qirghiz continued to remain true to their old customs and were hostile to the converted Mughals.[131] Saifi, who happened to be in Central Asia in 1582, says that the Qirghiz were neither *kafir* nor Muslim (Mahmud Ibn-i Wali says that the Kirghiz were infidels), that they did not have a Khan but *Begs* who were called *Kashka,* as with the Kalmuks.[132] The Qirghiz were subdued as early as 1218 by Juji, after whose departure for the west, the Qirghiz region came under the sway of Tuli,[133] whose headquarters were at Orkhan (and later in Peking) which became a great cultural and commercial centre.

The Qirghiz tribe in one way or another played an important role ever since the ascendancy of Chingiz Khan and particularly in the sixteenth century, along with Qazaqs. When Sultan Said invaded Kashghar in 1514, the Qirghiz under Muhammad helped him against their ruler Aba Bakr; Muhammad was rewarded by being sent to Moghulistan. He subjugated and united the Qirghiz there and organized nomadic raids against Sairam and Tashkent. In one of these raids Muhammad was involved in a pitched battle with Abdullah, the son of Uzbeg Khan Kuchum. Abdullah was captured by Muhammad, who released him and sent him back with other survivors to the Uzbeg Khan, along with apologies and presents. This infuriated Sultan Said, he invaded Muhammad's territories in 1517 and later threw him into prison for five years. The leadersless then retreated, joining Mansur in Chaligh Qirghiz often plundered Turkestan, Sairam, onwards, and Akhsi and carried into bondage many Muslim women and children.[134] The Qirghiz fought a number of wars (1522-4) against the Kalmuks. From 1511 onwards the Qirghiz made it impossible for the Mughals to live in Moghulistan which led to several wars between the two. The Mughals were already short of suitable pastures and grazing grounds in Kashghar, and thus planned a campaign against the Qirghiz in 1520. Muhammad Sultan was released and sent along with Rashid against the Kirghiz of Moghulistan. In the meantime Babajak Sultan attacked them.[135] Most of the Qirghiz joined the Uzbegs to save themselves from the onslaught of the Mughals. Henceforth it became impossible to punish the Qirghiz for fear of inciting the Uzbegs. Tahir Khan the Mongol leader then took them to Atbashi.[136]

Rashiduddin attributes 70,000 *khanawars* to Tartars whose *yurt* extended in the Chinese Turkestan (*Wilayat-i-Khatai*) with their headquarters at Manza uir Navwar. They were earlier subservient to

Chinese rulers. Since the Yasaq of Chingiz Khan was then unknown to them, they suffered from jealousy, anger and rancour. Since in the past they outnumbered and surpassed other Turks in the grandeur, all the Turkish tribes had adopted their name in the same way as all of them had now accepted the name Mongol seeing the ascent of Chingiz, and his, family. The Tartar women were much in demand and Chingiz, his family, and even the nobles sought their wives from Tartar tribes. The Tartars held high positions of exegete during region of Chingiz Khan and afterwards.[137]

In 1558, the Qirghiz again threatened Kashghar.[138] Haider Dughlat calls the Qirghiz 'the revening lions of Moghulistan'[139] and 'originators of all the revolts'. Even within Central Asia, they organized rebellions against Abdullah Khan in Aqsu in support of the Samarqand Sultans,[140] and in Farakat.[141] The Qirghiz were thus often a source of danger for the Uzbegs.

Tartars and Turks

After the disintegration of the Golden Horde and its division into independent, separate States, the word 'Uzbeg' disappeared from southern Russia and came to be applied only to those tribes which had reached Turkestan and Transoxiana. The Russians always used the name Tartar for the Golden Horde till the fifteenth-sixteenth centuries, identifying them as Crimean, Kazan, Astarakhan and Siberian 'Tartars'. Even the Ottomans, after subjugating Crimea in 1475, called its inhabitants the Crimean Tartars, though these Tartars preferred to call themselves Turks. The Russians began to use the word Tartar in the wide sense and 'Radloff often used it for Uzbegs or generally, to denote the Turkish speaking population of Central Asia. On the Upper Volga, however, the local intelligentsia finally adopted the name Tartar hence—later on we read of the Tartar Republic.'[142]

In Persian sources, too, the term Mongol of Tartar, and occasionally, Turko-Tartar, is used in a fluid sense, the word Tartar denoting Mongols or usually Turks. Although the Tartars rebelled under Timur and were ruthlessly suppressed by him and his successors, they do not seem to have been an effective opposition group under the Uzbegs presumably because they were of the same stock.

In the old Turkish language the word 'Sart' denotes merchants and its in this sense that this word has been used in Kuitadgu bilk bilkand in Mahmud Kashghari. The term 'Sart' is not found in the earlier sources, which refer only to Sartawul, Sartak, Sartaktan, etc., indicating Persians, not only traders but also cultured folk, irrigation specialists, etc. In medieval sources the term 'Sart' came to be used to denote settled Turkish speaking urban populations as distinct from the Tajiks and the nomadic Turks.[143] The word 'Sart' is probably derived from the Sanskrit word '*Sartavaha*' (leader of a trading caravan), who monopolized trade between nomads and Indians.[144] Whereas the Tajiks were Persian speaking and often settled as an agrarian community 'not entitled to sovereign rights' and 'alien to the methods of warfare',[145] the Sarts excited no such comments from chroniclers as they never had a regal past or present claims.

According to Mahmud Kashghari, the Sarts were the old trading community, admixture of Turks and Iranians, who resembled Tajiks although they usually spoke Chaghatai Turkish and were settled in Central Asia. Shergul found them lagging in education and culture, though they were forward in accumulating wealth.[146] Abul Ghazi applies the name Sart to the urban Central Asian in contrast to Uzbegs, Qirghiz and Turcomans, etc. Babur also used the word to indicate difference between Sarts and nomadic populations, and in the sense of a settled people. Brestchneider points out that the Chinese annals often used the term 'Sart' to denote Muslims.[147] Contradictory views are given by modern historians regarding the Sarts. Krader says that the Uzbegs and Qazaqs on settling down in farming communities came to be known as Sarts, in addition to the Tajiks who had long been so called.[148] Von Schwarz applies the term Sart to both sedentary and nomadic populations. Aristov calls them 'aboriginal' Turkish people different from Uzbegs not on an ethnographic or linguistic basis but in their socio-economic standards and way of life. Radloff says that the Sarts were a Turkish speaking urban population of Central Asia. Barthold's view, that the Mongols borrowed the word 'Sart' from Turks and that it did not signify any tribal or racial entity but only denoted merchants in general whether of Iranian or Turanian, Turkish or Mongolian origin, seems to be convincing. Barthold proves ably that the words *Sartawul, Sartaktai,* etc., were connected with the Sarts. Since the Turks were also involved in trade after the eleventh century, they too were included by Barthold in the Sart group,[146] though elsewhere he refers to the fact that most commercial activities were undertaken by the Tajiks.[150]

NOTES

1. V.V. Barthold, *Sochinenija*, V, Moscow, 1968, pp. 266-9; Barthold, *Sochinenya*, II, parts I, II, Moscow, 1963,1964; Ivanov Peter, *Ocherki pa istori*, Sredni Azi, Moscow, 1958; Lawrance Krader, *Peoples of Central Asia*, The Hague, 1966; Czaplica, *The Turks of Central Asia*, Oxford, 1918; N. Elias, Introduction, Eng. tr., *The Tarikh-i-Rashidi*, Patna, 1973, pp. 1-128; other eminent scholars who have done valuable work on the subject are: M. Wahabov, *Formirovanya Uzbegskovo Naroda*, Tashkent, 1961; *Ethnografichesk*, Ocherki, Moscow, 1962, I, II, edited by Tolstova Janko et al. Semenov, *K Vaprosu o proiskhazdeniya sostava Uzbegov Shaibani Khane, Material pa Istori*, Tajikove Uzbegov Sredni Azi, Stalinabad, 1954.
2. *T. Banakiti*, pp. 341-2; *Abdullahnama*, I, ff. 15-25; *T. Guzida*, pp. 562-80; *Jamiut Tawarikh*, pp. 40-71; *Aughuzu' lonqova wa Shaibani Nama*, MS no. IOST, *Oghuz Nama*, MS no. 185, IV; *Medieval Researches*, II, pp. 68-9; Dorji Banzarova, *Sobranija Sochinenija*, Moscow, 1955, pp. 178-86.
3. Ibn-i-Arab, Eng. tr., p. 78.
4. *Jamiut Tawarikh*, pp. 26-7, 47, 58, 62-71, 111-12, 129, 165-78; *T. Guzida*, pp. 563-73; Banakiti, pp. 341, 568-9; *Abdullahnama* I, ff. 15-16; *Tarikh-i Rashidi*, Eng. tr., Introd., pp. 80-90; Frye, pp. 111-13; E.H. Parker, *A Thousand Years of the Tartars*, London, 1895, pp. 303-4.
5. *T. Guzida*, pp. 562-80, Banakiti, pp. 341, 568-9; *Jamiut Tawarikh*, pp. 147-71; *JT*, pp. 24, 28, 110-12, 218; *Abdullahnama*, I, pp. 15-25; Bretschneider, *Medieval Researches*, Vol. II, pp. 68-9; Frye, pp. 113-15.
6. For an interesting account on Turks see Claude Cahen, pp. 1-15, preface.
7. Lamb, p. 78.
8. Banakiti, pp. 360-1.
9. *Abdn*, pp. 9-29.
10. *Sochinenija*, V, pp. 205, 208; also see Richard N. Frye, *Bukhara: The Medieval Achievement*, Norman, 1965, pp. 112-19.
11. Rashiduddin Fazlullah, *Jamiut Tawarikh* I, Tehran, 1338, pp. 47-71; also see Louis Bazin, 'Reflecions sur le Probleme Turco-Mongol', *Turcica*, Vol. XV, 1983, pp. 31-58; A.S. Kent, *The Call of Tartary*, Shanghai, 1919, pp. 4-7, 34-6, 42-50, 57-64; Suhraev, *Bukhara*, XIX-XX, Moscow, 1966, pp. 113-80. For details see Ignaz Goldziher, *Muslim Studies*, p. 245; Lewis Bernard, *Islam from the Prophet Muhammad to the Capture of Constantinople*, II, USA, 1974, pp. 207-28.
12. A dialect spread in the Zar Afshan valley, Qashqa darya region, between Samarqand and Khulj and part of Farghana and Tashkent, in Semireche, Chinese Turkestan in the trade colonies on the Silk Road in fourth-tenth centuries. The Sughdi alphabet were borrowed from Aramaic. In the first quarter of eighth century Sughdi was still the main language since Narshakhi says that in 713 Bukharians spoke both Sughdi and Arabic. Sughdi was preserved as an 'international trade language' in ninth-tenth centuries. Majority of the population had taken to the Tajik language as Muqaddasi at the end of tenth century still noticed the widespread use of Sughdi in the environs of Bukhara and Samarqand, and it continued to be used till thirteenth-fourteenth centuries in the hilly regions. Nevertheless the Turkicization of the Sughdi settlements in Semireche and Chinese Turkestan ended in complete disappearance of Sughdi

language. For details cf. *Ethnoocherki* I, pp. 135-8; Borovkov, *Vaprosi izuchenija turkoyazichni epaz narodi Sredni Aziie Qazugstan; Vaprosi Izuchenija epaza narodov* SSr, Moscow, 1958, pp. 66-100; for detailed study of Turkish speaking peoples of Central Asia and Qazaqstan cf. Ibn-i Hauqal.

13. *BN*, text, p. 2, Eng. tr., p. 4, also see *TR*, Eng. tr., p. 394; also see *Majma-ul Arqam*, text, p. 11, tr., p. 34; Frye, pp. 114-16, 185, 190.
14. Yezdi also refers to Turkish and Persian languages existing in Timurid court. *ZN*, I, p. 19.
15. Cf. A. Juwanmardaev, XVI-XIX *asrlarda Farghanada Yir Suv Mas'alalarida dair*, Tashkent, 1965.
16. Barthold, *Sochinenija*, IV, Moscow, 1966, pp. 343-65.
17. *Sochinenija*, III, Moscow, 1965, pp. 118-20; *Sochinenija*, V, pp. 162-209.
18. *Badaiul Waqai*; Dorji Banzarov (1822-55), *Dorji Banzarov*, *Sabranija Sochinenija*, Moscow, 1955, p. 208. Also see *Sochinenija*, VIII, pp. 205-9.
19. *Islam*, pp. 58-9. Also see Bonvalot, p. 246; for a detailed account of Arabs in Central Asia (nineteenth-twentieth centuries), see *Ethno*. II, pp. 582-96.
20. Ibn-i Khaldun, *Muqaddimah*, Vol. II, p. 307. For interesting details on early Arab settlement in Farghana and surrounding districts see Claude Cahen, *Ore Ottoman Turkey*, London, 1960-7.
21. Yezdi, *ZN*, I, pp. 25, 26, 71; *ZN*, II, p. 197. Vol. I, 2nd edn., 1349 AH, p. 68; *TR*, Eng. tr., pp. 137-8; also see Tura Khwaja b. Ziauddin, *Miratu'l futuh*, MS Asiatic Museum.
22. According to the *T. Guzida*, pp. 563-73, 580 and *Turkish Dictionary of Vakif Pasha*, the *Ulus* was divided into *English* (lit. comradeship) and El into Aimaqs with further subdivisions into *boi* and *urchiki*.
23. For a detailed description of Yurt see N. Znagvaral, *The Mongolian People's Republic*, Ullan Bator, 1956, pp. 22-3.
24. Marco Polo, *Travels*, pp. 90-1; Ibn-Battuta, pp. 142-7; John Smith, *Purchas*, VIII, pp. 337-9.
25. John Smith, pp. 337-9; for a detailed and very interesting account of various nomadic camps (*Yurts, Kibiteki*) and their construction cf. G.P. Vasileva and Makhova, *Programme Sbora Materiala pa shelishe selskoi nasileniya, Material K Istori Ethnograhicfeskoma atlasu*, Moscow, 1961, pp. 110-36; Ralph Rox, *Peoples of the Steppes*, London, 1925, pp. 154-5; Zhagovaral, pp. 22-4.
26. B.A. Obruchev, *Pa Gorame Pustiniyam Sredni Azi*, M-L 1948, pp. 18-19; Berg, *Pa Ozeram Sibiri e Sredni Azi*, Moscow, 1955. For an interesting account of these Yurts see Abbot, *Genghis Khan*, New Delhi, 1975, p. 24.
27. Yuldasheva, *Kistori Targovikhe Pasolskikh Svyazi Sredni Azi sa Rassiye*, Tashkent, 1964, pp. 7-9. Abbot, p. 31. Arabian Hoyy seem to be an equivalent to Khanwars.
28. N. Prejevalsky, *Mongolia*, tr. Delmar Morgan, Vol. II, p. 53.
29. See *Matla*, p. 717.
30. *TR* II, p.161.
31. For Beg see *Soch*. V, p. 502; *Ethno*, p. 173, *Ethno Glossary*, p. 707, for comments on Bai see Barthold V, p. 49.
32. D.E. Tikhonov, *Termin EL e Budun va drevnikh Uighurskikh documentakh*, Issledovaniya pa Istorii Kulturi Narodov Vastoka, Leningrad, 1960, pp. 250-5.

33. *Ethno*, pp. 314, 717; *Encyclopaedia of Islam* 1092 *Ain*, I, p. 506.
34. In Southern Mongolia four Aimaqs have been mentioned each after the name of their Khan. Similarly in Afghanistan too *Char Aimaqs* indicated four nomadic groups of people. *Soch* V, p. 489; Uzbegskoj-Russki Slavar, Moscow, 1959, p. 27, also see Banzarov, pp. 182-3.
35 *ZN*, I, pp. 30-3, 45, 53, 65, 100, 133, 160-3, 173.
36. *Ethno*, p. 173, also Glossary, pp. 707, 713.
37. Ivanov, pp. 23-4.
38. *Istorija Uzbegskoj*, p. 349; Barthold, V, pp. 396-7.
39. *TR*.
40. See *ZN*, I, p. 520; *ZN*, II, pp. 407-9, 450, 497; *Matla*, III pp. 34, 50, 54, 56; *Haft Aqlim* II, p. 35.
41. For an explanation of these terms see infra 'System of Taxation'.
42. *BN*, tr., p. 55; text, p. 33.
43. *Rodoslavanya Turk* I, p. 210; II, p. 225; *Soch* II, pp. 594-5; Abul Ghazi says that the tribes namely Ali and Tiviji paid the taxes on cattle and the tribe Adakal was to supply *naukars* to the Khan. Abul Ghazi, op. cit., II, p. 338; Barthold, *Sochinenija*, III, p. 78.
44. Babur, *Mubaiyyan*, MS Institute of Oriental Studies, AN SSR, nos. 1-104, ff. 56-8, 98.
45. *Rauzat*, p. 359.
46. Clavijo, pp. 186-7
47. *Haft Aqlim* II, p. 36.
48. *Abdn*, p. 262.
49 Cf. *Istorija Uzbegskoj*, p. 349.
50. See *Matla*, II, III, p. 416.
51. *Insha-i Abul Fazl*, Newal Kishore edn.; *AN*, III, Eng. tr.
52. Kradar, p. 157.
53. *Abdn*, p. 262.
54. See *ZN*, I, pp. 258, 302-4, 442, 468, 487, 543-4; *ZN*, II, pp.34-7, 357-9; 409-10, 417, 448-9; *IA*, Eng. tr. pp. 198-200, 213; Gulbadan, pp. 88-9; *BN*, Eng. tr., pp. 145, 160-3, 228, 250-3; *Matla*, II, pp. 1410, 1429; *Matla* II, iii, pp. 357-60, 371-4, 416-19, 421.
55. See *ZN*, I, p. 119; *Abdn*, pp. 160, 199, 380-1; *Rauzat*, p. 359.
56. Qirghiz had only once carved an empire, Spuler, *Muslim World*, pp. 239-42; also see *Manas*, pp. 1-112, *Soch* II, I, pp. 479-543.
57. *Purchas* XII, pp. 4-6; also see *Vaprosi Izucheniya epaza Narodov SSR*, Moscow, 1958, p. 85.
58. *Abdn*, pp. 380-1, see also *Rauzat*, p. 359.
59. Ibid., p. 160.
60. Ibid., p. 199.
61. Ibid., pp. 475, 482.
62. Ibid., p. 160.
63. Ibid., pp. 363, 483.
64. Ibid., pp. 122-42.
65. *Abdn*, pp. 417-20.
66. Ibid., p. 105.
67. *TR*, Eng. tr. pp. 153, 156.

68. Ibid., pp. 97-9; *Abdn*, p. 43.
69. Ibid.
70. *BN*, Eng. tr., p. 221, text, p. 140.
71. *BN*, pp. 2, 98, 105 fn. 2, 172, 362; *Abdn.* text, p. 64; for details cf. *TR*, p. 357.
72. *BN*, text, p. 64; Eng. tr., pp. 104-5, 254-5.
73. *TR*, Eng. tr., p. 148.
74. *TR*.
75. *BN*, pp. 104-5; also see Isfahani, p. 167.
76. *Matla*, pp. 386-9.
77. *BN*, Eng. tr., p. 140; text, p. 90.
78. Ibid., p. 64; *TR*, tr., pp. 261-2.
79. *TR*, Eng. tr., p. 358.
80. Ibid., p. 358.
81. *BN*, pp. 19, 20, 23, 101, 155, 161; *TR*, pp. 307-9.
82. *TR*, p. 308.
83. Juveni, text, p. 242; Eng. tr., pp. 505-6; Rashiduddin, p. 177.
84. *JT*, Vol. I, pp. 502-3.
85. Ibid., p. 82.
86. *BN*, Eng. tr., pp. 100, 155.
87. *TR*, Eng. tr., p. 242. Chingiz the '*Ssutu Bogdo*' (the god sent) had inculcated in them a new feeling of racial pride by detaining them, as Koko Mongols (the Heavenly Blue Mongols). Prawdin, pp. 86-7.
88. *TR*, Eng. tr., pp. 261-2.
89. Ibid., pp. 351, 307; Prawdin, pp. 86-8.
90. *BN*, text, p. 10; Eng. tr., pp. 19-20, 350.
91. *BN*, pp. 350-1.
92. *TR*, p. 156.
93. *TR*, tr., pp. 191-3, 241.
94. *FS*, I, pp. 157-8.
95. Khwand Mir says that this history was written by Shahrukh's literatures in the name of Ulugh Beg (*HS* III, p. 4; *FS* II, p. 136).
96. *TR*, tr., p. 148; Introduction, pp. 72-98 by N. Elias deals at length with these anomalies of nomenclature.
97. *BN*, Eng. tr., p. 320; also cf. fn. 2. *Taimurnama*, Eng. tr., p. 172.
98. *Mehn*, pp. 145-6, 156, 260; *IA*, p. 194; *TR*, Eng. tr., p. 172.
99. *TR*, Eng. tr., pp. 148-9; *Muzzakkira*, p. 89; Wasifi, old edn., p. 1114, also see *Mehmannama*, p. 260; Sanders, *IA*, Eng. tr., Appendix 333, XVI, also p. 33, XVI; *Ethno Ocherki* 171; *FS*, II, pp. 10-11; *Soch* V, pp. 169, 211-12; B. Lewis, Pehat & Schacht, *Encyclopaedia of Islam*, Vol. II, pp. 2-4.
100. Ibid.
101. *TR*, Eng. tr., pp. 148-9. For similar usage of the term *Chaghatian* see Badauni, I, Eng. tr., pp. 464, 572, 574 fn. 6, 575-6, Riazul Islam, *Calendar*, p. 422, *Maasir-ul Umara* II, pp. 429-37.
102. *Letters and Historical Documents*, f. 34.
103. Clavijo, pp. 190-1.
104. *IA*, Eng. tr., p. 4.
105. See *IA*, pp. 198-200, 313; *ZN*, I, pp. 302-4, 468, 487; *ZN*, II, pp. 34-7.

106. *Soch* V, p. 172.
107. *TR*, Eng. tr., p. 173.
108. Clavijo, pp. 195-6.
109. *TR*, Eng. tr., p. 206.
110. *Badaiul Waqai*, p. 1114.
111. *Abdn*, p. 181; *Muzzakkira*, p. 45.
112. Mirza Badi, p. 94.
113. Shergul, pp. 78-80; also see *FS*, III, pp. 91-170.
114. Shahnawaz Maasir, I, Eng. tr., p. 565.
115. Juvani, text, p. 242; Eng. tr. pp. 505-6; Rashiduddin, p. 177.
116. *JT* I, pp. 502-3.
117. *JT* I, p. 82.
118. *Ain Blochmanur*, pp. 480-1.
119. *Maasir-ul Umara*, Vol. I, Patna, 1979, p. 565; *AN* I, Eng. tr., pp. 178, 190.
120. Whssaf, p. 558.
121. *TR*, p. 294.
122. Ibn Khaldun, *Muqaddimah*, Vol. I, tr. From Arabic by Franz Rasuthal, New York, 1958, p. 295.
123. Marco Polo, p. 24.
124. Ibn Battuta, p. 145, for detailed description of horse trading cf. Ibn Battuta, p. 145; Marco Polo, p. 623.
125. *ZN*, I, p. 197.
126. *Histoire des Mongols*, text, p. 207, II, p. 221; *Soch* II, pp. 598-623.
127. Abul Ghazi, p. 253.
128. *FS*, III, pp. 130-8; *Tarikh-i Jahankusha-i Nadiri*, f. 4.
129. *BN*, pp. 49, 211-79.
130. *Rodoslovnaya Turka*, Vol. I, p. 1225, Vol. II, p. 241; *Soch*, Vol. II, pp. 585-623.
131. *TR*, Eng. tr., p. 148. According to Kent 'Kirghiz or eastern Kirghiz were trust representatives of Turanian turks (Kir-cultivated fields), agriculturists at least from sixth century. All Kirghiz were related by inter-marriage . . . quite a different nation. It must be noted that Kirghiz occurs also as a clan name among Uzbegs and Attains', Kent, pp. 48-9; Prawdin, p. 80.
132. Abdul Karim Bukhari, *Histoire de l'Asie Centrale*, ed. Schefer 16, Paris, 1876, pp. 302-3; *Soch* V, p. 216; *Manas*, pp. 143, 158; Kent says they were called Manap and Aga Manap (Kent, pp. 49-50).
133. *Soch* II, p. 517 for a detailed early history of Qirghiz and analogies between Qirghiz and Altaic people see Abramson, *Ethnographic ties of Kirghiz with Altaic People*, Moscow, 1960, pp. 1-15.
134. *Rauzat*, p. 326.
135. *TR*, Eng. tr., pp. 124-6, 254, 339, 348, 358, 367, 377-9, 388; also see *Soch* II, p. 511.
136. *TR*, Eng. tr., pp. 349-51, 358, 367-8, 377, 379, 388; also see *Soch* II, pp. 48-56, 511-19; *Manas*, pp. 142-4, 159-69, Abramson, pp. 1-25.
137. Rashiduddin, p. 157, for details information on Mongol-Tartar relations see Rashiduddin, pp. 58-71.
138. *TR*, Eng. tr., p. 254.
139. Ibid., pp. 124-6.

140. *Abdn*, pp. 260-1.
141. Ibid., pp. 481-3; *T. Sh.*, pp. 76-7.
142. *Soch*, V, pp. 142-4.
143. The term *Sart* has been used in the same sense in sources, e.g. *T. Shahrukhi*, p. 193.
144. *Soch*, II, pp. 310-14, 527-9.
145. Yezdi.
146. Shergul, pp. 50-90, 81; Mahmud Kashghari I, p. 91.
147. Bretschneider, Vol. I, pp. 268-9.
148. *Soch*, V, p. 109; Wheeler, p. 41.
149. *Soch*, V, p. 110; *Soch*, Vol. II, part II, pp. 310-14; also see Bretschneider, Vol. I, pp. 268-9.
150. *Soch*, II, part II, pp. 310-14; Wheeler, p. 41.

Agriculture and Agrarian Relations of Central Asia

The agrarian relations subsisting in the various states of medieval East, Central and South Asia offer interesting comparisons. The theoretical origins in Islamic law and the common terminology (the result of a close mutual intercourse and territorial annexations by one state at the expense of another) assist us in examining the conditions in each state, while there must, of course always be pitfalls in assuming that a particular term had the same connotation in one country as in another.

The Uzbeg Khanates in the sixteenth-seventeenth centuries appear to have represented a regime of transition. The rulers, themselves of nomadic or semi-nomadic origins, were called upon to govern a highly developed agricultural region. It was worth asking who won out, the settled agrarian order or the dissolving influence of nomadism. There are also other phenomena which, to a student of Indian history, would seem strange (unless one bears in mind the large temple grants of southern India), namely the large amount of land under the control of religious establishments. And yet the basic instrument of surplus extraction, i.e. the land tax, would seem quite familiar to any Indian historian.

It is generally assumed by most modern, historians that the steppe tribes who were known as Uzbegs and who had established themselves in Central Asia under the leadership of Shaibani Khan after displacing the Timurids were only half way through civilization. Before invading Central Asia, these tribes do not seem to have been very familiar with the advanced technique of agriculture and had mainly engaged in cattle breeding. Qazvini praises their pastures and plains (*shahari wa alfazaraha*) and categorically states that most of the steppe inhabitants were nomads (*sahra nashin*) and only a smali portion of people and the country was settled.[1] The same source states that most of the lands of the Uzbegs were deserts or plains, with only limited production of grain. Although millet and other edible grains were grown in some abundance in summer, grapes and melons were rare and cotton was not cultivated. Pastures, with access to water, and cattle formed the basis of their subsistence. While describing the characteristics of his Uzbeg kinsmen (viz., the sons of the Khan, Sultans, notables and elders of the Dasht-i-Qipchaq), Shaibani is reported to have said that, as soon as they reached puberty and achieved maturity, their entire effort was directed towards collecting herds of sheep which enabled them to amass worldly wealth in a short time. In addition, they were also interested in acquiring booty and thus they became *bais* and *bai-i-kalan* (rich magnates) rapidly.[2]

Historians of the early fifteenth and sixteenth centuries frequently refer to plundering excursions which were an established means of earning one's livelihood or a temporary engagement, till one attained power during the hard days (*darzaman-i-qazaqi*).

While giving a description of the Dasht-i-Qipchaq, the region where Shaibani was born, Binai Harwi and Isfahani mention its pastures, trees and flowers,[3] and Isfahani appreciates the fertility, prosperity and populousness of the region.[4] A modern Uzbeg historian, Bori Ahmedov, writes that the *ushr* tax was realized from the settled population of the steppe,[5] but he does not mention any source for this information. Elsewhere *yasaq* is mentioned as the most common tax of the time and it was realized by the *basqaqs* of Khans through enumeration. Hamza Bi Manghit's invasion of Uzgand and the realization of its *hasilat* by him is also described in the sources. Such stray information also confirms the existence of a few agricultural fields. The possibility is that at best only a small section of the Uzbeg population might have been engaged in agriculture. Bori Ahmedov goes on to assert that the Uzbegs indulged in frequent raids not only to secure booty but also for the acquisition of rich agricultural regions; and that they had individual ownership of lands, pastures, buildings and water.[6] However, again, no source has been quoted for this conclusion. The Uzbegs were undoubtedly in search of green pastures and water since these two were extremely essential for their nomadic life. Even as early as the second half of the sixteenth century there existed a struggle for pastures amongst the Uzbegs, Qazaqs, Kalmuks and Manghits in the steppes. It seems plausible that either a pressing need for pastures attracted the Uzbegs towards Khwarazm and Turkestan, or that their chiefs were increasingly drawn to the luxuries that the possession of the agricultural regions might yield. But it would be far fetched to suppose that the people of the steppes were shifting completely to agriculture and so sought agricultural lands.

But once the conquest of Central Asia had occurred, the rulers, in spite of their nomadic origins appear to have seen the connection between continuous agricultural production and their own wealth and power. Maulana Isfahani, writing in the first decade of the sixteenth century, describes the strenuous efforts made by Shaibani Khan to improve agriculture.[7] The steps taken by the early Shaibanids for the promotion of agriculture also show that at least a section of the Uzbegs had begun to interest themselves in the essentials of an agricultural society.[8]

It is possible that, while adapting themselves to the needs of an agricultural society, the Uzbeg rulers also initiated a process whereby their ordinary nomadic followers were gradually assimilated with the local population. The Uzbeg conquerors had appeared in Central Asia not in large hordes but in limited numbers, but leading vast forces comprising heterogeneous peoples. Simultaneously, they did not have any markedly advanced cultural traditions. It was no wonder, then, that the process of assimilation was hastened. The Uzbegs gave their tribal name Uzbegs to the whole population of the lands subjugated by them. In turn, they themselves probably began to take to settled life. The common Turkish language also helped this process of assimilation.[9]

The background of the Uzbegs as well as their performance in the earlier days was by no means conducive to the development of an agricultural economy. The accounts of contemporary historians are, therefore, full of complaints against Uzbeg atrocities and nomadic reprisals in the first few years of their regime. The Qirghiz, Qazaqs, Qara Qirghiz created trouble for the new Uzbeg rulers who, in return, attempted to destroy these nomadic opponents. Religious persecution in the Persian Empire, as well as the pressure of population in the steppes, turned the nomads towards the richer lands of Central Asia. This not only created an economic crisis but a cultural tug of war, ending in a temporary retrogression. The nomadic Turkish traditions were revived to a great extent with the inflow of nomadic elements. But this was a temporary phase which ended with the ascendancy of Ubaidullah Khan, whose campaigns in Persia neutralized the nomadic elements and revived the traditional culture of Central Asia.

A conflict between pastoralism and agriculture must certainly have occurred at some time. The Uzbeg leaders were first given *yurts* on the banks of rivers in the rich agricultural regions such as Zarafshan, Qashqa darya, and the Surkhan darya valleys, and a large number of them settled on the banks of the Oxus. In this process of settlement, some damage must have been caused to agriculture because it was necessary for the Uzbegs to convert arable lands into pastures for their cattle. The inhabitants of these regions suffered considerably and were forced to flee. While describing the northern side of Farghana, Babur says, 'at the present time all is desolate, no settled population whatever remaining, because of the Mughals and the Uzbegs'.[10] Abdussalam also refers to another tract of fifty *tanabs* of land which was destroyed and turned desolate due to Uzbeg incursions.[11] Constant wars in Central Asia, the plundering habits of the Uzbegs and their nomadic raids might also have affected agricultural life adversely.[12]

But the Uzbegs soon realized their error and, after the second conquest of Central Asia, their love for booty and spoils was restrained by their desire to creating an empire. They tried to encourage cultivation and also to rejuvenate the crippled economy through various methods. Within one decade, their efforts were partly rewarded. Wasifi, who visited Central Asia during the second decade of the sixteenth century, gives a vivid description of its relative prosperity in spite of the famine which had broken out in Central Asia in 1512-13. But quite a large portion of the Uzbeg tribal population seems to have still retained its nomadic habits. The process of settlement continued throughout the sixteenth and seventeenth centuries (if not up to the nineteenth century as believed by certain historians). According to some Soviet scholars the fact is proved by the evolution of a new term, *qishlaq nashin* (nomads turning to settled life), which came into vogue towards the end of sixteenth century by analogy with the two terms, i.e. *sahra nashin* (nomads) and *deh nashin* (the settled people), thereby denoting such Uzbegs as had started learning agriculture and become settled people.[13] The nomadic element howsoever sparse was present in the Uzbeg Empire even in the second half of the sixteenth century during the reign of Abdullah Khan. Barthold writes that the rule of Abdullah was beneficial to the settled population only because the nomads were still very diffident about a strong Central Government.[14] While writing in 1831-4, Burnes noticed an Uzbeg tribe called Lakay who were 'celebrated for their plundering propensities. A saying amongst them curses everyone who died in bed and not in forays, *chupao*'. They lived near Hesar. Their women also accompanied them and helped plundering even passing caravans.[15] Later ethnographic studies confirm the account of Burnes.[16] All this indicates that stray elements of nomadism in the Central Asian population were not completely eliminated and the tribal characteristics continued to dominate the mode of life of some of the Uzbegs long afterwards. Ivanov[17] suggests that Uzbegs' nomadic characteristics had disappeared for they were forced into textile and other handicrafts from cattle breeding and their pauper kinsmen soon found settled economy to be a sure way of removing economic crises. The nomadic dependants quickly followed richer kinsmen in wars and pursuits for booty and other benefits. Their ejection from their homeland was also a result of the struggle for pastures among Uzbegs, Qazaqs Nogai, Oirats (Kalmuks).

While discussing the agrarian conditions one must also bear in mind the geographical drawbacks of the region—even though it may not be a *natura maligna* par excellence. As has already been described, three quarters of Central Asia is a desert region with arid and semi-arid low lands notwithstanding the large rivers rising in the well-watered peripheral high lands and losing themselves in the desert sands or in Aral Sea. They left their local settlements in the midst of unreclaimed deserts. The Kuhik water, for example, flowed along the north of Samarqand at the distance of some 4 miles. The river was sufficiently large but often the hot weather reduced it considerably. Babur complains that 'the river is large but not too large for its dwellings and its culture; during three or four months of the years, its waters do not reach Bukhara.[18] The oases are formed by the streams which are not more than twenty seven and all the water was and is absorbed in irrigation.'[19] Babur expresses his surprise over the fact that 'though water goes into the fort of Andijan by nine channels, none comes out at even a single place'.[20] Jenkinson noted that the 'water that serveth all the country is drawn by ditches out of the river Oxus unto the great destruction of the said river and all that land is likely to be destroyed and to become a wilderness for want of water when the river Oxus shall fail'. The Russian travellers of eighteenth and nineteenth century confirmed that his fears came true.[21]

The rainfall is higher in the mountains than on plains. The

precipitation is low and erratic for the rainfall on plains ranges from about 3 inches or 4 inches to about 6 inches increasing to 14 inches at Samarqand and Tashkent. Crops can be cultivated without irrigation in the mountain valleys, but not on the plains where pulses, fruits, rice and fodder all depend upon artificial water supply. In certain areas like the villages below Khujand, it was sometimes so cold that even irrigation channels were frozen along both the banks though because of its swift current it was not ice bound only in the middle. Thus the fertile areas wherein most of the population is found covered less than 15 per cent of the surface of Central Asia. Consequently alongside agriculture, the pastoralism supported by a large number of livestock continued in Central Asia.[22]

The medieval chroniclers are, however full of praise for Central Asian lands. Not only the natives of Transoxiana but the contemporary external historians also admire its prosperity. Amin Ahmad Razi, an Indian historian of sixteenth century boasts about the prosperity and populousness of Transoxiana saying that it surpasses many *wilayats* in its excessive production of grains, fruits, dry fruits, and abounds in cattle. Its population is also very large. One of the signs of its prosperity in the estimation of Razi was that famines never occurred here and if it did occur, never lasted long (*chandan napayad*).[23] According to Qazvani there were about 20,000 villages and cultivated and arable lands (*deh o mazraa*) in the entire Transoxiana.[24] The 'numerous gardens of Samarqand with abundant grains, grapes, fruits, melons' and 'unlimited cultivable lands of Farghana' have also been appreciated by Qazvini.[25] Ibn-i Hauqal says that in Transoxiana the fruits were produced in such an abundance that even cattle subsisted on them.[26] Thus inspite of the vast areas of steppes and deserts, there was a large enough agricultural zone in Central Asia to sustain agriculture and urban life.

The first cultural region in the basin of Syr was Farghana. The entire area between Aush and Andijan and the valley of Aqbura was well-irrigated. The Andijan torrent Aqbura rud goes to Andijan after having traversed the suburbs of Aush and the orchards lay along both its banks in Babur's time so that all the Aush gardens overlooked it. Farghana was thus the most fertile valley in Transoxiana being 'at the limit of settled habitation'.[27] Although Farghana was not a very large district, it abounded in grain and fruits. It had nine *tumans* (districts) like Andijan with plenty of grain and fruits particularly excellent grapes and melons.[28] The melons for some months served as the staple food of Turkestan. In the melon season, it was not customary to sell them out at the beds. Pears of high quality were grown in Andijan. In the mountains round Farghana there were excellent summer pastures.[29] A number of rivulets falling into Syr namely Bugan, Chayan, Arslanliḳ and others have been described by Hafiz Tanish. Babur also refers to the Aqbura rud as a 'broad tossing river' which falls from the Kurdun pass and 'was the mother of all the running water in Andijan area'. The rivulet Shahjui also flowed from Barakuh mountains. There was the famous clover meadow by the canal flowing from Barakuh hills.

Babur condemns Khujand as a 'poor place' where 'a man with two or three hundred followers would have a hard time'[30] due to its small revenue. Nevertheless it was described in other sources as a very attractive place with plenty of fruits, particularly melons and pomegranates. Its fruits were carried as gifts to other lands.[31] The almonds of Kandi Badam, a dependency of Khujand, were excellent and exported to India and Hormuz in Babur's time.[32] Its pomegranates though formerly as famous as Samarqand apples were less popular than those of Marghinan in the early sixteenth century. Towards the south and south west of Marghinan was Asfara which had running water, beautiful little gardens and orchards.[33]

The pomegranates particularly the sort known as Danaikalan and palatable apricot called 'Subḥani' was famous. There was the famous shady and delightful clover meadow near Aush.[34] From Kashan Akhsi water 'comes in the same way as Andijan water comes from Aush. Kashan had beautiful little gardens. These gardens lie along the bed of the torrent hence people call them the fine front of the coat.[35] The river Syr flowed passed both Khujand and Akhsi. There were *tabalghu* (the red willow) trees with red bark in the mountains of Farghana. Another plant was called *Mihrigiyah* (plant of love) having the qualities of mandrake is found in Yitikent. The melons of Akhsi were excellent, one of which known as Mir-i Timuri was estimated by Babur as better than the Bukhara melons.[36] Amongst the agricultural zones of the Uzbeg Empire, Turkestan was highly admired by Isfahani who says that most of the forts in Turkestan were populous and prosperous. Although there were very few houses, the fort of Arquq was so surprisingly prosperous that the large army of Shaibani was able to receive here all the corn it needed in the middle of winter (when there should have been scarcity) and collected sufficient provisions (*zawada*) from the houses without giving any chance to the people for complaints. The same amount of provisions if demanded from other *baldas* of Transoxiana, Khurasan, Iraq or Azarbaijan, could have been collected only with great difficulty and much harassment of the people.[37] The same chronicler speaks highly of the richness of Sighnaq. The 300 *farsakhs* land in Turkestan was made so fertile by Syr that there were pastures and reedbeds along its banks. Isfahani says that if there had been no Qazaq invasions, probably Turkestan would have been the most prosperous land in the world. There were excellent forests which provided nice hunting spree and a lot of firewood.[38]

The region of Sughdiana commonly known as Samarqand was called Simiz Kent (the rich town) by the Turks and the Mughals.[39] Surrounded on three sides by the mountain ranges, Samarqand stands in a fertile valley with aqueducts, running springs, square basins and round ponds,[40] i.e. plenty of water and consequently full of innumerable fruit orchards, groves, gardens with abundant grapes, melons, apples and pomegranates. Its grapes (*sahibi*) and its apples were particularly famous.[41] Babur refers to the Kuhik water flowing along the north of Samarqand at the distance of some four miles and the Darigham water flowing along the south at the distance of some two miles. The latter was like a large river cut off from the Kuhik water. All the gardens and suburbs and some of the Tumans of Samarqand were cultivated by it. By the Kuhik water a stretch of 30 to 40 *yagach* by road is made habitable and cultivated as far as Bukhara and Qarakul. The river Qarasu or *Ab-i Rahmat* passed through it a stream (with driving power) for perhaps seven or eight miles[42] and which was bordered by a quagmire. Samarqand was a land suitable for all kinds of grain and corn.[43] Samarqand is reported to have 10,000 *jaribs* of fertile lands (*zamin-i mamura*). From one of its gate up to one *farsang* in the interior of the city the area is full of gardens, pastures and corn fields. There were 12 *farsangs* of such cultivated places. Apart from the meadows, Samarqand had seven fertile suburban districts (Tumans) like *sughd* which was so green that in the words of Babur 'there was not one single *yigach* of earth without its villages and its cultivable lands'. Savdar was also abounding in waters. The arable land in Samarqand was suitable for the cultivation of most kinds of corn except buck wheat and soyabeans, wheat ripened in the fourth month. The people in the eartly thirteenth century had their own way of harvesting it—simply stacking it in heaps and fetching a little to grind as they required it.[44] In his geographical account of Transoxiana, Yeh Lui Chutsai says that Khujand (Khoqand) abounds in pomegranates . . . they are as large as two fists and of a sour sweet taste. Their water melons weigh fifty pounds and two are a load for a donkey'.[45] There were mines of gold, silver, copper and sal-ammoniac in Samarqand. Clavijo not only appreciates the excellent cotton growing lands, melon beds, fruit trees, rich vineyards and magnificent livestock beasts and poultry of fine breeds but also confirms that Samarqand was fertile in producing wheat in abundance. Kash also stood in a plain with surrounding lands well irrigated by stream and water channels. On these lands, 'five crops yearly of corn are grown-vines also and much cotton cultivation for the irrigation is abundant'.[46] There were two major canals in Kash which made the place green and full of gardens.[47] Ibn-i Battuta found Qarshi surrounded by gardens and water channels.[48] Babur, however, describes it as 'scantily supplied with water though beautiful in spring and its grain and melons were reputed'.[49] Both Maqdisi and Istakhri confirmed that the country of Bukhara was so copiously irrigated that no tall trees were to be found there, the grass was so high that a horse would disappear in it.[50] Babur describes Bukhara as a fine town with plenty of fruit orchards, excellent melons of various kinds having no match for their quality, variety and quantity being plentiful.[51] Bukhara plum was also 'famous and unique', which they skin dry and carry it from land to land as rarities (*tabarruklar bila)*.[52] Isfahani also appreciates the abundance of melons and grain in Bukhara.[53] Hasan Nisari Bukhari says that there was hardly any land left uncultivated (*zamin-i-bezara*).[54] Such was the fertility of Bukhara that even if someone possessed one only *jarib* of land he could spend a comfortable life along with his family and horde of relatives.[55] In Babur's time Qarshi was reputed for its grain and melons.

Marco Polo describes Shibarghan as being plentifully supplied with every kind of provisions, 'celebrated for best melons' in the world which are dried and sent to various 'neighboring countries' for sale as they are 'eagerly sought for'. Yuan Chwang found Balkh being 'rich' in natural products. In Juvaini's estimation, Balkh by reason of the multitude of its produce and its manifold kinds of revenue was superior to other regions; its territory was more spacious than that of other countries; and in former times, it was in the eastern land as Mecca in the west and called the abode of Islam[56] (*qubbat-ul Islam*). In early nineteenth century in Balkh, the fruits were so abundant that apricots and apples were sold 'almost below value as 2,000 could be purchased for a rupee'.[57]

In Qunduz, wheat and barley were produced. The place was marshy and there was snow for three months resulting in inundations. Rice grew only in those regions where there were no inundations.[58] In Badakhshan good wheat was grown and a species of barley without husk was also found.[59] In Taliqan 'a great market for corn was held, it being situated in a fine and fruitful country'.[60] The apricots, cherries and mulberries of Khulm are also described.[61] An excessive produce of gram is noticed in Merv. Both Qazvini and Sultan Muhammad record that if one maund of grain is sown it yields 100 maunds in the first year, 30 maunds in the second year and 10 maunds in the third year.

The town of Tashkent, earlier known as Banakat, Binakent, Chach, Sajor, Shash called by Firdausi as 'Bihishti kebek'[62] has been highly praised by Wasifi in the early sixteenth century for its fruit orchards and trees.[63] Zamain had running water, pastures, gardens though in Ibn-i Hauqal's time it was in ruins and its inhabitants had migrated to some other place.[64] While describing the campaigns of Abdullah Khan in Zamain, in the course of 1578, Hafiz Tanish describes it as a nice place with a water reservoir between Jizak and Zamain. Another 'pleasant spot with plenty of water and good air' called *yailma* is also referred to in *Abdullahnama*.[65]

Khwarazm is placed in the fifth climate and described as a cold country. The town had an abundance of dry fruits, grains and particularly melons.[66] These melons surpassed others in east and west except the Bukhara melon and after it, Isfanan melon. According to Walters, 'Tashkent denotes the country or domain of Shih or Tash' (or *chesh*—the personal name of the brother of Ts'ung ling (the ruler of Samarqand). Tash ruled over this province of Tashkent in sixth-seventh century. The land here was noted for its fertility and its grain crops made it the granary of the country. Among its products are enumerated cotton, silk woollen stuffs and articles of leather.

Apart from wheat, barley, rice, millet, coarse grain, juar and other grains were sown in large quantity. From amongst the beans, *mash*, and peas were grown. Much place was occupied by clover.[67] Most of the cultivable lands in Bukhara had melons and wheat and barley. Presumably there were two crops winter and autumn as the dates of the sale deeds are between October and May and they speak of the 'twice irrigated' barley and wheat (i.e. winter crop) with two irrigations to follow in autumn. One interesting document of sixteenth century leads one to conclude that wheat and barley was sown on cultivable lands in equal proportions. In the Bukhara region a bitumen (about one big Bukhara maund)[68] of wheat or barley in one *tanab* was sown. The *tanab* had different extensions at various time. The bitumen mentioned in this document was equal to 26.5 kg. If nineteenth century measurement of *tanab* is accepted then 100 kg of wheat and barley was sown in one hectare. About the extent of cotton and silk no detailed information is available except that Maulana Arif was once reported to be busy in cultivating cotton (*pamba kashtan* and *kirmaz panba kashtan*).[69] The documents in Hujjatlar show that the population in Qarasakan Adaq, Kizil Rabat and Gaukashana was engaged in cotton cultivation and rearing of silkworms.[70] Clavijo describes 'the cotton growing lands' in Samarqand and Shergul refers to the increased cultivation of cotton and dry fruits[71] caught up intensively due to its being a lucrative trade item. Perhaps cotton and silk remained to be narrow specializations till the nineteenth century as indicated by later sources.[72]

In the documents of the Juibari shaikhs, orchards of apples, figs, apricots, almonds, raisins, guavas, *shaftalu, zardalu, sanjid, zarak* are mentioned.[73] From amongst the ordinary trees, *qaraghaj* and silver poplar were raised. The big gardens were usually divided into small parts. Some gardens were specially planned to have one or two kinds of fruit plantations. Each new plantation as a single or whole was organized. There were tree lined streets with *hauz* and often nursery gardens (*tulistan)* for rearing saplings.[74] Gardens for the rearing of silkworms are described. In sixteenth century, mulberry trees were much valued. In the purchase deeds, the number of mulberry trees and vines were carefully specified. The black berries are also mentioned in the documents.[75] The mulberry trees were sown in the gardens in small numbers and in the vineyards. But there were separate big mulberry gardens also.[76] In one of the documents it is described that one village in Qarakul bought by Juibari shaikhs in 1561-3 comprised 690 mulberry trees in each of the 6 parts of the garden. Much in vogue was market gardening, truck farming, melon cultivation. In the outskirts of the big cities there were vine yards and gardens for marketing purposes which indicate that they were very big. Even those gardens which had fruit trees other than vines are called vineyards in the sources. The quality of grapes is usually described in the documents but the number of vines is not indicated.[77] There were different types of grapes like *khalili* (of Bukhara), *Qara khalili*[78] (Turkoman lands), Sahibi, Husaini, Babaki, Kuzaki, Shakarangur.[79] Abul Fazl in his *Ain* 28 speaks of Turani fruits and also supplies a list of Turani fruits with the season and prevalent rates.[80] The gardens, *chaharbagh*, irrigation of hundreds of *tanabs* of arable lands and fruit trees sown at the order of Khwaja Juibari with plenty of dates, lemon, apple, guavas, *injir, unnab, bihi, jauz* have also been described.[81]

During the sixteenth century, no change in the instruments seems to have occurred. In one of the sixteenth century documents yoke, wooden plough, shovel, spade are enumerated. The same are depicted in the miniature paintings. Rashhat mentions the striking of a *chak* (a kind of wooden fork with several prongs of branches to agitate corn so that the wind may clear it of the chaff or a wooden mallet used in taking cotton out of the pods (separating the grain from the chaff) by a group of *muzarian*.[82] The only progress noticeable was in the field of irrigation as a number of new canals are mentioned in the sources.

While referring to agrarian system in the Uzbeg Khanates, Hafiz Tanish states that in 'most of the countries of Iraq and Azerbaijan the fiscal affairs and transactions (*muamlat-i diwani*) are based upon *Tarikh-i-Ghazani*.[83] Although some short-term planning is also occasionally visible some continuity in financial system is noticeable. The basis of economy in Central Asia was agriculture. The basic social unit of the Central Asian peoples both Turkish and Iranian is the village. The nomadic village is called *aul*, the sedentary agricultural village *qishlaq*.[84] The village of the nomads was generally small consisting of ten or twelve tents which contracted and expanded to a considerable degree during the year relative to the annual nomadic round. The winter camp of the *aul* is *kystau*; here the entire kin village gathers. During the summer, the village is dispersed.

In form the *qishlaq* had a closely knit settlement pattern with usually fifty or more houses.[85] The sources refer to a number of words like *deh qariya*, to denote the villages. These *dehs* were usually in the outskirts of the city, just 2 or more *farsangs* away from the town or surrounding it. The villages were of different sizes. The big village (*deh-i buzurg*) consisted of a few *dehs* and pastures (*muzraa*).

Qazvini says that there were about 20,000 villages in Samarqand.[86] The author of *Almuta-ul Fakhra* says that the region known as Miyankal (lit. the places in between) lying in Zarafshan valley between Samarqand and Khatirchi (at the confluence of Aq darya and Qara darya) there were well irrigated and excellent agricultural lands and nice villages, etc.[87]

As described in the documents[88] a group of *dehs* constituted a *qasba*. Bukhara is reported to have consisted of a number of populous and prosperous *qariyas* (*qariya-i mamura)* in its environs[89] Jam had 212 *dehs* and Jablaqa 50 *dehs*.[90] Another village Pushto is said to have comprised a hundred houses.[91] Some were big village (*deh-i buzurg*) comprising several small *dehs*, e.g. *wabkani*, a *deh-i buzurg,* which was situated 3 *farsangs* away from Bukhara consisted of a few small *dehs* and cultivable lands (*muzaraa*).[92] Besides, new settlements each with small population and an adjacent bazaar sprang up as conveniently on each river bed, lake-side or temporary rain water ponds as they were swept away through adverse circumstances.[93] It seems that the fertility of the surrounding area helped in the establishment of villages. There were other forms of settlements also which included the nomadic settlements or military forts (*rabat*) near the towns. *Rauzat-ur Rizwan*[94] refers to the forts and settlements of Turcomans spreading over 27 forts and more than 1,000 *qariyas* between Merv up to Simnan and Bustam. Babur says that in the whole of the district (Samarqand) there was not a single village without its defences because of the Mughuls and the Uzbegs.[95]

Although a detailed account of the medieval villages is nowhere available, Burnes, who happened to be in Central Asia in 1831 gives some idea of the villages. According to him the village of Khwaja Salu gave 'a better sign of a more tranquil country' as 'each peasant's house standing at a distance from that of his neighbour and in the midst of his own fields'.[96] Obruchev and Berg also refer to 'small earthen cob-houses', or clay walled cottages 'resembling a kennel'.[97] The number of inhabited places was yet great, and each different settlement was surrounded by a wall of sundried brick as in Kabul but the 'houses were neither so neat nor so strong as in that country'. The regions in the heartlands of Central Asia showed at once 'the extreme of richness and desolation'. The strip of cultivated land on either bank of Kuhik did not exceed a mile in breadth and was often less for the desert pressed closely in upon the river. Burnes describes a village 'Meerabad' which was 40 miles away from Bukhara and in the district of Qarakul which consisted of 20 houses.[98] Further Burnes describes Heibuk as a 'thriving village' having a 'castle of sun dried bricks built on a commanding hillock'. The valley opened there and 'presented a sheet of gardens and most luxuriant verdure. The soil is rich and the vegetation wsh. The snakes and scorpions were more numerous than in India. The construction of the houses at Heibuk arrested our attention: they have domes instead of terraces, with a hole in the roof as a chimney; so that a village has the appearance of a cluster of large brown beehives. The inhabitants adopt this style of building as wood is scarce.'[99]

The people engaged in agriculture (*ashab-i zirat wa harasat*) formed one class of have-nots who had a certain unity amongst themselves, irrespective of their Tajik, Uzbeg or Turkish descent. The bond of common grievances was stronger than the difference in descent. Within the agricultural population, three categories of the peasants namely *riaya, karindahs* and *muzarias* have been mentioned. Occasionally the sources refer to the terms *sharik*[100] and *burzgar*. It seems that the terms *muzariah* (Arabic) and *karinda* were used for the lease holder or *metayer*. The *riaya* is often used in a wider sense denoting subjects or in a specific sense indicating tax paying peasants, elsewhere described as *raiyyat* or *raiyyat-i reza*.[101] While presenting a description of extensive landed property of Khwaja Mushtari, Abul Abbas states that it was not possible even to count the names of *muzarean* let alone the question of enumerating the *riayas* and *karindas*. The manner in which the author of the *Matlab-ut Talibain*[102] refers to the three categories of peasants, i.e. *riaya, karinda* and *muzari*, suggests that the *muzaris* were intermediaries as lease-holders or *metayors*, whereas the *rayas* seems to be of the category of lower peasants. The sixteenth century *yirliqs* of the grants of any form of lands usually refer to the officials, functionaries and the population (who should know about the order) and simultaneously include *riaya* and *muzari* in the list which goes to signify here that *riaya* was probably a separate independent group of peasants. Davidovich says that *riaya* signified the peasant community. *Rauzat-ur Rizwan* refers to certain Mirak who had assigned his agricultural lands to one or two *barzgars* to work for him (*ki az barai ishan kar mi kunand)*.[103]

Either the lands were assigned in *kadewari*, *muqataeh*[104] (fixed lease), *muzareah* (*metayage?*) or *ba qarar-i mubaiyyan* (declared agreement). The *kadewars* (lit. landlords, village headman, farmer, gardener) were those who held their personal property also but were dependent cultivators working as *muzaris*[105] on the lands of big landowners. *Waqf* document of 1326 shows that *kadewari* existed till the fourteenth century and the *kadewars* lived near the palace of the landlords and not in a separate place. They had only partial control over the land.[106] The relationship between the landlords, *muzari* and *kadewar* is not clearly defined and probably varied with the agreement. Similarly the details about the agreement with the *sharik* are also not given. *Rashhat* refers to a certain Khwaja Ibrahim who had started agricultural activities in collaboration with someone (*ba kase sharik shudand*).[107]

Regarding the *karindas*, Maitley says that among Turcomans any surplus land whether belonging to villages or families could be given as *karinda* land, the revenues from which were devoted to communal needs.[108] According to Lokkegard under the fiscal type called *muqata'eh* a man enters upon a *qabala* contract and becomes a *zamin*. Like the Hellenistic location *qabala* is also a tenancy and tax farming. The tax farmer, the link between tax payers and the tax officials of the government supervised sowing and dike work. *Muqata'eh* was basis of a piece work for labourers which they undertook by contract. *Muqataah* is used of the dues paid by the one who undertakes the tax management of an entire province or a major area. It may also apply to small areas, soils, fields, mills, groves and the right to receive the taxes otherwise paid to the state. It is also applicable to such *iqta's* which are granted on the basis of a foregoing agreement upon a fixed due. Thus an *iqta* or *muzareah* of a district falls under the same category. According to Qalqashandi since *iqtas* were rare, the *amwal* were levied directly to the state's treasury from which expenses for the army were defrayed. Often, however, the village (*alqaryah*) was given in fief and fixed terms were stipulated for its feudal lord for which he was liable to the state treasury. This was called *muqata'eh*.[109] Whereas the methods of *ibrah* and the two *misahas* (measurement of whole area or of cultivated and sown area alone) are applied to the peasantry alone, the *muqata'eh* is reserved for the upper classes as *muqataah* is calculated according to *ibrah* and *misaha* both.[110]

The term *dihqan* is also a term evoking much controversy. The works of various scholars had proved that the class of *dihqans* enjoyed unconditional land grants and privileges. On the basis of Samanid and other sources, Barthold describes these *dihqans* as a superior class of nobles who remind us of ancient Greeek basilicans than Asian despots. They were called *Bukhar Khudata* (masters of Bukhara) in Narshakhi's time, as they belonged to the old *dihqan* class. They held immense landed and other property and most of the inhabitants of the place belonged to their land or were their servants. The most influential and rich rulers of Samarqand and Ferghana were also called *dihqan*. The Soviet scholar A. Mukhtarov rightly points out that this term was used in a fluid sense signifying big and small landowners, village elders, petty rulers, rural residents and sometimes even Persian in general in the Sasaanid period.[111] While discussing Qabala institution, Lokkegaard refers to *dihqans* as *sahib al qaryah* or rich man, who undertakes to guarantee a fixed amount of taxes while he himself receives the regular *kharaj* from the tax payers. The *dihqans* have also been described as 'a peculiar class of the Persian nobility' or as 'subordinate land-owners who stood at the head of the peasantry and varied in status from important chieftains to mere village headmen', entrusted even with the 'responsibility for the collection of revenue and for the maintenance of law and order particularly in the districts outside the towns' and that 'much of the substantial wealth of the country was in their hands'.[112] Watt defines *dihqans* as a 'kind of local gentry or squires'.[113] After the Arab conquest, the term *dihqan* signified a distinct class of big and small landowners. Not only Barthold[114] but several other scholars also concluded that the growth of conditional land grants, i.e. the *iqta* system, resulted in the disappearance of *dihqans* as a class of big landowners under the Qarakhanids owing to the former's persistent striving for political power. But Juvaini refers to the existence of '*dihqans* who competed with the kings and *amirs* of the times due to excessive wealth'.[115]

There is controversy regarding the disappearance of the date of this group of land owners. While Bertels places it in eleventh century,[116] Petrushevski believes that the term *dihqan* was gradually disappearing from the eleventh to thirteenth centuries.[117]

Nevertheless, Mukhtarov's study of the *kairak* inscriptions and the sources throw some new light on the problem.[118] The word *dihqan* occurs in three sixteenth century *kairaks* and seems to be an honorary title which often accompanied the title *amir*. Since under the Seljuqs the title of *dihqan* as well as land was allotted in Khurasan to Turks also, Mukhtarov concludes that the title *dihqan* was awarded not only to nomadic Turks but to local nobles also in

Zarafshan valley and was considerably widespread as is indicated by the two *kairak* inscriptions (nos. 39 dated 1537-8 and no. 139 dated 1544-5), in which the deceased have been designated with '*Raisul dihqan wal aizaz*'. Although the reason for the following conclusions is not given, Mukhtarov seems to believe that the *dihqans* in Match and Falgar owned most of the cultivated lands and cattle; some of them even enjoyed administrative posts and were therefore called *amirs*; thus the *dihqan* was not hereditary in Falgar. Mukhtarov further stresses that on the whole, the *dihqans* were privileged people the representatives of the more well-to-do strata and they existed in remote and isolated regions till sixteenth century. Mukhtarov contests Petrushevski's view that *dihqan* 'knighthood' disappeared in the Mongol epoch and is certain that 16 out of the 70 castles which were said by Qazvini to have survived, were actually in the hands of the *dihqans* in the fifteenth century. Some of these *dihqans* were deprived of their village, garden, land and house and remained proprieter without property. Wasifi also refer to a certain Haji Mahmud Farahi, a *dihqan* from Khurasan who was executed by Sultan Husain and describes in detail the property of this big feudal lord who called himself a *dihqan* twice while talking to an Iranian.[119] Mukhtarov maintains that *dihqans* continued to exist as a distinct group of big landowners in North Iran, Khurasan and other regions till fourteenth-fifteenth centuries and even in sixteenth century[120] though generally the term seems to have been applied to the peasants in fifteenth-sixteenth centuries.[121] According to the available information, the *dihqans* existed in Iran. To a great extent they seem to be a counterpart of Indian *zamindars* who owned land and property and were like the chiefs of the villages representing the land owning aristocracy. In sixteenth century Central Asian sources, such a term is not found frequently which suggests that probably the term *dihqan* was a local term in Iran which was limited only to one region and to a fixed period of history. Its extension in Central Asia, if any was too insignificant to present a full fledged group of the landowning aristocrats. Even the term *bai* (rich and honest Mughals) does not really give an exact corresponding meaning for the wealth of a *dihqan* depended upon land whereas those of *bai* could be from cattle or just from booty. In any case *dihqans* are not mentioned in the sources as a superior class after the end of sixteenth century. A few remnants of the same institution found in the *kairak* inscriptions or in the sources cannot prove it otherwise. Ali Sher Navoi frequently used the term *dihqan* in the sense of peasant cultivator. The Uzbeg aristocracy comprised *ughalns, noyons, begs* and *bais* but no reference to *dihqans* is found as part of any category of the rich landowners. Frye believes that as early as the Saljuqid period, the *dihqan* became more involved in trade and crafts as well as land and they gradually moved to the cities. In the oasis of Bukhara mostly the *dihqans* came to the capital and lived near the court as absentee landlords.[122] The change from such unconditional to conditional land tenure caused decline of *dihqans* and their eventual disappearance. The decline of the *dihqan* class, the backbone of Bukhara society, therefore, started in the second half of the tenth century though the process of deterioration lasted more than half a century. Among the reasons attributed to the fall of the *dihqans* are the urbanization under the Samanids and shifting of *dihqans* to the cities; centralization of authority in the Samanid bureaucracy to weaken the power of the *dihqan* class. Their loss of influence was a prelude to the Turkification of Transoxiana; economic crisis leading to decline in land values in the oasis, increase in state lands since members of Samanid family now held lands and *waqf* lands etc.[123]

Davidovich classified the peasants into three categories on the basis of evidence belonging to our period:

(a) The petty landowners holding independent but very small pieces of land.
(b) The peasants who followed a communal system of farming.
(c) The leaseholders of various categories.[124]

The first category of petty landowners themselves worked on their farms and socially they had a varied type of set up[125] and were in many ways better placed than the other two as they had to pay only to the State and not to any individual superior. They themselves held the land and as the State share on the *milk* land was only 20 per cent of the crop which sometimes rose to 30 per cent they had to pay 20-30 per cent of the produce together with other miscellaneous taxes.

But such lands were few as these petty *milkdars* were forced to give their land on lease or sell it to the big landowners on various pretexts particularly if it was situated near the farms of a big landlord. In the words of Davidovich these three categories are mentioned in the terms: *riaya, muzarean* (Arab) and *karandaha* (Tajik) and the context in which these appear indicates their real meaning. The terms *muzarean* and *karanda* in the sixteenth century indicated the leaseholder *metayor* whereas the term *riaya* was simultaneously used for all the tax paying peasants for the subjects in general as well as for a specific group of peasants referred to in the various documents along with the *muzarean.*[126]

The text of the *waqf* documents of Shaibani Khan categorically speaks of the situation where those associated with the *waqf* establishment did not work on the land themselves and gave it on lease. The *waqf* lands could be given in the form of *ijara, muqata'eh* and *muzareah.* No definite and clear definition of these three terms is available except the inference that they represented three different agrarian relationships. According to the analysis by Muqminova, the term *ijara* denoted the giving away of the shops and workshops on lease for money. As against this, *muzareah* indicated the giving away of cultivable lands on lease for a share of the produce.[127] *Muzaraa* was the peasant 'who had only his labour to offer and paid the owner a portion of his harvest generally in natural state'.[128] *Muqata'eh* signified a grant of land farmed out with complete control over it by the grantee. Not only the *waqf* lands but all other forms of land control (state, *milk*) were given on lease. The period of lease differed. In some of the documents, the period is specifically mentioned,[129] which made the leaseholder very vulnerable as the owner could at any time avoid renewal of lease and give it to some other person. Besides, the payment from leased lands was higher than other taxes paid by peasants. The analysis of a somewhat later period shows that the land was given on lease for half or even more than half of the crop. The terms and conditions of lease were not uniform and varied with the form of land and the agreement.

In certain legal documents of sixteenth century, there are references to situations where the land belonged to one person and the settlements (*sukniyat*), gardens or vineyards to another. Here the metayor appears to be the proprietor and owner of gardens and the indigenous dwellers of the *qariyas* united by common rights on all the lands of *qariya* or on their special parts. In support of her argument, Davidovich quotes a documents of seventeenth century where names of two groups of peasants are given as *karindagan* and *kuraviah* denoting the *metayers* and inhabitants of the (village) *qariya.*[130] In a document, Abdullah assigns the lands to Khwaja giving him the option either to cultivate the land or assign it to a *karinda* and receive the *hasilat (zira't ba khud kunand waya ba karinda andakhta hasilat i anra begirand)*. This again shows that the *karinda* was an agent.

The position of the leaseholder *metayor* was not a very enviable one. As the documents prove the position of such leaseholder was nearer to that of peasant, the rate of payment too was the same. The ownership of long-term settlements suggest a rather long period of lease. In other situations, *metayor* gave on lease gardens and lands in less cumbersome conditions. In this situation the owners of the lands (usually big landlords) attempted to buy the leased gardens. The examples of sublease are also available. From sixteenth century documents, it is apparent that owners of *sukniyat* (establishments on other lands be it state or *waqf*) were privileged people and therefore they used the lands of others as leaseholders. As they did not work upon the land themselves they subleased (the land and *sukniyat*) directly to the producers. The peasants, however, used the lands in *qariyas* for generations and by the change of owners their rights were not lost as they held constant rights over the land. Wasifi says that when they appeared with the *kuwwaras* (baskets) of grapes and presented themselves before the Uzbeg governor as the *burzgaran* of the former begum of Herat, the ruler stated that since the lands now belonged to him, the peasants also came under his jurisdiction.[131]

The *milkdars* (paying 20 to 30 per cent of the entire produce along with other taxes) were few in number. Some of them were compelled by the circumstances to give out lands on lease or to sell their lands to the richer neighbours.

Some indirect information available in the sale deeds indicates that some sort of a rural community existed in the sixteenth century even in highly developed agricultural regions and pastures. The communal lands (*jamaat*) which belonged to the village also existed. The extent of the land in *qariayas* was very high, e.g. in one of the documents of sixteenth century the names of the two *qariayas* are given consisting of 1,000 and 1,100 *tanabs* of lands.[133] Usually in legal documents the absolute and exact measurements of lands of *qariya* are not given and simply the boundaries are specified. The land of a *qariya* could be state land or *milk* or *waqf*. Very often they were sold only in bits and not as a whole (*mash'a)*. In one of the documents for example it is stated that in the beginning only 2/5 then 1/5 and later on again 1/5 of one village in the *wilayat* of *karmina* were sold in phases. Every time, the borders of the entire village were recorded in the same manner so that it is possible that the parts of the land alienated were not demarcated on the ground. The sale was actually of the right to rent. If the population of the village had common rights over the land or on any part of the land, e.g. pastures, etc., then the ownership rights were preserved and simply transferred to the next owner.[133] According to Davidovich this indicated the existence of the reallotment of lands or collective use of separate parts especially demarcated.[134] But the argument is open to the simple objection that the evidence at land suggests joint rent-collection rather than commercial agriculture. Conditions in India where village level or joint *zamindari* prevailed, did not necessarily (indeed did not have normally) any kind of communal cultivation.

Some kind of communal agriculture is, however, implied by scholars in the description of pre-revolutionary conditions.[135] Matley refers to the two groups of the landless labourers: one who helped with the harvests and secondly a group of farmers who did not own land and were share croppers (*charakar*) farming a landlord's acreage with tools he supplied in return for a third to half of the cotton harvest.[136] The farmer's claim to any waste land was limited by the number of ox teams he owned. The peasants appeared after the announcement by elders along with their teams at a certain place. The land was divided into as many plots of equal size as there were teams.The actual distribution was done by drawing lots, the owners of several teams being awarded adjacent sections. Such portions of lands were known as *cheks*.[137]

Although there existed various categories of land grants, it should be noted that the rate of demand from all forms of land grant was the same. But the peasants on various forms of lands paid taxes at different rates. Davidovich had proved that though the peasants paid different rates, the category of the peasant concerned was the only determining factor and not the form of land grant. A closer study of the sources and documents reveals the fact that from the cultivable lands the rate of payment by the peasant depended mainly upon the category to which he belonged. The peasants belonging to one of the three groups paid the same rate though they belonged to different categories of the land.

Despite many praises showered by the poets like Ali Sher Navoi on the peasants, e.g. that all prosperity and happiness in the country was due to them,[138] the condition of the peasants themselves was quite miserable. The peasants had to pay to the landlord a larger sum than the fixed rate of demand (usually 30 to 40 per cent of crop) plus other taxes. If the *qariya* belonged to the State, the taxes went to the State treasury. Otherwise the sum was divided between the landholder and the State. The straight sale and purchase of land grants or villages along with its population, forests, canals, irrigational facilities and arable lands always resulted in the long servitude and bonded labour on the lease, attaching the peasant with the land and forbidding any movement voluntary or otherwise. There were, therefore, forcible transmigrations of peasants with the consent of Khan.[139] Whenever the royal army crossed through a particular region the agricultural population had to supply them with provisions in the form of *tughar* tax which was realized with cruelty and force. Excess destroyed the prosperity.[140] Apart from financial obligations, the peasants were also required to give forced labour which was known as *hashr wa begar*. The burden of all forms of land assignments fell ultimately upon the peasants who had to take these lands on very exacting terms. The peasants under bondage lost all rights even the freedom of movement. The lower level of the development of productive strength, stagnation in the technique of the rural handicrafts and the possession on land and water resulted in the complete dependence of peasants on the land owners.[141]

The villages were exposed to several natural calamities. Sometimes floods destroyed the villages. The author of *Rashhat* mentions a big flood (*sail-i azim*) from the river Kuhik. Such was the torrent that the people of the village Deg-i Garan (in *qasba* of Hazara, 3 *farsangs* away from Bukhara) were frightened that the village would be washed away.[142] Sometimes severe cold, hailstorms and rains followed by floods and excessive cold destroyed the crop. *Rauzat-ur Rizwan*[143] refers to such an event in 999 AH. When extreme cold, snowfall and rains for continuous three months caused much distress to the people. Everywhere there sprang up rivers which flooded each corner of the country. Similarly, Wasifi records that in the year 1512, there occurred a very harsh winter with heavy snowfall which resulted in famine and pestilence. These natural calamities were exploited by the propertied classes to the maximum. Abdurrazzaq tells us of what happened during a scarcity in the following words 'when the royal army needed provisions, no grains were available as the *kalantars* had not left any for sale with the *raiyyat-i reza* (peasants) and the grains and corn were hoarded by all with the expectation of a flood or a famine'.[144] The epidemic of plague, drought, excessive winter, forced exile of tribal population, flight of peasants due to extortions were permanent features of Central Asian lands till the nineteenth century.[145] Some of the rivers (Amu for example), changed the course which must also have affected the villages and towns on the banks of rivers in that region adversely.

It seems that the civil wars always caused acute distress to the peasants. In one of the letters from Khudai Pirdi to Khwaja Juibari, the flight of most of the peasants (*riaya*) from the *tumans* of Shaikhin and Afrinkent (dispersed due to the disturbances of civil war) to Bukhara and Miyankal is recorded. In this connection the Khwaja's assistance was sought by the ruler to persuade the peasants to return to original places.[146] After new conquests the population's forcible migration to the other places must have caused economic and agricultural loss. Frequently after the building of a new village, town or even the task of punitive migration must have tremendously upset the agrarian set-up. Babur complains how during the siege of Samarqand in 1501 there was the 'time of ripening grain but no one brought new corn into the town' and how the peasantry became desperate'.[147]

The evil effects of the wars are well described by Muhammad Saleh who says that 'the toiling masses were reduced to poverty, cattle were taken away by the military leaders, bread was trampled down by the horses. In the winter and snow many died of hunger and destitution in Bukhara and Samarqand. People faded like tulips. Many died not only in this region but in Qarshi and Kash. The unshrouded corpses were scattered in streets.[148] This was the situation in the beginning of the sixteenth century. Similarly the destructions caused by the forces during Balkh campaign in 959 'transformed the prosperous town into dust'.[149] *Rauzat-ur Rizwan* refers to he old Chaharbagh extending over 50 *tanabs* of land which was ruined during the Uzbeg regime.[150] The Qazaq invasions which so frequently ravaged the agricultural regions also hampered the growth of stable agrarian economy and the process of urbanization. There were sometimes deliberate destructions of fields, canals, etc. During siege of Balkh in 1498, Khusru Shah sent Nazar Bahadur to destroy the water channels (*ariqlar*), *ashligh*, provisions, corns, etc.[151] In one of his letters an Uzbeg prince Darvesh Sultan wrote to Khwaja about the mutual rivalry and civil wars amongst the princes which 'if not checked in time could destroy and devastate Transoxiana an enviable place for all in the world'.[152] After his conquest of Samarqand, Babur says that Samarqand 'overran' and so long subjected to raid and rapine had been in such 'stress that it needed seed corn and money advances, what place was this to take any thing from?'[153] Hence Babur's men could get little booty and no incentive and homesick as they were, they started deserting him.[154]

Overburdened by excessive taxes, the peasants often fled to the other places abandoning their lands. This is evident from the discussion of Shaibani Khan at Kan-i Gil.[155] The exploitation of the peasants followed by their flight seems to be a more common phenomenon in the *milk* lands than the State lands. The owners of *milk* land tried to squeeze the maximum benefit from their property by making the peasants compensate for the loss which they had to incur as a result of the State demands. The situation was even worse under the *waqf* and *milk-i khur o khalis*. In the event of excessive tyranny the peasants had no option but to shift himself to some other land. In a *farman* which was presumably issued by Ubaidullah Khan in 1513 to Kamaluddin Masud Mir Hazara Arab, the position of the peasants had been described in the following words: 'Wherever in the *wilayat* or *tumans*, there are peasants (*riaya*) or *sharik)* they come under the control of their particular *yert* and they should be quietly engaged in their work. Let no one else give them protection nor hinder their work.'[156] The statement has been further corroborated through certain other *yirliqs* of the Khan issued in the sixteenth-seventeenth centuries in which an order was given for forcible return of fugitive peasants to their original lands through the intermediation of highly placed religious personages in the region of eastern Farghana, and the collectors were asked to abstain from realizing the taxes till the return of these peasants to their respective places and resumption of work by them had been secured.[157] Thus the peasants appear to have been seen largely as semi-serfs not capable of shifting from one area to another as they pleased.

Due to these exacting conditions and excessive taxes the peasants sometimes offered passive resistance like refusal to sow the lands of their masters or even to work on their own lands, as in Farghana and Samarqand, or even refusal to fulfil fiscal obligations, etc.[158] When the peasants were unable to flee, they had no choice except to place themselves at the mercy of usurers so that they could meet the demands set on them.[159] Exemptions from taxes were frequently given to the Juibari shaikh, *ishans,* nobility, merchants and other rich persons but the benefit of these exemptions did not go to the peasants who continued to force the exploitation under the multiple taxes. Although mention has been made about the existence of *awarijas* (account books, registers) and the *munshis* and *navisandas* (writers and record keepers). The rate of miscellaneous taxes does not seem to have been determined properly and the loopholes in the administration offered many opportunities for the exploitation of peasants.[160]

Main Forms of Agrarian Exploitation

The Uzbegs rulers were specifically called upon to decide how to distribute the resources from the agricultural surplus of their newly conquered territories. Under Timur, the lands were assigned to the members of the ruling family, the nobles and commanders in various forms which were known as *suyurghal, iqta, jildu,*[161] etc. During the regime of his successors, the system seems to have continued. Timurid sources enumerate *suyurghal, milk, waqf, jildu*, etc., as the main forms of land control. Apart from these and the conferment of large and small towns, Babur mentions various other grants assigned 'for the rest of Umar Shaikh's *begs*, e.g. district (*wilayat)* or land (*yir*) or office (*mauja*) or charge (*jirga)* or stipend (*wajh*)'.[162] The Uzbegs deviated slightly from the Timurid pattern and, by reviving certain old Turkish institutions, came closer to the Saljuqids of Central Asia. Except for the first few years of the sixteenth century, *suyurghal* ceased to be synonymous with *iqta*.

The Uzbegs had brought with them the old Mongolian concept of *yurt* and, therefore, in the first few years, the princes and nobles were assigned *yurts* and various places, along with the settled populations. The *yurt* was not a new term for Central Asia. It had been in vogue under the Mongols too. The word *yurt* occurs in the sources of the reign of Timur. Lambton renders the term as tribal pastures.[163] In the Uzbeg language, however, the term denotes 'country' or a place, which fits well when the term is read in the *Matla-us Sadain* or the *Zafarnama*.[164] Under the Mongols, the term specifically meant the 'appanage of a Mongol prince'. In the sixteenth-seventeenth centuries the term seems to have acquired much fluidity. It has been used in the sense of a territory or military post or land grant, camps, habitats and tents. Frequent references have been made to this term in the *Mehmannama*.[165] At one place, one hears of 'noted Uzbeg nobles' whose *yurt* was near the territories (*mamalik*) of Hazarat Sultan Timur (the son of Shaibani)[166] Soviet historians tend to take *yurt* to mean appanages assigned to the members of the ruling family, or leaders of the tribes.[167] As land grant, however, the term seems to have fallen out of use after the first two decades of Uzbeg rule. References to it are rarely found in later sources.

According to the Turko-Mongol traditions, the empire was divided into appanages called *wilayat, mamlakat* or *mulk* and these large provinces were assigned to various Sultans by the *khaqan*. The holder of each *wilayat* subassigned territories and distributed *iqtas* and other forms of land control to his relatives and nobles in his appanage.

The portion of the land which belonged to the Khan personally was known as *khassa*, or *khas*, and it was probably selected by the Khan himself. Abdullah had done so in Balkh.[168] Portions of the *khassa* lands of the sixteenth century were in turn assigned as *waqf* or alienated in some other form. Apart from the lands, the Khan also possessed palaces, handicraft workshops, shops, water mills, pastures, flocks of sheep, herds of livestock, etc., in the form of *khassa*.[169]

Krader describes the *mamlaka-i padshahi* or *mamlaka-i sultani* as the 'treasury land', the same as the '*diwan* land of middle ages'.[170] This land was owned by the State and its revenue went to its exchequer. The *mamlaka* was assigned to members of the royal family, the sheikhs, the *ishans* and the nobility. Legally, the *mamlaka* could neither be sold nor converted into any other category of land. But some times the immovable property existing on a *mamlaka* was given on lease either temporarily or for the lifetime of a person. The owners of *mamlaka* could, in turn, assign this land to the small landholders or to ordinary peasants for cultivation.

The conditional land grants known as *iqta* had started in Central Asia in the ninth-tenth centuries under the Qarakhanids, or perhaps even earlier,[171] and gradually started developing as the basis of military organization under Mongol rulers.[172] Under the Saljuqids, the *iqta* contributed to decentralization, combining civil and military authority in a fief to be enjoyed by its holder. In the middle of the fourteenth century, the term *suyurghal* appeared in Central Asia and with the Golden Horde, as synonymous with *iqta*. According to Bori Ahmedov, in the steppes too, the Uzbegs had this form of land assignment besides one other form *tarkhani*. Under Timur and his successors, *suyurghal* was granted to members of the royal family and to distinguished nobles. In a way, the Timurid *suyurghal* had replaced the Saljuqid *iqta*.[173] Apart from these large provincial grants, regions with tens of cities and 100 villages were also assigned and subassigned to persons of various gradations. The *suyurghal* was a hereditary land grant though subject to annual renewal, which, however, could be terminated at the will of the sovereign. In the fifteenth century, *suyurghal* was not only given in lieu of military service to commanders but was also bestowed upon musicians, religious divines, officials and learned men.[174] The *suyurghal* holder enjoyed several privileges. In the first place, no share of the income from a *suyurghal* could go to the state treasury; It was utilised entirely by the holder. Occasionally immunity from other obligations was also granted.

Nabiev believes that the conditional *suyurghal* grants continued down to the sixteenth-seventeenth centuries when the nomadic Uzbegs tried to occupy all the cultivable lands. Both Ivanov and Nabiev emphasize that, though a number of other forms of land control like *iqta, tankhwah, darubast* existed, they were all covered by the universal term *suyurghal*.[175] But *darubast* was not a form of grant at all, meaning, as it does 'complete' and 'entire'.[176] This literal meaning suits the contexts in which the word appears in documents and sources.[177]

In Central Asia, *suyurghal* was also used in a fluid sense, denoting occasionally a military grant or a subsistence allowance. Presumably the definition of *suyurghal* as given by Abul Fazl (who treated it as a 'subsistence allowance' like that prevalent in India) is nearer to the truth as far as sixteenth century Central Asia is concerned. In the sixteenth century *suyurghal* ceased to be synonymous with *iqta*—a military grant as under the Timurids. The *suyurghal* could be an independent grant or just part of a larger grant, from which a portion had been assigned to someone unconditionally for personal use. Nevertheless, some sixteenth century sources often refer to the *iqta* as *suyurghal*, though the two terms seem to carry different connotations in other documents. The authors of *Abdullahnama* and other sources occasionally refer to the term, which makes it seem similar to *iqta*, and involving certain military and financial obligations to the state. For example, Saghraj and its dependencies are said to have been assigned as *suyurghal* to Qalich Qara Sultan and later to Ibadullah Sultan; Khujand was assigned to Shighai Khan and the *wilayats* of Farghana from Khujand to Aush and Andijan to Isfandiyar Sultan.[178] The incident quoted by Hafiz Tanish about a noble, Shah Nazar Bi Qarluq, the holder of the *suyurghal* of Khujakat, whose men had driven away the few servants of Uzbeg Sultan who had come to collect the revenue (*zar-i tahsil*),[179] confirms that the holders of these *suyurghal* (in the form of *iqta*) were also required to make payments to the State. Such instances are confusing unless one notices the loose usage so common in medieval sources. Certain other sources, as well as the documents, conclusively prove that *suyurghal* holders were not required to fulfil any State obligations, as the sum of revenue from the land assigned to them was expected to serve as their subsistence allowance.

Shaibani granted *suyurghal* to the *ulama*, to *saiyids* and to learned men.[180] Nauroz Ahmad (1551-6) assigned the *yabisat-i shash* along with mines of turquoise, iron, etc., as *suyurghal* to Shamsuddin Muhammad Khurasani, a distinguished and learned man of his times, to enable him to use the revenue from these various sources as his subsistence allowance (*wujuh-i maash*)[181] Similarly Iskandar Khan (1560-83) granted certain fertile *mauzas* as *suyurghal* to Yar Muhammad, so that revenue from these lands could be used by him as his subsistence allowance (*sarf-i maishat*) for he was inclined towards asceticism (*darveshi*) and had also renounced the world.[182]

It is also surmised that the Uzbeg State owned or had a monopoly of mines. There are references to persons holding the *darughagi* of Kani Firuza as Ruhi Bukhari, a poet and a servant of Shaibak Khan who had the *darughagi* of the mines of turquoise. Nauroz Ahmad had also bestowed upon Saiyid Shamsuddin Muhammad, the most talented scholar of his times, the right to receive from all the mines and quarries (excepting the mines of turquoise, iron and steel in which presently the work is being done) the *hasilat* in entirety as *hudbari suyurghal* to serve as his (*wujuhi mash*) subsistence allowance.[183]

The documents found in the fundamental library of Kazan deal mainly with the *suyurghal* holdings of the Shaibanid and Ashtarakhanids and highlight a number of important facts regarding this grant. In the first place, *suyurghal* could be hereditary though subject to renewals at regular intervals. In 1595, Abdullah Khan Uzbeg renewed the old and new *suyurghals* of Qazi Burhanuddin and instructed the *gumashtas* not to demand *malojihat* and *ikhrajat* from him. One of such documents was issued by Imam Quli in 1621 referring to the fact that *urushana*, *rabat khas*, cultivable lands in Ipana, Qaratasha Sehgazi, Naushaba, etc., belonging to Qazi Abul-

Maani's ancestors from earlier times by continuous renewal grants issued by various sultans and *khaqans*; hence the renewal order by Imam Quli in 1621. It is interesting to note that the above mentioned grant was renewed again and again in 1636-7, 1647, 1657, 1669 and so on. The grant carried with it exemption from *ikhrajat, amilat, malojihat, alighat*, etc.

Secondly the *suyurghal* grants did not comprise lands only. Besides land, water, *khanawar,* servants, water mills *(asiyaha)*, mines, gardens, etc., could be declared *suyurghal* and were consequently exempted from all State demands. Whether the *suyurghal* lands were tilled by the holder himself or with any intermediary, whether the water was conrolled by him personally or through a *karinda*, no money was to be demanded from him. One of the *nishans* of Keldi Bahadur dated 1601 bestows Qaziship of Andijan as *suyurghal* and instructs the local population, officers and peasants to consider him (and not any other self-styled *qazi*) as the real *qazi* of Andijan. The local *qazis* of various places such as Jartak, Suzak, Nauqad, Rabatak, Jalabak, Sulatkand, etc., must look upon him as the real authority. The *Qazi-askar* was not to interfere in his affairs except in the affairs of Uzbegs and Chaghatais. The same document contained the details of his *ulufa* 1,000 *tangas* from Rabat-i Khas, Qaratash, 30 *khanawars*, etc., exempting him from 1/10 and 2/10 payments. Again after three years in 1603 the same Keldi Muhammad had to renew his own order.

The third and perhaps the commonest form of *suyurghal* was the granting of State share of taxes to an individual from a *milk* land. In a document issued in 1575-6 by Sultan Muhammad Hashim, it is categorically stated that the village of Faizlik which had since old times belonged to the *milk* lands of Haji Khan Qazi had been granted as *Suyurghal* by the Khan to Haji Khan Qazi and the grant was now being renewed. The document instructs to give 2/10 and 1/10 share of the crop to his trusted *gumashtas* without any deception. Another document dated 1578-9 of Sultan Muhammad Hashim refers to the hereditary *imlak* of certain Amir Ibrahim in Noshaba village. As a reward for his restoring the irrigational ditch, 2/10 part of the produce was given to him as a *suyurghal*. The documents ordered that no one was to interfere in the rights of Amir Ibrahim. Let those who work on the land and sow it give 2/10 of produce without resorting to fraudulent practices. Similarly, one more document issued in 1584 by Isfandyar Sultan grants *mauza* Qabizlik to a certain Amir Ibrahim instructs people not to demand 1/20 (*deh nim*) of the produce.[184]

At one place, *altamgha* grants have also been mentioned along with *waqf*.[185] The existence of such a form of land assignment in Central Asia is not confirmed by other statements. There are, however, certain interesting observations contained in the autobiography of the Indian ruler Jahangir. The Emperor writes that 'whoever wished to have his birth-place made into his land assignment should make a representation to that effect so that in accordance with Chingizi *tura* the estate might be conveyed to him by *altamgha* and become his property and he might be secured from the apprehension of change. Our ancestors and forefathers were in the habit of granting assignments to every one under proprietory title and adorned the *farmans* for these with *altamgha* seal which is an impressed seal made in vermilion (red ink).'[186] The reference to Chingizi canon leaves us in no doubt that the term had been used only to denote the vermilion seal attached by the Mongols to their documents and the reference of this term in the same connotation is found in *Jami-ut tawarikh* also.[187]

Certain Soviet historians have used the two terms, i.e. *iqta* and *tuyul*, as synonymous. The word *tuyul* does not appear in the sources for the reign of Abdullah Khan Uzbeg although it has frequently been mentioned in the *Waqfnama* of Shaibani Khan. The Soviet historians have referred to another form of land grant which was known as *tankhwah*. The *Abdullahnama* contains a reference to *tankhwah,* when it states that after the conquest of Nasaf certain *qariyas* (villages) of Nasaf were allotted to the victorious army as *tankhwah*.[188] Since the assumption of Soviet historians is based primarily on a reference to this incident in *Abdullahnama*, it is difficult to accept with any certainty the identification of *tankhwah* with *iqta*. The mere literal sense of salary would also suit the context. Another reference of *tankhwah* is found in one of the *Inayatnamas* land grant document of 9 Sept. 1626 where the *dihyak mauza* Taban was allocated in the name of Malik Muhammad Zaman and happened to be the *tankhwah* of son of a certain Chuq Chuq. It was again to be bestowed upon Muhammad Zaman as *tankhwah*. Another explanation of the term seems more convincing that: 'The state lands (*mamlaka*) were sometimes granted along with its population to an individual or to a group which entitled them to collect the taxes or levies in lieu of their salary or stipend hence the grant named as *tankhwah*. They were free from all forms of obligations.'

Another form of assignment granted by the Khan was known as *jildu* (reward). This was given to the princes and nobles for performing some outstanding deed. Ubaidullah Sultan had received Qarakul as *jildu* for his success against Babur and the Persians.[189] Shah Said Bi Qarluq was given Kahmard and certain *aimaqs* as *jildu* for his conquest of Kahmard.[190] Hafiz Tanish gives several examples of conferment of *jildu*.[192]

From the very beginning the *waqf* institution was often used for 'dodging tax assessors and to safeguard personal property in other ways',[192] since the legal status of the *waqf* land was different from that of other forms of land grants. The taxes from these lands were to be fixed and realized in accordance with the terms and conditions laid down in the documents concerned. The absolute rights over such lands and taxes from it, enjoyed by the *waqf* owners were not given to the holders of other land grants. In a way, the system of *waqf* provided a surety for the big magnates who retained and preserved their wealth and property without any interference by the State or by the *khwajas*. In other words, landownership could be made inalienable by the foundation of a *waqf* with the provision for the future subsistence of the administrator (*mutawalli)*.[193] From the beginning of the sixteenth century, the attempts of the royal family, big nobles and other dignitaries to convert their property into *waqf* holdings become quite noticeable. Apart from the land grants and other property of Mihr Sultan, Abdullah Khan Uzbeg also gave away much of his property in *waqf* for his *madrasa* in Bukhara. The three *waqfnamas* refer to several such properties. Even Qulbaba Kukultash in 1593-4 converted his 33 big stores, shops and workshops into *waqf* for his *madrasa*. A *timchik* (small market) and 22 stores were given as *waqf* to the *madrasa-i Ghazian* in Bukhara in 1535-6. For the *madrasa* of Fathullah Qush Begi in Bukhara one *timchik* and 52 stores were reserved.[194]

According to the terms of the *waqf*, the *waqf* lands could be given on lease on a period varying from one month to three years. These lands could not be held by one person for more than three years as this could entitle him (in accordance with the *sharia* rules) to appropriate the land. Such usurption must have occurred as the *waqf* document clearly forbids the assignment of *waqf* lands for cultivation (*zaraat)* or by way of *ijara* to various highly placed officers, nobles or sultans 'if there was any danger of their occupation by coercion for it was not possible to relieve the land from such hands'.[195] Again the fact highlighted is that the lease holders of the *waqf* lands were no other persons than the same magnates, *suyurghal* holders, big landlords, nobles and sultans who either occupied the land or did not pay the taxes to the *diwan*. On their behalf, these rich persons placed the peasant metayor as the direct producer instead of having their own personal economy.

The *waqf* property could be hereditary also as is indicated by the term *waqf-i aulad*. According to the conditions laid down in the *waqf*, the *mutawalli* from the family of the owner of the *waqf* was to receive 1/5 of the entire income. The Khans of Samarqand had a right to place new *mutawalli* from outside also. Such intruders were entitled to receive their allowance (*haqqut tauliya*) at the rate of 1/10 only.

It should be noted that though the property was given away in *waqf*, the original owner maintained the complete ownership rights over the lands and establishment, and also had the freedom to interfere in the internal administration. According to the conditions in the *Waqfnama* of Shaibani Khan, Mihr Sultan Khanam, the owner continued to enjoy the right to use the establishment, make amendments in terms and conditions of *waqf*, replace *mutawalli* and other officials arbitrarily and increase or decrease their privileges summarily. Even the sale of the land was also indicated in the clause authorizing the owner to sell it or use it for some other purpose and no one could interfere in that. This was applicable to the next generation also. The clauses in the *waqf* document discussed above indicate that Mihr Sultan gave it away in *waqf* only with a view to guard it against the encroachments of the representatives of holy men and preserve it for herself and her family.[196]

The scholars agree on one point that often the donation as *waqf* was mainly done to avoid taxes as there existed an agreement between the religious institutions and the owners which left him in the real ownership of *waqf* property for the payment of just a sum of money. In other types only part of income went to the institution or even the children of the owner were declared trustees and so on.[197] Apparently it seems that any property if assigned for some religious purposes was free of all encumberance and this arrangement protected the interests of the owners. The *tauliya* and *shaikhi* (the financial and administrative rights) of the tomb of Hazrat Ali were once given by Abdullah to Hasan Khwaja Naqib and the entire *mahsul* of that tomb was declared as an additional *ulufa* of his *iqta* (*zamimai sair ulufa wa iqta*).[198]

From the sources available for this period it is not clear whether *waqf* lands were free from the payment of taxes. On the contrary, the State share of each category of land has been mentioned specifically. The category of the land converted into *waqf* has also been mentioned in the *waqf* documents presumably to indicate the share of the state. In certain documents, it is also stated that immunity from State dues was granted on the *waqf* lands. For instance, the *waqf* document of Husain Khwarazmi issued in 1547, records a variety of taxes from which exemption had been granted. But, the entire money saved in this manner had to be utilized for the maintenance of mosque, *madrasas*, etc. Sometimes the *waqf* lands were sold away along with the taxes but such an action was not in conformity with state orders. Soviet historians stress the fact that if a *milk*-holder converted his land into *waqf* the state still retained its claim over the share of rent from this *waqf* land. But when a *milk-i khur o khalis* was given away for *waqf* the *milk*-holder became the sole claimant to all proceeds and the State disowned any claims on the *milk* land.[199]

Wasifi records the displeasure of one of the *mullas* over the suspected realization of *mal-i auqaf*. The context makes it clear that it was not considered to be a legal (*halal*) acquisition.[200] However, there is no doubt that the *waqf* lands were frequently exploited. Isfahani records that Shaibani had appointed him for making investigations into the *waqf* holdings of Samarqand with the assistance of the local *qazi*. Having scrutinized the income and expenditure of these lands and after assessing the extent of deterioration in the condition of *madrasas,* Shaibani reprimanded the culprits and attempted to stop the misadministration of the *waqf*.[201] To cite another example of the action taken against the exploitation of *waqf* land, Mihr Sultan Khanam at the time of assigning the land as *waqf* to the *madrasas* of Shaibani specifically mentions that these lands should not be given for cultivation to influential people, such as officers, servants of the *khaqan*, nobles or *suyurghal* holders. Mihr Sultan further stresses that this should not be given in the form of *ijara* to persons who might occupy it later on and start practicing tyranny.[202] Spuler says that 'since *waqf* properties were not exempted from taxes and were normally rented, peasants as far as possible avoided working on them'.[203]

Milk land has been mentioned frequently in the *waqfnama* of Shaibani Khan. A description of the two types of *milk* land, i.e. *milk-i ushri* and *milk-i kharaji* had been given by Isfahani in *Suluk-ul Mulk*. In *Milk-i kharaji*, the holder of the land was required to pay the amount of *kharaj* even while the *kharaji* land was not being cultivated but in the case of *milk-i ushri*, on which he was supposed to pay at the rate of one-tenth of the produce, payment depended on the cultivation and not on the land as for the *milk-i kharaj*.[204] Shaibani's reference to *milk-i kharaj* in his discussion at Kan-i Gil suggests that the two categories of the land holding might have existed under the early Shaibanids. According to the Hanafite laws, land tax was paid in accordance with two rates *ushr* 1/10 of produce or higher; yield of *kharaj* varying from one fifth 2/3 being often however half of the output. It was the right of Sovereign to decide in particular cases if the land is subjected to *ushr* or *kharaj*. *Ushr* land was to be irrigated by *ushr* water (by natural streams) and *kharaj* lands by *kharaj* water[205] (canals dug out by men).

The *milk* lands which existed before and after the Shaibanids have been a subject of much controversy. Some scholars have described them as the personal property of an individual. Others have stated it to be State land. Even for sixteenth century *milk* lands, there exist two different views. According to Ivanov,[206] the *milk* land was an unconditional personal property whereas in the opinion of Nabiev (who drew his conclusions from certain sixteenth-seventeenth century documents from Ferghana) the *milk* lands not only indicated personal property of land owners but also referred to the State lands which were granted as *suyurghals*.[207] Davidovich's conclusions that the *milk* land was an indivisible property with two joint proprietors—individual and the State[208] in her own opinion confirms the statement of Nabiev.[209] According to this analysis, the two owners of the *milk* land divided the taxes from the *milk* land and could even divide the lands proportionately in accordance with the taxes. Consequently one portion was categorized as *mamlaka-i padshahi* held in entirety by the State while another was individual property called *milk-i khur o khalis*.[210] Chekhovich refers to some sort of a process of 'collapse or disintegration' in the *milk* land which was followed by an intensive growth of the same in the next century.[211] The legal position of indivisible *milk* land implied the presence of the two proprietors each of whom could arrange for his own share of taxes. The individual *milk* land could be sold or converted into some other form. But the State retained its share of taxes irrespective of the change of ownership. The taxes on *milk* land were sold and not the land itself. Such partial sale of *milk* lands bought was at lower prices than the fully alienable lands (*milk-i khur o khalis*). In another form the indivisible *milk* land remained in the hands of the two owners, the individual and the State, either claiming a share of revenue from the land. Sometimes the State granted its share of taxes not to a third person but to its sharer in which case the entire revenue was realized by one and the same *milkdar* holding the land partly as its owner and partly as assignee of a conditional grant.[212] A document issued in 1575 shows that Amir Khwaja Kalan (*qazi* of the two regions of the *wilayat* of Andijan) was the proprietor of *milk* land in one village, where he held the royal grant of *milk* as well. Simultaneously another document of 1578-9 refers to a certain Amir Ibrahim who happened to be the owner of *milk* land and who restored the irrigational canal which was washed away by the river and who irrigated the land and was, therefore, subsequently assigned the State share of the revenue from the *milk* land. Thus proprietorship of a *milk* land belonged to two shares the owner receiving 1/10 of the harvest and the state/tax assignee, receiving another portion of the produce. In one such case (in 1626) when the assignee died, the *milkdar* was given the conditional ownerships of the state share of the revenue.[213] In all the situations, the State granted to the person the State share of the taxes and not the land. Nevertheless, categorizing the *milk* land as State land would not be correct as the assignee held the land as private property. The bestowal of *milk* lands as *suyurghal* meant unconditional personal land grant. Similarly, the *milk* land assigned in the form of other land grants also had almost the same position. The State assigned its share of *milk* land to some individual without in any way disturbing the right of the *milkdar* over the latter's share of taxes whereas the *milkdar* could give away his share to a third person without disturbing the rights of the State. Thus, theoretically both the owners enjoyed rights over the *milk* land and were capable of dividing it. It should be noted here that the above conclusions indicate another possibility that not only the *inju* or Sate lands called *mamlakat-i padshahi* were assigned in lieu of some military service or financial obligations but the *milk* land could also be a conditional land grant.

The state could at any time terminate the grant of such taxes from the *milk* land. It seems that under Abdullah Khan Uzbeg an attempt was made to discontinue or confiscate the *milk* lands also. One of the petitions addressed to Khwaja Juibar requests the Khwaja to recommend and to persuade Abdullah Khan Uzbeg to renew the *haq-i Malikana dehdui* (one/half) granted to a lady earlier and terminated recently. In another petition of Mahmud Sultan b. Sulaiman to Khwaja Qutub-ul Abrar, the former is said to have stated that his mother held two *kariz* as *milk* in Nur and that it was also exempted from the *dehdui malikana* and the petitioners stated that Khans and Sultans of Samarqand and Tashkent had exempted it from *dehdui*. Now if the Khwaja was kind enough he could get the *nishan* of *dehdui* issued in the (*atun*) petitioner's name.[214] The *dehdui* seems to be the half *ushr* tax. But the Khwajas were again safe from such encroachments. In one of the letters of Abdullah to Khwaja it has categorically been stated that 'out of infancy Abdulmomin Sultan had committed a rudeness of occupying (*mutassarif shud)* the *imlak* of Khwaja' and when admonished for the same he apologized and returned it 'as before by way of *peshkash* to the *wukla* of Khwaja'.[215]

In the legal document and sources of sixteenth-seventeenth centuries there are different terms attached to the *milk* land qualifying their type. Some of them are *deh yak, deh do, sals-o salsan.*[216] These terms indicated the rate of demand. The taxes on the *milk* land seem to be high as is evident from Shaibani's discussion at Kan-i Gul since it is explained that the *milk* land had been abandoned by the owners of these lands due to high taxes.[217] Presumably due to high taxes, the *milk* holder preferred to convert his land into a form known as *milk-i khur o khalis* according to which the holder had to give back the possession of two-thirds of his *milk* to the State in order to free the remaining one third of his *milk* from all State obligations. The holders of *milk* land (*kharaji*) were required to pay the taxes regardless of the fertility of the soil or the actual cultivation being done on the land. A remission from *kharaj* was granted only under certain unavoidable circumstances like the destruction of crops, etc. The *milk* lands thus abandoned were resumed by the State and reassigned to some other persons for proper utilization of the land so that the *kharaj* could be recorded.[218]

No definite information is so far available about the rate of taxes and income from the *milk* lands. Ivanov puts it as 3/4 of the crop as State share.[219] A later analysis puts it as 2/3 of the total produce in theory as in practice it was more. The remainder (1/3) was divided between the peasant and the *milkdar*. Davidovich explains that there existed varied types of *milk* lands hence the difference in their taxes. The tax rates from *milk* land as quoted by Davidovich and Ivanov from certain documents show that the state received 2/3 and the *milkdar* just 1/3; elsewhere the ratio is 3/4 and 1/4. Davidovich, however, points out that the above mentioned rate of tax does not give the exact quantity of produce. Instead it merely refers to the mutual ratio of the shares of the two joint owners. In certain cases, the share of the State is higher and in others it is less than that of *milkdar*. Usually the taxes were divided into two unequal portions, e.g. 1/3 and 2/3 or 1/10 and 2/10 of the produce.

Such cultivable *milk* lands from which a small portion like 1/10 of produce was realized by the state was called *milk-i ushri* or just *ushri*. The share of the individual *milkdar* from such lands was 2/10. Other forms of such cultivable *milk* lands present a completely different picture, the state receiving 2/10 and *milkdar* 1/10. In this arrangement, *milkdar* lost 1/10 (*deh yak) as* is shown in one of the documents dated 1556.[220] The state share in another document dated 1578-79 appears to be more, as the State assigned its share of 2/10 (*deh dui)* to someone as *suyurghalat*. In another document dated 1575/6 only one person was given all the taxes from the *milk* land, i.e. 2/10 and 1/10. Subsequently the rate of tax comes to about 3/10 or 30 per cent of the produce which was augmented frequently. The document dated 1556 refers to 20 per cent tax as State share. It is stated that there were 13,400 *tanabs* of cultivable lands in the vicinity of Samarqand out of which 3,600 *tanabs* happened to be *milk* land turned into *milk-i khur o khalis* (with complete exemption from all State obligations) where the *milkdar* lost his privilege. Till the division occurred, the individual *milkdar* was stated to have a share of 1/10 in addition to miscellaneous taxes which came to about 1/4 of the produce in 1556. The state received 3/4 of the taxes i.e. 3/10 of the crops plus other taxes. This again shows that in mid-sixteenth century taxes accounted for 40 per cent of the produce and there were certain other taxes which were not stated categorically. All the peasants had to pay these two taxes, i.e. the land tax and the miscellaneous taxes. The land tax was usually 30 per cent occasionally increased up to 40 per cent. The exact details about the amount of miscellaneous taxes is not available. Nevertheless the long list of the various taxes enumerated leaves us in no doubt that the amount must have been considerably high and only a very paltry sum must have been left with the peasant.

The land tax in sixteenth century was realized in cash, kind and in the form of corvee. The land revenue included not only the land tax but also miscellaneous taxes. The land tax was not only calculated on the basis of the produce but was sometimes even realized in kind.

It should be noted here that as in other Islamic states, the fiscal activities, based upon an annual budgetary evaluation had probably two main aspects: Although the taxes and salaries were not 'necessarily paid in cash but their level was always stated in terms of official monetary units'.[221]

The sources refer to the large establishment of Khwaja Saad who not only held a complete apparatus for realization of taxes but even employed executives and managers to collect taxes in cash and kind and to transport them. According to Davidovich, the individual land owners usually realized rent partly in cash and partly in kind. The reference to the transportation of grain indicates that the basic part of land revenue was collected in kind from the cultivable lands. The large and numerous granaries and underground stores of Khwaja Saad seem to corroborate the fact.[222] In each *anbar*, supposedly there were 1,00,000 *mans* of grain (big Bukhara weight, 2,560 tons) and in pits 1,000 *mans*.

The State also realized the taxes from *milk* lands (and probably from State lands) in kind. The *waqf* lands were also taxed in kind and cash both. The *Shaikh-ul Islam* and the *qazi* of Andijan both received the land as well as 1,000 silver *tangas*.[223] The land grant again speaks of payment in kind. The *waqf* documents refer to the payment in cash and kind both only in kind to various employees. In turn, this again proves that the realization from *waqf* land was also in kind.

However, produce of all kinds was brought from the villages to the cities in large quantities. According to Davidovich, these products were brought to the city either by the peasants themselves in order to pay the rent or they were marketed by the big landlords who received them as land revenue in kind and again converted them into money.[224]

As we have already noted, the generally prevalent view that the pastoral Uzbegs were not very familiar with agriculture is not quite accurate. On the other hand, the Uzbeg rulers seem to have done much to promote cultivation in their empire. Isfahani refers to several attempts made by Shaibani for the development of agriculture and for the amelioration of the conditions of his people.[225]

Orders were issued that revivification of dead lands should be undertaken and whosoever performs this task, would enjoy the ownership of the revived lands in accordance with the Muslim law. The revivification of *mewat* lands (waste or abandoned) with state's prior permission and subsequent settlement projects granting rights of ownership to the reviver as permissible in Islamic law was attempted by other Uzbeg Khans. Nauroz Ahmad had also issued a *manshur* to a great scholar Saiyid Shamsuddin Muhammad to the same effect that

> in the *wilayat-i mahrusa* (the province in the empire) of Shash (Tashkent) wherever the dead lands or waste lands (*arazi i maita*) are revived to cultivation by Shamsuddin (*Ihya farmayend*) by my order, in accordance with *sharia* rules it would be considered his land, free of all state obligations (*muaf o mussallam o marfuu'l qalam*) and none should interfere with that not even the brothers, sons, wise *amirs, sadrs, wazirs* and even *nawab's munshis*. The high and low alike should consider this as a permanent possession (*min haisu'l istiqlal*) and none should be considered as his partner (*shariki sahim*) and no annual renewals should be demanded from him.[226]

A network of irrigational canals had also been created. Although a chronological account of the irrigational measures undertaken by the different rulers cannot be attempted, some fragmentary information can be offered. Shaibani constructed a cause-way or dam over the river Zarafshan and divided it into two branches, Aq darya and Qara darya, which have survived up to the present times. Shaibani had arranged for providing irrigational facilities in Sauran also. Isfahani mentions that several canals were dug from the Syr river for providing irrigational facilities in the vicinity.[227]

Wasifi who came to Central Asia in 1512, states that Kuchum Khan dug canals in Turkestan; about 95 Indian slaves served in the work of excavation.[228]

It is stated that even such a pleasure-loving Khan as Nauroz Ahmad engaged himself constructing a dam over Ab-i Dargham when he died.[229] The *Waqfnama* of Shaibani Khan refers to several canals and *juis* whose owners have not been identified in the documents.[230]

While the Tejend and Murghab rivers had no surplus for the extension of agriculture, the Amu in south was an important source of irrigation. Abul Ghazi informs us that Ali Sultan Uzbeg (d. 1565) cut a canal from the south eastern part of old Urganj and named it *Tashli Yarmish* (stone). Some other canals namely the Zeharik crossed to north of Khiva en route *wazir*, the *yang i arik* not far from Urganj in its south Haikanik near Khanqah situated at the stone bridge for Khiva are also mentioned in the *Shajratul Atrak*.

The most outstanding irrigational ventures of Central Asia in the sixteenth century were undertaken by Abdullah Khan Uzbeg. In 1559, Abdullah had constructed a garden near Bukhara to the *mazar* (mausoleum) of Abu Bakr Sad. The garden was connected with the canal. Shady trees lined the banks of the canal. Under Abdullah Khan in 1578 a bridge was constructed on Zarafshan near Ghujdwan and another near Kermina in 1582. It is stated that the river was divided here into small chanels and each channel was led into small canals, on the banks of which were established villages.[231] Another canal ran between the villages of Shargh and Sikijkal (i.e. 4 *farsakhs* from Bukhara en route Samarqand) and was called Samjen or Haram on which there was a bridge of bricks. But the canal terminated at Paikand.[232]

A canal near Tashkent is also mentioned by Hafiz Tanish in 1580. After his conquest of Sauran in 1582, Abdullah took certain measures for constructing, excavating and repairing the canals and rejuvenating agriculture which had suffered a serious setback earlier.[233] In this connection, special importance is attached to his activities in the region of Nur below Nur Ata. Hafiz Tanish proudly describes how the irrigational facilities were provided by Abdullah from rain water collected in the reservoir Hazr Jushan. During his campaigns in the far north in 1582, on his way from Temur Kabuka in Nur, Abdullah came through the Aqchab valley in the vicinity of Hazr Jushan. In the spring season, much water used to accumulate in this valley due to the rains; but this could not be utilized for purposes of agriculture. Abdullah now ordered that Ahmad Ataliq Naiman should construct a dam on this ravine in the manner of the milky way so that accumulated water could easily be used by the population for agriculture.[234] Hafiz Tanish refers to a large canal which was built by Abdullah after the conquest of Badakhshan in 1584 from the river Amu for irrigating the steppe of Hazrat Imam which was situated in the south of Panj, a high place at the confluence of Wakhsh and Aqsarai. It is recorded that the Dasht-i Imam which happened to be devoid of water was a deserted place till that time, but now became so prosperous and populous that the increased cultivation yielded crops which were greater by a hundred times than before. Some of the people of Khutlan, Qunduz, Baghlan were ordered by Abdullah to migrate and settle down in that area after completing the construction of this canal. A part of *tahsil*, from this *juibar* was utilized by the *mujavirs* and the remaining amount was prescribed for travellers.[235]

Another famous canal in Samarqand was Abe Rahmat which was brought from Saib near Kan-i Gul. In the sixteenth century, the area irrigated by the canal Abe Rahmat was known as Naqsh-i Jahan.[236] In the region of Kashka darya valley, Abdullah Khan constructed Hauz-i Khan resettled 'Faizabad in the *wilayat* of Qarshi'.[237]

The Dargham dam, the *mai* source of irrigation in Samrqand, was sufficiently large[238] and needed repairs frequently. Sometimes, it broke down even during the sowing season which made Samarqandis call this dam the *dard-o gham*.[239] In 1593 Abdullah Khan had tried to bring out a canal on the left bank on Amu but failed. It was in 1602 that Arab Muhammad (father of Abul Ghazi) succeeded in bringing a canal from the upper borders of Tuka situated near the lower part of Nukus.

The Khwaja who dominated the arena in the sixteenth century and occupied most of the land were keen to oblige people by arranging for the digging of canals in various parts of Central Asia. In the *waqf* documents of Khwaja Ahrar, a number of canals are mentioned besides the *jui-shahr*. Wasifi records that Mir-i Arab, the famous saint of early sixteenth century had give to his native place, Sauran, a set of two *kariz* (dug up by two hundred Indian slaves). The sources of the two *kariz* were at a distance of one *farsakh* from Sauran in a strong fort in which a well was dug whose depth was 200 *gaz* of which 150 *gaz* were under water and the distance from the water level up to the upper surface of the land measured 150 *gaz*. The water was lifted through a *chigir* (a form of Persian wheel), the *chigir* being moved with the help of oxen. The author had prepared the documents regarding *kariz* and the buildings at the request of Mir-i Arab himself.[240]

Another Khwaja Shaikh Husain Khwarazmi arranged for the digging of a canal in the *qariya* of *shatri*. The stones for construction were supplied by Khan Abdul Aziz of Bukhara, a devotee of the Shaikh who was, therefore, later on lovingly called the Khan Kuhkan which was adopted by the Khan as his pen name also.[241] In the *wilayat* of Wakhsh another canal was dug. At the imperial order 10,000 *mardikar* were supplied to Khwaja for the construction and in 991 around ten deserted villages were repopulated.[242]

Rauzat-ur Rizwan gives a detailed account of such 'philanthropic' activities of the Khwajas. The author claims that within one decade, Khwaja Saad had arranged for the excavation of a number of canals so much so that within a decade from the borders of Sabran in Turkestan down to Darband in Khurasan, there was no city, plain or corner where a hundred *juibars* had not been dug up at Khwaja's order.[243] The cultivation (*tarh-i zaraat* and *kisht o kar kardan*) in *baldas* of Transoxiana, Merv, Akhsikat, Turkestan, Badakhshan, Balkh, Herat and Khurasan developed so much that two thousand pairs of oxen (*juft gao*) were employed.[244] Similarly in 964 another canal (brought from the Rud-i Shahr-i Bukhara) in the plains of Samarjuq converted a dreary place into a green verdure.[245] In 967 Khwaja Qasim Shawari ordered the digging of another canal from river Kuhik, designed to run through waterless plains and deserts.[246] Khwaja Amir Kalan Shawari had built another canal (*juibar*) bringing water from a *rud* of Tuman-i Ramtain which flowed just below the Qariya of Sewanj and turned the saline land (*shorazar*) into a cultivable land. Still another canal was brought from river Amu (Oxus) in 970 which flowed just below Feasar-i Charjiu. In 976, Khwaja ordered that a canal should be cut from the canal of the upper city of Merv to pass through the old city, falling ultimately into the lands below. This attempt to rejuvenate agriculture was made by Khwaja 'though the lands remained devoid of water for the past 318 years' (beginning with the Mongol conquest). The availability of the water not only created gardens but also facilitated the working of a number of water-mills (*asiya-i gardun*) in the old city.[247] In 987 again the *juibars* were constructed in Wakhsh[248] which made at least ten deserted villages prosperous. Khwaja Mushtari founded a town known as Tahsinabad and constructed a large dam for the canal which was brought from Kuhik and for whose construction many labourers were engaged. When minor damage occurred a group of 10,000 labourers and 10,000 asses, were used to strengthen the dam. The people of the *deh* had become tired of doing the work on this dam. After making incessant efforts for several days, the water still flowed out.[249] At another place mention is made of the *juizgah* of Tashkent which was occupied by Khwaja's men. Khwaja Mushtari also arranged for the canals to be taken to several places in the desert, bringing them under cultivation.[250] In the Kalas steppes, the arable lands of Khwaja Ahrar's father have been mentioned which shows that some water supply must have been available there also. In *Abdullahnama* the route of Kalas is described as a verdant place irrigated by the Ata canal.

The existing *juibars* were also repaired. The *Rauzat-ur Rizwan* says that in 979, the *juibar* in Samanjuq was rebuilt with stones.[251]

In Transoxiana, an ideal material loess was available for construction of the canals. When moistened loess was as plastic as clay and dried in sun it became as hard as stone.[252] The canals were often even multistoreyed, one above the other and frequently crossing each others. It may be noted that these canals which were owned by the Khans and Juibari sheikhs had to be constructed and repaired by the people through unpaid labour. In April 1585, Abdullah Khan Uzbeg entrusted the task of digging the canals of Khwaja Juibari in Wakhsh to a trusted person, Mulla Muhammad Bi, who was supposed to look after the work as well as arrange for 10,000 labourers who were brought by Abdullah from the *wilayat* at Hesar. Mulla Muhammad Bi was ordered to see the Khwaja and to carry out his orders.[253] In this connection, another *souzomiz* of Abdullah Khan (dated Jumad I 993) ordering the officers, *arbab, kalantars, reaya* of Deh-i Nau, Hesar, Qubadiyan and *aimaqs* of Shahr-i Safa to supply 10,000 *mardikar* for digging the canal of Khwaja at Wakhsh was also issued. Simultaneously, Ahmad Ali Ataliq was also asked to supervise the construction of Khwaja's canal in Rabi II 993.[254] The inability to supply labourers was treated as offence against the State and harsh punishment was meted out to such offenders.[255]

The *farman* of Abdullah Khan Uzbeg contained in the *Rauzat-ur Rizwan* also testify to the fact that building of canals was carried out by labourers who were supplied by the officers in a particular locality where the canals had to be dug.[256] Although the work remained unpaid, it was compulsory on the ground that the peasants themselves needed the water; the use of this same water, however, was subject to tax. Even on the lands on which there were no taxes, the peasants had to pay the tax for using the water which was known as *mirabana*.[257] For the use of this water, the peasants had to depend very largely upon the sweet will of the rulers. At the beginning of the seventeenth century under Baqi Muhammad, the canal in Nasaf was closed down as a punishment to the inhabitants of Nasaf for their participation in an uprising against the new dynasty; as a result of this closure the region was faced with an acute scarcity of water.[258]

In Transoxiana there were certain water rights dating from extreme past with the old irrigational system prevailing over the centuries. The irrigation system was usually supervised by a local ruler with the help of an organisation which was called *miraba* or *mirab-i shahr*. When the water reached the corners of the town, its use inside the city was supervised by certain officers.[259] Generally the cooperation of the local population (other than nomads) was requisitioned for constructing new canals or for maintenance and repairs of irrigation works. The irrigation economy also necessitated agreement on water distribution choice of crops, allocation of costs of irrigation works, etc.[260] Dobson who visited Central Asia in 1888 says that 'at present and as for many years past there exists both in Bukhara and Turkistan a very important body of water police named Mirab the ruler of the water with others of subordinate rank whose duty is to see that every person gets his fair share of the precious fluid and does not suffer from the greediness or enmity of his neighbors. The Amil and the local ruler simply had a written record of the use of water and its distribution. The wealth and social position of a native in these parts are estimated to a great extent by the quantity of water to which he is entitled'.[261] The *Majma-ul Arqam* says that the *Ataliq-i kalan* controlled the distribution of water. During flood times as well as during shallow waters they let the water go through 21 *rawaq* to reach the places and people in accordance with the need and in rightful amount (*haqqaba*). The 21 canals carry the water sufficient enough for irrigating about 1,00,000 *tanabs* of land; 518 waterways (went through one canal) given to *hazara* lower Kermina, Tashirabat upto Takhti kir, one *rawaq* [262] with 1/4 of water irrigated Shafurkam and Mirabad (3/5 for the population of former and 2/5 for the latter) and so on. The information given by Istakhri and others regarding 'the water bureau, with a chief and 10,000 subordinates to help him in which the unit of measurement was the quantity which issued from an apertures one *shairah* square' is also mentioned by Obruchev in nineteenth-twentieth centuries which shows a continuation of the same system. The amount to be distributed was divided into 60 parts, water meter was placed at a distance of one *farsang* from *merv*—this was a board with a longitudinal slit. If the gauge stood at 60 barley corns—a fruitful year, if no higher than 2 barley corn—a famine. The state of the gauge was, at each time reported to the water bureau which then fixed the ration and sent it to all, sluice keepers.[263]

Since water was seen as God's gift which could not be owned or controlled by a private person, the distribution of water to the fields was managed at the village level by a water controller (*mirab*) who in turn was supervised by the elder (*aqsaqal*) elected from the villages using the canal. If the extent of the irrigational network requires two or more elders to supervise it one elder was designated senior and in charge of the whole system. The officials were also responsible for the cleaning and maintenance of the canals.[264] In theory, the water was to be supplied equally to all. Not only the measure of water called *qulaq* was gauged only by the eye but the final judgement to determine how much water was needed by an individual farmer was also determined by the elders. Consequently, the rich land owners through bribery could draw greater benefit than the poor from the supply of water.[265]

NOTES

1. V.V. Barthold, *Sochinenija*, Vol. VI, Moscow, 1969, p. 202; N. Elias and E. Denison Ross's preface in English translation of *Tarikh-i-Rashidi* of Mirza Haidar Dughlat, *A History of the Mughals of Central Asia*, London, 1895, p. 56; Lawrence Krader, *People of Central Asia*, Indiana University Publication, Vol. 26, rpt., the Hague, 1966, p. 92; G. Ghaffurov, *Istorija Tajikskovo Naroda va kratkom Izlozeni*, Moscow, Leningrad, 1949, 1952, 1955, p. 331, Ivanov, *Ocherki pa Istori Sredni Azi*, Moscow, 1958, p. 57. Qazvini, *Nazhat-ul Qulub*, Bombay, 1311, p. 234.
2. Fazlullah Ruzbehan Isfahani, *Mehmannama-i-Bukhara*, Tehran, 1962, p. 149.
3. Binai Harwi, *Futuhat-i Khani*, Institute of Oriental Studies, Tashkent, MS no. 14/1, f. 53. Ibn-i Battuta found the Qipchaq desert green and verdant, but flat and treeless. There was no firewood so they made fires of dung. Ibn Battuta, *Rehla*, Eng. tr., p. 142; Persian tr., p. 359.
4. Isfahani, p. 141.
5. Bori Ahmedov, *Gasudarstova Kochevikh Uzbegov*, Moscow, 1965, pp. 148-50.
6. Ibid.
7. Fazlullah, p. 100.
8. Barthold, II, p. 273.
9. *Istorija Uzbegskoj SSR*, Tashkent, 1956, pp. 392-3.
10. *Babur Nama* (*BN*), Eng. tr., Beveridge, London, 1922, p. 2.
11. Amin Ahmad Razi, *Haft Iqlim*, Vol. III, p. 440.
12. *Rauzat*, pp. 295-6.
13. *Istorija Uzbegskoj SSR*, op. cit., p. 393.
14. Barthold, *Soch*. V, p. 184.
15. Burnes, p. 255.
16. For such references and details see Mansura Haidar, *Central Asia in the Sixteenth Century*.

17. P. Ivanov, *Ocherki pa Istorii Sredni Azi*, Moscow, 1958, pp. 49-52.
18. *BN*, p. 3.
19. Deniel R. Bergzmark, *Economic Geography of Asia*, New York, 1937, pp. 585-92; G.B. Cressey, *Asia's Lands and Peoples*, New York, 1955, pp. 345-52; D. Stamp, *Asia*, 3rd edn., London, 1935, pp. 679-88.
20. *BN*, p. 3.
21. Jenkinson, p. 14.
22. Bergzmark, pp. 585-92; Stamp, pp. 679-88, Cressey, pp. 345-52.
23. *Haft Iqlim*, III, p. 331; Ibn-i Hauqal, *Surat-ul Arz*, pp. 193-4. Ibn-i-Hauqal further adds that if at all some natural calamity befalls in summer/or winter, the helpfulness and immense cooperation of the people from the vicinity enables to tide over the situation.
24. Qazvini, *Nuzhatu'l Qulub*, pp. 228-9.
25. Ibid., p. 235.
26. Ibn-i Hauqal, pp. 194-5, 202-3.
27. Ibid., pp. 228-9.
28. *BN*, text, p. 45; Eng. tr., p. 76.
29. *BN*, p. 11.
30. *BN*, pp. 97-8.
31. Qazi Habibullah, *Ajaib-ul Gharaib*, MS Ouseley 47, Bodleian Library, Oxford f.55, *BN*, pp. 1-9; *IA*, Eng. tr., p. 17.
32. *BN*, pp. 1-9; Ibn-i Hauqal, pp. 236-8.
33. Ibid., p. 7.
34. Ibid., p. 6.
35. *BN*, Eng. tr., p. 10.
36. Ibid., pp. 9, 10, 12, 82.
37. *Mehn*, pp. 66-7; Razi, *Haft Iqlim*, III, p. 472.
38. Isfahani, pp. 86-7.
39. E. Bretschneider, *Medieval Researches*, Vol. I, 1887, pp. 21-2; also see Clavijo, p. 287.
40. Ibn-i Hauqal, pp. 220-8; Bretschneider, pp. 21-2.
41. *BN*, Eng. tr. pp. 74-7, 81; *Haft Iqlim*, III, p. 334; Hasan Nisari, pp. 45-6; *Mehn*, p. 281; Clavijo, pp. 284-7.
42. *BN*, p. 81.
43. Ibn-i Hauqal, pp. 228-9.
44. *Travels of an Alchemist*, p. 105.
45. Lamb, p. 133.
46. Clavijo, pp. 284-8.
47. *Ajaib-ul Gharaib*, p. 47.
48. Ibn-i Battuta, op. cit., p. 172.
49. *BN*, p. 84; *Abdn*, p. 87; *Soch*, p. 460.
50. Maqdisi, p. 283, Istakhri, p. 312; Ibn-i Hauqal, pp. 201-2, 211-16; Adam Mez, p. 448.
51. *BN*, pp. 82-3.
52. Ibid.
53. *Muzzakkira*, pp. 32-8.
54. Ibid.
55. Ibn-i Hauqal, p. 215.
56. *Majma-ul Gharaib*, f.98; Thomas Walters, p. 108, Juvaini, text, p. 103; tr. 130.

57. Marco Polo, p. 57.
58. Burnes, pp. 228, 230.
59. Marco Polo, p. 62.
60. Ibid., p. 58.
61. Burnes, pp. 228-30.
62. Abul Ghazi and Shergul say that this name was given by an ancestor of Chingiz Khan (*Turkestan*, pp. 149-50) (see 214 b).
63. Wasifi, *Badaiul Waqai*, 2nd edn., Iran, pp. 297-307, also see Ibn-i Hauqal, p. 233.
64. Ibn-i Hauqal, p. 230.
65. *Abdn*, pp. 86-7.
66. Ibn-i Hauqal, p. 209; Qazvini, p. 234; Ibn-i Battuta, Persian tr., p. 411. For a very interesting discussion on the name 'Tashkent', see Walters, *On Yuan Chwang's Travels in India AD 629-645*, edited by Rhys Davids and S.W. Bushell, New Delhi, 1961, pp. 85-90.
67. Ibid.; *Iz Arkhiv Shaikhov Juibar*, Docs. 120, 127, 159, 213, 240, 362.
68. Ibid.
69. *Rashhat*, p. 56.
70. Hujjatlar 42/61, cf. Muqm, p. 204.
71. *Sherul Turkestan*, pp. 137-8.
72. Docs. 109, 117, 118, 130, 139, 155, 157, 159, 213, 216, 317, 318.
73. *Iz Arkhiv Shaikhov*, Docs. 310, 320, Chang Chun's *Travels*, pp. 105-6.
74. *Arkhiv Shaikhov Juibar*, Docs 164-5.
75. Ibid., Docs. 310, 312, 317, 318, 320.
76. Chang Chun spent the night under such a huge mulberry tree which could have sheltered a hundred people (*Travels*, p. 91).
77. *Arkhiv Shaikhov Juibar*, Docs. 109, 110, 111, 118, 123, 126, 146, 159, 162, 163, 164, 214, 215, 216.
78. Ibid., Docs., pp. 118, 159.
79. Wasifi, p. 297; *Mehn*, p. 281.
80. *Ain-i-Akbari*, Eng. tr. by Blochmann, Delhi, 1965, pp. 68-9.
81. *Rauzat-ur Rizwan*, MS 253, IOST, no. 2094, pp. 296, 355-6.
82. *Rashhat*, p. 352; even as late as eighteenth-twentieth centuries. The same age old instruments were being used (Shergul, *Turkestan*, pp. 133-4; *Bcemernaya Istoriya*, p. 577; Obruchev, p. 40.
83. *Abdn*, p. 405, for details of these reforms cf. *Cambridge History of Iran*, pp. 483-538.
84. *Bolshaya Sovetskaya Entsiklopedia* II, Netherlands, 1963, p. 229.
85. Kradar, *Peoples of Central Asia*.
86. *Nuzhat-ul Qulub*.
87. *Al mataul Fakhri*, f. 207 b.
88. *Rashhat*, pp. 35, 37, 44, 49, 52-4, 56, 80.
89. For detailed account see *Ajaib-ul Gharaib*, p. 30.
90. Ibid., p. 35.
91. *Tazkira-i Daulat Shah*.
92. Examples: *Rashhat*, pp. 1-35, 37.
93. See Mansura Haidar, 'Glimpses of Central Asian Rural Life in Russian Explorer's Works', *CAJ*, 1984, p. 2.
94. *Rauzat*, p. 512.

95. *BN*, p. 98.
96. Burnes, p. 249.
97. Obruchev, pp. 45, 65, 70; Berg and Ignatov, p. 53. See Mansura Haidar, 'Glimpses of Central Asian Rural Life in Russian Explorer's Works', *CAJ*, Nov. 1984.
98. Burnes, pp. 330-6.
99. Ibid., pp. 204-5; for details on later villages see Mansura Haidar, 'Glimpses of Rural Life in Russian Explorer's Works, *CAJ*, Nov. 1984, pp. 16-26.
100. Burnes, Vol. I, pp. 204-5.
101. For *Sirkah* see Lokkegaard, p. 100.
102. *Matla.*
103. *Rauzat*, p. 319.
104. According to Lambton, *muqata'eh*, was the assessment of the tax of a district at a fixed sum; the farming of the revenue of a district by the inhabitants for a fixed sum. Lambton, *Landlord and Peasants Glossary*, p. 435.
105. For details see O.D. Chekhovich, *Bukharski dokumenti*, Tashkent, 1965, pp. 14-20. In classic period *muzaraun* were liable to an amount lying between half and two thirds of the output but frequently less (*Islamic Taxation*). The share of the *metayer* might be half of the produce which is the same as in Sasanid period. Tenancy against a fixed rent as well as *metayage* has its roots far back in Babylonian times. The *muzara'ah* tenancy in most cases seems to have been in force for one or two years. The stipulations connected with it are, at least according to some traditions, somewhat less profitable than those of the *musaqah* (crops sharing contract for the trees). The tenant might be warranted a third or a fourth of the output and apparently the owner was able to decide which kind of crops should be grown. This might be due to the fact that the term *muzareah* is used for all types of tenancy even the less favourable ones, and the tenants are collectively called *muzaraun* (*Islamic Taxation*, p. 69) entrusted in return for a share of the crop under a crop sharing contract (see Lambton, *Landlord and Peasants Glossary*, p. 435).
106. *Bukharski documenti*, XIV, pp. 14-20.
107. *Rashhat*, pp. 261-2.
108. *Matla.*
109. Lokkegaard, *Islamic Taxation in the Classic Period*, Copenhagen, 1950, pp. 93-108.
110. Ibid., pp. 110-11.
111. Mukhtarov, *Nagrobni Kairaki, XIII-XVI C Upaminanya termin 'Dihqan', Epigrafika Vastoka XVIII*, Leningrad, 1967, pp. 80-93, for similar conclusions see Barthold, *Turkestan Down*, pp. 180-1.
112. Reuben Levy, *The Social Structure of Islam*, pp. 70, 380; *An Introduction to Sociology*, pp. 224-6.
113. Watt, *Islam and the Integration of Society*, p. 115.
114. Barthold, *Turkestan va Epakhe Mangolov*, Vols. I-II, St. Petersburg, 1900.
115. Juvaini, *Tarikh-i Jahankusha.*
116. A.E. Bartels, *Nasir-i Khusrau and Ismailism*, Moscow, 1959 (Russian tr.), pp. 18-26.
117. Petrushevski, *Agrarnikh otnosheniya va Irane*, XIII-XIV, Moscow, Leningrad, 1960, pp. 75-6; *Bolshaya Sovetskaya Entsiklopedia*, p. 129.

118. Mukhtarov, *Nadgrobni Kairaki XIII-XVI C. Upaminanya termin 'dihqan', Epigraphika Vastoka XVIII*, Leningrad, 1967, pp. 80-93.
119. Wasifi II, pp. 12-15; Belenitski, pp. 113-14.
120. Mukhtarov, *Nadgrobni Kairaki XIII-XVI C. Upaminaniye termin 'dihqan'* (Concerning the development of the social category of '*dihqans*' in the middle ages), paper presented by USSR Delegation at 26th International Congress of Orientalists, Moscow, 1963.
121. *Bolshaya Sovetskaya Entsiklopedia*, p. 129.
122. Frye, *Bukhara: the Medieval Achievement*, Norman, 1965, pp. 74, 156-7.
123. Ibid., pp. 74, 156-7.
124. *Izvestia*, p. 36.
125. Ivanov, *Khazyaistova*, pp. 31-2.
126. Davidovich, *Izvestia*, p. 38.
127. Ibid.
128. *Cambridge History of Islam*, Vol. 2, Cambridge, 1970, p. 519.
129. Chekhovich, *Novie Istochniki pa Istori Bukhari va Nachale*, XIV, 1959, no. 5, p. 158; Davidovich, p. 38.
130. Davidovich, *Izvestia*, p. 38; Ivanov, *Khazyaistova*, p. 44.
131. *Waqfnama*, Abdullah Khan State Lib. An UZ SSR, no. 24/2, f.323, also cf. Davidovich, *Izvestia*, p. 37.
132. Ibid.
133. *Iz Arkhiv Shaikhov Juibar*, nos. 333, 334, 363, 365, 366 ff.
134. *Izvestia*, pp. 36-7.
135. Ghaffurov, *Istorija Tajikskovo Naroda*; *Matla*, pp. 277-80.
136. *Matla*, p. 279.
137. Ibid., p. 280.
138. Ali Sher Navoi, *Mahbub-ul Qulub*, Academy of Sciences USSR, Moscow, Leningrad, 1948, p. 46.
139. *Narod Sredni Azi*, II, p. 93.
140. *Mehn*, p. 89.
141. *Narod Sredni Azi e Kazakhstane*, pp. 93-4; S.E. Balshaya, *The Turkic Peoples*, The Netherlands, 1963, p. 116.
142. *Rashhat*, pp. 52-3; *Nafhat-ul uns*, MS. Aligarh, *Farsiya Akhbar*, 28, f. 557.
143. *Rauzat*, pp. 485-9.
144. *Matla*, II, III, pp. 379, 387-8, 400-1.
145. Ibid.; also Muhammad Abdus Saad Khan, *Tarikh-i Qahet*, MS Aligarh Farsiya 4, Abdussalam Collection 272/42, ff. 65-9, 83-6; see Obruchev, p. 37; Berg and Ignatov, pp. 53-86; also see Mansura Haidar, 'Glimpses of Central Asian Rural Life in Russian Explorers Works', *Central Asiatic Journal*, Nov. 1984.
146. *Rauzat*, pp. 108, 157-8.
147. *BN*, pp. 144-6.
148. *Shaibani Nama* by Muhammad Saleh, pp. 66-7, 71, 82.
149. *T. Raqim*, pp. 90-1; *Rauzat*, p. 203.
150. *Rauzat*, p. 296, also see pp. 345-6.
151. *BN*, pp. 93-4.
152. *Rauzat*, p. 345.
153. *BN*, Eng. tr., p. 86.

154. Ibid.
155. *Mehn*, pp. 295-9.
156. S.A. Wallin, *Sochinenija Kistori Sredni Aziatski Arabov*, 2nd edn., Arab Association, 1937, p. 120.
157. *Istorija Uzbegskoi SSR*, Tashkent edn., 1967, p. 533.
158. Ibid.
159. Qazi Docs., Tashkent, 1937, pp. 28-41, 44, 59; Davidovich, *Izvestia*, pp. 33-4.
160. A somewhat brighter picture of peasants plight in Central Asia is depicted by Spuler who says that 'peasants were free men, not legally bound to the soil'. In the event of natural calamities they could get loans of livestocks, etc., without any return unless the donor himself met with adversity. If then the peasants were unable to pay they were to be placed in bondage for debt and would not for the time be able to leave the land but they did not even so lose all their rights. When 'land hunger appeared in consequence of population growth, portions of state land (*amlak-i padshahi*) or royal domain *camlak-i sultani*) were regularly made available. The area in private possession grew in this way and not only large proprietors but also small cultivators benefited. *The Islamic World: Central Asia in the Last Centuries of Independence*, p. 241).
161. Examples *ZN*, pp. 58, 347, 352, 390, 444, 485.
162. *BN*, text, Eng. tr., pp. 32-3.
163. *Landlord and Peasants*, Glossary, also p. 100.
164. *ZN*, p. 733, *Matla*, pp. 14, 15, 353, 483.
165. *Mehn*, pp. 46, 60, 91.
166. Ibid., p. 91.
167. *Istorija*, p. 525.
168. *Abdn*, p. 454.
169. *Istorija*, pp. 525-6.
170. Krader, p. 94.
171. According to Lokkegaard (*Islamic Taxation*, p. 14) the original meaning of *iqta* is the act of bestowing or allotting a *qatiah* or cut off piece; its genuine Arabic origin can be traced back to the times of the Prophet when it was simply a grant or bestowl of property without any other obligations (called by the latter jurists as *iqtai tamlik*). Lokkegaard, *Islamic Taxation*, 62-72. From the very beginning of Islamic period, *iqta* with its various categories (*tamlik, istighlala, tadmin*) and even institutions of *fay* and *hima* are mentioned. The military fiefs originated in frontier regions (*ribat* and *masatih*) and military fiefs were known already in Babylonian period; the lack of cash or supply of coined metal could be one of the several reasons cash for its existence (Petrushevski). It was in vogue in Persia too and could be a result of several influences. For interesting details on the origins of *iqta* cf. Frye, pp. 125-8; Lambton, *Landlords . . .*, pp. 31-77.
172. Petrushevski, *Ikaz Soch*., p. 232; R.N. Nabiev, *Izvestia*, p. 24.
173. Ahmedov, p. 148-50; Belenitsky, p. 113; for Saljuqid *iqta* see Tusi, pp. 44, 203.
174. Nabiev, *Izvestia*, Acadim Nauk Uz SSR 3, 1959, p. 24.
175. Ivanov, *Khazyaistova*, p. 26; Nabiev, p. 25.

176. See Yasin's Glossary, under *Darubast.*
177. *Abdn*, p. 377.
178. Ibid., pp. 370, 395, 480-1.
179. Ibid.
180. *Silsilat*, p. 269.
181. Wasifi, pp 1327-8.
182. *T. Raqim*, p. 125.
183. *Lataifnama-i Fakhri*, p. 269.
184. Nabiev, Novi Documentalni Material K Izuchenie Feudalnovo Instituta Souyurghal va Ferghane XVI-XVII, *Izvestia*, 1959, no. 3, Tashkent, pp. 23-32.
185. M. Salim, *Tarikh-i Raqim*, p. 121; *Silsilat*; Yasin's Glossary, also refers to *altamgha* as 2 separate words, *al* (official assurance) and *tamgha* (*hasil o baj*) and also as red seal (Yasin's Glossary under *altamgha*) on the *farmans.*
186. *Tuzuk-j Jahangiri*, tr. Alexander Rogers, Delhi, 1968, p. 23.
187. *Jamiut Tawarikh*, Eng. tr. by John Andrew Boyle, *The Successors of Genghis Khan*, New York & London, 1971, p. 83; *Glossary*, pp. 39, 340 under *al-tamgha.*
188. *Documenti Kistorii agrarnikh atnashenija Va Bukharskom Khanstave*, Vol. I, Tashkent, 1954, p. 13.
189. *Abdn*, p. 34.
190. Ibid., p. 419.
191. Ibid., pp. 350, 377.
192. Lokkegaard, *Islamic Taxation*, p. 54.
193. Spuler, p. 241.
194. Tsgee a UZ SSR, f. 323, no. 24/1/2, no. 55/69, no. 1188/7, no. 13; cf. *Izvestia*, p. 41; for the origin of the *waqf* land cf. Levy, also Z.E. Yampolski, *K. Vaprosu o proiskhazdenija Vakfa*, pp. 110-12; *Narod Azii e Afriki*, 4, 1964.
195. *Waqfnama-i Shaibani Khan.*
196. Ibid.
197. *Matla*, p. 279; Schuyler, *Turkestan*; Muqminova, *Iz istori Wuqufnovo Zemlevladeniya va Sredni Azi* XVI, *Isledovaniya ka Istori Kulturno Narodov Voctoka*, Moscow, Leningrad, 1960, pp. 215-18.
198. *Abdn*, p. 198.
199. *Istorija Uzbegskoj*, p. 526.
200. Wasifi.
201. While discussing the dishonest practices in various grants noticed in subsistences allowances, Abul Fazl mentions that Iranian and Turain women were also convicted of fraud, and the order was passed that every excess of land above 100 *bighas* held by them should be inquired into whether it was correctly held or not, *Ain* I, Delhi, 1977, pp. 279-81.
202. Muqminova, *Waqfnama*, Tashkent, 1966, pp. 81, 196, 197-8; also see Yasin's Glossary for *ijara.*
203. Spuler, p. 241.
204. *Suluk*, BMMS, 253, f. 80.
205. *Suluk*, p. 80. Lokkegaard, pp. 72, 85-6.
206. Ivanov, *Khazyaistova*, p. 40; Ivanov, *Ocherki*, p. 60; Davidovich, p. 28.
207. Chekhovich, p. 223; Razia Muqminova, p. 72; Davidovich, p. 28.

208. E.A. Davidovich, 'Rezentsia na kneegu P.P. Ivanov, Khazaaistova Juibari shaikhov', 1954; *Sovetskaya Ethnografia*, 1955, no. 3, pp. 188-90.
209. Nabiev, *Novi, Documentalni Material*, pp. 23-32.
210. Davidovich, *Masterial dlya charcteristiki, economiki e socialnikh otnoshenye va sredni Azi* XVI Izvestia 1 (24) Stalinabad, 1961, pp. 28-9.
211. O.D. Chekhovich, *Bukharski pazemelni acti*, XVI-XIX, Problem Istochnikovedeiny, IV, 1955, p. 223 onwards; Davidovich, *Izvestia*, pp. 28-9.
212. Davidovich, *Izvestia*, p. 29.
213. Nabiev, *Novie Documentalni Material*, p. 26, Doc. 2, p. 27, Doc, p. 4; *Documenti Kistori agrarnikh atnashenija va Bukharskom Khanstova*, Vol. I. *Feudalni substvennosti na zemliu XV-XIX podbor documentov*, tr. by Chekhovich, Taskhet, 1954, p. 13, Doc. no. 4.
214. *Rauzat-ur Rizwan*, MS 77, Oriental Institute, Tashkent, no. 2094, f. 115.
215. Ibid., pp. 255-6.
216. Cf. A.A. Semenov, Ocherk pod zemelnoi padatnova e nalogave ustroistova, Tashkant, 1929. Davidovich, *Izvestia*, p. 31.
217. *Mehn*, pp. 295-9.
218. Ibid., pp. 295-8.
219. *Khazyaistova*, p. 45; Davidovich, p. 30.
220. Qazi Docs., XVI, Tashkent, 1937, Doc. 60, p. 37; ibid edited by Chekhovich, *Bukharski pazemelni acti*, pp. 228-31; *Tarikh-i Qahet*, pp. 83-6. Spuler says that agricultural land tax was levied as a rule in kind but increasingly in cash, it should legally have been 10 per cent of the crop but higher rates were in practice often charged probably around 20 per cent (Spuler, *Muslim World*, op. cit., p. 241).
221. Cook, *Studies in the Economic list of the Middle East*, p. 40; *Monetary Aspect of Medieval Near Eastern Economic History* by Andrew S. Ehren Kreuts, p. 40.
222. *Majma-ul Arqam*; pp. 28-9; *Mubaiyyan*, no. A-104f-63; *Suluk*, pp. 97-100; *Matlab*, p. 261; also see *Izvestia*, Davidovich, p. 34; Ivanov, *Khazyaistova*, p. 60.
223. Docs. 1550-1 and 1601 quoted by Nabiev, *Izvestia*.
224. *Izvestia*, pp. 34-6.
225. *Mehn*, p. 100.
226. Also see Dennet, *Ottoman Economic Mind*; Cook's *Studies*, pp. 200-9; Wasifi, *Badaiul Waqai*, old edn., Moscow, pp. 1327-34.
227. *Mehn*, pp. 86, 199.
228. *Badaiul Waqai*, p. 119.
229. *Abdn*, p. 87; *Rauzat*, pp. 169-71.
230. Muqminova, *Waqfnama*, pp. 48, 61, 63, 65, 69, 70, 77.
231. *T. Raqimi*; *Soch*, p. 200.
232. *T. Raqimi*, p. 186; *Soch*, Vol. III, pp. 113-15.
233. *Abdn*, p. 366.
234. Ibid., pp. 369-72.
235. Ibid., pp. 432-3.
236. *Istorija Samarqanda*, ed. by E.M. Mominov et al., Tashkent, 1969, pp. 282-7.

237. *Soch*, p. 226.
238. *BN*, Eng. tr., p. 76, f.45.
239. *Istorija*, pp. 282-7.
240. *Badai-ul Waqai*, pp. 348-55.
241. *Muzzakkira*, p. 84; *Silsilat*, p. 50.
242. *Rauzat*, p. 355.
243. Ibid., pp. 305-6, 356.
244. Ibid., p. 356.
245. Ibid., p. 253.
246. Ibid., p. 253.
247. Ibid., p. 253.
248. Ibid., pp. 312-18.
249. Abul Abbas, f. 261.
250. Ibid., p. 103.
251. *Rauzat*, p. 294.
252. Adam Mez, *The Renaissance of Islam*, Eng. tr. by Salahuddin Khuda Bakhsh and Margoliouth from German, Delhi, 1979, pp. 451-2.
253. *Rauzat*, p. 316.
254. Ibid., pp. 311-12, 316.
255. Ibid., p. 88; *Taj-ut Tawarikh*, f.35.
256. *Rauzat*, p. 88.
257. Ibid., p. 305; *Istorija Samarqanda*, pp. 283-7.
258. Barthold, III, p. 161.
259. *Matla*, p. 279.
260. Spuler, *The Islamic World: Central Asia in the Last Centuries of Independence*, Vol. III, p. 241.
261. Dobson, *Russian Railway Advance into Central Asia*, London, 1890, p. 232.
262. Literally *rawaq* means filtered, purified. In this context *rawaq* refers to channels through which the water reached in the regular direction of irrigational canals (cf. *Majma-ul Arqam;* Glossary, under *Rawaq*).
263. For details regarding irrigation system cf. *Majma-ul Arqam*, pp. 90-3; also see Şemenov, *Bukharski Trakat*, pp. 146-7; Istakhri, p. 261; *Mufatihu ulum*, ed. by Van Vloten, p. 68; Adam Mez, pp. 449-50; Obruchev noticed this 'real hermitage in sand' in the form of 'telegraphic lines' on the tables in Qaraqum deserts and on enquiry he was told by some very old Turcomans that these were water tunnels for supply of water from distant nice wells on the caravan routes between Merv and Charjui. Since there were only sanity wells in the region and the shifting of far off good wells was also not possible, they had built pump houses and had provided a mechanic and two other workers for this purpose (Obruchev, p. 55; Dobson, pp. 336-7).
264. *Matla*, pp. 279-80. Spuler considers *mirab* and *aqsaqal* as one and the same water controller (*IslamicWorld*: *Central Asia*, p. 241).
265. *Matla*, pp. 280-1; also see Khamid Inoyamov, *Central Asia and Kazakhistan before and after the October Revolution*, Moscow, 1966, pp. 13-18; for interesting detail about irrigation and watering taxes, cf. Lokkegaard, pp. 120-4.

System of Taxation Under the Uzbegs

Notwithstanding ceaseless efforts by various Uzbeg Khans and the Shaikhs of Juibar to arrange for irrigation, Central Asia in the first half of the sixteenth century witnessed deteriorating agrarian conditions. The decline in agriculture could not but affect tax realization. Jenkinson records in 1558 that 'the revenue of the ruler of Bukhara is but small and he is most maintained by the city taxes'.[1] In the second half of the sixteenth century, royal tax resources improved owing to large-scale confiscation of lands by Abdullah and also thanks to his efforts to improve agriculture. The rate of demand also seems to have increased.

Land revenue under the Uzbegs was known under various names, such as *kharaj, ikhrajat, matalibat-i sultani, amwal-i diwani, tahsilat, mahsulat* and *mal-i ghallat*. The rate of *kharaj* varied with various categories of land. However, the standard rate is said to have been more than half of the produce.[2] From the analysis attempted by Davidovich after a study of various sources and Russian works, it seems that the land tax amounted to 30 to 40 per cent of the crop.[3] This does not to include a variety of other taxes like *zabitana, jaribana* or *tanabana* (measurement tax, from the technical sense of *zabt, jarib* or *tanab,* all meaning measurement), *mawannat-i diwani* (requisitions of the *diwans*), *muhassilana* (collection tax), *mushrifana* (fee of the *mushrifs*), *amilat,* and other miscellaneous taxes, which could substantially raise the amount, making it more than a half of the produce.

Abul Fazl, writing at the end of the sixteenth century confirms that 'in Iran and Turan from ages past, they have exacted a tenth (of the produce) but the exactions have increased to more than a half, which, he avers, does not appear exorbitant to a despotic government'.[4]

According to Hanafite law, the land tax was of two types, namely, *kharaj-i maqasima* (crop-sharing payment in kind at the rate of ½, or ¼, the remainder was to be used by the holder for his personal needs); and *kharaj-i muazzaf* or *wazifa* (payment in cash fixed after the measurement of each *jarib*), as mentioned in the *Suluk-ul Mulk.*[5] In his *Mubaiyyan* Babur also indicates that the *kharaj* was realized in both cash and kind.[6] This is further proved by the fact that the *tahsilat* of the Juibari Shaikhs have also been given in cash and kind.

Semenov shows that *kharaj-i muazzaf* was realized in cash in one region at the rate of one *tanga* at another place, the rate was one *tanga* in spring and one *tanga* and 15 kg of grain in autumn, and so on.[7] This fluctuation is explained when we look into the account of *kharaj-i muazzaf* in the *Suluk-ul Mulk,* where it is stated clearly that the *kharaj-i wazifa* varied according to the quality of the crop and the fertility of the soil. For example, it was 5 *dirhams* on each *jarib* of grapes and 10 *dirhams* on each *jarib* of saffron, and so on.[8] Taxes on the gardens and vineyards known as *mal-i baghat* and *tanabana* were, however, paid only in cash,[9] presumably because the produce was usually marketed. The tax on water (*mirabana*) was also realized in cash.

The *hshr* tax was imposed upon fruits and *milk* lands and pastures (*zar'a wa samar*) at the rate of *deh yak* (10 per cent) if the land was naturally irrigated and *nisf ushr* (5 per cent) if artificially irrigated.[10] Most jurists agreed that irrigated lands had rivers. Amu and Syr were *kharaji.*[11] There were separate *Baitulmal* for *ushr* and *kharaj.*[12]

Apart from the land tax, there were a number of other taxes and sources of revenue for the state treasury. According to Abul Fazl in every kingdom, the government taxes the property of the subjects over and above the land revenue and this they call *tamgha.* In Iran and Turan, they collect the land tax from some, from others the *jihat* and from others again the *sair-i jihat,* while other cesses under the name of *wujuhat* and *faru'at* are extracted. In short, what is imposed on cultivated lands by way of land-tax is termed *mal.* Imports on manufactures of respectable kinds are called *jihat* and the remainder *sair-i jihat.* Extra collections over and above the land tax, if taken by revenue officers are *wujuhat;* otherwise they are termed *furuaat.*[13]

A careful study of Central Asian sources supports the above statement, though such terms categorizing various taxes are rarely found. In addition to these, some more forms of extra-canonical taxes are noticed. Here the description of some taxes is given in order of importance and the volume and extent of the amount raised by them. These include *jaziya, peshkash, mal-i amani,* taxes on merchants and artisans, collections for the benefit of the army and the steppe and some unidentified taxes.

In his discussion at Kan-i Gil, Shaibani is reported to have justified the imposition and collection of *jaziya* (poll tax) from non-Muslims.[14] Again, in 1593, Abul Ghazi refers to the collection of a poll tax.[15] Although Burnes noted that 'peaceful and pleasant toleration' was practiced in Central Asia, he refers to the fact that the Hindus paid *jaziya* or poll tax which 'they only rendered in common with others, not Mohammedans.[16] Muhammad Fazil says that *jaziya* was imposed upon everyone excepting Sunni Muslim; and the Jews and Hindus paid the amount annually according to their capacity, from one to four *tangas* each month (*ba qadri instead haryak tanga ta chahartanga*).[17]

The dues which were offered to higher authorities in the form of presents were known as *sawuri, tansuq, peshkash* or *padnashini* and could be made in the form of cash, valuables, slaves, horses, clothes or cattle. The great provincial governors, nobles as well as traders, artisans and even petty landlords were expected to bring such presents on special occasions, including the king's arrival in their vicinity. The presents were to be offered preferably in *tuquz* (numbered in nines). The *peshkash* would sometimes be distributed among the distinguished princes or nobles or even amongst the army.[18] But this was not a common practice. This form of obligation was considered to be essential—'a primary indicator of faithfulness, a vow or a promise as expression of devotion'.[19]

An indemnity called *mal-i amani,* was usually imposed upon conquered peoples. The amount was determined after negotiations. After the conquest of Herat, Maulana Abdur Rahim Sadr and Khwaja Kamaluddin Mahmud along with a group of *tahsildars* and soldiers were appointed by Shaibani for the acquisiton of *amwal o jihati ghaibi* in accordance with the concurrence of the notables (*akabir*). The collections (*tahsilat*) were written down and all the exactions (*wujuh*) realized from the *akabir* and *reaya* by force within a week. For *mal-i amani, peshkash* and *sawuri* were agreement by which populations (*amma-i reaya)* and the artisans (*muhtarifat*) were to pay about 1,00,000 *tangcha* of one *misqal*. The nobility and *suyurghal* holders were to pay in all about 20,000 *tangcha* as *peshkash-i khasa* to the Khan and 15,000 *tangcha* to Maulana Abdur Rahim.[20] According to Muhammad Salih the *ashligh* tax was collected only during wartime.[21] It was like a ration or food tax levied during an emergency. The amount of this tax varied according to the intensity of the Khan's needs as also the capacity of the payers.[22] In 1504, Shaibabni burdened the people so heavily with this tax that the towns of Shahrukhia and Khujand were completely ruined.[23] Another military tax, a continuation of steppe traditions, was *ghalla-i tughar* or *tughar,* which was prevalent in Central Asia even prior to the Shaibanids. *Tughar* was a kind of levy for the supply of foodstuffs to the army. Shaibani imposed it during his campaigns against the Qazaqs.[24] The amount realized is not specifically mentioned anywhere, but presumably the Khans and the other magnates decided the amount. Sometimes arbitrary collections for military expenses had devastating effect.

Whenever the *kharaj* did not suffice for the payment of the army, the government 'resorted to imposition of military levies', their extent and amount depending upon the capacity of the payer and the need of the government.[25] *Mirhazari,* a tax for the maintenance of the rural *mir* (chief) of military or administrative regions (*hazari*) has been mentioned in several documents of the sixteenth century. The *darughas* sitting in the *mauzas* (village and town fields) also realized *darughana*, often causing much harassment to the people. According to Semenov, the *madad-i lashkar* was a special cash tax levied for purposes of the maintenance of the army. Another military tax was known as *hashr,* involving forced labour of any kind, and *hashr wa begar-i qila*, which was met in the form of corvee, including the obligation to build or repair forts, etc.[26]

Kazu was a kind of forced labour. Peasants who were unable to pay their dues had to engage in construction work or wells, etc., without payment. Peasants could even be recruited against their will for unpaid services in the army and for revenue collection. But peasants were not the only victims: the exploitation of masons in building palaces, bridges, highways, etc., was widespread. For subsidiary works, unskilled labour was also employed and dealt with severely. The burden of expenditure for the repair of mosques and *khanqahs* also fell on the shoulders of neighbouring population of the region concerned. Not only artisans, but other categories of civil population were also generally asked to appear for military service. In 1501, Shaibani ordered all the people of Bukhara 'from 7 to 70 years of age, master or slave' to serve in the army.[27]

Besides, the Khan could demand that any number of unpaid labourers known as *mard-i kar* render all kinds of physical services. Kuchum Khan was once provided with Indian slaves.[28] The fate of the *mard-i kar* was completely in the hands of the ruler. Abdul

Momin (1598) ordered the reconstruction of the fort of Balkh within six months. It was proclaimed that if any *mard-i kar* was found behaving lethargically he would be buried alive within the walls. The author of the *Taj-ut Tawarikh* informs us that the bones of people were still visible in the walls of the fort of Balkh.[29]

The word *qupchur* in Mongolian literally means pastures. In the thirteenth century the nomadic Mongols were unaware of any other form of economy except pastoral. Since cattle were their chief wealth, the tax on heads of cattle was naturally the most important sources of revenue. According to the *Dastur-ul katib fi taiyyun ul maratib,* the rate was one head from per hundred heads of cattle. *Qupchur* was realized not only from nomads but also from the settled population and soldiers. Barthold says that the tax covered all the straight taxes levied on agriculturists and nomads and was different from the *tanga* or city taxes. Barthold holds that *qupchur* was of two types, one imposed upon nomads (*reayai dehnashin*) twice a year, and the other upon the steppe population in the beginning of a year. In the Uzbeg Empire of Abulkhair the rate of this tax is reported to have been 70 gold coins on one hundred head of cattle, which is said to have replaced the earlier rate even though it was equally imposed upon the nomadic as well as settled populations.[30]

In sixteenth century documents a number of unidentified taxes have also been mentioned. The steppe tax on land was known as *yasaq,* which was collected by the Khan's *basqaqs* by a census.[31] The word *yasaq* has been used in an Uzbeg document of Abdullah Khan's reign, where not only *yasaq* but also another tax, *alban,* has been mentioned.[32]

A number of steppe taxes existing in the Empire of Abulkhair are also of some interest. The *saimzakat* or *sawaimzakat* was paid at the rate of 1/40 or 2/5 per cent of the general number of cattle.[33] Another obligation was *saan* (the tax on milch animals).[34] It had been a nomads custom since ancient times to store meat for the winter. For this purpose the nomads drove in a part of their animals every autumn, a ritual called *sogum sochi* (the killing on *sogum*). At the time of the *sogum sochi* every nomad had to bring to the Khan, Sultans and local ruler some cattle as *sogum.* Similarly, when migrating to the summer pastures of the Khans, *ughlans* and others, the subjects brought cooked meat or other foodstuff for them.[35] This was called *shibaghun.* But these taxes were imposed in the steppe

Empire of Abulkhair and are seldom mentioned in the sixteenth century sources of Central Asia. Exemption from taxes like *taufir, tafavut, taqabbuli* (i.e. the surplus amount in addition to the *jama-i muqarrari*—stipulated money[36]) is reported to have been granted by Khan Abdul Aziz in 1541. The amount realized by these measures was quite high (81,000 *tangas*), which shows that they were important taxes.

The terms *gavzakhira*,[37] *amwali taqabbul,* and *dudi* are frequently found in lists of taxes. But their purpose remains undefined. Similarly, the *ayenda wasrawanda*, literally the tax on entrance and exit, is not explained anywhere, though it may have been a tax on travellers. The available information further indicates that there were a number of obligations and various local taxes exclusively levied in a particular region and not elsewhere. Occasionally, the same term could represent different taxes in different places.

Another tax was *qunnulgha* (called elsewhere *nuzul, qira* or *ziafa,* i.e. the billeting of soldiers), which was a levy for the entertainment of envoys, etc. This could be either in cash or kind or in the form of corvee. The rural population was duty bound to supply the necessaries to envoys and officers. The *Matlab-ut Talibain* refers to the *qunnulgha* in these terms: 'in each *sarkar,* wherever you happen to pass, let them provide you *qunnulgha* and also *kharj* to enable you to go from one sarkar to another'.[38] The tax on pastures, hunting grounds (reserved for the Khan and his family) known as *qurughmal* was realized both in cash and kind.[39]

It seems that the imperial *elchis, qushji tuwaji* and other state officials could demand from merchants en route the *ulagh* tax in the form of draft or taxed cattle and use them for administrative purposes on the grounds that merchants had to supply the facility for transportation or *ulagh*. The *ulagh* (levy for postal couriers or for animals for the post) was paid not only by agriculturists but also by traders. The available data indicate that *ulagh* was realized several times in the year. From the civil population, *ulagh* was realized during the army's march when provisions were collected by *diwans* and *yasawuls* in the name of the *'aliq-i ulaghan*.[40] Under Abdullah Khan, provisions known as *ulufa* (fodder for the horses of officials) were demanded. A certain Khwaja Raziuddin Ahmad, *diwan*, had been asked to collect *ulufa* (for the army[41]) which tempts one to infer that the term *ulufa* might be a synonym for *ulagh*. The term *ulagh* is also found.

Another tax was known as *tarh,* by means of which both farmers and artisans were compelled to sell their products to the state at lower than market prices. Simultaneously, the *tarh* forced merchants and craftsmen to buy the same products from the state at four to five times the market rates. An example of this tax is *tarh-i sabun* mentioned in the *Waqfnama* of Shaibani Khan, or *tarh-i ghalla.*

The various taxes imposed upon merchants and artisans are nowhere so profusely described as in the *Tarkhani* grants issued individually to merchants and nobles, where the names of these taxes are frequently mentioned, and in the documents of endowments, etc., where, in connection with the fiscal rights of the assignee, the various taxes are enumerated. In one of the *nishans* in *Maktubat wa Asnad,*[42] taxes on passage by road (*rahdari*) and river (*kishtibani*), and tolls at ferries are mentioned. For officers and servants a present (*khidmatana*) was demanded.[43] In a *manshur*[44] issued to a certain Khwaja Iliyas Chelebi officers are instructed not to take anything from the goods of the Khwaja in the form of *kharj, tamgha, saughat, salamana, peshkash* or *khidmatana.*

The list of taxes and the conditions imposed upon the sale of goods amply prove how difficult it was for artisans and peasants to market their goods. The accounts of travellers like Jenkinson and Sidi Ali Reis and, at a later date, Burnes, show how merchants and travellers were harassed by officers for presents.

Jenkinson says that the 'King of Bogher' (Bukhara) 'is most maintained by the city for he taketh the tenth penie of all things that are there solde as well by the craftsmen as by the merchants, to the great impoverishment of the people, whom he keepeth in great subjection, and when he lacketh money, he sendeth his officers to the shoppes of the sayd merchants to take their wares to pay his debts, and will have credit of force, as the like he did to pay me certain money that he owed me for ten pieces of Kersey'.[45]

The documents elsewhere show that in Turkestan and Khurasan all the above taxes were demanded from those who did not possess. In some cases, *rahdari, kishtibani, tamgha* and *zakat* as well as the opening of goods and the payment of an 'unforeseen' tax is forbidden. But there were no hard and fast rules in black and white, and the exploitation and harassment of ordinary subjects must have been considerable.

There were also the rents paid for urban properties (*mustaghallat,* such as on markets, mills, workshops) to the central exchequer, from which money was given for public endowments. Although the workshops of big merchants were exempt from taxes, such as the uratiba mills, as they all belonged to the category of *milk-i khur o khalis*,[46] taxes were still often demanded for them. The *Waqfnama* of Shaibani Khan refers to a tax imposed upon the square adjoining the mills.[47] The tax was known as *teg-i joi* or *taht joi*, to which was added the specific name of the area taxed, e.g. *teg-i joi*, *asiya ba khan* or *teg-i joi hanman*[48] and also specific places in the bazar. The tax for a place was given to its owner, be it the state, waqf holder or an ordinary citizen. This continued down to the nineteenth century.

Taxes on mills (*asiya*), sugar mills, and oilpresses, etc., known as *tigirman* (mills), were collected partially in cash at a later date and presumably in the sixteenth century also. In medieval and later medieval Bukhara, the owners of water mills using water from imperial canals were subjected to cash payments of *asiya pulli* and *abjawaz pulli*.[49] In accordance with the *yirliqs* given to the Saiyids of Karasakan a mill and oilpress were freed from tax obligations so as the money could help their owners. Officers were instructed not to collect *tigirman, asiya* and *juwaz khana*.[50] A special technical tax was also imposed upon artisans. The *chitgars* or chintz makers paid for using water. The tax on the preparation of chintz seems to have continued down to Abul Fazl's time, whose order of 1723 categorically mentions the 2½ *tanga* (instead of the 2 *tangas* as formerly paid) daily on the preparation of chintz in Bukharas.[51] Transcribers also had to pay *haqq-i kitabat* to persons appointed by the ruler.[52] Another tax frequently mentioned in the sources is *toujihat*. Barthold and Ivanov describe it as an entrance and maintenance tax on artisans.[53] The manuscript 210 in the Tashkent Library and *Abdullahnama* mention *taujinat* as a general tax on artisans and cultivators.[54] The *Ajaib-ul Gharaib*, a sixteenth century source, refers to an amount of 30,000 *dinars* paid as a *taujih* by the people on Sultan Husain's arrival in Balkh.[55]

Among other trade duties, *baj* seems to have been an important tax. Barthold explains it as city tax, or duties.[56] In the literature of the time, *baj* is treated as a road tax or, at times, a tribute. In a *nishan* issued to a merchant Haji, he is awarded *tarkhani* or exemption from *baj, kharaj, tamgha, zakat, saughat, salami, peshkash, rahdari* and *kishtibani*.[57] In Central Asia, the practice of realizing *baj* from merchants on their arrival from one region to another seems to have been common. At the order of Abulkhair in 1579-80, collectors, carters, ferrymen, imperial officers and others were ordered not to realise *baj* from *mutawalli* Saiyid Ali who had been sent to Andijan from Akshikat.[58] Presumably *baj* (like *tamgha*) was realized from merchants as well as artisans and also from peasants transporting cotton, silk, wool, bread, fruit, vegetables, etc., from villages to the city. This tax was imposed on all articles carried by the seller from one region to another or transported from neighboring places.[59] *Baj* and *kharj* are reported to have been demanded at the border of India also.[60]

One of the main taxes was *tamgha,* first introduced by the Mongols and realized by the *tamghachis.* It was levied on handicrafts, artisans, workshops, on trade, both wholesale and retail, and even on goods brought for sale in towns from nearby villages, be they products of cottage industry or agricultural produce. Barthold calls *tamgha* a tax on trade and handicrafts. Under the term *tamgha* was included the levying of all taxes in cities from trade, artisan establishments to public houses.[61] Since *tamgha* was charged on transit of goods it brought in a large income from Samarqand and Bukhara in the fifteenth to sixteenth centuries; hence its repeal was invariably followed by its renewal.[62]

The available information shows that *tamgha* was realized not only on the sale 'but before and during the transportation of the goods'. Babur observes that '*tamgha* was realized on the roads, cities, villages, avenues, bridges and crossroads'.[63] Similarly, Hafiz Tanish says that *tamgha* was realized from merchants on the borders of India.[64]

Nishans given to the pilgrims Khwaja Saifuddin and Khwaja Nizamuddin, who were sent to Mecca, *tamgha* and *zakat* and exemption from fulfilling *ulagh*. The *Habib-us Siyar* also describes *tamgha* and *zakat* as separate taxes.[65] From *Maktubat wa Asnad* and other sources, it appears that *zakat* was a tax on trade imposed along with other taxes, including *tamgha*. Both Petrushevski and Muqminova think that the terms *zakat* and *tamgha* in the fifteenth and sixteenth centuries were used for different kinds of tax collections and that each was important.[66] In certain documents the terms *tamgha* and *zakat* have occasionally been used as synonymous. According to other explanations, *zakat* was a tax on recurring property or productive income paid by Muslims, whether landlords or traders.[67] It should have been taken at the rate of 2½, but was often higher in practice.[68] In accordance with Islamic law, it was charged on cows, horses, bullocks and sheep if they exceeded the minimum number required and were meant for sale. Similarly, *zakat* was also imposed upon a variety of agricultural produce and on cash crops of fruit, vegetables and precious grains; gold and silver metals from mines, though not on iron, copper, etc., and also levied on commercial stocks and merchandise (*amwal-i tijarat*). Thus *zakat dar amwali zahir* (*ushr-ikharaj*), *izakat-i sawaim* and *zakat-i amwal-i tijarat* were its various forms.

Petrushevski says that the official calculation and assessment of taxes on artisans was stated in money and based on prices fixed by the state, though they were actually levied on produce in kind.[69] Muqminova, however, contends that only part of a city's collection was realized in cash.[70] The sources and documents prove beyond doubt that realization from all kinds of taxes was made in both cash and kind, depending upon the commodity and the convenience of the payer and state. One of the *nishans* contained in *Maktubat wa Asnad* and issued to a certain Kamaluddin Zikri, requires that every one who brought silk from any quarter for trade was to bring his goods to Zikri so that it could be weighed and the payment determined. The tax on silk was in kind which went to the benefit of the *nazir* and which was determined by weight. Burnes saw the minister in Bukhara levying duties on merchants 'who are most liberally treated in this country'. Burnes describes that the 'webs of cloth are produced and every fortieth piece is taken in place of duties, which gives the merchant his profit, without distressing him for ready money'. Burnes further says that, on declaring himself to be poor, a Mohammedan could have his 'goods returned without an iota of charge', though he may have committed a falsehood. However, Burnes mentions that in the previous monarch's reign the duties on goods were never paid till they were sold, as in the bonding system of a British custom house.[71]

The taxes on cotton and bread were realized in cash. The *yirliqs* issued to Saiyids grant them some money from taxes. Saiyid Zahid Khwaja, for example, was assigned a number of taxes along with *guzapulli* (tax on cotton) in 1599-1600, which was collected in money.[72] Another example of a draft on *pilla* (collection from rearing silk worms) given to the same person further attests to realization being made in cash.

Attempts at evasion are frequently noted as the *nishans* invari ably include a clause forbidding an attempt to conceal anything.

Simultaneously, custom officers overseers, controllers and other administrative staff were forbidden to open goods, of merchants who were given special privileges. Customs officers and merchants could detain merchants and artisans not holding immunity grants and could even inflict physical punishment on them. The documents given to the privileged few specifically enjoin officials to allow the merchant to go safely and to give him assistance in all dangerous spots. Such merchants must have been closely associated with the Khan and presumably might be carrying even the King's own goods. The attempts of the Khans and rulers to subjugate trade (particularly international) and to exploit the traders is borne out by the order contained in the *Maktubat wa Asnad*[73] directing traders 'from wherever they may be' to bring their valuable goods and precious things for inspection by the King's nominee, who could acquire the goods at dictated rates for the Khan. The traders were asked 'not to conceal anything', and 'no one could buy anything from the merchant till the inspection was over'.[74] Generally speaking, in sixteenth century there was no guarantee of immunity and safety in respect of personal property of artisans and traders. Barthold[75] rightly concludes that absence of all guarantee from new and unforeseen taxation gravely injured commerce.

Due to political, religious or personal reasons, amnesty from taxes was occasionally granted to sections of the population. For example, when Shaibani was pleased with the people after his victory in Arquq, he ordered the remittance of the *taklifat-i diwani*.[76] Another *farman* issued in 1541 and later inscribed on a marble plate which was fixed on the portals of the Bukhara Mosque under Abdul Aziz proclaimed the granting of amnesty to the people from *tafaut taqabbul* and *taufir* and several other taxes.[77] The total amount mentioned as remitted was 81,000 *tangas*. Abdullah Khan granted amnesty to the people of Farab from the *taklif-i ahdi*.[78] Still another amnesty *amwal-i wajibi* was granted to the people of Bukhara.[79] Such occasional benevolence shown to the common people was nothing compared to the *Tarkhannamas* (*farmans* for relief from taxes) to the rich and propertied people like the Khwajas and nobles. The *Rauzat-ur Rizwan* and other manuscripts contain a number of *farmans* granting *tarkhani* or exemption from all taxes. These exemptions from taxes were given frequently to the Juibari Shaikhs, Ishans, nobility, merchants and other rich persons.[80] By such methods, the state treasury was considerably weakened and favoured individuals flourished at its expense. No benefit from these exemptions was transferred to the common man who continued to face the exploitation under multiple taxes.

Although an exhaustive list of the taxes and the names of the officers has been given, it is not possible to describe precisely the actual machinery and the system of revenue collections because of lack of material. Nevertheless, it is possible to have some idea of the working of the assessment and machinery of collection through the *Tarkhannamas* (amnesty grants) and stray information scattered in various sources. Besides, a valuable source for the subject is Mirza Badi Diwan's *Majma-ul Arqam* (compiled in 1789) which deals at length with intricate details of Uzbeg chancery, imperial exchequer, art of account keeping and maintenance of registers as well as the assignment of various landgrants and system of taxation.

It is difficult to describe precisely the exact methods of assessment. The *Suluk-ul Mulk* refers to the *jarib* (measurement, lit. measuring rod). The amnesty grants also frequently warned the officers not to measure the rent free land (*tanab na kashand*) or demand fee for measurement (*tanabana*).[81] Mirza Badi refers to *masahat* (measurement), *qismat* (cropsharing) and *qiyas* (assessment).[82]

Under Abdullah Khan Uzbeg, the tax on agriculture and handicrafts was fixed after investigations and scrutiny (*tahqiq*). Hafiz Tanish states that Abdullah had ordered his deputy Qulbaba to go to Samarqand in March-April 1586 for a *tahqiq* (verification or ascertaining) of the conditions in the *wilayat* and its dependencies. Thereupon Qulbaba proceeded to Samarqand along with the *diwaniyan-i uzzam* and *wazirs* who held the charge of the management of affairs in their own hands. The *wazir-i azam* Khwaja Muhammad Qasim the *diwan-i sultani* who held the *wizarat* in that region for years was summoned alongwith the *arbabs* (mayors or chiefs of the town) and *kalantars* (elders of the artisan groups). From early spring down to the month of *tir* the *tahqiq* of the *wilayat* and its dependencies was completed. They fixed the amount of demand upon the artisans and agriculturists (*ahl-i hirfa wa san'at wa arbab-i zera'at wa harasat*) according to what they could afford to pay (*anche dar adai aan qudrat dasht* and *mutaiyyan sakhati*). Thereafter Qulbaba along with *wazirs* came to the emperor and presented to him the register (*daftar-i tahqiq*) of investigations for perusal.[83]

Mirza Badi says that a number of registers had been maintained at the Centre in earlier times, namely, *daftar-i maqasama, daftar-i mu'azzaf, daftar-i taujih, daftar-i diwan-i sarkar, daftar-i zargarkhana* and so on though in his times (1789), *daftar-i navisi* had been replaced by *tumar* and the *daftars* were being maintained only in accordance with the latest rules (*nasq-i jadida*). There registers contained full details regarding all sorts of land grants so that the *hasil* of the entire empire could be known only by adding the total amount of the revenues in cash and kind from all the *tumans, qariyas* and *wilayat.* Specifically speaking, the extent of the land grant given in *alufa* by *amirs* was to be described by the *mudabbir* (scribe) in *tanabs, arrows, juft gao* or even by amount of irrigation water. The name of the assignees along with the details of his *urugh* and dependencies, the assigned *qariya*, approximate produce in cash and kind were also given. The taxes from the gardens and melon beds (*mal-i bagh, mal-i charbagh, mal-i faliz*) were entered with the names of fruits and grains, mode of payment and rate of demand and amount of the income and expenditure, the remainder or excess. The area of each category of land—*kharaji* or *mamlaka* and its allocation—was written in separate registers. There were usually seven copies of each register.[84]

The highest officer in the sphere of revenue collections was the *diwan-i kalan* (*diwan-i aala, dastur-i aazam* or *diwan-i sultani*), who was appointed by the king personally from amongst his confidants. The *daftar-i aala* was in charge of the preservation of all the above mentioned *daftars* and was also to ensure that no excuses, overlooking or mistakes occur deliberately or inadvertently in the registers (*daftars*) of *daftardars, diwan-i tanabana, diwan-i taujih* and *diwan-i sarkar.*

There were *shariks* in every village, Jami refers to Amir Qiwamuddin Sanjani (Khwafi) one of the well known saints who had earlier served as one of the *shariks* of the *qariya* of Sanjan Khwaf and held under his charge, all the records (*nuskhai*) of *jama o kharji taujih o tahqiq* of that *qariya*[85] of Sanjan.

The division of the realized money from *kharaj* (*taqsim-i mahasila az kharaj*) was to be spent in accordance with *sharia* and the *diwan-i aala* was expected to ensure that this was done.

It is mentioned in the *Matlab ut Talibain* that Juibari Shaikhs who owned much property maintained a full *daftar-i buyutat* consisting of several *wakils*, 4 *daftardars*, 17 *diwans* and 40 *navisandas*.[86] Such a daftar alongwith various diwans existed at the centre also. The *diwan-i tanabana* was *mutasaddi* (accountant) of *kharaj-i muazzaf,* whereas the *diwan-i sarkar* who was incharge of imperial exchequer also controlled the registers of taxes in cash and kind (*daftar-i ghallat o naqud-i sarkari padshahi*). The *mushrif-i kalan* was in charge of army, arms and military grants; *alufa, wazifa, saropa*, etc., of the envoys, *tuwajis*, warriors and the learned men. The *daftardar* was the incharge of salary grants (*tankhwah*).[87] Frequently *barats* (drafts) on these hereditary grants were issued by these *Khwajas* and very often the assignees landed in exile or prison due to non payment of these high demands.[88]

In 616 the *maliqarari* (the fixed or stipulated amount) of sultan from *mauza* Nur near Bukhara amounted to 15,00 *dinar*.[89] Only the fifteen *parganas* of Qandahar belonging to the Great Moghul are said to have yielded to Aurangzeb a rental of 19,92,500.[90] In the pre-Mongol Central Asia (under the Samanids) the revenues of various places were allocated for the expenses of a particular office, e.g. expense of the wardrobe was paid from the revenues of Khuzistan, the office of *tashtdar* (basin holder) met its expenses by the revenues of Khwarazm.[91] Under the Mongols this specification did not continue.

The Mughal chronicler Muhammad Sadiq Khan who had accompanied the imperial army to Badakhshan claims to have enquired about the amount of *mahsul* (including *mal* and *peshkash*) of the entire territories of Badakhshan and Balkh which was written down in the registers as being 122 millions of *khanis* (equivalent to 3 million rupees).[92] Even the taxes imposed on city population were excessive. From Samarqand itself the annual collections of only two taxes *taufir* and *tafavu* were between 18,000 and 27,000 *tangas* (silver coins)[93]. Burnes[94] says that *jaziya* was paid annually at the rate which 'varied from four to eight rupees per head'. The *mal-i amani* fetched large sums as this punitive levy imposed in Herat under Shaibani yielded, 1,00,000 *tangchas* of one *misqal* (of 6 *dinar-i kepeki* each) from general public and craftsmen and 20,000 *tangchas* from nobles and *suyurghal* holders.[95] Similarly, after the fall of Urganj, Abdullah had ordered his officers to collect from each of the *raiyyat* a sum of 30 *tanga-i Bukhari* (one *tanga-i Abdullah Khani* was more valuable than a golden *ashrafi*[96]) which shows that special levies were also quite large.

Mention has been made of the existence of *awarijas* (account books) and the *munshis* and *navisand* (writers and record keepers). But the rate of miscellaneous taxes does not seem to have been determined properly and the loopholes in the administration offered many opportunities for the exploitation of peasants. The officers were often dishonest. By exacting money from the people through dubious means, they overburdened them heavily. Ubaidullah's *wazir* Khwaja Nizam, while trying to increase the revenue of the state, had to deal severely with the dishonest and tyrannical officers.[97] Maulana Muhammad Amin Zahid, a divine for whom Ubaidullah had deep regard, was compelled to draw the attention of the Khan to the high handedness of the corrupt officials and tax collectors and to secure relief for the poor. Discussing the general taxes *taujihat* (levy on peasants) and *kharj i lashkar* (military taxes), the Maulana claimed that 'it had four improper and inappropriate points. In the first place it is realized and demanded from those from whom it should not be demanded, secondly, it is not imposed upon those on whom it should be imposed. Thirdly, they give proceeds from its income to those whom it should not be given and fourthly they do not reach it to those whom it should actually go to.'[98] Under Abdullah Khan also, Khwaja Shaikh Azizan was reputed to be ever seeking relief for the suffering people from *matalibat i sultani* and *ummal i diwani*.[99] Even a poet like Mushfiqi Bukhari through his eulogy presented to Abdullah and entitled *shikayat uz zulm,* appealed to the Emperor against a tyrannical officer.[100] The provincial diwans were allegedly involved in embezzlement. Tanish refers to the fate of Khwaja Muhammad Qazsim Diwan who had held the diwanship of Balkh for several years. When he failed to produce sufficient income (*mublagh i Karamand*) and upon audit expressed his inability to do so, the *shahnai qahr* alongwith the qalmaqs tortured him to death.[101]

NOTES

1. Jenkinson, *Purchas and his Pilgrims*, Vol. XII, pp. 22-3.
2. Abul Zazl, *Ain-i Akbari* (*Ain*), Eng. tr. Blochmann, Calcutta, 1877, pp. 55-6.
3. Davidovich, *Izvestia*, pp. 1-45; B.J. Ghaffurov, pp. 336-8.
4. *Ain*, Eng. tr., p. 56.
5. Fazlullah, *Suluk*, pp. 80-8, 97-8, elsewhere it is stated that *maqasama* was the 5th or 6th produce 'of the soil and *wazifa* is any amount stipulated or agreed upon', *Ain*, Eng. tr., p. 62.
6. Babur, *Mubaiyyan*, MS Oriental Institute Library, Tashkent, no. A-104, f. 63.
7. A.A. Semenov, *Ocherki podzemelnoi padatnoi e nalognoi istori va Bukharskom Khanstave,* Tashkent, 1929, p. 22.
8. Fazlullah, *Suluk*, pp. 80-100.
9. *Iz Arkhiv Shaikhov Juibar*, p. 220.

10. *Suluk*, p. 82.
11. Ibid., p. 83.
12. Ibid., p. 80; also see, Athar Husain, *The Glorious Caliphate*, pp. 214-15.
13. *Ain*, pp. 57-8, Eng. tr. Sarkar and Jarret, p. 63. Momin openies that *mal* and *jihat* appearing in combined forms simply mean land taxes and revenue charges. *Far* was imposed in addition to the *mal*, the rate being 10 per cent of the *mal* (Bausani, *The Persians*, p. 114).
14. *Mehmannama* (*Mehn*), pp. 12-13, 91, 132.
15. Abul Ghazi, *Tarih-i shajra-i Turk*, Kazan, 1891, p. 172; Fazil, p. 15.
16. Burnes, p. 285.
17. Muhammad Fazil Khan Hafiz, *Risail-i Manazil*, Bukhara, Aligarh MS, Salam 154/20, f.15.
18. *Mehmannama*, pp. 262, 281, 308-9.
19. Bori Ahmedov, *Gasudarstova Kochevikh Uzbegov*, p. 96.
20. *H. Siyar* IV, pp. 377-8.
21. *Shah Nama*, p. 71.
22. Mirza Badi, p. 92.
23. Muhd. Saleh; Ahmedov, p. 95.
24. *Muzzakkira*, pp. 278-9; *Mehmannama*, p. 89.
25. Badi, p. 92.
26. Ivanov, pp. 38-9; Ghaffurov, p. 339.
27. Mulla Shadi, *Fathanama* 385.
28. Wasifi, p. 348.
29. *Taj-ut Tawarikh*, p. 19, also see *Tazkira-i Muqim Khani*.
30. Ahmedov, pp. 94-5.
31. *T. Guzida*, p. 57; Ahmedov, p. 94.
32. MS 210, f. 95.
33. *Sawaim* (lit. a pasturing animal) *zakat* was 'paid on animals which are pastured in order to be sold later on for other purposes'. This tax was realized not only in the Glorious Caliphate but also in the Empire of Timur. For details see Babur, *Mubaiyyan*, ff. 56-7; Athar Husain, *The Glorious Caliphate*, Lucknow, 1980, pp. 207-8.
34. Ethno Ocherki, Vol. II, Glossary, p. 726.
35. Ahmedov, pp. 95-6.
36. Yasin's Glossary, p. 63; *Jamiut Tawarikh*.
37. For similar taxes (*gav bahreh*, *gavband*, *gavdaran* and *gavran*) cf. Lambton, *Landlords and Peasants in Persia*, Glossary, p. 428.
38. *Matlab-ut Talibain*, pp. 454-5.
39. There were about 20 other taxes like *qachu*, *alghut*, *salghut*, *bashpuli*, *qurughmal*, *barcha*, *ummal*, *tunqutar* and others found in various documents of sixteenth-seventeenth centuries. For details cf. M.U. Usmanov, *Termin Qurughmal*, pp. 107-10; *Narod Azii e Afriki* 4, 1964.
40. *Mehmannama*, p. 69.
41. *Abdn*, p. 48. For a detailed description of term *tarh* as a tax see Barthold, *Soch* IV, pp. 335-6; also Bausani, *The Persians*, p. 116; A.K.S. Lambton, *Landlord and Peasant in Persia*, p. 85.
42. *Maktubat wa Asnad*, p. 171.
43. *BN*, p. 241; *Maktubat wa Asnad*, pp. 77, 78, 170, 171.
44. *Maktubat wa Asnad*, p. 172.

45. Jenkinson, Hakluyt Society Series, p. 464. A similar example is given by Ali Ibn-ul Hasan Alkashifi, *Rashhat-i Ainul Hayat,* MS Bodleian Library, no. 122, f. 140.
46. *Material pa Istori Uratibe*, p. 47; Muqminova, p. 204.
47. *Waqf Nama*, pp. 180-7; Muqminova, p. 205.
48. *Jamiul Wasaiq*, Loiv AN SSR A-933, ff. 79-80; also see *Ethnograficheski Ocherki*, Vol. I, Glossary, p. 720.
49. Cf. Muqminova, p. 204, Semenov, Ocherk pod zemelnoi padatnovo e nalogavo ustroistova va Bukharskovo Khanstave, Trud Sagu II, I, Tashkent, 1929, p. 25.
50. *Hujjatlar*, Doc. nos. 45/78, 47/113; Muqminova, p. 204.
51. Muqminova, p. 204.
52. *Maktubat wa Asnad*, p. 37, *Ajuwaz maijuwaz* in Ferghana was a butter churner thus the tax may be on butter (cf. Zaharova, *Sredni Aziatski Sbornik* II, Moscow, 1959, pp. 240-3).
53. *Khazyaistova Shaikhov Juibari*, Doc. 37; Barthold, *Nadpisi*, p. 33.
54. MS 210/116; *Abdn*, p. 379; Lambton, Glossary, p. 441.
55. *Ajaibul Gharaib*, p. 32.
56. *Nadpisi na Stene Ainski mechet*, pp. 318, 319, 333.
57. *Maktubat wa Asnad*, p. 171.
58. *Hujjatlar*, Docs. 110/85.
59. Juwan Mardaev, *Asrarlarda Ferghana da yir* XVI-XIX, p. 68; *Termin Baj wa Tamgha*, p. 68.
60. Hafiz Tanish, p. 451.
61. Barthold, IV, pp. 332-4; Bausani, *The Persaians,* tr. by J.B. Donne, London, 1971, pp. 116-17; *Termin Baj wa Tamgha, 66* .
62. *Rashhat-i Ainul Haiyat*, pp. 298, 300-1; *BN*, p. 185; Barthold, *Ulugh Beg e evo vremiya*, pp. 133, 156, 171; Nabiev, *Iz Istori palitiko economicheski shizni Mawaraunnahra*, XV, pp. 33, 38-9; Muqminova, p. 208.
63. *BN*, p. 360.
64. *Abdn*, p. 451.
65. *H. Siyar* III, p. 157. For details cf. *Suluk-ul Muluk*, pp. 66-82. The rates of *zakat* varied according to the quality of the taxed object. Since Caliph Usman's time all the caliphs are said to have demanded *zakat* on merchandise (*Suluk*, p. 78).
66. Petrushevski, *Zemlevladeniva e Agrarnikh Otnasheniya*, p. 386; Muqminova, p. 210.
67. A. Ben Shamesh, *Taxation on Islam*, pp. 15, 77-9, 103; Spuler, *The Islamic World: Central Asia in the Last Centuries of Independence*, Vol. III, p. 241.
68. Ibid., Hafiz Muhammad says that the *zakat* tax in Bukhara was realized at the rate of 1/40 *chehloyak* annually. A trader was supposed to pay only once in an year even though he may come to Bukhara for buying and selling a Salam, 154/20 f. 15.
69. Petrushevski, *Zemlevladeniva e Agrarnikh Otnasheniya*, p. 386.
70. Muqminova, p. 210.
71. Burnes 290-1.
72. *Hujjatlar*, 42/61.
73. *Maktubat wa Asnad*, p. 30.
74. Ibid., p. 30.
75. Barthold, *Nadpici na Ainski*, p. 327.

76. *Mehmannama.*
77. *Tirmin Tamgha wa Baj*, p. 66; Muqminova, pp. 202, 203.
78. *Asar-us Salatin*, pp. 24-6.
79. *Abdn*, pp. 270-5.
80. *Rauzat-ur Rizwan*, pp. 306, 316-17, 477, 479; MS 210/189a; *Matlab-ut Talibain*, p. 263.
81. *Rauzat*, pp. 311-17.
82. For system of measurement and fractions see Mirza Badi, text, pp. 45 onwards.
83. *Abdn*, pp. 464-5.
84. Mirza Badi says that there existed four different *bait-ul mals* where the entire *mahsulat* of the *wilayats* were deposited and spent. The *zakat, khums ushr* and taxes on mills (*tahuna*), shops and workshops (*dukan*) ferries tolls (*kashti bani*) were collected in one *bait-ul mal*. The *zakat* was spent on charities and it was recommended that the proceeds of the other taxes be used in the same manner (*bahaman masraf sarf sazand*). To the second *bait-ul mal* belonged the money from *kharaj, jaziya*, booty, indemnity and commercial taxes and extractions from the non-muslims and *zimmiz*. Under the supervision of *qazis, muftis, muhtasibs, ghazis, muezzins*, the money was to be utilized for public works like construction of mosques, canals, bridges or harbours, *gari* (division of water of big rivers). The third *bait-ul mal* was for escheated property, the money from which was to be spent on uplift of the backward, burial of the unclaimed bodies of the poor, treatment of the sick and also on other items of social welfare which were considered necessary by the *imam*. Similarly, the fourth *bait-ul mal* dealt with the *luqtat* (treasure trove. . . the property found on the ground and preserved in trust). The *qazi* and the *imam* were to ensure that the amount was consumed properly 'the way *zakat* was consumed'. The seven registers were one original called *jaiza* with six other copies called *dula, sqhla, paimuza, zam, qite*, etc. (Badi, pp. 9-37).
85. Jami, *Nafhat-ul Uns*, pp. 494-6; *Tarikh-i Nuhzathai*, p. 6810.
86. *Matlab*, p. 335.
87. Badi, text, pp. 34-6; Russian tr., pp. 53-5.
88. *TR; Ubaidullahnama*, f. 229.
89. *JT*, I, p. 360.
90. Bernier, p. 456.
91. Juvaini, part II, pp. 2-3; Eng. tr., pp. 277-8.
92. Muhammad Sadiq Khan, *Tawarikh-i Shahjahani*, pp. 8-9; Khafi Khan, *Muntakhab-ul Lubab*, p. 403, part I, Calcutta, 1869, says it was Rs. 30 lakhs which was equal to 1 crore and 20 lakhs *khanis*.
93. *Nadpisi Shashkin*, p. 25.
94. Burnes, p. 285; Muhammad Fazil says the rate was one to four *tangas* monthly.
95. *H. Siyar*, pp. 376-8; *T. Sh.*, pp. 22-4.
96. Abdul Ghazi, *Tarikh-i Shajra-i Turkazan*, 1891, p. 172.
97. Wasifi, p. 359.
98. *Muzzakkira*, pp. 278-80.
99. Hafiz Tanish, p. 237.
100. Jan Rypka, p. 503.
101. *Abdn*, p. 381.

Workshops and Markets

Historians have believed that the development of handicrafts increased during Uzbeg rule. It has been considered by some to be the direct result of the fusion of pastoral and settled people.[1] Others presume that due to the decline of the international commerce of Central Asia, more emphasis came to be laid on internal handicrafts.[2] The sale of commodities was one of the chief sources of revenue, as the rulers 'were most maintained by the city taxes'.[3] As early as the thirteenth century, there were said to be more than one hundred thousand artisans in Khwarazm alone.[4] After their campaigns Chingiz, Timur and later some Uzbeg rulers like Mahmud, Shaibani, Ubaidullah and Abdullah took special care to save captive artisans 'the master craftsmen of all nations' and take them to Central Asia.[5] Consequently, the resultant possible expansion in the artisan population and a refined development of handicrafts was almost inevitable at every level. Babur appreciated Central Asian workmanship and criticized Indian handicrafts for 'having no form or symmetry, method or quality'.[6]

Under the Uzbegs, the significance of trade and handicrafts is very well-reflected in Jenkinson's observation that 'two parts of Bukhara are the king's and the third part is for merchants and markets'.[7] The large-scale purchase of workshops and trade centres, mills and other productive enterprises by nobles and *khwajas* alike, amply indicate the lucrative prospects of such investments—the evidence for this coming from the *waqf* documents of Shaibani Khan. From eighty shops in the complex comprising ten trade centres in Samarqand, forty belonged to the *madrasa*, fourteen to other *waqf* establishments and twenty-six to private owners from the aristocracy. Mehr Sultan, the daughter-in-law of Shaibani, herself placed her property in private hands. Aq Begam, the daughter of Ahmad Mirza, Shamsuddin the Shaikh-ul Islam, and such other dignitaries extracted income from commercial handicraft centres, assigning them on lease to immediate producers. Many of the shops were given by them in *waqf*. As discussed elsewhere in detail, the urban economy and life could well be described as a complicated interplay of the interests of the aristocracy and struggling artisans.

Bukhara and Samarqand were the principal commercial centres. Then came the following towns which could be described as centres of handicrafts: Qarshi, Shahr-i-Sabz, Tashkent, Andijan, Marghilan, Akhsikat, Uratippa and Khujand.[8] In the Syr darya region, there were towns like, Arquq, Sighnaq, Sauran and Yasi;[9] the production techniques, however crude and 'at a primitive level',[10] evoked the admiration of chroniclers. The role played by artisans in literary, academic and social life is borne out well by Wasifi.[11]

As early as 1221, Chang Chun noticed that there was 'much merchandise' in the bazaars of Samarqand and that 'the whole town was full of copper vessels, shining like gold'.[12]

Travellers and the chroniclers from the fourteenth to nineteenth centuries express admiration for the well-organized markets of Bukhara, Samarqand and Tashkent. Among the products of Tashkent are enumerated cotton, silk, woolen stuffs and articles of leather. Babur says of Samarqand that 'different trades are not mixed up together in it but each has its own bazaar, a good sort of plan.[13] Wasifi refers to 'different quarters (*kui*) and bazaars for different things'[14] and in the mid-sixteenth century Jenkinson reported that 'every science hath their dwelling and markets by themselves'.[15] Obruchev, a nineteenth-century traveller, reports the continuance of specialized market places[16] in various parts of Central Asia. The account has its echoes in the travelogues of Polovtsoff, Burnes, Vambery, Berg, Igniatev and several others. Typically, Islamic 'concentric arrangement and strict organization of various elements of trade and crafts'[17] existed in urban areas of Central Asia also. Documentary evidence attests that in Samarqand alone there were more than ten small and big markets and trade centres, each with shops dealing in certain special types of goods, with separate quarters for each specialized branch. Streets were named after particular professions, e.g. the *muhallah, kucha, kui,* bazaar of *sangtarashan* (stone cutters), *sim kash* (wire drawers), *qannad* (confectioners) *kamangaran* (bow makers), *namad malàn* (felt makers), *sartarashan* (barbers), *shakkar farushan* (sugar sellers), *bazazan* (clothiers), *burabafan* (sellers of ropes and strings), *zargar, jewelers* (goldsmiths), *adrasbafan* (*adras* weavers), *attârân* (perfumers), *angushtgaran* (ring makers), *abginagar* (glass makers), *shamma* (wax chandliers), etc. In the cities, the bazaars traditionally comprised covered market building *(charsu)* of bricks with multi-cupolas and criss cross arches. Timur, Shahrukh, Ubaidullah had constructed the luxury markets (*tim*) in large towns. The three markets of Abdullah Khan built in 1586, namely, *taqi zargaran* (dome of jewellers and goldsmiths), *taqi sarrafan* (dome of shroffs or money changers) and *taqi tilpaq farushan* (dome of milliners) have survived to this day in Bukhara built in 1586-7.[18] In Khwarazm, Jenkinson found a long, covered street serving as a market place.[19] Under the Shaibanids, the covered markets were divided into certain sections.

Thus, the professional handicrafts inside the city and often in distant villages had, at different periods of Shaibanid rule, contributed to the development of internal markets with two strong centres at Bukhara and Samarqand. Apart from the shops and workshops, the bazaars had caravansarais and bath houses.[20] Attached with particular streets were residential quarters where people of the same profession lived. Badruddin Kashmiri refers to the two caravansarais in Charsu in the *darun-i shahr* (inner urban centres) and streets of *sarrafan* (money changers) in the *berun-i shahr* (outskirts of the city) where merchants and traders from all over the world assembled for transactions.[21] Similarly, also existed houses in various markets. The leather workers worked and lived in Bukhara in the following quarters; Charmgaran, Khalfa Khudaidad at Sherigaran Gate; Isham-i-Pir (Araban Pir Massu at the gate of Soleha Khan and Iskandar Khan) and finally in Old Shahristan. The *kasagaran* (potters) lived in another special quarter in the western part of Bukhara.[22] The matmakers (*burobofan*) lived in the *amiri* quarters[23] of Bukhara and also in the centre of the *tiplaq* at Tioaq Farushan. At times, bazaars occupied only a part of a street.[24]

The place where the medieval artisans worked as already mentioned was the workshop (*karkhana*) which often served as the *dukan* (shop) of the finished products also. The *dukan* was usually built of earth and not of burnt bricks. Clavijo says that usually in Samarqand 'each shop had two chambers front and back and streetway arched over with a domed roof with windows and water fountains'.[25] Occasionally, it was double storeyed with a *balakhana*. The shops were valued according to their situation and those shops situated in busy streets were far more valuable. The shops mentioned in legal documents were of various sizes, e.g. 40 square *gaz*. The shops had an entrance, a *takhtadan* with which it was closed at night. The sixteenth century documents refer to the markets marked for their various ceilings with cross beams (*wasa*), e.g. in *bazaar-i bazazan* of Samarqand there were four such ceilings (*balar*) hence the name *balar chahar poshishi* bazaar.[26] The workshops and shops were not very big. The sale deeds of the shops enumerate sets of instruments or stocks of goods, as for example wire drawers (*sim kashi*)[27] in a shop of silver.

A beautiful market which was constructed in the second half of the sixteenth century for the sale of luxury goods was known as *tim*. Wasifi refers to a market *timibazazân* where expensive kinds of cloth like *parcha, zarbaft, abyari, atlas-i khitai, diba, aksun*, etc., were sold.[28] The big and small market places with cupolas, called *suq, chaharsu, taq or tim* differed from each other in the organization of public services and amenities. Sometimes various allied specializations were mixed together in one area, e.g. the quiver makers, the shoe makers and the saddle makers. Some bazaars were protected by fences of reeds, poles and wooden beams. The artisans chose the area according to the needs of the profession. The metal workers usually occupied the central place, working near big roads and the city gates. The skinners, the soap makers, the candle makers lived in the outskirts of the town; the chintz printers settled down near running water. Horse markets needed space and were, therefore, in the outlying areas. The bread and loaf markets were spread throughout the city.

In the *waqf* documents and other sources, varied types of shops in the cities are mentioned.[29] The rural economy, however, also played an important role in the process by supplying the raw material and the labour forces.[30] There were certain kinds of handicrafts which flourished only in the villages, whereas other handicrafts were mainly developed in the cities. The *abresham* (silk thread), *tabidi safid* (white goat skin) and such other raw material was brought from the villages.[31]

The striking feature of sixteenth century seems to be an attempt at improving the specialization in various handicrafts. The *Arais-ul Jawahar* (compiled in 1300) refers to only nine important handicrafts.[32] In the Qazi documents of the Shaibanid period about 60 handicrafts are mentioned. Towards the end of seventeenth century, Said Nasafi, a Bukhara poet refers to the existence of about 200 handicrafts.[33] It seems probable, however, that even the specialized branches have been counted as separate and independent crafts.[34] During sixteenth-seventeenth centuries, specialization in each craft had increased considerably. For example, in the workshops for cloth weaving, the artisans made various types of cloth. Hence we find in existence separate specialities and specialists like *makhmal bafan, kimkhabagaran, alachabafan, chahar gul bafan, chalmabafan*. Even in the sphere of ready made garments, we find various specialists like *jamaduzan, khalatduzan, pustinduzan pupakduzan* and others. Similarly, the *kaghazgars* prepared various kinds of papers. One variety of paper was silk paper, the *sultani*, which enjoyed a reputation for its smootheness and lightness; another was *mir ibrahimi* containing white rings.

In her pioneering work on the artisans, Muqminova says that there were about 130 handicrafts existing in sixteenth century Central Asia, the manufacture flourishing during the 'peaceful phases' of short periods between intermittent civil wars throughout sixteenth century. The unification of *khanates* by Abdullah was supported and desired by artisans, merchants, civil population and the religious personages alike; but in turn it began to tell heavily upon the economy and commercial enterprise of the country.[35] The craftsmanship of Central Asia had reached a higher degree during the reign of Timur and his successors.[36] Ibn-i Arab Shah writes that the craftsmen in Central Asia were 'a more than can be counted and too numerous for all to be reckoned. In short, Timur gathered from all sides and collected at Samarqand the fruits of everything and that place accordingly had in every wonderful craft and rare art some one who excelled in wonderful skill and was famous beyond his rivals in his crafts'. The traditions continued during the Uzbegs to a great extent. A short account of the varied types of handicrafts which flourished in Medieval Central Asia is being offered here.

Paper Manufacture

Babur claims that 'the best paper in the world' was made in Samarqand.[37] This is confirmed by his compatriots like Sultan Ali Meshhedi (in his work on calligraphy compiled in 1514), Jami and Ali Sher Navoi[38] and by the Arab and Indian chroniclers[39] and European travellers.[40] Various kinds like *kaghaz-i abri* for manuscripts, *kaghaz-i sultani* or silken paper, *kaghaz-i abreshmi, kaghaz-i nakhudi, kaghaz-i mir ibrahimi*, etc., were manufactured. The process of production of paper hardly changed during sixteenth-nineteenth century. The evidence in *Waqfnama* shows that *kaghazgar* and *muhrakash* (polisher of the paper) were two separate specialists, though unpolished paper could also be found in the market. The manuscripts of the *Waqfnama* of Mehr Sultan, *Majma-ul Wasaiq, Badai-ul Waqai, Rauzat-ul Ahbab, Mehmannama, Anis-us Salatin* transcribed on the *Sultani* paper are excellent proof of the quality of paper manufactured.

For preparation of paper were needed cotton, torn clothes of old *khalats*, blankets, quilts, etc. After moulding on the form with the net for several days, it was shifted to the board to be wrung out. The prepared sheet was posted with the starch, dried, glossed and polished by *muhrakash* through roller. Vegetable and certain mineral colours were applied in the production of papers.[41] According to Sultan Ali Meshhedi paper colouring was done by myrtle, saffron,[42] etc. The rich Central Asians loved to write on papers decorated with floral patterns, self designed papers of different colours, i.e. cream, pink, red, blue and green. The colour play is visible in book illustrations, miniature paintings and even in architectural patterns.[43]

Excellent ink was prepared with complicated recipe described in *Jawami-ul Ulum* and also in a sixteenth century source.[44] Sultan Ali also gives the 'professional secret recipe' of ink which he himself prepared.

In the environs of Samarqand were water mills and on the canals brought from Siab were workshops for manufacture of paper. The water for the paper mortars (pulping) all came from Kan-i Gil.[45] Mihr Sultan's *waqf* lands had two paper mills supplying paper to the market. A document of 1589 shows that another *kaghazgar* Ustad Saifi had one flour grinding mill also which shows that he took to this profession only partly.[46] Dyer's shops, dyeing and cloth painting (*rangrezi, sabbaghi*) were professions found both in Samarqand and Bukhara. Samarqand was famous for producing certain types of colours and paints. The *rangrezi* shops were also in line as *Waqfnama* shows. There were three shops in bazaar-i Amirzada Muhammad and two shops each on bazaar-i Khwaja Muhammad Qasim Chap and *dar-i mukhma-i kuhna* in Samarqand.[47] In Bukhara there were two shops belonging to Juibari Shaikhs with *hujras* on streets of Masjid-i gao kushan and Sukniyat. The dyer's shops with an *aiwan* on bazaar-i darwaza-i nan on the streets of Masjid-i Maulana Rahmatullah are also mentioned. Saifi Bukhari (1582) says that Qazaqs used to prepare caftans from sheep skin decorated with different colours.[48] The suede sheep skin was dyed by *ruiyan* (a madder, red dye). The wooden saddles were also coloured by it in golden colours such as those sent by Abdullah to Feodre Ivanovich. *Ruiyan* was cultivated in the environs of Namanghan in less fertile areas where no other crop could possibly be grown.[49] For colouring clothes, paper skin, etc., *ruiyan, buzgun,* myrtle (*henna*) indigo (*neel*), saffron, *bugam* (a kind of wood), *qirmiz* (kermes, crimson), tea, granite peels, rinds and onion peels were used.[50] Hafiz Tanish refers to black finger like stones found in the mountains which was burnt and its ashes were used for whitening the cloth.[51] *Qirmiz* was used for dyeing expensive cloth. *Buqghun* (pistachio tree) a colouring agent was sold in packets in Bukhara and Tashkent. Saffron was used for dyeing silk, woolens, textiles and also in the preparation of medicines and ink. Myrtle was applied for dyeing hair, beard, hands and also paper. It also served as a medicine base. There was a *hammam-i hena farushan* in Samarqand in the beginning of sixteenth century.[52] The Brazilian wood (*chobi beqam*) producing dark violet, black and red colour was used for dyeing silk and suede. *Beqam* was boiled with alum for desired results.[53] Before preparation of colours, its weights and measures by *misqal* were carefully determined. The dye was used in ceramics and pottery also and potters worked in close collaboration with the dyers. Certain dyer's shop with *dukan khana* (where clay pottery was made) was included in the immovable acquisitions of Juibari Shaikhs in Ghujdwan. On the streets of *kasagaran* were prepared cups and wares, which were also sold there, whereas the dyeing process was undertaken by the masters (*ustakars*) in the *cheetgar khana.*[54]

Weapons

There were special imperial workshops (*zarrad khana-i-khas*) for the manufacture of arms. Clavijo appreciates 'the excellent workshops of arms maintained by Timur.[55] Timur had brought with him bowmakers from Damascus who produced cross-bows and gunsmiths from Turkey who made arquebus, and artillery men—both engineers and bombardiers besides those who make the rope by which these engines work.'[56] A description of various types of swords, sabers, pole axes, cuirasses, hatchet, helmet, daggers, etc., used by the sixteenth century fighters is found in the chronicles and travelogues. Their specimens preserved in the museums confirm that excellent manufactures were undertaken in Samarqand, Bukhara and Tashkent, each place having its own specialists.

The shields preserved in the museums at Tashkent and Samarqand were of wood and skin often decorated with metal or having metal sheet lining or metal rings.[57] Most of the skin shields were decorated with floral designs of red, black or multicolours.[58] The shield makers knew the art of painting the shields as well. Some of the skin shields were of oblong shape, thin at centre and wide at corners. The ornamented metal shields of different sizes depicted in the miniature paintings of sixteenth century are also found in the stores of museums. Wooden shields could be prepared during sieges by the artisans who accompanied the army. The varied forms of shields (*tora qalqaan*) are noticed though they could be pierced with arrows particularly if cannons were there in the army. The arrows were flung so nicely that not only once but often twice they exposed the shield to fire.[59] They wore metal circular rings running through each collar like a shirt with short sleeves, striped skins, ordinary cloth or *barkhat* guaranteeing the vertical forms like those covered with thick felt or metal or chain mail of net or without it are also found in museums and miniatures though some of them were brought from Europe to Central Asia and were called *firangi*.[60]

There were separate specialists and masters for making each kind of equipment and had big and small bazaars for the same in Samarqand and Bukhara. There are mentioned in the sources *kamangar, tirgar* (bow and arrow makers), *rekhtagar* (artillery men), *tarkash duz*, *shamshirgar.* Bows often served as export objects particularly *kamani tillakari.* For the bows and arrows nice covers and quivers of skin decorated with self designs or metal were prepared.[61] *Majma-ul Wasaiq* contains an agreement between future learner and a *jebatab* in 1590. One of these Mulla Timar, son of Mulla Jan Muhammad gave his brother Ibadullah under the training of Ustad Muhammad Jebatab so that the latter taught his brother the art of manufacturing armour so that he surpassed his teacher. In accordance with second agreement, Nauroz Jebatab was to teach his specialization to Shah Muhammad for a period of four years.[62] The bows of Tashkent and Khwarazm (Chachi wa Khwarazmi), arrows of Mawaraunnahar called *khudang* were other specialities. Babur refers to *khwarazmi* arrows (of mail and of wadded cloth) which 'pierced shield and cuirass, sometimes the two cuirasses'.[63] The *rekhtagars* (artillery founders) prepared a fusion of copper with alloy from which they manufactured various products.[64]

Although the weapons of Central Asia were usually made of steel,[65] in some areas of Central Asia (e.g. Kesh Southern Hills near Amu) there were large bamboo with pith inside which were used by the soldiers to make lances and spears.[66]

In this task they were helped by the auxiliary force from Bukhara and Samarqand. The introduction and expansion in the use of firearms changed the character of metal arms. The iron armour first underwent a change in form and ultimately lost its importance.

Samarqand was the centre of manufacture of arms and armaments like swords, dagger, lances (*sungu*, *pichaq*, qilich dagger), in the first decade of the sixteenth century. The arms were sold in Samarqand and made also to order. The sabre of one of the Farghana Beg Noyon Kukultash was prepared by a Samarqand master at his special order.[67] In the following decades upto the end of sixteenth century, Bukhara became the main production centre of arms where not only most of imperial army's needs were fulfilled but even a *darukhana* (gunpowder store) also was situated. Hafiz Tanish records how a sudden fire engulfed the first and second storeys of the store resulting in an explosion. In the disaster which followed, many died including the artisans and for several hours there were in the air, fragments of the debris, timber, bricks, stones and even men's limbs and feet as the store was in a residential area.[68]

Usually all kinds of weapons were manufactured in Central Asia. Nevertheless the imported arms and armaments were also frequently used. Sidi Ali Reis refers to the Ottoman arms and armour being supplied to Nauroz Ahmad.[69] Hafiz Tanish records the arrival of certain camel loads of armours (*saut* and *joshan*) which came to Bukhara from Moscow.[70] Similarly the Kalmuk *jeba* and Derbend *jebaci* are also mentioned. Hafiz Tanish refers to *johanha-i firangi* (European armour) and *kajim* (horses' armour).[71] Wasifi described a *karad-i firangi* (European dagger) in the early years of sixteenth century.[72] Another document of 1589 mentions the steel knife of European make for cutting meat being deposited by its owner Mulla Baqi in the safe custody of a group of master artisans. The value of the knife was fixed and for each day of its deposit an advance money of 100 *tanga-i khani* was given by the owner at the rate of 7 *dinars* per day.[73] Muqminova thinks that the works of Western master specialists in arms manufacture were important into Central Asia through Russia and that the mutual influence on Russian and Central Asian handicrafts is also visible. During Abdullah Khan's reign, not only Derbend top arms and European coats of mail (*joshnahai firangi*) are mentioned but also an Uzbeg envoy Muhammad Ali is reported to have brought 10 coats of mail from the Czar in June 1589 [74] though coats of mail were prepared in Central Asia also.[75] The evidence of Egelberg Kempfire and Evliya Chelebi proves that goat skins filled with naphtha were sent romping from Apsherana to different countries including Central Asia.[76] Merchants coming to sell naphtha stayed in a separate caravansarai.

Wine and Liquor

Excellent wine was distilled in Central Asia from ancient times. In sixteenth century too wine-making supported a class of professionals and even the Khwajas engaged themselves in this lucrative business. Muhammad Saleh informs us that more than half of the grapes from Shaikh-ul Islam Khwaja Abul Mukaram's vineyards was utilized for wine whereas the remaining part was used for preparing *uksus* and *dushab* (grape syrups). There were special places in Samarqand for storage and preservation of grapes.[77] In documents and sources varied kinds of wine (*sharab*), *muskir mussalas, chagir*,[78] etc., are mentioned. Bubur writes about the Bukhara wine which was considered to be the 'strongest' in Transoxiana.[79] Babur tasted this wine in Samarqand which confirms that internal transport was common. Distilled liquor (*araq*) was prepared with barley and honey and was used mostly by Turkish population. *Kumis* a special mild intoxicant of soured milk of sheep was a popular drink of Qazaqs. Wine was distilled both in the villages and cities but was brought from villages to city. There were other distilleries like the one at Herat too.

In Samarqand wine was sold openly in wine shops. Not only Ali Sher Navoi refers to the bars and gambling houses (*maikhana* and *qumarkhana*) in his times but also Wasifi refers to the noise of drunkards and *mastans* reaching the skies in one of the famous taverns (*sharabkhana*) of Khurasan.[80] Neki Maqsud a *khammar* (wine distiller) who had opened his wine shop in Pul-i Safed had invited Samarqand merchants, students, poets along with Wasifi to a wine party.[81] The wine was usually taken in gold cups and procelain containers (*altun aiyagh*[82] *chini qad*) by the nobles and the rich.

Religious personages condemned drinking and almost continuously an attempt at prohibition was made by the rulers. Often wine was not allowed to be sold in the market.[83] Timur is said to have avoided intoxicants[84] though the wine was served in the assemblies openly 'in the Mongol fashion'.[85] In 844 Shahrukh tried to impose prohibition and not only his associates and nobles abstained from it but Shahrukh had even once poured out the entire quantity of wine in the bars (*khumkhana*) of Mirza Jugi and Abdullah.[86] Under the later Timurids, however, wine drinking was a way of life and many of them died of 'bibbing and bibbing' wines.[87] From the *waqf* documents of Mihr Sultan Khanum, we learn that *qazis* and *wazirs* were forbidden from drinking and the offender was to be turned out of the *madrasa* in the early sixteenth century.[88] Jenkinson in 1558 says, 'whosoever is found to break the law is whipped and beaten most cruelly through the open markets and there are officers appointed for the same who have authoritie to go into any man's house, to search if he hath Aquanita, wine or brag and finding the same break the vessels, spoyle the drink and punish the masters of the house most cruelly. . . .'[89] The *Maktubat wa Asnad* also contains a copy of such an order.[90] Notwithstanding these restrictions, drinking seems to have been a popular pastime at all levels.[91] The Uzbeg Sultans do not seem to have indulged in excessive drinking: wine was served on special occasions and in *kornish-i amma* even in seventeenth century.[92] Indeed in our sources officers connected with the distribution of wine (like *sauchi*), the royal bar (*sharabkhana-i khas*) and various kinds of drinks are mentioned.[93] The Uzbeg Sultan Keldi Muhammad used the wine so excessively that he fell terribly sick. Nauruz Ahmad also had been fond of drinks Influential and rich parents and their children drank wine and easily escaped the punishment from the *muhtashib*. Some women also consumed liquor as is indicated by both Babur and Ali Sher Navoi.[94]

Textiles

Extensive manufacture of cotton and silk fabrics was carried on in Central Asia.[95] The cloth manufacturers were of three kinds, those who made it for their own consumption; those who prepared it for sale and sold it themselves; thirdly those who sold through merchants.[96] While referring to silk manufacture in Samarqand Clavijo comments in the following words: 'This land of Samarqand was not only rich in foodstuffs but also in manufacture such as factories of silk both the kinds called *zaytuni* and *kimkhob* also crapes, taffetas and stuffs we call *tercenals* in Spain which are all produced in great numbers'.[97]

According to Rice there developed a style which was wholly and completely Persian out of the mixed styles of the Ilkhan period and that 'it was really thanks to the enthusiasm of Tamerlane and his descendants that the most important developments took place' under Timur, Samarqand was 'certainly an important centre, and there are records of garden pavilions adorned with frescoes and of exquisite painted textiles that was admired there' though no examples have survived. Gulbenkian collection prepared for Iskandar Sultan and particularly the works of artists like Muhammad Husain speak of the complete maturity of the school. This and the fact that the Chinese motifs such as the *kilin* or stylized cloud form were almost invariably present without any Chinese style in actuality[98] suggest that the textile paintings too must have felt its impact.

The fine fabrics, special type of wool, delicate and varied kind of silks and cotton, printed, plain striped, gold woven were reportedly prepared in Merv, Bukhara, Samarqand and Khwarazm. Samarqand was a famous centre of production for a cloth of silver called *simgun*.[99] In the above mentoned cities were manufactured certain types of linen woven in Egyptian styles.[100] The Egyptian linen (*katan-i misri*) is mentioned in an Ishrat Khana *waqf* document.[101]

Clavijo informs us that Timur had carried away with him all weavers of that city (Damascus) who 'worked at silk looms'.[102] The *katan* both ordinary and expensive was widely used in Central Asia by all sections of population. The dresses from silk and linen were often studded with precious stones or decorated with gold thread embroidery.[103]

The *katan* (linen) cotton or cloth, both ordinary and expensive was used by the rich for it served as excellent dinning sheets (*dastarkhwani katan*) and bed covers, as well as for clothes (*jama*). Wasifi says that all the dignitaries of Herat in Jami's time were dressed in woolen red *suqurlat* or *katan* and even Amir Haji Pir in Sultan Husain's time is said to be clad in *khalat* of *katan*.[104] *Katan* was often multicoloured.

Taffeta (*tafta, silk*) was rarely mentioned as once in the *waqf* grant of Husain Khwarazmi according to which taffeta was used for turban (*dastar*).[105] The *zendani* (*zaytumi*) so highly appreciated by Narshakhi and was much in demand even in seventeenth-eighteenth centuries in Iraq, Fars, Kirman and India continued to be popular notwithstanding the changes in style, texture and quality during one decade. We get references to varied types of *zendani* red, with floral designs, *zendani semendi* (manufactured in village Semend near Samarqand, mentioned by Barthold[106]), *zendani dubandi*, *pubandi* and *du nimbandi* (probably denoting thicnkness and quality of the cloth as suggested by Muqminova[107]). Both Barthold and Muqminova think that *zendani* was only a common name for all sorts of cloth[108] which were produced in zendan a small city near Bukhara.

The rich wore clothes of *katan, suf* (wool), *suqurlat*, Chinese silk (*atlasi khitai*), *diba aqsun* and these were studded with precious stones. Wasifi refers to one such *khalat* in Amir Yadgar's box costing 30,000 *tangas*.[109]

In the sixteenth century, Bukhara far surpassed Tabriz in the art of the minature paintings and in silk weaving best miniatures were at first produced in Bukhara, Samarqand and Shiraz where such schools had been established over a long period.[110]

Cotton cloth (*kurpas* also called *bayazi*, *buz*, *baz*) was prepared in both villages and towns; it was dyed in at least eight colours. The manufacture was undertaken for consumption in the Uzbeg dominions and outside.[111] Rashidudin refers to *kurpas* for which Chingiz is reported to have paid one silver *balish* for each *parcha* (piece).[112] Isfahani says that the nomadic population acquired cotton cloth, through traders or even through incursions.[113] Wasifi used cotton bag for carrying the precious ornaments of the fugitive Timurid Mirzas[114] in 1507. *Kurpas* was included among the presents sent by the Khan of Khiva to the Czar in 1641.[115] In Tawais, a city near Bukhara prepared excellent cotton cloth known as *bukhari* in large quantity and was exported to Iraq. Such was the demand of the cloth that people from Khurasan rushed especially to this place at a fixed time of the year to buy the stuff.[116]

Clavijo says that in Samarqand special fur linings for silk garments were prepared besides 'stuffs in gold and blue with other colours of diverse tints dyed'.[117] Wasifi refers to the use of thin red coloured woolen *suqurlat* (scarlet) which was manufactured in Samarqand.[118] In 1590 an agreement was signed for teaching the art of *suqurlat* weaving (*sanat-i suqurlatbafi*)[119] another agreement signed in 21 September 1589 refers to the specializations in *jamabafi* and *chahargulbafi*.

Barkhat (bakhmal, makhmali qirmizi) used by the aristocracy for shawls, curtains, pillows,[120] etc., was appreciated by Clavijo. Babur says that 'another article of Samarqand trade carried to all sides and quarters is the cramoisy velvet'.[121]

Other popular textiles included *chobtari khairabadi, malmali shahi*, *mandili sunar kaim* and *katan-i Gujarati*[122] some of which of course, must have come from India. There were other stuffs which were imported. Jenkinson refers to the import of white cloth for turban.[123] The chronicles also mention *futa-i zarbaft-i yezdi* (from Yezd) sold for 50 *tangas*, and *futai Banarasi* (from Banaras in India) for 2 *tangas*.[124]

It seems that *futakars* (turban weavers) often prepared the stuff at home also since a number of agreements for imparting skill in this art to an apprentice within a period of four years were signed in Samarqand during the sixteenth century.[125]

As is evident from the archival documents of the Sheikhs of Juibar, the manufacture of *alacha* (*alachabafi*) was equally developed in both Bukhara and Samarqand. In the environs of Bukhara there were the workshops of *alachabafan* also known as *tukanchi*.[126] In 1590 three agreements were signed between the *ustad* (master) and *shagird* for teaching *alachabafi*.[127] *Alacha* was a striped cloth in cotton or semisilk woven from a high quality thread of varied colours of bright and dark shades. Najmuddin Kubra is said to have been the founder of this art.[128] The cloth was cheap and durable.[129] Three agreements (1589-90) for imparting training in weaving of *alacha* have come down to us.[130] In one of the documents of 1561, a village of *alachabafan* is mentioned, this being situated in Rukhshabad near Bukhara.[131] It was presumably inhabited mainly by manufacturers of *alacha*.

The technique for *alacha* apparently originated and developed in Turkestan from where these *ikat* fabrics were introduced into Persia and India and taken westward by the Mongol conquerors. Another type of stripe in segmented panels of lattice fret patterns was also presented in a Parthian tapestry in Central Asia.[132]

The *qazi* documents refer to the finest quality of silk *shahi* being produced by *shahi bafan* (royal weavers). The pure silk *barkhat* was prepared in the quarters of Juibar and mixed silk-cotton weave like *adras* and other varieties were manufactured in the *karkhana* quarters of Bukhara. Striped cloths, *bekasam*, *alacha*, etc., were produced in the *pukhtabafan* quarters and to some extent in *khanaka* quarters near Juibar. The Bukhara ambassador to Czar Mikhailovich, Mulla Farrukh reported in 1671 that in Bukhara, they prepared 'kindyak, zendeni, kamakand atlas not much in quantity but excellent in quality'.[133] In the seventeenth century, the demand for silk from Bukhara exceeded its capacity of manufacture. According to the merchant Pazuhina 'the consumption and outlay of silk in Bukhara is greater and though the silk manufactured in Bukhara is not exported, the Bukhara natives have to go all the way to Khiva to buy the silk there'.[134]

The Chintz-printing (*sanat-i cheetgari*) was an important specialization of Samarqand. Muqminova refers to a number of sixteenth century documents containing agreements between the apprentices and the master artisans, some of whom had apparently come from India. In accordance with a decision taken in Samarqand *qazikhana* in February 1590, a certain Neki Maddud Kazar Multani, son of Mulla Muhammad Multani, acknowledged the debt of a sum of 120 *tanga-i khani* which after the expiry of the fixed time (2 months), he was bound to return to Mulla Fathullla Multani. The sum appears to be the cost of forty pieces (*parchas*) of *cheet* namely *purband, cheet mulun.*[135] A 'Lahiri' *cheetgar*, son of Lalu, was mentioned in a promissory receipt of 13 October 1589. He was to pay back the borrowed money (150 silver *tanga-i khani* of one *misqal* each) to Darya Khan son of Shaikh Saadi.[136] Amidst the presents delivered by the Khivan envoy Muhammad Amin Bukhari in 1641 were mentioned 100 pieces of Indian *cheet*,[137] which were either imported from India or were made in Central Asia after the Indian technique or design.

The master printers did not weave but simply trimmed and prepared the finished cloth simply as artisan clothiers of local printers. They prepared a solution of colours. There is a detailed account of the printing of Bayazi cloth, which shows that printing by hand was both complicated and technical. The cloth was first boiled then soaked into *ishkhar* (potash) water, dried and then designed with decorations and ornamentations with the boiling solution of colours.[138] The designs were stamped pressing the *qalib* (the stamp for printing) left in colour solution before hand.[139]

We derive considerable information about Samarqand chintz-printers from sixteenth century documents. Document at the end of 1589 refers to a certain, Ustad Jauhar son of Abdullah and his wife Bibi Sausan who received a promissory receipt (*tamassuk*) in return for 14 different pieces of cloth, 7 pieces of *purband haftrang* (7 coloured) *cheet*, 3 pieces of red *purband cheet*, 3 *gaz* of red *shahri cheet* and one *gaz* with 4 *gazimuqassiri* red *beekchi cheet*.[140]

One Mulla Jamal *cheetgar* (as appears from an agreement of apprenticeship signed on 26 September 1590) was to teach this art (*sanat-i cheetgari*) in four years to a boy called Khudai Quli son of Tengari Quli. Since chintz printers did not have enough money, they had to borrow money settled for 32 pieces of *cheet purband* of seven colours (*parhca cheet purband haft rang*) after the expiry of four months.[141] The Central Asian *cheet* was sent to Russia also.[142]

Readymade garments included various types of *qaba* (robe), e.g. *qabai parchagi, quba-i purpanba; chapan* (coat), *chikman* (a kind of long robe) or upper garment, *saropa, tunipustin* (fur covers), *suqurlat chikman* with buttons (*tugmalik*). Special *khalats* could be bought for 30,000 *tangas*.[143] There were different kinds of shirts (like *kuilak pairahan kunglak*), caftans, *dakala, nimcha* (minishirts), *kurta, izar* (trousers), belt (*kamarband*) with metal decorations made by *tagbandbafan*, headgear or cap (*buruk, taqiya, qalpad*), *keshik qalpaq* (fur cap), *dastar, futa* (turban), *faraji, pustin kash* with a Chinese silk cover on fur coat. For each article were skilled artisans like *kurtakar*, *jamakar*, *futakar.*[144] There were different dresses for summer and winter. The *Waqfnama* of Husain Khwarazmi instructs the *mutawallis* to give away in charity four *usual khalats* or robes (2 for summer, 2 for winter), two *kurtas*, two *pyjamas*, one taffeta turban, one *taqiya* (Uzbeg cap), *futa*, shoe and socks. The nomads and seminomads used upper garments over their shirts.[145]

Muhammad Saleh reports that the Uzbeg nobility and rulers usually wore fur caps, mink coats of fox skin, *tulki*, red mink *tuni aidi*, a*ltai, surar*, olter, ermine squirrel (*eteen*), *kesh* (sables) and also special fur caps (*keshik qalpaq*). Isfahani also refers to the ornamented dresses of silk used by the steppe nobility.

Saifi Bukhari says that the Qazaqs prepared caftans from sheepskins decorated with floral designs resembling *atlas*. They were bought and sold in Bukhara at the same price as *atlas* and were extremely beautiful. Isfahani says that from Astarakhan to Turkestan the mink and fur coats of sables and squirrel were brought.

The furs were prepared by *pustin duzan* and *muinduzan*. The training of cap sewing (*taqiya duzi*) was imparted usually to menfolk for a period of three years as is indicated by sixteenth century contracts.[146]

Other Handicrafts

The wood carving and artistic ornamentation (*ou makr* or *sarkarlik*) on railings, doors, columns, capitols, cornices carved wood cornices, and wooden decorations on walls were a handsome feature of Uzbeg building. There were wood workers like *shana tarash, khargah tarash, duktarash, kharrat, najjar* (respectively comb maker, tent pitcher, spindle maker, turner and carpenter). In Samarqand delicate *duktarashi* is noticeable in the *aivancha* (balcony) on *bazaar-i risman.*[147] There existed *bazaar-i chub farushi* where wood and building materials were sold.[148] Near the *bazaar-i chub* was another market called *bazaar-i dar* where readymade gates, doors, wardrobes, etc., were sold. In Samarqand there was a street of carts (*arabachiyan*). Different wooden articles like saddle, cages for birds, oars, *qalibs* for printing, wooden staffs, boxes and two-wheeled *arabas* (carts) were sold in these markets.[149] Babur refers to the Masjid-i Maqata with ceilings and walls covered with *islimi* (carved ornamentation) and Chinese pictures formed of segments of wood. The same chronicler describes Tabalghu—'a tree with red barks they make staves of it; they make bird cages of it; they scrape it into arrows'.[150]

Clavijo says that Timur had brought with him 'craftsmen in glass and porcelaine from Damascus who are known to be the best in all the world'.[151] In sixteenth century also glasswork was undertaken and cups, bottles, containers, pots and vases, etc., were prepared. Glass from Haleb and Aeppo (*Haleb shisha si*) was sold in Samarqand.[152] The floral designs on panes of windows in varied colours of violet, blue, yellow green and red are still to be seen in medieval Central Asian buildings. Wasifi refers to Maulana Muhammad *abgina gar* who collected embossed and raised pieces of glass for Faulad Sultan, son of Shaibani.[153]

Jahangir in his memoir refers to a jug of jasper prepared in the reign of Ulugh Beg with the name of the said prince carved on the neck of the jar in *riqa* characters. Its 'stone was exceedingly white and pure' and the jar 'was a very delicate rarity and of a beautiful shape'.[154]

In Samarqand the leather workers worked and lived in the region of Abi Mashad near Shahizinda and in Kaftar Khana[155] from sixteenth-nineteenth centuries. The *kafash duzan* (the shoe makers) and *kafash farushan* (sellers of shoes) prepared leather footwears. Both Wasifi and Hasan Nisari mention 'excellent and renowned' leather workers (*charmgar*) at Samarqand. One such *sarraj* Maulana Maili was so unique in leather work that his workshop served as a light house for leather workers and his saddles were carried by the traders to Bulgaria and China not only for sale but as a specimen of fine workmanship.[156] From leather were prepared purses, cases for knives, shoes, belts, straps, thongs, harness, arrowbags, *shagreens* (*keemukht*), files for papers (called by Wasifi as *makawa sazi*), folders, dustwrappers, etc. There were book binding shops also near the *bazar-i attaran*. The felt served as floor covering; for defence against arrows, headgear for the poor and even as partitions within rooms. The felt makers (*namadmalan*) also had a separate area for themselves. The *lajam duzan* prepared bridles.[157] In sixteenth century Maulana Taleyi was famous for his fine manufacture of bows and arrows (*sanaati tirgar*) and Mulla Shaikhi for his excellent shoe making.[158]

Engraving was also well-developed. The epitaph of Shaibani preserved in Ermitaz is an excellent specimen of delicate ornamentation. The Samarqand engravers usually worked on order. Wasifi says that Sultan Muhammad, the ruler of Tashkent ordered them to prepare an epitaph for his father Souyunch Khan.[159] In Samarqand, there was one whole street known as stone-cutters or, engraver's street (*sangtarashan*[160]). Abdullah once presented to Khwaja Saad four captive slave stone-cutters (*ghulam sangtarashan*) from northern India.[161] According to Babur a number of other articles like knives, handles, clasps for belt, etc., were made of beautiful red and white stone found in Barakuh.[162] The famous engraver of sixteenth century were Maulana Navedi Suni,[163] Sultan Husain and Muhammad Sharif.[164]

The metal workers of Samarqand were also famous.[165] The sources refer to varied types of bath-tubs (*taas hammam*) weighing a maund and five *seers* or 75 kgs, copper buckets (*sital*), *deg-i lahori, tabaq* (large dish), *degcha*,[166] bronze *aftaba, uudsoz* (incense burning stand), candle stand, *khulanchi* copper *qandils* (chandeliers), *shah kasa* (large cups, bowl), *kasa* (bowl, cup), and *kafgir,* cast iron *degs* (*deg-i chuyan*). The ironsmiths of Samarqand and Bukhara are often mentioned in the sources with their *dukans* (shops) consisting of wooden *aiwans* (wooden stalls) and work-yards as in the Qarakul documents of 1566.[167] The miniature paintings show the furnaces, bellows, instruments, hammer, pair of tongs, pincers among their tools. Among such workers may be included *mekhchagir* (iron-pig makers), *naalbandan tagachiyan* (horse shoe makers) in Samarqand and-Bukhara, *karadgar* (knife makers), *chilangar* (saw makers) *suhnagar* (makers of pincers and pair of tongs), *miqrazgar* (makers of scissors), *misgar* (coppersmiths) and *rekhtagar* engaged in bronze casting. There was a separate area for needle makers and needle work (*sana't-i suzangari*) and a place for them known as *darwaza-i suzangaran*.[168]

The pottery famous as 'Samarqand wares' was manufactured in a number of different centres and remained in use for quite a long time. These were related to those of Nishapur but in design they were generally less harsh and angular. The 'peasant wares' made at Samarkand, Bukhara and elsewhere in Turkistan down to quite recent times belong to the same family. The bodies of the vessel were red or pink and were covered with a whiter, red or black slip, over which the designs were executed. The result comprises patterns in white, pink, red, black, brown and yellow under a thick colourless transparent glaze. The forms were mainly restricted to simple plates and bands though a few jugs and jars are known also. The designs were in general of a basically geometric character but were balanced and sophisticated; kufic scripts was freely used, with very fine effect.[169]

In Samarqand there was an area known as *chuyanchiyan* (ironsmith's ward). One of the legal documents of 1563 refers to a *rekhtagar's* shop and home in an alienated strip. Another document refers to an area called *chuyanchi* where iron casters lived; and in one of these houses 4 maunds of cast iron costing 16 *tanga-i khani* were found. In Samarqand a shop was sold in 1589 having implements like *kunda gaodum*, etc. The shop is said to have various blocks called *ahankashi, atishkari, barikkashi* referring to different processes.

In *charkhkari* (metal decoration) Ustad Kamal of Samarqand is described by Wasifi as a unique expert.[170] There were about sixty styles of metal decoration one of which was filigree. Bukhara Mongol was prepared with an iron blade and copper handle.[171] In Bukhara there were shops for cloth-embossing, braiding or plaiting of a garment (*dukan-i uttukashi*) using heated metal.[172]

In sixteenth century ceramics the traditions of Timurid pottery were continued in every respect except that the Uzbeg pottery in comparison to that of the Timurids was somewhat crude in form and primitive in its ornamentation and subdued in colours. There seems to be the same Chinese influence of white and blue designs on porcelain with the same cobalt as used by the Chinese and initiated by Timurids. The usual style was that in place of earlier polychromy, single coloured bright blue designs preferably on snowy white background, the pattern not covering the entire base, submerging at the end without any prominent ornamentation at the bottom. The designs were usually free of miniature techniques either in subdued or on bright blue hues, often depicting Chinese phoenix bird fin or lotus or other floral designs. The Timurid style is reflected in sixteenth century Samarqand cups through its cobalt, dark green colours on white background. The fragments of a dish from Samarqand (preserved in Samarqand Museum) shows a sparrow sitting on a branch. Although its upper borders show cracks, the figure of the bird, the details of the painting, the treatment of branches prove the skill with which the work was completed. Apart from pottery, the polished bricks, multi-coloured majolica on glazed earthen ware, tiles of different form and sizes, water tubs, containers for grain and *tandur* for baking were also prepared.[173] The *kasagar* and *kasatarash* were specialists of different art. The relief ornamentation which was blown up in the form, or embossed designs were stamped in decorating the glass work or the pottery. The motives were not very complicated. We have the diamond shaped signs, trees rosettes, birds, etc., engraved on the glass. The stone matrix was made of dark green stone (*qalib tash*) for moulding and casting metal objects with embossed designs.[174]

Alkashifi refers to a large village (*dehibuzurg*) comprising several villages and agricultural fields, which was 3 *farsangs* away from Bukhara and where the entire population depended for its subsistence on the pottery, clay work and flower painting (*kasbi-gilkari*).[175] The clay used for pottery was found in Kuhik the hillock near Samarqand.[176] The decoration brickwork, stuccoes both carved and moulded motives like five lobed vine scrolls, bud like designs, etc.

There were three main centres of both plain and glazed pottery—the street Khumdanak in Samarqand, Guzar-i Kasagaran in Bukhara,[177] and Ghujdwan for its own characteristic pottery.[178] The pottery with blue and black decorations of flowers and bright colours was a especiality of Samarqand.[179] The art of building construction also progressed considerably. Voronina rightly points out that the 'sixteenth century architects had full appreciation for the ensemble, which explained why so many beautifully arranged complexes emerged at the time in the city itself, and in the suburbs. Particularly numerous were ensembles of the *kosh* (literally, pair) type, out of two buildings placed on the same axis and overlooking each other, although dating sometimes from different epochs'. Although the décor executed in tiled mosaic was basically true to the fourteenth century tradition, certain new features emerged in sixteenth century such as majolica inserts into the alabaster moulded semi-cupolas and decorative flat cupolas. Of the exterior facades, only those with portico (*aivan*) had mono coloured stuccoed décor in sharp contrast to the interior irridesence, of colourful glazes and the regal *kundal*[180] (a feature of the deorating style in the epoch of the Timurids). The *kundal* ornamental technique consisted of brushing over the wall surface and preferably against the background of the blue, a solution of red earth that formed a convex design or an inscription, to be subsequently guilded.

In the Buland Mosque for example the hall was oblong in shape with a decorated wooden cutting suspended on chains to the old beams of the ceiling, its roof made of earth. It seems that in the later half of the sixteenth century the 'aseisimic qualities of the building enhanced. . . . It was a period of the rapid development of forms with criss-cross arches and shield shaped pendants which multiplied gradually to form a smooth web-like transition to the calot of dome.' Another novel feature was a broad variety of decorative cupolas with the herring-bone pattern of ground brickwork, and fine and exquisite facets and tiled mosaic inserts. Certain sixteenth century buildings had no tiles or mural. *Chaspak,* a two colour stuccoed, mosaic was successfully applied to the interior surface of the cupola. Majolica, previously a component of the facade décor, gave place to new decorative styles such as sectional mosaic, either tiled or of ground brickwork with glazed dark or light blue seams.

The Madrasa-i Abdul Aziz was richly designed with mosaics and majolica and indeed relief decorated in some spots, with exuberant polichrome ornamentation and fine landscape motifs of the murals.[181] The stalactite of Samarqand and Bukhara differed from each other. In Bukhara the most popular style being 'Iraqi' which came into existence in sixteenth century by combining the then prevalent different styles. The style *muqannas* was used in capitals and the Iraqi *muqannas* in half cupolas and lower portals.[182]

The epitaphs with genre paintings and elegy, the carved, the fretted niches, the inscriptions decorated uniformly on both sides with diamond shaped embossed or geometrical or wattled patterns, the carved columns with animal forms with human heads, snakes, etc., were other prominent features of sixteenth century artistry.[183]

Another artistic introduction in the decoration of buildings was *usta shirin* which had varied designs like charzamin, vaulted or arched roofs with *sharafa tossaq, madakhil, munabat baf, ishini, berg Islimi, gulnari, charhasht, shashduazda, zaminkar*. Some of these are found in Madrasa-i Burraq Khan. Special and technically sophisticated instruments like the basic *shuturgardan, kalan-i shukufta* (for engraving and levelling), *minakari* (for surface concavity), *kalam puh* (for preparing rollers), *lula kashak* (for drawing spiralling lines or cylinders), *marpech*, etc., have come down to us and prove the highly developed art of construction and décor.[184]

Building construction employed a number of workers. There were specialists like the *kashi tarash* (mosaic), *qulkaran, tarrahan* (floral painters, designers), *muhandisan* (engineers), *durudgran, kardaran diwarzan, kajpazan, khishtmalan* (brick makers) have been mentioned in the sources. Banai's father was a *sabz bana* (an architect, a good builder). For supervisory work *darughas* or often *kutwals* were appointed by the ruler. Copies of the *nishan* of the construction of *waqf* buildings in Samarqand and its entire *amla* and other orders for irrigational canals by *mard-i kar* and bridge construction by soldiers show an elaborate and systematic arrangement for construction work.[185] Babur says that many stone cutters were brought from India.[186] Certain Maulana Saiyid Ghiyas who excelled in the art of construction and had planned a nice garden for Ubaidullah Khan in Bukhara was so indispensable that no one carried the construction work without discussing it with him or bringing it to his notice.[187]

The work of the jewellers of Central Asia has been highly appreciated by Clavijo and Ibn-i Arab Shah. Wasifi also records that Mirak Zargar (goldsmith) in sixteenth century was an expert in his field and could assess the value of various gems.[188] The jewellery shops were usually found in Samarqand and Bukhara where the rich and highly placed members of the ruling class clustered. The ruling group and nobles used gold and silver utensils (*altun iyagh* and *nuqra jam*). The ornaments changed hands from generation to generation. The sources refer to bracelets (*datwana*), finger rings (*angushtari*), ear rings (*halqa-i qushwar*), *halqailila* (gold rings), nose rings (*khalkhal*), pearl necklace (*gardruimarwarid*). The pearl necklace with a nose ring could be had for 90 *tanga-i khani*.[189] Wasifi refers to the immense riches in the form of precious stones and says that Mir Shah Wali had ten boxes, two of which were full of rubies, emeralds, and other precious stones. Sultan Husain's wife is reported to have boxes of precious stones and ornaments.[190] Excellent gem polishers and decorators are mentioned by Ibn-i Arab Shah.[191]

The jewellers of Bukhara had their markets in Taqizargaran and were famous for making ornaments from precious stones inlaid in gold and silver. Apart from ornaments, even sabres, knives and bows of gold and silver were made there. Embroidery with gold, silver and silken thread was another speciality of Bukhara.[192]

The sources[193] refer to mines of gold, silver and lapis lazuli, *wahi*, rubies, turquoise, agate, saralik and emerald. There were *simkash* (silver wire drawers) and *zarkash* (gold wire drawers) who produced works of filligree and such other pieces of workmanship. Usually the rulers and the nobles had close connections with their own jewellers. Sultan Murad Master Zargar was a close associate of Amir Shah Mansur, a confidant of Sultan Husain.

As discussed earlier, the ethnic composition of the artisan class was quite varied. Sources refer to the Turk and Tajik artisans alongside the Uzbeg artisans of Dasht Qipchaq. Apart from them, artisans from other places are also mentioned, viz., Khwarazmi, Kashghari, Khurasani, Tirmizi, Arabi, Multani, Lahori, etc. After each new conquest the captive artisans were sent to the ruler.[194] There was one separate quarter, the Kui Tarasiyan, in Samarqand occupied by Christians. The artisans did not belong to one social stratum. Some of them were very poor, others rich.[195] There was no simple single pattern of relations in craft production. Several kinds of artisans can be identified such as the affluent master artisans, artisans engaged in handicrafts in conjuction with the usurers, artisans with their own workshops, artisans working in their homes, artisans serving in master's shops, lease holder artrisans, artisans working on borrowed material, and finally captive and slave artisans.[196] Certain artisans were attached to the court and served there. The products of such artisans were never dispatched to the markets, but directly sent to the state department.

The requirements of the imperial household, high officials and religious groups were served by public workshops. The orders contained in the *Maktubat wa Asnad* show that activities of these craftsmen were restricted to the fulfillment of the needs of king and his close circle.[197] Under the Mongols, such royal workshops, where captive artisans worked, was known as *karkhanas*.[198] Clavijo speaks of state workshops of Timur where more than a thousand captives were held 'within walls in duress and captivity'. They were kept at work throughout the year for preparing bows, arrows, artillery plate armours, helmets, clothes and other things.[199] They were probably not subjected to taxation.[200]

The sixteenth century documents, however, refer only to the artisans belonging to the royal family or to *waqf* holdings and to other highly placed individuals. The bulk of artisan population appears to have consisted of free artisans.[201] Unlike Turco-Mongol times, the labour employed in the royal workshops now no longer comprised slaves.

The other social categories of the artisan population mentioned in the sources are *karigar* (craftsman) and *mazdur* (wage labourer) who must have provided the labor force. A more prominent category was that of the petty independent artisans who had his own tools and workshop. The artisans could at anytime set up their own workshop though they continued to maintain their relations with their mother workshop for selling articles. Those possessing their own workshop were certainly in an advantageous position than those holding it on lease.[202] There were special but primitive tools for the various professions and it depended only upon the skill of the masters to make the manufactures perfect.[203]

In the workshop, there were three sets of persons: the master artisan or the owner of the workshop the *ustakar,* the hired master *khalifa* and the *shagird* or apprentice. A singnificant point is that the basic work in both types of workshops was done by the *khalifa* or the dependent masters.[204] The *khalifa*, though qualified to be a master, did not possess the means to start an independent shop and had to work for some other craftsman. To start his shop, the *khalifa* did not require any new initiation.[205]

The son usually adopted the profession of his father as from the very beginning the family helped the master in running the workshop. Not only the older sons but women too helped in the work. One of the legal documents (mentions a decision at the end of the sixteenth century) in which the name of a woman Saadat Sultan Muinaduz appears.[206] Although in certain professions like *sabbaghi* (dying) or *qassabi* (meat selling) hereditary Practice of a profession is mentioned.[207] The change of profession was not an uncommon phenomenon. We hear of a blacksmith, son of a plasterer, or the sons of candle makers, saddle makers, skinners and weavers becoming artists, calligraphists, poets and even nobles. Muqimnova says that such instances often occurred when the head of the family died a premature death.[208] Such cases are enough to suggest that there were no 'caste' restrictions, the hereditary practice, wherever found, was a matter of convenience only. Babur's amazement that in India 'every artisan follows the trade that has come to him from forefathers to forefathers',[209] shows how strange this seemed to a man from Central Asia. Certain other documents written in the name of Mulla Fazlullah, son of Mulla Rustam Naqqash, indicate that different professions could be chosen by various members of the family simultaneously. Fazlullah offered his younger brother to a *namedmal* (feltmaker) for a period of three years for 5,000 *dinars*. In another document a fuller was engaged to impart the art of fulling to the brother of Mulla Fazlullah.[210] One Maulana Safai is said to have continued not only the profession of his father, who was an excellent porcelain maker, but also his own profession, i.e. the manufacture of *suqurlat* also.[211]

The traditions of skill and artistic professions were not only transmitted from one generation to another but the master could teach his art to his relatives or even to those who wished to acquire excellence in a particular profession. Such an apprentice served his master and learnt all the work which was assigned to him by the master so as to gain the necessary skill himself.[212] Darvesh Muhammad Khurasani Turk, who received instruction in painting from Behzad, started his preliminary work by preparing colours. Gradually he was able to learn the art.[213] It was only in the final stage that independent work was entrusted to him.[214]

The apprentice was supposed to enroll himself officially under an expert master for training. During the period of training, the trainee lived in the house of the master and his board and lodging was paid for by the guardian of the trainee in accordance with the financial agreement. The *Khutut-i Qaza* refers to such contracts.[215] To avoid unnecessary delays and other complications, a formal agreement between the master and apprentice used to be prepared in the *qazikhana. The Majma-ul Wasaiq* contains 25 such documents (*wusqai shagirdi*). Of these 11 date from the period August 1589 to January 1591. Each document contains the date, month and year of the agreement, the names of the trainee and of his father or guardian, the probable age (minor or major), period of training, nature of specialization, the duties of the trainee during the period of apprenticeship and the financial obligations (to be borne by the guardians), including the fee payable to the master. For some reason which is not clear, the surviving documents tend to exaggerate the amounts of payments. It is possible that they represent formal specimen rather than actual contracts. A document of 17 December 1589 refers to a woman Raushun Bakht who entrusted her son Yakhshi Buldi to Khwaja Baqi Sarraj, son of Nauruz Qassab, for five years for 6,000 *dinars* out of which 3,000 were to be spent on the needs of apprentice and the remaining to serve as the fee for the master. Two such agreements are included in the *qazi* documents.[216] In the first documents written in the name of Tursun Muhammad in 1587, Tursun offers himself as an apprentice to the weaver of *alacha* Kichik for 3,000 *dinars* for half a year during which he was required to complete all the work assigned to him by the master and to learn the art of *alacha* weaving (*sanati alachabafi*). The master's fee of 1,000 *dinars* was included in the above amount. The remaining 2,000 *dinars* were to be spent on the maintenance of the apprentice.[217] The other documents written in the name of Mulla Fazlullah, son of Maulana Rustam Naqqash, indicates that the money was paid in return for an agreement of obligation to give the apprentice such training that even experts might appreciate his work.[218] The documents were probably drafted to protect the interest of the apprentice against exploitation or ill treatment by the masters. Neverthelesss after the agreement, the trainee was fully under the control and at the mercy of the master and his wife who could demand any kind of work from him (including domestic work) and could provide any condition of living.[219] The period of training even in one particular field depended upon the age and, ability of the trainee, the quality of training required and the complexities of the art. The dealy in the completion of the training was, however, frequently caused due to the use of the trainee's employment in domestic work. As the independent work by an artisan without the supervision of a master was forbidden so was any protest or ventilation of grievances against the master. Stern punishments were meted out to offenders. The entire artisan corporation not only governed the occupational and professional but also the personal affairs of the apprentices. The difficult situation of the apprentice often led to his flight from the house of the master. In such cases strict penalties or punishments[220] were prescribed. Although the period of training was specified it was not so firmly adhered to. The master demanded the trainee to learn by heart the *risala* (text or rules) of each profession. One of the clauses in the *risala* specified said that 'if the trainee attained majority and did not settle down as a married man he was not to be respected'. The apprentice could not start his own work without the permission of the master.

The *qazi* documents show that in eighteen out of twenty-five cases, the apprentices were minors. Only one was an adult. The remaining six too must also have been adults as they enrolled themselves on their own. A youngman needed 6 months to learn the same art for which a teenager needed 3 or 4 years. If the economic condition of the trainee was poor the period of training was shortened at the request of the guardians. To be accepted as a master, each trainee had to pass an examination which included practical use of instruments and oral display of his knowledge. If the master judges (*akabiran*) refused to given their pproval for the work, the master was deprived of his right to accept more trainees. For setting up as a master, the apprentice had to arrange for entertainment, etc., for the master and his followers.

Although the sources refer to masters or heads of artisan guilds, e.g. *kalantars, peshwas* and *akabir,* no statements regarding the number of such persons are available. We are told that the Imam-i Muhalla, Kalantari-Qariya or *peshwa-i jamaat* engaged in the defence of the city and in the decoration of the town and place on special occasions (the birth celebrations of Baisunghur). Khwaja Ali Ardgar Isfahani prepared a glass vessel for rose water in which were depicted '32 groups of artisans (*jamaat-i muḥtarifa*) which are at work in the workshop of the world'. Each artisan was engaged in his own special handicraft. There were 32 shops and workshops and each was settled at its particular place. These artisans who were on the move and did not keep shops (like *khayyat*, *naddaf*, *najjar* and *huddad*) had been depicted in the same manner.[221] One may infer that there were 32 *asnaf* (artisan groups) in Timurid Central Asia which might have continued down to the Shaibanid period.

There is no detailed information regarding the daily earnings of an artisan. Both Ali Sher Navoi and Sultan Ali Meshhedi stress that an artisan had to work from sunrise to sunset without giving rest to his hands or without raising his head.[222] A later work, the

Risalabafandchik, says that if an *ustad* earns 3 *tangas* a day he should give part of it to the *pir,* religious persons and *faqirs.*[223] The artisans of the imperial court had a fixed income whereas those engaged in *waqf* holdings were also paid in cash or in kind in accordance with the rules of the concerned *waqf.* For other artisans, even exhaustive labour could not guarantee them minimum subsistance as the taxes on trade and craft and lease payment of the workshops left them with little in hand.[224] The work of a small craftsman in many ways depended upon the middleman who bought the finished goods.

No detailed information is available regarding the existence or organization of the guilds. In the sources there are ambiguous references to *kuloyan* (judges of the market), and *isnaf* (artisan groups) and *kalantara.*[225] Certain historians, however, conjecture a well-organized guild system.[226] The term used for professional organizations (guilds or corporations) are *hirfa*, *sinf, taefa, kasba wa isnaf, sunna wa muhtarafat* and *jamaat.*[227] Whether these were craft-based religious fraternities like Ottoman *futuwwa* or *akhi* organizations or simply professional corporations cannot be stated with precision. Presumably the *jamaat* was a collection of several guilds (craft guilds) formed on the pattern of communes inviting all artisans of various specializations. The existence of some sort of a council of elders or of control is very likely. All those associated with the clay work (like *najjaran, gulkaran, kashitarashan, gajpazan, khishtmalan*) were united into one craft guild or group. Similarly other evidence shows that *memar*, *najjar, kharrat, ahlitisha, shana tarash* were included in one corporation. All the specialists engaged in construction work 'wherever they may be' were placed under the Kalantar Ustad Ghulam Ali.[228] Another order issued to Kamaluddin Bahzad gives him the *kalantaarani* (headship) of all the people employed in the imperial library, e.g. *katibs, naqqash, muzahib, judwalkash, halkaran, zarkoban, lajaward shoyan* as well as the entire group of people engaged in this work throughout the region.[229] Wasifi also gives the text of a letter in which Husain (and his predecessor Ali) were appointed as the *kalantars* of the tailors of *wilayat* of Shahrukhia.[230]

Although no written regulation of the guilds survive, it seems that the traditional norms which regulated and bound the artisans were so well known that there was felt to be no need for such records. In the documents and the *nishans* to *kalantars*, there are certain instructions to the artisans 'to adhere to the established order and set forms' as well as 'to behave in a responsible, customary manner'.[231]

The master artisans and the artisans joining the guild had to offer unquestioning obedience. They were 'not to go against the orders of the *kalantars* and to act towards him in the same manner as they have acted and transacted with his predecessors'.[232] Heavy punishments were given to those who did not comply with his orders. Yusuf Munshi speaks of inefficient workers being put to death by being bricked up.[233]

Thus, a special position was held by the elders of the artisan corporations who were called by different names, e.g. *mihtar, sahab, kalantar.* They were not elected and the *kalantars* of state artisans and free artisans were both appointed by the king or ruler directly. The *Maktubat wa Asnad* contains a numbers of *nishans* issued in favour of various persons for appointment as heads of the corporations of musicians, tailors, cloth merchants and others.[234] Certain *nishans* indicate that not only the weavers but the *bazaz* (cloth merchants) also came under the jurisdiction of the *kalantar* which inclines one to presume that these were simultaneously territorial, merchant and craft guild. Whereas the *kalantars* were the overall guild supervisors of the entire region the *akabir* were the supervisors of the town guilds. A certain Husain Khayyat (tailor) was appointed as the *kalantar* or *mihtar* of tailors of the entire *wilayat* of Shahrukhia.[235] Similarly Kamaluddin Zakaria was the *nazir* and *kalantar* of the weavers.[236] The duties enumerated in the *nishans* of the *kalantars* throw light on the functions of these *kalantars*. The *kalantar* was supposed to be 'an obedient person who feared to make mistakes, excelled in work and avoided violation of royal mandates'.[237] The *kalantar* enjoyed superiority over all the departments, shops and workshops within his jurisdiction, he was expected to supervise the quality of production, estimate its quantity and oversee the actual sale of finished products.[238] Kamaluddin Zakariya the *kalantar* of the weavers was instructed to regulate the prices of cut pieces and costly cloths of local manufacture as well as the imported articles, weigh the silk and other material brought in from outside, arrange for their storage, collect taxes from the artisans engaged in the preparation of silk and other costly stuffs.[239] All those coming to the city for selling craft products were registered as tax payers. In fact these *kalantars* controlled trade and handicrafts and held local markets in their hands. The privileges given to these *kalantars* made them so powerful that not only the petty artisans but the merchants and the high royal officers too had to pay some respect to them.

Although a general control on the market places, weights and measures were entrusted to *muhtasibs* who had to manage the prices and check weights, etc., the prices of articles were fixed by *kalantars* which presumably enabled the middleman to buy the finished goods from the petty artisans at very low rates.

The social and economic position of the artisans in sixteenth century Central Asia as reflected through the various sources gives a very gloomy picture of the life of this class of people. The documentary evidence of sixteenth century shows that many of the small traders and artisans of Samarqand did not possess their own shops or workshops and were compelled to take *waqf* shops or the shop of big men on rent. Even amongst the 80 shops situated in the area of ten Samarqand bazaars (like *bazaar-i naalbandani qadim, bazaar-i shamma, bazaar-i darbikapan, bazaar-i masjidnuma*) 40 belonged to the Madrasa-i Shaibani, 14 to other *waqf* holdings and 26 to certain individuals. These 26 shopowners who had given their shops on lease or sublease were really members of the aristocratic elements, e.g. Mihr Sultan Khanam (daughter-in-law of Shaibani), Aq Begum (daughter of Ahmad Mirza), Shaikh-ul Islam Shamsuddin Muhammad and such others.[240] There were some magnates who owned 10 to 100 premises of workshops. The sale documents preserved in the archives of shaikhs of Juibar introduce us to Khwaja Islam who purchased premises of 104 shops in Bukhara in sixteenth century.[241]

Some master producers owned shops alongwith the artisans and craftsmen. In the *waqf* documents of Mihr Sultan Khanam ten such shops of papers, paint, watermills, bathhouses, etc., were given away in *waqf*. In return, these shops were rented out to certain rich citizens who subleased them to the poor artisans.[242] From the *waqf* documents of Shaibani Khan, we learn that certain workshops had been given away in *waqf* alongwith the tools of production. The owner sometimes provided on lease along with the shop some other tools and goods for use by the lessee.[243] It is clear from the *waqf* documents that small traders and artisans had to pay to the king or to the leaseholder a number of taxes on the production, sale, place in the bazaar as well as on the lane itself.[244] Due to their scanty means many artisans could not buy the material necessary for work. The nobility and the bureaucracy having money could serve as the usurers giving loan to urban and rural artisans in the form of cash or kind.[245] Even Qulbaba the deputy of Abdullah worked as a creditor. From the legal decisions of 1590 in *qazikhana* of Samarqand it is learnt that the bail or guarantee of receiving loan included the additional percentage rate to be paid after a specified time.[246]

From the documentary evidence of the last quarter of sixteenth century, it appears that mortgaging of workshops, trade centres and property was a common feature. One *qazi* document records that 'Neki Khwaja Hakim mortgaged a part of his caravansarai, another person Mulla Muhammad had mortgaged his own house and, a vegetable shop in the vegetable market. Still another Mulla Nazar had mortgaged his shop of stretching wires at the bazaar-i khurdad farushan. The supplementary documents also confirm the fact that some of the mortgaged property of small owners was lost to the big owners.[247]

The custom of *dadni* (advances putting out system) prevailed among the small artisans of Central Asia. Since some of the artisans and masters had only limited means and some of them could not even buy the necessary material, they had to borrow the required sum which they were supposed to return after the sale of articles. According to some documents of 1590, one Maddud Kazar Multani was to pay to Mulla Fathullah Multani 40 pieces of *purband* for 120 silver *tangas* within a period of two months. Another document of 1589 which contained the decisions of the *qazi* informs us that one Neki Darya Khan Multani took 32 pieces of cloth on the promise of repaying the debt within a period of four months. Since the word Multani is attached to the names of these artisans, it is probable that they were Indian traders.

According to a documentary evidence, Khwaja Mir Qasim Haravi of Samarqand, son of Amir Dust Zargar, lent 200 silver *tanga* to Daulat Qadam Qusht Kash, the interest was at the rate of three copper *dinars* for every passing day. Since charging of interest was prohibited according to the Islamic tenets, the money was realized by keeping certain articles like metal basin or even a turban as a surety. Not only money but also goods were lent by the usurers. Being everburdened with heavy debts, the artisans had either to pawn their property and workshop or to serve as bondsmen.[248]

In a document, one Lahori (*cheetgar*, a chintz printer of Lahore) was to pay 150 silver *tangas* to Darya Khan. The records of a supplementary document show that the decision was taken in the same *qazikhana* a little later on 3 October 1589, that Lahori *cheetgar* and his wife were henceforth to serve Darya Khan owing to the former's failure to repay the loan.[249] This is significant in that it shows that the creditor could buy his claim, not only on the debtor's own labour but also on that of his family.[250]

Certain other interesting documents contained in the *Majma-ul Wasaiq* speak of collective debts. In one of the documents of 1590, a loan was given to a group of seven master craftsmen (*ustads*). The creditor was to get 100 *tanga-i khani* with interest from the seven *ustads* who had borrowed the money for personal needs (*hawaij-i khud*). Another document[251] refers to six artisans who had borrowed 3,333 *khan-i tangas*, the price of 5,000 maunds wheat. They had to return it in a span of two years. A third document of 1590 indicates a loan jointly taken by four persons (called *mullas*), of the sum of 133 *khan-i tangas* for five months. Each was collectively responsible (*kafil bilmal*) for the payment. The debtors were not to leave their places of their own free will.[252]

Disputes among artisans often arose. Wasifi drafted one such complaint on behalf of an important dignitary, Maulana Ghayas-uddin Turbati whose associate Ustad Kamal, *charkhkar*, was being harassed by his fellow artisan, a *coppersmith*, Ustad Husain. Turbati criticised the work done by Husain as 'presenting incomplete work and destroying not only the charm of his own art but also spoiling the grace of the entire market in this profession'. He avers that 'since he can not serve his master well, he had resorted to a competitive attitude and quarrelsome behaviour towards him'. It was, therefore, prayed that he 'be checked and made to pursue his own work'.[253]

While the prevalence of usury considerably affected artisan labour, the artisans also suffered from the custom duties and arbitrary collection of taxes described by Jenkinson.[254]

A document referring to the distribution of property among the relatives of the deceased *chuyanchi*, of Tuman-i Sughd Kalan describes the movable and immovable property belonging to Mulla Nauroz alongwith his workshop of iron ware. The Mulla possessed immense wealth. Such examples indicate that not only the ruling class and the Khwajas but certain other individuals also obtained wealth from engaging in trade and organizing manufacture.[255]

The *Waqfnama* of Shaibani Khan refers to the two paper shops (*jawaz-i kaghaz*) of Mihr Sultana Khanam which were situated on the river Siyab. It consisted of iron, stone and wooden implements alongwith a workshop with two rolling stones (*sarkar-i sangin*). While referring to the Chingizid workshops, the sources refer to the basic difference which distinguished the Shaibanid workshops from the earlier ones in that no slave labour was now used. The artisan establishments were given on lease as *ijara, muqateah* and *muzareah* for a period of three months to three years. The owner of workshop often himself participated in the work. The list of implements shows that at least in paper workshops several persons were simultaneously engaged in different type of work during the process of its manufacture. Apart from the master and specialists there was another category of amateur workers without any particular qualifications.

The *karkhanas* were the production centres and the *dukans* were for the sale of finished goods. The *karkhanas* were usually sited on the outskirts. Badruddin Kashmiri refers to only one *hauz-i karkhana* in Bukhara.[256] The *dukans* were inside the cities where the artisans themselves sold the finished goods. Often the production and sale were both undertaken in the *dukan*. Sometimes the manufacturer could be a trader also who traded not only in Central Asia but also abroad. In certain cases public sale was separated from manufacture, e.g. in the case of paper makers and paper sellers, clothiers, dress makers and dress sellers, *futa* weavers, potters and dish makers, shoe makers, furriers and fur garment sellers and so on.[257]

The fact that for Waqf documents, the *mutawallis* had to allocate an amount for buying paper shows that these shops were stores and that paper was bought by individuals from these stores.[258] Similarly the *kaac* cloth was prepared in rural areas usually and was sold in the cities by the *birpasfarush*.

Some of the artisans prepared goods on order and were closely connected with the buyers. Some were employed in imperial workshops. There were handicrafts which were marketed by the artisans themselves such as the *diwan-i jamabaf* (the intinerant cloth merchants).

The legal documents, show that agreements between artisans and merchant-creditors were quite common. Having borrowed raw material from Darya Khan, Mulla Husain was required to supply finished goods after seven months. From the value of the finished goods was extracted the rate to be paid for the supply of material on loan. In the same way, the *cheetgars* (chintz-makers) were also obliged to supply finished goods in a given time after having received the material.[259] The resourceful and the rich could however deal in various goods simultaneously, as Ali Sher Navoi speaks of one such dealer: 'Except conscience everything is available at his counter.'[260]

The middleman buying from the producer directly and selling it used to exrcise considerable influence. Two such middlemen were Darya Khan and Tangari Berdi who provided petty manufactures with some raw material (429 pieces of *futa-i tululi* costing 3,432 *tanga-i khani*, 15 *futa-i nabafta* (unwoven *futa*) costing 75 *tanga*, 5 *maunds* of silk 62½ maund *samarqandi*, *chobi baqam* (Brazilian wood from which red dye is extracted costing 120 *tanga-i khani*. Presumably the middleman gave away partly finished goods to the artisans and later on passed these to wholesale buyers. Thus the connection between petty producers preparing half-finished goods and the master preparing finished goods and craftwares was controlled by the merchant buyer. Obviously, the latter was in a position to dictate his own terms over the artisan and control production generally. The foreign merchants also had such connections. Tangari Berdi not only acted as a local producer but supplied raw material to various regions through merchants.

The few traders often monopolized the entire wholesale trade occupying a significant place in city trade, e.g. the whole supply of cloth, part of which was sold on its way from other countries (e.g. India) was first purchased by Mirza Salim, son of Maulana Ibrahim Sadr, whose stamp was placed on all the varieties of cloth in which he traded.[261] This system of monopoly aggrarated popular misery. The situation is best summarized by Ali Sher Navoi: 'The profiteer who in the town outbids all in buying the good, wishes an advantage for himself and disappointment and failure for the people. The people's loss brings him profit, he buys on cheaper rates and sells at higher rates. When he buys it he calls it canvas; when he sells it he calls it line.'[262]

A considerable sector of craft production was controlled by the religious personages nobility and the ruling family. They owned commercial centres, workshops, caravansarais, mills, oil mills and paper mills. They served as usurers who gave loans, advance money and grains to, the rural and urban poor and sometimes even provided raw material to the artisans. To cite an example, Qulbaba Kukultash, an influential deputy of Abdullah, engaged in usury as is shown by a legal document of 1590 affirmed in Qazi Khan of Samarqand.[263]

As for merchant usurers they often brought and stored large quantities of raw material and half finished goods.[264] Gunpowder stores of Qulbaba are mentioned by Hafiz Tanish[265] and the stores of *chobi baqam* (Brazilian wood) and raw material for *futa* are mentioned in various documents.[266]

NOTES

1. Ghaffurova, *Istrorija Tajikskova Nardoa*, 1952, pp. 339-40.
2. Pugachenkova, *Istorija Iskustova Uzbegistana*, pp. 320-1.
3. Jenkinson, Hakluyt Society Series, I, p. 21; Juvaini, pp. 135, 162, 177; Clavijo, pp. 286-91.
4. Juvaini, Eng. tr., p. 127.
5. Juvaini, pp. 21-100, Clavijo, pp. 201-4, 286-8; Ibn-i Arab, Eng. tr., pp. 151, 161-2, 188, 215-18, 313-14; *T. Shahrukh*, f. 19; *Rauzat*, ff. 275, 375; Muqminova, p. 31.
6. *BN*, Eng. tr., p. 518.
7. Jenkinson, p. 21.
8. Suhraev, *Pozdni feudalni gorad Bukhara*, Tashkent, 1962, p. 24; *Istorija Uzbegskoj*, pp. 534-6.
9. *Mehn*, pp. 85, 199-200
10. Spuler, *The Islamic World: Central Asia in the Last Centuries of Independence*, Vol. III, p. 242.
11. Zainuddin Mahmud Wasifi, *Badaiul Waqai* (2 vols.) are full of such details.
12. V.V. Barthold, *Turkestan Down to Mongol Invasion*, London, 1958, pp. 451-2.
13. Watters, p. 87; *BN*, p. 81.
14. Wasifi, pp. 44, 384, 399.
15. Jenkinson, p. 21.
16. Obruchev, pp. 31, 37, 63, 69.
17. *Cambridge History of Islam*, Vol. II, 1970, p. 454; also see Grunebaum for such specailized bazaars in all other Islamic countries, *Islam*, London, 1955.
18. Varonina, *Architectural Monuments of Middle Asia*, Leningrad, 1969, p. 30.
19. Jenkinson, p. 450; also see *Matla*, p. 108.
20. *Istorija Samarqanda*, p. 267.
21. *Rauzat-uz Rizwan*, p. 201; Ibn-i Hauqal also refers to the markets in and outside the town of Bukhara which were organized on times where transactions of *chaharpa* (quadrupeds), slaves dresses and other necessities like copper utensils, cotton clothes famous as Bukharim, blankets, floor covers, beddings, etc., which were even exported to Iraq, were carried out (Ibn-i Hauqal, pp. 209-20).
22. Suhraev, p. 30; *Iz Arkhiv Shaikhov Jaibar*, no. 41, p. 60.
23. *Iz Arhkiv Shaikhov Jaibar*, no. 27, p. 21; Suhraev, pp. 30, 134.
24. *Majma-ul Wasaiq* (*M. Wasaiq*), pp. 140-1.
25. Clavijo, pp. 278-9.

26. *M. Wasaiq*, p. 129.
27. Ibid., p. 25; *Waqf Nama* 234; Muqminova, p. 179.
28. Wasifi, pp. 121-8; also see *Istorija Iskustova*, p. 325; *Istorija Samarqanda*, p. 267.
29. Apart from the shops and handicrafts mentioned above there were the following: *rangrez* (dyers), *sibagh* (dyer), *khishtkar* (brickworkers), *sufalfarosh* (seller of earthen wares), *misgar* (coppersmith), *sakkak* (cutler), *khammar* (wine merchant), *raughangar* (oil pressers), *abreshamkar* (silk weavers), *rekhtagar* (melter of brass and copper), *naddaf* (cotton dresser), *kirpas farush* (muslin seller), *charmgar* (skinner), *suzangar* (needle workers), *kharratan* (turner), *zinsaz, zingaran* (saddle makers), *mushkfarush* (sellers of musk), *nassaji* (making of coats mail with iron rings), *mujjalid* (book binder), *sharbatdar* (syrupsellers) (Wasifi, pp. 98, 107, 114, 115, 196, 199, 527, 1222; *Muzzakkira*, pp. 168, 361, 399, 442, 446, 456; *Waqf Nama*, pp. 120, 121; *Istoriji Samarqanda*, p. 281.
30. *Maktubat wa Asnad*, p. 116.
31. They were *abginagar, zargar, suzangar, shamshergar, durudgar, kashigar, kuzagar, minagar, kuhgar. AJ*, pp. 63, 72, 137, 210, 212, 230, 236, 237, 328, 338, 342, 246, 404.
32. *Istoriji Uzbegskoj*, new edn., Tashkent, 1967, p. 534.
33. Ibid.
34. *Waqf Nama-i Shaibani*, p. 131; Wasifi, pp. 107-8; *BN*, p. 81, *Istorija Samarqanda*, pp. 31, 148-50; Spuler, p. 262 .
35. Muqminova, pp. 31, 148-50; Spuler, p. 262.
36. Clavijo, pp. 201-4, 286-8; Ibn-i Arab, Eng. tr., pp. 215-18, 313-31; *T. Shahrukh*, f. 19.
37. *BN*, text, pp. 47-8; Eng. tr., p. 81
38. Sultan Ali Meshhedi, *Traktat*, p. 131; Muqminova, p. 96.
39. Ibn-i Hauqal, p. 194; *Burhan-i Qate*, Lucknow, 1888, p. 53.
40. Vambery, p. 351.
41. Muqminova, pp. 95-103.
42. Meshhedi, pp. 129-33
43. Basil Gray, *The Arts of the Book in Central Asia 14th-16th Centuries*, 1979, pp. 50-3, 249-71.
44. This was a proper blend or mixture of lamp black, soot, *samgh, mazum, zag, ziya* (gum of tree), *qaraz, gall* or oak apple, alum, vitriol. Timur's letters to the Khwarazm ruler Yusuf Sufi were written adding *mushk* to the ink so that works emerged clearly on silk cloth.
45. *BN*, text, pp. 47-8, 81, also f. 3.
46. *M. Wasaiq*, p. 142.
47. *Waqf Nama*, pp. 119-38; *Istorija Uzbegskoj*, p. 534; Muqminova, pp. 84-7.
48. Quoted by Barthold, *Sochinedija* II, i, 1963, p. 96; Muqminova 86.
49. Muqminova, p. 88.
50. *Waqf Nama*, pp. 89-90, 129.
51. *Ajaib-ul Makhluqat*, p. 265; Razi, p. 467.
52. Muqminova, pp. 89-90.
53. Ibid.
54. Ibid., pp. 88-90.
55. Clavijo, pp. 285-90.
56. Clavijo, pp. 287-8.

57. Specimens are still available in Aibak Museum.
58. *Abdn*, p. 423.
59. *Sh.N.*, Saleh, p. 58; *BN*, pp. 163, 189, 234; *Abdn*, pp. 423, 445.
60. Muqminova, p. 117.
61. *Iz Arkhiv Shaikhov Juibar*, Doc. 45; *M. Wasaiq*, p. 127.
62. *M.Wasaiq*, pp. 120, 122.
63. *BN*, text, p. 163; Eng. tr., p. 255; *Adabul Harb wa Shujaat*, Oriental College Magazine I, Nov. 1937, pp. 51, 1466-73.
64. *Iz Arkhiv Shaikhov Juibar*, Docs 40-5, *Abdn*, pp. 88, 482a.
65. *Travels of an Alchemist*, p. 107.
66. Ibid., p. 108.
67. *BN*, p. 97.
68. *Abdn*, pp. 450-1.
69. Sidi Ali Rais, *Mirat-ul Mamalik*, Tashkent, 1963, p. 100; Vambery, p. 80.
70. *Abdn*, p. 335.
71. Ibid., p. 465.
72. Wasifi, p. 1100.
73. *M. Wasaiq*, p. 185.
74. *Muytt*, text, p. 432.
75. *Muzzakkira*, p. 361.
76. Evliya Chelebi, pp. 4, 189; Muqminova, pp. 114-26.
77. *Shah Nama*, pp. 53, 81; *Istorija Samarqanda*, p. 271.
78. *BN*, pp. 83, 385-8; Wasifi, p. 573.
79. *BN*, p. 83.
80. Wasifi, old edn., pp. 412, 970. Chang Chun was also served wine every where (*Travels*, pp. 92, 97.
81. Ibid., pp. 196-7, 557-8.
82. *Shah Nama*, p. 3.
83. Mingshi Bretschneider, *Medieval Researches*, Vol. II, p. 270.
84. *IA*, Eng. tr., pp. 130, 188, 220.
85. Ibid.
86. *Matla*, pp. 739-741.
87. *BN*, Eng. tr., p. 265, *BN*, pp. 557-8.
88. *Waqf Nama*, 4; *Istorija Samarqand*, pp. 271-2.
89. Jenkinson, pp. 22-4.
90. *Rauzat*, p. 171.
91. *Muzzakkira*, pp. 267-8; *Rauzat*, p. 171.
92. *Bahrul Asrar*.
93. *Badaiul Waqai*, pp. 571-2.
94. Ali Sher Navoi, *Soch*, II, p. 42; *BN*, pp. 31, 76.
95. Ibn-i Hauqal, p. 194.
96. Cf. Muqminova, pp. 72-8.
97. Clavijo, p. 287; Ibn-i Arab, Eng. tr., pp. 216-20.
98. David Talbot Rice, *Islamic Art*, London, 1975, pp. 214-19.
99. Pope A.U. and Ackermann, *A Survey of Persian Art*, Vol. V, London; *Textiles of the Islamic Periods* by Ackermann, p.1997.
100. Ibid.
101. *M. Wasaiq*, p. 2229; Muqminova, p. 57.
102. Clavijo, p. 287.

103. Ibid., p. 254; also see Muqminova, pp. 57-8.
104. Ibid., pp. 623, 553.
105. Ibid., p. 58.
106. Barthold, *Khlop kavodstova va stredni Azi*, p. 443.
107. Muqminova, p. 61.
108. Ibid., pp. 61-2.
109. Wasifi I, p. 553; II, p. 1127.
110. Rice, pp. 236, 246.
111. Navoi, *Mahbub-ul Qulub*, p. 41; Wasifi II, p. 1127; *Mehn*, p. 84; *M. Wasaiq*, pp. 96, 119; Muqminova, pp. 46-7.
112. Isfahani, p. 47.
113. Wasifi II, p. 1123.
114. Muqminova, p. 47.
115. *JT*, II, p. 4.
116. Ibn-i Hauqal, pp. 216-17.
117. Clavijo, p. 287.
118. *M. Wasaiq*, p. 120.
119. Ibid., p. 118.
120. Muqminova, p. 69.
121. *BN*, Eng. tr., p. 81; text, p. 48.
122. *M. Wasaiq*, p. 182.
123. Jenkinson.
124. Wasifi, pp. 341, 623; *M. Wasaiq*, p. 26.
125. *M. Wasaiq*, pp. 119-20. The 'coarsely woven stuff of Merv of domestic manufacture each strand accompanied by a creptius ventris' which was 'prized for turban' is also mentioned by other chroniclers (see Talibi's *Lataif-ul Maarif*, p. 119; Ibn-i Hauqal, 316; Ibn-ul Faqih, p. 320, also see Muqminova, p. 316; Khuda Bakhsh, p. 463.
126. *Iz Arkhiv Shaikhov Juibar*, Doc. 200.
127. *M. Wasaiq*, pp. 18-21.
128. *Iz Arkhiv*, Docs. 10, 12, 52, 58, 200.
129. Vambery, pp. 154, 351.
130. *M. Wasaiq*, pp. 118-21; Muqminova, p. 51.
131. *Iz Arkhiv*, p. 200; Muqminova, p. 52.
132. Ackermann, op. cit., pp. 2043-5, 2048-63.
133. Suhraev, p. 24.
134. Ulyanitski, *Snashenija Russia sa Indi e Sredni Azi*, XVI-XVII, Vol. 3, 1889 43; Suhraev, p. 60.
135. Qazi Documents, Tashkent, no. 14, 1937; Muqminova, pp. 62-7.
136. *M. Wasaiq*, p. 182; Muqminova, pp. 62-7.
137. Muqminova, pp. 62-7.
138. Ibid., pp. 62-7, 92.
139. *Risala-i Cheetgari*, no. 1900/23; Muqminova, pp. 62-7.
140. Muqminova, pp. 62-7; *M. Wasaiq*, p. 184; Qazi Doc., no. 57, *Istorija Samarkanda*, pp. 534-6.
141. *M. Wasaiq*, p. 182.
142. Muqminova, pp. 62-7.
143. Wasifi, II, p. 1127.
144. Muqminova, pp. 127-34.

145. *Waqf Nama* of H. Khwarazmi, p. 27; Muqminova, p. 129.
146. Muqminova, pp. 48-54.
147. *Iskustava Uzbegistan*, Tashkent, 1962, p. 242; Muqminova, pp. 140-1.
148. *Rashhat*, p. 197.
149. Muqminova.
150. *BN*, text, pp. 11, 46, Eng. tr., pp. 5, 79.
151. Clavijo, pp. 287-8.
152. M. Saleh, p. 3.
153. Wasifi, p. 414.
154. Jahangir, Eng. tr., Vol. I, p. 146.
155. Suhraev, p. 27, also fn. 22.
156. *Muzzakkira*, pp. 167-8, 275.
157. *M. Wasaiq*, p. 17.
158. *Muzzakkira*, pp. 219, 275.
159. Wasifi.
160. *M. Wasaiq*, p. 102.
161. *Rauzat*, p. 261.
162. *BN*, Eng. tr., p. 11.
163. *Muzzakkira*, p. 227.
164. A. Mukhtarov, *Rezba pa derevu va daline zarfshan*, Moscow, 1966, pp. 5-17.
165. *Istorija Uzbegskoj*, new edn., pp. 534-5; Muqminova, p. 104.
166. *M. Wasaiq*, pp. 22, 28, 77, 229; Muqminova, p. 104.
167. *M. Wasaiq*, p. 177; *Iz Arkhiv*, Docs 40, 43, 280, 308, MS.LoIV AN SSR 6-1654, f. 212; O.C. Galerkina, *Rukapisi Sochinenija Navoi*, 1521-2; Iz sobranija GPB Im M.E. Sattikova shedrina, Leningrad trud TxL11 Institute Istori e Arkhyalogye, ethnografi. AN Tajikskoj SSR, 1956, pp. 228, 230-2; Muqminova, pp. 185-6.
168. *Iz Arkhiv*, Doc. 40.
169. Rice, *Islamic Art*, London, 1975.
170. Wasifi, I, p. 108.
171. *Maktubat wa Asnad*, 216; *M. Wasaiq*, p. 116; Wasifi, p. 1138; *Iz Arkhiv*, Doc. 48.
172. G.A. Pugachenkova and L.E. Rempel, *Vidayushiya Pamyatnik Iz obrazitelnova Iskustova Uzbegistana*, Tashkent, 1960, pp. 120-2, also see illustration 126.
173. Muqminova, p. 135, Pugachenkova, pp. 16-30.
174. *Iskustova Uzbegistana*, pp. 120-4.
175. Ali Ibnu'l Hasan Alkashifi, *Rashhat-i Ainul Hayat*, no. 122, Bodleian Library, f. 35.
176. Ibn-i Hauqal, p. 222.
177. *M. Wasaiq*, p. 99; *Rauzat*, p. 206; *Arkhiv Shaikhov Juibar*, p. 283; Muqminova, p. 135.
178. Ibid.; *Istoria Uzbegskoj*, p. 320.
179. *BN*, p. 179; Eng. tr., p. 286.
180. Varonina, p. 29.
181. Ibid., pp. 6-23.
182. Mukhtarov, *Rezba pa deerevu va daline zarafshan*, Moscow, 1996, pp. 5-17; E.E. Notkin, *Bakharskaya rezba pa ganchu*, Tashkent, 1961, pp. 15-39, also illustrations.

183. Varonina, pp. 6-32.
184. Mukhtarov, *Rezba pa dereva va daline zarafshan*, pp. 5-17; Notkin, *Bukharskaya rezba pa ganchu*, pp. 15-39, also illustration; Voronina, pp. 6-32.
185. *Rauzat*, pp. 265, 301-2, 316; *Maktubat wa Asnad*, pp. 53, 54, 55, 79, 175; *T. Muqim Khani*, f. 68.
186. *BN*, p. 45; Eng. tr., p. 77.
187. *Muzzakkira*, pp. 283-4.
188. Clavijo, p. 200; Ibn-i Arab, pp. 216-17; Wasifi, p. 851.
189. *Majma-ul Wasaiq*, p. 81; Wasifi, p. 180.
190. Wasifi, p. 180.
191. Eng. tr., pp. 216-17, 313-16.
192. Suhraev, p. 54; *Istorija Uzbegskoj SSR*, pp. 534-5.
193. *Ajaibul Maktubat*, pp. 232, 235; *BN*, pp. 1-4; Qazvini, p. 215; Chandra Bhan Brahman, *Chahar Chaman*, MS Abdussalam Collection 293/63, Aligarh, f. 57; Ibn-i Hauqal, pp. 193-244.
194. Ex. *Rauzat*, p. 275.
195. Mukminova, p. 175.
196. *Istorija Samarqand*, pp. 274-76.
197. *Maktuba wa Asnad*, p. 72.
198. Muqminova, p. 180.
199. Clavijo, pp. 285-90.
200. B.J. Ghaffurov, *Tajiki*, p. 498.
201. Ibid.
202. Muqminova, pp. 163-4.
203. Ibid., pp. 163-4; Spuler, p. 242.
204. Suhraev, pp. 162-3.
205. *Goncharnovo Proizvodstava va Sredni Azi*, Moscow, 1959, pp. 313-72.
206. *M. Wasaiq*, p. 75.
207. *Iz Arkhiv*, pp. 4, 7, 22; *M. Wasaiq*, p. 171; *Maktubat wa Asnad*, p. 52.
208. Mukminova, p. 152.
209. *BN*, Vol. I, pp. 7, 192; *Istorija Samarqand*, pp. 275-6.
210. *Istorija Samarqand*, pp. 275-6.
211. *Muzzakkira*, p. 399.
212. *BN*, pp. 117, 192; *Istorija Samarqand*, p. 244.
213. *Iskustova Uzbegistana*, p. 244.
214. *Istorija Samarqanda*, p. 244.
215. *Khutut-i quza*, pp. 179, 180.
216. Muqminova, p. 154.
217. Qazi Documents, Tashkent, 1937, nos. 24-5, 35.
218. Ibid., nos. 4-25; Suhraev, pp. 161-2, *Istorija Samarqand*, pp. 275-6.
219. Muqminova, pp. 100-60.
220. Ibid., p. 160.
221. *Matla*, p. 424.
222. *Tazkira-i Khalatan-i Bukhara*, p. 43.
223. *Risala*, pp. 46-7.
224. Ali Ibnul Hasan Kashfi refers to one Maulana Pir Ali who owned a shop of clothes and describes how a tax collector came as a foot soldier and presented him with a *barat* (cheque). Maulana was not in a position to fulfil the demand and consequently invited wrath and violence of the collector (*Rashhat*, p. 140).

225. *Matla* II, p. 96; *Rashhat*, p. 2590, calls them military.
226. Ghaffurov, *Tajiki*, pp. 497-8; Simkin, pp. 60-1.
227. *BN*, p. 288.
228. *Maktubat wa Asnad*, p. 175.
229. Ibid., pp. 169-70.
230. Wasifi, pp. 696-7.
231. *Maktubat wa Asnad*, p. 175.
232. Wasifi, pp. 696-7.
233. *Tazkira-i Muqim Khani.*
234. *Maktubat wa Asnad*, pp. 79, 116-17, 169-70, 175.
235. Wasifi, pp. 696-7.
236. *Maktubat*, p. 116.
237. Wasifi, pp. 696-7.
238. *Istorija Samarqanda*, p. 272; *Tajiki*, pp. 497-8; Pugachenkova, p. 91.
239. *Maktubat*, p. 116.
240. *Waqf Nama-i Shaibani*, p. 118; *Istorija Samarqanda*, p. 273; Muqminova, p. 163-4.
241. Ivanov, *Khazyaistova Juibarski Shaikhov*, Moscow, 1954, p. 52; Izarkhov, nos. 4, 5, 6, and others; Suhraev, p. 178; *Istorija Samarqanda*, p. 274.
242. Ibid.
243. *Waqf Nama*, pp. 120-1, 136.
244. See chapter on taxation for taxes on artisans.
245. George Dobson however says that in his times (1888) there were a few Hindus with red smudges on their foreheads who were all usurers like the Jews. The Jews ran after Dobson at every turn with offers of services in negotiating for his purchase of curiosities and although cursed and reviled by the stall keepers and repulsed by Dobson they nearly always managed to get some little trifle out of our bargains (*Russian Railway Advance into Central Asia*, London, 1890, p. 224).
246. *M. Wasaiq*, p. 186.
247. *Istorija Samarqanda*, pp. 272-6.
248. Ibid., p. 274; Muqminova, p. 167.
249. *M. Wasaiq*, p. 812, *Istorija Samarqanda*, p. 274.
250. *Istorija Samarqanda*, p. 274.
251. *M. Wasaiq*, pp. 185-6; Muqminova, pp. 160-7.
252. *M. Wasaiq*, pp. 185-6.
253. Wasifi, p. 107.
254. Jenkinson, p. 23.
255. Muqminova, pp. 190-2.
256. *Rauzat*, p. 291.
257. *Waqf Nama-i Shaibani*, p. 135.
258. Ibid., p. 205.
259. *M. Wasaiq*, p. 182.
260. Vazlibulenni Sirdsa, *Soch*, X, p. 32.
261. *M. Wasaiq*, p. 182.
262. Vazliublenni Sirdsa, p. 31.
263. *M. Wasaiq*, p. 186.
264. Ibid., p. 229.
265. *Abdn*, pp. 420-51.
266. *M. Wasaiq*, p. 229.

Money, Wages and Prices

Centre Asia had a trimetallic currency, but the coinage in each metal had alloys of varying proportion. The currency had nevertheless attained considerable uniformity. Generally from the nineteenth to the twelfth centuries the *dinar* denoted a gold coin, the *dirham* a silver coin and *fuls* copper coins.[1] Under the Saljuqids, however, the *dinar* denoted a silver coin. In the Mongol Empire of Centre Asia, silver coins of higher denominations were *dinars*, while smaller silver coins were called *dirhams*. In the Steppe state established by Juji, his successors are said to have fixed the weight of the *dirham* as of the gold *misqal*, and this was the weight adopted thenceforth in Central Asia and Persia. The coins bore different inscriptions and ornamentation.[2] Kebek (1318-26) occupies important place in the history of Centre Asian coinage. His *dinars* (*dinar-i kebeki* or *kepeki*), consisted of 6 *dirhams*. Strangely enough, these coins, like those of the Golden Horde, were anonymous, carrying only the Turkish inscription *Qutlugh Balsun* in the Uighur script. More surprising still is the fact that Mongol words are never to be seen on the coins of the Chaghatai Khans, whereas Timur's coins contained the Mongol word '*oog manu*' (lit. 'my word'; decree—a Turkish equivalent of word would be *sozum* or *souomiz*)[3] in the Arabic script, besides other Turkish and Arabic words. In the fifteenth century under the Timurids, silver coins were known as *dinars* and copper coins as *dinar-i fulus*.

From the end of the fifteenth century to the end of sixteenth century, silver coins bore the name *tanga* when alloyed; when pure, this was specified.[4] These coins usually carried the name of the Khan, the place and date of the mint[5] and sometimes even the weight of the coin. Copper coins were usually designated as *puls*.

The monopoly over coinage could serve as a tool in the hands of kings to exploit the people. Under the Timurids and the Shaibanids the so-called monetary reforms had this effect. Each new Khan devalued the currency of his predecessor by 10 per cent and introduced his own coins which were deemed proportionately greater in value. After sometime, he would increase the value of the old coins. By this method, on the one hand the state treasury gained 10 per cent on each coin, and on the other, an additional amount was earned by the state through seigniorage (fee for converting the old coins into new ones), thus gaining substantially on both counts.

The minting charge accounted for the difference between its real value (i.e. cost of metal and minting fee) and the face value. To augment its fiscal income the government in the fifteenth to sixteenth centuries frequently practiced the 'immobilization' of one kind of coins, substituting them with another. Even the coins recently minted and in circulation (*sikka-i jadida raijul waqt*) were easily declared 'old' and 'immobile' to ensure a profit for the state when exchanging 'old' coins for 'new' ones. According to Davidovich, who has studied the numismatic evidence, the rulers employed three methods here:

1. The mint issued coins with new inscriptions and designs differing from the so-called old coins. This was the most expensive method of the three.
2. The appearance of the old coins was changed by stamping them on the obverse and reverse. The method was quick and cheap.
3. A smaller stamp was prepared and each coin was 'branded' with it. Such branded coins were held to be as good and mobile as new ones.

The first method was rarely applied while the last two were common.[6]

Amongst the Timurids, Ulugh Beg, Khusru Shah and Babur had noted such 'monetary reforms' with some degree of success.

Inherent in these measures was the capacity of mints to supply new coins to replace the old ones. Earlier, only one mint was needed to guarantee the supply of enough coins to the market. After Ulugh Beg's reforms in 1428-9, when the minting of copper was centralized in Bukhara, the mint of that city supplied copper money throughout Central Asia, and no temporary mints were needed. In the period from the end of the fifteenth to the beginning of the sixteenth century, however, mints worked not only in big but small towns, suburbs and even in villages thanks to the need to coin enough copper money.

After the reforms in 1500-1, Khusru Shah withdrew from

circulation all the earlier coins of diverse types and gave to the market new, uniform coins. In a period of several years, the minting and circulation of these new coins did not change. The improved coins of Khusru Shah are found in large numbers in the territory of southern Tajikistan. The Shaibanid Sultans revived the earlier traditions; old coins were not melted down, but reissued by branding or stamping. This implies the survival of earlier coins. Davidovich says that the surviving coins of Ulugh Beg are found in larger quantities than those of certain other Timrid and Shaibanid rulers.

According to Davidovich, the existing norms and traditional system of silver currency became more complicated during the sixteenth to seventeenth centuries. A classification of silver currency brings to light two different kinds of measures: the first referring to the regimes of Shaibani, Ubaidullah and Abdullah, which are characterized by genuine currency reforms, i.e. these were issuing the monetary policy of minting new coins and withdrawing from circulation old coins (which were bought by the mint at five-sixth of their face value) thereby a uniform type of *tanga* (silver coins) from various mints. Simultaneously, the adjustment of the silver and copper ratio was also an important item of currency reform. The second kind, marked by political and financial instability that affected the currency in myriad ways, occurred during the second, fourth and sixth decades of the sixteenth century and show by the rulers regular exploitation of the monetary system.[7]

Although some information about Shaibani's reforms is to be found in the *Tarikh-i Shaibani, Habib-us Siyar* and *Rauzat-us Safa,* many details of the subject are revealed only by Shibani's *Waqfnama* and numismatic evidence. The three historical texts give us an identical passege: 'It was decreed that half a *dang* (*nimdang*) should be added to all the former *tangas* (silver coins) (or *tangajati sabiqa*) and, as the coins were issued, each of the (new) *tanga* was to consist of 6 *dinar-i kepeki* as against the earlier *tangas* of one *misqal* which were to be considered now as equal to 5 *dinars* only.[8] But on the basis of Shaibani's *Waqfnama*[9] and collections of coins in museums at Moscow, Samarqand, Tashkent and Ashkabad, Davidovich[10] sets Shaibani's monetary reforms in three phases.

The first phase (1501-4) shows Shaibani's efforts to eradicate decentralized minting, to streamline the issue, determine mutual relationship of various currencies and also distinguish them from earlier coins by distinct designs. He was helped in this task by the immense stocks of silver in Timurid treasuries now under his possession. Special types of copper coins were issued and a part of the Timurid copper coins were returned to the market in the form of smaller denominations.

In the second phase (1504 to 1507-8) Shaibani was engaged in his decisive struggle with the Timurids in Hesar, Qunduz and Khwarazm and his urgent need for finances to raise an army compelled him to undo what he had done earlier: he too opted for fiscal profits through monetary manipulation.[11] By 1507-8 the financial condition and their position of silver had improved thanks to the acquisition of booty, *mal-i amani* and various treasures falling into the hands of Shaibani. In Herat alone 1,00,000 *tangas* were demanded from artisans.

The period from 1507 to 1509, i.e. the third phase of Shaibani's reform is marked by a return to the successes of the first phase. Out of thirteen coins of one type numismatic catalogue number 62 published by Davidovich and 65 specimens of silver coins in southern Turkmenistan and various other collections in Samarqand, only 60 full-bodied coins were found in excellent condition. An intensive minting of silver coins (*tanga*) in 1508-9 is proved by a number of available coins and the functioning of a large number of mints. About 70 per cent of Shaibani's silver coins issued from six out of eight mints are dated 914 AH (1508-9), though a systematic minting of silver coins in Herat, Samarqand, and other towns is noticed in 1507 too.[12]

Shaibani introduced his major reforms in 1507-8 after the conquest of Herat, when a declaration was made in the mosque that one *tanga* would henceforth command 6 *dinars.*[13] Shaibani also increased half a *dang*[14] on each *tanga* of one *misqal* for this purpose. The Timurid coins were allowed to be exchanged with the newly minted *tanga* at the new ratio of 1:6.[15] The centralized minting obviously needed a considerable quantity of metal which Shaibani Khan had brought from the various territories he had conquered. The Timurid copper coins were not allowed to circulate except those of smaller denominations and silver coins were devalued in accordance with their metal content, though they continued to be in circulation till the reign of Kuchikunji Khan (1512-28). According to Davidovich the 'monetary reform's were as much intended to herald a new regime as to ensure a fortune to royal exchange by exploiting the financial potentiality of the mint, following the examples of rulers like Muhammad II of Turkey, Ulugh Beg and others. Shaibani used the diminishing value of the coin to earn in two ways—through seigniorage and by way of discarded silver. The systematic minting of silver coins was started by Shaibani around 1507-8 after which a uniformity in weight, etc. was maintained though they were issued from different mints. The coins were subject to a certain discount on the basis of age. The medium weight of large coins of Shaibani and the golden coins of the Ashtarakhanids prove that one *misqal* was more than 4.7 gm and that Shaibani in 1507-9 put one *misqal* as equal to 4.8 gm. The 4.8 gm *misqal* and *dirham* of 4.8 gm in sixteenth-seventeenth centuries was used not only in Bukhara during the time of the Shaibanids but also under the Janids and the Manghits. This does not mean that these regions did not have their own *misqal* or *dirham*, but in minting the above mentioned two units formed the basis. Thus around 65 per cent of coins of Shaibani preserved in Ashkhabad and another 60 full-weight coins of Shaibani showed that in 95 per cent cases their basic weight was 5.06 gm, 5.30 gm, medium 5.18 gm and usually 5.2 gm,[16] i.e. *yak misqal* 4.8 gm, *nimdang* 1/12 *misqal* = 0.4 gm), as is proved by the available full weight coins of Shaibani Khan. The average weight of these coins came to about 5.20 gm. The copper and silver currency both were minted from state metal under Shaibani Khan.[17]

In the beginning, the new reforms undoubtedly benefited the state which earned a considerable seigniorage. The bulk minting of silver currency fetched a large sum, e.g. from the big Samarqand *bitumen* of 19.2 kg were minted 3,692, 3 *tangas* of 5.2 gm each by which the state earned about 2 kg silver, out of which another 400 *tangas* could be minted.

In the wake of the reform in silver currency a corresponding reform was needed in copper currency as well. The copper coins minted too were now of 5.2 gm. One silver *tanga* comprised 24 *dinars* and one *tangcha* 6 *dinars*. The unitary and strong weight of both coins (copper and silver) were bound to create illusion of correctness and of mutual relationship, i.e. 1:24. These reforms were neither detrimental to the interests of treasury nor did they actually affect the fiscal resources.

The corrective measures taken to reform the currency system were directed to promote trade and to bring at par the intrinsic and face value of the coins. Shaibani's reforms were thus spread over five years and were neither arbitrary nor casual but in consonance with the then prevalent market; and there existed a definite equality between copper and silver coins fixed by the state.

The death of Shaibani in 1510, the loss and recovery of Central Asia by the Uzbegs and subsequent unsettled financial and political conditions told heavily upon its currency. Central minting was no longer possible. The decentralization and opening of 'free' mints created fresh problems. Highest rate of minting is recorded between 917-18. Out of 611 dated coins minted in Bukhara and found in Samarqand, 580, i.e. 97.7 per cent were minted in 917-18 after Shaibani's death and 31 coins, i.e. more than 3 per cent only from previous years. Similarly from Samarqand issue of 1229 dated coins, 1212 or 99 per cent were minted between 917-19 and only 17 coins or little less than 1 per cent from former years. From Tashkent horde of 44 dated coins 42 were minted in 917-19.[18]

Havoc had been created by the increased money circulation in accordance with the quantity theory of money and stagnation in supply of commodities. As the mints had been opened at several places, the supply of money increased rapidly. With this, the purchasing capacity of the people had also improved. But at the same time, the price level too had become proportionately high. In addition, since the coins of Shaibani Khan were of pure metal, the traders were tempted to carry the money outside Central Asia. Ming Shi says that 'in trade the Samarqandis used silver coins minted in the country which might have led to the crisis'.[19] The people were also encouraged to deceive the state by melting the coins in their homes and selling them as metal in open market. As there was free minting, people hesitated to bring silver to the state mint due to the lack of trust in the government and to avoid discount. Thus, after some time, the state also started losing its seigniorage.[20] The copper coins lost their value and silver coins disappeared from circulation. Now the situation deteriorated owing to an artificial lack of silver currency.

Chaggi Memet, a Persian traveller from Tabas (Gilan) who visited Central Asia in the sixteenth century says that in Samarqand and Bukhara 'the money which they have are not coyned but gentleman and mechant makes thin rods of gold and silver as is before said of campion and succuir'.[21]

In the following decade, civil wars and unsettled economic and political conditions further contributed to the problem. A severe famine broke out in Samarqand and other places and food grains were scarce.[22] In view of the increasing prices and the shortage of silver, Kuchikunji was compelled to introduce further monetary reforms, according to which the exchange ratio of silver coins for copper coins was fixed at 1:5 instead of 1:6 as under Shaibani Khan. Like under the Timurids, the weight of the coins was determined as 4.8 gm, and one silver coin was equal to 20 copper coins. Although these reforms could be introduced only very gradually, stretching over a decade (i.e. 1515-25), due to the interference of Ubaidullah Khan, the desired improvement in the economy was noticed. By raising the value and weight of copper coins and forbidding the reminting of old copper coins, Kuchikunji dealt with the problem of mounting prices. The shortage of silver had also been temporarily overcome by increasing the use of copper coins. By 1520 a uniform weight of silver and copper coins was fixed. According to Davidovich since then the *tanga* (silver coin) under the Uzbegs came to be one *misqal* standard, down to Abul Ghazi Khan.[23]

The effects of Kuchikunji's reforms do not seem to have lasted very long. The period extending from the demise of Kuchikonji (1528) to that of Abdul Latif is marked by continuous minting of coins as proved by the specimen of the coins bearing the dates 937-48 and issued from the mints of Balkh, Bukhara, Samarqand, Tashkent and other places.[24] There are some coins minted at Meshhed (923-4, 934), Herat (940-3, 945), Astarabad and Tun[25] presumably to commemorate the Uzbeg conquest of these places.

Towards the middle of the sixteenth century the exploitation through the so called monetary reforms appears to have been revieved, for Jenkinson (1556-8) tells us that deliberate fluctuations in silver money were created artificially by Uzbegs Khans to oppress the subjects:[26] 'their money is silver and copper. . .; they have but one piece of silver which the king causeth to rise and fall to his most advantage every other moneth not caring to oppress his people'.[27]

Moreover during this phase (1540-83) one is bound to come across many provincial ruler declaring independence and issuing silver coins in their own names. In this category we have Burhan Sultan, Yar Muhammad, Abdul Aziz and Timur Sultan. Thus the forms of minting, norms of circulation and basic value of the coin differed within the Empire at a given period.[28] Such provincial currency carried the name of its ruler along with the name of his provincial capital. One such coin is mentioned as '*tanga-i Bukhari*' in sixteenth century documents.[29]

The norms of circulation of silver coins in this phase of political disintegaration were bound to differ affecting uniformity and circulation and enforcing frequently changing exchange ratios. During civil wars, these provincial rulers preferred the circulation of the *tangas* of their own mints and accepted the *tangas* of other *khanates* only under favourable exchange rates. The difference between various provincial coins lay only in their outward appearance and designs. These variegated type of coins issued from various mints were equal and usually static in weight even if suffering loss of value when taken to other areas. The so-called new coins of 9/10 weight circulated on forced exchange value and declared as 'old', lost 10 per cent of their purchasing capacity whereas the 'new' *tangas* of the same weight of 9/10 carried with them a 10 per cent higher exchange value.[30] The owners of the 'old' coins thus lost ten per cent on each head of the coin. Jenkinson's reference to these fluctuations in silver currency is corroborated by the legal documents of that period which mention two kinds of *tangas*, i.e. 'new' ones (called as *Mazruba-i jadida* (newly minted) *jadidaul zarb, jadida-i aan 'asr, jadida, nau, raijul waqt* currently in circulation) and the 'old' coins (called as *sabiqul zarb, kuhna*, i.e. formerly minted, old). These devices shook people's faith in the coinage. The problem was aggravated during Iskandar Khan's regime (1560-83) but was sought to be resolved by Abdullah in the last quarter (1583-99), only to be aggravated in seventeenth century again when the owners of old *tangas* had to lose not only 10 but 20, 30 or even 40 per cent on each coin.

The chaotic political situation had taken its toll from 1540 onwards. Davidovich says that when Iskandar Khan came to the throne (1565), the scarcity of silver was being felt even in essential quantity. This crisis was caused not due to the exploitative measures of 'immobilization' of coins but because silver started disappearing from circulation, and became immovable by hoarding or was taken away from Central Asia through trade. The supply thus exported was bound to affect coinage for which sufficient billion would not be available.

Abdullah's large conquests, booty and organizing capacity however helped him to normalize the currency system. In the last quarter of sixteenth and till the beginning of seventeenth century, the currency issued was said to be of 'pure' silver and any case of debasement was the result of illegal falsification or forgery.[31]

There existed a definite equality between copper and silver coins by the state fixed not arbitrarily but on the basis of commercial and market relationship of the two metals. Even the slightest change in this relationship forced the ruler to change the ratio between silver and copper coins. The values of the coins in the three metal fluctuated with the values of the respective metals. Again the monetary reforms of Abdullah Khan ended the crisis. One of his main reforms was the fixation of a new ratio between silver and copper coins. The conclusions of Davidovich on the basis of numismatic evidence suggest that the market attitude and the relationship of monetary metals changed. The reforms of Abdullah Khan brought into accord official and market course of silver currency. The 'new coins' of Abdullah Khan were equal to 30 copper *dinars* whereas earlier the 'old coins were equal to 20 or 21 *dinars*. Although assaying of the new coins was done frequently, the position on the whole was stabilized and the same ratio continued till the third quarter of seventeenth century.[32] The documentary and numismatic evidence suggest that only 'new coins' (silver) comprised thirty *dinars*, the older *tangas* still carried a lower value. The old coins of lesser ratio included not only the coins of preceding ruler but even some of the coins of the new ruler as well. Accordingly some of the documents of the third quarter of seventeenth century refer to these coins not only as 'new' or 'old' but as '30 *dinar* coins'.[33] Another term appearing in sixteenth century documents in *dehnuhi* (i.e. 9/10) applied to the 'old' *tangas* determining in some way its relationship with the new *tangas*. In the two documents of the end of sixteenth century, before writing the 'old' *tanga* it is clearly stated that they were equal to 27 *dinars*, hence the term 9/10 x 30 = 27.[34] Davidovich has, however, conclusively proved that all the Shaibanid coins were minted on the basis of *dehnuhi* or 9/10 in sixteenth century, i.e. silver amounted to 9/10 of the weight.

Although the silver coins of seventeenth century were often so debased as to have the purity ratios of 8/10, 7/10, 6.5/10, 6/10, and even 3/10, 2.5/10 and 0.25/10, the Shaibanid coins maintained the 9/10 ratio.[35] To these Shaibanid coins were almost always designated two terms *sirra* (highly tested, fully valued—of pure silver) and *pakiza* (pure). The four legal documents of the time of Wali Muhammad (1605, 1611) (e.g. sale deeds and *waqfnama* of mosque and *madrasa* of Charbaqqal (1608) contain references to *tangai nuqra sera pakiza masku* (or *mazruba) i yak mesqali si dinar raiju'l waqt*, i.e. the silver currency of unalloyed pure metal of one *misqal* current for 30 *dinars* (copper coins).[36] Even early Ashtarakhanid coins of 9/10 and 8/10 *tangas* are described as '*pakiza*', but the term was not applied to coins of lower quality, e.g. 3, 5/10x, 3/10x, etc., the term is not applied.[37] It appears that though described as 'pure' the silver in the currency from end of the sixteenth to mid-nineteenth century consisted of some quantity of alloy. Some consider it to be a result of paucity of silver. In the Russian sources of sixteenth century there is some evidence that Central Asian Khans lamented the deficiency of silver and requested the Czar to send silver to them which led Peter Ivanov to conclude that the alloyed lower quality silver currency was a result of lack of silver.[38] Davidovich, however, contends that neither was there any lack of treasure in the state treasury nor lack of precious metals in the country in the first two and last quarter of sixteenth century. The supply of precious metals in each period was determined by three items: (1) the treasures inherited from preceding century, (2) booty, and (3) movement of precious metals through state frontiers and circulation of foreign and indigenous currency. In all the three respects the Shaibanids were successful. The insufficiency of silver, if any, did not affect the minting of currency as the general availability of silver in the country was sufficient to sustain and guarantee the essential quantity of metal.[39] A highly 'pure silver' currency was current not only in Khorezm in the fourteenth century but also under the Timurids at the end of the fifteenth and beginning of the sixteenth century when the ratio of silver and gold was 1:10 and silver currency was considered as highly pure. Even the Ashtarakhanids inherited rich silver stocks from their predecessors. Moreover under the Ashtarakhanids the position of silver further improved but the quality of money certainly declined. If the incessant changes in the assay of coins and the exploitation through money are taken into consideration, the Ashtarakhanids were far more extracting than the Shaibanids.[40] Carson says that the silver currency of the Shaibanids in Bukhara during sixteenth century were 'of a similar spread fabric' as of Ashtarakhanids dynasty (1599-1785).[41] But the numismatic evidence and the study undertaken by Davidovich conclusively prove that the Shaibanid coins were of standard quality and finer in mould then those of Ashtarakhanids. From among the numismatic collections at Ermitajsh, only the silver coins of Abdul Momin seem to be somewhat crude in form and diminutive in size:

very thick (though of 4.8 gm only), looking like a copper coin in shape and type and different altogether from the silver coins of the Shaibanids and Ashtarakhanids.[42]

The minting of silver money under Ashtarakhanids up to the reform of Abul Ghazi was also not 'free'. Davidovich, therefore, describes Ivanov's assessment as 'an unrealistic and pessimistic analysis'. According to her the deficiency of silver occurred only from 1540 to 1575 and she argues that the quality and quantity of silver currency depended in this context not only on the stores of metal in the country but on the position of the treasury. The Ashtarakhanid treasury was more depleted than those of the Shaibanids owing to the extension of *milk i khur* and tax-free lands and diminution of state and *milk* lands leading to a fall in the state share's of revenues.[43] Philip Efremov (1774-82) notes that in his times the Bukhara '*tanga* comprised copper nearly half of its weight'.[44] By the end of the seventeenth century the Uzbeg coins had deteriorated considerably in quality carrying only 25 per cent of silver and the rest being copper. Subhan Quli's coins were particularly poor though they were of one *misqal*. The documents prove well that the proportion in seventeenth century *misqal* silver coins was 10 *nakhud*[45] out of a maximum of 24 *nakhud* thus the alloy was 58 per cent. But in sixteenth century the silver dominated and alloy was only nominal, i.e. 9/10.[46] Abul Fazl (1595) confirms that 'in Iran and Turan they call the highest degree of pureness of silver *dahdahi* 10/10' and further adds that in Persia 'they do not know above 10 degrees of fineness whereas in India they had *barahbani* (12 degrees) or even *bist biswa* (20)'.[47] It should, however, be borne in mind that even sixteenth century 9/10 silver coins of the Uzbegs were inferior to Indian silver currency. The Central Asian silver was not considered to be very pure at least in Akbar's time. While discussing the mints in India, Abul Fazl says that 'out of 100 tolas of *lari* and *misqali* (silver) which are current in Turan, there are lost three *tolas* and one *surkh* they become then of Imperial standards'.[48] Thus the Indian standard was probably 3.01 per cent higher as Central Asian silver was mixed with 3 per cent alloy. This difference could be noticed in the prices of the two qualities of silver. Abul Fazl says that the '*lari*' silver and other 'baser coins' could be bought for one rupee a *tola* and that 950 rupees could buy 989 *tolas* whereas for the same money only 969 *tolas* of Indian silver could be purchased.[49] These comments of Abul Fazl are confirmed by a later source.[50] While discussing the method of recording the proceedings of the mint (*tariqa-i tahrir-i darul zarb*), Mirza Badi describes the varied aspects of minting of *tanga* 'in former times' and gives valuable information regarding not only the working of the mint, assaying, etc., but also about the forging of the coins, minting of alloyed coins, etc. The passage is reproduced here:

'The minting of mixed coinage was not an easy job since the documents of *darul zarb* (mint) were maintained with necessary precision. If the government orders the minting of *tilla* or *ashrafi* (pure gold coins) or *tanga-i sir-i pakiza nuqra-i khani* (pure silver coins) then the matter was simple. But if the minting of mixed, adulterated and falsified (*maghshush*) *dirhams* was ordered, then the recording was a bit difficult as it could not be done without disturbing the *sharia* (*khalal-i shara'i*) and was against the principle of *Nisabu'l ihtisab* (a Hanafite law book). In such circumstances the names of *Bayaan-i ba'i sarf* (merchants money changers?) *tahwil* and *tahwildar* (consignments, cash keeper/ treasurer) and the staff of the *sarfa* should be written alongwith the terms of the deal with *sarfa*. To find out or differentiate the extent of copper from silver in the old *tanga* could be done in the following manner (which could serve as an example for guessing the rest of the ratio): In the old *tanga* the *deh dahum* ratio is to be multiplied by 2½ in this manner:

5520 x 2½ = 13800 13800:10 = 1380

The value of the *tanga* could be determined in this manner:

5520	4300	3660	5800
———	———	———	———
1104	1075	1830	1450
———	———	———	———
5555	4444	222	444

If the need for assaying or probing (*chashni giriftan*) through a furnace is felt then the liquid (*qudaz*) or melted coin metal of *tanga* could be tested by fire ('*iyar*). The liquid of the coins of the weight of ten *tangas* should be examined by a broker (*Kora, Kahbud)*. If full 30 *tanga* weight is recorded the purpose is fulfilled. Usually in the old coins silver was found in a small quantity due to blending (*makhlut*) or forgery. The striking of coins was never free from cheating (*qaliḇ*). In the given example, in 10 *tangas* after its *kahbudi* (examination and assessment by a broker), a clear weight of 30 *tangas* of pure silver should be acquired. If, for example, a deficiency of 1½ *nukhud* was discovered and supposedly considering it as the deficiency of silver—it is tested in a furnace then in each lot of 1,000 *tangas* there would be a total deficiency of 150 *nukhud* silver. In connection with this, one may refer to the ratio of copper—i.e. 150 *nukhud* to 80½ on each 21 *tanga* thus comes about approximately 11 ½ *tangas*. Subsequently the aggregate of deficiency in assaying of silver amounted to 334½ *tangas*. This sum should also be included in the income and expenditure. However, in the *darulzarb* there are many swindlers and cheats and the *darugha* ought to be extremely alert for full preservation and safety.[51]

The art of minting too is said to have been inferior than that of India. In *Ain* 7, Abul Fazl describes that the Indian *zarrab* used to cut off the gold, silver and copper ingots as exactly as was possible and criticizes Central Asian and Persian *zarrabs* saying that: 'In Iran and Turan they cannot cut these pieces without a proper anvil; but Hindustani workmen cut them without such an instrument, so exactly that there is not the difference of a single hair, which is remarkable enough.'[52]

The Central Asian silver currency thus was not only a coinage tainted by an element of debasement and less finely coined currency in the contemporary world to the stronger currency of Persia, India and other places. While describing the currency of the Uzbegs, Jenkinson says that 'they have but one piece of silver and that is worth twelve pence English'.[53] Badauni mentions that four lacs of *tangas* were equal to 500 Persian *tumans*.[54] Similarly Lahori says that the current 4 corers of *khanis* of Transoxiana were equal to 100 lacs Indian rupees and 3,33,000 *tumans* of Iran.[55] Sadiq Khan confirms that one crore and twenty lacs of *khanis* were equal to thirty-one lacs of Indian rupees.

Nevertheless the silver *tangas* of sixteenth century have a broader variety and form since the accession of each new Khan was marked by a completely new set of variegated designs of coins. Apart from the silver coins of Shaibani preserved in the British Museum (dated 910/1504 and minted at Merv),[56] there are large collections of Shaibanid coins available in various museums of Central Asia. The 13 coins included in the catalogue and 62 available and published already, seem to be of uniform type and with similar inscription. The term '*sher mard*' appears the on obverse of the coins with names and epithets of four caliphs and on the reverse is noticed the name of the ruler with his titles *Khalifat-ur Rahman* and *Imamuzzaman*. The coins also carried the date and place of mint and their weight.[57] The *kalima* is put in a circle.

Apparently each new Khan introduced some distinct features to his coins to distinguish them from those of his predecessor and to herald the new regime.[58] Some of the coins of Abdul Latif bore the title introduced by Ubaidullah Khan which was continued by Iskandar Khan in accordance with the tradition of the house of Jani Beg though certain coins of Iskandar carry the word '*qaan-ul aadil*' also.[59] The coins of Abdulmomin and Yar Muhammad carried the same title. Most of the Shaibanid silver coins are oval shaped.[60] Interestingly enough the names of three Caliphs appear on one set of coins which do not bear the name of the mint and the name of fourth Caliph Ali alone was inscribed on the coins minted in Balkh presumably due to its proximity with Persia. The Kalima is seen on all the coins though either in double and quatrefoil area or in ornamented pentagon.[61]

Incidentally, in Central Asia gold coins seem to be quite a rarity. The study undertaken on the basis of archival and numismatic material by Baronin, Davidovich Markov and Lunin proves beyond doubt that silver and copper coins were far numerous than the gold pieces. The coins of Chaghatai Khans of Central Asia may illustrate the point. From the valley of Qaraul tebe, a large vessel of coins was excavated. As compared to 3,700-3,800 copper coins and 1,860 silver coins of 1271-1300, from various mints, only forty full gold coins of 1350 have come down, two of which carried the names of Mangu Khan/Munke Khan.[62]

Although, the gold coins of Timur and Shahrukh are available and *tilla* and *ashrafi* are mentioned in the sources of early sixteenth century,[63] no gold coins of early Uzbegs seem to have been minted. In 1558, Jenkinson observed that 'their money is silver and copper for gold there is none currant'.[64] It was only during the reign of Abdullah Khan Uzbeg that we hear of rare and precious gold coins which were good for trade and particularly valuable in medieval East. The design was not peculiarly special except that its five sided figure doubled by the *kalima* and the title *Abdullah Bahadur Khan* was carrying a quatrefoil in *nun* of Khan.[65]

As Abdullah insisted on complete purity of gold for minting the metal into standard coins, neither the public nor the state could expect any extra gains in this process. Thus, the money supply matched with the demand for money in the market. As a result of this, the price stability could also be maintained largely during the time of Abdullah. Hafiz Tanish records his appreciation of the wise decision of the Khan to corelate the value of the coins by declaring their intrinsic and the face values as being equal to one another.[66] Since Abdullah had ordered that a *pul* (copper coins) should be one *misqal*, attempts for false coining were also discouraged. Chances of error and fraud were further eliminated because Abdullah 'personally supervised the weighing' of the coins.[67] It is interesting that some of the copper coins of Abdullah Khan excavated on 14 October 1894 and studied by Markov do not bear the name of Abdullah though they carry the date of their mintage (955-1001/ 1586-92) and the names of the mints (Tashkent, Samarqand, Andijan). They were found buried in Sardabin near Namanghan.[68]

Thus, it was only under Abdullah Khan Uzbeg that monetary reforms had been carefully planned and enforced in the empire. The Khan chose gold both as a measure of value and as a medium of exchange and adopted full bodied gold coins whose intrinsic and face value were declared as being at par with each other. A detailed account of these measures is given by Hafiz Tanish in the following words:

> For the welfare of the subjects who are the deposits of God, a *farman* was issued that gold (*zar*) should be purified of alloy (*ghash*) *pul* should be struck of one *misqal* each and this the basis of coining false money (*asasi qallabi*) should be exterminated. His Majesty personally turned his attention towards the problem, summoned the assayers (*iyaran*) and their gold was tested under the eyes of the Emperor, assayers were identified and though not much of a difference was discovered between the assaying of yellow and *nakud* (*iyar-i zard o nakhud*) they were all subjected to imposition of fine and exemplary punishment. The Khan stayed in the city for correcting the weight of gold and repairing *pul* (*islah-i iyar-i zar o tadaruk-i pul*) which had been delayed and personally attended to this business carefully.[69]

The copper money during the fifteenth-sixteenth centuries not only served as fractional money in relation to the silver but was a major medium of payment. Jenkinson who lived in Bukhara for about two and a half months (1556-8) recorded that 'the copper money are called pooles—and is more common payment than the silver'.[70] The copper money at that time, therefore, can be a good index of money-commodity relationship in the sphere of retail trade and products of daily requirement. The term *fulus* or *fuls* was applied to all kinds of copper coins (ninth-eighteenth century) generally. The basic nominal copper coins during the period tenth-fifteenth centuries were called '*adli*' the term '*dinar*' or *dinar-i fulus* replaced it from the sixteenth century onwards. A study undertaken by Davidovich shows that the development of monetary system from second half of the fifteenth century was directed towards an augmentation of numbers divisible by 3 and 5, i.e. coins of two denominations—the basic face-value and its half. At the end of fifteenth and beginning of sixteenth century in the markets of Central Asia one came across copper coins (*fuls*) of 6 denominations, viz., basic *dinar* of face value, double, one and a half, half of *dinar*, 2/3 and 1/6.[71] Such fractions of copper coins are the evidence of a significant rise in the use of copper, possibly because of a world-wide scarcity of silver, not relieved until the Spanish acquisition and export of American silver later in sixteenth century.

From the time of the Samanid (tenth century) upto mid fifteenth century the two copper denominations of coins *dinar* and *pul*, were issued by one and the same mint at Bukhara. The minting of *dinar* in our period was probably on a much smaller scale as they are rarely found in hoards or museums. Jenkinson does not mention the *dinar* but numismatic evidence suggests that they were minted though in an irregular and unsystematic manner as compared to the first quarter of sixteenth century. From the third quarter of sixteenth to eighteenth centuries, the leading role in small scale retail trade was taken by copper coins of half or one *dinar*. The number of mints decreased and copper coins were issued only by big town mints, testifying to the return of silver at the expense of copper.[72] Davidovich, it is true, argues that the contraction of copper coinage marks a contraction of trade. But this is doubtful, since the scale of copper-circulation has to be set by the side of silver-circulation. The silver influx from Europe after 1540 and the high price of copper owing to demand for artillery naturally reduced the size of copper coined into money. An exactly similar process took place in India where very few mints continued issuing copper money in the seventeenth century.

The legal documents and the sale deeds and *Waqfnama* show that Shaibani's copper coins were of one *misqal nimdang*, i.e. 5.2 gm and twenty-four of these were with one silver *tanga* of the same weight. But the weight and intrinsic and face value of copper money in different years from the end of fifteenth to the sixteenth century was not constant. From 1491-2 to 1507-8, the coin's weight value varied and it fell from 5.2 to 5.1 gm and even to 4.6 gm, i.e. losing 0.5 gm (2.5-3 *nukhud*). In 1508-9, it rose again to 5.2 i.e. 13/12 *misqal*. From 1512 onwards, the copper coins were of 4.8 gm and 20 of these were equal to one silver *tanga*. A uniform weight of copper coins throughout Central Asia was enforced from 1520 onwards. In *waqf* documents of 1535-6 of Madrasa-i Ghaziyan in Bukhara it is recorded that each *tanga* comprised 40 *fuls* and each *fuls* weighed 1 *misqal* and 2 *nukhud* (1/24 part of *misqal*). Twenty-seven to thirty of Abdullah's copper coins were worth 1 *tanga*.

In sixteenth century, Central Asian copper money circulated on the basis of the metal, and the relationship between the two metals—silver and copper—was determined by their prices. The reductions in weight of coins thus introduced a great element of instability.

The weight of the coins was sometimes inscribed on it. The numismatic evidence in the second half of the fifteenth century shows an augmentation of small denominations of copper coins, the half-copper coin being uttered as well as the unit coin. Later on, there was a coin representing a sixth of the unit.

The minting of copper coins (from the end of the fifteenth to the beginning of the sixteenth century) along with its fractions shows an enlargement of the circulation of copper currency—this being a special feature of the period.

According to Davidovich, the minting of copper coins was never done on such a big scale as in the last quarter of the fifteenth and the early sixteenth century. In the Khanate of Hesar alone there was a simultaneous issue of copper coins from Hesar, Qunduz and Tirmiz mints. Another lot of coins was issued at one time from nine mints of Hesar, Tirmiz, Chaghaniyan, Khutlan, Qabadian, Wakhsh, Nauband, Naubazar.[73] In the same period, the mints worked at Samarqand, Bukhara, Tashkent, Shahrukhia, Miyanakal, Zamain, Kufian, Qarshi, Merv and Nesa.

In 1505, even temporary mints cropped up as in the valley of Chirchik which guaranteed a supply of money to Tashkent and other places. Such temporary mints existed even in the second decade of the sixteenth century in a Samarqand *tuman* Shavdar and in a Bukhara *tuman*, Bab-i Kapi or Babi Kani, though the mints in these towns also were working simultaneously.[74]

A network of 'free' mints spread throughout Central Asia extending from Samarqand, Otrar, Tashkent, Herat, Kashan, Yezd,

Shiraz, Tirmiz, Astarabad, Lahijan, Bukhara, Akhsikat to Balkh and Khwarazm in the preceding few centuries.[75] In the sixteenth century also various mints at different periods issued a single type of coins in silver and copper.

Shaibani's coins bear the names of at least eight town-mints, namely, Herat, Nishapur, Meshed, Merv, Balkh, Bukhara, Tashkent and Samarqand. Although the extent of payment to the mint and the treasury and the waste of metal is nowhere available, the research undertaken by Butaner at a later period may give some idea about the working of the mint and the amount charged as seigniorage. According to him the minting in Bukhara in mid-nineteenth century followed the following system: those who brought gold received coins from that very metal, but the state took 1½ *tangas* for each *tilla* (gold coin), i.e. 1/42 parts of the whole in value. For the silver coins too the minting charges were the same. Thus in Central Asia in mid nineteenth century the expenditure on minting along with the income of the state treasury amounted to about 2.4 per cent.[76] There existed an interesting system of giving the mints on lease as happened in Astarabad in the nineteenth century. Each citizen desirous of getting his coins minted supplied pure silver to the leaseholder and paid to him the two hundredth part of the metal; later on this was put at a hundredth part of silver with a heavy (two-thirds) alloy of copper. The bullion owners had to pay 2 per cent exchange on the alloy.

These revenues enabled the lease of the mint to make a profit after he had paid the lease charges. The income received by Shaibani Khan from each mint is said to have been quite considerable almost 10 per cent (0.56 gm out of a weight of 5.2 gm). Thus, after meeting the minting expenditure, whatever remained with the treasury under Shaibani was much higher than that received by the state in free minting during nineteenth century.

During Ogedei's regime the cost of pearls varied between one *dinar* and two-sixths of a *dinar*.

In Ibn-i Battuta's time (733) a horse could be bought for 35 silver *dinars*, a dress or robe for 10 *dinars* and a sable coat (*pustin-i samur*) for 100 *dinars*.

In fifteenth-sixteenth centuries, the prices were high and rose much faster than the salaries. In the last decade of fifteenth century, a good bow with Kalliaiqand could be purchased for 27 *tangas*, a copy of the Koran for 100 *tangas*, one dress of cotton (*qabai parchagi*) for

20 *tangas* and one brocade *futa* of Yezd (*futa-i zarbaft-i yezdi*) for 50 *tangas*, the Arabian *tikmadari* (gold embroidered silk shoes) for 10 *tangas*, a dagger with cover for 10 *tangas* and one cap of black fur for 20 *tangas*.[77] Food grains and other necessities were also expensive. One Khurasan maund of copper could be bought for 5 *tangas* and 1 *misqal* of tin could be purchased for 2 *puls*.[78] A small place near the tomb could be rented out for 20 *misqal*,[79] whereas a plot of land (where a *khanqah* could be constructed) in Samarqand could cost 500 *tanga-i khani*.[80] Clavijo says that the land in Samarqand was generally very expensive.[81]

In times of scarcity or inflation the recorded rise in the prices showed that the rates could go up to an extent of 30 *tangas* and 20 *dinars* for 1 Khurasan maund of copper and 1 *misqal* of tin respectively.[82] During siege of Tashkent when the scarcity of provisions created inflationary conditions, 1 Bukhara maund of grain could be bought for 250 *khanis* and one camel load of the same for 1,000 *khanis*.[83] During famines, pestilence, war or floods such inflation frequently occurred though it was short lived.

Compared to these prices, what of the income, the salary of each of the two *sadrs* of Ubaidullah Khan is reported to be 30,000 *khani*.[84] An efficient and loyal servant of Ali Sher Navoi, a wealthy noble, could receive only 500 *khani* annually.[85] The salaries of a *piyadah* in the court or a servant of a provincial ruler were 100 *tangas* annually.[86] Equally rich were the occasional rewards and charities given by the rulers to their favourites. An acrobat was rewarded by Sultan Husain with 10,000 *tangas*.[87] Wasifi himself received 10 fat sheep, 20 maunds of maize, 100 *khani* and 4 trees for fuel only for writing a eulogy for Sultan Abu Said.[88]

When Abdullah Khan Uzbeg fell ill, his deputy Qulbaba distributed 20,000 *khanis* among the needy in Samarqand and 15,000 *khanis* were sent to the students of Bukhara. Similar donations were sent all over Transoxiana.[89] One royal assembly (*majlis-i aazam*) used to cost 100,000 *tangas*.[90] But this affluence was enjoyed only by a small section of population. The majority lived in abject poverty.

As is proved by various *waqf* documents, the salaries of the staff connected with *waqf* establishments were very low. The *waqf* document of 1527-8 of Madrasa-i Mir-i Arab in Bukhara show that the *imam* received a daily allowance of 6 copper *dinars*, the *muezzin* 3 copper *dinars*.[91] Another *waqfnama* of 1535-6 of Madrasa-i Ghaziyan of Bukhara recommended that the students should get

3 grades of stipends though the salary to the *mudarris* came to about 500 *tangas*.[92] Similarly, the *waqfnama* of 1569-70 of Madrasa-i Gaokushan in Bukhara fixed the salary of the cook as 5 *dinars*.[93] In some of the *madrasas* in later years, the rate of salary seems to have improved as the *waqfnama* of 1593-4 of Madrasa-i Qulbaba Kukultash in Bukhara says that *imam* received 11½ *dinars* and *muezzin* 5½ *dinars* per day.

If the salaries were accompanied by benefits or payments in kind the money-salaries were still more meagre as in the *madrasa* of Shaibani Khan, the *imam* received 1½ *dinars* and 2.5 kg of wheat. The same *waqfnama* further shows that the *hafiz* (readers of the holy book) received 2⅓ of copper *dinars* along with 5 kg of wheat or 2 copper *dinars* and 4,380 gm of wheat. The cook, *farrash* (chamberlain) and such other servants received only 1 *dinar* and 1,644 gm of grain; the *muezzin*, water carrier and servants got 5/6 *dinars* and 1,644 gm of wheat. The students of three categories received 1½ *dinars* and 3,288 gm wheat; 1 *dinar* and 2.5 gm wheat; 5/6 *dinars* and 1,644 gm of wheat respectively. In accordance with the *waqfnama* of Madrasa-i Ghaziyan (1535-6) in Bukhara the slaves especially bought for cleaning the *madrasa* earned 1⅓ copper *dinars* and 1.7 kg wheat. A similar situation is noticed in the *waqfnama* of the *madrasa* of Abdullah Khan (1570-1) where a little more than 3 copper *dinars* and 2.8 kg wheat is allocated for the *imam* and a half of the same for *muezzin* and *farrash*. In the *waqfnama* of Qulbaba Kukultash in Bukhara (1593-4), the *farrash* got 3$\frac{7}{10}$ *dinars* and 1.4 kg wheat.[94]

The legal documents (1588-90) pertaining to cases of divorce fixed the minimum subsistence allowance for a child somewhere between 2-3 copper *dinars* per day or even slightly higher, inclusive of food, dress and other necessities. If the dress was to be supplied by the father the amount was further reduced.[95]

The scanty information found in the *waqf* documents relates to the monetary earnings and subsistence wages of the lower and even middle income groups. The minimum subsistence allowance can be deduced from these accounts though the rate of wages were not the same everywhere as they largely depended upon the richness of the endowments concerned.

In *waqfnama* as a rule the annual salary and payments to various persons are given in silver coins (*tanga*) usually and daily wages in copper coins. But the relationship between the two changed from time to time apart from the simultaneous existence of silver coins of varied types. Interestingly, a gradual increase in the amount of wages is noticed if one compares the *waqf* documents of Ishrat Khana with that of Abdullah's *madrasa*. The *waqf* document of Ishrat Khana[96] in Samarqand (1463-4) gives the wages as follows: *hafiz* (reader of Koran) 1 copper money a day, slave 1.3 copper money and 0.650 kg grain, servant 2.3 copper money and 1.315 kg grain. Similarly, in the *waqf* documents of Khwaja Ahrar (1488-9) following wages are recorded:

1. *Muezzin* ½ *dinar*
2. *Hafiz* 1 copper *dinar*.

As against these the sixteenth century *waqf* documents have the following rates:

Waqfnama Madrasa-i Miri Arab (1527-8) in Bukhara: *imam* 6 *dinars* (copper), *muezzin* 3 copper *dinars*. In the *waqf* document of Abdullah Khan (1570-1), the *imam* received more than 3 copper *dinars* and 2.8 kg grain, the *muezzin* and *farrash* half of that. Simultaneously in 1593-4 in *waqf* documents of Madrasa-i Qulbaba Kukultash, the salary of *imam* is given as 11 $\frac{1}{10}$ *dinars* and that of *muezzin* as 5½ *dinars*. Whether the slight rise in the wages signifies an inflationary trend or simply a difference of standards in various *madrasas* can not be dertermined.

Apparently it seems that the *khanis* of Tranosiana were much less in value in the global market. Shahnawaz Khan says that the cost of crore of rupees was equivalent to 3,33,000 *tomans* of Persia and 4 crores of *khani* coinage of Transoxiana.[97]

NOTES

1. Ibn-i Hauqal, *Surat-al Arz*, Iran, 1345 AH, p. 217.
2. Barthold, *Sochinnija* V, Moscow, 1968, pp. 138, 162.
3. Ibid., pp. 138, 162.
4. Such coins are mentioned in the sources as *tanga-i nuqrai-i Sir-i pakeezah-i khani.*
5. Certain coins did not bear the name and date of mint.
6. Davidovich, *K organizatsia obmena mednikh monet i va Sredni Azi Kontse XV nachale XVI, V*, Trud AN Tajikskoj SSR, 1960 TC XX; also Davidovich, *Tovarnavo deneshni otnashenija va Sredni Azi*, narod Azi e Afriki, 6, 1965.
7. Davidovich, *Deneshnaya reforma Shaibani Khana*, Trud AN Taj. SSR,

Vol. 2, XII, 1954, pp. 85-108; Davidovich, *Nekotori Cheorti Obrashenija Mednikh Monet va Sredni Azi XV-XVI e role nadchekanov*, *Izvestia*, Otdeleniya obshestvennikh Nauk, AN Tajikskoj SSR, III, Stalinabad, 1953, pp. 49, 53, 69 and also Table 6.

8. *H. Siyar*, p. 379; *Tarikh-i Shaibani*, no. 75, MS Oriental Institute, Tashkent, no. 1505, f. 25; *R. Safa*, p. 86.
9. Davidovich, *Nekotori Cheorti Obrashenija Mednikh Monet*, pp. 49-53, 69.
10. Davidovich, *Deneshnaya reforma*, pp. 84-9; Davidovich, *Nekotori Cheorti Obrashenija*, pp. 49-53, 69.
11. According to new silver and copper coins aiming at an intensive exploitation through large scale circulation and minting of copper coins. (*Deneshnaya*, pp. 84-9; *Nekatori*, pp. 149-69.)
12. Davidovich, *Pa Pavodu Yushno Turkmenistanskoi Archeologieheskoi Kompleksnoii Expeditsia*, issue I, Ashkabad, 1949, pp. 144-9, 171-2, Tables 4-5, also see Davidovich, K Organizatsia.
13. *H. Siyar*, p. 379; *Tarikh-i Shaibani*, f.25.
14. The term *dang* signifies 1/6 part of any weight or *misqal* in the sources of fourteenth-nineteenth centuries, e.g. Bukhara *misqal* was 4.8 gms and *dang* was equal to 0.8 gm and Khwarazm *misqal* of fourteenth-nineteenth centuries was 4.53-4.55 gms for 0.76 gm. For details cf. Davidovich, *Material pa metrology srednevekovoi Sredni Azi*, Moscow, 1970, pp. 81, 94, 116, 122; also V. Khinz, *Musulmanski meri e vesa sa perevodom va metricheskui systemu*, tr. from German by U.E. Brejchaya, Moscow, 1970, pp. 1-15 for weight of *misqal* in various countries; Dokladi AN Uz SSR, 1951, nos. 5, 50. Also Davidovich, *K Vaprosu a razmerakh misqal e batmana va smarkand e Bukhari.*
15. *H. Siyar*, p. 379; *Tarikh-i Shaibani*, f. 75, MS Oriental Institute, Tashkent, no. 1505, f. 25.
16. Davidovich, *Deneshnaya Reforma Shaibani Khana*, Trud AN Taj, Vol. XII, 1954; also see Davidovich, *Istoriya Monetnovo dela Sredni Azi*, Dushambe, 1964, pp. 293-5, Khinz, pp. 1-15.
17. Ibid.
18. For details cf. Davidovich, *Deneshnaya Reforma*, Vol. XII, pp. 85-108.
19. Bretschneider, II, p. 270.
20. Davidovich, *Deneshnaya Reforma*, Vol. XII, 1954.
21. Chaggi Memet, *Purchas and his Pilgrims*, Vol. XI, pp. 473-4.
22. Zainuddin Mahmud Wasifi, *Badaiul Waqai*, Tehran edn., 1349 AH, pp. 62-73.
23. Davidovich, *Deneshnaya Reforma*, Vol. XII, 1954; also see Davidovich, *Istorjia Monetnovo dela Sredni Azi*, Dushambe, 1964, pp. 293-5. Even Ashtrarakhanid gold coins were of one *misqal*.
24. B.V. Lunin, *K topographic apisaniya drevnikh monetnikh Kladov otdelnikh montenikh nakhodko na territory. Uzbegistana Istorija materialnova i Kulturi Uzbegistana*, Tashkent, 1969, pp. 169-92.
25. Ibid.
26. Jenkinson, p. 23.
27. Ibid.
28. Davidovich, *Istorija Monetnovo dela Sredni Azi*, pp. 147-50, 159-61. Cheklar Doc. 5.
29. Institute Vastokavediniya AN Uz SSR.

30. Davidovich, *Istorija Monetnovo dela*, pp. 124-32; *Tajiki*, pp. 537-40.
31. Ibid., *Baljuanski Klad*, pp. 75-85.
32. Ibid., *Istorija Monetnovo dela*, pp. 145-6, 190.
33. Ibid., pp. 63, 85, 86; also see Davidovich, *Dve denejshni reforma va gasudarstova shaibanidov*, Trud, Sagu, new edn., Vol. XXVIII, 1951, pp. 126-41.
34. Ibid., *K Vaprosu o kurse*, pp. 141-4; *Istorija Monetnovo dela*, pp. 90-1.
35. Ibid., *Istorija Monetnovo dela*, pp. 90-1; *K Vaprosu o kurse*, pp. 141-4.
36. Ibid.
37. Ibid., pp. 82-92, 103, 136-40.
38. P.P. Ivanov, *Kistoriya razvitiya gornovo promisla va*, Sredni Azi, LM, 1932, p. 45.
39. Davidovich, *Istorija Menetnovo dela*, pp. 82-92, 192-200, also see *Baljuanski Klad, XVII veke-nekatori osobennosti serebryannoi obrasheniya pre Ashtarakhanidakh*, *Isbornik statiye phylogi*, Narodov Sredni Azi, Stalingrad, 1953, pp. 69-89.
40. *Istorija Monetnovo*, pp. 82-92, 103, 190-200, 203-10.
41. Carson, *Coins of the World*, Great Britain, 1962, pp. 483-7.
42. Davidovich, *Istorija Monetnovo*, p. 60 fn. 28.
43. Ibid., pp. 82-92, 103, 190, 203-10.
44. *Stranstoveo Vanija Philip Efremov*, 3rd edn., Kazan, 1811.
45. In sixteenth-seventeenth century Bukhara *nakhud* was = 0.2 gm, 1/24 *misqal*, see Miles, *Early Arabic Glass Weights*, p. 5; Davidovich, *Pa Metrology Sredni Azi*, p. 96.
46. *Istorija Monetnovo*, 82-92, 103, 190, 203-10.
47. *Ain*, p. 23.
48. Ibid.
49. *Ain*, p. 39; also see Davidovich, pp. 93-8.
50. Badi, pp. 37-40.
51. Badi, Persian text, pp. 37-9; Russian tr., pp. 55-7.
52. Abul Fazl, *Ain-i Akbari*, Vol. I; Eng. tr. Blochmann, Delhi, 1965, p. 22.
53. Badauni, *Muntakhab-ut Tawarikh*, II, Eng. tr. by Lowe.
54. Jenkinson, p. 23.
55. Lahori, *Badshah Nama*, Calcutta, 1867. Davidovich says that *khani* and *tanga* were synonymously used for one and the same silver coin (cf. *Istorija Monetnovo*, p. 84). Presumably Lahori chose *khani* in order to avoid confusion and to distinguish it from Indian *tanga*.
56. *Muzzakkira*, p. 14.
57. Davidovich, *Deneshnaya Reforma*, pp. 85-108; also Davidovich, *Nekotari Cheorti*, pp. 49-53; Davidovich, *K Vaprosu*, pp.2 137-70.
58. Kuchikunji Khan changed the title from *Imamuzzaman* and *Khalifat ur Rahman* to *Alsultanul a'azam abrar*. From the time of Ubaidullah Khan, the title *Alkhaqanul aadil wa Malikul Kamil* came into vogue and was inscribed on the coins alongwith the title Abulghazi. Abdul Latif additionally adopted the high sounding title of *Alkhaqanul khaqan* even though in his own empire most of the provincial rulers had declared independence and minted their own coins.
59. Ibid.

60. Ibid. Some of the coins of Ubaidullah are, however, different. Kuchikunji's coins bear the term *sher mard* and the *kalima* in a circle exactly like that of Shaibani Khan except that the name of the mint Samarqand was in six unlike the quaterfoil area of Shaibani's coins. The coins of Ubaidullah bear the name of the king and date in a quaterfoil whereas the *kalima* appears in ornamented quadrilateral with the names of the four caliphs in the margins. Some of his coins carry the name and title of the king in a square area with pointed projection on each side and the *kalima* in a circle. In the coins of Abdul Latif, the name of the ruler is found either in Mihrabi area or in oblong area with angular projection in middle of each side. The *kalima* too was either in double circle with one of the dots between or in square with knot in the middle of each side. On Iskandar Khan's coins also the name of the ruler appeared either in ornamented area or in oblong with projection at each side (Rodgers, pp. 148-51).
61. For details, cf. C.J. Rodgers, *Catalogue of the Coins*, Calcutta, 1894, pp. 147-52.
62. Lunin, pp. 169-92.
63. Wasifi, pp. 227; Rodgers, p. 141.
64. Jenkinson, p. 23.
65. Cf. Rodgers, p. 150.
66. *Abdn*, pp. 315, 317.
67. Ibid.
68. Lunin, p. 181.
69. *Abdn*, 315, 317. Although the ratio of exchange between silver and copper coins of sixteenth century is not clearly mentioned, a document of 1695 describes 60 coins of one *misqal* silver coins to be equal to that of one *misqal* gold (IOST, AN Uz SSR, Cheklar Doc. no. 7; Monetnovo, p. 197).
70. Jenkinson, p. 23. As early as tenth century, Istakhri says that in Transoxiana, the *dirham* is familiar, the *dinar* is not in use or current only in chief towns (Istakhri, pp. 314, 323.)
71. Davidovich, *O Vremeni maximalni razvitiya*, pp. 80-95.
72. Ibid.
73. Davidovich, *Material dlya characteristiki chekani e obrashenija Sredni Aziatski Mednikh monet*, XVI, *Numismatiki Epigrafiki*, V.M., 1965, pp. 225-34; also see Davidovich, *O Vremeni maximalni razvitiya tovarno deneshnikh otnashenija*, pp. 86-7.
74. Davidovich, *K organizatsia obmena mednikh monetov Sredni Azi Kontsa XV nachale XVI*, V, Trud AN Tajikskoj SSR, 1960, TC XX, pp. 61-4, also see *Tovarnovo deneshni atnashenija*, pp. 86-7. The Chaghatai mints include Balad Taraz, Kenje Otrar, Khujand, Binkent, Marghilan, Almalik, Farab also. For details see Lunin, *K topography*, pp. 176-7.
75. S. Lanepool, *Catalogue of Muhammadan Coins*, Oxford, 1888, p. 16; Carson, *Coins of the World*, Great Britain, 1962, pp. 483-7; C.J. Rodgers, *Catalogue of the Coins* II, Calcutta, 1894, pp. 140-7; Barthold, *Sochinenija* IV, p. 348; *Sochinenija* V, p. 162.
76. Butener, *Monetnovo dela va Bukhare, gorni jurnal*, 1842, IV, Kneega, p. 159. Juvaini, Eng. tr., pp. 233-4; text, pp. 189-90. Ibn-i Battuta, Pers. tr., pp. 410, 411, 422; Eng. tr., p. 170.

77. Wasifi, p. 415, new edn., p. 491.
78. Ibid., p. 1294.
79. Alkashifi, *Rashat-i ainul Hayat*, Bodleian Library, f. 259.
80. *Sochinenja*, VIII, p. 150.
81. Clavijo, *Travels*.
82. Wasifi, p. 491.
83. *Abdn*, p. 301.
84. Wasifi, p. 955.
85. Ibid., p. 415.
86. Wasifi, pp. 1028, 1033.
87. Ibid., p. 415.
88. Ibid., old edn., pp. 1221, 1233; new edn., pp. 55, 68, 69-71.
89. *Abdn*, p. 376.
90. Wasifi, p. 529.
91. Uy NA UZ SSR, f. 323, Doc. 16.
92. Ibid., Doc. 12.
93. Ibid., Doc. 115.
94. Ibid., Doc. ff. 1186-7, Doc. 24/1, I; also see Davidovich, *Tovarnovo deneshni atnashenija va Sredni Azi*, Narod Azi-e Afriki 6, 1965, pp. 84-5.
95. *Majmaul Wasaiq*, Oriental Institute UZ SSR, no. 1386, Docs. 257-302; also Davidovich, pp. 84-5.
96. V.L. Vyatkin, *Wuqufni documenti Ishrat Khana*, 'Mausoleum tovarno geneshni', pp. 84-5; TSGEA UZ SSR, f. 323, 1202/1, Doc. nos. 1, 12, 16, 115.
97. *Maasir-ul Umara* I, Patna, pp. 197, 397.

Index